THE HISTORIC
FOR THE RES
OF JESUS
THE DEIST CO

THE HISTORICAL ARGUMENT FOR THE RESURRECTION OF JESUS DURING THE DEIST CONTROVERSY

William Lane Craig

Texts and Studies in Religion
Volume 23

The Edwin Mellen Press
Lewiston/Queenston

Library of Congress Cataloging in Publication Data

Craig, William Lane.
   The historical argument for the Resurrection of Jesus during the
Deist controversy.

   (Texts and studies in religion ; v. 23)
   Bibliography: p.
   1. Jesus Christ--Resurrection--History of doctrines. 2. Deism. I.
Title. II. Series: Texts and studies in religion ; 23.
BT481.C695   1985   232.9'7'09033   85-21570
ISBN 0-88946-811-7 (alk. paper)

This is volume 23 in the continuing series
Texts and Studies in Religion
Volume 23 ISBN 0-88946-811-7
TSR Series ISBN 0-88946-976-8

All rights reserved. For more information contact:

The Edwin Mellen Press   The Edwin Mellen Press
Box 450   Box 67
Lewiston, New York   Queenston, Ontario
USA 14092   CANADA L0S 1L0

Printed in the United States of America

To

PI

CONTENTS

xi

PREFACE

During the first half of the present century, the importance of the historicity of the resurrection of Jesus for Christian faith was obscured by the predominance of dialectical and existential modes of thinking in theology, both of which depreciated the value of history for faith. But in the second half of this century, a remarkable revolution seems to be taking place in resurrection studies. The Marburg conference of 1953 marked a turning point against Bultmann's position on the irrelevancy of history to faith, and several of his pupils began to seek ways of re-tying the Christ of faith to the Jesus of history. Inevitably this sparked renewed interest in the event of the resurrection. Von Campenhausen's Der Ablauf der Osterereignisse und das leere Grab (1952) and Hans Grass's Ostergeschehen und Osterberichte (1956) were landmarks in the revival of attempts to investigate and defend the historicity of the resurrection of Jesus. Von Campenhausen argued for the essential historicity of the Markan narrative of the women's discovery of the empty tomb of Jesus, while Grass, though rejecting the empty tomb, argued that the post-resurrection appearances of Jesus cannot be explained away as subjective visions, but ought to be understood as objective (veridical) visions of the risen Lord.

Sceptical treatments of the resurrection also continued, of course, but by the late 1960's the Barthian/Bultmannian approaches to the resurrection appeared to have spent their force. Scepticism reached a faltering apogee with Marxsen's popular book Die Auferstehung Jesu von Nazareth (1968) and began quickly to recede. Gutwenger comments on the self-reversal of critical scholarship in this area:

It appears that a few years ago the attack on Jesus's resurrection . . . reached its climax. This situation was created through modern rationalism, which wants to explain everything through immanent causes, through a weariness with the divine, and a massive, hedonistic materialism. Bultmann's poorly understood teaching of demythologization and the open confession of some theologians that they cannot believe in the resurrection of a corpse helped to bring about a crisis of faith in Easten . . . Reaction came, and from the Catholic as well as the Protestant side the theme of the resurrection of Christ was taken up anew.[1]

During the past decade a continuing stream of works from German, French, and English-speaking scholars has flowed forth, defending anew the resurrection of Jesus historically. Perhaps the most striking indication of the new appreciation of the historical evidence for the resurrection is that one of today's most prominent Jewish theologians, Pinchas Lapide, has declared himself convinced on the basis of historical evidence that God did, indeed, raise Jesus of Nazareth from the dead.[2]

In the realm of systematic theology, probably the most significant development with regard to the resurrection is Wolfhart Pannenberg's attempt to construct his entire Christology "from below," that is, based exclusively on the historical evidence for Jesus and his resurrection. His historical approach has been hailed as ushering in a new era in European Protestant theology.[3] Arguing against Bultmann on the one hand that a kerygmatic Christ utterly unrelated to the real, historical Jesus would be "pure myth" and against Barth on the other that a Christ known only through dialectical encounter would be impossible to distinguish from "self-delusion," Pannenberg contends that the reports of Jesus's empty tomb and appearances are most plausibly accounted for by the explanation that he really did rise from the dead and that this supplies the foundation for faith.[4]   After the predominance of the Barthian/Bultmannian approaches to the resurrection, Pannenberg's program is a startling development that several years ago one could hardly have held for possible in German theology.

But although the historicity of the resurrection of Jesus has become one of the most discussed theological themes in recent years, most authors writing on this subject seem for the most part unaware that they stand at the end of a long tradition of debate on this subject. Although it was anticipated in earlier Christian thought, the historical argument for the resurrection of Jesus became the crowning element in the evidentialist apologetic for Christianity during the years of the Deist controversy, and the seventeenth and especially the eighteenth century also saw a flood of books, both pro and con, flow from English, French, and German presses. In this study I seek to bring to light again the principal issues in the debate of that period, with a view toward assessing what arguments of lasting value may be discovered therein for the contemporary discussion. This was an extremely fertile and exciting period of thought, fascinating in its own right, but also rich in lessons for our own time.

I wish to express my gratitude to the Alexander von Humboldt Foundation for the generous fellowship and extension thereof which funded my research at the Universität München and at Cambridge University. The Foundation's efficiency, broadness of mind, and personal concern for Fellows were much appreciated, and the West German government may be rightly proud of its clear-sightedness in establishing so fine an organization to bring research scholars to Germany.

I also wish to thank Prof. Dr. Wolfhart Pannenberg for serving as the supervisor of my research and Prof. Dr. Ferdinand Hahn for his reading and criticisms of my work.

Finally thanks are due to my wife Jan for her initial typing and re-typing of the manuscript, and to Mary Dalton for the production of the finished typescript, and to Janet Gutman for preparing the typescript for publication.

William Lane Craig

München, Bundesrepublik Deutschland

NOTES

[1] E. Gutwenger, "Auferstehung und Auferstehungs-leib Jesu," _Zeitschrift für Katholische Theologie_ 9 (1969): 32.

[2] Pinchas Lapide, _Auferstehung_ (Stuttgart: Calwer Verlag, 1977; München: Kösel Verlag, 1977).

[3] Wolfhart Pannenberg, _Jesus: God and Man_, trans. L. L. Wilkins and D. A. Priebe (London: SCM Press, 1968). See B. A. Willems, "W. Pannenberg, _Grundzüge der Christologie_," _Tijdschrift voor theologie_ 7 (1967): 322; René Marlé, "Comincia un'era nuova nella teologia protestante tedesca'?" _Civilta Cattolica_ 119 (1969): 214-25; Daniel P. Fuller, "A New German Theological Movement," _Scottish Journal of Theology_ 19 (1966): 160-75.

[4] Pannenberg, _Jesus_, pp. 27-8, 88-106.

PRE-MODERN ANTICIPATIONS OF THE HISTORICAL
ARGUMENT FOR THE RESURRECTION OF JESUS

Although the historical argument for the resurrection of Jesus is for the most part a development of modern Christian apologetics, the thinkers who employed this argument--and those who opposed it--during the seventeenth and eighteenth centuries were indebted to earlier disputants concerning matters of both structure and substance in their argumentation. Not only do various arguments pressed by these early Christian writers and their opponents often crop up again in the later centuries, but the modern evidentialist approach to apologetics owes a great deal to the system worked out by medieval scholastics, as we shall see. Therefore, in this section I propose for purposes of background to survey briefly several of the important figures in the history of Christian thought who foreshadowed the modern development of the historical argument for the resurrection of Jesus.

Primitive Christianity

Whether they defend or deny the witness of the New Testament writers to the resurrection of Jesus, virtually every modern critic or theologian acknowledges that at least the belief that Jesus had risen from the dead lay at the heart of primitive Christianity. This is the true import of Bultmann's words: "All that historical criticism can establish is the fact that the first disciples came to believe in the resurrection."[1] The Bultmannian disciple Schubert

Ogden similarly holds that the resurrection is the faith of the first disciples.[2] New Quester James M. Robinson agrees that historically the content of early Christian preaching was God's eschatological action centering in the cross and resurrection.[3] Willi Marxsen, though himself believing that Jesus is dead, admits that Paul and the early disciples obviously believed that the resurrection actually occurred.[4] The message is, after all, written throughout the pages of the New Testament. When Paul wrote, "If Christ has not been raised, then our preaching is in vain and your faith is in vain" (I Cor 15.14), he spoke not for himself alone. The fact that Christ "was raised on the third day" was one of the essential elements of the gospel message received by Paul from those who were in Christ before him and delivered by him to the recipients of his preaching (I Cor 15.1-5).[5] According to Paul, this was the common message proclaimed by all the apostles (I Cor 15.11). All the gospels climax with the proclamation of Jesus's resurrection. In Acts, the chief duty of an apostle is to serve as "a witness to his resurrection" (Acts 1.22), and all the evangelistic sermons in Acts find their climax in the announcement that God raised Jesus from the dead. Not only do references to Jesus's resurrection abound in the epistles, but so do citations of early Christian formulas encapsulating the fact of the resurrection (for example, Rom. 1.3-4; 4.24-5; 10.8-10; I Cor. 15:3-5; I Tim. 3.16)[6], thus demonstrating the importance of belief in the resurrection to the earliest Christians. "It is everywhere clear that the event of Easter is the central point of the New Testament message," writes Gerhard Koch; "Resurrection by God and appearing before his disciples constitute the basis of the New Testament proclamation of Christ, without which there would be virtually no witness to Christ."[7]

But while this fact is widely recognized, it is perhaps not so widely appreciated that early Christians argued for the fact of the resurrection as well as proclaimed it. In the New Testament books themselves we find clear examples of first century Christian apologetic for the fact of the resurrection.

The Gospels and Acts

Matthew

Early Christian apologetic for the resurrection is evident in each of the gospels. Perhaps the clearest example is Matthew's use of the story of the guard at the tomb (Mt 27.62-6; 28.4, 11-15) to counter the allegation that the disciples had themselves stolen Jesus's body. In relating this story, which is unique among the canonical gospels (John does mention a guard in connection with Jesus's arrest [Jn 18.3,12; cf. Mk 14.44]), Matthew's intention is to provide a Christian counter-response to the Jewish polemic concerning Jesus's resurrection. Besides the clear statement in 28.15, this is indicated by the designation of Jesus as an "imposter," an earmark of Jewish anti-Christian polemic.[8] The Jewish allegation that the disciples had stolen Jesus's body by night is also mentioned by Justin Martyr in his Dialog with Trypho 108, but he does not refer to a guard. This should not lead us to think, however, that Matthew's story of the guard at the tomb was a Matthean creation. For evidence of pre-Matthean tradition may be found in the many words which are hapax legomena for the New Testament:

ἐπαύριον, παρασκευή, πλάνος/πλάνη, κουστωδία, ἀσφαλίζω, σφραγίζω.
Moreover, the expression "chief priests and Pharisees"
(cf. 21.45) is unusual for Matthew and never appears in
Mark or Luke, though it is common in John (7.32,45;
9.47, 57; 18.3).[9] Moreover, the Gospel of Peter also
relates the story of the guard at the tomb, and its
account, while much later than Matthew's, may well be
independent of it, since the verbal similarities
between them are virtually non-existent.[10]   That
Matthew did not invent the guard story also seems
evident from the fact that behind it there would appear
to lie a tradition history of Jewish and Christian
polemic, a developing pattern of assertion and
counter-assertion:[11]

> Christian: "The Lord is risen!"
> Jew: "No, his disciples stole his body away by
> night."
> Christian: "The guard at the tomb would have
> prevented any such theft."
> Jew: "No, his disciples stole away his body while
> the guard slept."
> Christian: "The chief priests bribed the guard to
> say this."

The Jewish charge that the disciples had stolen
the body was probably the Jewish reaction to the
Christian proclamation that Jesus was risen.   This
proclamation may well have been in the words repeated
twice in Mt 27.64; 28.7: " ἠγέρθη ἀπὸ τῶν νεκρῶν ."[12]
To this the Jews answered with the charge of
body-snatching by the disciples. At this point, there
was no need to mention a guard, so that the origin of
the guard cannot be attributed to the Jewish polemic.[13]
Rather the first mention of the guard comes in the
Christian response to the Jewish slander: the guard
posted by the Jews would have prevented theft of the
corpse. Note that at this stage of the controversy

there is no need to mention the bribing of the guard, for this presupposes their falling asleep. But this lapse on the guards' part cannot be attributed to the Christian apologetic, since it would be self-defeating. The assertion that the disciples stole the body while the guard slept originates in the next response of the Jewish polemic. This is the rumor which Matthew reports (28.15b). Only now does it become necessary to relate the story of the bribing of the guards by the chief priests. At the most then, only the final response in the above pattern of assertion and counter-assertion could, it seems, be plausibly attributed to Matthew. It is interesting to note in this connection that Matthew's story falls into two parts, the setting of the guard and the bribing of the guard. All the traditional material noted above appears in the first section. Also in the Gospel of Peter, the story of the bribe is missing. The guard report, not to the chief priests, but to Pilate, and he simply commands them to remain silent. There is no mention of the guards' falling asleep or of the bribe. It may be that the apocryphal writer only knew of the tradition in Matthew's first section; on the other hand, however, he could not have included the second section in any case, for he has multiplied the witnesses at the tomb and described the resurrection, so that the guards' falling asleep and being bribed must be omitted. At any rate, it seems evident that it is misleading to speak of the story of the guard at the tomb as a "Matthean apologetic," for Matthew probably contributed at most only the story of the bribe.

In Matthew's employment of the guard story, then, we have a good illustration of how early Christians argued for the fact of Jesus's resurrection, upholding it against the Jewish polemic. It is interesting to note that the first counter-explanation of the resurrection with which Christians were apparently forced to deal was the conspiracy theory, which was revived by eighteenth century Deists. Their opponents would again have recourse to Matthew's guard story in response. Ironically, the chief value today of Matthew's account of the guard lies not in the guard itself, which nearly all contemporary critics reject as unhistorical, but in the incidental information that Jewish polemic never denied the empty tomb, but rather sought to explain it away.[14] Thus the early opponents of Christianity themselves bear witness to the fact of the empty tomb.

Mark

Mark's simple narrative of the discovery of the empty tomb lacks the obvious apologetic motifs which Matthew's story contains. Bultmann comments, ". . . Mark's presentation is extremely reserved, in so far as the resurrection and appearances of the risen Lord are not recounted."[15] Nauck points out that many theological motifs that might be expected are lacking in this story: (1) the proof from prophecy, (2) the in-breaking of the new eon, (3) the ascension of Jesus's spirit or his descent into hell, (4) the nature of the resurrection body, and (5) the use of Christological titles.[16] Despite this, however, the early Christians do not seem to have been completely oblivious to the apologetic value of the empty tomb. The prominent place it occupies in the pre-Markan passion story and the careful recounting of the women witnesses, scorned and un-qualified though they were in Jewish society,[17] shows that the empty tomb had some

positive evidential value, at least for Christians.
Were this not the case, it seems odd that the
evangelists should have given it such a place of
prominence in the gospels rather than skipping over it
to the appearance traditions. Mark wants to emphasize
that the tomb of Jesus was found empty and that this is
a significant sign of the resurrection.

Another interesting feature of Mark's narrative
which may be of apologetic significance is the story,
peculiar to him, of Pilate's wonder at Jesus's quick
death and Pilate's interrogation of the guard to
determine the reality of Jesus's death (Mk 15.44-5).
It could be that this interchange is meant to
counteract or forestall the objection that Jesus was
not actually dead, so that his resurrection was merely
a resuscitation. If so, this would be an anticipation
of the rationalist attempt to explain Jesus's
resurrection as a merely apparent death. Death by
crucifixion was very slow, and since it was difficult
to determine precisely the time of death, the bodies of
crucified victims were usually left on the cross until
they decayed or were eaten by birds or animals,
although the corpse was usually handed over if
relatives or friends requested it.[18] If the body was
to be taken down, the Roman executioners could ensure
death by means of a lance thrust into the victim, as
John records (Jn 19.34).[19] Mark may have wished to
refute or preclude the idea that Jesus was taken down
unconscious but alive. This is uncertain, however,
since we have no evidence that this explanation was
propounded by opponents of the early Christians. It
could be that this is a piece of tradition that is only
obliquely apologetic. Stylistically, v. 43 does not go
with v.46, for this leaves a gap in the story

concerning Pilate's decision. In leaving out vs. 44-5
of Mark, Luke creates such a gap in Lk 23.52-3, whereas
Matthew fills the gap with Mt 27.58b. The two verses
in Mark contain Markan expressions (θαυμάζω, προσκα -
λέομαι, κεντυρίων, ἐπερωτάω), but γνοὺς ἀπὸ is a
unique construction here, and δωρέομαι and πτῶμα are
technical terms, together reflecting perhaps the
official language of the governor's order: donavit
cadaver. So there could be traditional material here.
Grass, Taylor, and others have, moreover, found the
story plausible and feel that it does not merit
Bultmann's appellation as legendary.[20] Of course, that
an account is historical does not preclude its being
apologetical as well, since the question of apologetics
concerns only the purpose for which the account is
related, not its facticity. In the present case the
apologetic intent is not sufficiently obvious for us to
conclude that this is the raison d'être for the two
verses; certain is only that, for whatever purpose,
Mark wished to underline the fact that although Jesus's
death was quick, it was sure.

Luke-Acts

It is the evangelist Luke, however, who in his
double work of Luke-Acts has composed the apologetic
treatise par excellence on the historical evidence for
the resurrection. Of all the evangelists, Luke is the
most self-consciously a historian, and he seeks to
provide a firm basis for Christian faith in historical
facts. In his prologue to his double-work, Luke
insists that what he relates is squarely based on the
testimony of those who experienced the events
first-hand:

> Inasmuch as many have undertaken to compile a
> narrative of the things which have been

accomplished among us, just as they were delivered
to us by those who from the beginning were
eyewitnesses and ministers of the word, it seemed
good to me also, having followed all things
closely[a] for some time past, to write an orderly
account for you, most excellent Theophilus, that
you may know the truth concerning the things of
which you have been informed.

_____

[a] Or accurately (Lk 1.1-4).

The prologue is composed in excellent Greek, some
of the finest in the New Testament; after this initial
sentence Luke reverts to a more popular style. It is
as though he were trying to demonstrate to any reader
that he is capable, should he so desire, of writing in
the style of the most eloquent Greek historian.[21] In
the prologue he refers to the first-hand nature of his
sources and to his long and careful procedure in his
research. His use of   is meant to underline
the historical reliability of his narrative (cf.
Josephus Contra Apion 1.53-5; idem Jewish War 6.134).[22]
He makes it clear that he intends to construct an
orderly or chronological narrative of what has taken
place so that his reader might know the certainty or
reliability of the facts of the gospel. That Luke
takes this intention seriously is evident from his
elaborate synchronization of events in the style of the
classical historian to fix the date of the beginning of
John the Baptist's ministry (Lk 3.1-3).[23] Luke is
manifestly very much concerned with establishing the
factual basis of what Christians believed, and the
historical resurrection is the key event on which his
double-work hinges. Luke adduces two lines of argument
for the historicity of the resurrection: the proof
from prophecy and the proof from eyewitness testimony.
Both are found already in the gospel: In the Emmaus

appearance, Jesus says, "'Was it not necessary that the Christ should suffer these things and enter into his glory?' And beginning with Moses and all the prophets, he interpreted to them in all the scriptures the things concerning himself" (Lk 24.26-27; cf. 24.44-47). In the appearance to the eleven, Jesus, after displaying from the Old Testament that the Christ must suffer and rise on the third day, gives this charge to his disciples: "You are witnesses of these things" (Lk 24.48). Both these lines of argumentation, which Luke portrays as stemming from the risen Jesus himself, are then carried out in the book of Acts. As Luke represents them, the apostles continually reinforced their message by the appeal to eyewitness testimony and to Old Testament proof-texts:[24]

1. Peter's sermon at Pentecost: Peter draws upon his hearers' own knowledge of Jesus's miracles; he accuses them of murdering Jesus; and he announces that God has raised him from the dead. He then proceeds to quote Ps 16.8-11 that God's Holy One would not see corruption, and he shows the inapplicability of this psalm to David. Therefore, it must be that David

'foresaw and spoke of the resurrection of the Christ, that he was not abandoned to Hades, nor did his flesh see corruption. This Jesus God raised up, and of that we are all witnesses' (Acts 2.31-32).

2. Peter's speech in Solomon's portico:

'. . . the God of our fathers glorified his servant[c] Jesus, whom you delivered up and denied in the presence of Pilate, when he had decided to release him. But you denied the Holy and Righteous One . . . and killed the Author of Life, whom God raised from the dead. To this we are witnesses.'

_____

^c Or <u>child</u> (Acts 3.13-15).

3. <u>Peter and the apostles' answer to the Council</u>:

'The God of our fathers raised Jesus whom you
killed by hanging him on a tree. God exalted him
at his right hand as Leader and Savior, to give
repentance to Israel and forgiveness of sins. And
we are witnesses to these things and so is the
Holy Spirit . . .' (Acts 5.30-31).

4. <u>Peter's speech to Cornelius's household</u>:   In
preaching to outsiders the appeal to eyewitness
testimony becomes more extensive:

' . . . Jesus of Nazareth . . . went about doing
good and healing all that were oppressed by the
devil, for God was with him. And we are witnesses
to all that he did both in the country of the Jews
and in Jerusalem. They put him to death by
hanging him on a tree; but God raised him on the
third day and made him manifest; not to all the
people but to us who were chosen by God as
witnesses, who ate and drank with him after he
rose from the dead. And he commanded us to preach
to the people . . .' (Acts 10.32-42).

5. <u>Paul's speech in Antioch of Pisidia</u>:   Paul also
finds it necessary to inform his listeners more closely
as to who Jesus was and what he did. After reciting
God's great acts in the history of Israel, Paul
announces:

' . . . God has brought to Israel a Savior, Jesus,
as he promised . . .' . . . those who live in
Jerusalem and their rulers, because they did not
recognize him nor understand the utterances of the
prophets . . ., fulfilled these by condemning him.
Though they could charge him with nothing
deserving death, yet they asked Pilate to have him
killed. And when they had fulfilled all that was
written of him, they took him down from the tree,
and laid him in a tomb. But God raised him from
the dead; and for many days he appeared to those
who came up with him from Galilee to Jerusalem,
who are now his witnesses to the people . . . what

God promised to the fathers, this he has fulfilled
to us their children by raising Jesus . . . And as
for the fact that he raised him from the dead, no
more to return to corruption, he spoke in this
way, . . . "Thou wilt not let thy Holy One see
corruption." For David . . . fell asleep . . .
and saw corruption; but he whom God raised saw no
corruption' (Acts 13.23, 27-37).

6. Paul's Areopagus speech: In Athens Paul
"preached Jesus and the resurrection" (Acts 17.18), but
is cut short by mockers before witnesses are mentioned:

' . . . God . . . has fixed a day on which he will
judge the world in righteousness by a man whom he
has appointed, and of this he has given assurance
to all men by raising him from the dead' (Acts
17.30-31).

Thus in the Acts speeches we find Jesus's commission in
the gospel carried out: the resurrection is not simply
proclaimed but there is also the attempt to provide
credibility to the proclamation by the use of scripture
proofs and eyewitness testimony that Jesus had been
raised. Were a sceptical antagonist to have demanded
of them how they knew Jesus was raised, the apostles,
as Luke represents them, would have confidently
responded that they had seen Jesus alive again, talked
with him, and eaten and drunk with him over a period of
many days.

The repeated emphasis in the speeches on
eyewitness evidence shows that Luke was concerned about
the historicity of the resurrection and was prepared to
argue for it on the basis of the testimony of the
apostolic eyewitnesses. Indeed, the concept of witness
plays a leading role in Luke-Acts.   The word
and its derivatives occur nine times in the gospel and
39 times in Acts.   In his important study of the
missionary sermons in Acts, Ulrich Wilckens has

contended that it is a special Lukan trait to emphasize
the role of the apostles as witnesses (Lk 24.48; Acts
1.8, 22; 2.40; 4.33; 8.25; 18,5; 20.21, 24; 22.15,20;
23.11; 26.16; 28.33) and that it is undoubtedly the
case that Luke has a developed, peculiar theory of
witness (eine ausgebildete, eigene Zeugen- und Zeugnis-
theorie).[25] Although Wilckens, in dependence upon Hans
Conzelmann's "Mitte der Zeit" conception of Luke's
program, maintains that Luke's theory of witness is
theologically motivated, could not his motivation in
stressing the witnesses be primarily historico-
apologetical, not theological? In this case Luke's
repeated emphasis on witnesses would be intended to
underscore the historical reliability of his account of
Christian beginnings. Allison Trites in his study of
the concept of witness in the New Testament has argued
that this is in fact the case. He points out that
Luke-Acts presents the claims of Christ against a
background of hostility, contention, and active
persecution, which accounts for the large place given
to juridical terminology and ideas drawn from the
lawcourt.[26] Luke wants to present the evidence,
especially the evidence of the resurrection, which
vindicates Jesus over against his condemnation by the
Jewish court. The resurrection brings, as it were,
fresh evidence which serves to re-open his trial.
Hence, Luke often emphasizes double witnesses to the
facts he records, in accordance with the Jewish rule of
evidence laid down in Deut 19.15. According to Trites,

        . . . the only testimony Luke means to offer is
    that which would satisfy a court of law, and this
    demands twofold or threefold testimony; this is
    the significance of his repeated use of the
    principle of twofoldness. By this device Luke
    seeks to provide evidence for the truth of the

events which have transpired, thereby giving
Theophilus 'authentic knowledge' (ἀσφάλεια , . . .
the same word used by Thucydides in the preface to
his historical work, 1.22) and vindicating his own
name as a historian. His whole book is meant as a
witness to the truth. He uses the historical
material for the Book of Acts according to the
standards of his time as they are expressed by
such ancient historians as Herodotus, Polybius,
Thucydides and Josephus, and certainly intends to
offer evidence that will stand the test of the
closest scrutiny . . .[27]

If this is the case, then we have in Luke-Acts a
sophisticated, historical apologetic for the Christian
faith centering on the resurrection. The operative
question for Luke, contends Trites, is: on what
grounds or evidence can people have faith; hence, the
greatest possible stress is placed upon the factual
content of the preaching.[28] The testimony concerns
God's great acts in Jesus and the resurrection
constitutes the very heart of this. " . . . the
Christian faith rests upon historical facts, and Luke
in both his Gospel preface and Acts stresses the
importance of the apostolic witness for this reason."[29]

In addition to this thread of continuity which
runs through his double-work, Luke also graphically
describes the appearances of Jesus to which the
apostles bear witness in such a way as to preclude
their being hallucinations or ghostly visitations (Lk
24.36-43). The demonstration of corporeality through
eating is underlined in the preaching in Acts (Acts
10.41; cf. 1.4: συναλίζομαι [30]). Noteworthy is Luke's
summary statement in the prologue to the second volume
of his double-work: "To them he presented himself
alive after his passion by many proofs, appearing to
them during forty days, and speaking of the kingdom of
God" (Acts 1.3). Luke's singular use of "proofs"

(τεκμηρίους   ) demonstrates again, not only his
preoccupation with historical facts, but also his
insistence on the realism of Jesus's resurrection.
Once again, however, one must be careful in speaking
about "Luke's physicalism" or "Luke's apologetic," for
while it is true that only Luke mentions Jesus's eating
(but cf. Jn 21.9-14), the showing of the wounds is part
of the tradition he received, granted John's
independence from Luke, for John also narrates this (Jn
20.20). Moreover, the words βρώσιμον and ἰχθύς ὀπτός are
unique here, indicating that even Jesus's eating before
the disciples is not a Lukan redaction, but part of the
tradition he received. Thus, the physical
demonstrations, which serve the two-fold purpose of
showing corporeality and continuity with the crucified
Jesus, cannot simply be set down to Lukan creativity.
The emphasis in Luke and John on the demonstrations of
corporeality and continuity are perhaps best viewed as
an attempted proof that the disciples were not just
"seeing things," as Celsus was later to allege. This
would be an anticipation of the hallucinatory
explanation of the resurrection appearances, championed
by the nineteenth century liberal school of theology
and still propounded by several critics today.

    In Luke-Acts then we have a sophisticated example
of early Christian argument for the resurrection.
Indeed, in a sense Luke stands like a rock far out at
sea, as the first systematic attempt to establish the
resurrection through historical evidence; for with
Luke's lengthy and close scrutiny of the facts, his
research into eyewitness reports, his descriptions of
unmistakeable appearances of Jesus alive from the dead,
and his repeated emphasis on the first-hand testimony
of the apostolic preachers, a historical proof for the

resurrection, among other things, is exactly what he is about.[31]   We must wait until the fourth century for another Christian historian to arise, and then Eusebius will also employ his skill as a historian to attempt to establish the resurrection through historical reasoning.

John

    In John's gospel like Luke's we find an emphasis on the concept of witness. According to Trites, the witness in this gospel is apologetic and juridical in nature.[32]   John like Luke seeks to root the resurrection narratives in eyewitness reports. Thus, after recording that one of the soldiers pierced Jesus's side and that blood and water issued forth, an incident peculiar to John's gospel, this insertion follows: "He who saw it has borne witness--his testimony is true, and he knows that he tells the truth--that you also may believe" (Jn 19.35). Similarly at the end of the epilogue to the gospel we find this note: "This is the disciple who is bearing witness to these things, and who has written these things; we know that his testimony is true" (Jn 21.24). This testimonium is attached to a resurrection appearance in Galilee and is therefore particularly noteworthy. It is clearly an attempted authentication of what is therein related by appealing to the eyewitness status of its author. Like Luke, John lays great emphasis on the disciples' role as witnesses. Perhaps the most striking example is Jn 15.27, a sentence which could just as easily have come from Luke's hand: "and you also are witnesses, because you have been with me from the beginning" (cf. Lk 24.48; Acts 1.21-22). John's use of the signs also shows his interest in providing evidence substantiating Jesus's claim. Jesus offers these signs as evidence: " . . . these very works which I am doing, bear me witness that the Father has sent me" (5.36); " . . . even though you do not believe me, believe the works, that you may know and understand that the Father is in me and I am in the Father" (10.38); "Believe me that I am in the Father and the Father in me; or else believe me for the sake of the works themselves" (14.11). In John's portrayal the signs can actually serve as the foundation for faith in Christ. Hence, he can conclude his gospel by stating that these signs have been recorded in order that the reader may believe that Jesus is the Christ (20.31). So John's gospel as well as Luke's is at pains to underscore the fact that its narration of the events surrounding the death, burial, and resurrection of Jesus stand on a solid historical basis.

A second indication of John's concern with the historical basis of the resurrection is his manner of dealing with the problem of believers who did not see Jesus risen from the dead. John handles this problem through the appearance to Thomas, who would not believe unless he personally saw and touched Jesus. When Jesus appears to Thomas and Thomas believes, Jesus says, "Have you believed because you have seen me? Blessed are those who have not seen and yet believe" (Jn 20.29). The same problem is similarly dealt with in I Peter, whose author describes himself as "Peter, an apostle of Jesus Christ" and therefore an eyewitness of "the resurrection of Jesus Christ from the dead": "Without having seen him you love him; though you do not now see him you believe in him and rejoice with unutterable and exalted joy" (I Pet 1.1, 3,8). This problem of believers either temporally or geographically removed from the original events could only arise in a context in which the historicity of the original events was valued. Were the resurrection not treasured in the mind of the early church as a historical event, the problem of believers at a distance would never arise. The fact that the problem does arise within John shows how highly the historicity of the events in the resurrection narratives and the apostolic testimony thereto was valued. The Thomas story heightens, not diminishes, John's emphasis on the historical. Indeed, in the next breath after Jesus's words to Thomas, John states,

> Now Jesus did many other signs in the presence of the disciples, which are not written in this book; but these are written that you may believe that Jesus is the Christ, and that believing you may have life through his name (Jn 20.30-31).

In other words, those who do not have Thomas's first-hand knowledge may nevertheless believe confidently because of the reliable eyewitness testimony recorded by John to the signs, including the resurrection, of Jesus. Thomas himself should have believed without seeing because he possessed the word of the ten other disciples who had seen. The Thomas story is not at all meant to play down the importance of the disciples' having seen Jesus alive (as though because it was not important for the disciples, it ought not to be important for subsequent believers); on the contrary, the story teaches that subsequent believers are blessed because they believe without the advantage of seeing which the disciples enjoyed and that it is precisely because of the disciples' sure witness to what they experienced with their own senses that subsequent believers' faith is confident and secure.[33] Thus for John every bit as much for Luke is the apostolic witness to the resurrection the means by which our faith is supported.[34]

Paul

Turning from the gospels to Paul, we find that because his letters were written to Christian churches which presumably needed no convincing, the resurrection is widely mentioned, but not contended for. If a certain heresy had never arisen in the church of Corinth, we should not have possessed one of our most valuable testimonies to the historicity of the resurrection. In the Corinthian church, certain persons were maintaining that " . . . there is no resurrection of the dead" (I Cor 15.12). This prompted a brief treatise on the subject of resurrection by the apostle Paul. He begins by reminding the Corinthians "in what terms I preached to you the gospel" (I Cor 15.1), whereupon the following summary is given:

> For I delivered to you as of first importance what I also received, that Christ died for our sins in accordance with the scriptures, that he was buried, that he was raised on the third day in accordance with the scriptures, and that he appeared to Cephas, then to the twelve. Then he appeared to more than five hundred brethren at one time, most of whom are still alive, though some have fallen asleep. Then he appeared to James, then to all the apostles. Last of all, as to one untimely born, he appeared also to me (I Cor 15.3-8).

Why does Paul want to remind the Corinthians of the content of the gospel he preached to them? The answer seems to be that Paul saw that their denial of the doctrine of the resurrection would imply that Christ himself did not rise from the dead, which would

invalidate the Christian faith. If, however, Christ
rose from the dead, then the general denial is
necessarily false. The crux of Paul's argument,
therefore, is to show that Christ did rise from the
dead (v. 20). For this purpose, he cites the formula,
which culminates in Jesus's resurrection and
appearances, and adds his own comment in v. 6b, the
appearance to himself in v. 8, and perhaps the
appearances in vs. 6-7. Pannenberg draws attention to
the fact that the method employed by Greek historians,
such as Herodotus, in proving a historical event was
the naming of witnesses, a method which Paul follows
here.[35] With regard to Paul's comment in v. 6a, Dodd
observes, "There can hardly be any purpose in
mentioning the fact that most of the 500 are still
alive, unless Paul is saying, in effect, 'the witnesses
are there to be questioned.'"[36] In short, Paul is
arguing historically for the resurrection of Jesus.
"The intention of this enumeration is clearly to give
proof by means of witnesses to the facticity of Jesus'
resurrection," concludes Pannenberg; " . . . one will
hardly be able to call into question Paul's intention
of giving a convincing historical proof by the
standards of that time . . ."[37]

Conzelmann's objection that Paul cannot be trying
to prove the resurrection since the Corinthians already
accepted the authority and content of the formula (vs.
1-2, 13)[38] misses the point. Of course, he is not now
trying for the first time to convince the Corinthians
of Jesus's resurrection, but he is reviewing the
evidence which underlies the crucial assertion of v.
20. Weiss also seems to misunderstand Paul's argument,
declaring it to be purely ad hominem: if Christ is not
raised, then our faith is in vain; but this cannot be

affirmed because our experience is too real.[39] Though
Paul does draw out the disastrous consequences of
denying Christ's resurrection,[40] perhaps to bring home
the gravity of just what the Corinthians were
asserting, he does not then argue, "But our experience
is too real . . ." Rather he states, "But in fact
Christ has been raised from the dead . . . (v. 20). He
appeals, not to subjective experience, but to
objective, historical fact. On Weiss's view there is
no reason to cite the formula at all; the chapter could
have begun at v. 12. The logic of Paul's argument and
his insertions and additions to the formula show that
he is recounting the historical evidence for the
resurrection of Jesus in order to undergird his
statement that Christ has been raised.

   That this understanding of the passage is correct
is evident from the famous Barth-Bultmann debate over I
Corinthians 15.[41] Barth asserted, ". . . it must be
emphasized that neither for Paul nor for the tradition,
to which we see him appealing here, was it a question
of giving . . . a 'historical proof of the
resurrection.'"[42] The expression "according to the
scriptures" twice repeated would have no meaning in a
historical proof. The "he was seen" is connected to
the "he rose again" by "and," not "then," as would be
the case if the passage aimed at historical
demonstration. The most serious objection to the
historical interpretation is that the historical fact
of Jesus's resurrection, if it occurred, is according
to verse 13 dependent upon the general resurrection of
the dead. Barth asks incredulously, "What kind of
historical fact is that reality of which [sic], . . .
is bound up in the most express manner with the
perception of a general truth, which by its nature

cannot emerge in history . . .?"[43]   The point of the
passage is actually to demonstrate the continuity of
Paul's preaching with that of the primitive church.[44]
Paul adduces the witnesses "not to confirm the fact of
the resurrection of Jesus, not for that purpose at all,
but to confirm that the foundation of the Church, so
far as the eye can see, can be traced back to nothing
else than appearances of the risen Christ."[45]   Barth
means by "appearances," not optical phenomena, but the
incomprehensible revelation of Christ.[46]   Paul's
mention of the 500, most of whom were still alive
though some had died, was intended to show that though
some of these men who had seen the Lord nevertheless
died, the ultimate victory over death would be won
through Christ's resurrection. Bultmann responded that
Barth's interpretation of I Cor 15.1-11 was simply
false exegesis.[47]   In the mind of Paul and the whole
Christian community, a historical account would be the
more meaningful if it were "in accordance with the
scriptures."   And since Paul also accepted the final
resurrection of the dead as a historical event, the
truth of Christ's resurrection could be said to depend
on the fact of the resurrection of the dead.   That
Christ's appearances were localized is evident from the
expressions "most of whom are still alive" and "last of
all" (I Cor 15.6, 7). Says Bultmann, "I can understand
the text only as an attempt to make the resurrection of
Christ credible as an objective historical fact."[48]
Although Bultmann characterizes such historical
argumentation as "fatal" because it tries to adduce
proof for the kerygma,[49] he acknowledges that Paul does
"think he can guarantee the resurrection of Christ as
an objective fact by listing the witnesses who had seen
him risen."[50]

More recently R.H. Fuller has resupported Barth's
position.[51] He acknowledges that Paul uses the list of
witnesses as evidence. But they are cited as proof,
not of the resurrection, but of the appearances. Paul
proves the appearances to show that his gospel is
identical with the original disciples', whom the
Corinthians insisted preached a gospel with no future
resurrection (I Cor 1.12;3.4). But the artificiality
of Fuller's distinction between appearances and
resurrection seems at once apparent. Of course, the
witnesses are cited as proof for the appearances--and
thereby for the resurrection. Once it is known that a
man "died" and "was buried," what better way to prove
that he "was raised" than by adducing reliable
testimony that he"appeared" alive to people after his
death (cf. Acts 1.3)? Thus, in Acts to be a witness of
the appearances is bluntly said to be a witness of the
resurrection itself (Acts 2.32; 3.15; 5.30-32).
Moreover, Paul's primary aim does not seem to be to
show continuity with the disciples' doctrine, a wholly
tangential truth which appears only incidentally in
verse 11. Paul's foremost aim is to refute the
Corinthian heresy by a step-by-step argument.[52] His
first point is to remind the Corinthians of the content
of the gospel preached to them by Paul. Then from
verse 12 he proceeds to show that the content of this
preaching would be false if the dead were not raised.
If the content of the preaching is false, then all
sorts of rueful consequences follow, with the final
result that we are of all men most to be pitied. But
the content of the preaching is true: "But in fact
Christ has been raised from the dead . . ." (I Cor
15.20); therefore, the dead are raised: ". . . the
first fruits of those who have fallen asleep. For as

by a man came death, by a man has come also the
resurrection from the dead" (I Cor 15.20b-21).
Therefore, the rueful consequences do not follow either
(I Cor 15.22-28).   It is in establishing that the
content of the preaching is not false (= Christ has
been raised) that harks back to verses 5-8; it is the
historical evidence for this fact upon which the entire
argument depends.   Hence, Paul seems to be definitely
citing these witnesses as empirical evidence for the
resurrection.[53]   Finally, there is no evidence that the
Corinthians believed the other apostles preached no
future resurrection. The bickering church described in
the first chapter is so fractionalized (with even Paul
and Jesus parties) that the problems are clearly not
reducible to the rather black-and-white issue of
whether the dead are raised.   The source of the
Corinthian heresy most likely lies in Greek secularism,
not apostolic proclamation. Whether we regard it as
fatal or not, it seems clear that Paul, as Bultmann
admitted, is definitely arguing for the historicity of
the resurrection in I Cor 15.   Dodd has drawn an
interesting comparison between the gospels and Paul on
this count: both wish to provide historical evidence
to the resurrection, the gospels by appealing to
corporate apostolic testimony, Paul by focusing on the
availability of individuals to be questioned.[54]

The Earliest Christian Apologetic

It appears to be undeniable therefore that the
first attempts to provide historical arguments for the
resurrection of Jesus are found within the pages of the
New Testament itself. But we can go further. For it
seems very likely that such an approach to the

resurrection was also characteristic of primitive
Christianity prior to the composition of the New
Testament. It is generally recognized that I Cor
15.3-7 contains a very old formula(s) reciting the
death, burial, resurrection, and appearances of
Christian.[55] Although the exact extent of the formula is
disputed,[56] it must have at least included the
appearances to Cephas and the Twelve:

. . . ὅτι Χριστὸς ἀπεθανεν ὑπὲρ τῶν ἁμαρτιων ἡμῶν κατὰ τὰς γραφάς,
και   ὅτι ἐτάφη,
και   ὅτι ἐγήγερται τῇ ἡμέρᾳ τῇ τρίτῃ κατὰ τὰς γραφάς,
και   ὅτι ὥφθη Κηφᾷ εἶτα τοῖς δώδεκα.

Now according to Paul the elements of this formula were
part of the kerygma preached by all Christian
missionaries (I Cor 15.11), part of the tradition which
Paul received (I Cor 15.3), and part of the Gospel
preached to the Corinthians when Paul evangelized
Achaia (I Cor 15.1). This means that the adduction of
witnesses to the resurrection was from earliest times
on an integral part of the Christian kerygma.[57] This
is also a prominent feature of the Lukan speeches in
Acts.[58] In this particular, Paul and Luke's
representations of the apostolic preaching are in
complete harmony.[59] This mutual confirmation strongly
suggests that the use of witnesses as confirmatory
evidence of the resurrection was no late development,
but actually characterized the apostolic preaching.
"Jesus is in fact risen from the dead, because after
his death he "appeared" to definite witnesses. That is
the post-Easter argument of the Christian community,"
concludes Mussner.[60]

    The first attempts therefore to provide historical
evidence for the resurrection were those of the
primitive gospel preachers themselves. We have
discovered that the appeal to witnesses was an

important part of the kerygma and that in the gospels
we find stress laid on the facts of the empty tomb and
appearances of Jesus, as well as apologetic motifs
countering or anticipating what would later be called
the apparent death theory, the conspiracy theory, the
subjective vision theory, and the legend theory.
Dulles's judgement appears well-founded: "A critical
sifting of the New Testament materials makes it
indubitable that the resurrection of Jesus held a place
of unique importance in the earliest Christian
apologetic."[61]

The Early Church
Early Apologists

Subsequent to the New Testament we have no
apologetic literature until 125, the church fathers of
the sub-apostolic age being more concerned with matters
of faith and practice in the churches.[62] But the need
for apologetics arose when Christians found it
necessary to defend themselves against allegations of
social crimes, and early apologists were primarily
concerned with gaining civil toleration of the new
religion. According to Dulles the shift from
intra-church literature to apologetic writing may be
largely attributed to the influence of four groups:
(1) converts often felt as educated men the need to
come to grips with the pagan philosophy they formerly
espoused and to give a justification for their
conversion; (2) philosophers began to attack
Christianity, and believers saw the necessity of a
response; (3) emperors and other civil magistrates had
to be persuaded of the legality and social
acceptability of Christianity; and (4) Jews were a

prime target for literature aimed at their conversion or condemnation.[63] As a body the apologetic literature was of two sorts: (1) political apologies, aimed at securing civil toleration, and (2) religious apologies, aimed at securing the conversion of either (a) pagans or (b) Jews. Political apologies primarily dealt with clearing up absurd rumors lodged against Christians, such as cannibalism and Dionysian banqueting. Religious apologies to Jews followed the New Testament pattern and relied most heavily on the proof from prophecy, of which Justin's D̲i̲a̲l̲o̲g̲ ̲w̲i̲t̲h̲ ̲T̲r̲y̲p̲h̲o̲ ̲t̲h̲e̲ ̲J̲e̲w̲ (ca. 155-60) is the prime example. Religious apologies to pagans were primarily critiques of the follies of popular mythology or syntheses of the best of pagan philosophy with the revealed truth of Christianity.

Arguments for the resurrection of Jesus were not often used during the first three centuries. The argument from fulfilled prophecy was considered much more effective than proofs from miracles because, according to Justin Martyr in his F̲i̲r̲s̲t̲ ̲A̲p̲o̲l̲o̲g̲y̲, the pagans simply wrote off the miracles of Christ to magic.[64] Hence, the evidential value of the resurrection lies almost exclusively in the fact that it was predicted.[65] He emphasizes that the fact that these prophecies were fulfilled in Christ can be proved by eyewitness testimony, and he challenges unbelievers to conduct a careful and thorough examination.[66] Justin does mention in his D̲i̲a̲l̲o̲g̲u̲e̲ the theory of the Jews in Matthew 28 that the disciples stole the body and adduces a purportedly official report of the Sanhedrin in this regard. ". . . Ἰησοῦ τινος Γαλιλαίου . . . , ὅν σταυρωσάντων ἡμῶν, οἱ μαθηταὶ αὐτοῦ κλέψαντες αὐτον ἀπο τοῦ μνήματος νυκτός, ὁπόθεν κατέθη ἀφηλωθεις ἀπο τοῦ σταυροῦ, πλανῶαι τους ἀνθρώπους λέγοντες ἐγηγέρθαι αὐτον ἐκ νεκρῶν και εἰς οὐρανον ἀναληλυθέναι."[67]

This document is not known today. In his Apology
(197), Tertullian mentions a report by Pilate to the
Emperor concerning Jesus's execution and the empty
tomb, as well as the rumor that the disciples had
stolen the body.[68] In another work Tertullian
derisively refers to the theory that the body of Jesus
had been removed by the gardener, who, surmises
Tertullian, feared that the trampling crowds of
visitors sure to come to the tomb would destroy his
lettuce patch![69] These brief comments are the closest
that one comes to arguments for the resurrection of
Jesus.

Apologies for the Resurrection of the Flesh

Nevertheless there is a continuous tradition
running through early church fathers which forms a
backdrop to the argument for Jesus's resurrection,
namely, the justification, over against pagan
conceptions of death and immortality, of the idea of
the resurrection of the body. The early apologists
make it evident that pagans knew of and derided this
Christian view of immortality, and the Christian
apologists briefly refer to arguments for the notion of
physical resurrection which would be later systematized
by Irenaeus, Tertullian, and others, especially in the
refutation of Christian heretics. The root of the
rejection of the resurrection of the body lay in
Greco-Roman pagan philosophy. According to Tertullian,
the heretics borrowed the pagan arguments and would not
in the absence of these be able to support their view
from Scripture.[70] In Tertullian's analysis, the
philosophers either denied immortality altogether, such

as Epicurus or Seneca, or else they adhered to the
immortality of the soul and its reincarnation in other
life-forms, as with Pythagoras, Empedocles, and the
Platonic thinkers.[71]   This had led to the popular
depreciation of and revulsion for the physical body, an
attitude which made the idea of the resurrection of the
flesh absurd and repulsive:

> Itaque haeretici inde statim incipiunt et inde
> praestruunt, dehinc et interstruunt, unde sciunt
> facile capi mentes de communione favorabili
> sensuum. an aliud prius vel magis audias [tam] ab
> haeretico quam ab ethnico, et non protenus et non
> ubique convicium carnis, in originem in materiam
> in casum, in omnem exitum eius, immundae a
> primordio ex faecibus terrae, immundioris deinceps
> ex seminis sui limo, frivolae infirmae criminosae
> molestae onerosae, et post totum ignobilitatis
> elogium caducae in originem terrae et cadaveris
> nomen, et de isto quoque nomine periturae in
> nullum inde iam nomen, in omnis iam vocabili
> mortem? 'Hancne ergo, vir sapiens, et visui et
> contactui et recordatui tuo ereptam persuadere vis
> quod se receptura quandoque sit in integrum de
> corrupto, in solidum de casso, in plenum de
> inanito, in aliquid omnino, de nihilo, et utique
> redhibentibus eam ignibus et undis et alvis
> ferarum et rumis alitum et lactibus piscium et
> ipsorum temporum propria gula? adeone autem eadem
> sperabitur quae intercidit ut claudus et luscus et
> caecus et leprosus et paralyticus revertantur, ut
> redisse non libeat, ad pristinum: an integri, ut
> iterum talia pati timeant? . . . . nimirum haec
> erunt vota carnis recuperandae, iterum cupere de
> ea evadere.' et nos quidem haec aliquanto
> honestius pro stili pudore: ceterum quantum etiam
> spurciloquio liceat, illorum [est] in congressibus
> experiri tam ethnicorum qual haereticorum.[72]

The pagans and heretics could in this light only regard
the message of the resurrection of Jesus as foolish and
offensive. Hence, early Christian thinkers found
themselves embroiled in the controversy to justify the
concept of bodily resurrection überhaupt.

Justin Martyr

Justin Martyr in his first Apology sounds a note which would characterize later defenses of the resurrection: the resurrection is vital to God's judgement of men for their deeds in this life.[73] Justin states that Christians believe with Plato that the wicked will be punished, but that in their very bodies, united with their souls, they will be tormented eternally and not merely for a thousand years, as Plato had said. In chapter 18 of that work Justin asserts that Christians believe in God more than Empedocles and Pythagoras, Plato and Socrates, because Christians expect that their bodies, though dead and buried in the earth will be revived--for nothing is impossible with God. This appeal to Jesus's word in Matt 19.26 would become a frequent citation among the defenders of the resurrection. Justin's following argument also proved influential: if it is possible that from a drop of human sperm a man composed of bones, muscles, and flesh should develop, then why should it be thought incredible that God should by His power produce from the earthly body an immortal resurrection body? It is unworthy of God's power to maintain that He is unable to do anything more than allow everything to revert to the original elements from which it was produced.[74] In Justin's Dialogue with Trypho we find an allusion to the pagan objection, noted above by Tertullian, that in the resurrection bodily infirmities and diseases would persist. According to Justin, Christ raised the dead, thus compelling men of his day to recognize him. But though they witnessed these miraculous deeds with their own eyes, they attributed them to sorcery. Jesus, however, performed these deeds in order to convince his future followers that if anyone were faithful to his teaching, then, no matter how maimed his body might be, Jesus would raise him up at his second coming entirely sound and deliver him forever from death, corruption, and pain.[75]   Later in the Dialogue Justin denounces so-called Christians, who are really godless and impious heretics, who do not espouse this doctrine.[76] These persons hold that there is no resurrection of the dead, but that the soul is taken up to heaven at the very moment of death.   One should not, Justin warns, consider such persons to be real Christians.   Here we have reference to apparently Gnostic Christians who had absorbed the pagan disdain for the physical body into the Christian religion.   It will be against such heretics as well as against the pagans that later apologists will have to defend the resurrection.

Athenagoras

Athenagoras in his Supplicatio to the Emperors Lucius Aurelius Commodus and Marcus Aurelius foreshadows another issue that would become extremely important in the controversy over the resurrection.   In rebutting the charge that Christians participate in cannibalism, he asserts that it is ridiculous to charge with cannibalism people who believe in the resurrection of the dead.[77] For if the earth will give up its dead, so will men give up the dead they have swallowed. People who believe in the resurrection believe that the body which carried out the irrational impulses of the soul will be punished with it for a man's evil deeds. Hence, it is more likely that those who do not believe in immortality would commit cannibalism than those who believe in the resurrectiton of the body.   Athenagoras admits this doctrine of resurrection may sound novel, but at least it is innocuous.   It is interesting that

we see here not only the connection between
resurrection and judgement, but also the foreshadowing
of the knotty problem of how God will raise the bodies
of those eaten by cannibals, since the same elements
are constitutive of both men's bodies.

Theophilus

In Theophilus of Antioch's Ad Autolycum, the
apologist refers to the analogy of human seed to show
that if God could create a man from nothing then surely
He can raise him from the dead.   "καὶ ἔπλασέν σε ἐξ
ὑγρᾶς οὐσίας μικρᾶς καὶ ἐλαχίστης ῥανίδος, ἥτις οὐδὲ αὐτὴ
ἦν ποτε˙ καὶ προήγαγέν σε ὁ θεὸς εἰς τόνδε τὸν βίον. . . .
τῷ δὲ ποιήσαντί σε θεῷ ἀπιστεῖς δύνασθαι σε καὶ μεταθὺ ποιῆσαι;"[78]
Here the analogy is employed somewhat differently than
by Justin, for the notion is now introduced that it is
easier to recreate something than to create it. Since
God has the power to create the body in the first
place, it follows that He has the power to recreate it
at the resurrection of the dead.   Therefore the
doctrine is not incredible. Theophilus also connects
the idea of resurrection with the judgement of God.[79]
If the unbeliever should come to believe in God now,
then God will raise up his flesh with his soul, and he
will see that he had spoken unjustly of God. To the
unbeliever's challenge to show even one person raised
from the dead, Theophilus replies: (1) one's belief
would then have no importance after having seen the
event, (2) pagans believe that Heracles and Asclepius
were raised from the dead, (3) if one disbelieves what
God says then one would be apt to disbelieve even if he
saw a dead man raised and alive.[80] Moreover, continues
Theophilus, God has given many indications for
believing Him. Here he appeals to analogies in nature,

which were to become popular in defenses of the
resurrection, such as the resurrection of seeds and
fruits and the monthly resurrection of the moon as it
waxes and wanes. Even when one is ill and loses
weight, then recovers and regains his former health, he
does not know where his flesh went and whence it came
again. Certainly it came again from food converted
into blood, but this is also the work of God. The
analogy would seem to be that as God can reconstitute
the body from foodstuffs, so He can restore it again at
the resurrection. Theophilus adds the personal note
that once he too did not believe in the resurrection,
but now having considered the matter he believes.[81]
Interestingly, the basis of his new-found faith is not
the resurrection of Jesus, but fulfilled prophecy.

Irenaeus

In Irenaeus's great Adversus haereses he deals at
length with those heretics who deny the bodily
resurrection. Irenaeus makes the link between our
resurrection and Christ more explicit. As Christ was
raised in the flesh, states Irenaeus, so shall we be.[82]
But the main link between our resurrection and Christ
is not his resurrection, but his incarnation.[83] If our
flesh were not in a position to participate in
salvation, then the Word would not have become
incarnate. But because he really took on flesh, not in
appearance but in fact, and shed his blood for us, our
flesh has received the capacity of salvation. Much of
Irenaeus's case, being directed against heretics,
concerns properly understanding the Scriptural teaching
on this doctrine, especially concepts like "spiritual
body" and the Pauline phrase, which had become a
watchword among the heretics, "Flesh and blood cannot

inherit the Kingdom of God." He shows that the
heretics misinterpret these expressions in substantival
terms, rather than in terms of spiritual orientation.[84]
These arguments, however, need not concern us, for our
interest lies in Irenaeus's contribution to the defense
of the concept of resurrection.

On this score he eloquently presses the argument
that since God created man from the dust of the earth
originally, and since it is easier to recreate than
create, then God is powerful enough to raise man from
the dead.

> Sed quoniam potens est in his omnibus, de initio
> nostro contemplari debemus, quoniam sumpsit Deus
> limum de terra et formavit hominem. Et quidem
> multo difficilius et incredibilius est, ex non
> exsistentibus ossibus et nervis et venis et
> reliqua dispositione quae est secundum hominem
> facere ad hoc ut sit et quidem animalem et
> rationabilem facere hominem, quam quod factum est
> et deinde resolutum est in terram, propter causas
> quas praediximus rursus redintegrare, licet in
> illa cesserit unde et initio nondum factus factus
> est homo . . .[85]

If God gives life to this flesh now, then why not also
in the resurrection? Irenaeus maintains that if there
is any external cause why God does not raise the dead,
then this impugns His omnipotence and freedom.[86]

He also defends a wholistic anthropology against
his opponents. A perfect and complete man consists of
body and soul together. A disembodied soul is thus not
a glorified man, but a truncated man.

> Anima autem et Spiritus pars hominis esse possunt,
> homo autem nequaquam: perfectus autem homo
> commixtio et adunitio est animae assumentis
> Spiritum Patris et admixtae ei carni quae est
> plasmata secundum imaginem Dei.[87]

Irenaeus flatly contradicts thereby the idea that the

soul ought to be released from the body for the
perfection of human nature. Rather human nature
involves the body as well as the soul and spirit, and
hence resurrection is necessary for complete human
realization.

Tertullian

Tertullian was indebted to Irenaeus in the writing
of his own treatise De resurrectione carnis, and much
of this work as well is dedicated to Scriptural
interpretations, which need not detain us. But
Tertullian does argue carefully against the pagan
objections to the resurrection, and many of his
arguments can already be found in his earlier
Apologeticus. There he ridicules those philosophers
who can believe that man can become reincarnate as an
animal or an animal as a man and yet who sneer at and
persecute a Christian who thinks that a man will return
to life as a man.[88] Like Justin, he believes that one
cannot be a Christian and deny the resurrection or use
the objections of non-Christians to that doctrine.[89]

He first attacks the notion that the flesh is
somehow unworthy of God's resurrecting it.[90] The flesh
is worthy because it is the creation of God, and while
He was fashioning it God did so with the thought of the
incarnation in mind; that is to say, man's being made
in the image of God means in the image of the incarnate
Son--a point alluded to by Irenaeus. Hence, why should
we deprecate the flesh when the Artificer by choosing
it judged it worthy and by handling made it so?
Tertullian also points out that the flesh as well as
the soul participates in sanctification during this
life and so is worthy of resurrection.

Tertullian next defends the resurrection against

anyone who should say it is outside God's power.[91]
Here again we find the important argument from God's
power to create.[92]   Almost all the sects recognize
God's creation of the world, and they should therefore
know that He has sufficient power to raise the dead.
Even in the case of those philosophers who say that God
only constructed the universe out of pre-existent
matter, it remains true that He created out of the
matter things which did not formerly exist.   So in
either case, God's power to raise the dead should be
acknowledged.

> sive enim ex nihilo deus molitus est cuncta,
> poterit et carnem in nihilum prodactam exprimere
> de nihilo: sive de materia modulatus est alia,
> poterit et carnem quocumque dehaustam evocare de
> alio. et utique idoneus est reficere qui fecit,
> quanto plus est fecisse quam refecisse, initium
> dedisse quam reddidisse. ita restitutionem carnis
> faciliorem credas institutione.[93]

We also find repeated the argument of Theophilus from
analogies in nature, such as day and night or the
seasons.

> semel dixerim, universa conditio recidiva est:
> quodcumque conveneris fuit, quodcumque amiseris
> erit: nihil non iterum est: omnia in statum
> redeunt cum abscesserint, omnia incipiunt cum
> desierint: ideo finiuntur ut fiant: nihil
> deperit nisi in salutem. totus igitur hic ordo
> revolubilis rerum testatio est resurrectionis
> mortuorum: operibus eam praescripsit deus ante
> quam litteris, viribus praedicavit ante quam
> vocibus.[94]

Tertullian even appeals to a natural analogy in the
phoenix, which he apparently accepts as a real bird:
"sed homines semel interibunt, avibus Arabiae de
resurrectione securis?"[95]   Thus, creation and analogies
of resurrection in nature make it evident that God has

the power to raise the dead.

Finally, as to the rationale for the resurrection, Tertullian lays down the entire purpose of the resurrection to the fact of judgement.[96]

> igitur si deo et domino et auctori congruen-
> tissimum est iudicium in hominem destinare de hoc
> ipso an dominum et auctorem suum agnoscere et
> observare curarit an non, idque iudicium
> resurrectio expunget, haec erit tota causa immo
> necessitas resurrectionis, congruentissima
> scilicet deo destinatio iudicii.97

Tertullian emphasizes that the plenity and completeness of God's judgement necessitates that the whole man appear before Him. It is entirely appropriate that the flesh be judged with the soul, for the flesh and the soul are in this life partners in all a man's deeds. Tertullian has a peculiar view of the soul, that it is a corporeal substance. Therefore he makes it clear that the flesh is not necessary in order for the soul to suffer in the after-life.[98] But as the soul cannot act completely without the flesh, neither can it suffer completely without the flesh. Since the flesh has also participated in sins, then it is appropriate that it be involved in suffering as well. Hence, for judgement to be equitable and complete, the flesh must be raised to life.

Later in his treatise Tertullian handles some of the typical pagan objections to the resurrection of the flesh.[99] To the objection that this would re-instate bodily diseases and infirmities, he replies, like Justin, that if in the resurrection we are changed into glory, how much more into health! It might also be demanded what good certain bodily parts will be when in the resurrection they will no longer have any function. Tertullian responds that they are retained for the

purpose of being judged. Besides, he adds, they can
have different functions, for example, the mouth will
no longer serve for eating but for praising God.
Hence, even in the resurrection these bodily parts will
glorify God.

Pseudo-Athenagoras

Perhaps the high point of argument for the
doctrine of the resurrection came in the treatise De
resurrectione attributed to Athenagoras.[100] The author
distinguishes two types of argument: one on behalf of
the truth (ὑπὲρ τῆς ἀληθείας) and one concerning the
truth (περὶ τῆς ἀληθείας).[101] The former is directed
toward those who disbelieve the doctrine of the
resurrection, the latter to those who receive the truth
gladly. He first discusses arguments on behalf of the
truth of the resurrection. Those who deny the
resurrection must prove that God is either unable or
unwilling to raise dead bodies and to restore them, if
they be decomposed.[102] The author argues first that
God is able to do this.[103] He maintains that when the
body decomposes, God knows where all the parts go, such
that He can reassemble them, and that even in the case
that men's bodies should be consumed by wild beasts,
God has the power to restore them. In this context he
has recourse to the familiar argument from creation:

> Καὶ μὴν καὶ τὴν δύναμιν ὡς ἔστιν ἀρκοῦσα πρὸς τὴν
> τῶν σωμάτων ἀνάστασιν, δείκνυσιν ἡ τούτων αὐτῶν
> γένεσις. εἰ γὰρ μὴ ὄντα κατὰ τὴν πρώτην σύστασιν
> ἐποίησεν τὰ τῶν ἀνθρώπων σώματα καὶ τὰς τούτων
> ἀρχάς, καὶ διαλυθέντα καθ᾽ ὃν ἂν τύχῃ τρόπον,
> ἀναστήσει μετὰ τῆς ἴσης εὐμαρείας ἐπ᾽ ἴσης
> γὰρ αὐτῷ καὶ τοῦτο δυνατόν.[104]

The argument from creation suffices to prove that God
can raise the dead, but here a new objection crops up:

what about men who are eaten by cannibals, such that
the same elements belong successively to two different
men?[105] The author's response to this question is to
assert that in the power and wisdom of God each species
has its own proper food and that things which are eaten
which are not proper to the species are therefore not
assimilated, but are passed on. And even if some
element were assimilated into the flesh of the eater,
it might well be non-essential to it and worked off in
time. Thus, the opponents of resurrection cannot prove
that human bodies eaten by others are fused with the
bodies of the others.[106] God is therefore able to
raise the dead.

But is He willing? For the resurrection to be
foreign to God's will it would have to be either unjust
or unworthy of Him.[107] It is unjust neither to
creation nor to man, in either body or soul, to raise
the dead. Nor is it unworthy of God, for if it is
worthy of Him to create a corruptible body, how much
more to create an incorruptible body? The resurrection
is therefore both possible for and willed by God and
ought therefore to be believed.

Turning now to arguments concerning the truth
addressed to believers, the author expounds two
Irenaean arguments. First, the nature of man involves
both body and soul.[108] God created man for his own
sake and man is properly composed of body and soul,
each having its respective functions. God made man
that he might participate in rational life and
contemplate God forever.

ἡ μεν τῆς γεωέσεως αἰτία πιστοῦται την εἰς ἀει διαμονήν, ἡ δε
διαμονη την ἀνάστασιν ἧς χωρις οὐκ ἀν διαμείνειεν ἄνθρωπος. [109]

Since man qua man is soul and body together, man cannot

survive death apart from resurrection. Secondly, the
judgement requires the resurrection of the body.[110] It
would be unjust to punish either the soul or the body
alone for deeds done with respect to the other member.
It is the man who, as the combination of both, receives
justly the judgement for his deeds. Since each man is
an individual, he must receive again at the
resurrection precisely the same body he possessed
during his lifetime. Hence, the very nature of man and
the judgement of man provide a basis for the
resurrection of the dead.

　　With these sorts of arguments, the early church
fathers sought to make the Christian doctrine of the
resurrection of the body intelligible to the
Greco-Roman world. Certain themes run throughout the
literature, indicating a continuous tradition of
apologetic argumentation. It is noteworthy how rarely
the resurrection of Jesus himself is mentioned. It
seems odd, for example, that Irenaeus should say that
the clearest proof that the resurrection concerns one's
identical earthly body is the resurrection of those
raised by Jesus, rather than Jesus's own
resurrection;[111] or again, that Theophilus, when
challenged to show one person raised from the dead,
turns not to Jesus but to Heracles and Asclepius! But
perhaps an appeal to the resurrection of Jesus would
have been question-begging, since it was by implication
the point under fire. If resurrrection in general is
impossible, then so is the resurrection of Jesus.
Hence, most thinkers concentrated their energies on
justifying even the notion of resurrection. It was not
until Celsus unleashed his attack specifically on
Jesus's resurrection that a defense of that event was
called forth.

Origen

So although the early church writers referred to
the resurrection of Christ and argued at length for the
concept of the resurrection of the body, the first
substantial apology employing arguments for Jesus's
resurrection was Origen's Contra Celsum (246), written
in response to Celsus's polemic against Christianity
True Doctrine (178). Celsus's treatise, now lost but
largely reproduced in Origen's frequent citations, was
divided into two parts: in the first, Celsus argues
against Christianity from the standpoint of a Jew; in
the second, he assumes his true role of a Hellenic
philosopher. Origen's reply to the Jewish objector
contains a lengthy defense of the miracles and the
resurrection of Jesus, which Origen calls "the greatest
of all miracles."[112] Because it is a response to
Celsus's objections, Origen's arguments cannot be
called a positive case for Christianity; nevertheless,
if his arguments are successful a positive result is
achieved, for he acknowledges as correct Celsus's
statement that believers regard Jesus as the Son of God
because he performed miracles, to which fact Origen
adds the confirmation of fulfilled prophecy.[113]

Celsus presses six objections against the
resurrection: (1) The only reason Christians believe
in the resurrection is because Jesus foretold that
after his death he would rise again.[114] Origen replies
to this rather odd reasoning that one might equally
demand of Celsus's Jew, what led you to believe except
that Moses foretold his own death and burial? The
point is apparently that both the Jewish and Christian
religions alike appeal to fulfilled prophecy. (2)
Others, as recorded for example by Herodotus, have

claimed to have returned from the dead; why then is Jesus extra-ordinary?[115] Origen replies that Celsus has here dropped the guise of the Jew, for these arguments, which could be pressed with equal force against Moses's deeds, stem from the Greek mind. At any rate Celsus admits that these Greek stories are "fantastic tales" and that the heroes probably slipped away for a time, only to reappear claiming to have returned from the dead.[116] But Jesus's case is not analogous, for he was publicly executed; had he not died on the cross before all the people, the objection might have some force. But as it is, there is no comparison between Jesus's resurrection and the Greek heroes' reappearance. But the most clear and certain proof of Jesus's resurrection, adds Origen, is the behavior of the disciples, who risked their lives for their teaching. Had they invented the story that Jesus had risen from the dead, they would not have taught this with such spirit, nor prepared others to despise death as they themselves did. This exchange between Celsus and Origen foreshadows important aspects of the contemporary debate on the resurrection. Celsus's objection raises the question of the relationship between Jesus's resurrection and the Hellenistic θεῖος ἀνήρ figure--could the resurrection accounts be no more trustworthy than and indeed influenced by such legends? And Origen's reply concerning the post-resurrection behavior of the disciples is still regarded by many who accept the historicity of the resurrection as the most convincing argument for the reality of that event. (3) The witnesses of Christ's appearances are unreliable: who saw him?--a hysterical female![117] Origen reminds his opponent that there were others as well who saw the risen Jesus. Besides, there

is no foundation in the biblical account for describing
Mary as hysterical. (4) The appearances of Christ
could be visions due to a dream or to hallucination
brought on by wishful thinking.[118] Origen rebutts this
as unconvincing, since the visions occurred in broad
daylight and the persons involved were neither mentally
unbalanced nor delirious. When Celsus states that
Jesus produced only mental impressions of his wounds in
the disciples' minds (again a remarkable anticipation
of modern para-psychological explanations of the
appearances) but did not actually appear with these
wounds, Origen retorts that Celsus selects arbitrarily
from the gospels what he wishes to believe, for the
appearance to Thomas proved the physical reality of
Christ's wounds.[119] Origen adds that prophecy
harmonizes with the fact of the risen Christ's having a
real body, although this body was of a sort in between
a solid body and a disembodied soul.[120] (5) Christ
should have appeared to the very men who executed him
and to everyone everywhere.[121] To this objection,
which was to be tirelessly batted back and forth by
succeeding generations of polemicists, Origen proposes
two solutions: (a) The unbelieving Jews lacked the
capacity to see the risen Christ, and (b) had Jesus
appeared to them they would have been smitten with
blindness.[122] (6) There is a discrepancy between the
number of angels at the tomb.[123] Origen responds that
the accounts are not contradictory. Matthew and Mark's
one angel is the one who rolls back the stone; Luke and
John's two angels are described only as standing by or
sitting in the tomb. But in drawing attention to the
discrepancies in the resurrection narratives, Celsus
has grasped the end of a thread that would eventually
threaten to unravel the whole fabric of the accounts,

as we shall see.

In book three, Celsus again raises the question of Jesus's resurrection, comparing it to Greek apotheosis stories and remarking that Jesus appeared only as a phantom.[124] By contrast, many confess that they have seen and still see today real appearances of Asclepius, not just a phantom.[125] Some have wondered whether Celsus does not contradict himself here, since in book two such tales were dismissed as fantastic.[126] If he is here asserting that these events really occurred, then a contradiction would seem unavoidable. However, despite Andresen's insistence that Celsus regards the events in 3.22-33, not as legends, but as actual events in history confirmed in the past and present, it seems questionable whether Celsus commits himself to their historicity. He always reports these events in the third person, as believed by other people.[127] As Origen notes, Celsus carefully words the objection so as not to commit himself to saying whether these heroes were gods or not.[128] One possible way of reconciling Celsus's argument would be by viewing it as a dilemma: either the stories of the Greek heroes are true or not. If they are not true (assumption of book two), then why should any more credence be given to the stories of Jesus? If they are true (assumption of book three), then why is Jesus unique? Hence, Celsus urges that though they have done such deeds, no one regards Aristeas as a god,[129] nor does any one think Abaris is a god,[130] nor do men think even Clazomenian was a god.[131] Whether this enables Celsus to escape the contradiction or not, it remains true that "In both cases analogies to the resurrection of Jesus out of the history of religion are brought forward, and they in each case serve the polemic purpose of sapping the

Christian   faith   in   the   resurrection   of   its
strength."[132]   Origen,   for   his   part,   sticks   by   his
defense in book two:

> καὶ συνεξεταζέσθω γε τὰ τῶν περὶ ἐκείνων ἱστοριῶν τῇ περι
> τοῦ ᾽Ιησοῦ. ῞Η ἐκεῖνα μὲν βούλεται ὁ Κέλσος εἶναι ἀληθῆ,
> ταῦτα δὲ ἀναγραφέντα ὑπὸ τῶν τεθεαμένων καὶ τῷ ἔργῳ
> δειξάντων τὴν ἐνάρυειαν τῆς καταλήψεως περι τοῦ τεθεωρη-
> μένου, καὶ παραστησάντων τὴν διάθεσιν ἐν οἷς προθύμως ὑπὲρ
> τοῦ λόγου αὐτου πεπόνθασιν, εἶναι πλάσματα;[133]

He goes on to upbraid Celsus for accusing others of
believing irrationally in Jesus's miracles, while he
himself appears to believe in such tales without
adducing any proof for them or any evidence that they
really happened.[134]   By contrast the gospel writers
give evidence of their veracity by their willingness to
die for the truth of what they wrote, which no one
would do for inventions or myths and incredible tales.
Look at the result in the lives of those who have been
changed by these stories, and one will find the answer
as to which records the truth.

  With Origen, then, we begin to find arguments from
a standpoint once removed from that of the New
Testament: instead of the claim "We are witnesses of
these things," we now find arguments for the
credibility of the witnesses themselves, most notably
the argument from the behavior of the disciples. The
exchange between Celsus and Origen, as Brown observes,
strikingly anticipates the classic debates of the
eighteenth century. "It illustrates the perennial
dilemma that appears to confront the believer. If the
miracles of Jesus are not unique, what then is so
special about Jesus? But if they are unique, how can
we accept them without incurring the charge of blind
credulity?"[135] With regard to the resurrection, Origen

sought to answer this dilemma by arguing for the historical credibility of the biblical accounts as over against those contained in pagan mythology and legend.

Arnobius

Arnobius of Sicca, a convert from paganism, also appealed to the resurrection of Christ, as well as his other miracles, in his The Case against the Pagans (297) in order to justify the worship of Christ over pagan deities. He, too, emphasizes that Christ's miracles were seen personally by the best witnesses and the surest authorities who handed them down to us their descendants with confirmation of no small weight.[136] To the objection that these events may never have taken place, that the men of that time were deceivers and liars, Arnobius responds that in such a case it is inexplicable that in so short a time the whole world would become filled with their religion.[137] Here we have the argument from the rapid expansion of Christianity for the historicity of the events at its roots. Arnobius also appeals, like Origen, to the behavior of the disciples, for men would not give up their lives for bare, unsubstantiated reports. Therefore, the gospel accounts of Christ's miracles and resurrection ought to be accepted as historically credible.

Eusebius

The great historian of the early church Eusebius of Caesarea composed an apology for the Christian faith entitled Demonstratio evangelica (314-18), of which book three contains a historical proof for Jesus's divinity on the basis of miracles, including the resurrection.[138] In order to provide evidence for the deity of Christ, Eusebius lists a whole catalogue of marvellous works wrought by Jesus, culminating in his resurrection, appearances, and ascension. These proofs of his divinity, states Eusebius, we have received only after subjecting them to the tests and inquiries of critical judgment.[139] Eusebius's most significant contribution to the discussion of the historicity of the resurrection is his refutation of the conspiracy theory, a refutation that would be emulated by generations of later Christian apologists.[140] He begins by arguing that it is inconsistent with the moral teaching of Jesus for the disciples to have invented the stories of their Master's miracles. It makes no sense to say that those who learned and then imparted such teaching should be base deceivers. Moreover, how could so many--that is, the twelve apostles plus the 70 disciples--agree together to lie? Suppose Jesus was an imposter who taught the disciples to deceive for selfish advantage, so that they banded together to invent all the miracles. Would such an enterprise engineered by such men ever hold together? In fact, these men went to their deaths testifying unanimously to what they had seen. Why after observing Jesus's miserable death would they stand their ground? Why would they die for him when he was dead, after they had deserted him when he was alive? Furthermore, they were unlearned men. How could they go out into all the world to preach the gospel in foreign lands? And how is it that the different testimonies of these shifty deceivers all agree? Eusebius composes a delightful speech supposedly delivered when the disciples joined together in this conspiracy: let us band together, the

speaker exhorts his fellows, to invent all the miracles
and resurrection appearances which we never saw, and
let us carry the sham even to death. Why not die for
nothing? Why dislike scourging and torture inflicted
for no good reason? Let us go out to all nations and
overthrow all their institutions and denounce their
gods. And even if we convince nobody, at least we
shall have the satisfaction of drawing down upon
ourselves the punishment for our deceit! Eusebius asks
if we can really believe that the disciples would
suffer and die for nothing. To suggest that Jesus and
the disciples were deceivers is like saying that Moses
was actually putting on a pretence to a holy life when
he gave the law or that the Greek philosopher's life
was a hypocritical show. On this sort of reasoning,
all the records of the ancients would be turned upside
down. In reality, what happened was that the disciples
gave up family, worldly pleasures, and money for what
they proclaimed. In the gospels, Matthew describes
himself in debasing terms as a publican, while Mark's
gospel, based on Peter's preaching, neglects to record
Jesus's blessing upon Peter at his great confession,
but does recount his three-fold denial of Christ. Can
such self-effacing men be thought to be rank deceivers?
As a historian Eusebius emphasizes that if we distrust
these men, then we must distrust all writers who have
compiled lives and histories and records of men. The
gospel history and secular history stand or fall
together. Eusebius also protests against those who
selectively accept the passion narratives, but reject
the miracles. If the aim of the writers was to
deceive, then they would never have recorded Jesus's
weaknesses or their failings. They would have invented
fabulous stories telling of Christ's miraculous escape

from his executioners (much as the Docetists were later
to do). Eusebius then cites the famous passage from
Josephus as confirmation of the gospel accounts and
concludes by observing on the evidence of Acts that
since myriads of Jews and Greeks believed in Christ, he
must have really done the extraordinary works
attributed to him.

Eusebius appears to have been the last great
champion of the historical argument for the
resurrection of Jesus until the dawning of the
Renaissance. As the events connected with the origin
of Christianity receded further and further into the
past, arguments from miracles and the resurrection
rested necessarily more and more upon faith in the
accuracy of the biblical documents. Already in Origen
we find a certain perplexity as to how one can
establish the historicity of events in the remote past:

> . . . σχεδὸν πᾶσαν ἱστορίαν, κἂν ἀληθὴς ᾖ, βούλεσθαι
> κατασκευαζειν ὡς γεγενημένην, καὶ καταληπτικὴν ἐμποιῆσαι
> περὶ αὐτῆς φαντασίαν, τῶν σφόδρα ἐστὶ χαλεπ ωτάτων, καὶ ἐν
> ἐνίοις ἀδύνατον. Φέρε γάρ τινα γέγειν, μὴ γεγονέναι τὸν
> Ἰλιακὸν πόλεμον, μάλιστα διὰ τὸ ἀδύνατον προσπέπλεχθαι
> λόγον περὶ τοῦ γεγνῆσθαί τινα Ἀχιλλέα θαλασσίας θεᾶς
> Θέτιδος υἱὸν καὶ ἀνθρώπου Πελέως, ἢ Σαρπηδόνα Διὸς, ἢ
> Ἀσκάλαφον καὶ Ἰάλμενον Ἄρεος, ἢ Αἰνείαν Ἀφροδίτης· πῶς
> ἂν κατασχευάσαιμεν τὸ τοιοῦτον, μάλιστα θλιβόμενοι ὑπὸ τοῦ
> οὐκ οἶδ᾽ ὅπως παρυδανθέντος πλάσματος τῇ κεκρατηκυία
> παρὰ πᾶσι δοξῃ περὶ τοῦ ἀληθῶς γεγονέναι τὸν ἐν Ἰλίῳ
> πόλεμον Ἑλλήνων καὶ Τρώων;[141]

The same difficulty applies to the gospel accounts of
Christ, he acknowledges.[142] He confesses that

> αἱ μὲν τεράστιοι δυνάμεις τοὺς κατὰ τὸν χρόνον τοῦ κυρίου
> γενομένους προκαλεῖσθαι ἐπὶ τὸ πιστεύειν ἐδύναντο· οὐκ ἔσωζον
> δὲ τὸ ἐμφατικὸν μετὰ χρόνους πλείονας ἤδη καὶ μύθους εἶναι
> ὑπονοηθεῖσαι. πλεῖον γὰρ τῶν τότε γενομένων δυνάμεων ἰσχύει
> προς πειθω ἢ νῦν συνεξεταζομένη ταῖς δυνάμεσι προφητεία,
> κἀκείναις ἀπιστεῖσθαι ὑπὸ τῶν ἐρευνώντων αὐτὰς κωλύουσα.[143]

But of course even the proof from prophecy presupposes

that the prophesied events occurred, and this is a
historical matter. Origen, as well as Arnobius and
Eusebius after him, felt that he was able to argue
historically for the miracles and resurrection of
Jesus. Their arguments were mainly refutations of
theories advanced to explain away the testimony of the
New Testament writers. According to Origen, Arnobius,
and Eusebius, those who denied Christ's miracles
dismissed them on either of two grounds: sorcery or
deceit.[144] The allegation that Jesus was a sorcerer
would soon become only a curious relic of antiquity,
but the second charge, which was urged against the
resurrection, that Jesus or his disciples were
charlatans, was to assume a predominant role, along
with the natural explanations of the resurrection
suggested by Celsus, in the rationalistic attacks of
the Enlightenment upon Christianity. The arguments of
Origen, Arnobius, and Eusebius would then be taken up
and restated in order to turn back these objections.
Their insistence on the credibility of the witnesses,
the moral integrity of the disciples, their unflinching
testimony even unto death, and the rapid spread of
early Christianity was to be the mainstay of the
Christian response to the Deistical attacks of the
seventeenth and eighteenth centuries.

The Middle Ages
The Dearth of Historiography

As we move into the Middle Ages and the events of
the New Testament sink into historical obscurity, we
find less and less reliance on historical reasoning to
establish the truth of the Christian faith. This lack
of historical argumentation reflected the dearth of

historical methodology in general. In contrast to the
Byzantine lands, the West saw a period of intellectual
and cultural decline that lasted from the fifth to the
eleventh centuries. Only in ecclesiastical circles
were literacy and learning preserved, for the populace
at large was to a great extent illiterate. Most
medieval histories of this time, of which Bede's
Ecclesiastical History of the English People covering
the years 597-731 probably ranks as the greatest,
consisted of chronicles simply listing events and their
dates. During the decades around 900 historiography
almost completely disappeared. For the medieval
historians, the biblical writers and the church fathers
on the one hand with the classical writers and poets on
the other counted as "authors," that is to say,
authorities, whose testimony was not questioned. Their
successors counted merely as "writers" or "compilers,"
who adduced the testimony of authorities. Thus,
verbatim reiteration became a virtue, and a writer
describing the history of the recent past, for which no
authorities could be adduced, often felt obliged to
apologize for writing in his own words. The character
of medieval historical writing as reiteration of
authorities was largely determined by Isidore Bishop of
Seville (d. 636), who argued in his Etymologies that
since history, as contrasted to both fable and myth,
narrates what truly took place, it must be an
eyewitness account. Therefore, the narration of past
events is simply a matter of compilation of the
testimonies of authorities, who were taken to be
eyewitnesses. Writing history consisted of copying
one's sources. This viewpoint naturally discouraged
the writing of history of the remote past during the
Middle Ages, but instead channeled energies into the

writing of contemporary history, which would end in the
present and for parts of which eyewitnesses could still
be found. While the eleventh and twelfth centuries
experienced a revival of culture and learning, this had
little effect on historiography. Although there were
important exceptions, such as the forerunner of modern
historians William of Malmesbury (d. 1143), history
continued in the main to be a recapitulation of
authorities; by the thirteenth century history as a
literary form had collapsed back into chronicle, and
the historians of the thirteenth century made no
progress over those of the twelfth. It is interesting
that when in 1286 the authorities of the University of
Paris drew up a booklist of all the texts necessary for
basic reading at the university, only three texts out
of 140 were historical. It was not until the Italian
Renaissance and the humanists of the fifteenth century
that modern historiography was born and not until even
later that history would become a widely read literary
type. Beryl Smalley sums up the situation:

> To write the history of the past in the Middle
> Ages meant copying and compiling: it was not
> creative. A critical study of the remote past, as
> distinct from mere compilation of earlier sources,
> called for tools and equipment which were lacking
> in the Middle Ages.[145]

Thus to expect a historical proof on the part of
medieval writers of the events narrated in the gospels
would be to expect an anomaly. Indeed with rare
exceptions medieval scholars could not even read
Greek.[146]

What then could be done to commend rationally the
truth of the Christian faith to unbelievers? Some
thinkers, epitomized by Anselm, sought to prove the

Deity and incarnation of Christ (and hence the truth of
the biblical books authorized by him) from a priori
reasoning alone. As Anselm's dialogue partner at the
end of cur Deus homo confesses,

> Rationabilia et quibus nihil contradici possit
> quae dicis, omnia mihi videntur; et per unius
> quaestionis quam proposuimus solutionem, quidquid
> in novo veterique testamento continetur, probatum
> intelligo. Cum enim sic probes deum fieri hominem
> ex necessitate, ut etiam si removeantur pauca quae
> de nostris libris posuisti . . . , non solum
> Iudaeis sed etiam paganis sola ratione
> satisfacias, et ipse idem deus-homo novum condat
> testamentum et vetus approbet: sicut ipsum
> veracem esse necesse est confiteri, ita nihil quod
> in illis continetur verum esse potest aliquis
> diffiteri.[147]

Anselm's deductive approach circumvented the need for
any investigation of historical facts, since everything
was proved by a rational necessity. On the other hand,
we also find very early on and then with increasing
sophistication in the thirteenth century a
philosophical framework developed which was amenable to
historical argumentation, even if devoid itself of such
argumentation. According to this approach, one
supported the authority of Scripture by the empirical
signs of credibility, mainly miracle and prophecy. We
find this framework enunciated in a rudimentary way in
Augustine and developed more fully in Aquinas.

Augustine

The Bishop of Hippo adhered to a strong view of
biblical authority, taking the Bible as the inspired
and hence inerrant Word of God. He believed that if it
were admitted that there is one false statement in the
Scriptures, their authority would be destroyed.[148] The

authority of Scripture he held even above the
pronouncements of the Church, declaring that of the
canonical books of Scripture alone does he hold the
authors to be completely free from error.[149]
Everything recorded in the Scriptures must therefore be
absolutely believed.[150] Augustine's attitude toward
biblical authority was to guide thought on the question
of authority throughout the Middle Ages. Küng
observes,

> . . . it was above all St. Augustine who . . .
> regarded man as merely the instrument of the Holy
> Spirit; the Spirit alone decided the content and
> form of the biblical writings, with the result
> that the whole Bible was free of contradictions,
> mistakes and errors, or had to be kept free by
> harmonizing, allegorizing, or mysticizing. St.
> Augustine's influence in regard to inspiration and
> inerrancy prevailed throughout the Middle Ages and
> right into the modern age.[151]

Given such a view of biblical authority, one might
expect that for Augustine and the medievals the truth
of the Christian faith was simply given by authority.
Sometimes Augustine does give such an impression. He
asserts that one must first believe before he can
know.[152] This sentiment is expressed in his frequent
reference to the LXX Isaiah 7:9: "Unless you believe,
you shall not understand." The Augustinian principle
of fides quaerens intellectum was to guide all medieval
thinkers in the Augustinian tradition. On the other
hand, Augustine makes it clear that he is neither a
fideist nor a simple authoritarian. He holds that
reason and authority co-operate in bringing a man to
faith.[153] Authority demands belief and prepares man
for reason, and reason leads in turn to understanding
and knowledge. But at the same time reason is not
entirely absent from authority, for a person has to

consider whom to believe, and the highest authority belongs to truth when it is clearly known. Elsewhere Augustine, extrapolating on Isaiah 7:9, advises, understand that you may believe; believe that you may understand.[154] This suggests that authority and reason are not separate and successive, but concomitant and complementary in leading a person to faith. Augustine's statements that imply that belief precedes knowledge should probably be understood in terms of full-orbed, saving knowledge of God, not in terms of intellectual knowledge of certain truths about God. Copleston explains:

> It is not that Augustine failed to recognize, still less that he denied, the intellect's power of attaining truth without revelation . . . He knew quite well that rational arguments can be adduced for God's existence, for example, but it was not so much the mere intellectual assent to God's existence that interested him as the real assent, the positive adhesion to the will of God, and he knew that in the concrete such an adhesion to God requires divine grace . . . If there was a question of convincing someone that God exists, Augustine would see the proof as a stage or as an instrument in the total process of the man's conversion and salvation: he would recognize the proof as in itself rational, but he would be acutely conscious, not only of the moral preparation necessary to give a real and living assent to the proof, but also of the fact that, according to God's intention for man in the concrete, recognition of God's existence is not enough, but should lead on, under the impulse of grace, to supernatural faith in God's revelation and to a life in accordance with Christ's teaching. Reason has its part to play in bringing a man to faith, and, once a man has the faith, reason has its part to play in penetrating the data of faith; but it is the total relation of the soul to God which primarily interests Augustine.[155]

In this sense, belief precedes the saving knowledge of

God and true understanding, but it does not precede
intellectual grasp of truths about God.

As Augustine indicates, reason is involved even in
the use of authority as a basis for faith, for a man
must determine which authority to believe. According
to Augustine, it is our duty to consider what men or
what books we are to believe in order to rightly
worship God.[156] As Gerhard Strauss in his analysis of
Augustine's doctrine of Scripture explains, for
Augustine the Scripture is absolutely authoritative and
inerrant in itself, but that does not mean it carries
credibility in itself.[157] Therefore, he must find
certain signs or _indicia_ of credibility to make its
authority evident. On the basis of these signs, it is
credible to believe that Scripture possesses divine
authority and therefore, as the authority, can demand
belief. One indication of Scripture authority which
Augustine mentions is the doctrine of monotheism. He
argues that we ought to believe those who summon us to
worship one God rather than man.[158] But while this
would eliminate polytheistic religion, it would not
vindicate Christianity over against Judaism. So
Augustine must have additional signs if he is to show
that the New Testament possesses divine authority. The
principal signs adduced by Augustine on behalf of the
authority of the whole of Scripture are miracle and
prophecy.[159] Strauss explains that while the
Scriptures are only one among many offering the way of
salvation, the Scriptures alone have miracles and
prophecies which make it clear that they have genuine
authority.[160] These signs make it credible to believe
that the Scripture is the true authority. Now this
seems to imply that reason for Augustine actually
precedes authority, for it is by reason of the signs

that we accept Scripture as authoritative. But this
seems to flatly contradict what Augustine says
concerning the precedence or at least concomitance of
authority with regard to reason. The solution to this
discrepancy seems to lie in the concept of authority
possessed by the medievals. For us history stands
within the realm of reason as one of the human
sciences, but for the medievals, who lacked the
historical method, this cannot be said. As Lang points
out, the medieval concept of auctoritas embraced the
whole authoritative tradition of past knowledge, which
must be re-digested in the present by reason.[161]
Gradually in the course of the development of
scholasticism, auctoritas became confined to
theological traditions alone, to the supernatural
truths of faith. Originally, however, the
auctoritas/ratio problem was not just the relation of
faith and reason, but of the whole spectrum of past
knowledge and our present understanding. It seems that
for Augustine knowledge of the past still belonged to
the realm of authority. According to Augustine,
knowledge consists in what is (1) seen or (2)
believed.[162] To see that something is true may be
either (a) by means of physical perception or (b) by
means of rational demonstration. To believe that
something is true is to accept it on the testimony of
others. Belief is knowledge based upon the witness of
others of something which is not present. Hence, with
regard to God's acts in history and prophecy, Augustine
says that the trustworthiness of temporal things either
past or future can be believed rather than known by the
intelligence.[163] But what this seems to imply is that
believing upon the basis of historical testimony
belongs not to the realm of reason, but authority.

This is in fact what Augustine says. For just prior to
his assertion that one must believe before he can know,
Augustine states that one should believe in God because
this is taught in the books of the men who have left
their testimony in writing that they lived with the Son
of God and saw things which could not have happened if
there were no God.[164] Dulles comments, " . . .
Augustine proposes an approach to the existence of God
that is integral with and inseparable from his belief
in miracles and in the Christian testimony. The normal
order is first to believe such matters, and then later
to arrive at some rational understanding of them."[165]
Hence, to accept the authority of Scripture on the
basis of the fact of miracles is to accept its
authority on the basis of another authority, since for
Augustine historical testimony lay in the realm of
authority, not reason. We today, because we do not
regard history as part of authority, would probably say
that Augustine's position is that one accepts the
authority of Scripture on the basis of reason (the
historical facts of miracle and prophecy) and that on
the basis of the authority of Scripture one places
one's faith in God and that in the light of that faith
one acquires ever deeper saving knowledge of God. This
is not to re-interpret Augustine, but simply to
recognize a linguistic difference in the way we use the
words "authority" and "reason." We would say that to
provide grounds in miracle and prophecy for accepting
Scripture as the one true authority among competing
authorities is to accept it on the basis of reason, but
Augustine, while agreeing with the procedure, would
still say authority precedes reason, since historical
testimony is authority.

Of course, the inevitable question arises, why

ought one to accept the historical testimony of the
gospel writers to miracle and fulfilled prophecy? The
same question could be asked of the classical writers.
That is to say, Augustine did not place the testimony
of the gospel writers in the realm of auctoritas
because their writings are Scriptures, but because they
are history. It is the fact that the miracles and
fulfilled prophecies are not in the present but in the
past that makes testimony to them authority.
Therefore, the question might be asked of all
historical testimony whatever why one should accept its
truth. Now clearly, if Augustine is to avoid
circularity, he cannot appeal to the authority of
Scripture to guarantee these events, since it is to
these very events that he appeals to establish the
credibility of Scripture's claim to authority. That
means that he must either come up with some basis for
accepting the truth of the evangelists' testimony to
miracles and prophecies or else abandon the point.
Given the medieval lack of historiography, however, the
first option was not greatly open to him. Therefore,
he chooses the second.

He frankly admits that the books and documents in
which the story of Christ is told belong to ancient
history, which anyone may refuse to believe.[166]
Therefore, he leaves these and turns to the miracle of
the Church as the basis for accepting the credibility
of Scripture.[167] He extols the universality of the
Church, the sufferings of its martyrs, the chastity and
moral earnestness of its members. He states that while
visible miracles were at first necessary, now that the
Catholic Church has been founded and diffused
throughout the world, miracles are no longer
necessary.[168] He maintains that we should still

believe those who proclaimed miracles, though only a
few actually saw them, for miracles were then necessary
because the people were not yet fit to reason about
divine and invisible things. But now the very
existence of the mighty and universal Church is an
overwhelming sign that what the Scripture says is true.
One must be careful here not to think that Augustine in
now basing the authority of Scripture upon the
authority of the church. As we have seen he held the
authority of the Bible above even that of the church.
His appeal for the credibility of Scripture authority
is still to miracle, only now he has made the miracle,
not those of Jesus and the apostles, which are
irretrievably removed in the past and thus incapable of
being established, but the contemporary miracle evident
to all, the Church itself. This miracle actually
serves in a way to prove the others as well. For as he
says in De civitate dei, even if the unbeliever rejects
all the biblical miracles, we are still left with the
one stupendous miracle, which is all one needs, of the
whole world believing, without the benefit of miracles,
the miracle of the resurrection.[169] This would seem
the closest Augustine comes to historical argumentation
for the resurrection. Interestingly, by turning to the
contemporary miracle of the church as the chief sign of
Scripture's credibility, Augustine, according to his
conception of reason and authority, implicitly based
Scripture's credibility on reason, for the sign was no
longer in the past, in the realm of authority where it
could only be believed, but was now in the present
where it could be seen. Be that as it may, however, we
find in Augustine, coupled with his strong view of
biblical authority, the rudiments of the philosophical
framework of the signs of credibility which Aquinas

shall develop.

Thomas Aquinas

Early scholasticism followed the Anselmian pattern
of trying to provide credibility for the Scriptures by
systematically demonstrating by means of reason the
coherence and intelligibility of the Christian
faith.[170]   During the twelfth century, however, it
became increasingly evident that this a priori approach
often failed to carry full conviction. Thus, in the
thirteenth century, we find growing weight given to
external signs of credibility. Aquinas rejected the
Anselmian approach of proving truths of faith through
the employment of natural reason and adopted instead
the philosophical framework of the signs of credibility
for Scripture. Aquinas's Summa contra gentiles
(1258-64), composed to combat the challenge of
Greco-Arabic philosophy, is the greatest apologetic
treatise of the Middle Ages and so deserves our careful
consideration.

In this work Aquinas begins by making a
distinction within truths about God.[171] There are
truths about God that wholly surpass the capability of
human reason, such as the doctrine of the Trinity. On
the other hand, there are truths about God which lie
within the grasp of natural reason, such as the
existence of God. In the first three volumes of his
Summa Aquinas attempts to demonstrate by means of
natural reason this latter body of truths, including
the existence and attributes of God, the structure of
creation, the nature and end of man, and so forth. But
in the fourth volume, when Aquinas turns to the
subjects of the Trinity, the incarnation, the

sacraments, and the final things, he abruptly alters
his methodology: such things are to be proved by the
authority of Holy Writ, not by natural reason.[172]
Because these doctrines surpass reason, they are
properly objects of faith.[173] But it is very important
to understand why. according to Aquinas, these truths
surpass natural reason. Although one is apt to take
Aquinas to mean that these truths are mysteries,
doctrines "above logic" as it were, this is not the way
he defines his terms. Thomas holds that truths of
faith surpass reason in that they are empirically
indemonstrable.[174] He makes no suggestion that these
doctrines somehow transcend Aristotelian logic; it
seems to be primarily a matter of lack of empirical
data that distinguishes truths of faith from truths of
reason. Thus, while the existence of God may be
demonstrated from His effects, the truth of the Trinity
cannot be so demonstrated. Similarly, the
eschatological resurrection cannot be empirically
proved because there is no empirical data for this
future event. Thomas elsewhere makes it clear that
neither can truths of faith be demonstrated by reason
alone. He maintains that only strictly demonstrable
arguments must be used to prove truths of reason and
that arguments (such as Anselm's in Cur Deus homo?)
which attain no more than a degree of probability must
not be used to prove truths of faith, for the very
insufficiency of these arguments is counter-
productive.[175] Aquinas's position is thus reminiscent
of Augustine's distinction between seeing and
believing. Truths accessible to natural reason must be
capable of strict, rational demonstration from
empirical premisses and can therefore be said to be
objects of knowledge, while truths neither empirically

evident nor rationally demonstrable surpass reason and
are therefore objects of faith.

But this implies for Aquinas neither fideism nor
blind authoritarianism, for he proceeds to argue that
in the realm of truths that surpass reason, God
provides signs in the form of miracles and fulfilled
prophecy that serve to confirm these truths, while not
demonstrating them directly.[176] Thus, the truths of
faith taken together as a whole share in the quality of
credibility; "Et sic sunt visa ab es qui credit: non
enim crederet nisi videret ea esse credenda, vel
propter evidentiam signorum vel propter aliquid
hujusmodi."[177] These signs, which later theology was
to call the "motives of credibility," are described by
Aquinas as confirmations of truths of faith:

> Sed quia sermo propositus confirmatione indiget ad
> hoc quod recipiatur, nisi sit per se manifestus;
> ea autem quae sunt fidei, sunt humanae rationi
> immanifesta: necessarium fuit aliquid adhiberi
> quo confirmaretur sermo praedicantium fidem. Non
> autem confirmari poterat per aliqua principia
> rationis per modum demonstrationis: cum ea quae
> sunt fidei, rationem excedant. Oportuit igitur
> aliquibus indiciis confirmari praedicantium
> sermonem quibus manifeste ostenderetur huiusmodi
> sermonem processisse a Deo, dum praedicantes talia
> operarentur, sanando infirmos, et alias virtutes
> operando, quae non posset facere nisi Deus . . .
> Fuit autem et alius confirmationis modus: ut, dum
> praedicatores veritatis vera invenirentur dicere
> de occultis quae postmodum manifestari possunt,
> eis crederetur vera dicentibus de his quae homines
> experiri non possunt. Unde necessarium fuit
> donum prophetiae, per quod futura, et ea quae
> communiter homines latent, Deo revelante, possent
> cognoscere et aliis indicare . . . [178]

Aquinas went so far as to speak of these signs as
arguments and proofs:

> Haec enim divinae Sapientiae secreta ipsa divina

Sapientia, quae omnia plenissime novit, dignata est
hominibus revelare, quae sui praesentiam et doctrinae et inspirationis veritatem convenientibus
argumentis ostendit, dum ad confirmandum ea, quae
naturalem cognitionem excedunt, opera visibiliter
ostendit, quae totius naturae superant facultatem;
videlicet in mirabili curatione languorum, mortu-
orum suscitatione, caelestium corporum mirabili
immutatione, et, quod est mirabilius, humanarum
mentium inspiratione, ut idiotae et simplices, dono
Spiritus Sancti repleti, summam sapientiam et
facundiam in instanti consequerentur.
Quibus inspectis, praedictae probationis efficacia, non armorum violentia, non voluptatum
promissione, et, quod est mirabilissimum, inter
persecutorum tyrannidem, innumerabilis turba non
solum simplicium sed etiam sapientissimorum
hominum ad fidem christianam convolavit; in qua
omnem humanum intellectum excedentia praedicantur,
voluptates carnis cohibentur, et omnia quae in
mundo sunt haberi contemni docentur . . . 179

In his later _Summa_ Aquinas even states that Christ's
miracles are sufficient to demonstrate his divinity.[180]
These remarks make it clear that there are for Aquinas
good reasons to accept the truths of faith as a whole.
The proofs of miracle and prophecy are compelling, but
indirect. That is to say, the Trinity, for example,
remains a truth of faith because it cannot be
demonstrated directly by any argument; but insofar as
all the truths of faith together have the signs of
credibility, there are sufficient reasons to believe in
the Trinity. Hence, an opponent may be convinced of
the truths of faith on the basis of the authority of
Scripture as confirmed by God with miracles.[181] Thus,
Aquinas's doctrine may be exhibited in three steps:
(1) Fulfilled prophecy and miracles make it credible
that the Scriptures taken together as a whole are a
revelation from God. (2) As a revelation from God,
Scripture is absolutely authoritative. (3) Therefore,
the doctrines taught by Scripture that cannot be proved
demonstratively by empirical reasoning, such as the

Trinity and incarnation, are accepted by faith on the authority of Scripture. Hence, for Aquinas it is on the authority of Scripture that we accept truths of faith, but it is the role of prophecy and miracle to identify that what we have is, indeed, divine Scripture. In this sense, they are signs that make it credible to believe that the Bible is Holy Scripture, is revelation, and is therefore authoritative.

According to Van Hove and Lang, a miracle was Aquinas's most important sign of credibility.[182] For Thomas a miracle is something that is wonderful (that is, naturally inexplicable) in itself, and not merely with reference to this person or that.[183] This implies that a miracle is an event caused by God; indeed, Aquinas states that properly speaking, miracles are works done by God outside the order usually observed in things.[184] Since God acts by free will and not as a mechanically operating cause, He can produce effects in the world without intermediate causes, and hence miracles are possible for Him.[185] The fact that He sometimes works independently of the natural order displays that the order of nature is the result of His free will and not a determined system emanating from Him with natural necessity. When God performs a miracle, He does not act contrary to nature strictly speaking, for nature as His creation is disposed to be acted upon by God.[186] His acts may be outside the ordinary course of events, but not contrary to nature. Of God's miracles, Aquinas lists three orders: (1) miracles that only God can do, but never nature (for example, making the sun stand still), (2) miracles that nature can do as well as God, but not in the same order (for example, causing life after death), and (3) miracles that nature and God can both perform (for

example, causing rain).[187]   The first two orders admit
of miracles of differing degrees of magnitude. Aquinas
points out that only God can be properly said to
perform miracles.[188]   Since all created beings are part
of nature, and a miracle has no natural cause, it
necessarily follows that only God can work miracles.
Even invisible creatures such as angels or demons can
only produce effects that are proper to their created
natures. They may do works that appear to be miracles
to us, but this is only because we do not discern their
causal activity.[189]   At the same time, Aquinas hastens
to add, God may do a miracle through an angel or saint
by His power.

How do miracles serve to confirm the truths of
faith? Aquinas answers,

> Respondeo dicendum, quod divinitus conceditur
> homini miracula facere, propter duo. Primo
> quidem, et principaliter ad confirmandam veritatem
> quam aliquis docet: quia enim ea quae sunt fidei
> humanam rationem excedunt, non possunt per
> rationes humanas probari, sed oportet quod
> probentur per argumentum divinae virtutis: ut dum
> aliquis facit opera quae solus Deus facere potest,
> credantur ea quae dicuntur, esse a Deo . . .
> Secundo ad ostendendam praesentiam Dei in homine
> per gratiam Spiritus Sancti . . .[190]

With this in mind, Thomas affirms, "Respondeo dicendum,
quod miracula facta sunt a Christo propter
confirmationem doctrinae ejus, et ad ostendendam
virtutem divinam in ipso."[191]   But do Christ's miracles
demonstrate his divinity?[192]   Aquinas answers
decisively that Christ's miracles demonstrate his deity
in three ways: (1) The very nature of the works he
performed totally surpasses the capability of any
created power and therefore could have been wrought
only by divine power. (2) He worked miracles through

his own power and not through prayer as did others.
(3) His teaching, confirmed by his miracles, was that
he was God.   To the objection that others have done
miracles of equal magnitude with Christ's, Thomas
replies that in his virgin birth, resurrection, and
ascension he did what no other has done.   With this
remark, we may see how closely Aquinas's apologetic
approximates an argument for Christianity based on the
resurrection.

     In fact, Aquinas, in answering the question
whether the proofs offered by Christ sufficiently
manifested the truth of his resurrection, answers that
they did so in two ways: (1) by the evidence of
witnesses and (2) by proofs or signs.[193] By witnesses,
however, Aquinas means the angelic witnesses and the
testimony of prophecy used by Christ, not historical
witnesses. By signs, he means the empirical reality of
Christ's risen body and the miraculous properties it
possessed.   Taken together in a cumulative way, these
arguments   are   sufficient   proof   of   Christ's
resurrection.   It is evident that Aquinas means
sufficient for the disciples, not for us. Only if one
accepts the Scriptural account are these evidences
proof today of the resurrection.   Aquinas simply
asserts the fact of the miracles which serve to confirm
the truths of faith.

     Thus   the   crucial   problem   for   Aquinas   is
historical: how to prove that fulfilled prophecy or
miracle ever occurred.   There is the danger of
reasoning in a circle: fulfilled prophecy and miracle
confirm that the Scripture is from God; therefore what
it teaches is authoritatively true; therefore the
miracles and fulfilled prophecy taught by Scripture
actually occurred.   In all fairness, it must be said

that Aquinas never closes this circle; he leaves the
historical question unanswered. But it is a very short
step from here to adding historical arguments for the
historicity of these signs of credibility. Dulles has
observed,

> Doubtless the undeveloped state of textual
> criticism and of historical science at the time
> would have made it impossible to construct a
> full-blown apologetic for Christianity through
> miracles, prophecies, and other historical signs
> of revelation. This approach, which became
> prevalent in the 19th century, fits well with the
> theory of credibility worked out by the
> scholastics . . .[194]

It might be thought that such an approach would be
barred for Aquinas, since events like miracles lie in
the past and so are not any more perceptible to the
sense than future events. Thus, the resurrection of
Jesus would have to remain as much a truth of faith as
the eschatological resurrection. This conclusion,
however, would seem hasty. For Aquinas does not
maintain that an object must be directly perceptible by
the senses in order to be demonstrated empirically. It
can be demonstrated to exist by means of its empirical
effects, as with the case of God. But this would seem
to leave the door open for a historical proof. For
past events, unlike future events, have traces in the
present, such that one could reason from certain
effects back to an event as their historical cause.
Aquinas himself actually adumbrates such argumentation,
for referring to the miraculous signs of credibility,
he says,

> Haec autem tam mirabilis mundi conversio ad fidem
> christianam indicium certissimum est praeteritorum
> signorum, ut ea ulterius iterari necesse non sit,
> cum in suo effectu appareant evidenter. Esset

> enim omnibus signis mirabilius, si, ad credendum
> tam ardua et ad operandum tam difficilia et ad
> sperandum tam alta, mundus absque mirabilibus
> signis inductus fuisset$_{195}$a simplicibus et
> ignobilibus hominibus . . .

Taken over from Augustine, this argument--that without miraculous events at its inception, it is impossible to explain the origin of Christianity and the transformed lives of its adherents--is still pressed by many Christian thinkers today.

The Middle Ages, therefore, did not argue historically in a substantial way for the resurrection of Jesus. Rather the theologians of this period progressively elaborated a framework within which miracles such as the resurrection possessed evidential value for the truth of the Christian faith. Natural reason can establish certain of the Christian truths without aid from revelation. Those truths that cannot be demonstrated by reason are to be accepted by faith on the authority of Scripture. We can be sure that the Bible is truly divine Scripture because of the various signs of credibility. So the medieval thinkers did not advocate a blind submission to the authority of Scripture without attempting to provide a warrant. It is noteworthy that although they did not presuppose the authority of the Scripture, they did assume the unity of Scripture in their argument. Scripture <u>as a whole</u> receives the signs of credibility. The notion that some parts of Scripture might be false and other parts historically accurate was foreign to them. Scripture was taken as a block, and the signs confirmed it as an entirety, not just at the point of confirmation. The concept of treating the Scripture as one would any ordinary fallible document was yet to come.

About the only proof offered by the medieval

thinkers of the historial signs, such as Jesus's
miracles, was the origin and growth of Christianity.[196]
Because they lacked the historical method, they could
not argue in any substantial way for the historicity of
the events recorded in the gospels. Lang concludes,

> Even though the goal of grounding the faith was
> already seen in the proof of the external
> credibility of revelation and securing the faith
> fell to the criteria of credibility, the
> scholastics did not occupy themselves thoroughly
> with their development. The reliability of the
> gospels and the correctness of their traditional
> exegesis admitted of no doubt. The reports of
> miracles were also generally recognized as
> certain. One only needed to allude to them; they
> had no need of a critical guarantee. Therefore,
> one could usually content oneself with a list of
> the criteria of cerdibility without having to
> verify more closely their historical facticity or
> their philosophical power of demonstration.[197]

Later thinkers, such as Scotus, sometimes included
signs of credibility which were historical in
character.[198] During the fourteenth century Galfridus
Hardeby in De vita evangelica (1360) argued for
Christianity from miracles, but his only proof that
miracles had occurred was that the miraculous spread of
Christianity was a visible miracle to all men.[199]
Similarly Heinrich von Langenstein in 1396 listed
historical signs of credibility, but stopped short of
historical argumentation because, according to Lang,
Christianity had not yet encountered opposition on that
score. Nor was there as yet a genuine historical
consciousness. But by the time Christianity will have
emerged from the Reformation, both of those
deficiencies will have been remedied, and modern
apologetics will be born.

SECTION II

THE MODERN PERIOD

The Eighteenth Century Flowering of the
Historical Argument for the Resurrection

The eighteenth century, writes John Orr, "was
undoubtedly the richest period for apologetical works
in all the long history of Christianity."[1] In terms of
sheer quantity of output, this verdict can hardly be
disputed. Year after year in England, France, and
Germany, scores of books and pamphlets flowed from the
presses boldly proclaiming and defending the truth of
the Christian religion. It was during this outpouring
of apologetic treatises that historical apologetics and
in particular the historical argument for the
resurrection of Jesus evolved as a means of defending
Christianity and assumed the predominant role in that
defense. Indeed, Dulles speaks of the eighteenth
century's "almost exclusive insistence on Biblical and
historical evidences" in support of the truth of
Christianity.[2] The use of historical arguments in a
substantive way to defend the historicity of Jesus's
resurrection and biblical faith in general appears,
however, to reach at least as far back as Hugo
Grotius's De veritate religionis christianae published
in 1627 and then, after suddenly gaining momentum
around the turn of the century, to have climaxed 167
years later in the eighteenth century with William
Paley's A View of the Evidences of Christianity in
1794. The little more than a century and a half
separating these two works saw the case for
Christianity based on the historical evidence for

Jesus's miracles, of which his resurrection was always
taken to be the supreme instance, become the principal
mode of defense on the part of the proponents of
Christianity.

Its Provocation by Deism

What accounts for the remarkable productivity of
Christian apologists during this period?   To those
familiar with the literature of the era, there can be
little doubt of the answer: Deism, and especially,
English Deism.   Roughly coinciding with this same time
span, there arose the movement of modern free thought,
which, as a part of its rejection of all forms of
authoritarianism and traditionalism, assailed the
Christian religion in favor of a religion of nature.
Their attacks called forth a deluge of apologetic
literature, and it was in the crucible of this
controversy with Deism that the historical argument for
the miracles and resurrection of Jesus was worked out.
Although Deism is generally associated with
eighteenth century England and its inception traced to
Lord Herbert of Cherbury (pronounced by Thomas
Halyburton in his Natural Religion Insufficient (1714)
to be the father of English Deism) and his treatise De
veritate,   prout distinguitur a revelatione,   a
verisimili, a possibili, et a falso (1624), the roots
of this movement are actually Continental and extend
all the way back into the sixteenth century.   In note D
of his article on Viret, Pierre Bayle observes that in
the dedicatory epistle dated December 12, 1563, to
Viret's two volume work L'instruction chrétienne, Viret
specifically mentions the Deists and, deploring their
infidelity, describes their tenets:

There are many who confess that while they believe
like the Turks and the Jews that there is some
sort of God and some sort of deity, yet with
regard to Jesus Christ and to all that to which
the doctrine of the Evangelists and the Apostles
testify, they take all that to be fables and
dreams. . . .There is much more difficulty with
these than there is even with the Turks, or at
least as much. For they hold opinions with regard
to religion that are just as or more strange than
the Turks and all other miscreants. I have heard
that there are of this band those who call
themselves 'Deists', an entirely new word, which
they want to oppose to 'Atheist.' For in that
'atheist' signifies a person who is without God,
they want to make it understood that they are not
at all without God, since they certainly believe
there is some sort of God, whom they even
recognize as creator of heaven and earth, as do
the Turks; but as for Jesus Christ, they only know
that he is and hold nothing concerning him nor his
doctrine.

These Deists of whom we are now speaking, adds Viret,

ridicule all religion,

notwithstanding the fact that they adapt
themselves in outward appearance to the religion
of those with whom they must live and whom they
want to please or whom they fear. And among them
are some who have a certain belief in the
immortality of the soul; some regard this as did
the Epicureans and in the same way the providence
of God: as if he took no hand at all in the
governing of human affairs, just as if they were
governed by fortune or prudence or the folly of
men as things happen to occur. I am horrified
when I think that among those who bear the name of
'Christian' there are such monsters. But my
horror doubles when I reflect that many of those
who belong to the profession of literature and
human philosophy and are even many times deemed to
be the most learned and acute and subtle minds are
not only infected with this execrable atheism, but
also make it their profession and teach it and
poison many people with such poison.[3]

Prior to 1563 Pierre Viret was serving as a Reformed

minister in Lyon, and he probably heard of the Deists'
beliefs there; it seems that he had no first hand
contact with them. His description could just as
easily have been written of the English Deists of the
late-seventeenth and early-eighteenth centuries. The
characteristics noted by Viret remain the same: the
belief in one God transcending all particular
religions, His creation of the world and aloofness from
it, the rejection of Jesus Christ and his doctrine as
any special revelation from God. The difference of
opinion among the Deists concerning immortality of the
soul was later preserved in the distinction between
so-called mortal Deists and immortal Deists.
Particularly interesting is Viret's note concerning the
Deists' insistence on the distinction between
themselves and atheists, for later Deists were
constantly charged with atheism and so labeled by their
orthodox opponents. In fact, Viret after noting the
distinction turns around and himself accuses them of
execrable atheism (a label which he repeats in the
sequel). This ought to alert us to the fact that
apologetic works of the sixteenth and seventeenth
centuries purportedly aimed at atheists may in fact
have as real targets thinkers more properly regarded as
Deists.

The fact that we do not hear of this early Deism
more overtly is not surprising when one remembers the
rigid censorship laws in Catholic France that
prohibited publication of unorthodox opinions. The
official policy of suppression, however, only prolonged
the period of gestation and ultimately proved
counter-productive, as Robertson explains:

> . . .the clerical policy had the result of leaving
> them all unanswered when they nevertheless got

into private circulation. It was impolitic that
an official answer should appear to a book which
was officially held not to exist; so that the
orthodox defense was mainly confined to the
classic performances of Pascal, Bossuet, Huet,
Fenelon, and some outsiders such as the exiled
Protestant Abbadie, settled in Germany. These
having been written to meet the mostly unpublished
objections of previous generations, the Church
through its chosen policy had the air of utter
inability to confute the newer propaganda, though
some apologetic treatises of fair power did
appear, in particular those of the Abbé Bergier,
which, however, all appear to date from 1770
onwards.[4]

Similarly in England the press laws resulted in
the curious circumstance that prior to Herbert of
Cherbury, Deism is only obliquely represented by
published answers to unpublished opinions.[5] When the
Licensing Act of 1662, which required works to be
approved by the censor, was allowed to lapse in 1679,
Charles Blount seized the opportunity of a temporarily
free press to publish his Anima mundi (1679), Great is
Diana of the Ephesians (1680) and his influential Life
of Apollonius of Tyana (1680), a translation with notes
of Philostratus's work in which Blount compared Jesus
and his miracles with the wonder-working Apollonius.[6]
Upon his accession to the throne in 1685, James II had
the law re-instated, and it was renewed again in 1693
for two more years. When the lid was finally taken
permanently off the press in 1695, John Toland's
epochal Christianity not Mysterious (1696) almost at
once appeared.[7] But even after the freedom of the
press had been ensured, the Blasphemy Law of 1696
probably sufficed to make any Deist think twice before
publishing his opinions. Indeed, some later Deists
such as Woolston and Annet actually suffered fines and
imprisonment for their writings. Besides this, it was

not always easy for Deist authors to find a printer for
their material, and they often had to content
themselves with miserable little pamphlets that paled
by comparison to the handsome volumes of their orthodox
opponents.   Nevertheless, Deist opinions were
widespread, as is evident from the founding of the
Boyle Lectures in 1692 "for proving the Christian
religion against notorious infidels, viz., atheists,
theists, pagans, Jews, and Mahometans, not descending
lower to any controversies that are among Christians
themselves,"[8] as well as from the many works aimed at
refuting Deist tenets.[9]

Thus,   given   these   circumstances,   it   is
understandable why Deism is not easily charted prior to
Lord Herbert.   It is really quite amazing that this
movement, which peaked in the eighteenth century,
should be already a matter of concern to Viret, a
contemporary of Calvin and compatriot of Guillaume
Farel in Geneva in 1534; his comments on this menace
were written within 25 years of the establishment of
Calvinist rule in Geneva and more than 60 years before
Lord Herbert broached his theological system.

In any case it seems evident that the earliest and
most significant treatises on the historical evidences
for the Christian faith were written with an eye toward
Deist opinions.   In 1581 the French Calvinist leader
Philippes de Mornay, Lord Duplessis-Mornay, writing in
his mother tongue instead of Latin, penned at Anvers
his De la vérité de la religion chrestienne.   Mornay
subtitled his work Contre les athées, Epicuriens,
Payens, Juifs, Mahumedistes, & autres Infidèles.   In
his preface Mornay like Viret decries the spread of
contempt of religion which one encounters at every
step, even among those who make a profession of piety.

His mention of atheists, Epicureans, and other infidels
as threats is especially interesting. He uses the term
atheist to describe one who denies the existence of
God, so that he cannot designate by this term Deists.
Viret had used the term Epicurean in describing French
Deists less than twenty years earlier. Mornay also
seems to associate Epicureanism with persons who sound
very much like Deists:

> The Epicureans are cut from this cloth because,
> sensing that their soul is guilty of so many
> crimes, they think to have declined the justice
> and providence of God in denying it. And of them
> we can say that reason has been swept away and
> ravished by the course of this world to which they
> adhere in order to have no other discourse and no
> other course than the world's. Some go a bit
> further and with regard to God and with regard to
> themselves hold that there is a God and that man
> has from him an immortal soul, that God governs
> all, and that man must serve him. But they see
> the Gentiles, the Jews, the Turks, the Christians
> in the world; among diverse peoples and diverse
> religions each one thinks to serve God and to find
> his salvation in his own religion. Just as at an
> intersection so many ways meet, so they, instead
> of choosing the correct one by the judgement of
> reason, stop, wonder, and conclude in this
> bewilderment that all go back to one, as if the[10]
> South and the North lead to the same place.

Although the statement concerning God's governance of
the world appears somewhat puzzling, it may be that
this is to be taken in the most general of senses and
implies no specific acts of God in the world. Grotius
will speak of persons who regard God's governance of
the world in such general terms, as we shall see, and
Pascal in his notes specifically associates such a view
with Epicureanism: "The God of Christians is not a God
who is simply the author of mathematical truths, or of
the order of the elements; that is the view of pagans

and Epicureans."[11] This makes it likely that Mornay's Epicureans are in fact Deists. The further belief noted by Mornay that man must serve God is characteristic of Lord Herbert's Deism. The rest of the description seems to echo Viret's: the divided thinking concerning the immortality of the soul, the denial of God's providence, the appeal to one God transcending all the claims of particular religions. Mornay's system also seems to favor the identification of some of his opponents as Deists. In his effort to find a common ground, he observes that Jews and Christians share a common belief in the Old Testament; hence, the efficacy of the proof from prophecy. The Gentiles and Jews share a belief in one God and immortality, which constitutes a common ground. As for the atheist, he may be convinced by the proof from motion. Those who deny the divinity of Christ may be convinced by philosophy and history. Philosophy proves that miracles are evidence of Deity (since something cannot come from nothing), while history proves that miracles have occurred. Of the opponents enumerated in the subtitle, this last argument seems best directed against the Epicureans and other infidels, which makes it likely that they are Deists, since the denial of Christ's deity was also characteristic of Deist beliefs. Thus it seems plausible to think that Mornay's apologetic system is in part directed against Deists in its use of miraculous evidences for Christianity.

Similarly Grotius's treatise De veritate religionis christianae (1627), while not explicitly mentioning Deists, seems well-designed to refute their tenets. Grotius does tell us specifically that the work is intended to be a handbook for world travelers,

who would encounter the opinions of pagans, Muslims,
and Jews in the course of their journeys. But he also
adds this note:

> Neque deesse impios, qui abditum metu venenum ex
> occasione apud simplices prodant: adversum quae
> mala optare me, ut recte armati sint nostrates, &
> qui ingenio praestant, incumbant pro virili
> revincendis erroribus, caeteri saltem id caveant,
> ne ab aliis vincantur. [12]

These "impios" could well have included Deist thinkers.
It is not until Books four, five, and six that Grotius
gives detailed refutations of paganism, Judaism, and
Islam respectively. In Books one through three he
follows the logical order of Mornay, establishing first
the existence of God, then showing the divine character
of Judaism, and finally proving at length the truth of
the Christian religion. In the course of his argument,
Grotius finds it necessary to prove that God governs
not only the universe at large but also the affairs of
the mundane world: "Multum autem errare eos, qui
providentiam hanc coeli orbibus includunt. . . . "[13]
Nor is God's governing of the world to be conceived in
a vague, general sense: "Neque minus falluntur, qui
universalia ab eo curari volunt, non & singularia."[14]
It could well be that Grotius is here interacting with
Deist sentiments. We have noted the denial of God's
providence that characterized Deists, and Grotius's
comment on those who allow only the most general
government of the world by God is reminiscent of
Mornay's opponents. In refuting these opinions Grotius
asserts that the most certain proof of Divine
providence is from miracles and fulfilled prophecy,
which can be established historically:

> At certissimum divinae providentiae testimonium
> praebent miracula, & praedictiones quae in

historiis exstant. Referuntur quidem multa id
genus fabulosa: sed quae testes sui temporis
idoneos habuerunt, id est, tales quorum nec
judicium, nec fides laboret, rejicienda non sunt,
quasi omnino talia fieri non possint.[15]

When it comes to proving the Christian faith, it is to
Jesus's miracles and resurrection that Grotius will
turn. Thus, his arguments are well-suited for
combatting Deist beliefs. We know that Grotius was
familiar with such beliefs, for between the first
publication of De veritate in Dutch in verse form in
1621 and the greatly expanded Latin edition of 1627,
Grotius was visited in Holland by Lord Herbert of
Cherbury, who gave to the Dutchman a copy of his own De
veritate.[16] Hence, it is not at all unlikely that
Grotius's apology aimed to combat, not only paganism,
Judaism, and Islam, but also Deism.

Among the papers left behind by Blaise Pascal upon
his tragic death in 1662 we find specific references to
Deism in his embryonic L'Apologie de la religion
chrétienne. Speaking of those who reject Christianity
because they misunderstand it, he comments:

> They imagine that it consists simply in the
> worship of a God considered as great, powerful,
> and eternal; which is strictly Deism, almost as
> far removed from the Christian religion as
> atheism, which is its exact opposite. And thence
> they conclude that this religion is not true,
> because they do not see that all things concur to
> the establishment of this point, that God does not
> manifest Himself to men with all the evidence
> which He could show.
>   But let them conclude what they will against
> Deism, they will conclude nothing against the
> Christian religion, which properly consists in the
> mystery of the Redeemer. . . .
>   All who seek God without Jesus Christ, and
> who rest in nature, either find no light to
> satisfy them or come to form for themselves a
> means of knowing God and serving Him without a

mediator. Thereby they fall either into atheism
or into Deism, two things which the Christian
religion abhors almost equally.[17]

For Pascal not only is Deism religiously empty because
it provides no personal knowledge of God, the living
God of Abraham, Isaac, and Jacob, but also because it
is rationally inferior to Christianity.[18] The rational
foundations of Deism are comprised of philosophical
arguments for the existence of God, which lack force
and cogency. By contrast the Christian religion is
supported by the proofs of Jesus Christ, namely, the
evidential proofs from prophecy and miracle. Pascal's
famous wager and his emphasis on reasons of the heart
should not obscure the fact that he was fundamentally
an evidentialist. Christianity is rationally, not
simply religiously, superior to Deism because the
proofs for Christianity are more evident and give
sufficiently clear proof that God has revealed Himself
in Christ. Thus, Pascal's Apologie, too, appears to be
designed in part to show the superiority of
Christianity to mere Deism.

By the time we get to Jacques Abbadie some twenty
years later, Deism is fully in view as an enemy of the
Christian faith. A Reformed thinker like Mornay and
Grotius, Abbadie, after first proving the existence of
God, devotes volume one, section two of his Traité de
la vérité de la religion chrétienne (1684) to proving
"the truth and necessity of religion against Deism."[19]
He wants to show that mere belief in God is
insufficient and that specific religious claims and
practices must be embraced. He will then follow the
familiar pattern of first proving the truth of the
Jewish religion and finally the Christian.

With the turn of the century and the flowering of

English Deism, orthodox divines turned all their
weapons against this foe. It was during this century
that the most sophisticated treatments of the
historical evidences for the miracles and resurrection
of Jesus were written in direct refutation of Deist
tracts and books. As the English controversy spilled
over into France and Germany about the middle of the
eighteenth century, it was again this threat of Deism
that evoked the most important historical apologetic
treatises in those nations. Thus, it would seem that
the modern historical approach to Christian apologetics
and particularly to the question of Jesus's
resurrection arose as a result of the threat of Deism.

Factors contributing
to the rise of Deism

In order to better understand the nature of this
threat and the response to it, it might be helpful to
delineate more sharply some of the factors contributing
to the rise of Deism. The root causes of this movement
are various and multi-faceted:

Geographic expansion
The rise and spread of Deism was due in no small
measure to the great transformation wrought by the
"Expansion of Europe." H.E. Barnes explains,

> By this term is meant the extended movement of
> exploration and discovery which occurred in the
> three centuries from 1450 to 1750, and its almost
> incalculable intellectual and institutional
> consequences. The isolation, repetition,
> stability and provincialism of the old order could
> not endure in the face of the widespread contact
> of contrasting cultures--that most potent of all
> forces in arousing intellectual curiosity and

promoting striking changes of every sort.[20]

The effects of this broadening of Western man's horizons is particularly evident in the enormously popular travel literature of that era.[21] As early as the thirteenth and fourteenth centuries we find works such as the Travels of Marco Polo, dictated from 1298 in a Genoan jail after its author had spent twenty years in the East; also the fictitious, but popular Travels of Sir John de Mandeville, which appeared about the middle of the fourteenth century. The discovery of the New World by Christopher Columbus in 1492 and his subsequent accounts thereof and the voyage of Magellan, which was related by one of his sailors Antonio Pigafetta in Magellan's Voyage Around the World, fired the curiosity and imaginations of Portuguese, Spanish, and Italian writers. Important historical works on the New World such as the Decades of the New World (1516-30) of Pietro Martire d'Anghiera (known as Peter Martyr), A Brief Account of the Destruction of the Indies by Bartolome de Las Casas (whose descriptions of Indians inspired the "noble savage" image in eighteenth century Europe), and the General History (1601-15) of Antonio de Herrera y Tordesillas (an important history of Hispanic America) acquainted readers in Europe with the discoveries and conquests made throughout Central and South America. The first important French collection of voyages was Melchisedech Thevenot's Accounts of Various Curious Voyages (1693-96). Marquette's Voyages and Discoveries (1681) told of French explorations along the Mississippi River, and Pierre François Xavier de Charlevoix's The General History and Description of New France became the most popular account of French explorations in America. The first English work on the Expansion of Europe was

Richard Eden's <u>Decades of the New World</u> (1555), which drew upon the work of Peter Martyr. Richard Hakluyt's <u>The Principal Navigations, Voyages and Discoveries of the English Nation</u> appeared in 1588. The first prominent account of English colonization in the New World was Captain John Smith's <u>General History of Virginia and New England</u> (1624). In addition to these works on the New World, travel literature and histories concerning the East also appeared. Avid interest in particularly Muslim culture was stimulated by popular works such as Richard Knolles's <u>General History of the Turks</u> (1603) and Jean Chardin's <u>Travels into Persia and the East Indies</u> (1686).

The Expansion of Europe with its attendant travel literature rocked belief in traditional Christian orthodoxy. La Bruyère toward the end of the seventeenth century in his description of the impiety of the <u>esprits forts</u> laments, "Some of them manage to corrupt themselves by long voyages and lose the little religion that they had; they see one day after another a new cult, diverse customs, diverse ceremonies," or, if they have not traveled themselves, the accounts of a Tavernier or of a Chardin display these things to them.[22] They remain therefore incapable of fixing their choice; besides, their laziness leaves them in a state of indifference, which is worse than hostility. "They neither deny these things nor concede them; they just do not think about them."[23]

Grotius's treatise on the truth of the Christian faith, it will be remembered, had been specifically designed not only to help voyagers and sailors propagate their faith, but also to insulate them against the paralyzing effects on faith of observing such religious pluralism:

Propositum enim mihi erat omnibus quidem civibus
meis, sed praecipue navigantibus, operam navare
utilem, ut in longo illo marino otio impenderent
potius tempus, quam, quod nimium multi facuint,
fallerent. Itaque sumpto exordio a laude nostrae
gentis, quae navigandi solertia caeteras facile
vincat, excitavi eos, ut hac arte, tanquam divino
beneficio, non ad suum tantum quaestum, sed & ad
verae, hoc est, Christianae Religionis
propagationem, uterentur. Neque enim deesse
materiam, cum per longinqua itinera passim
incurrerent, aut in paganos, ut in Sina & Guinea;
aut in Mahumetistas, ut sub imperio Turcae,
Persae, & Poenorum; tum vero Judaeos, & ipsos jam
Chritianismi professos hostes, dispersos per
maximas partes terrarum ...: adversum quae mala
optare me, ut recte armati sint nostrates, & qui
ingenio praestant, incumbant pro virili
revincendis erroribus[24] caeteri saltem id caveant,
ne ab aliis vincantur.

The impact of the increasing familiarity with
foreign lands and religions promoted Deism in at least
two respects: (a) It tended toward the relativization
of religious beliefs. Christianity could no longer be
regarded as the triumphant and universal religion, but
was now seen to be but one competing creed among many,
largely confined to a corner of the world. The great
and ancient proof for the church's authority based on
universal consent now became an embarrassment, for the
majority of the world's peoples had apparently never
even heard of Jesus Christ. The plethora of competing
religions, all claiming to show the way to God, created
scepticism concerning all of them and promoted belief
that all particular religions are corruptions of some
one, overarching natural religion. Diderot, for
example, cleverly drew upon an ancient argument of
Cicero in order to prove the superiority of natural
religion. To prove that the Romans were the most
war-like people, Cicero asked the Gauls, Parthians, and
Africans who, after themselves, were the bravest,

strongest, and so forth--and the answer always came
back: the Romans. Similarly, says Diderot, ask all
the world's religions which, after themselves, is the
best, and they will all reply: natural religion.
"Now, those," concludes Cicero, "to whom the second
place is unanimously awarded and who in their turn do
not cede the first place to anyone--it is those who
incontestably deserve that place."[25] The belief in the
primacy of natural religion logically stimulated both a
critical and a constructive element within Deism, to
borrow a convenient distinction from Stephen.[26] For
the construction of a natural religion proper to all
men implicitly entailed a rejection and critique of all
particular religions. Hence, we often find in Deist
writings Christianity classed along with and played off
against other particular religions, as Charles Leslie
explained in his A Short and Easie Method with the
Deists (1697):

> And they say, That there is no greater Ground to
> believe in Christ, than in Mohomet: That all
> these Pretences to Revelation are Cheats, and ever
> have been among Pagans, Jews, Mohometans, and
> Christians: That they are all alike Impositions
> of Cunning and Designing Men, upon the Credulity,
> at first, of Simple and Unthinking People; till,
> their Numbers increasing, their Delusions grow
> Popular, come at last to be establish'd by Laws,
> and then the force of Education and Custom gives a
> Byas to the Judgments of after Ages, till such
> Deceits come really to be Believ'd, being receiv'd
> upon Trust from the Ages foregoing, without
> examining into the Original and Bottom of them.[27]

The comparison between Christ and Mohammed,
Christianity and Islam was a favorite of the Deist
authors, and works on both sides of the controversy are
filled with references to "the Turks" and discussions
of the merits of "Mohometanism." The brash Woolston

even went so far as to assert in his Third Discourse on the Miracles of Our Saviour (1728) that Mohometanism is in fact more reasonable than Christianity.[28]

To replace the cacophony of competing creeds, Deists proposed to construct a single, harmonious religion of nature. Rousseau in the profession of faith of the vicaire savoyard in his Emile (1762) appeals to natural religion as the only solution to the problem of competing religious claims.[29] Look at the mutually exclusive religions of the world, he exclaims. To find the true faith, it would not suffice to examine one; it would be necessary to examine them all, and not only their proofs, but also the objections to each one. To assess only Judaism, Christianity, and Islam it would be necessary to be a scholar in comparative religions. And how can people investigate these impartially, given national prejudices and differing resources? Toujours des livres! quel manie! Just because Europe is so full of books, Europeans regard them as indispensable, forgetting that three-fourths of the world have never even seen them. And how many millions have never even heard of Moses, Jesus Christ, or Mohammed? How can men be held responsible to discern the one true religion revealed by God? Rousseau draws a breath and concludes,

> I take as witness this God of peace whom I adore and announce to you that all my researches were sincere, but, seeing that they were and always would be without success and that I was being swallowed up in an ocean without shores, I retraced my steps and confined my faith to my primitive notions. I never could believe that God could command me under pain of hell to be so wise. Therefore, I have closed all the books. There is only one open to all eyes: that of nature. It is in this great and sublime book that I learn to serve and adore its divine author. No one is

excused for not reading it because it speaks to
all men a language intelligible to all minds. If
I were on a desert island, and if I had seen no
man other than myself, if I had never learned what
happened long ago in a corner of the world, yet if
I exercise my reason, if I cultivate it, if I
utilize correctly the immediate faculties that God
gives me, I will learn of myself to know him, to
love him, to love his works, to want the good he
wants, and to fulfill in order to please him all
my duties upon the earth. What more will all the
knowledge of man teach me?[30]

Rousseau's attitude toward particular religions
was more sympathetic than most of his English forbears.
Rather than impostures and delusions, they are salutary
institutions honoring God in each country according to
the genius and customs of each particular people.[31] Le
culte essentiel est celui du coeur. God rejects no
hommage, so long as it is sincere, regardless of the
form in which it is offered. In any case, whether
their attitudes toward particular religions were
sympathetic or condemnatory, the Deists were moved by
the new appreciation of global religious pluralism to a
relativization of all particular religions, criticizing
them and offering a religion of nature in their place.

Not only did the Expansion of Europe promote Deism
in the relativization of particular religious claims,
but also (b) It tended to make Christianity's claim to
exclusiveness unjustly narrow and cruel. It was
painfully obvious that if Christ's claim to be the only
way to God was true, then since the vast majority of
the world had not heard of him, most of the human race
was condemned to eternal damnation. What made the
situation even more embarrassing was the fact that some
of the pagan cultures were found to posseess a moral
rectitude that put the corrupt Christian West to shame.
Stephen explains,

As distant countries, whose existence had scarcely
touched men's thoughts in former ages, or which
had been conceived as lying in some dim borderland
rimming the bright circle of Christendom, came
daily into closer contact with ordinary life, the
true proportions of human history became manifest.
Christendom was but a fragment of the world.
Millions upon millions of human beings had never
even heard of its existence; they knew nothing of
the one true faith, which to know was life
everlasting, and not to know was to incur
everlasting torment. Could all the Chinese, for
example, be damned because they knew nothing of an
event which, so far as they were concerned, might
as well have happened on the moon? If not damned,
and if, in fact, they were about as happy and
virtuous as Christians, could the Christian faith
be necessary either in this world or the next?
Throughout the eighteenth century, the deists are
always taunting the orthodox with this startling
fact of three hundred million Chinamen whose case
cannot be squared with the old theories.[32]

The medieval appeal to the greatness and universality
of the Church as a testimony to her divine authority
had now become counter-productive, an awkward
circumstance which could not escape the acerbic wit of
Voltaire. He concludes the article on Christianity in
his _Dictionary_ by noting matter of factly that of the
estimated 600 million people in the world, the Roman
Catholic church possesses about 16 million of them--or
about one twenty-sixth of the inhabitants of the known
world.[33] In mock piety, he confesses,

> God himself came down from heaven and died to
> redeem mankind and extirpate sin forever from the
> face of the earth; and yet He left the greater
> part of mankind a prey to error, to crime, and to
> the devil. This, to our weak intellects, appears
> a fatal contradiction. But it is not for us to
> question Providence; our duty[34] is to humble
> ourselves in the dust before it.

Voltaire's contemporary Rousseau was also scandalized
by the exclusiveness of Christianity. He maintains

that no one can be obligated to recognize the special
revelation of God because ". . .this pretended
obligation is incompatible with the justice of God,
and, far from removing obstacles to salvation, it
multiplies them, since it renders them insurmountable
for the greater part of the human race."[35] It is said
that Christian missionaries go everywhere. But, asks
Rousseau, have they gone to the still unknown heart of
Africa, where no European has yet penetrated? Have
they gone to the immense continents of America, where
whole nations do not yet know that people from another
world have set foot on their shores? Have they gone to
the harems of the princes of Asia to preach the Gospel
to their thousands of slaves? And what of their women,
to whom missionaries may not speak? Are they condemned
to hell for their isolation? And even if missionaries
had reached all these, there would undoubtedly have
been someone who died the day before the missionaries
arrived. If there is one man in the whole universe who
has never heard of Jesus Christ, then the problem is
every bit as great for this one man as for a quarter of
the human race.[36]

Natural religion, by contrast, was available to
all men of all generations. Matthew Tindal, whose
Christianity as old as Creation: or the Gospel a
Republication of the Religion of Nature (1730) became a
sort of Bible of English Deism, argues that, given
certain premises, the sufficiency of natural religion
can be the only logical conclusion:

> If God never intended Mankind shou'd at any Time
> be without Religion, or have false Religions; and
> there be but One True Religion, which ALL have
> been ever bound to believe, and profess; I can't
> see any Heterodoxy in affirming, that the Means to

> effect this End of infinite Wisdom, must be as
> universal and extensive as the End itself; or that
> All Men, at all Times, must have had sufficient
> means to discover whatever God design'd they
> shou'd know, and practice.[37]

Since the only means universally available to men are
their rational faculties, it follows that the true
religion must be a religion based wholly upon the
exercise of natural reason.   Given the further
premises that God is perfect and that He willed from
the beginning that all men follow this one true
religion, it follows that this original religion is
also perfect and because perfect, unalterable.   From
this it follows that any subsequent revelation of God
can only be another method of communication of the same
religion.   This means that since Christianity is true,
it is as old as creation and in its essence adds
nothing to the natural religion of reason; they are the
same and the gospel is simply a republication of that
original religion.[38]   Günter Gawlick comments that
behind Tindal's subtitle lies a radicalizing that
becomes most apparent when the phraseology is inverted:
what in historical Christianity is not as old as
creation, that is, not in the rational nature of things
or binding a priori, is not really part of the one true
religion nor of God's will, but is superstition and the
work of man.[39]

 Wherein consists, according to Tindal, this
natural religion?

> By Natural Religion, I understand the Belief of
> the Existence of a God, and the Sense and Practice
> of those Duties, which result from the Knowledge,
> we, by our Reason, have of him, and his
> Perfections; and of ourselves, and our own
> Imperfections; and of the Relation we stand to
> him, and to our Fellow-Creatures; so that the

Religion of Nature takes in every Thing that is
founded on the Reason and Nature of Things.[40]

Anything in Christianity beyond this is superflous and
even deleterious.   Because it is founded only on
universal reason and the nature of things, natural
religion avoids the scandal of an unjustly narrow and
cruel Christianity and offers salvation equally to all.

Thus, the Expansion of Europe during the three
centuries prior to 1750 greatly abetted the rise and
spread of Deism because (a) it tended toward the
relativization of religious beliefs and (b) it tended
to make Christianity's claim to exclusiveness unjustly
narrow and cruel.

Scientific revolutions

During roughly the same era, a number of
scientific revolutions occurred which changed
drastically the prevailing conception of God, man, and
the universe.   If the geographic expansion enlarged
men's conceptions, then the breakthroughs in astronomy
were even more impressive.   The universe of medieval
man was a comfortable and secure home for man, the
earth the center of the cosmos, enclosed by the
Aristotelian spheres containing the planets and fixed
stars.   It is probably difficult for moderns to
conceive the disorientation experienced when, under the
impact of advances in astronomy, this geocentric model
of the universe began to fall apart.   Orr comments that
with the possible exception of the demonstration that
the earth is a sphere, no scientific achievement did
more to lessen men's respect for the old ways and to
discredit the authority of the Church and the Bible
than the revolutionary advance in astronomy begun in
1543 with the publication of Copernicus's De

revolutionibus, for which the Polish scientist was
excommunicated by the pope.[41] Copernicus's theories,
however, had little impact on Continental Europe for
fifty years (though Giordano Bruno sided with
Copernicus in his Oxford lectures of 1584); the first
edition of De revolutionibus never sold out. For
although Copernicus revived the heliocentric hypothesis
first propounded by Aristarchus of Samos, he could not
rid himself of 48 Ptolemaic epicycles necessary to
account for planetary motion. It was up to Kepler to
discover on the basis of Brahe's observations that by
coupling the geocentric hypothesis with elliptical
rather than circular planetary orbits, one might
eliminate the elaborate system of cycles and epicycles.
In 1609 he published his work on the new astronomy and
so demolished the very structure of the medieval
universe with its spheres, its wheels, and its angelic
movers. In place of spiritual forces, he introduced
into astronomy purely physical forces and so severed
the tie between theology and astronomy. Kepler's three
laws of planetary motion mark a turning point in the
history of thought, for they were the first "laws of
nature" in the modern sense, and he compared the
universe to a clock, whose operation obeyed his three
laws. The same year that Kepler's magnum opus
appeared, an Italian mathematician named Galileo,
having heard of the invention of the telescope by
Janson, duplicated and improved the device for use in
astronomical observation.[42] In 1613 he published his
work on sunspots, in which he embraced the Copernican
heliocentric hypothesis. Attacked by certain
philosophers and ecclesiastics as a heretic, Galileo
maintained that the Bible had no authority in matters
of science and ought to be interpreted in light of

man's knowledge of natural phenomena based on reason
and observation. Despite Galileo's interventions, the
Church moved officially in 1615 to condemn the
heliocentric hypothesis as contrary to the Scriptures.
When in 1632 Galileo again expounded the theory, he was
summoned by the inquisition to Rome and in 1633 forced
under the threat of torture to recant. Of course, the
force of evidence gradually brought about the general
acceptance of the heliocentric hypothesis. As a
result, the Church and the Bible on whose authority the
Church had condemned the modern, scientific picture of
the universe were badly discredited in this matter.
The association of the Christian religion with the old
and the false, with blind authoritarianism rather than
observation and experiment, served only to promote the
spread of infidelity.

More importantly, however, this revolution in
astronomy not only served to discredit the authority of
the Church and the Scriptures, but it promoted Deism
more directly in that it brought about a radical
conceptual shift in relationship between God and man.
Formerly, man had occupied center-stage, so to speak,
but now the scenery had become too wide for the drama.
Man's horizons had expanded out to infinity, and the
earth was discovered to be but a speck circling a star
itself lost amid myriads of other stars and other
worlds. "It was possible, indeed, verbally to promote
the Jewish deity to rule over the vast territory which
had thus sprung into existence," admits Stephen, "But
though the traditionary mythology was not forced by a
clear logical necessity to postulate a limited earth
and heavens, it became more shadowy and dim when
confronted with the new cosmology."43 The utter
insignificance of man in an oblivious universe governed

by purely physical forces promoted belief in a Deity
who master-minded the great creation but who took no
personal interest in the petty affairs of men. It
simply seemed incredible to think that God would
intervene on this tiny planet on behalf of some people
living in Judea. Voltaire exemplified this incredulous
attitude. For him men are like ants, crawling,
fighting, disputing on this little atom of mud. In his
Dictionary article on miracles, he asserts that a
miracle is, properly speaking, something admirable;
hence, "The stupendous order of nature, the revolution
of a hundred millions of worlds around millions of
suns, the activity of light, the life of animals, all
are grand and perpetual miracles."[44] But according to
accepted usage, "A miracle is the violation of
mathematical, divine, immutable, eternal laws"[45];
therefore, it is a contradiction in terms. But, it is
said, God can suspend these laws if He wishes. But why
should He wish to so disfigure this immense machine?
It is said, on behalf of mankind. But it is impossible
to conceive that the divine nature should occupy itself
with only a few men in particular; He would have to act
for the whole human race, which itself "is less than a
small ant-hill, in comparison with all the beings
inhabiting immensity."[46] But is it not "the most
absurd of all extravagances" to imagine that the
Infinite Supreme Being would on behalf of three or four
hundred emmets on this little atom of mud "derange the
operation of the vast machinery that moves the
universe?"[47] Voltaire's God, indeed the God of all
Deists, was the cosmic architect who engineered and
built the machine, but who would not be bothered to
interfere in the trivial affairs of men. In this light
Christianity simply became unbelievable.

A second scientific crisis began to take shape in
what would become the field of geology. In the same
way that astronomy had expanded man's horizons outward,
geology pushed them backward. A literal reading of the
Biblical account of creation indicated a relatively
young universe created by God in six successive days.
By calculating a chronology based upon Biblical
genealogies, Bishop Ussher was able to determine the
date of creation as 4,004 B.C. Of course, the presence
of fossil forms imbedded in the earth was known, but
these were not taken to be evidence of an ancient
earth. Tertullian had explained them as the result of
Noah's flood. During the scholastic age, they were
attributed by ibn Sina to a stone-making force in
nature and similarly to formative quality in the earth
by Albertus Magnus. Some thinkers believed they grew
from seed, and others ascribed to them powers of
reproduction like ordinary plants and animals. In
general, the belief prevailed for centuries that these
curiosities were strange sports of Nature, serving some
unknown purpose of the Creator. The Genesis accounts
of creation and a young earth were fundamentally
accepted as literal history, and universal history,
such as Bossuet's, tracing the course of the world from
the origin of man to the present day was a common and
accepted genre. But doubts began to arise. Da Vinci,
about the beginning of the sixteenth century, suggested
that fossils might be the remains of ancient plants and
animals, and his contemporary Fracastoro also accepted
this idea. Toward the end of the century Palissy
propounded the theory. Near the beginning of the
seventeenth century, French thinkers such as De Clave,
Bitaud, and De Villon espoused the same belief,
provoking a protest from the theological faculty at the

Sorbonne, which resulted in the condemnation and destruction of their works and the authors' banishment from Paris. The most incendiary work, however, came from the pen of Isaac de La Peyrere of Bordeaux, who explicitly sought to re-interpret the Scriptures in favor of an old earth. Popkin writes,

> The flood, and the descendants of all mankind from Noah and his family provided serious difficulties when examined in the light of new geographical, anthropological, meteorological, and mechanistic physics. . . . And, at just about the same moment that Menasseh ben Israel and Ussher had reconstructed man's history from Noah to the world of 1650, in a possible chronology, and with conceivable migrations to put people in China, Polynesia, America, etc., the whole enterprise of reconciling Scripture and the new science was blown apart by a mad genius, Isaac La Peyrere (Pereira), who, I believe, really set off the[48] warfare between theology and science.

Through a disastrous exegesis of Rom 5.12-14, La Peyrere had become convinced that the human race existed prior to Adam. Retiring to the safety of the Netherlands, he composed his Prae-adamitae (1655) in defense of his theory. Scandal immediately erupted; the insensed Parliament in Paris ordered the book burned. La Peyrere was arrested in Brussels and only released after he renounced his heretical opinions.

La Peyrere argued that since, according to Paul, sin was not imputed before the law, the law in the passage must refer to the law broken by Adam, since sin was in fact imputed from Adam to Christ.[49] Death came into the world through Adam's transgression, but sin was in the world previously. La Peyrere points to Gen 2.6 as proof that laws and ceremonies existed before the Mosaic law, and he adduces numerous examples of the imputation of sin before Moses, such as Adam, Cain,

Sodom, and so forth. The triumphant conclusion is that
since sin was in the world, though not imputed, prior
to Adam, there must have existed men before Adam:

> Si lex illa intelligebatur de lege data Adamo:
> statuendum erat peccatum fuisse in mundo ante
> Adamum, & usque ad Adamum: peccatum vero ante
> Adamum non fuisse imputatem. Ponendi ergo erant
> alii homines ante Adamum, qui quidem peccavissent,
> sed qui non peccavissent imputative; quia ante
> legem peccata non imputabantur.[50]

The men who lived prior to Adam sinned, but their sin
was not like the transgression of Adam. Nevertheless,
after Adam's fall, there was a sort of retroactive
imputation of sin to these men as well.[51]

La Peyrère's exegesis was dangerous enough. But
he augmented his heresy by arguing that his
interpretation better accorded with the facts of
ancient history and astronomy than did the traditional
viewpoint.[52] He maintained that recent discoveries in
America, Greenland, and China indicated that men
existed as long ago as 50,000 years before Christ.[53]
He argued for a merely local flood, the independent
origins of different cultures, and the descent of
Judeo-Christian people alone from Noah. This was a
threatening move in the seventeenth century, when
orthodox Christians were attempting to ward off the
implications of the new geographic and scientific
discoveries. Pascal dismissed La Peyrère as a crank,
and the eminent apologist Huet sought to refute him.
But even if La Peyrère's exegesis could be shown to be
fanciful, that only brought more clearly into focus the
contradiction between the Bible and the new science.
La Peyrère thereby undermined confidence in the
credibility of Genesis and of the Bible as a whole. In

this he influenced Spinoza's criticism of the
Pentateuch and, along with Spinoza, the French Catholic
biblical scholar Richard Simon, who not only
corresponded with La Peyrere, but also met with him
personally.[54] The increasing evidence for the
antiquity of the earth and against the literal
interpretation of Genesis promoted Deism not only in
casting doubt on the reliability of the Bible, but also
in disclosing the relative newness of the
Judeo-Christian religion. If the earth and mankind
existed long before the origin of these revealed
religions, then, if Christianity be true, millions of
people in the past must have been passed over by God in
silence, left in spiritual darkness without hope or
possibility of salvation from eternal damnation. But
this seemed unconscionable. The antiquity of the human
race and the goodness of God seemed to demand a natural
religion that was, in Tindal's words, as old as the
creation.

A third scientific revolution of profound impact
occurred in 1687 with the publication of Isaac Newton's
Philosophiae naturalis principia mathematica, a work
which grew out of Newton's attempt to connect Kepler's
first law of planetary motion with an inverse-square
law of force.[55] The _Principia_ begins with eight
definitions and Newton's famous three laws of motion,
from which theorems and corollaries are then deduced:

> I. Every body continues in its state of rest, or
> of uniform motion in a right line, unless it is
> compelled to change that state by forces impressed
> upon it.
> II. The change of motion is proportional to the
> motive force impressed; and is made in the
> direction of the right line in which that force is
> impressed.
> III. To every action there is always opposed an

equal reaction; or, the mutual actions of two bodies upon each other are always equal, and directed to contrary parts.

By regarding the world in terms of masses, motions, and forces operating according to these laws, Newton's Principia gave rise to a picture of the universe aptly characterized as the "Newtonian world machine." Newton's model of mechanical explanation was enthusiastically received as the paradigm for explanation in all fields and reached its height in the outlook of Laplace that a Supreme Intelligence, equipped with Newton's Principia and knowing the present position and velocity of every particle in the universe, could deduce the exact state of the universe at any other point in time. Such a view of the world promoted the Deist conception of God as the Creator who created the world machine, wound it up like a clock, and set it running under the laws of matter and motion, never to interfere with it again. We have already seen the outworking of such a conception of God and the world in Voltaire's attitude toward miracles. He argues that it is impossible that an omniscient and omnipotent God should perform miracles, for it is obvious that God originally made the universe, "this immense machine," as good and perfect as He could; since He could also foresee any future imperfections that might arise. He provided for that in the beginning. Hence, He will never change anything in it. To say that God performs miracles, charges Voltaire, actually denigrates him:

> He would then, in reality, be supposed to say: 'I have not been able to effect by my construction of the universe, by my divine decrees, by my eternal laws, a particular object; I am now going to change my eternal ideas and immutable laws, to

endeavor to accomplish what I have not been able
to do by means of them.' This would be an avowal
of His weakness, not of His power; it would appear
in such a being an inconceivable contradiction.
Accordingly, therefore, to dare to ascribe
miracles to God is, if man can in reality insult
God, actually offering Him that insult. It is
saying to Him: 'You are a weak and inconsistent
Being.' It is, therefore, absurd to believe in
miracles; it is, in fact, dishonoring the
divinity.[56]

Voltaire's frequent metaphor of the universe as a huge
machine operating according to immutable mechanical
laws well illustrates the eighteenth century concept of
the Newtonian world machine with whose workings God did
not interfere. Such a view was not Newton's own, for
in the Scholium to his work, he maintained that God did
need to periodically intervene in the world to preserve
the stability of the cosmos. But as the gaps in
scientific knowledge began to be filled, these
"adjustments" by God were seen to be no longer
necessary, and the "God of the gaps" was gradually
squeezed out. In any case, the Newtonian world machine
of the eighteenth century, governed by inexorable laws
laid down initially by the Creator himself, permitted
no miracle, for such an incursion into its clock-like
operation could only be a "violation of the laws of
Nature" and as such inadmissable.

Incipient biblical criticism

During the seventeenth century we discover the
beginnings of the science of biblical criticism.
Though not appreciated or utilized to any degree of
sophistication by the Deists, this new movement tended
to foster Deism by treating the Bible like any other
historical book, thus removing its aura of holy
"untouchability," and by creating doubts concerning the

reliability of the Scriptures, especially the Old
Testament. It is intriguing to note that the founder
of modern apologetics was also the founder of modern
biblical criticism: Hugo Grotius.

Grotius inaugurated the method of handling the
Scriptures not as inspired writings, but as ordinary
historical documents. In this radical departure from
the accustomed procedure of adducing signs on behalf of
the inspiration of the Scriptures taken as a whole,
Grotius anticipated and indeed influenced the French
biblical critic Jean Le Clerc, as is evident from Le
Clerc's several references to him. Grotius contends
that there is no need for historical narratives to be
dictated by the Holy Spirit:

> Sed a Spiritu Sancto dictari historias nihil fuit
> opus: satis fuit scriptorem memoria valere circa
> res spectatas, aut diligentia in describendis
> veterum Commentariis. . . .Si Lucas divino afflatu
> dictanto sua scripsisset, inde potius sibi
> sumpsisset autoritatem, ut Prophetae faciunt, quam
> a testibus quorum fidem est secutus. . . .[57]

All that is necessary to ensure the authority and
trustworthiness of a historical account is that it be
attested by reliable witnesses. Thus, in his
Annotationes in libros Evangeliorum (1641), his
Annotationes ad V.T. (1644) and his Annotationes in
N.T. (1646, 1650), Grotius freely treats the biblical
books as he would any other historical work of
antiquity.[58] In his apology for the Christian religion
he follows the same procedure. He nowhere tries to
prove that the New Testament is inspired or inerrant;
it is enough to establish its authenticity and
credibility to ensure its authority.[59] He argues that
the received authors of these books are correct and
that, since they were eyewitnesses and had no reason to

deceive, their accounts are dependable. Subsidiary
confirmation of the authors' credibility comes from the
apostolic miracles and fulfilled prophecies; but even
here Grotius does not conclude more than a general
historical reliability.[60] The objection that the
gospel accounts sometimes appear to be mutually
inconsistent is turned by Grotius to his advantage:

> Imo hoc ipsum Scriptores illos ab omni doli
> suspicione liberare debet; cum soleant illi qui
> falsa testantur, de compacto omnia ita narrare, ut
> ne speciem quidem quicquam diversum appareat:
> Quod si ex levi aliqua discrepantia, etiam quae
> conciliari nequiret, totis libros fides decederet,
> jam nulli libro, praesertim Historiarum, credendum
> esset; cum tamen Polygbio & Halicarnassensi, &
> Livio & Plutarcho, in quibus talia deprehenduntur,[61]
> sua apud nos de rerum summa constet auctoritas.

With regard to the Old Testament, he argued similarly
for a general historical reliability.[62] Grotius was
confident that by treating the Scriptures as ordinary
histories it could be shown that the biblical accounts
of the miracles and resurrection of Christ are factual
and that therefore the doctrine taught by Christ is
true. He did not anticipate the quite different use to
which his countryman Baruch Spinoza would put the
fledgling science of criticism nor the havoc that would
then ensue.

"In the history of religious ideas," writes Albert
Monod, "the eighteenth century begins with
Spinoza"[63]--not indeed with his Ethic, in which he
exhibited his pantheistic system in geometric form, but
rather with his Tractatus theologico-politicus (1670).
Spinoza's Ethic, it seems, was not generally understood
and its impact confined to philosophical circles.[64] By
contrast the arguments of the Tractatus stirred fires
of controversy on at least two fronts: the problem of

miracles, to which we shall return in the sequel, and
biblical criticism, especially Pentateuchal criticism.
Farrar believes that no work of free thought, except
for the work of Strauss, had more influence than the
Tractatus on friend and foe alike.[65]

Spinoza was not without his predecessors, however.
During Spinoza's day verbal inspiration of the
Scriptures was taken so rigidly that the question of
the date of the introduction of the Massoretic vowel
points was hotly debated by many under the impression
that the doctrine of inspiration would be overthrown
should it be admitted that they were added subsequent
to the closing of the canon. In Rabbi Elijah Levita's
Massoret ha-Massoret (1548) the author speculated that
the Hebrew vowel points had been added several
centuries after the beginning of the Christian Era.
The Reformed Protestant Cappel concurred in Arcanum
punctuationes (1624), and in his Critica sacra (1650)
pushed the argument even farther by showing that the
Hebrew text without vowel points was not exempt from
faults. So troubled were Protestant theologians by
these developments that several such as Buxtorf, Owen,
François Turretin, and others resisted the arguments of
Cappel for the late-dating of the vowel points and
maintained instead that the vowel pointing was, like
the text, inspired by the Holy Spirit. In the Formula
Consensus (1675) of the Helvetic church this position
was actually given credal status. If these disputes
over the Hebrew text of the Old Testament formed the
background for Spinoza's criticism, the work of Abraham
ibn (Aben) Ezra provided the immediate impetus. In his
Commentaries on the Old Testament (1526) Rabbi Ezra
muses over six objections to the Mosaic authorship of
the Pentateuch. Spinoza, who, as the son of Jewish

refugees to Holland, was well-acquainted with Jewish writings, borrows all six and adds four more. Spinoza believes that Aben Ezra did not pronounce decisively against Mosaic authorship out of fear of persecution; but, living in tolerant Holland, no such fear constrains him.

Along with the commentaries of ibn Ezra, the work of Thomas Hobbes was also an important influence. It is interesting to note that Hobbes traveled often on the Continent, visiting Galileo in 1636, from whom he learned the laws of inertia, which undercut the accepted Aristotelian physics. From 1640-51 he was exiled in France, where he became close friends with Gassendi, whose materialism seems to have strongly influenced Hobbes. His classic political treatise Leviathan appeared in 1651, the year of his return to England. Hobbes had been attacked in France for atheism, which is an understandable interpretation of the religious views expressed in Leviathan. For it is not altogether clear whether those views are really Hobbes's own or serve merely as a veneer to give an appearance of orthodoxy so as to avoid persecution. The philosophical argument of the work seems to lead in precisely the opposite direction of the religious confessions, but the latter are finally rescued by the authority of the Sovereign, who appears almost like a deus ex machina. There is no point, advises Hobbes, in trying to sift a philosophical truth out of mysteries by means of logic. "For it is with the mysteries of our Religion, as with wholesome pills for the sick, which swallowed whole, have the virtue to cure; but chewed, are for the most part cast up again without effect."[66] These mysteries are "swallowed whole" simply upon the Sovereign's decree.[67]

Hobbes's personal philosophical persuasion may well have been materialism. He argues that all substances are bodies and that, therefore, "incorporeal substance" is a contradiction in terms.[68] Neverthe- less, when Scripture speaks of God as a Spirit, faith consists not in our opinion, but in our submission. "For the nature of God is incomprehensible; that is to say, we understand nothing of what he is, but only that he is . . . ."[69] Similarly, when discussing the origin of religion, Hobbes contrasts belief in Gods with belief in one infinite, omnipotent, and eternal God. The former were conceived by men to be "invisible Agents" possessing "aereall bodies"; while men who arrived by meditation to acknowledge the latter "choose rather to confess he is Incomprehensible, and above their understanding; than to define his Nature by Spirit Incorporeall, and then confess their definition to be unintelligible."[70] When these words are applied to God they are not to be understood dogmatically as informative descriptions of the divine nature, but piously as expressions of devotion seeking to honor God by removing him from the "grossenesse of Bodies Visible."[71] In the same section, Hobbes contends that belief in Gods is the product of human fear; but belief in one eternal, infinite, and omnipotent God he attributes to the causal argument for a First Mover propounded by the Heathen Philosophers, without committing himself to the argument and knowing full well from his discussions with Galileo that the Aristotelian prime mover argument had been completely undercut by the new astronomy and physics.[72] It is hard to resist the conclusion that while Hobbes may have thought religion necessary for the well-being of the State, for him the concept of God involved

self-contradiction and the existence of God was
rationally unjustified.

When turning to the subject of revelation, Hobbes
similarly took back with one hand what he gave with the
other. He says that while his discourse on the
Christian Commonwealth will be based greatly on the
Prophetical Word of God, "Nevertheless, we are not to
renounce our Senses, and Experience; nor (that which is
the undoubted Word of God) our natural Reason."[73] He
grants that a man to whom God has spoken will
understand what it means for God to speak to a man, but
for anyone else, this notion is "hard, if not
impossible" to understand.[74] Not only does Hobbes
thereby imply that the concept of special revelation is
unintelligible, but he goes on to argue that even if
God did speak to a man there appears to be no way to
verify this claim. What certainty is there then of
knowing the will of God other than by Reason? queries
Hobbes. He proposes to resolve the difficulty by
applying the tests of a true prophet in Holy Scripture:
miracles and fidelity to accepted doctrine. But once
again Hobbes implicitly undercuts his proffered
solution by arguing that the two signs taken
individually are inadequate and that they therefore
have cogency only when taken in conjunction. The
problem is that he never shows, nor is it at all
obvious, that the weaknesses of the two individual
signs are mutually compensated for when they are
conjoined. Since miracles have now ceased, concludes
Hobbes, it is impossible that we should ever deviate
from the accepted doctrine taught in Scripture.

Hobbes then turns to a discussion of the
authorship of the biblical books, observing that
because there is insufficient testimony on this from

other histories, we must determine our judgement from
evidence in the books themselves.[76] With regard to the
Pentateuch, the attribution of this book to Moses may
indicate not its author, but rather its subject matter.
There are many problems with Mosaic authorship. The
statement of Deut 34.6 concerning the whereabouts of
Moses's grave was clearly written after his interrment.
The observation of Gen 12.6 that Canaanites were then
in the land was written by someone living when they
were not. Since Num 21.14 refers to the book of the
Wars of the Lord, which registers the acts of Moses,
Numbers must have been written later on. Hobbes grants
that Moses wrote what he is said to have written,
namely, the Volume of the Law. Similar chronological
anomalies occur in the other historical books of the
Old Testament. Hobbes surmises that the Scripture was
set forth in the form we have it by Ezra. Proceeding
to the New Testament books, Hobbes recognizes their
apostolic origin. Noting that the first complete
listing of the books of the canon came not until the
Council of Laodicea (364), Hobbes thinks nevertheless
that the Doctors of the church did not corrupt them,
though only they possessed them and were trying to palm
off frauds on people to make them more obedient to
Christian doctrine. Having thus created more doubts
about the books of Scripture than he has resolved,
Hobbes nonetheless concludes, "He therefore, to whom
God hath not supernaturally revealed, that they are
his, nor that those that published them, were sent by
him, is not obliged to obey them by any Authority, but
his, whose Commands have already the force of laws,
that is to say, by any other Authority, than that of
the Common-wealth, residing in the Sovereign, who only
has the Legislative power."[76]

The _Tractatus_, written in defense of religious
toleration[77], has no such deference for authority. The
history of the Bible, states Spinoza bluntly, is not so
much imperfect as untrustworthy; the foundations are
not only too scant to build upon, but they are also
unsound.[78] In examining the Mosaic authorship of the
Pentateuch, Spinoza explicates the six objections of
ibn Ezra: (1) Since Moses never crossed the Jordan, he
could not have written the preface to Deuteronomy.
(2) The "mystery of the twelve" mentioned by ibn Ezra:
perhaps that the book of Moses was written at full
length on an altar of twelve stones (Deut 27; Josh
8:32), thus implying it was short; or perhaps that the
last chapter of Deuteronomy, containing twelve verses,
speaks of Moses's death. (3) The statement of Deut
31.9 that Moses wrote the Law could not have come from
Moses himself. (4) The author of Gen 12.6 lived when
Canaanites were no longer in the land. (5) In Gen
22.14 Mount Moriah is called the mount of God, which is
a later name. (6) The relic of the iron bed in Deut 3
points to a later date. To these considerations
Spinoza adds: (1) The whole Pentateuch gives details
about Moses in the third person. (2) Moses could not
have written about the thirty days of mourning after
his death nor written that there was never in Israel a
man like Moses. (3) Many of the place names are of
later origin; for example, Dan (Gen 14.4). (4) The
narrative is prolonged after Moses's death (Ex 16.34;
Josh 6.12). It is as clear as the sun at noonday,
concludes Spinoza, that the Pentateuch was not written
by Moses, but by someone who lived after Moses. Moses
wrote only the War against Amalek (Ex 17.14; Num
21.12), the Book of the Covenant (Ex 24.4), and the
Book of the Law (Deut 1.5; 29.14; 31.9). After briefly

examining the other historical books of the Old
Testament, Spinoza infers that they were all written by
a single historian, who, he thinks, was probably Ezra.

Spinoza declines a comparable investigation of the
authenticity of the books of the New Testament, but he
does add some very significant remarks on the nature of
inspiration.[79] The prophets, he observes, were only
inspired when speaking directly the words of God; when
they spoke in ordinary conversation as private
individuals, their discourse was not inspired. Now
when we read the writings of the apostles, it is
evident that they are not speaking as inspired
prophets. They use reasoning to convince their readers
and employ modes of expression that are incompatible
with immediate revelation from God. Therefore, their
writings are not given by divine command, but are the
product of the natural powers of their authors.
Moreover, it is evident that the apostles often
disagreed among themselves, as we see in the books of
Acts and elsewhere. The implication would seem to be
that if the apostles could err privately, then, since
their writings are not inspired, they could also err in
them. In this way Spinoza undermined the authority of
the New Testament while not denying its authenticity.

The rudimentary biblical criticism expounded by
Spinoza served indirectly to promote the Deist cause.
Although Spinoza himself was a pantheist, as the Ethic
makes evident, the Tractatus is nevertheless in
substance a Deist work.[80] Its attacks on the
authenticity of biblical books and the doctrine of
inspiration, which were brought to the reading public
by the debates they engendered between Simon and Le
Clerc, were sufficient to topple the faith of many.
Lamenting the libertinism and impiety that everywhere

prevailed, Le Clerc declared,

> This is undoubtedly a great Mischief, and to which
> those who are any ways able to bring Remedy are
> oblig'd to do it.   It has been endeavoured to
> overthrow the Authority of the holy Scriptures, by
> making appear that the Stile of the sacred Writers
> was not inspir'd, and that they did not receive
> everything they said from immediate Inspiration.
> And in effect it has happen'd that many people
> have hereupon believ'd, that the Authority of the
> Scripture was intirely ruin'd; And imagining the
> reasons brought by Spinoza to prove this Opinion
> was unanswerable, they have fall'n into Deism or
> into Atheism.[81]

Spinoza's influence in this regard, however, was
largely brought to bear indirectly via the attempts of
Simon and LeClerc themselves to turn back the force of
his arguments.   Simon inaugurated the science of Old
Testament criticism with his Histoire critique du Vieux
Testament (1678), in which he treats in three books the
Hebrew text of the Bible from Moses to the present, the
various translations of the text, and the method for
translating the Scriptures.   In grappling with the
objections of ibn Ezra mediated by Spinoza to the
Mosaic authorship of the Pentateuch, Simon acknowledges
that it can no longer be maintained that Moses wrote
these books personally.[82]   But he does not adopt the
position of Hobbes and Spinoza; rather he contends that
Moses wrote part of the Pentateuch and that at his
order scribes assembled the rest of it from public
records.[83]   In order to retain the authority of the Old
Testament books, Simon opposes to Spinoza this
fundamental principle: it is not important who wrote
the books of the Old Testament because those who did so
were all prophets who were guided by the Holy Spirit in
compiling their books out of the ancient acts kept in
the registry of the republic.[84]   Simon concludes,

> We may by this same principle easily answer all
> the false and pernicious consequences drawn by
> Spinoza from these alterations or additions for
> the running down the Authority of the Holy
> Scripture, as if these corrections had been purely
> of humane Authority; whereas he ought to have
> consider'd that the authors of these alterations
> having had the power of writing Holy Scriptures
> had also the power of correcting them.[85]

Simon underlined his case in his Traité de
l'inspiration des livres sacrés (1687). He argues here
that criticism ought to be applied to the Scriptures as
to any other profane work and that God has not
preserved the text by a special providence, as certain
Jews and Protestants maintain. He reiterates that it
is a matter of indifference whether Moses or his
scribes wrote the Pentateuch, for these scribes, like
the New Testament evangelists, wrote under inspiration
of what they had seen and heard. But Simon's main
point is that only the scribal hypothesis can save the
authority of the Pentateuch; here he lists the
objections of Spinoza and shows how his hypothesis
resolves them.[86]

Jean Le Clerc, while professor at Amsterdam
(1684-1728), sought to blunt Spinoza's critique in an
even more radical manner, foreshadowed by Hugo
Grotius.[87] In his Sentimens de quelques théologiens de
Hollande sur l'Histoire critique du Vieux Testament
(1685), he, under the guise of reporting the opinions
of Dutch thinkers, boldly advocates a doctrine of
limited inspiration of the Scriptures. Purportedly
relating the opinions of one Monsieur N., Le Clerc
asserts that far from being a Deist, M.N. claims that
only he has the answer to their objections.[88]

He begins his case by dividing the Scriptures into
prophecies, histories, and doctrines. As to

prophecies, Le Clerc asserts that these need not always
be inspired. For example, the reporting of visions and
voices from God may be done by giving back the sense of
what was seen and heard in one's own words.[89] The fact
that prophets do differ in style disproves the
dictation theory of inspiration. Similarly, the
Evangelists give back only the sense of what Jesus
said, since they, too, differ in precise wording. As
to doctrines, Le Clerc appears to believe that the
doctrine taught by Christ was inspired as well as
certain doctrines taught by the apostles.[90] But he
denies, like Spinoza, that the apostles were always
inspired; for example, Paul before the High Priest was
quite clearly not inspired in the words he spoke.[91]

It is in his treatment of histories that Le Clerc
laid the goundwork for the eighteenth century English
Deist controversy over the credibility of the miracles
and resurrection of Jesus. He maintains that since it
can be shown that the gospel accounts are historically
reliable, the notion of inspiration becomes wholly
superfluous. To establish the truth and authority of
the Christian religion, it is enough to prove the
credibility of the narratives of Jesus's miracles and
resurrection in attestation to his doctrine:

> An historian that is honest, and well-inform'd of
> that which he relates, is worthy of Credit. And
> if you add thereto, that he has also suffer'd
> Death maintaining that they had seen and heard,
> that which the Gospel tells us of Jesus Christ;
> then not only that History will be worthy of
> Credit, but they who shall refuse to believe it,
> can pass for no other than Fools or obstinate
> Persons. In this manner we may be fully assur'd
> of the Truth of the History of the New Testament;
> that is to say, That there was a Jesus who did
> divers Miracles, who was rais'd from the Dead, &
> ascended up into Heaven, and who taught the[92]
> Doctrine which we find in the Gospels.

Against those who maintain that the Evangelists were inspired, inspired even to the very words they use, Le Clerc urges five objections: (1) There is no positive proof of such inspiration.   Those who support inspiration do so only because they think that if it is denied, we cannot be perfectly certain of the truth of the gospel history.   To which Le Clerc retorts: (a) An unpleasant consequence cannot disprove the truth of the fact from which it is drawn.   (b) The misgiving is in fact entirely ungrounded:

> . . . I affirm that it is false, that we cannot be perfectly certain of the main substance of a History unless we suppose it inspired. We are, for Example, perfectly certain that <u>Julius Caesar</u> was kill'd in the Senate by a Conspiracy, whereof <u>Brutus</u> and <u>Cassius</u> were the Chiefs; without believing that they who have inform'd us hereof were inspired. . . .[93]

In the same way, we can be perfectly certain of the truth of the gospels without supposing them to be inspired.

(2) The supposition of inspiration posits a miracle without any warrant.   The Scripture gives no indication that the Evangelists were inspired.   So there is no warrant to posit the miracle of inspiration.   "To relate faithfully a matter of Fact, which a Man has seen and well observed, requires no Inspiration.   The Apostles had no need of Inspiration to tell what they had seen, and what they heard Christ say.   There needs nothing for that but Memory and Honesty."[94]   People object that this is only human faith.   But Le Clerc responds that it is the same faith that tells us that Matthew's Gospel is really his, namely, faith in the power of historical evidences.   So with Christ: the only reason we believe in him is

because we are convinced, on the basis of testimony by
eye-witnesses who died for the truth of their
testimony, that the history we have of him is true. Le
Clerc has no reservations about drawing the conclusion:
"So that Human Faith is found to be the ground of
Divine Faith."[95] But, he hastens to add, there is no
reason to fear that this foundation is not firm enough.
One would have to be no more than a brute in reasoning
to deny this foundation, as the many writers on the
truth of the Christian religion have shown.

(3) The testimony of the sacred writers themselves
is contrary to their being inspired. Citing Luke
1.1-4, Le Clerc comments, "You may observe in these
words a Confirmation of what I have been saying, and a
full Proof that St. Luke learn'd not that which he told
us by Inspiration, but by Information from those who
knew it exactly."[96] Thus the Evangelists themselves
give evidence that they are not inspired.

(4) The contradictions in Scripture make it plain
that the Scripture Historians were not inspired.
Although the Evangelists agree in the main among
themselves, there are circumstantial details in which
they disagree, which proves that every particular was
not inspired. These details are of no consequence with
regard to the authority of the Evangelists; in fact
they are positive proof that they did not conspire
among themselves to fabricate the gospel story.
Nevertheless, if the Holy Spirit had dictated the
gospels to them, they would have agreed perfectly in
every detail, since God knew these as well as the main
facts of the story. An example of the sort of
circumstantial detail which Le Clerc is discussing is
the differing accounts of Judas's death, which stand in
"manifest Contradiction."[97]

(5) The Evangelists often show their ignorance of
certain facts. They often use phrases like "about a
certain time" or "about a certain number" (Luke 1.56;
3.23; John 2.6; 6.10, 19; 19.14) which show that they
were not inspired by the Holy Spirit, who would have
known exactly what time or what number was in question.

On the basis of these objections, Le Clerc holds
that it is unnecessary to believe that the Evangelists
were inspired. He is anxious to emphasize that because
the Scriptures are historically reliable, he has in no
way undermined the authority of Scripture:

> Thus then, according to my Hypothesis, the
> Authority of Scripture continues in full force.
> For you see I maintain that we are obliged to
> believe the Substance of the History of the New
> Testament; and generally all the Doctrines of
> Jesus Christ; all that was inspir'd to the
> Apostles; and also whatsoever they have said of
> themselves, so far as it is conformable to our
> Saviour's doctrine, and to right Reason.[98]

We believe the doctrines on the authority of Christ,
established by his miracles, resurrection, and
ascension. This hypothesis has the advantage of
focusing attention on the essence of religion:
applying ourselves wholly to obey the precepts of
Christ. Moreover,--and here Le Clerc no doubt thinks
of the Tractatus--we can answer objections that the
Scripture has low style, contradictions, little order,
and so forth. We have seen that Le Clerc was concerned
with Spinoza's attacks on Scripture and the plunging of
many persons into Deism or atheism. What remedy, he
asks, is there for this?

> For my part, I confess, I see but one of these
> three. Either a way must be found to burn all the
> Copies of these impious books . . . and to blot
> out of Men's Memory the Arguments of these

libertines; or else there must solid Demonstration
be made of the falsity of the Arguments they make
use of to maintain their Opinions; Or, lastly, in
granting to them that the sacred Pen-Men were not
inspir'd, neither as to the Stile, nor as to those
things which they might know otherwise than by
revelation, it must be yet demonstrated that the
Authority of the Scriptures ought not for all that
to be esteemed less considerable.
   It is plain that the first of these three is
absolutely impossible. . . .For my part I could
wish with all my heart that somebody would try the
second. . . .But since nobody has yet done, nor
that I know has undertaken to do it, why should it
be ill taken that Mr. N̲ has made use of the third
method . . . ?[99]

In order to prove that the third method does not

lead to Deism, Le Clerc constructs his own mini-apology

for the truth of the Christian religion on its basis.

He presents the basic dilemma found already in Grotius

and characteristic of anti-Deist apologetic for more

than a century to follow: <u>for the gospels to be false,</u>

<u>the apostles</u> <u>would have to be either</u> <u>deceivers or</u>

<u>deceived, both of which are impossible.</u>   In order to

prove that the disciples are not deceivers, Le Clerc

appeals to early extra-biblical sources that describe

the sufferings of Christians for their faith.   Peter

and Paul were martyred for their faith.   The apostles

had simply nothing to gain from preaching this new

religion.   From this he concludes no more than "that

the Apostles were sincere Persons, who believed their

own Doctrine, as were also those who by their Example

dy'd for it."[100]   Nor can it be said that the apostles

were themselves deceived concerning all the miracles of

Christ which they relate.   They saw these things with

their own eyes, heard them with their own ears.

Therefore, can we not believe them when they relate the

death and entombment of Jesus?   So why should we not

equally believe them when they assert they saw him

alive?

There are two possible ways to object to a fact,
continues Le Clerc; either by impugning the quality of
the witnesses or by demonstrating the inherent
impossibility of the fact in question. But in this
case, the disciples have been proved to be excellent
witnesses. And as for the a priori objection of
Spinoza to the impossibility of miracles, the fact is
that his theoretical arguments "are not comparable in
evidence and force to the Principles we have
establish'd."[101]   In other words, the empirical
evidence that the miracles and resurrection of Christ
did occur simply breaks the back of the a priori
argument that they could not have occurred. The force
of the factual arguments is greater than the force of
the philosophical arguments. According to Le Clerc,
over against the abstract arguments of the Spinozists,
we have direct proof of the truth of these events
"which are infinitely more clear than their Reasons,
which no body can understand, as perhaps neither do
they themselves."[102]   The conclusion of all this,
states Le Clerc, is that Christ must be a teacher sent
from heaven to set men right that were gone astray.

Simon responded to Le Clerc in his Histoire
critique du Texte du Nouveau Testament (1689), in which
he inaugurated the scientific criticism of the New
Testament. In his chapter on the inspiration of the
New Testament, Simon goes after Spinoza and the author
of the Sentimens. His fundamental principle on which
he aims to refute Spinoza and Le Clerc is that
inspiration should not be understood woodenly in terms
of dictation: "Il n'est pas necessaire qu'un Livre
pour être inspiré ait été dicté de Dieu mot pour
mot."[103]   The Evangelists in composing the gospels were

not divested of reason and memory by the Holy Spirit.
Rather God directed them in their work and so kept them
from falling into error.   In a later chapter on
Spinoza's objections (which Simon traces to Grotius),
the French critic maintains that Spinoza's problem was
that he could not conceive how a man could use his
reason and yet be inspired by the Holy Spirit.[104]
Spinoza's whole reasoning is predicated on the false
idea which he has formed of the nature of inspiration.
As for the Sentimens, they are merely a popularizing of
Spinoza's reasoning. If inspiration is understood in
terms of direction, not dictation, then the fact that
the apostles speak not as prophets but as doctors in no
way destroys the inspiration of the Holy Spirit.   As
for the grounds for belief in inspiration, Simon points
to II Tim 3.16, which he believes Protestants have
correctly interpreted ("all Scripture is inspired by
God"), though this does not exclude the addition of
Catholic traditions.

Le Clerc responds to such objections by retreating
to a more cautious position: "My Argument proves not
directly that there was no Inspiration on these
occasions, but only that there was nothing in the thing
itself to induce us to believe that there was any; and
consequently, that such Inspiration is suppos'd without
any Necessity."[105]   As for II Tim 3.16, this should be
translated "all Scripture inspired by God is
profitable, etc.", leaving open that some Scripture may
not be inspired. As for Simon's notion of inspiration
as guidance, this is unobjectionable, so long as the
direction extends no further than the selection of the
subject matter. With regard to Simon's contention that
reasoning and inspiration are not mutually exclusive,
Le Clerc argues that either the Holy Spirit gave the

apostles full-framed arguments or only general principles. If complete arguments, then there was no need for reasoning. But if he gave only general principles, then the apostles were still dependent on fallible reason to make their deductions, and hence nothing is gained.[106]

Simon and Le Clerc debated the issue back and forth, thereby arousing grave doubts in the minds of many thinkers concerning the reliability of the Scriptures.[107] But as Monod points out, biblical criticism did not really assume the importance one would expect after Spinoza and Simon.[108] This may be, says Monod, because of the apologies of respected authors who determined the opinions of most ecclesiastics. Since biblical criticism was done by churchmen, the new movement was arrested. In any case, we find little use of such critical studies on the part of the Deists. Perhaps the closest example would be Anthony Collins, a close friend of the elderly John Locke.[109] Collins became one of the leading Deists of England, publishing his A Discourse of Free-Thinking, Occasion'd by the Growth of a Sect Call'd Free-Thinkers in 1713 and his A Discourse on the Ground and Reason of the Christian Religion in 1724. The first of these, which provoked thirty-four responses in England, is an apology for free thought, which Collins tries to show stretches from Socrates to Herbert of Cherbury and Locke. He also charges on the basis of Mills's catalog published in 1707 of 30,000 variations in the biblical text that the Old Testament is fatally corrupted.[110] Collins was answered by the esteemed scholar Richard Bentley in what was by all accounts a thorough refutation.[111] The second work, which called forth thirty-five replies, is a withering attack on the

traditional proof from prophecy. Collins maintains
that no Old Testament prophecy has been literally
fulfilled in the New Testament, and the prophecies can
therefore only be taken allegorically. He also
reiterates that the Old Testament text is badly
corrupted,[112] and he impugns the canon and inspiration
of the New Testament.[113] This is, however, the extent
of his use of criticism. As Monod says, Simon and Le
Clerc would have been embarrassed about Collins, who
substituted impassioned polemic for criticism.[114]
Stephen points out, however, that Bentley's reply to
Collins was significant in that Bentley, by treating
the text critically like any other ancient manuscript,
tended to reduce the Bible to the level of an ordinary
book. Bentley could himself claim to be a free-thinker
"because the destructive agency of science and
criticism could be as yet but dimly suspected. Those
who ventured, like Collins, to foretell the coming
deluge could be safely ridiculed, when as yet there was
but a cloud as big as a man's hand. And, for the time,
their defeat was crushing."[115]

Thus, no true disciple of Simon and Le Clerc is to
be found until Jean Astruc and Johann Semler in the
latter half of the eighteenth century. The influence
of these early biblical critics upon Deism consisted in
their removing the aura of sanctity from the Holy
Scriptures by handling them like any other historical
work and in the doubts they created concerning the
reliability and authority of the Bible. The rough and
ready handling of the Scriptures was an earmark of
Deist writings, as John Leland observes in his A View
of the Principal Deistical Writers (1754),

    In their treatment of the Scriptures, they have
    everywhere discovered an eager desire and

resolution to expose and run them down at any
rate. In examining the writings of venerable
antiquity and authority, a man of candour and an
impartial inquirer after truth, would be inclined
to put the most favourable interpretation upon
them that they will bear: But instead of this,
these writers seem only solicitous to find out
something that may make the scriptures appear
ridiculous. They take pains to wrest and pervert
them, as if they thought it meritorious to treat
those sacred writings in a manner that would not
be born with regard to any other books of the
least credit. Of this many instances might be
produced: If they meet with any passages of
Scripture that have difficulty in them, and which
at this distance it is not easy to explain; and
some such passages must be expected in books of so
great antiquity, written in times and places, as
well as dialects so different from our own; this
is immediately improved, as if it were sufficient
to shew that the whole sacred volume is false, or
so corrupted, as not to be depended upon. . . .[116]

The running battle between Simon and Le Clerc in the
seventeenth century undoubtedly aided the cause of
incredulity and thereby Deism. Monod explains,

Deism is going to reign supreme. Spinoza has
lasting influence on a few through the Ethic, on
many through the Tractatus. Whether the Tractatus
exercises this influence directly or through the
intermediary of Simon and Le Clerc matters little.
When these last tried to institute a rational
exegesis, when R. Simon adopts the principle that
in matters of philosophy (science) one need not
follow the Scriptures to the letter because they
are in accord with popular ideas (3), when Le
Clerc exhausts the inspiration of the apostles in
following the way which Spinoza only indicated
(4), one understands that the influence of the
Jewish philosopher was by means of them
reverberated and amplified. And that is exactly
how the traditional Christians took him (5). The
whole rationalist movement, Deist or Socinian, was
strengthened by him.

----

3. "Bibliothèque critique," Amst., 1708-10, 4

v.12; t. IV, p. 94, n.2.
4. "Sentimens de quelques théologiens de
Hollande," Amst. 1685, 2 v. 8°. Let. 11 and
12.
5. . . .Groteste de la Mothe: "Traité de
l'inspiration," p. 4.[117]

But there is also one other fascinating respect in
which this movement affected the course of English
Deism. Le Clerc's discussion of the inspiration of the
Scriptures in the Sentimens is widely thought to have
been trtanslated into English as Five Letters
Concerning the Inspiration of the Holy Scriptures in
1690 by John Locke. The English philosopher could not
resist the force of Le Clerc's argument. Embracing the
new view for his own, Locke states, ". . .apply unto me
the Author's Apology. Our case is the same, and, I
think, he has said all that is needful upon it."[118]
Locke saw around him, too, the prevalence of unbelief
and realized that the Bible could no longer be presumed
to be reliable without further ado: "The Doctrine of
Implicit Faith has lost its Vogue. Every Man will
judge for himself, in matters that concern him so
nearly as these do. And nothing is now admitted for
Truth, that is not built upon the foundation of Solid
Reason."[119] Five years later in 1695 Locke published
his Reasonableness of Christianity in which he employs
the method of M.N. to establish the truth of
Christianity. Locke's work marked the beginning of the
great Deist controversy in England and helped to
determine the course of that debate by the apologetic
method he employed. In this way the seeds sown in
Continental Europe during the seventeenth century came
to harvest in eighteenth century England.

Religio-social effects
of the Reformation

In his account of the history of English Deism,
Orr lists seven effects of the Protestant Reformation
which contributed to the rise aand spread of Deism:
(1) The Reformation gave a less important place to
orders, ordinances, and rituals; (2) The reformers
lessened the miraculous content of religion; (3) The
reformers gave an increased importance to the use of
reason in religion; (4) In the Reformation, clergy
became targets of criticism on the charge of
corruption; (5) The Reformation greatly multiplied the
number of rival sects, each claiming to have the true
religion; (6) The evils of the religious wars that
followed the Reformation tended to produce bitter
antagonism to Christianity; and (7) The hardships
suffered by nearly all men as a result of a policy of
religious intolerance wrought a backlash of sympathy
for the Deist cause.[120]   A word ought to be said on
each of these.

1.   Diminished importance   of ecclesiastical
additions to religion: The Reformers opposed the pomp
and wealth of the Roman Church, reduced the number of
sacraments, abolished observance of most special days,
simplified the ritual, and removed all these from the
essence of true religion. Orr should have mentioned,
however, that this was only part of the wider critique
of the reformers that the Roman church had overlaid the
true gospel of primitive Christianity with layer upon
layer of human doctrines, such that the original gospel
had been all but lost; hence, their emphasis on sola
gratia, sola fides, sola Scriptura. The reformers
criticized the church for obscuring the simple gospel
not only with ceremony and pomp, but also with

unbiblical doctrines and false practices. It is only
natural that many should have subsequently gone beyond
the reformers in a desire to divest true religion of
all ecclesiastical forms and abstruse doctrines. This
would lead eventually to a simplified natural religion,
owing nothing to the church and possessed of few
doctrines.

We find a good example of this in Lord Herbert's
Deism. The five principles which he laid down as
constituting the essence of religion, the notitiae
communes, remained characteristic of most Deists:

    I. That there is one supreme God.
   II. That he ought to be worshipped.
 III. That virtue and piety are the chief parts of
      Divine Worship.
  IV. That we ought to be sorry for our sins and
      repent of them.
   V. That Divine goodness doth dispense rewards
      and punishments both in this life and after
      it.[121]

Herbert considered that these principles were entirely
sufficient for salvation and piety; Christian doctrines
such as the Trinity, the atoning death of Christ,
justification by faith, and so forth are implicily
regarded as superfluous.[122] With regard to the third
principle, Lord Herbert contrasted natural religion
with the religion of external forms and ceremonies.
The proper means of worshipping God is to lead an
upright life, not to submit to the regimen of
performing ritual actions. He attributed the
corruption of natural religion to a religion of mere
form in the hands of power-hungry priests.[123]

Although English Deists were to re-iterate Lord
Herbert's sentiments, it must be said that the Deists
of authoritarian Catholic France were much more bitter
in their denunciations of the church and its system of
dogmas and rites, which they invariably denoted by the

word "superstition", than their English counterparts.
At the same time, however, they were more willing to
retain an element of external form in their natural
religion, along with a minimum of dogmas.

Rousseau, for example, substitutes for all the
doctrines of the church three simple articles of faith:
(1) that there is a will which moves the universe and
animates nature, (2) that the laws of nature evince an
intelligence behind them, which we call God, and (3)
that man is free in his actions.[124] Rousseau also
accepts the goodness of God, the immortality of the
soul, and the dispensing of rewards in the
after-life.[125] Conscience is the divine guide for
leading a moral life on earth.[126] Any dogmas beyond
these only serve to degrade religion: "Rather than
illuminating the notions of the great Being, I see that
particular dogmas confuse them; far from elevating
them, they debase them; to inconceivable mysteries they
add absurd contradictions; they render man proud,
intolerant, cruel; instead of establishing peace on
earth, they bring iron and fire."[127] A special object
of ridicule by French Deists was the doctrine of
transubstantiation; Rousseau mocked the doctrine by
stating that it proves that the part is greater than
the whole, since at the Last Supper Jesus held his
whole body in his hand and put his head in his
mouth!--a remark which delighted Voltaire.[128] As for
the external ceremonies and ritual of religion, these
are cultural and relative, not divine; had all men
listened to God's voice in nature and conscience, there
would be only one religion on earth:

> There had to be a uniform worship I grant it: but
> was this point therefore so important that it
> necessitated all the magnificence of the divine

power to establish it? We must not confuse the
ceremony of religion with religion. The worship
which God asks is that of the heart; and that
worship, when it is sincere, is always uniform.
It would be to have a foolish vanity indeed to
imagine that God takes such a great interest in
the form of the priest's habit, in the order of
the words which he pronounces, in the gestures
that he makes at the altar, and in all his
genuflections. . . .God wants to be adored in
spirit and in truth; this is the duty of all
religions, of all lands, of all men. As for the
external form of worship, if it must be uniform
for good order , that is purely a police matter;
one certainly does not need revelation for that.

---

* it must be uniform, it is true, but it is up to
the government to prescribe it.[129]

For Rousseau, then, ceremony stood on the
periphery of true religion. But it is interesting to
note that he acknowledged its importance for what he
calls "civil religion," that is, the religion of the
citizen qua citizen. Since the citizen cannot be
separated from the man, he cannot be expected to give
his allegiance to laws unrelated to moral and religious
principles. Therefore, it is necessary to have a civil
religion administered by the state. Rousseau admitted
frankly that his natural religion was incapable of
constituting such a civil religion.[130] In the first
place, since natural religion (or as Rousseau calls it,
"theism" or "the religion of man") has no relation to
the body politic, it can give no added sanction to the
laws. Secondly, far from inspiring the hearts of the
citizens to allegiance to the state, it, more than
anything else in the world, draws them from it,
transcending as it does national and cultural
limitations. Declares Rousseau: "Je ne connais rien
de plus contraire a l'esprit social. . . .une société

de vrais chrétiens ne serait plus une société
d'hommes."[131]   Therefore, one must institute a purely
civil religion, and it is up to the sovereign to
establish the articles thereof.   These articles of
faith, says Rousseau, are not precisely like dogmas of
religion, but more like feelings of sociability without
which it is impossible to be a good citizen or loyal
subject.[132]   As to their content, Rousseau explains,

> The dogmas of civil religion must be simple, few
> in number, enunciated with precision, without
> explanation or commentary. The existence of the
> powerful, intelligent, beneficent, provident and
> providing Deity, the life to come, the happiness
> of the just, the punishment of the wicked, the
> holiness of the social contract and the laws:
> these are the positive dogmas. As for negative
> dogmas, I restruct them to one: that is
> intolerance: it returns in the forms of worship
> we have excluded.[133]

Rousseau's civil religion thus, in effect, gives his
natural religion the force of law and adds to it the
notions of sanctions and of the divine nature of the
state and its laws. He thus reintroduces, albeit on a
diffferent level, some of the external trappings of
religion.

Voltaire also took a similar tack. He describes
the ideal religion as the adoration of the supreme,
only, infinite, eternal Being, the former of the world,
who gives it motion and life.[134]   Voltaire would
substitute a pure morality for all the vain ceremonies
as the means of worshipping and reaching God.

> I say to you: 'Continue to cultivate virtue, to
> be beneficent, to regard all superstition with
> horror, or with pity; but adore, with me, the
> design which is manifested in all nature, and
> consequently the Author of that design--the
> primordial and final cause of all; hope with me

that our monad, which reasons on the great eternal being, may be happy through that same great Being.'[135]

The reward of our virtues would be to be re-united with this Being; the chastisement for our crimes, separation from Him.[136]   Voltaire believed that this simple religion was that taught by Jesus which was then corrupted by the church. "There is not a single dogma of Christianity that was preached by Jesus Christ," he proclaimed.[137]   Jesus was born as a Jew and lived as a Jew. He never revealed the mystery of his incarnation nor his virgin birth. He never baptized anyone, never spoke of the seven sacraments, never instituted an ecclesiastical hierarchy. He concealed from his contemporaries that he was the Son of God, begotten from all eternity, consubstantial with his Father, and that the Holy Ghost proceeded from the Father and Son. He did not say that his person possessed two natures and two wills. So long as he lived, he departed in nothing from the ways of his fathers. In the eyes of men, he was simply a just man, pleasing to God, condemned by prejudiced magistrates. "He has left His holy church, established by Him, to do all the rest."[138]

Like Rousseau, however, Voltaire recognized the need for some sort of institutionalized religion with a priesthood and ritual. But, he insisted, the ideal religion would have "august ceremonies, to strike the vulgar, without having mysteries to disgust the wise and irritate the incredulous."[139]

2. Diminished miraculous content of religion: The reformers generally regarded Catholic miracles, such as those associated with saints, shrines, and relics, as entirely spurious. But while they denounced these

popish miracles as frauds and exposed them to ridicule,
they retained a belief in biblical miracles. But once
scepticism and incredulity had been aroused concerning
miracles that had been solemnly authorized by the holy,
catholic church itself, it was unrealistic to expect
these grim visitors to halt suddenly at the threshhold
of the biblical miracles. If the Catholic miracles
appeared ridiculous and unvelievable, then, by the same
token, to many minds so did the biblical miracles.

This incredulity reaches its most vitriolic
expression in Thomas Woolston's Discourses on the
Miracles of Our Saviour (1727-9). In Woolston's
analysis, Anthony Collins had dealt so crushing a blow
to the proof from prophecy in his Grounds and Reasons
of the Christian Religion that some orthodox writers
were seeking refuge in miracles as the justification
for Christianity.[140] Therefore he proposes to examine
the miracles of the gospels with a view toward proving
three propositions: (1) Healing miracles do not prove
Jesus's Messiahship. (2) The literal history of
miracles implies such absurdities, improbabilities, and
incredibilities that the miracle stories should be
understood as prophetic or parabolic narratives of what
Christ would do. (3) When Christ appealed to miracles
as proof, he meant mystical miracles which he would do
in the Spirit.[141] For Woolston the gospel miracles
appear every bit as ridiculous as did Catholic miracles
to the reformers, and he denounces them as frauds, just
as the reformers did the objects of their attack.

The weapon employed by Woolston, indeed, by many
of the Deists, in his attack upon miracles was mockery.
Ridicule, he says, should take the place of sober
reasoning in these matters.[142] His strategy was simply
to make the biblical miracles look so silly that no

amount of scholarly reasoning could generate belief in them. An example of his approach: in the story of the resurrection of the saints at Christ's crucifixion the evangelist should have mentioned "whether there were any Women among those Saints; and whether they appear'd naked (as Jesus modestly did to Mary Magdalen, unless he slip'd himself by stealth into the Cloths of the Gardner, . . . for she suppos'd she saw the Gardner). . . . "[143] The only way to preserve the miracle stories of the gospels from degenerating into absurdity, opined Woolston, was to interpret them allegorically as the Fathers did. But his attempt to salvage the gospel miracles, of course, implicitly removes any evidential value they could have possessed for Christianity.

About 1731 there began in Paris a remarkable sequence of events which had a profound effect upon the eighteenth century discussion of miracles and probably did as much as any polemical treatise to destroy belief in the gospel accounts of miracles.[144] At the tomb of the Jansenist abbé François de Paris in the cemetery of St. Médard, a series of purported healing miracles began to take place. The healings were accompanied by violent bodily convulsions, so that the participants in these wonders became famous as the convulsionnaires. Things eventually got so out of hand that in January of 1732 a guard had to be stationed at the cemetery to keep out the crowds, who sometimes even tried to eat the dirt of the cemetery. The spectacle of healings that were incomplete or accompanied by wrenching convulsions and sometimes obscene or ridiculous gestures and words discredited the genuineness of these miraculous cures. Yet the witnesses to these miracles were abundant, and the Jansenists defended their authenticity, even comparing them to the gospel miracles. That, of course, only served to cast doubt upon the genuineness of the gospel miracles as well. When a counselor to the Parisian Parliament Carré de Montgeron, a man versed in judicial affairs, sought to prove the veracity of the miracles at St. Médard by a detailed investigation complete with interviews, witnesses, and illustrations, which are unavailable for the gospel miracles, it became painfully obvious that if evidence could be so abundantly accumulated for miracles which everyone of good sense knew were false, then the weaker evidence on behalf of the gospel miracles proved nothing. By the same token, if the Jansenist miracles should be shown to be fraudulent, then a fortiori the gospel miracles are undermined as well. The pseudo-miracles of St. Médard constituted for many a decisive disproof of the argument from miracles to which Deist writers would refer again and again. They showed graphically the impossibility of discerning the supernatural, the ease of illusion, and the contagious credulity of the witnesses. Why should one accept evidence for miracles done 16 or 17 centuries ago, demanded Marie Huber, when one would not accept the same evidence for miracles done only a few years ago?[145] Diderot ridiculed the miracles of St. Médard, comparing them to pseudo-miracles of the past, and sneered at Montgeron's conversion through the Jansenist wonders.[146] Conyers Middleton repudiated the miracles of St. Médard in his effort to prove historically that all miracles ceased after the New Testament.[147] Middleton's attempt to discredit the miracles of the Catholic church recalls most clearly the efforts of the reformers, but now there is a radical difference: by demonstrating the insufficiency of the evidences and testimony to the Catholic

miracles, Middleton implictly robs the evidence for the
even further removed gospel miracles of all force.[148]
David Hume pointed to the Jansenist miracles at the
tomb of the abbé Paris as one of three examples of
miracles every bit as well attested as the gospel
miracles.[149]   Hume's point was simply that if no
reasonable man ought to accept the absurdities of St.
Médard despite the evidence, then neither should he
believe in the miracles of the Bible.   Rousseau used
the miracles at St. Médard to disqualify the evidence
for the gospel miracles.   If someone were to come to
the archbishop of Paris, claiming to have seen the abbé
Paris risen from the dead, he would respond, "I know
that two or three witnesses, honest and of good sense,
can attest the life or death of a man, but I do not yet
know how many it would take to establish the
resurrection of a Jansenist.   Until I learn, go, my
child, and try to strengthen your hollow head."[150]
Voltaire in his dictionary article, "Convulsionnaires"
ridicules the Jansenist miracles and in his article on
miracles he borrows Middleton's argument comparing
well-attested pagan and church miracles to biblical
miracles.[151]   How wonderful it would be, he sighs, if a
miracle could be performed before the Royal Society of
London or the Academy of Sciences at Paris with the
assistance of an armed guard to keep back the
crowds![152]

Of course, the orthodox did not take this lying
down. They sought to show that the pseudo-miracles of
St. Médard lacked any resemblance to the gospel
miracles.[153] The convulsions were contagious and the
witnesses fanatical. Analogies to the healings could
be found. Desperate efforts were made to bring on the
miracles, which were often incomplete, though this was

not immediately obvious. For these and other reasons,
one was perfectly justified in rejecting these false
miracles, yet adhering to biblical miracles.

In any case, in Deism the reformers' critique of
Catholic miracles was extended to include the biblical
miracles as well. The dividing wall between sacred and
profane history had been broken down. This is, agree
Stephen and Brown, the true significance of Middleton's
argument.[154]   He asks, in effect, why should you
believe Matthew if you will not believe Augustine? If
you believe Augustine, do you disbelieve modern stories
of miracles?   The orthodox divines, contrary to
Stephen, did try to answer these sorts of questions,
usually by drawing up lists of criteria for the
authenticity of miracles and arguing that only the
gospel miracles passed those criteria. It must be said
that the orthodox were, as Brown observes, often
hampered in effectively answering these questions
because of one presupposition under which they labored:
the cessation of miracles. During the seventeenth
century, it had become almost a dogma of Protestantism
that miracles had ceased early on in the church. Thus,
they felt compelled to argue against any modern miracle
while accepting the gospel miracles, a procedure which
gave the appearance of special pleading. It did not
seem to occur to them that the admission of a genuine
modern miracle would in no way logically undercut the
truth of the gospel stories.

3. Increased importance of the role of reason in
religion: When Luther, having already admitted at
Leipzig that Popes and Councils could err, declared at
Worms that unless he were dissuaded by Scripture or
sound reason he would not nor could not recant, he set
in motion a revolution in religious epistemology. In

place of the infallible authority of the church as a
test for religious truth Luther substituted Holy
Scripture and reason.   Scripture he held to be
immediately authenticated to the believer by the
witness of the Holy Spirit, which is self-authenti-
cating.[155]   Reason when used ministerially in
submission to Scripture could correctly ascertain
truth.   Similarly, Calvin maintained the primacy of
Scripture as authenticated by the witness of the Holy
Spirit, but he also accepted reason's proper role in
confirming and defending the truths of Scripture.[156]
Their opponents in the Roman church charged that this
appeal to Scripture and reason as the tests for
religious truth would ultimately land one in utter
scepticism. Basing the authority of Scripture on inner
subjective experience makes it impossible to adjudicate
between similar competing claims to divine revelation
and could lead, in fact, to self-delusion.   Nor is
reason an infallible guide, for Scripture is not
sufficiently clear that its interpretation can be left
to the subjective decisions of the individual, unaided
by the objective and infallible guide of the church.
This was already manifestly apparent by the
fragmentation and discord within Protestantism itself.
Against the bickering factions of Protestantism, the
Catholic theologians opposed an objective, infallible
criterion for truth: the authority of the Roman
church. As legitimation that the church's authority
was, indeed, the test for truth, they produced lists of
the notae ecclesiae, the marks or evidences of the
church.[157]   Bellarminus enumerated as many as fifteen
marks of the church, the most important being
catholicity, antiquity, eternal duration, and amplitude
or multitude and variety of believers.[158]   The

remaining included apostolic succession, the conformity
of doctrine to that of the primitive church, unity,
sanctity of doctrine, efficacy of doctrine, the
sanctity of the Fathers, church miracles, its lumen
propheticum, the admission of its adversaries, the
miserable deaths of its opponents, the temporal
felicity of its defenders.   The heirs of the
reformation countered that it was the Catholic
theologians, not they, who were on the road to
scepticism. For in order to establish the authority of
the church, its defenders had to turn to some other
authority, namely, the marks of the church. But these
were obviously inadequate. For as Du Moulin pointed
out, to be true marks of the church, they must be valid
at all times.[159] But obviously, at one time the church
did not possess antiquity, nor amplitude, nor
catholicity. At the inception of Christianity,
believers were a recent, tiny, and despised minority.
Thus, the implication was that either the notae are
inadequate warrants for the church's authority or else
at one time the church would be proved to have been
false. Therefore, the crucial question was not whether
the Catholic church possessed certain external
characteristics, but whether the doctrine it taught was
true. And the only way to determine that was by the
light of Scripture and reason. If these are denied,
one is lost in scepticism. In this way, the Protestant
Reformation gave to reason a new and significant
emphasis in religious espistemology.

     At about the same time that these theological
disputes were going on, a philosophical crisis began to
swell. The rediscovery of Greek Pyrrhonic philosophy
during the sixteenth century brought about a wave of
"new Pyrrhonism" that threatened to sweep away all

certainty of rational truth claims. The publication of
the text of the classic Greek sceptic Sextus Empiricus
by Henri Estienne in 1562 initiated the rediscovery of
Pyrrhonical philosophy. Francisco Sanches, professor
of philosophy and medicine at Toulouse, wrote in 1576
and published five years later his Quod nihil scitur,
in which he utilized Pyrrhonical arguments to show the
impossibility of acquiring certain scientific knowledge
of any object. He, for this reason, exalted faith
above reason in attaining truth.

The greatest sceptic of the sixteenth century,
however, was Sanches's distant cousin Michel de
Montaigne. The scepticism of Montaigne appears to have
been stirred by the Expansion of Europe, which he
experienced first hand as he traveled widely and spoke
with persons of other religious faiths.[160]   As he
studied Sextus Empiricus, he passed through his own
crise pyrrhonienne, out of which developed his
"Apologie de Raimond Sebond" (1575-6; published 1586).
Raimundus Sabundus was a teacher of theology at
Toulouse who wrote in 1436 the rationalistic treatise
Liber creaturarum, or, as it came to be later known,
Theologia naturalis. In this work Sabundus tries to
prove almost every article of the Christian faith on
the basis of reason, with reference neither to the
Bible nor to the Church. He argues for the existence
of God, the incarnation and deity of Christ, and the
authority of the Scriptures and Church authorized by
him.[161] Montaigne's essay is a purported defense of
Sabundus's strained arguments, showing that
Christianity is properly based on faith alone and that
since all reasoning is ultimately unsound, Sabundus
should not be blamed for his fallacies.[162] He grants
Sabundus the right to support faith by rational

arguments, but he insists that reason can never be the
foundation for faith.[163] He then proceeds to demolish
all attempts at sound reasoning, under the guise of
defending Sabundus for his weak arguments. He compares
man's powers of reasoning to those of mere animals,
showing man to be little better than they in his
ignorance and weakness. He expounds the conundrums
posed by classic Greek Pyrrhonism, concluding that
everything is so doubtful, I cannot even assert that I
do not know--since that would itself be a positive
assertion of knowledge--but can only ask, "What do I
know?" These words--"Que sais-je?"--became Montaigne's
personal motto. Montaigne, drawing upon the new
discoveries in geography and history, hammers home the
ethical, legal, and religious relativism that
ensues.[164] He points to new opinions in astronomy to
show the uncertainty of scientific knowledge.[165] He
attacks all empirical knowledge as uncertain because of
our inability to check if our sense impressions
correspond with reality. For our senses may be
inadequate, deceived, or distorted.[166] Finally, any
suggested test for truth will itself require a warrant,
and this another warrant, ad infinitum. Thus, if we
follow the course of reason, we end in complete
scepticism. In such a quandary, the Pyrrhonist will
suspend judgement on all propositions, since all are
doubtful, and live according to nature and custom.[168]
But in a Catholic nation like France, this could only
mean that the Pyrrhonist will also be a Catholic.
Since he opposes all assertions, he will also oppose
the viewpoints of the Reformation. Moreover,
Pyrrhonism actually prepares the heart for religion by
clearing the way for faith:

There is nothing in man's invention that has so
much verisimilitude and usefulness. It presents
man naked and empty, acknowledging his natural
weakness, fit to receive from above some outside
power, stripped of human knowledge, and all the
more apt to lodge divine knowledge in himself,
annihilating his judgement to make more room for
faith; neither disbelieving nor setting up any
doctrine against the common observances; humble,
obedient, teachable, zealous; a sworn enemy of
heresy, and consequently free from the vain and
irreligious opinions introduced by the false
sects. He is a blank tablet prepared to take from
the finger of God such[169]forms as he shall be
pleased to engrave on it.

Thus, Pyrrhonism is actually the friend of the true
Catholic faith.

According to Richard Popkin,[170] in Montaigne we
see three aspects of the sceptical crisis that came to
a head in the seventeenth century: (1) The theological
crisis: No rational way exists to discover the rule of
faith. Therefore, one must simply acquiesce to the
accepted norm of Catholicism. With Montaigne thus
begins the appropriation of Pyrrhonism on the part of
Catholic thinkers as a means of defense against
Protestantism. (2) The humanistic crisis: The
rediscovery of the ancient world coupled with the
discovery of the New World displays the relativity of
culture and beliefs. What trans-cultural standard
exists by which one may pronounce the noble savages of
the American wilderness inferior to the cultivated
Christian man of Europe? (3) The scientific crisis:
Aristotle's science, accepted by the Church, can no
longer be touted as an indubitable body of knowledge
about the real world or natures of things. All that we
can know of the world is how it appears to our fallible
senses. Popkin concludes, "By extending the implicit
sceptical tendencies of the Reformation crisis, the

humanistic crisis, and the scientific crisis, into a total crise pyrrhonienne, Montaigne's genial Apologie became the coup de grâce to an entire intellectual world."[171]

The scepticism of Montaigne, mediated by his disciples Pierre Charron in Les trois véritez (1594) and De la sagesse (1601) and Jean-Pierre Camus in Essay sceptique (1603), was, of course, a double-edged sword. It could be and was taken up by Catholic apologists as a weapon against the reformers' rule of faith in Scripture and right reason. Veron and other leaders in the Counter-Reformation blasted away at the strongholds of Protestant rationalism by means of the new Pyrrhonism, as we shall see. But the sceptical philosophy might also be taken up by those less friendly to the cause of religion. After all, there could be no logical compulsion to take the step from scepticism to fideism. Thus, around the beginning of the seventeenth century we find in Paris a clique of free-thinking, young men known as the libertins érudits, among them Gabriel Naudé, Guy Patin, François de La Mothe Le Vayer, and Petrus Gassendi. According to Popkin, "As the avant-garde intellectuals of their day they led the attack on the outmoded dogmatism of the scholastics, on the new dogmatism of the astrologers and alchemists, on the fanatic enthusiasm of the Calvinists, and, in general, on any type of dogmatic theory."[172]

Then, during the 1620's the response to the nouveau pyrrhonisme began. Among the host of thinkers who strove to provide a way to knowledge immune to the Pyrrhonian attacks was Edward Lord Herbert of Cherbury, who was the English ambassador to France from 1618 to 1624. Lord Herbert came to know Gassendi during his

ambassadorship and presented him with a copy of De
veritate. He also knew Diodati, a diplomat who
belonged to the society of the libertins érudits, the
Tetrade; he probably also became acquainted with the
Pyrrhonist Mersenne during this time. Two-thirds of De
veritate is given over to a discussion of
epistemological issues, in which Lord Herbert emerges
as a thorough-going rationalist. It is in this context
that his notitiae communes play their proper role. He
grants the sceptics that the senses and reason alone
are insufficient to provide certain knowledge of the
real world because by means of them alone we have no
way of knowing whether the appearances they present to
us have any correlation to the independently existing
world. These notitiae communes are innate principles
which furnish accurate knowledge of the extramental
world, thereby enabling us to check on the veracity of
our judgements based on sense and reason. These
notions are characterized by prioritas, independentia,
universalitas, certitude, necessitas, and modus
conformationis (Assensus nulla interposita mora). The
universal consent to these principles among sane and
normal people makes it evident that they are innate.
We have already mentioned Herbert's five notitiae
communes in the area of religion. These foundational
principles preclude all scepticism concerning religion:
"Yet the five above-mentioned truths ever were, and
always will be, of that divine nature, that like
sunbeams, which no weight can depress, nor any wind
blow out, they have darted their glorious rays into the
minds of men in all parts of the earth, where they did
but exercise their natural use of reason."[173] Thus,
Herbert's De veritate, wtitten with an eye to the
Pyrrhonism of early seventeenth century France, in

becoming the charter document of English Deism helped
to set the epistemological course for that conflict.
Although John Locke in his Essay Concerning Human
Understanding took issue with Lord Herbert for his
innatism, he agrees with the truth of the
principles,[174] thereby dismantling Lord Herbert's
philosophical rationalism but leaving his theological
rationalism intact. Later Deists were to follow the
epistemological empiricism of the great Locke, but all
remained faithful to the theological rationalism
inherited from the Continent.

Two other English divines deserve comment in this
regard. William Chillingworth was well acquainted with
the scepticism of Sextus Empiricus, and it was
Pyrrhonical uncertainties that caused each time his
shift from Protestantism to Catholicism and thence
again to Protestantism. In moving back to
Protestantism, Chillingworth argued that the Catholics
were insisting upon too rigid a standard for what
constitutes knowledge. Once one abandons the
unrealistic quest for absolute rational certainty, he
realizes that we do have sufficient grounds for making
reasonable and therefore morally certain judgements.[175]
In the sphere of religion, the Bible is the authority
to which Protestants turn. If it be asked what is the
legitimation for that authority, the answer will be
natural reason. Another Protestant controversialist of
seventeenth century England, Archbishop of Canterbury
John Tillotson also attacked Rome in the name of
natural reason. His essay on transubstantiation, from
which Hume drew the inspiration for his own argument
against miracles, attacks the Catholic doctrine as
absurd and contrary to all our senses.[176] He maintains
that no revelation contrary to the principles of

natural religion should be accepted, that no doctrine or revelation should be embraced without good proof, and that no argument for a doctrine or revelation is successful unless it is clearer and stronger than the objections to it. The arguments of Chillingworth and Tillotson were all of a piece with the Continental dispute between Catholics and Protestants over the efficacy of reason in religion. Like their Protestant brethren on the Continent, they maintained the sufficiency of natural reason to provide a basis for religion. But the English divines did not perhaps appreciate that their indictments of Rome were furnishing ammunition to Deists operating on the same epistemological presuppositions and would soon be turned against them. Stephen remarks,

> . . . the great Protestant divines of the seventeenth century are rationalist in principle, though they might long receive as equivalent . . . the authority of the Scriptures or of the early Fathers. Thus, in many of their arguments it is sufficient to substitute Revelation for Rome to make the attack upon Catholicism available for an attack upon all supernatural authority. Their reasoning has a wider sweep than they imagine. Striking at the most prominent embodiment of the hostile principle, they are striking at tenets which they would themselves regard as sacred. . . The Protestant writers against Rome were forging the weapons which were soon to be used against themselves. The assumptions which were common to them and to their antagonists naturally escaped any strict scrutiny, though it was presently to appear that they were equally assailable by the methods employed against assumptions actually disputed.[177]

Hence, the crisis in the epistemology of religion precipitated by the Reformation helped to stimulate Deism by the response of rationalism which the crisis elicited. Once the epistemological foundations of

theological rationalism were laid, it could only be
expected that reason would turn to criticize the
revelation it had formerly served.

Meanwhile in France the crise pyrrhonienne
continued. Both Gassendi and Descartes attacked Lord
Herbert for failing to provide any grounds for taking
the notitiae communes as the basis of knowledge. Not
only were these principles not universally held, but
more fundamentally it is possible that false principles
might be universally believed. The seventeenth century
saw the formulation of the great rationalist systems of
Descartes, Spinoza, and Leibniz in the attempt to build
a view of reality on foundations which even the most
radical scepticism could not shake. But for our
immediate purpose, an even more important and
influential figure for the course of Deism was Pierre
Bayle.

Bayle's Dictionnaire historique et critique (1695)
made him the most significant sceptical thinker of the
late seventeenth century. The dictionary found its way
into more private libraries of the eighteenth century
than any other book of that time. Though the work is
purportedly a biographical dictionary, a sort of Who's
Who of obscure and curious personages throughout
history, the notes to the various articles consume ten
times as much space as do the articles themselves, and
it is in these notes that Bayle expounds his own
philosophical viewpoints on subjects only distantly
related to the text. Sensing a kindred spirit there,
the eighteenth century French Deists and philosophes
ransacked the notes of the dictionary for arguments
supporting their own outlook, ignoring anything Bayle
might have said to the contrary. Hence, Bayle became
one of them, himself a libertine or atheist.

Bayle, however, must be read in terms of the seventeenth century, not in retrospect of the eighteenth. As Walter Rex has persuasively argued, the traditions out of which Bayle worked were neither atheist nor libertine, but Calvinist.[178] Bayle was born and raised a Protestant, but became a Catholic at age 22 during his years of study at the Jesuit college in Toulouse. A year later he re-converted to Protestantism and, as this act was severely punishable under law, fled to Geneva. His letters of this time express a genuine religious conviction. At Geneva he sat under Tronchin and Chouet, from whom he imbibed rationalism and Cartesianism. Thereafter, he worked closely with the Reformed theologian Jurieu, whom Bayle idolized, at Sedan (1675-81); when the Academy there was closed by the authorities, he fled to Holland. He and Jurieu assumed posts at the Ecole illustre at Rotterdam and became members of the Reformed Church there, which Bayle never left.

Once in Rotterdam Bayle published an essay which he had written on the comet of 1680, Pensées diverses sur la comète. In the Pensées diverses Bayle attacks superstition and intolerance, purportedly concerning the comet, but with obvious implications for religion as well.[179] But as Rex argues, the work is not subversively intended to undermine the Christian religion, but rather Catholicism. The polarity for Bayle is not Christianity versus libertinism but Catholicism versus Protestantism. Bayle's essay is a point for point refutation of the reasons for which he became a Catholic. In the Pensées diverses, he exposes the fallacies of appeals to the authority of persons, the authority of the traditions of antiquity, and the authority of the multitude of witnesses--all of them

Catholic _notae ecclesia_.   Like   the   Protestant
polemicists, Bayle repeatedly draws parallels between
Catholicism and paganism. All of his arguments in the
first part of the work are drawn from the Calvinist
polemics against Catholicism.   In part two, Bayle
develops his influential thesis that superstition is
worse than atheism.   In showing how it is paganism and
idolatrous Christianity,   not   atheism,   that   are
responsible for the crimes against humanity, Bayle's
target is again Catholicism, not Christianity.   Bayle
does criticize Protestants for being as superstitious
concerning heavenly bodies as anybody and because their
morals are as low as the Catholics';[180] but the first
is a matter of practice, not principle, and the second
point was often made by Calvinist divines themselves.
Bayle also remarks that the argument from tradition was
used by pagans against the Catholic church and by
Catholics against the Reformers, and, he predicts, will
be used by the Reformers against their schismatics.[181]
Rex points out that Bayle is not here equating
Protestantism and Catholicism or attacking religion _per
se_, but seeking to preserve religion from the spurious
appeal to tradition.   "For it is not as a sceptic, or a
deist, or an atheist that he warns the Protestants: he
threatens them in the name of the principles which
justified their Reformation, of their own concept of
the Church, of their own theology, of their own
doctrine of truth."[182]   Thus, the _Pensées diverses_ is
really an anti-Catholic, Calvinist-inspired polemic
justifying Bayle's departure from the Catholic church
by destroying its claim to authority.   "There is not
the faintest suggestion in the _Pensées diverses_ that
Bayle is trying to undermine the divinity of Christ,
nor that he is attacking all religion, nor showing the

inherent immorality of Christianity."[183]   When Bayle
sent copies of his work to his professors at Geneva,
they complimented him on it; Jurieu's only fear was
that some people might read false opinions into it.
for most of a decade, no Calvinist protested against
the book.

While in Rotterdam, Bayle grew increasingly
distant to Jurieu as the latter became more and more
intolerant and politically revolutionary.   From 1684
Bayle edited the literary review Nouvelles de la
République des Lettres, which brought him into contact
with the most prominent thinkers of his day.   As a
reviewer Bayle read Le Clerc's Sentimens de quelques
théologiens and was shaken in his own conviction of
biblical authority as a result.   He had also been
reading widely in the libertine Pyrrhonists, and a
personal crise pyrrhonienne was culminating.   Perhaps
decisive in this regard, as one reflects on the
significance of the problem of evil in Bayle's analysis
of religion in the Dictionnaire, was the tragic death
of Bayle's beloved brother Jacob, a Calvinist minister
in France, in the religious persecution attending the
Revocation of the Edict of Nantes.   Arrested in June of
1685, Jacob was sent to the wretched hole Chateau-
Trompette in Bordeaux and in November died there,
refusing to abjure his faith to obtain release.   The
pain for Bayle was particularly bitter because Jacob's
incarceration was touted as a reprisal against Bayle
himself for his writings.   During the months following
his brother's death, Bayle composed Ce que c'est que la
France toute catholique sous le règne de Louis le
Grand, a vivid description of religious persecution in
France.   Then in 1686 he published his defense of
general toleration, Commentaire philoso-phique sur ces

paroles de Jésus-Christ "Constrains-les d'entrer". Rex
argues that like the Pensées diverses this work is best
understood in light of Calvinist traditions.   In the
Eucharistic   controversy   over   transsubstantiation,
French Calvinist rationalism had long maintained that
transsubstantiation was absurd and that therefore
Jesus's words "This is my body" must be taken
figuratively.   Jurieu set forth four general
hermeneutical principles on which to judge when any
given text is to be taken figuratively.[184] (1) If the
passage says something literally absurd, it must be
taken figuratively.   (2) If the passage is literally
impossible and full of contradictions, one must take it
figuratively.   (3) If the passage commands us to commit
a crime, it must be interpreted figuratively.   (Jurieu
like the Calvinist theologians Du Moulin, La Place,
Blondel, and Claude appeal to St. Augustine for this
principle.)   (4) If the passage attributes to God
things unworthy of him, it must be taken figuratively.
The first two are principles based on reason, the
second two on conscience.

Now Bayle in the first part of his Commentaire
Philosophique argues that Jesus's words "Constrain them
to come in" must be taken figuratively precisely on the
basis of the third principle listed above by Jurieu:

> I rely, in order to refute this invincibly, on
> that principle of natural light, that any literal
> meaning which entails the obligation to commit
> crimes is false.   St. Augustine gives this rule
> and, so to speak, this criterium for discerning
> the figurative meaning from the literal
> meaning.[185]

Since intolerance entails the commission of crimes
against the persecuted, Christ's words cannot be taken
to command religious intolerance.   The natural light of

reason makes it evident that acts of persecution are
crimes and that God cannot command crimes; therefore,
natural light compels us to take Scripture figuratively
here. Bayle thus asserts the pre-eminence of reason
over Scripture when the two conflict. He maintains
that there are certain principles of natural light
which are so obvious that all the Scripture passages
and miracles in the world could not cause one to
disbelieve them; one would instead take the passages
figuratively and interpret the miracles as demonic.
Catholics and Protestants alike implicitly follow this
procedure in their disputations. The upshot of this is
a thorough-going theological rationalism:

> Thus all theologians, whatever faction they belong
> to, after having exalted as much as they pleased
> revelation, the merit of faith, the profundity of
> the Mysteries, come away from all that to pay
> hommage at the foot of the throne of Reason, and
> they recognize though they do not say it in so
> many words (but their conduct is sufficiently
> expressive and eloquent a language), that the
> supreme tribunal and one who judges in the last
> resort and without appeal everything which is
> presented to us is Reason, speaking by the axioms
> of natural light or of Metaphysics. Let one say
> no more, therefore, that Theology is a Queen for
> whom Philosophy is but the servant, for the
> Theologians themselves testify by their conduct
> that they regard Philosophy as a Queen and
> Theology as the servant, and thence come the
> efforts and contorsions which they deliver to
> their minds in order to avoid being accused of
> being contrary to good philosophy. . . . [186]

Rex calls this passage a milestone in French thought,
"a turning point in the intellectual history of
seventeenth-century France" perhaps exceeded in
importance only by Descartes's _Discours sur la
méthode_.[187] Bayle asserts boldly in a manner as yet
unheard the supremacy of reason over matters of

religion. On the basis of God-given natural light we can see that it is wrong to take "Constrain them to come in" as a literal command to force people under threat of torture, execution, or exile to believe in the Christian faith; hence, deviant religious views must be tolerated.

In the second part of this work, we begin to see a different Bayle, closer to the sceptical Bayle of the _Dictionnaire_. He now argues for toleration on the basis of the inviolability of conscience. This tenet had also been a plank in the Calvinist case against transsubstantiation. Jean Daillé had argued that Protestants cannot be compelled to adore the host in the eucharist because such an act would be for them idolatrous, since they would be worshipping bread.[188] To violate the dictates of one's conscience is inherently sinful. Jurieu likewise argued that it is wrong to force people to believe contrary to conscience because an act of belief not reflecting the judgement of the intellect is hypocritical and blasphemous.[189] Jurieu therefore defended acts of ignorance done in good conscience that would otherwise be immoral. Bayle follows this lead, but seems to lose control of the argument: (1) He draws not only upon Calvinist traditions, but now also upon the arguments of La Mothe le Vayer concerning the cultural relativity of all beliefs. He thereby appears to sacrifice the truth of the Christian religion. We see here the intrusion of Pyrrhonical arguments to supplement those from the Calvinist arsenal. (2) He presses the argument from conscience so hard that he is driven, not only to defend immoral acts and crimes which were done in ignorance and good conscience, but also to affirm the paradox that if a man's conscience tells him to

persecute, then he is morally obliged to carry out the
dictates of conscience and persecute![190] Thus, the
argument from conscience for toleration of divergent
viewpoints leads paradoxically to a moral justification
of intolerance. (3) Bayle extends the sceptical
tradition of Montaigne, Charron, and La Mothe le Vayer
in arguing that God does not require man to find the
true faith. How can God require all men to be
Christians when the multitudes of Asia, Africa, and
America have never heard of Christ? Besides this,
persons are largely determined by heredity and
environment in what they believe. And God has not made
the evidence for true revelation clear enough to
distinguish it from false.

Thus, in the second part of the Commentaire
philosophique, Bayle completely undermines all that he
has said in the first. The certain guide of natural
light in ethics gives way to fallible, relative
conscience; rationalism gives way to fideism; certainty
gives way to fallible persuasion; ethical absolutism
gives way to a sincere conscience; and Christian
orthodoxy dissolves into religious relativism. Yet
despite these tendencies which seem to lead directly to
the Deism of the next century, Bayle does not in his
last chapter draw this logical conclusion. Natural
religion is insufficient, he maintains, and most of
humanity is lost in sin because men have not followed
conscience. But although Bayle will not embrace Deism,
he has logically worked himself into a position whence
the only escape, if his arguments be sound, is a leap
of faith in the face of reason. That brings us to the
Bayle of the Dictionnaire.

In 1687 Bayle's health broke and, forced to resign
his editorship of the Nouvelles de la République des

Lettres and to take a leave of absence from the Ecole
illustre, he left Rotterdam for a time of recuperation
at Aix-la-Chapelle. The illness seemed to bring to a
head all the doubts and inner struggles which had been
gnawing at Bayle, and he returned to Rotterdam a
chastened and more sceptical man, ready to undertake in
earnest his most monumental project yet: the
Dictionnaire historique et critique, which after many
years of extensive research and intense labor appeared
in Rotterdam in 1695.

Although it is difficult to know whether Bayle is
speaking sincerely, the religious epistemology of the
Dictionnaire is prima facie a rational scepticism
supplemented by fideism. Throughout the dictionary,
Bayle attacks various philosophical systems and even
the coherence of theism itself, only to espouse a
religious faith independent of reason as the single
answer to scepticism's doubts. Richard Popkin remarks,

> The Dictionary was allegedly a biographical one. .
> . . The heart of it, however, was the digressive
> footnotes in which theory after theory was
> dissected, criticized, and refuted, and the whole
> world of seventeenth century thought torn
> assunder.   In the longest article in the
> Dictionary he attacked Spinoza.   In another
> ("Rorarius") he attacked his friend Leibniz. The
> theories of Descartes, Hobbes, Locke, Malebranche,
> Newton, Aristotle, Plato, and anyone else were
> examined, dissected, and found to be "big with
> contradiction and absurdity." A whole series of
> problems--for example, the problem of evil, the
> nature of mind or matter, the problem of the
> relation of mind and matter; and the like--could
> not be successfully solved by any rational system.
> Over and over again, Bayle insisted, as he
> dissolved one theory after another, what this
> showed was the hopeless inadequacy of reason to
> make sense of the world.   Reason should be
> abandoned for faith.   And the faith Bayle
> portrayed was blind, unintelligible, and
> amoral.

He thus arrives at a position precisely contrary to
that of the Calvinist rationalism out of which he grew.

Bayle once remarked to the abbé of Polignac, "I am
a good Protestant, and in the full sense of the word,
for from the bottom of my heart I protest against
everything that is said and everything that is
done."[192] The point of Bayle's wide-ranging attacks on
various philosophic solutions to the problems of mind
and body, space, time, matter, and so forth, was
apparently to expose the utter inadequacy of natural
reason to make sense out of the world. He wants to
show that reason--or philosophy, as he sometimes calls
it--inevitably goes astray and ultimately degenerates
into a self-stultifying scepticism. In his article on
Pierre Bunel, Bayle reports that Reginald Polus had
written to Sadolet, asking him to encourage Lazare
Bonamicus to study the Scriptures, or at least
philosophy. Polus believed that Bonamicus would
perceive that philosophical light could only lead man
to admit that he knows only that he knows nothing, from
which one must necessarily conclude that the mind of
man has need of another light to dissipate the darkness
of his ignorance; what could this be but revelation?
Sadolet responded that he found so scornful an attitude
toward philosophy strange, since without philosophy
theology could not subsist, and he outlined the
advantages of philosophy. Sadolet's position recalls
Bayle's own remarks on philosophy and theology in the
first part of the Commentaire philosophique. But now
we find a different viewpoint expressed by Bayle:

> Be that as it may, I find that Polus's judgement
> is the most sensible that one can make about
> Philosophy, and I am delighted that such an author
> should furnish me with confirmation of that which
> I establish in various places, that our reason is

not suited but to confuse everything and to create
doubt about everything; she has no sooner built a
work than she shows you the means to destroy it.
She is a true Penelope, who during the night
destroys the curtain she had made by day. Thus
the best use one can make of the studies of
Philosophy is to know that it is a way that leads
one astray and that we must seek another guide,
which is revealed light.[193]

According to Bayle, reason seems to operate very well
in its critical function, but seems incapable of
establishing any positive truth. In his later Réponse
aux questions d'un provincial (1703-07), Bayle
reiterates these sentiments:

If reason were consistent with herself, one would
have to be sorrier that she accords so uneasily
with certain of our articles of religion, but she
is a runner who does not know where to stop, and
like another Penelope, herself destroys her own
work: diruit, edificat, mutat quadrata rotundis.
She is more suited to demolish than to build; she
knows better what things are not than what they
are.[194]

Since reason is self-destructive, it matters little
whether it can be brought into accord with faith;
hence, Bayle's many attempts to show how reason pulls
it apart if one lets it go. Bayle's metaphor of the
coureuse is reminiscent of another comparison of reason
that he made in note G to his article on Uriel Acosta:

Be that as it may, there is no one who in
employing reason does not have need of God's
assistance, for without that she is a guide who
loses her way; and one can compare Philosophy to
powders so corrosive that after having consumed
the pus of a wound, they will eat away the living
flesh and rot the bones and pierce all the way to
the marrow. Philosophy refutes first errors, but
if one does not stop her there, she attacks
truths, and when one lets her do as she pleases,
she goes so far that she no longer knows where she
is and can no longer find where to sit down. It

is necessary to attribute that to the weakness of
man's mind or to the wrong use he makes of his
would-be powers.[195]

Once reason begins its course, it will, unless it is
halted, continue all the way into complete scepticism;
but this is self-refuting, as Bayle realized:

> [This subtlety] confounds itself, for if it were
> solid, it would prove that it is certain that it
> is necessary to doubt. There would thus be some
> certainty; one would thus have a sure rule for the
> truth. Now this ruins the system; but do not fear
> that one will come to that. The reasons for
> doubting are themselves doubtful; therefore, it is
> necessary to doubt if it is necessary to doubt.
> What chaos and what torture for the mind! It
> seems therefore that this unfortunate state is the
> most appropriate of all to convince us that our
> reason is a way that leads us astray, since when
> she displays herself with the greatest subtlety,
> she casts us into such an abyss.[196]

Reason thus reaches a state in which even scepticism is
doubtful, but this tends to confirm scepticism! Bayle,
in his clarification on Pyrrhonism added to the second
edition of the <u>Dictionnaire</u>, observes that the
Pyrrhonists delight in this muddle, since it tends to
confirm their views.

Bayle, who had earlier championed natural light
and the supremacy of philosophy, now seems intent on
showing that reason left uncontrolled will run itself
out into scepticism. He tries to show that
philosophical systems erected by reason are themselves
destroyed by reason. But reason is not content to
expose falsehood; it even gobbles up what we know to be
true. It finally reaches complete self-stultification.
Therefore, we ought to recognize that reason is a way
that leads us astray (<u>une voie d'égarement</u>). It is a
false guide; it will not lead us to truth. We ought to

renounce it.

Why was Bayle so intent on exposing the complete inadequacy of reason as a guide to truth? After all, he could have had recourse to a sort of mitigated scepticism, arguing that granted certain general presuppositions commonly held by all men, he could show the Christian or at least the theistic world view to be the most rational scheme of things. The answer seems to be that he did not in fact believe this to be so. Bayle had become convinced that the problem of evil constitutes an insuperable objection to the theistic world view and that an individual following the dictates of reason would eventually become an atheist. That is to say, Bayle became convinced that atheism is rationally superior to theism. Therefore, he had at all costs to destroy reason if he was to remain a believer. Hence, in his article on Acosta, he explains in note G that Acosta left the Catholic church because he could not agree with its decisions, as they did not accord with reason. He then became a Jew because Judaism conformed better to his lumières. But he then rejected the infinity of traditions in Judaism because they were not found in Scripture; he renounced the immortality of the soul because it was not taught in the Old Testament; eventually he rejected the divinity of the books of Moses because their laws did not conform to the truths of natural religion. Acosta thus apparently slid into Deism. Had he lived longer, muses Bayle, he would have rejected even natural religion because he would have discovered difficulties in the free will of an eternal and necessary being, providence, and man's free will.[197] Then follows Bayle's comparison of reason to the corrosive powders. Similarly, in his article on Pierre Charron, Bayle

defends Charron against the charge of atheism. Charron
could, according to Bayle, respond to this allegation
by asserting: "I would be such as you say if I went by
the small light of my reason, but I do not at all rely
on such a guide; I submit to the authority of God; I
captivate my understanding to the obedience of
faith."[198]   Again Bayle seems to imply that the
rational man will be an atheist, and only faith can
save him from that end.

In the dictionary Bayle defends the bold thesis
that Manichean dualism is a more satisfactory
explanation of the problem of evil than traditional
theism.[199]   It must not be overlooked, however, that
Bayle regards this dualism as rationally impossible.
He states plainly that a priori reasoning shows that it
is absurd to have two eternal, independent beings, one
of which is without goodness and which may halt the
designs of the other. Nevertheless, Bayle contends, a
system must also be able to account for experience, and
here the question arises, can our experience be
satisfactorily explained on the basis of one first
principle? Bayle answers that in man and man alone do
we find decisive objections to the unicity of the
Supreme Being. Man knows evil both in himself and in
the world, intermingled with good. Zoroaster might
therefore maintain that dualism provides a more
satisfactory explanation of man's experience than does
theism: ". . . you surpass me in the beauty of ideas
and in a priori reasons, and I surpass you in the
explanation of the phenomena and in a posteriori
reasons."[200]   Since a system must explain experience to
be good, it follows that theism despite the beauty of
its ideas is no good. Bayle thus proposes a sort of
antinomy: a priori reasoning supports theism, but a

po_s_te_ri_or_i reasoning supports dualism. Reason
demonstrates that if God exists, He is one; but the
doctrine of one God shatters on the hard facts of
experience. Dualism gives a better account of
experience; but it is rationally absurd. The implicit
conclusion would seem to be that therefore God does not
in fact exist; hence, the antinomy cannot arise. Thus,
we are led to atheism.

But the theist could respond that the existence of
evil is not incompatible with one Supreme Being. Moral
evil is the result of man's free choices, while
physical evil is God's punishment for man's sins.
This, however, cannot turn back the force of the
objection, according to Bayle. For if we say that God
made man absolutely neutral with regard to evil such
that man's choices are entirely of himself, then (1) we
have no idea of a being which can act of itself unless
it also exists of itself. This would imply that only
God could have free will. (2) But more importantly, an
irresolvable dilemma arises as a result of God's
foreknowledge. For either God foreknew that man would
fall into sin or He did not. If it is said that He did
foreknow, then the problem arises that it does not at
all appear possible to foreknow future free acts.
Since these are the result of an inderterminate cause,
how could they be known in advance? But even more
difficult, if God did foresee man's fall into sin, why
did He not prevent it? On the other hand, if God could
not foresee man's fall, then He at least knew such a
wrong choice was possible. Therefore, he would have
created in man a proclivity to do good and would not
have allowed anything to draw him into evil.

Elsewhere, Bayle sharpens this dilemma by means of
a poignant illustration.[201] What would we think of a

mother who allows her daughters to attend a ball where
she suspects that they will be seduced and lose their
virginity? Would a loving parent permit them to go?
Suppose furthermore that the mother has a potion which
would render her daughters insusceptible to the
seductors' influence, but she refuses to give it to
them before they go. How can she be called a good
mother? Suppose finally that the mother secretly goes
to the ball and actually watches her daughters being
seduced, but does not interfere. Is she not also
responsible for her daughters' fall? Bayle later
responds to the objection that such interference would
violate a person's freedom. He maintains that it is
morally justifiable to violently interfere with a
person's action if by so doing one will save him from
harm. If doing a lesser evil to a person prevents a
greater evil from happening to him, then one may
interfere to prevent his action. And in any case, God
would have no necessity to interfere, for He has the
power to create good volitions in man's soul in the
first place.

It might be objected that the creation of such a
predisposition to do good would remove man's freedom of
will. Bayle appears to grant this, but regards this
loss as of little consequence.[202] Against Origen, he
maintains that being determined to do good and having
no so-called free will does not make one God; for
example, the angels are so constituted. Foreseeing
man's free choice, why did God not turn man to good?
After all, the blessed in paradise worship God without
having freedom of the will. Bayle suggests that God's
so acting need not be coercive, for if His grace can
help Christians to do good without coercing them, why
can He not similarly turn man to the good?

Bayle was thus convinced that anyone who reflected long and hard on the problem of evil, especially with regard to God's foreknowledge, would become an atheist.[203]   What solution did he therefore propose to this problem? Appealing to the scholastic principle <u>ab actu ad potentiam valet consequentia</u>, Bayle maintains that we accept on the basis of Scripture that God is one and that the fall of man occurred and that therefore no matter how impossible the Manicheans say this is, we know it is possible because it happened.[204] Thus, Bayle advises the Christian disputant:

> . . . he should prove by the word of God that the author of all things is unique and infinite in goodness and in all strength of perfections, that man, coming from His hands innocent and good, lost his innocence and his goodness by his own fault. That is the origin of moral evil and physical evil. Let the Marcionites and all the Manicheans reason as much as they please in order to show that under an infinitely good and holy providence this fall of innocent man could not have occurred. They will be reasoning against a fact, and will consequently make themselves ridiculous.[205]

Bayle emphasizes that in dealing with someone who objects to Christianity on the basis of the problem of evil, it is fatal to try to reason with him. Once this is done one can never lead him back to truth.[206] It is better not even to enter into a dispute with such a person; let the philosophers' objections run like vain chicanery and oppose nothing to them but silence with the shield of faith.[207] Bayle states that the best thing to say to someone who demands why God permitted man to sin is, "I know nothing about it; I only believe that He had very good reasons from His infinite wisdom, but which are incomprehensible to me." In this way, says Bayle, you cut the discussion short; but if you get into the free-will defense, I do not know how you will ever get out.

Bayle's scepticism thus ends ostensibly in fideism. There is no rational solution to the problem of evil. But reason is a false and fatal guide anyway. Thus we are led to the Scriptures as the source of true knowledge:

> Human reason is too weak for that; it is a principle of destruction and not of building; it is only suitable for forming doubts and for turning toward the right and toward the left in order to perpetuate a dispute, and I do not believe I err if I say of natural revelation, that is to say, of the light of reason, what Theologians say of the Mosaic dispensation. They say it was only suitable to make known to man his impotence and the necessity of a Redeemer and of a merciful law. It was a pedagogue (these are their terms) to lead us to Jesus Christ. Let us say similarly of reason that it is only suitable to make known to man his darkness and his impotence and the necessity of another revelation. It is that of Scripture.[208]

In this sense Pyrrhonism can actually be of some service to religion. Though it is rightly detested in the schools of theology, comments Bayle, nevertheless it has its uses in obliging man, when reason has failed, to call on help from above and to submit to the authority of faith.

> The natural conclusion of this must be to renounce this guide and to ask for a better from the cause of all things. This is a large step toward the Christian religion, for it wants us to look to God for the knowledge of what we must believe and must do; it wants us to captivate our understanding to the obedience of faith. If a man has convinced himself that there is no good promise in his philosophical discussions, he will feel more disposed to pray to God to ask Him for the persuasion of the truths which one must believe than if he flatters himself with a good success in

reasoning and disputing.[209]

Bayle asserts that Pascal saw this and that Calvin, too, agreed with this. He cites La Mothe le Vayer that it is the sceptic who is the most receptive to revelation. In his clarification on Pyrrhonism added to the second edition of the Dictionnaire, Bayle pushes the tension between faith and reason a notch further. Denouncing the Pyrrhonists as unworthy opponents, Bayle contends that the Gospel should not be exposed to their attacks. One must choose either philosophy or the Gospel. To try to combine them is like trying to have a square circle. The true Christian will only laugh at the Pyrrhonists. His faith places him on a mountain top above the disputes, and from that vantage point he will see the weaknesses of reason and the hopeless wanderings of those following this guide. What is faith according to Bayle? The essence of faith, he says, consists in binding us to revealed truths by a strong conviction solely on the basis of God's authority. In fact, the more we must sacrifice reason in order to believe, the stronger faith is. Bayle does not hesitate to draw the obvious inference: the highest faith is that which embraces truths most opposed to reason simply on the basis of divine authority.

Such is Bayle's religious epistemology--at least at face value. Perhaps one of the most intriguing questions for students of Bayle is whether he was sincere.[210] On the one hand, it seems almost unbelievable that anyone could be so naive as to think that after one has thoroughly demolished the rationality of Christian theism people will respond to the rather facile appeal to faith. Bayle's interest seems to be much more to show the irrationality of Christianity than to inspire faith, judging by the proportionate space and intensity given to each. His tepid confessions of faith lack the passion of a Pascal and have the appearance of dutiful concessions to orthodoxy. Worse yet, they often appear ironic. It is hard to believe Bayle is serious when in his clarification on Pyrrhonism he cites with approval the fulminations of a priest against all reason. And in his article on Acosta, Bayle's approval of those who condemn the freedom to think philosophically about religion seems to align him with those who persecuted the wretched man and drove him to suicide. Bayle's denunciations of reason also ring rather hollow, since it is precisely by the power of reason in its critical function that he demolishes constructive philosophical systems. It is hard to believe that Bayle thought it would be the Manicheans who would look ridiculous, arguing by means of the same critical reason against an opponent who contends that theism is possible because it is true, and that we know it is true simply because the Bible says so. It is also difficult to believe that a sincere Christian could write the sort of destructive things that Bayle wrote in an article like "David," for example, whatever his motivations. It must be remembered that Bayle himself had gone through a crisis of faith that seemed to rob him of the vitality of his earlier religious experience. Perhaps he lost faith entirely.

On the other hand, Bayle claimed to the end to be a true Christian. In an apparently authentic note penned only a few hours before his death, Bayle wrote to Terson

My dear friend . . .

I sense that I have no more than a few moments to
live; I die as a Christian Philosopher, persuaded
and pervaded with the goodness and mercy of God,
and I wish you a perfect happineess.[211]

Bayle's faith had gone through a crisis and may have
become not extinct but intellectualist; that is to say,
while Christianity lacked the vitality it once had for
him, it survived as an intellectual conviction based
not upon reason but upon faith. If the appeal to faith
appears naive, this may be because we look back on
Bayle across the century of the philosophes, who did
make such an appeal insincerely. But many of Bayle's
predecessors evidently regarded fideism as the true
remedy to Pyrrhonism, and Bayle may have shared this
view. It is interesting to note that in his article on
Pyrrho, Bayle tells how a "learned theologian"
arbitrated a dispute between two abbés over Pyrrhonism:
"He concluded that it was wrong to waste time disputing
with the Pyrrhonists or to imagine that their sophisms
can be easily eluded by the mere force of reason; that
it was necessary above all to make them feel the
infirmity of reason so that this feeling might lead
them to have recourse to a better guide, which is
faith."[212] In Bayle's last work Entretiens de Maxime
et de Thémiste (1707), he reveals that this learned
theologian was Bayle himself. The sentiments expressed
seem to encapsulate perfectly Bayle's approach to
religious epistemology. Of course, to grant that Bayle
was both a sceptic and a fideist is not to say what he
believed. Even sympathetic interpreters of Bayle's
religious opinions such as Labrousse and Popkin concede
that his beliefs may have only slightly resembled
orthodox Christianity.

Fortunately, the dispute among Bayle scholars on this head need not be resolved for our purposes, for whatever Bayle's personal views may have been, it is clear how the Deists of the eighteenth century perceived him. The philosophes saw him as one of themselves, at most a Deist, if not an atheist. They viewed Bayle as a rationalist at heart, who like themselves submitted everything to the searching light of reason; but they overlooked Bayle's critique of reason itself as an errant guide. They plundered the dictionary for arguments they could employ in their critique of the religion of the ancien régime and adopted the style of the dictionary article. Bayle's fideism was taken as a subterfuge to placate the ecclesiastical authorities. In short, Bayle, whatever his own views may have been, helped to usher in the Eclaircissement and its religion of reason. Not only did Bayle set the course for eighteenth century French Deism, but he was also a significant influence in English thought. Shaftesbury actually lived for a time with Bayle, and Mandeville studied under Bayle at Rotterdam. Collins made several trips to Holland, where he became acquainted with Bayle. Hume was also an avid reader of Bayle. Thus, through the Deists' perceptions of Bayle's thought, reason, which had since the Reformation come to play an increasingly significant role in the epistemology of religion, assumed an overweening importance for both the criticism and construction of religion.

4. Anti-clericalism: It would be very misleading to give the impression that the causes of Deism were purely intellectual. The corruption and immorality of ecclesiastics which was ridiculed by Erasmus in his In Praise of Folly and which fueled the Protestant

Reformation of the church were undoubtedly one of the major factors contributing to the distrust or even hatred of institutionalized religion and to the development of a purely natural religion uncorrupted by greedy, self-seeking clergy. As much as by any other factor, the Deists are all characterized by their disgust and denunciation of the hypocrisy, luxury, lust, and abuse of power on the part of ecclesiastical authorities. Anti-clericalism runs all through their writings.[213] According to Cragg, "This is one of the constant and staple ingredients in the Deists' attack on religion. It is sarcastic in Collins, suave in Tindal, abusive in Woolston, but constant in all of them."[214] The very existence of particular religions was sometimes blamed on the selfish designs of priests, who corrupted the original, pure natural religion into organized structures in order to manipulate the people for their own ends. Sometimes the text of the Bible was assailed as doubtful because it had been handed down through the hands of generations of clergy. Similarly, the doctrines of Christianity were often regarded as inventions of ecclesiastics, not characteristic of Jesus's own teaching. The English Deists, among whom Woolston stands as the most bitterly anti-clerical, had no use for clergy in their natural religion. French Deists, by contrast, might allow for a priesthood of the Supreme Being. Voltaire, in specifying the restrictions on such a priesthood, provides a typical sample of anti-clerical sentiment characteristic of Deist writings:

> But where is the harm of employing a citizen, called an 'elder' or 'priest', to render thanks to the Divinity in the name of the other citizens?--provided the priest is not a Gregory VII, trampling on the heads of kings, nor an

Alexander VI, polluting by incest his daughter,
the offspring of a rape, and, by the aid of his
bastard son, poisoning and assassinating almost
all the neighboring princes: provided that, in a
parish, this priest is not a knave, picking the
pockets of the penitents he confesses and using
the money to seduce the girls he catechises;
provided that this priest is not a Letellier,
putting the whole kingdom in combustion by
rogueries worthy of the pillory, nor a Warburton,
violating the laws of society, making public the
private papers of a member of parliament in order
to ruin him, and calumniating whosoever is not of
his opinion.[215]

Although there is no necessary connection between the
truth of a system of beliefs and the quality of the
lives of its practitioners, there can be little doubt
that the sort of corruption painted by Voltaire was one
of the chief motivating factors causing people to turn
their backs on the church and orthodox religion and to
embrace instead a religion of nature not dirtied by the
hands of the clergy.

    5. Proliferation of Sects: The Protestant
Reformation did not split the Roman Church cleanly in
two, but just as the Catholic authorities predicted, it
shattered it into a myriad of splinter groups, each
professing to embody the true faith.   The decades
following the Reformation not only witnessed the
battles between Catholic and Protestant, but also the
infighting of Lutherans, Reformed, and Anabaptists, as
well as Socinians, enthusiasts, Deists, libertines,
atheists, indifferent, and other factions.   This
spectacle of competing sects, coupled with the
increasing awareness of Islam, oriental and heathen
religions, and classical paganism, intensified the
crisis of conviction concerning any religion's claim to
exclusive truth. Ostervald wrote in 1700,

> The ecclesiastics, having their minds filled with nothing but disputes, contemplate and labor only on this; in their sermons and in their works they talk only of these matters which occupy them and appear essential to them. . . . The unbelievers on the other hand, seeing that the Christians are not at all in accord among themselves, find therein occasion to doubt everything, and they judge that there is only uncertainty and obscurity in a religion where there are only controversies and different sentiments.[216]

The religion of nature and reason took only those elements which are common to all religions and thus transcended this bickering sectarianism. Rousseau writes,

> I considered this diversity of sects which reign on earth and mutually accuse each other of falsehood and error; I asked: Which is the right one? Each one responded: Mine, each one said: I alone and my adherents think correctly; all the others are in error. And how do you know that your sect is the right one? Because God says so.(i) And who tells you that God says so? My pastor, who well knows. My pastor tells me so to believe, and so I believe; I am certain that all who say otherwise than him are lying, and I do not listen to them.
> What! I think, is truth not one? And what is true for me, can it be false for you? . . .
> Either all religions are right and acceptable to God, or if there is one which He prescribes for men, He has given it certain and manifest marks so that it can be distinguished and known as the only true one. These marks are at all times and in all places equally perceptible to all men, large or small, wise or ignorant, Europeans, Indians, Africans, Savages.

(i) . . .217

Of course, only natural religion could bear such universal marks of authenticity. Thus, Deism offered an attractive solution to the bewildering multiplicity of cults that sprang up after the Reformation.

6. Religious wars: Another factor of social
rather than intellectual character that provided
tremendous impetus for Deism was the bitterness and
disenchantment generated by decades of religious wars
following the Reformation. Prior to the Edict of
Nantes (1598), which guaranteed freedom of worship for
Huguenots, France was torn by eight religious wars in
which the fate of French Protestantism seesawed back
and forth for a generation.[218] The years 1562-70 saw
three wars in one protracted struggle in which the
Huguenots were defeated; they were victorious in the
fourth (1572-3) and fifth (1574-6) wars, but lost again
in the sixth (1577) and seventh (1580) wars, though
obtaining favorable terms. The final war (1585-9) saw
the victory of the Catholic party. Probably the most
infamous incident during these terrible years was the
Massacre of St. Bartholomew on the 24th of August,
1572.[219] The Calvinists had flocked to Paris to
celebrate the marriage of the King of Navarre to the
daughter of Catherine de Medicis. But the Court
decided for a pre-emptive strike against the Huguenots,
and, in a sudden and treacherous action, some two to
three thousand Huguenots were massacred in Paris;
another six to eight thousand were probably killed in
the provincial towns. This incident, commemorated in
verse in Canto II of Voltaire's Henriade, became a sort
of symbol of all that was evil in religious
intolerance. Even after the Edict of Nantes, there was
war between Huguenots and Catholics again between
1625-8, which ended with the final subjugation of the
Huguenots in the Siege of La Rochelle. Lechler remarks
that as a result of the Huguenot wars, France during
the time of the visit of Herbert of Cherbury was a seed
bed of deistical and sceptical thought.[220] Sixteenth

century Germany experienced similar conditions to
France. The Peasant's Revolt was crushed in 1525 with
the destruction of 100,000 lives. In 1535 the leaders
of the Anabaptists were executed by public torture and
with them perished many of their followers. Emperor
Charles V tried in 1546 to crush Protestantism by war
and so began the Schmalkaldic War, which was halted in
the battle of Muhlberg the next year. But war broke
out again in 1552 between Charles and Henry II of
France, ending in the religious peace of Augsburg in
1555. At length, after a half century of instability,
came the long-drawn horror of the Thirty Years' War
(1618-48), "which left Germany mangled, devastated,
drained of blood and treasure, decivilised, and
well-nigh destitute of the machinery of culture."[221]
Meanwhile in England Catholicism had been restored
under Mary (1553-4) and Protestant leaders, including
Cranmer and Latimer, burned at the stake (1555-6). But
during the subsequent reign of Elizabeth (1559-1603),
the Catholics found themselves the victims of
persecution. Charles I (1625-49), through his bungling
war with Scotland and incompetent dealings with a
Puritan controlled parliament, provoked the parliament
to vote for war against the King, thus throwing England
into civil war (1642-6; 1648-9), which ended with the
establishment of Puritan rule under Cromwell. Though
religious concerns played a dominant role in the
subsequent restoration of the monarchy under Charles II
(1660) and especially in the revolution against
Catholic James II led by William of Orange (1688),
England was spared significant further bloodshed from
religious strife, such as was seen again in France upon
the Revocation of the Edict of Nantes (1685). These
wars, in which religious interests aligned themselves

with political, left people bitter and disenchanted with religions that commanded adherence through the sword. By contrast Deism offered a religion based not on passion but on reason, a religion whose dogmas were so few, so evident, and so generally accepted that it could never be a contributory cause to war for the sake of religion.

7. Policies of Intolerance: Undoubtedly one of the most counter-productive strategies employed by the church subsequent to the Reformation was religious intolerance. Only in Spain did the Inquisition succeed in utterly exterminating free thought. Elsewhere the attempt to clamp a lid on dissent only postponed the inevitable explosion. It is interesting to compare England and France in this regard. If it is true that religious toleration permitted Deism to come to full bloom in England, though its seeds were first sown in France, it is also true that it was in some measure due to the same attitude of toleration that Deism withered away in England of the eighteenth century while it flourished and overran France. In England the champions of orthodoxy, especially in the Low Church, were also advocates, even if sometimes grudgingly, of religious toleration. They agreed, as we shall see, when Anthony Collins asserted in his Discourse on Free-Thinking that men should freely investigate the rational grounds of religion; but they simply came to a different conclusion about Christianity's rationality than Collins. It was a defender of Christianity, John Locke, who in England set the pattern for religious toleration. In his four letters concerning toleration, Locke argued that since the church is an organization of voluntary membership comprised of people who had attained the age of discretion, it had no jurisdiction

over the beliefs of those who did not choose to become
members.[222]   An attempt to control the beliefs of
non-members would be inconsistent with the nature and
purpose of the church and would constitute an
usurpation of power.   Therefore, the church must
exhibit an attitude of toleration toward the opinions
of those outside its pale.   Locke also maintained that
the State had no business trying to suppress divergent
opinions.[223]   Since the sovereignty of the State is a
sovereignty delegated by the individual who possesses
it by natural right, it follows that the State can
exercise its authority over the individual in matters
of religion only when the individual's beliefs
constitute a positive danger to the State, as with
atheism.   Otherwise, the individual is free to think
and believe as he sees fit.   Locke had no fear that
toleration would undermine Christianity.[224]   On the
contrary, since truth will always triumph when a free
spirit of inquiry reigns, the removal of constraint
actually serves to promote the rise of the true
religion.   It is only error and false sects that need
the use of force to maintain supremacy.   Argument, not
force, should be used to inculcate the true religion in
men's minds.   In his Reasonableness of Christianity
Locke himself sought to demonstrate the rational
superiority of the Christian religion.   His appeal to
reason and his advocacy of toleration of divergent
views became the model for the subsequent conduct of
the Deist debate on the part of orthodox thinkers.

Contrast France, where in 1685 Louis XIV brought
about the Revocation of the Edict of Nantes in a
misguided attempt to secure by force of arms the
conversion of the Huguenot population to
Catholicism.[225]   Prior to the Revocation, thousands of

conversions were forced under the threat of quartering
dragonades in Protestant homes. Though with the
Revocation the borders were officially closed to them,
some 200,000 Huguenots managed to flee the country.
Those who remained behind were faced with the threat of
torture and death, if they refused to convert. We find
no Catholic counterpart of John Locke in France.
Instead we have the great Bossuet arguing in his
Histoire des variations that all opinions except the
true one must be eradicated from the land. The
proponents of toleration on the Continent are not those
in power, as in England, but heretics like Spinoza in
his Tractatus or members of the Protestant Refuge like
Bayle in his Commentaire philosophique, secure in
Holland's tolerant haven. From Voorburg Spinoza
eloquently and severely denounced the corruption and
pride of the clergy, exclaiming that if they were more
concerned for their opponents' souls instead of their
own reputations, they would no longer persecute them,
but be filled with pity and compassion.[226] Religious
intolerance may have delayed the impact of infidelity
in France, but the policies of suppression and coercion
could only foster unbelief, and when the explosion
finally came, the extent and depth of infidelity far
exceeded anything England had seen. Stephen observes,

> From the variation of opinions Bossuet inferred
> that all, save one, should be stamped out. The
> inevitable tendency of such a method was already
> seen by the more acute minds. To support a
> religion by force instead of argument is to admit
> that argument condemns it. In other words, it is
> to sanction scepticism; and before the end of the
> coming century, Bossuet's countrymen had to reap
> the harvest of which the seeds were sown by this
> desperate policy. The English theologians,
> accustomed to trust in reason, though with some
> heterogeneous admixture of tradition, and to

practise toleration, though with many limitations,
adopted a different course. Since men differ
hopelessly on many points, let us take that in
which all agree. That surely must be the essence
of religion and the teaching of universal reason.
Thus, we shall be able to found a reasonable
Christianity.[227]

When Deism finally did sweep France about the middle of
the eighteenth century, it was evident that the
bitterness generated by years of intolerance had
contributed to its appeal. Here the incomparable
figure of Voltaire comes to mind. In 1762 he undertook
the defense of Jean Calas, a Protestant who had been
tortured and put to death by Catholic persecutors.
Voltaire's campaign to exonerate Calas received
contributions from all the Reformed parts of Europe and
finally triumphed in having the verdict of the Toulouse
court reversed. So began Voltaire's personal war
against fanaticism, and for the remaining fifteen years
of his life he devoted himself to destroying
institutional Christianity. "Ecrasez l'infame!"
became his angry motto, the initials of which he penned
after his signature on letters to other free thinkers.
Besides the case of Calas, Voltaire also spoke out
against the cases of Sirven, who had been unjustly
condemned in 1762 on suspicion of having caused his
daughter's death to prevent her from becoming a
Protestant, and of La Barre, who on suspicion of having
damaged a crucifix on the bridge of Abbeville was
condemned in 1763 to be tortured on the rack, to have
his tongue cut out, and to be killed. Voltaire's
renown spread all over Europe for his championing the
causes of such victims of intolerance. Fanaticism,
asserted Voltaire in echo of Bayle, is a monster a
thousand times more dangerous than philosophical
atheism.[228] Spinoza, in contrast to the church, never

hurt anybody. True religion is serving one's neighbor
for the love of God, not butchering him in the name of
God.[229] Voltaire in his dictionary article on religion
tells of a vision in which he saw the remains of those
killed in religious persecution and spoke with the
righteous pagans. Finally he meet Jesus, a man also
killed by hypocritical priests. He learns that Jesus
was a godly Jew who said and did nothing to instigate
his execution. His only crime was that he exposed
hypocrisy. He contributed nothing to the remains of
those slain in persecution nor to the monuments of
pride and avarice that mark religion today. Voltaire
asks him wherein true religion consists. Love God and
your neighbor as yourself, comes back the reply.
"Well, if it be so," responds Voltaire, "I take you for
my master."[230]

In the hands of Voltaire and Rousseau[231]
toleration became a mightly ally of Deism, making
natural religion an attractive alternative to the
superstition and ugly fanaticism of the church. In
England the relative freedom after 1695 helped Deism to
develop more quickly to maturity than in France, but
the attitude of toleration prevented the terrible
recoil to orthodoxy that took place in France.

The Protestant Reformation thus set in motion a
variety of religio-social forces which tended to
promote Deism: the diminished importance of
ecclesiastical additions to religion, the diminished
miraculous content of religion, the increased
importance of the role of reason in religion,
anti-clericalism, the proliferation of sects,
subsequent wars of religion, and policies of
intolerance. Meanwhile the Expansion of Europe was
forcing a relativization of religious beliefs,

fostering a sense of the unjust narrowness and cruelty
of Christianity's claim to exclusive truth.
Revolutions in science blew away the whole world-view
of medieval man, thus discrediting the authority of
Church and Bible and revealing the utter insignificance
of man; the providence of God would be replaced by the
mechanical world-machine. And incipient biblical
criticism not only shook confidence in the authority of
the Bible, but reduced the Scriptures to the level of
an ordinary book. It was an age of uncertainty and
upheaval, a time when a natural, universal religion
based on reason seemed to many a structure more secure
than the tottering edifice of the Christian religion
resting on the rotted timbers of the old order.

Deism's instigation of the historical
argument for the resurrection

The attack on revealed religion
I have said that the historical argument for the
resurrection of Jesus developed in the orthodox
response to Deism, but at this point, we may wish to
know precisely what it was in Deist challenge that
called forth such a response. The answer to this
question lies in a distinction to which I have
frequently alluded: the distinction between natural
religion and revealed religion. By natural religion
was understood the religion based exclusively upon what
can be known about the being and attributes of God by
the operation of reason based on the created order, or
nature. By revealed religion was understood the body
of truths unattainable by natural reason, but
communicated to man by the Divine Being in the form of
special revelation. For many, such as Mornay, Grotius,

Malebranche, Abbadie, and especially the paradigm examples of Clarke and Paley, natural religion served as the foundation upon which the superstructure of revealed religion could be built. Now from one perspective, the whole Deist project might be viewed as the attempt to shave off the superstructure of revealed religion, thus laying bare once more the foundations of natural religion. Indeed, for many Deists natural religion had not only a logical priority to revealed religion, but also a chronological priority, and the Deist program sought to wipe away revealed religion, which they viewed as a sort of excrescence, from the pure and primeval natural religion. Operating as they were in the Western tradition of Christianity, this attack on revealed religion and special revelation naturally took the form of an assault upon the credibility and authority of the Bible. The point is already made by the contemporary historian of English Deism, Leland: "No man that is not utterly unacquainted with the state of things among us can be ignorant, that in the last and especially in the present age, there have been many books published, the manifest design of which was, to set aside revealed religion."[232] According to Leland, this design was the one unifying theme that characterized all Deist authors:

> From such a view, the reader might be enabled to form some notion of the several turns this controversy hath taken, how often the enemies of revealed religion hath thought proper to change their methods of attack, the different disguises and appearances they have put on, and the several schemes they have formed, all directed to one main end, viz. to set aside revelation, and to substitute mere natural religion, or, which seems to have been the intention of some of them, no religion at all, in its room.[233]

We find this attitude evident already in Lord Herbert
and Hobbes. We have already seen that Lord Herbert
regarded the five notitiae communes of religion as
innate principles, self-evident to all men and fully
sufficient for religion. Accordingly, any special
revelation from God in addition to these truths of
natural religion would be simply superfluous. Thus
Lord Herbert lays down stringent conditions for any
purported revelation: there must be proof that God was
accustomed to speaking with an articulate voice and to
deliver oracles, that the hearer was sure that it was
God who spoke and that he was not delirious, that the
revelation be recorded so immediately that any
intrusion of later changes would be corrected by its
authority, and that it be apparent that the doctrine in
it be absolutely necessary.[234] It is evident that Lord
Herbert doubted that any claimant to revelation could
meet these conditions. For Hobbes's part, we have
already seen his attempt to undermine the verifiability
of any claim to special revelation. There is no way,
he maintains, to prove that God has spoken in a dream
or a vision or by a voice or inspiration. Later Deists
delighted in Hobbes's remark: "To say that he hath
spoken to him in a Dream, is no more than to say that
he dreamed God spake to him . . ."[235] Since Hobbes
also rendered the signs of miracle and prophecy
ineffective, his only recourse was to appeal to the
authority of the state to determine religion. Though
Hobbes's answer was authoritarian and therefore
rejected by subsequent thinkers, nevertheless, he like
Lord Herbert undercut the authority of the Scriptures
in favor of some other authority. As Lechler comments,
"Both agree in this point, that they oppose to the
immediate authority of revelation another standard,

which in their view ought to be more obvious."236
Hence, in these two early and influential figures, the
attack on revealed religion has already begun.

One year after Locke had published his
Reasonableness of Christianity, the English Deist
controversy burst into the open with the appearance of
John Toland's Christianity not Mysterious (1696).
Toland attempted to pass himself off as Locke's
disciple--an association which Locke repudiated--and
his work as the logical extension of the great
philosopher's. As Locke had shown Christianity to be
reasonable, so Toland will show it to involve no
mysteries, nothing above reason. He begins by laying
out reason as the only rule of faith, since popes and
councils are contradictory.[237] He argues that we
should therefore not only refuse to believe anything
contrary to reason, but also anything for which there
are no positive proofs. Toland thus contends that
there must be demonstrative reasons in support of any
claim to special revelation; with regard to the Bible
it would be "blamable credulity and a temerarious
opinion" to accept "the divinity of Scripture or the
sense of any passage thereof without rational proofs
and an evident consistency."[238] Not only that, but
Toland goes a step further and asserts that one should
not believe anything above reason. Biblical mysteries,
rightly understood, are not above reason, but are
simply truths later disclosed that were previously
unknown.[239] Anything actually above reason would be
meaningless and cannot therefore compel our assent.
Toland did not dare spell out which elements in
traditional Christian theology he would let go by the
board, but his non-mysterious Christianity would
probably have looked very much like Lord Herbert's

Deism. Toland's book, says Stephen, was "the signal
gun which brought on the general action, and . . . gave
articulate expression to a widely diffused, but as yet
latent, sentiment."[240]   Substituting reason for
scripture as the rule of faith, Toland had implicitly
sought to reduce the amount of excess baggage brought
by revelation to natural religion. Now Deists after
him would attempt to show that natural religion needed
nothing of revealed religion and that the latter was
indeed irrational.

    Perhaps one of the most influential figures in the
ensuing controversy was Samuel Clarke, a vigorous
philosophical thinker perhaps best known for his
correspondance with Leibniz, who in his Boyle lectures
of 1704 sought to demonstrate the being and attributes
of God and in his Boyle lectures of 1705 the truth of
the Christian revelation. Inclined like Locke toward
Unitarianism, Clarke stood as a sort of half-way house
between Deism and orthodoxy, and like Locke he
influenced both sides of the dispute.[241] Deists tended
to overlook Clarke's clear defense of miracles and
revelation in his second set of lectures in favor of
his first, with which they could agree, and in the same
way that Toland attempted to ride Locke's coattails, so
Matthew Tindal portrayed his work as the logical
conclusion to Clarke's. Tindal's Christianity as Old
as the Creation (1730) is probably the most elevated
statement of constructive English Deism. The title of
the book is pregnant with import, for it implies the
reduction of revealed religion to natural religion. It
was inspired by a sermon of Sherlock's in which the
bishop proclaimed, "The Religion of the Gospel, is the
true original Religion, which was as old as the
creation."[242] We have seen how Tindal argued, starting

from the presupposition that since God is perfect the primeval religion He revealed was also perfect and unalterable, that any revealed religion can only be a republication of the original natural religion. In his fourteenth chapter, he takes on Clarke's attempt to build revealed religion on the foundation of natural religion. He argues that since Clarke is a natural law moralist, he would have to agree that should external revelation differ from the demands of the moral law, the moral law must be the supreme obligation. But this implies that revelation could only duplicate what we might know by unaided nature. Similarly, since Clarke is a rationalist, external revelation can add nothing to the dictates of reason. For if it is in accord with reason, it does not differ from natural religion; and if it diverges from reason, then it is false.[243] Clarke contends that sin obscured the law of nature and that hence God needed to do something extraordinary to recover men from their fallen state. But, retorts Tindal, this means God left mankind destitute of the means to do their duty for 4,000 years, all the while demanding of them that they do the impossible. This is contrary to the wisdom and goodness of God.[244] Clarke argues that Christianity possesses miraculous evidences that attest its divinity. Tindal urges the problem of demonic miracles. Clark's answer is that no miracle can prove a doctrine which is contrary to the moral law, but that miracles can substantiate an indifferent doctrine. But, Tindal shoots back, how on Clarke's principles can any doctrine be indifferent to God, since He does everything according to reason and nothing out of sheer arbitrariness?[245] Since all doctrines must be rationally necessary, it follows that natural religion is entirely self-sufficient and

revealed religion only redundant. Or as Tindal puts
it: "Tho' I pay a due Deference to the Dr's deep
Penetration in Matters of Religion, I dare not say,
there's the least difference between the Law of Nature,
and the Gospel, for that would suppose some Defect in
one of them, and reflect on the Author of both. . . ."246
Thus, Tindal and, it may be said, Deists in general
accepted the same foundations as Clarke, but sought to
destroy the structure of revealed religion built upon
it. As Leland says, "That which properly characterizes
these Deists is, that they reject all revealed
religion, and discard all pretences to it as owing to
imposture or enthusiasm. In this they all agree, and
in professing a regard for natural religion, though
they are far from being agreed in their notions of
it."247

When English Deism spilled back again into France,
the French Deists also found inspiration in Clarke.
Rousseau nearly idolized him, proclaiming that after
all the philosophers ancient and modern,

> . . .the illustrious Clarke illuminated the world,
> announcing at last the Being of beings and the
> disposer of things:+ with what universal
> admiration, with what unanimous applause was this
> new system not received, so great, so comforting,
> so sublime, so suited to elevate the soul, to give
> a basis for virtue, and at the same time so
> striking, so luminous, so simple, and it seems to
> me, offering less things incomprehensible to the
> human mind than it finds absurd in any other
> system! . . .Must not this one alone, which
> explains everything, be preferred when it has no
> more difficulties than the others?++

+the illustrious Clarke announcing first to the
world the true theism or natural religion

++for last sentence: Only Clarke's system crushes

all others; therefore it must be preferred by reason.

----

[4] 'He's right about Clark's (sic) 1st volume; the second is ridiculous, as is[248]the subject' (Voltaire, [Marginalia], p. 276).

Voltaire, who had lived in England, also had a grudging admiration for the English divine. Commenting that Clarke "is so totally absorbed in problems and calculations that he is a mere reasoning machine," Voltaire records that "He wrote a book, which is very much esteemed and little understood, on the 'Existence of God'; and another, more intelligible, indeed, but pretty much condemned, on the 'Truth of the Christian Religion'."[249] As this remark and the marginal note above make evident, Voltaire thought extremely little of Clarke's attempt to erect a structure of revealed religion atop the foundations of natural religion. So did Rousseau, who simply passes over his hero's second volume in benign silence, while presenting his own case against revealed religion. "The greatest ideas of deity come to us from reason alone," wrote Rousseau. "Look at the spectacle of nature, listen to the inner voice. Has not God said everything to our eyes, to our conscience, to our judgement? What more will men say to us? Their revelations only serve to degrade God . . ."[250]

Thus engaged as they were in an all-out assault on revealed religion, Deists relentlessly attacked the Scriptures, which communicated the purportedly revealed religion to man. They charged that the appeal to the authority of the church or Scripture was circular, and proposed to try the biblical religion before the bar of reason. There they felt sure it would be condemned.

<u>Orthodox defense of revealed religion</u>
<u>on the basis of the facts</u>

To take a step back and assume a broader
historical perspective, what had happened, in effect,
was that Deists were denying the existence of that body
of truths which scholastics like Aquinas had placed
atop truths of reason and called "truths of faith."
Truths founded on reason were acceptable; but farther
than this Deists would not go. When the orthodox flew
to the defense of revealed religion, it is interesting
that they did so precisely by appealing to the two
scholastic signs of credibility for truths of faith:
prophecy and miracle. But this time there is a
difference: the medieval use of these signs, as the
Deists charged, came dangerously close to circularity:
fulfilled prophecy and miracles prove that the
Scriptures are divine revelation; we know that prophecy
was fulfilled and miracles occurred because divine
revelation says so. But the defenders of the Christian
religion during the seventeenth and eighteenth
centuries avoided this circle by striking out in a new
direction: they proposed to establish these signs by
reason, too, or, to use their expression, <u>by the facts</u>.
By this time history had become a field of rational
inquiry, and since the Scriptures were a historical
revelation, the defenders of orthodoxy turned to
history to repel the Deist attack on Scripture and to
justify revealed religion.

The rise of historical consciousness. Such an
approach could only have taken place after the rise of
historical consciousness. It is probably no
coincidence that the revival of historical
argumentation for the resurrection paralleled the rise

of modern historiography. It was the Italian Renaissance that gave birth to the modern science of historical study. The first stirrings of the Renaissance spirit in Italy found expression in the search for ancient manuscripts. The humanists cultivated the use of classical Latin and Greek and found their greatest delight in the discovery of documents of antiquity in these languages. They learned the skills of historical criticism; on the basis of internal criteria alone Lorenzo Valla was able to expose the famous Donation of Constantine, by right of which the Catholic Church had asserted much of its secular authority in Italy, as a forgery. In spite of this embarrassment, for nearly a century the papacy supported the humanist writers, and learning and the arts flourished in Rome. In search of ancient manuscripts, Italian humanists visited the monasteries of Northern Europe, and their new learning spread, eventually making its way permanently into the university seats of learning in Germany and cultivated circles elsewhere. France, after the invasion of Italy by Charles VIII in 1494, thoroughly absorbed the spirit of the Italian Renaissance. Before the end of the fifteenth century, Oxford University was already offering courses in classical Greek and Latin, and Cambridge University soon followed suit. The embodiment of the ideal Renaissance humanist was Erasmus (1446-1536), who occupied much of his life translating classical works into Latin and editing the Greek New Testament. Other Renaissance humanists touched on matters of theology as well. Lorenzo Valla sought to restore the original Greek text of the New Testament through the use of ancient manuscripts. Erasmus published Valla's corrections as annotations on

the New Testament in 1505, and they provided the model
for Erasmus's edition of the Greek New Testament in
1516.   John Reuchlin, the most famous of early German
humanists, was proficient not only in Latin and Greek,
but also in Hebrew, which he learned to study the
scriptures in their original languages, by means of
which he was able to expose many a fallacious
interpretation. The Italian humanist Marsilio Ficino,
who devoted himself to Platonic studies and was the
first head of the Platonic Academy in Florence,
authored   De religione christiana et fidei pietate
(1474) in which he sought to bring Platonic philosophy
to the defense of the Christian faith.   The Spanish
humanist Juan Luis Vives also wrote a defense of
Christianity De veritate fidei christianae (1543), in
book two of which he defends the resurrection of Jesus.

      The Protestant Reformation spurred the development
of the science of history by turning attention to the
patristic age in order to accentuate the historical
accretions to as well as the departures from the faith
of the Fathers on the part of the Roman Church. In
their efforts to demonstrate that Catholic doctrines
and institutions were not after all of divine origin,
but could be humanly accounted for, the Reformers
stimulated historical research. Luther himself was
concerned to show that it was the church and not he
that had departed from the original doctrine of the
Fathers, and he was delighted to see the accord of
Scripture and history in exposing the pretences of the
Catholic Church.   And of course, the Catholic
Counter-reformers had a tremendous stake in the study
of history because, since Catholicism rested to such a
great degree on tradition, a defense of historical
tradition was a defense of religion.   Hence, James

Westfall Thompson can write,

> Modern historical scholarship had its inception in the Reformation and Counter-Reformation. Lutheranism and Calvinism alike were attacks upon the historical foundations and historical claims of the Roman Church. What Lorenzo Valla had done with the forged donation of Constantine might be done with many other traditions and documents upon which the Church rested its authority. Historical criticism became a Protestant weapon and documents were made missiles in the hands of the Magdeburg Centuriators. The Roman Church was slow to take alarm over the Protestant appeal to history. It vainly endeavored to confine the dispute to questions of theology. But the historical attack finally became so effective that Rome was compelled to fight history with history. Since the Reformation was an appeal to history, the counter-Reformation was forced to use the same instrument, with incalculable importance for the development of historical scholarship.[25]

By the end of the seventeenth century the most successful proponents of the science of history were Catholics of the scholarly orders; perhaps the most noteworthy example is Jean Mabillon's De re diplomatica (1681), in which he vindicated the authenticity of the charters of the Benedictine monasteries Saint-Denis and Corbie, at the same time advancing the science of historiography by the use of paleography, official seals, vocabulary studies, and so forth. Every class in European society took interest in the new historical scholarship and sought thereby evidence to support its contentions and interests. During the sixteenth and seventeenth centuries, historical writing became one of the most popular types of literature, avidly sought by a growing reading public. Between 1460 and 1700 it has been estimated that in excess of 2,500,000 copies of seventeen of the most prominent ancient historians were published in Europe. France excelled all others in the

depth of its historical scholarship, while England
ranked second. This interest in history continued to
grow during the next century. According to Thompson,
"No other age had such a voracious interest in
historical literature as the eighteenth century.
Everyone read and talked history."[252]

Without this rise of modern historical
consciousness, the orthodox defense of Scripture
authority on the basis of the facts could never have
occurred. In fact it appears to have been the
Protestant Reformation's stimulus to historical study
that helped to generate the historical defense of
revealed religion against the Deists. As Dorner points
out, when the Reformers placed the authority of
Scripture above that of the church, the question
necessarily arose, why accept the authority of
Scripture? The Reformers took Scripture as
authenticated by the Holy Spirit, and they had an inner
certainty of the truth of its contents. But
subsequently, the effort was made to ground the
authority of Scripture in the facts of history.[253]
Hence, the early proponents of the historical argument
for Christianity are by far predominantly Protestants.
Catholic apologists, following in the train of
Montaigne, tended to be more Pyrrhonic and fideistic.

Modern appropriation and development of the
medieval signs of credibility. It seems curious that
it should thus be the Protestants who employed an
apologetic system for Christianity so akin to the
medieval scholastic framework of the signs of
credibility, only now filled out with historical
argumentation. This becomes more understandable when
one examines the rise of modern apologetics. I have
called Hugo Grotius the father of modern apologetics;

but he himself acknowledges that he had important
precursors in Philippe de Mornay and Juan Luis
Vives.[254]

A veteran of Huguenot persecution who escaped from
Paris during St. Bartholomew's massacre, Mornay was one
of the most important Reformed leaders of his day,
respected as the "pope of Calvinism."[255]   As the
founder of the Protestant Academie de Saumur, he helped
set the course for French Calvinist rationalism.
Gentleman, scholar, theologian, diplomat, and royalist,
he was an austere Christian, loyal to his God and his
King. In 1581, writing in his mother tongue instead of
Latin, Mornay composed his treatise De la vérité de la
religion chrestienne as an antidote to various forms of
infidelity, including infant Deism. The book is a
systematic case for Christian theism: Mornay argues in
three steps for the existence and attributes of God,
the truth of the religion of Israel, and the divinity
of Christianity on the basis of fulfilled prophecy.[256]
But in addition to these arguments, we encounter,
however fleetingly, a new element in Mornay's
apologetic: a final chapter demonstrating that "the
Gospel truly contains the history and doctrine of
Jesus, Son of God."[257] Here is an appeal to historical
evidence, primitive though it may be. We saw earlier
that Mornay claimed to prove the divinity of Christ by
means of philosophy and history. He observes: "The
philosopher thinks only of nature; the historian only
of his documents. And from the two we have concluded
the deity of Christ and the truth of our
Scriptures."[258] Hence, his case is based on argumens
and tesmoings.[259] In his closing chapter, he explains
that the gospel accounts were written during the
lifetime of those who could testify as to their

accuracy, proclaimed before the eyes of the enemies of the faith, and signed in blood by the apostles' suffering and death.[260]   He elaborates an argument which Eusebius alluded to: the gospels graphically portray the weaknesses and ambitions of the disciples and even the physical weaknesses of Jesus himself, which speaks for their historical credibility, since one might expect such negative images to be suppressed.[261]   With regard to the topic of our interest, the resurrection, Mornay appeals to the great number of witnesses who saw Jesus after he had been raised, to the changed lives of the disciples, and to the conversion of the Apostle Paul as evidence for the historicity of the resurrection.[261] As the first major Protestant systematic apology for Christianity, the main importance of Mornay's work, according to Dulles, "is perhaps that it introduces into Protestant circles the same kind of apologetic writing that had been customary for centuries in the Catholic world."[262] True, but better would be to say that its importance lies in the advance it makes on Catholic apologetics in its appropriation of the scholastic framework and its introduction thereto of historical argumentation.   One still might wonder, however, how it should come to pass that the great Protestant controversialist should adopt the form of Catholic apologetics.

To better understand this, we need to go back yet another step to a more distant precursor of modern apologetics, the Spanish humanist Juan Luis Vives. Educated in Paris, Vives lived very much in the mainstream of Europeaan life; he traveled so frequently to England and throughout the Continent that Erasmus called him an amphibious animal!   After his fifth sojourn in England, he left for the Netherlands, never

to return to Spain. From 1538 to 1540 he labored on
his apology De veritate fidei christianae, but died in
that year; the book was published in 1543. According
to Graf, in Vives we find "a happy merger of the new
methodological advances of Humanism with the solid
principles of the old theology."[264] That is to say,
Vives is a dedicated Thomist who accepts the framework
of the signs of credibility, but as a humanist he also
begins to provide historical reasons for the
credibility of the Scriptures.[265] He attempts to deal
critically, for instance, with the question of why
Christ is mentioned mainly in Christian sources.[266] He
reasons: (1) Some passages in Jewish and Gentile
writings do refer to him; (2) Most works from antiquity
have been lost, and Vives furnishes a long catalogue;
(3) The Gentile authors were contemptuous of the Jews
and, hence, any Jewish sect; (4) It is only natural to
expect Greeks to write about Greeks and Romans about
Romans, not about Jews; (5) Writing about Christ
entails a unique problem, namely, if one approaches the
subject honestly and diligently, one becomes a
Christian; (6) Divine providence desired that
revelation be mediated by sacred, not profane, writers.
Vives also speaks of the true history of Christ and
provides a list of historical facts about Jesus. He
adduces both external and internal evidences for
authenticity of the gospels.[267] As external evidence,
he argues that as witnesses, the authors of the gospels
both could and would tell the truth. Under internal
evidence, Vives mentions the style and content of the
gospels in contrast to pagan works, the Koran, and the
Talmud. He stresses that there is no exaggeration or
ostentation in the gospel accounts and nothing
ridiculous. Finally he notes that there is no

doxological praise in the gospels, which speaks for the
factual nature of their reporting. In his chapter on
the resurrection, Vives appeals to the empty tomb and
appearances as evidence for Jesus's being raised.[268]
He even has a very rudimentary form of the dilemma
developed by subsequent apologists that the disciples
were neither deceivers nor deceived. He refutes the
first allegation by asserting that no one would be
crazy enough to die for the resurrection, were it
false. As to the second, he draws attention to the
palpable nature of the appearances and their extended
duration. Vives's arguments are primitive and little
more than assertions, but they are among the first
glimmerings of a historical approach to the credibility
of Scripture.

Now what is interesting for our purposes is that
Mornay, while never quoting Vives, nevertheless appears
to have been influenced by him. Zöckler points out
that chapters 27-31 of Mornay's book are derived from
book III of Vives's apology on prophecy.[269] Graf goes
even further and claims that Vives's work actually
served as the model for Mornay's, and he provides
several parallel passages to prove the point.[270] This
conclusion is highly significant, for it means that in
Vives we discover two very important links: (1) the
link between the rise of modern historical consciousness in Renaissance humanism and the appropriation of
historical arguments in defense of Christianity and (2)
the link between the scholastic framework of the signs
of credibility for revealed truths and modern
historical apologetics. As a Catholic traditionalist
Vives retained the scholastic framework, and as a
humanist he brought to it historical concerns. Mornay
borrowed Vives's approach and expanded the role of

historical argumentation in his case for Christianity.
As the attacks of Deists and other infidels on revealed
religion grew, this facet of the case would assume an
increasingly prominent role, eventually becoming itself
the entire case.

Seventeenth century development of the historical
argument for Christianity. Apart from Vives and
Mornay, however, Grotius had other unacknowledged
predecessors in the development of the historical
argument for the resurrection.[271] In what is surely
the most ironic twist in the history of the argument,
the most developed early form of this apologetic is to
be found, not in the writings of some champion of
orthodoxy, but in a Socinian catechetical document,
the Catechism of the Churches of Poland, commonly
called the Racovian Catechism. Polish Socinianism
originated, like Deism, in northern Italy during the
mid-sixteenth century, and seeking a tolerant haven for
the expression of its doctrines, migrated to Poland.
The doctrine of this school was vigorously anti-
Trinitarian and afforded a sort of half-way house
between orthodoxy and Deism. While adhering to
theological rationalism, these thinkers preserved the
authority of Scripture and validity of revealed
religion; though they denied the deity and incarnation
of Christ, they held to his miracles and resurrection;
while holding that Jesus had only a human nature, they
nevertheless enjoined worship of him in view of his
exaltation. Harnack characterized the movement as a
"Supernatural Rationalism," "a thorough-going
development of Nominalistic Scholathicism under the
influence of Humanism."[272] It was Fausto Sozzini
(1539-1604) (Socinus), whose name the movement bears,
who built anti-Trinitarianism into a church. Arriving

in Poland in 1579, he welded the diverse anti-
Trinitarian communities together and shaped their
doctrinal thinking into his mold. The center of
Socinianism in Poland was Racow, home of a Socinian
theological college and press. It was this city which
lent its name to the Catechism, which Sozzini had begun
sometime around 1603 and which was completed
posthumously by Schmalz, Volkel, and Moskowrowski in
1605. This Polish version was rendered into Latin in
1609 and reprinted with notes by Socinian divines in
1680. The Catechism is a remarkable document,
rationally apologetic rather than merely instructional
in character, laying out a defense of revealed religion
on rationalistic grounds focussing on the resurrection.

The oddity of a Socinian apologetic for the
resurrection of Jesus becomes more understandable once
it becomes clear what a central and essential role the
resurrection plays in Socinian doctrine. The catechism
revolves around the three offices of Christ as Prophet,
Priest, and King. But the first office is of
overwhelming importance, the discussion of the
prophetic office growing to about 17 times longer in
the 1680 version than the discussion of either of the
other offices. For Socinianism the work of Christ was
the work of a Teacher; he revealed to men the divine
will. But in addition to declaring the divine will,
Jesus confirmed it by his sinlessness, his miracles,
and his death, this last being the most important.[273]
His death confirmed the will of God, first, because he
was not deterred from inculcating his doctrine even by
the most painful and ignominius death and, second,
because his death was interrupted by his resurrection,
which also serves to guarantee our own.[274] Thus, it is
not so much Christ's death as his resurrection that

confirms his prophetic message. Indeed, the Catechism
tersely declares that more therefore depends upon the
resurrection of Christ than upon the death of
Christ.[275] Moreover, the resurrection is essential to
the worship of Christ as God which Socinianism
commanded. Once Christ is reduced to a prophet, it
would appear that worship of him would be idolatrous.
Indeed, Transylvanian anti-Trinitarianism under the
leadership of Franz David had arrived at precisely that
conclusion, and Sozzini, prior to coming to Poland, had
been instrumental in the arrest of David and the
suppression of this form of unitarian doctrine. In the
Racovian Catechism, the worship of Christ as God is
defended and enjoined.[276] The crucial consideration
justifying such worship is Christ's resurrection and
exaltation by God to His right hand. Jesus is called
the Son of God in virtue of his virgin birth, his being
sent by the Father, his resurrection, and his
exaltation.[277] These last two warrant our worship of
him as God, for by the resurrection he became like God
immortal and by his exaltation to a position of
dominion and supreme authority over all things he came
to resemble, or indeed, equal God.[278] Therefore, in
trying to preserve worship of Christ while denying his
divine nature, Socinianism laid great weight on the
resurrection of Christ, for principally his
resurrection declared him to be God.[279] All this is,
as I said, contained within the prophetic office of
Christ: the resurrection is the key confirmation of
Christ's divine teaching and the crucial justification
of regarding him as in fact more than a prophet.

The priestly office of Christ also stands or falls
with his resurrection. For Christ's priestly role is
exercised only after his death and resurrection--his

death on the cross is not seen as the locus of Christ's
priestly ministry. His suffering and death were not
themselves a sacrifice, but a way and preparation to
its completion, which comes only after his resurrection
with his ascension into heaven.280 In construing the
priestly office as essentially post mortem, Socinian
doctrine once more brought the resurrection of Jesus to
the fore. Finally, the office of King also hinges on
Christ's resurrection, for God, having raised him from
the dead and taken him up to heaven, has placed him at
His right hand, having given him all power in heaven
and on earth and put all things in subjection under his
feet that he might eternally govern, protect, and save
his faithful.281 The major part of the rest of the
chapter on the kingly office is devoted to proving that
Christ did not raise himself from the dead, but was
raised by God.

The importance of the resurrection for
Socinianism, therefore, may be understood, generally
speaking, in light of the fact that having denied the
pre-existence of Christ and yet wanting at the same
time to preserve the distinctiveness of the Christian
religion, Socinians were compelled to attribute the
divine in Christ chiefly to his post-existence, for
which the resurrection was the sine qua non.

But the doctrinal centrality of the resurrection
does not suffice to explain its apologetic employment
in the Catechism, were it not for one other feature of
Socinianism--its theological rationalism. For while
Socinianism held to the credibility and authority of
Scripture, it also maintained that it was reason which
makes evident to us that the Bible is divine
revelation. Thus, in the 1680 version in the chapter
on the sufficiency of Holy Scripture, it is said, in

response to a question concerning the use of right
reason, that it is of great service. Since without it
one could neither perceive with certainty the authority
of the Scriptures nor understand and apply its
contents.[282] Neither Catholics nor the Reformers would
have agreed with the first of these assertions, since
appeal could be made to tradition or the Holy Spirit
respectively. But the Catechism rejects Roman Catholic
traditions as either unnecessary or injurious. If the
traditions are false they are injurious, but if their
origin may be deduced from historical writings or other
authentic testimonies independent of the authority of
the Church, then they are unnecessary. There is,
states the Catechism of 1680, a certain medium between
Sacred Scripture and tradition.[283] That medium would
appear to be historical evidence, in the absence of
which the tradition is spurious and in the presence of
which the tradition becomes superfluous. The same
could be said by implication of the testimony of the
Spirit. Given this commitment to theological
rationalism and to the historical approach to the
Scriptures' truth; Catechism's opening chapter on the
authenticity of the Holy Scriptures constitutes a
rational apologetic for belief in the Scriptures.
Hormack has characterized the Socinian understanding of
religion as on the one hand the Book, on the other hand
the human understanding. This latter he calls the
second principle in Socinian dogmatics. This opening
chapter "is the first, and therefore it is an
important, attempt to establish the authority of Holy
Scripture, without making an appeal to faith . . . What
an undertaking it was for a church to provide itself
with such a Catechism: we must go back to the times of
Abelard, nay, even, of the Apologists, to find

something similar in church history!"[284]   When we
recall the centrality of the resurrection for Socinian
doctrine, especially its role in confirming Christ's
all-important prophetic office, then we may see why the
historical argument for the resurrection of Jesus
should play so important a role in the Socinian
atttempt to carve out a middle ground between Deism and
orthodoxy.

        The chapter on the authenticity of the Scriptures
falls into two parts and might better be titled "Of the
Credibility of the New Testament," since the aim of
these two parts is to show the credibility of the New
Testament.   The first argument, is that there is no
reason to doubt the New Testament's veracity.   The
approach here prefigures the apologetic argumentation
of the next two centuries: it is said that there are
four reasons to deny a book's veracity, none of which
apply to the New Testament: (1) the author is unknown,
(2) the author is suspect, (3) the text is corrupted,
or (4) there is testimony which detracts from the
book's credibility. Contra (1), it is pointed out that
Christians have from the first agreed that the New
Testament books were written by their received authors.
With respect to (2), it is maintained that an author is
suspect if (a) he is not thoroughly acquainted with his
subject, (b) he writes of things which are products of
his own invention, or (c) his writings exhibit
indications of doubtful veracity.   But the New
Testament writers cannot be so characterized, for they
were eye-and-ear-witnesses of what they record (or
depended on those who were), and they could not be
liars since their faith prohibited this. It therefore
follows that contraditions and falsehoods do not exist
in their writings.   Contra (3), the text of the New

Testament cannot be entirely corrupted or the received
authors would not be their authors after all. Nor can
it be corrupted in part, for if it were corrupted in
matters of great importance, this would be easily
detectable as at variance with the rest, and if it were
corrupted in insignificant matters, this is
insufficient to call into question the basic veracity
of the New Testament writings.[285] Moreover, it is
inconceivable that God would have permitted the
Scriptures to be in any way corrupted. Contra (4),
there simply are no conclusive and sufficient
testimonies by credible men which disprove the New
Testament.

The second argument declared to be of far greater
weight is that there is positive evidence for the
veracity of the books of the New Testament. This is
the evidence for the truth of the Christian Religion
itself. For since the Christian Religion is what the
New Testament teaches, it follows that if Christianity
is true, then the New Testament books are credible.
The Catechism now proceeds to prove that the Christian
Religion is true. Two considerations are proposed to
prove the truth of Christianity: (1) the divinity of
Jesus Christ and (2) the divinity of the religion
itself.

Turning to the first consideration, Jesus's
divinity, it is argued that Jesus was divine because of
(a) the truly divine miracles that he wrought and (b)
God's raising him from the dead on account of the
religion that he taught. Concerning (a), it is argued
that we know Jesus wrought miracles because this is
acknowledged not only by those who believed in him, but
also by his enemies, the Jews. We know Jesus's
miracles were divine because this is proved by his

resurrection: "Nam cum is affirmaret, se miracula
virtute divina fecisse, perspicuum est, postquam is
mortuus, a Deo vitae restituts est, verissimum fuisse,
quod affirmarat, nempe miracula ipsius fuisse
divina."[286]

This looks forward to (b), and already the
prominence of the resurrection has emerged, since the
divinity of Christ's miracles is proven by God's
raising him from the dead.   The Socinian emphasis on
Christ   the   teacher   is   also   clear,   since   the
resurrection is God's confirmation that the doctrine
taught by Jesus is true.   Two arguments are now offered
in support of the fact of Jesus's resurrection: (i)
many persons almost immediately after his death
insisted that they had seen him alive from the dead,
and they along with a great multitude of persons who
believed on the basis of their testimony submitted to
great suffering and horrid deaths in attestation of the
fact of the resurrection.   (It is interesting that this
apologetic thus makes no reference to the empty tomb,
but appeals only to the resurrection appearances.)
Therefore, the following dilemma arises: either Jesus
was actually raised from the dead or these men
voluntarily submitted to misfortune and death for what
they knew to be false.   Common sense shows the second
horn of the dilemma to be false; therefore, the first
is demonstrated.   Missing from this argument is the
alternative   that   the   disciples   were   themselves
sincerely mistaken, which later appologists would
incorporate into the dilemma.   (ii) Moreover, it is
incredible that, in view of the sacrifices involved, so
many nations should have received this religion, unless
it had been confirmed by Jesus's resurrection from the
dead.   By means of Jesus's miracles and resurrection,
therefore, it has been shown that Jesus is divine and

that therefore the religion taught by him is true.

Turning now to the second consideration in support of the Christian Religion, the divinity of that Religion, the Catechism argues, first, that the nature of the religion, as displayed in its precepts and promises, is so sublime and so surpasses the inventive powers of the human mind that its author must be God himself; and second, that the circumstances of the religion, as seen in its rise, progress, power, and effects, are such that only God could account for its success. With regard to its rise, the founders of this religion were poor and contemptible, having neither power, wisdom, nor authority to help in converting others to their doctrine. As to its progress, Christianity spread rapidly and widely among a diversity of nations and persons though it offered no worldly advantage, but only persecution. Finally, with regard to its power and effects, it could be suppressed by no power or authority, and it supplanted all other religious systems it encountered. Hence, these circumstances together with the nature of the Religion show it to be of divine origin.

The Racovian Catechism is remarkably advanced for its time with regard to its use of historical aplogetics, especially in its use of the resurrection. It is noteworthy that the proof from prophecy is altogether absent, the sign of miracle and the argument from the existence of the church bearing nearly all the weight. But we also find the more subjective consideration of the sublimity of the Christian religion, a consideration which would become prominent after the demise of the more objective, historical aplogetic. That the apologetic argument encapsulated in the Catechism influenced Grotius's formulation of

his own case for Christianity is not improbable.[287]
Although he does not acknowledge such influence, he
could hardly afford to confess his indebtedness to
heretical Socinian authors. The parallels between the
argument of book one of the Catechism and books two and
three of De veritate are striking. Grotius reproduces
in book two the reasoning of the Catechism concerning
the divinity of Jesus and the nature and circumstances
of the Christian religion. Noting in section three
that Jesus was worshipped after his death, Grotius in
section four accounts for this on the basis of Jesus's
miracles, which he in section five maintains cannot be
ascribed to the devil. In section six the evidence of
the resurrection is adduced as further confirmation of
Jesus's miracles and doctrine; this section includes
considerations parallel to those in the Catechism's
first argument for the veracity of the New Testament
and the argument from the circumstances of the
religion. Then in section eight and following, Grotius
appeals to the sublime nature of the Christian
religion, both in its promise of immortality and its
precepts of a holy life. Finally in sections eighteen
and nineteen come the arguments from the effects of
Christ's doctrine: its wonderful propagation, the
weakness and simplicity of the disciples, and the great
obstacles facing those who embraced it. In book three
we find Grotius's defense of the authenticity of the
books of the New Testament. He advances here the
arguments for the authenticity of the received authors
(section two), for their credibility on the basis of
their being eyewitnesses (section five), the
impossibility of their being liars (section six), and
their miracles (section seven), and for the purity of
the New Testament text (section fifteen). Perhaps most

interesting is the fact that the view of Christ presented in De veritate never rises above the Socinian understanding: Christ is the Teacher, the truth of whose doctrine is proved by his resurrection.[288]   In fact, Grotius's work was criticized at the time for its failure to make any mention of either the Trinity or the atonement.   Indeed, De veritate could be called a Socinian aplogetic par excellence, and it is noteworthy that in the Racovian Catechism of 1680 Benedict Wissowatius in an appended note commends, along with Socinian apologies, Grotius's De veritate.   I do not mean to suggest that Grotius was himself a Socinian; but his apology does not rise above that level, and Socinian divines seem to have expanded the apologetic argument of the 1680 Catechism by drawing on Grotius's treatise.   We know that Grotius was acquainted with Socinian writings prior to his composing De veritate,[289] and it is not unlikely that De veritate reflects their influence.   Grotius's silence on the deity of Christ may be due, not to his own lack of conviction on that score, but to his desire to present an apology useful to all facets of Christendom.   An eager ecumenist, Grotius was deeply distressed by the fragmented front presented by Christianity to other religions and irreligion, and the avowed purpose of De veritate is to present an apology for Christianity in general, not to adjudicate internecine debates.[290] Grotius was prepared to admit into an ecclesiastical alliance not only Calvinists and Arminians, but Catholics and Socinians as well.   It is interesting to note that the Polish Brethren or unitarians hoped for union with the Dutch Arminians or Remonstrants, with whom Grotius was politically aligned.   After his imprisonment in 1618 for his alliance with the

Remonstrants, Grotius escaped to Paris in 1621, where he was in contact with Martin Ruarus, a Socinian divine whose emendations of the Racovian Catechism were adopted into the 1680 version by Wissowatius. Grotius and Ruarus concurred in the policy of religious tolerance of all views. This broadness of mind is expressed in De veritate, which offends neither Socinian nor orthodox Christian, since it argues for the lowest common denominator among them and, hence, could be used by all. Since Grotius never actually explains what it is that Christ claimed and taught about himself, any sect looking to Christ as its teacher and admitting his miracles and resurrection could look to De veritate for support.

For his own part, Grotius was the first to provide a sophisticated historical argument for the truth of Christianity in his De veritate, and his treatise became known as the aureus libellus of Christian apologetics.[291] De veritate is divided into six books: in book one Grotius defends a cosmological argument for the existence of God and demonstrates how God is revealed in Israel's history; in book two he presents historical proofs for Jesus's miracles and resurrection; book three treats the authority of Scripture; in book four he demonstrates the superiority of Christianity to paganism; in book five Christianity is vindicated against Judaism and shown through the proof from prophecy to be the fulfillment of the Old Testament promises; book six contains a refutation of Islam.

Himself the author of a history of the wars of the Dutch against Spain, Grotius was one of the first to appreciate the importance of the science of history for the truth of the Christian faith. Hence, he observes

in book two that there are a variety of ways of proving
something to be true.[292]   For example, different
methods are employed in mathematics, physics, and
ethics.   When we come to matters of fact, we must rely
on testimony free from all suspicion of untruth;
otherwise the whole structure and use of history
collapses.   Many historical narrations are commonly
accepted as true on no other ground than authority, but
the history of Christ, on the other hand, is attested
by strong proofs which declare it to be true.   These
proofs are the evidence for Jesus's miracles and
resurrection.

Grotius begins by pointing out that it is certain
that Jesus of Nazareth was an actual historical person
living in Judea under the reign of Tiberius, a fact
acknowledged in historical writings from Christians,
Jews, and pagans alike.[293]   Further he was put to death
and thereafter worshipped by men.[294]   The reason for
this worship was that he had performed various miracles
during his life.[295]   Many of the early Christians such
as Polycarp, Irenaus, Athenagorus, Origen, Tertullian,
Clement of Alexandria, and so forth were raised in
other religions, yet came to worship this man Jesus as
God because they had made a diligent inquiry and
discovered that he had wrought many miraculous deeds.
Moreover, none of their opponents--neither Celsus nor
Julian nor the Rabbinic doctors--could deny that Jesus
had done these miracles.   It is not possible to explain
away Jesus's miracles as either wrought by nature or by
the devil.[296]   With regard to the first, it is not
naturally possible that terrible diseases and
infirmities should be cured by the sound of a man's
voice or his mere touch.   As to the second, Christ's
teaching was diametrically opposed to Satan, so that

his miracles could hardly be attributed to demonic
power.

Grotius then argues that Christ's resurrection can
also be proved by credible reasons.[297] He points out
that the apostles claimed to be eyewitnesses of the
risen Christ. They even appealed to the testimony of
500 brethren who had seen Jesus after his resurrection.
Now it would have been impossible for so many to
conspire together to perpetrate such a hoax. And what
was there to gain by lying? They could expect neither
honor, nor wealth, nor worldly profit, nor fame, nor
even the successful propagation of their doctrine. If
they lied, says Grotius, it had to be for the defense
of their religion. But in this case, they either
sincerely believed that this religion was true or they
did not. If not, then they would never have chosen it
for their own and rejected the safer, more customary
religions. But if they believed it to be true, then
the resurrection of Jesus cannot be avoided. For had
he not risen, contrary to his prediction, that would
have destroyed the very foundation of any faith the
disciples had. Moreover, their own religion prohibited
lying and any bearing of false witness. And besides
this, no one, and especially so many, would be willing
to die for a lie which he himself had made up, a lie
that would bring him absolutely no worldly good. It is
clear from their writings that the apostles were not
madmen. And finally, the conversion of the apostle
Paul bears witness to the reality of the resurrection.

Grotius concludes by handling two theoretical
problems: (1) To those who object that the
resurrection is impossible, Grotius simply replies that
it involves no logical contradiction to say that a dead
man has been restored to life.[298] (2) The significance

of the resurrection Grotius finds in its confirming the
new doctrine taught by Jesus, especially in light of
Jesus's prediction that he would rise from the dead.[299]

What Grotius had done in his case for the
resurrection of Jesus is confront his opponents with a
dilemma. Given the authenticity of the gospels and I
Corinthians, the apostolic testimony to the event of
the resurrection can be denied only if the apostles
were either lying or sincerely mistaken. Most of
Grotius's arguments go to disprove the first horn of
this dilemma ([1] the impossibility of conspiracy, [2]
the lack of motivation to lie, [3] the preference for
customary religion, [4] Judaism's prohibition of lying,
and [5] the unwillingness to die for a lie); but he
also argues against the second ([1] the disciples were
not mad, [2] the disciples' faith would have been
destroyed without the resurrection, and [3] the
conversion of Paul). We find here in rudimentary form
the dilemma which would be sharpened and urged by
subsequent generations of orthodox polemicists against
their Deist opponents.[300]

Another important seventeenth century figure in
the development of this historical approach to the
defense of Christianity was the brilliant French
mathematician and scientist Blaise Pascal, who strove
during the last years of his life (d. 1662), despite
the effects of a debilitating disease to which he
finally succumbed at only 39, to complete his fondest
project: L'Apologie de la religion chrétienne. From
the hundreds of notes and fragments left by Pascal, a
rough draft exists of what the Apologie was to look
like. Unfortunately, the evidentialist side of the
Apologie is often overlooked. While it is true that
Pascal eschewed philosophical proofs for God as

abstract and unconvincing, he was no mere fideist, but
placed his main emphasis upon miracle and especially
prophecy.[301]   From 1656-58 Pascal struggled with the
function of miracle in establishing faith, and his
papers left from this time are quite interesting.   In
defining a miracle, Pascal maintained that any effect
is miraculous which surpasses the natural force of the
means employed to produce it.[302]   Thus, healing disease
by a spoken word would be miraculous, but exorcism by
Satanic power would not.   The difficulty of demonic
miracles particularly bedeviled Pascal.   The problem
here is the relationship between miracle and doctrine:
If miracle judges the truth of the doctrine, then how
can one adjudicate between Christianity and demonic
deception, since both can produce at least apparent
miracles in support of their claims?   But if one says
that doctrine shall judge the authenticity of a
miracle, then miracles lose all evidential value for
faith.   In at least one fragment, Pascal suggests that
the solution is not in terms of either/or but in terms
of a reciprocal relationship between the two: "It is
necessary to judge doctrine by miracles.   It is
necessary to judge miracles by doctrine.   Both are
true, but they do not contradict one another."[303]
Pascal emphasizes that while the evidence of miracle
and prophecy is not "absolutely convincing," still it
is sufficient to condemn those who reject it, as doing
so not out of reason, but out of sinfulness.[304]   There
are two foundations of religion, he says, one interior
and one exterior: grace and miracles, both of them
supernatural.[305]   In his notes for his Apologie he
later writes that God puts religion in the mind by
reasons and in the heart by grace.[306]   In the Apologie
Pascal apparently intended to deal with the

resurrection of Jesus, for in a fragment entitled
"Proofs of Jesus Christ," he satirically portrays the
apostles assembling together after the death of Jesus
to conspire to say that he is resurrected, a picture
which Pascal ridicules as "truly absurd."[307]
Unfortunately that is all we hear from Pascal on the
evidence for the resurrection, and we must wait for
later writers to develop these themes.

The period between Pascal and Bayle, embracing
such figures as Malebranche, Huet, Bossuet, and
Abbadie, has been described by Monod as the golden age
of classical French apologetics.[308] Cartesians wedded
to Pascal, these thinkers do not forget the importance
of Pascal's role of the heart, but " . . . they all
remain convinced that the truth of religion is
demonstrable by reasoning and by the facts."[309] It was
a disciple of Pascal, Filleau de la Chaise, who in his
Discours sur les preuves des livres de Moyse (1672) set
the tone for this era. According to Monod, Filleau is
important because he inaugurates the method of proof
par les faits.[310] It would probably be better to say
that he inaugurates this approach as a self-conscious
methodology in apologetics, for certainly Grotius
employed the method, if he did not label it. In his
Discours Filleau essays to prove the authenticity of
the Mosaic books, which, as we have seen, had come
under attack in the second half of the seventeenth
century. He reasons that if Moses wrote the
Pentateuch, then the Jewish religion is true; if the
Jewish religion is true, then Jesus must be the
Messiah; if Jesus is the Messiah, we must believe what
he said, which guarantees the truth of such mysteries
as the Trinity, incarnation, real presence, and so
forth. Thus, by this "divin enchainement de vérités"

God leads men to true faith, and they can see "that
there is nothing more reasonable than the submission
which they render to the most incomprehensible
mysteries."[311]   Thus, the way in which to persuade
people who doubt the truth of the Christian religion
and cannot understand its mysteries is not by trying to
explain or comprehend the mysteries, but by showing
that they are conjoined with other truths which are
more readily received by the human mind. This is the
method of proving Christianaity by the facts:

> If men know anything with assurance, it is the
> facts; and of everything that falls within their
> knowledge, there is nothing in which it would be
> more difficult to deceive them and over which
> there would be less occasion for dispute. And
> thus, when one will have made them see that the
> Christian Religion is inseparably attached to
> facts whose truth cannot be sincerely contested,
> they must submit to all that it teaches or else
> renounce sincerity and reason.[312]

The method of proving Christianity by the facts was
thus, in French thought, a logical extension of
function of the scholastic signs of credibility in
attesting truths of faith. Since truths of faith are
above reason, they cannot be directly proved, but can
nevertheless be indirectly confirmed by miracle and
prophecy. In the same way, Filleau contends that we
may prove the mysteries of the faith, not directly, but
by the facts which entail their truth. Thus, there is
a turn toward the empirical among French apologists.
As Monod points out, there is made during this time a
bifurcation between the contenant and the contenu of
the faith.[313]   Roughly rendered, the distinction is
between the container of the faith and the content of
the faith. Though the content of the Christian
religion, that is, the body of truths constituting its

doctrines, might be above reason, nonetheless the container of this religion, that is to say, the historical events of the gospel story, is demonstrable by the facts; hence, the contenu is indirectly proved by empirical verification of the contenant.

Of the principal figures of this period, undoubtedly the most significant for our purposes is Abbadie. His contemporaries only touch on the historical evidences for faith. Malebranche's Conversations chrétiennes (1677) is an attempt to supplement a Cartesian philosophical system with the method of proving things by the facts.[314] In these ten conversations Malebranche sets out to prove: (1) that there is a God and that it is only He who truly acts upon us and can render us happy or unhappy, and (2) the truth of the Christian religion proved by two other reasons of which the first is metaphysical and the second dependent upon the facts. The first is Malebranche's occasionalism, according to which God is the only operative cause, so-called secondary causes being merely the occasions upon which God acts.[315] As to the second point, Malebranche's proof by the facts comprises only a brief discussion of the authenticity of the books of Moses.316 Huet's Demonstratio evangelica (1679) is also determined by philosophical rationalism, this time by Spinoza's, and is arranged, like the Ethic, in a deductive sequence of definitions, axioms, and propositions.[317] Although in the first two propositions, Huet attempts to prove the authenticity and contemporaneity of the New Testament books and, hence, their reliability (prop. three), the bulk of the Demonstratio is given over to the proof from prophecy, the heart of the book lying in prop. nine, that Christ fulfilled the Old Testament prophecies. The same may

be said of Bossuet's classic Discours sur l'histoire
universelle (1681), a paradigm of the genre of
universal history. Beginning with Adam, Bossuet sweeps
through twelve epochs of history to Charlemagne,
showing the unfolding of biblical prophecy, especially
the Messianic predictions.[318]

It is Jacques Abbadie who provides for us the
proof par excellence of Christianity by the facts.
Having already earned his doctorate at age 17, Abbadie
began his masterpiece Traité de la vérité de la
religion chrétienne (1684) at age 22. A Huguenot, he
fled France upon the Revocation of the Edict of Nantes
and became the pastor of a French congregation in
Berlin. From 1689 he pastored a church in London,
eventually retiring to Killalow, Ireland, where he died
in 1727. Abbadie's Traité, which was translated into
German and English, is perhaps the finest apologetic
work of the century. In the Nouvelles de la République
des Lettres, Bayle wrote, "It has been a long time
indeed since there has been a book in which there is
more force and greater reach of mind, more fine
arguments and more eloquence."[319] According to Monod's
survey of the catalogues of 73 private libraries of
French aristocrats published between 1775 and 1789,
Abbadie's Traité was found more frequently than any
other apologetic book (30 times), outstripping even
Pascal (29 times) and nearly doubling Bossuet (17
times).[320] The Traité continued to be reprinted until
1864 and exercised tremendous influence in France,
England, and Germany on the opponents of Deism.

The Traité fuses the same intimacy with God found
in Pascal's Pensées with the rigorous thinking of
seventeenth century Protestant scholasticism. In the
first volume he argues for (1) the existence of God on

the basis of nature and mind, (2) the truth and necessity of religion against Deists (loosely construed), (3) the truth of the Jewish religion based on the Old Testament contra Spinoza's objections, and (4) the function of Jewish religion in leading to Christianity (proof from fulfilled prophecy). In the second volume, Abbadie turns to historical evidences for Christianity, reminding his reader that he has already demonstrated the existence of God and Jesus's fulfillment of the Messianic promises.[321]

In the first section of volume two, he argues for the truth of the New Testament history on the basis of the character and suffering of its principal witnesses.[322] Secular records establish the suffering and martyrdom of early believers; but it is impossible that the apostles could have tricked men like Clement and Polycarp into believing that the apostolic miracles were genuine to the point that they would become martyrs for this truth. It would be as if someone today were to publish a book full of great moral precepts accompanied by the deeds of an extraordinary and divine man who lived at the beginning of this century and who is said to have raised the dead, healed the sick, calmed the winds and tempests, and gave to his disciples the power to perform many miracles; this man was taken and killed in Germany, but his disciples (listing their names) came to France, spread throughout Europe, and all died for the defense of their faith. No one would believe such a fable. So it is with the gospels. But in addition, unless the events of the gospels are factual, it is impossible to explain the transformation in the disciples themselves such that within a few weeks after Jesus's crucifixion, they fearlessly looked death in the face, boldly proclaiming

his resurrection. Grotius's dilemma now reappears in
sharpened form: a witness is reliable when he is
neither fooled himself nor attempting to fool others.
In the case of the disciples, it is impossible that
they be deceived by what they saw and heard and
touched.   But it is equally impossible that they be
intentionally trying to deceive: their simplicity
precludes their conceiving such a design; their loss of
hope after Jesus's death, the shame of public
appearance, and their conscience would stop them from
carrying it out; and the poverty and suffering they
subsequently experienced would have made at least one
of them divulge the truth.

        In section two Abbadie examines more closely the
reliability of the New Testament documents.[323]   One
might suspect the gospel evidence on three grounds:
(1) the writings might not be authentic, (2) their text
might be corrupted, and (3) the apostles themselves
might have filled them with glorious fictions.   In
laying the first suspicion to rest, Abbadie argues:
(1) as far as one regresses in history, there was no
time for a forgery to be written because even the most
ancient external testimony regards these writings as
divine; (2) the amount of intense interest in these
writings, since standing for them could lead to
martyrdom, would assure a thorough scrutiny of their
authenticity; (3) the forgers would have been early
believers, but no one dies for a fiction which they
have invented; (4) the fact that the epistles claim to
have been written to specific congregations prevents
them from being spurious; and (5) even if only the
epistles were genuine, we would then still have
adequate evidence for the miracles, resurrection, and
ascension of Jesus.[324]   Abbadie concludes that there

was simply no occasion for false writings to appear:
not during the lifetime of the apostles certainly, but
also not immediately thereafter, since by then the New
Testament writings are already known.

Turning to the second suspicion, that of a
corrupted text, Abbadie states that the citations of
the New Testament in the writings of the Fathers, as
well as the many exemplars of the biblical documents,
assures us that the text we have is pure.[325]

Abbadie argues at length against the third
misgiving, that the gospels could contain fables.[326]
He lists the external testimony to each of the four
gospels to show their authenticity. The differences
between the gospel narrations show clearly that they
were not written in concert. In fact, when one
considers the sufferings the disciples endured, it is
absurd to imagine that these simple men could conspire
together to write the gospels. The fact that the
gospels are not inventive fictions becomes even more
evident when one compares them to heretical writings.
Had the gospels been of the nature of these sort of
writings, the disciples would have sought to glorify
themselves; their writings would have been speculative
like the heretics', not simple empirical reports of
what they saw and heard. Moreover, six considerations
make it absolutely impossible that the disciples could
have invented the content of what they wrote and
preached.[327]   (1) The preaching occurred in the very
city in which the events took place. (2) It was only a
few weeks after the resurrection that the disciples
began to proclaim the miracles, death, and resurrection
of Jesus. (3) Many eyewitnesses were about who had
been with Jesus. (4) The facts of Jesus's life were
empirically verifiable and miraculous: the sick

healed, the dead raised, and so forth. (5) The number
of such attested miracles was enormous. (6) The
disciples themselves claimed to have received
miraculous powers which one might witness in
attestation to their message.

Abbadie further maintains that the simple,
unaffected style of the gospel narratives show that
they are not inventive pieces intended to deceive.[328]
The fact that they do not shrink from passages that
could be interpreted as showing imperfections in Jesus
displays their candor and sincerity. Of all things
reported in the gospels, it is certain that Jesus
performed miracles, and that the circumstances of his
death and resurrection are true.[329] For the disciples
had ample opportunity to observe his miracles, and if
he was a mere imposter then why did Judas and Peter
both repent? The public nature of the wonders
attending his death preclude their being inventions.
And the story of the guard at the tomb (which precluded
theft by the disciples) could not be 'false since it
reports what was already public rumor. Thus, the third
suspicion as well is groundless, and the evidence of
the gospels for the divine nature of Christianity must
be accepted.

In section three Abbadie examines more closely
Jesus's miracles, resurrection, and ascension, and the
outpouring of the Holy Spirit; our attention will be
directed toward the first two. Abbadie first explains
the presuppositions ingrained in the disciples when
Jesus made himself known to them.[330] (1) The reign of
the Messiah would be accompanied by temporal
prosperity. (2) The Messiah would reestablish the
kingdom of Israel and the reign of the house of David.
(3) The law would endure forever. (4) The sacrifices

were the most sacred and inviolable element in their
religion. (5) The Gentiles were entirely execrable in
their sight. How could these prejudices be changed so
quickly, among so many, and of one accord, unless there
were supernatural events involved, unless Jesus was
more than a human malefactor put to death by the Jews?
With specific regard to the gospel miracles, Abbadie
contends that these were of too public a character to
be fictitious.[331] Using the four examples of the
dumbness of Zachariah, the visit of the Magi, the
feeding of the thousands, and the wonders accompanying
the death of Christ, Abbadie maintains that all these
incidents were so openly observed that the gospel
stories could not be false. To illustrate the points
Abbadie composes an entertaining passage in which he
imagines us transported back to the time of Pentecost
such that we could talk with the citizens of Jerusalem
and inquire of all those who saw or were even subjects
of the public ministry of miracles performed by Jesus
Christ.[332]

Turning to the subject of the resurrection, [333]
Abbadie first notes that this event and the miracles
hang together: If the resurrection is true, so are the
miracles; similarly, if the miracles are true, then
what reason have we to doubt the resurrection? Abbadie
argues that Jesus did predict his own death and
resurrection. These prophecies were probably not
written back into the text because they are sometimes
found in contexts that could not have been products of
the disciples' own invention. For example, one such
prediction is found in connection with Jesus's harsh
rebuke of Peter, "Get behind me, Satan!", a passage
that, following upon the heels of Peter's great
confession, no disciple would probably invent. Again,

Jesus foretold his death in establishing the practice
of the Lord's Supper, but this would have been a
gruesome ritual holding no hope had it not been
accompanied by the prediction of the resurrection. But
finally the story of the guard at the tomb shows
decisively that Jesus predicted his resurrection. For
had Jesus never predicted his resurrection, the Jews
would never have set the watch; had they never set the
watch, then Matthew could never say that the story that
the disciples stole the body while the guards slept is
"spread among the Jews to this day." Matthew could not
and would not have written this passage had in fact no
such story been widespread at his time. And the
widespread story that the disciples stole the body
while the guards slept can not be accounted for if in
point of fact the guard had never been set. Thus,
Jesus must have predicted his resurrection.

Now if the watch was set at the tomb, the question
then arises, why did they not prevent the theft of the
body? If the guards' story were true, then why were
they not punished for their negligence? Why did the
Sanhedrin not confront the disciples with the guard
when the disciples were apprehended for preaching the
resurrection? Besides, if the disciples did steal the
body by night, it is unthinkable that they should be so
audacious as to stand up in Jerusalem without fear
preaching that Jesus had been raised. If the incident
occurred as the guards' story goes, then why were the
disciples not charged with fraud by the Sanhedrin? And
is it not contrary to all reason to suppose that the
guards were plunged into such sleep that the disciples
had the leisure to break the seal, move the stone,
remove the corpse, and carefully fold all the grave
clothes?

Futhermore, if the disciples stole the body, it must have been by collusion; otherwise the plot would never have endured. But the conspiracy hypothesis is fraught with difficulties: (1) no one will die for a lie he has himself invented; (2) even should one person venture upon such a course, it is extravagant to believe so great a number would do so, particularly after having conducted themselves on all previous occasions in so contrary a manner; (3) some would have believed lying and treachery to be contrary to salvation and would not have gone along; (4) someone would have divulged the truth under the threat of torture or death; (5) if the disciples' unity in fidelity was so weak, their unity in perfidy would only be still weaker. In addition to all these points, proceeds Abbadie, we must keep in mind that we are not speaking here of just the eleven apostles, but of all the disciples, including the women and the 500 brethren mentioned by Paul. With regard to these latter, the apostle would not dare to give false information, since he mentions so many who are still alive. Abbadie emphasizes again the incredible change in the disciples, such that if there were no resurrection, one could explain this transformation only by saying that they had ceased to be merely human!

After discussing the public nature of the ascension and miraculous gifts of the Holy Spirit given to the disciples, Abbadie sums up his argument in three principles:[334] (1) The apostles and other disciples of Jesus Christ actually testified to the miracles of Jesus Christ, his resurrection, his ascension, and the outpouring of the Holy Spirit on the apostles. (2) They believed in good faith what they testified. (3) Since they believed that Jesus Christ had done

miracles, was raised from the dead, had ascended to
heaven, and had sent his Spirit to his disciples, all
of which were events to which they were witnesses, it
necessarily follows that all these things are true.

Abbadie was the last great figure in France's
golden age of classical apologists, and his empirical
method helped set the course for the eighteenth century
French response to English Deism. With the advent of
Pierre Bayle, however, this golden age came to a halt,
and from around 1695 until about 1734 England led the
way in the defense of the faith. Bayle had brought a
formidable new threat, and this time there was no
Pascal or Abbadie to answer him. The orthodox
apologists began to lose ground. "Theologians
honorable and mediocre, in the most worthy sense of the
word, they start to become inferior to a task more and
more heavy."[335]

Eighteenth century English development of the
historical argument for Christianity. In England the
charter for the orthodox response to Deism was written
in the 1690's. The influence of French evidentialist
apologetics, as we have seen, may have been mediated to
John Locke via Jean Le Clerc. Already in his Essay
Concerning Human Understanding, Locke had defended
revealed religion in asserting that God can provide us
with special revelation as assuredly as He has provided
us with the natural light of reason.[336] According to
Locke, God can reveal to us truths which are also
attainable by reason (though reason gives greater
certainly of these) as well as truths unattainable by
reason. But revelation cannot be contrary to reason,
for the fact that something is revelation or that we
have interpreted it correctly will always be less
certain than our own intuitive grasp of the truth of

reason which the purported revelation contradicts.
Therefore, no proposition contrary to reason can be
received as divine revelation, for to do so undermines
the very basis upon which one accepted the revelation
as divine.[337]   Hence, although we know that a
revelation from God must be true, it still lies within
the province of reason to determine if a purported
revelation is indeed genuine and to determine its
meaning. Should any profferred revelation contradict
reason, it must be rejected. In matters where reason
cannot judge or can only attain probability, revelation
ought to be given the epistemic priority.   But in
matters where rational certainty is possible, reason
takes precedence over revelation. Locke concludes,

> Whatever God hath revealed is certainly true; no
> doubt can be made of it.   This is the proper
> object of faith: but whether it be a divine
> revelation or no, reason must judge; which can
> never permit the mind to reject a greater evidence
> to embrace what is less evident, nor allow it to
> entertain probability in opposition to knowledge
> and certainty.   There can be no evidence that any
> traditional revelation is of divine original, in
> the words we receive it, and in the sense we
> understand it, so clear and so certain as that of
> the principles of reason: and therefore nothing
> that is contrary to, and inconsistent with, the
> clear and self-evident dictates of reason has a
> right to be urged or assented to as a matter of[338]
> faith, wherein reason hath nothing to do.

Locke agrees with the Deists that we must accept the
dictates of reason as fundamental, that natural
religion is in accordance with reason, and that no
revelation contrary to reason can be admitted; but he
denies that this precludes God's revealing truths to
man which are not contrary to reason.

In his Reasonableness of Christianity Locke
enumerates some of the reasons why revelation is

necessary.[339] Although reason is sufficient to inform
man of the existence of God and of man's duty toward
Him, it is a simple fact that because of sin and
ignorance most men do not gain a knowledge of these
truths. Therefore, revelation is necessary to inform
them of what they should have known by nature.
Revelation is also necessary for the laying down of
ethical standards for the mass of humanity, since so
few are sufficiently enlightened to pursue the virtuous
life apart from the authority of revelation.
Revelation provides encouragement to live the moral
life and sanctions in the life to come as incentives.
Moreover, revelation is required if one is to acquire a
complete system of ethics that is authoritative and
without any admixture of human error.

But how may we know if a genuine revelation has
been made? In his Discourse on Miracles, Locke lays
down three criteria for revelation: (1) it must
deliver nothing dishonoring to God or inconsistent with
natural religion and the natural moral law; (2) it must
not inform man of things indifferent, insignificant, or
easily known by natural ability; (3) it must be
confirmed by supernatural signs. Thus, for Locke
miracles were the chief evidence for revelation.[340] On
the basis of Jesus's miracles, we are justified in
regarding him as the Messiah and his revelation from
God as true.

As the fountainhead for both Deist and orthodox
works, Lock's thought helped determine the character of
the eighteenth century Deist controversy in England.
In this I think one may see a subtle and yet decisive
difference between the French method of proving
Christianity par les faits and the English empirical
methodology. Both agree that revelation may be

discerned by what was once called the signs of
credibility, miracle and prophecy, but herein they
differ: by making a distinction between the contenant
and the contenu, the French thinkers underscored the
bifurcation between truths of reason and truths of
faith, the latter being in themselves rationally
incomprehensible and only indirectly verifiable by
entailment in certain empirically ascertainable facts;
the English divines tended to dissolve the distinction
between truths of reason and of faith, the upper story
collapsing down into the lower, so that all truths,
whether natural or revealed, become in a sense truths
of reason, rationally demonstrable whether by
philosophy, science, history, or what have you. True,
Locke granted that revelation might convey truths
"above reason"; but what he meant by that term was
radically different from the meaning given the phrase
by French thinkers. They understood "above reason" to
mean mysterious, rationally incomprehensible; Locke, on
the other hand, took it to mean simply not discoverable
by reason.[341] For Locke, the problem appears to be
primarily a lack of information, not intrinsic
incomprehensibility; the examples he gives of truths
above reason are the fall of the angels and the future
resurrection of the dead. Again, it is easy to see why
Toland considered himself a disciple of Locke. Of
course, as a man with Unitarian leanings, Locke did not
have to be bothered with doctrines like the Trinity and
incarnation, nor did transsubstantiation trouble anyone
in Protestant England. But even later divines who did
adhere to the deity of Christ tended to leave the
metaphysical aspects of these doctrines in the
background or to ignore them altogether and
concentrated, like Locke, on proving the rationality of

Christianity. Thus, English thought in contrast to
French emphasized much more vigorously the inherent
reasonableness of Scripture, of revealed religion, of
Christianity. Hence, Farrar writes of the English
Deists and their opponents: "Both alike travelled
together to the end of natural religion. Here the
Deist halted, willing to accept so much of Christianity
as was a republication of the moral law. The
Christian, on the other hand, found in reason the
necessity for revelation, and proceeded onward to
revealed doctrines and positive precepts."[342]

In the attempt to show the reasonableness of
revealed religion <u>contra</u> the Deists, the English
divines followed Locke's lead in trying to prove the
historicity of miracles, along with fulfilled prophecy.
Leslie's short and easy method with the Deists
published in 1697 corresponds with Filleau de la
Chaise's method <u>par les faits</u>: maintaining that
miracles would prove Moses and Christ to be true, he
pronounces, "Therefore the Whole of the Cause will
depend upon the Proof of these <u>Matters of Fact</u>."[343]
Accordingly, to facilitate this proof Leslie lists four
rules governing the demonstration of any matter of
fact:

> 1. That the Matter of Fact be such, as that Men's
>   outward Senses, their Eyes and Ears, may be
>   judges of it.
> 2. That it be done Publickly in the Face of the
>   World.
> 3. That not only Publick <u>Monuments</u> be kept up in
>   memory of it, but some outward <u>Actions</u> to be
>   perform'd.
> 4. That such <u>Monuments</u> and such <u>Actions</u> or
>   Observances be Instituted, and do commence from
>   the <u>Time</u> that the <u>Matter of Fact</u> was done.[344]

The first two rules prevent imposture, the last two

prevent legend. Leslie argues that when these criteria
are applied to Scripture, it will be proved that the
gospel story is true. Thus, on the basis of this
demonstration by the facts, Christianity may be
embraced. "I receive the Scriptures upon the
testimony, not authority, of the Church; and I examine
that testimony as I do other facts, till I have
satisfied my prior judgement there is no other way."[345]
Leslie thus restored the dilemma stated by Eusebius:
either reject all the works of classical history or
else admit the gospel accounts along with them. He
exclaims,

> And yet our Deist, who would laugh any Man out of
> the World, as an Irrational Brute, that should
> offer to Deny Caesar, or Alexander, Homer or
> Virgil, their Publick Works and Actions; do, at
> the same time, value themselves as the only Men of
> Wit and Sense, of Free, Generous, and Unbyast
> Judgements for Ridiculing the Histories of Moses
> and Christ, that are Infinitely better Attested,
> and Guarded with Infallible Marks, which the
> others want.[346]

Following in Locke's footsteps, Leslie by means of his
empirical method helped to determine the nature of the
orthodox response to the Deists'attack on revealed
religion. Stephen agrees as to his importance:
"Leslie gives in its early form the argument which was
to serve Christian apologists for the next
generations."[347]

    Eighteenth century French development of the
historical argument for Christianity. While eighteenth
century Englishmen were defending the rationality of
the Christian religion, Frenchmen were increasingly
deserting it. After Bayle the contenu de la foi was
not regarded as simply above reason, but actually
contrary to reason, as Bayle himself had said. But the

eighteenth century thinkers shared neither Bayle's
professed scepticism concerning reason nor his fideism,
as Lewis White Beck explains,

> Their guiding thought was that human reason was
> adequate to human needs, that it was an instrument
> slowly developed by nature and history or given
> ready-made by God, perfectly fitted for the wise
> conduct of life. There is no paradox in the fact
> that there were skeptics, among them the greatest;
> for skepticism at that time was not concerned to
> point out insurmountable obstacles in the way of
> getting worthwhile knowledge, so much as it was
> concerned to show the illusoriness and
> worthlessness of what could not be got by reason
> and experience . . . Skepticism was chiefly an
> instrument for the redirection of inquiry . . .
> There was no skepticism of reason bent upon its
> proper work.[348]

If Bayle was willing to abandon reason for faith, the
eighteenth century _philosophes_ decidedly were not. If
faith was to be saved, the orthodox apparently
reasoned, then the unbelievers had to be shown that
even granted that the _contenu_ of the Christian religion
appears to be irrational, nevertheless the sure facts
supporting the _contenant_ imply that its doctrines are
true. Hence, the apologists did not defend the
rationality of the faith, but the authenticity of the
facts.

Thus, the rift between truths of reason and truths
of faith grew even wider. Before, truths of faith were
regarded as above reason; but now they are admitted to
be in appearance contrary to reason. Perhaps the
boldest statement of this bifurcation comes from
Sylvestre Bergier, nemesis of Rousseau and about the
only French apologist of note in the second half of the
eighteenth century, who single-handedly combatted the
whole array of French Deists. In Bergier's analysis,

Rousseau's objections to Christianity all rest on one fundamental axiom: "God can only reveal to us and we can only believe that which is demonstrated to be true."[349]   But at the same time, Bergier charges, Rousseau in his profession of faith affirms that he believes in God, though He is incomprehensible.   Such belief is inconsistent with the above axiom:

> From this striking testimony which you render to the glory of God, one may infer a very simple argument. According to you and according to the truth, we cannot comprehend the attributes of God; yet He has revealed them to us, the Holy Scriptures publish them and extol them in a thousand places, but men never had a correct idea of them until God revealed them.   God can therefore reveal to us that which we cannot comprehend. There are even many of His attributes which, it appears to us, are impossible to reconcile with one another and which seem to us contradictory: for example, the freedom of God with His immutability, His perfect unity and His immensity, His infinite goodness and His justice. Yet God has revealed them to us; it is the Scripture which instructs us about them, and on these subjects the philosophers could only stammer.   God can therefore reveal to us that which appears contradictory, that which revolts our reason.[350]

Since God is infinite, states Bergier, I cannot understand all His nature, works, or decrees. Therefore, to refuse to believe because I cannot understand is itself contrary to reason! To strengthen his case Bergier appeals to the illustration of a blind man.   On Rousseau's axiom he should not believe in colors on the basis of the testimony of others because to him they are inconceivable.   It does no good to appeal to the hoary distinction between things above reason and things contrary to reason.   According to Bergier, things above reason appear to us as contrary

to reason. To a blind man a mirror is an inconceivable
contradiction, since the ideas of flatness and depth
are contradictory to one born blind. In the same way
many Christian truths appear contradictory to us. The
Trinity, for example, confesses Bergier, presents to us
palpable absurdities.[351] But since we have no clear
idea of "nature" or "person" we cannot say it is
self-contradictory; on the basis of revelation we know
that the absurdity and contradiction is only in
appearance. Bergier's point, especially clear in the
case of the blind man, is that reason itself can oblige
us on the basis of human testimony to believe in what
appears to be absurd; hence, God can reveal to us
something apparently absurd. Bergier even cites Bayle
himself to show that the strongest faith is that which
is based on the ruin of reason. Said Bayle in Réponse
aux questions: "The testimony of God is preferable to
the testimony of men. So believe God rather than
natural light."[352] In general faith does not conflict
with reason because it proceeds by the principle: it
is more certain to believe in the word of God than in
our own natural light.

        Of course, the question arises, how do we know a
purported revelation is the word of God? Here Bergier
responds that the principle "we can only believe that
which is demonstrated to be true" is correct in the
sense of external proofs. By "external proofs" he
appears to mean argument or evidence for a conclusion,
as opposed to the analytic consistency of a concept or
proposition. An apparently contradictory proposition
may actually be true, but to believe in any proposition
without proofs would be fanaticism and mere obstinacy
of faith.[353] Something may thus be incomprehensible
and yet still demonstrated to be true. Bergier

presents four such methods of demonstration: (1) A
proposition may be a deduction from evident principles;
for example, the attributes of God. (2) A truth may be
guaranteed by a sentiment intérieur; for example, the
spirituality and freedom of the soul against
materialists and determinists. (3) Something may be
proved by empirical experience; for example, the
existence of bodies, space, and motion despite Zeno's
paradoxes. (4) A fact may be demonstrated by external
testimony; for example, the reality of colors to a
blind person.

   As is no doubt clear by now, Bergier's intent is
to present Christianity as an example of the last
category. God can reveal apparent absurdities.
Suppose He has done so. How would one prove it?
Bergier responds, by testimony; revelation is a fact
and so it should be proved by the testimony to that
fact.[354] Only two facts need to be established to
prove Christianity: that Jesus and the disciples
preached and that they performed miracles in
attestation of their mission.[355] And these are both
provable by history.

   Thus, Bayle's destruction of the rationality of
the contenu of the faith only caused later orthodox
thinkers to redouble their efforts to prove the
contenant of the faith, that is, the historical facts
of the gospel. This, coupled with the influence of
English apologists, produced a rising tide of
apologetic literature in France stressing the proof par
les faits. The paradigm example of this approach is
abbé Claude François Houtteville's Vérité de la
religion chrétienne prouvée par les faits, which
appeared first in 1722 and in a superior, revised
edition in 1740. Shunning all other methods of

demonstration, Houtteville focuses exclusively upon the
method par les faits: "I want to prove by the facts
alone that the Christian religion is true and
divine."[356] This is the most solid of all foundations:
the facts.[357] There are different sorts of
proof--metaphysical proofs, proofs of sentiment, proofs
of fact--, but proofs based on fact are the most
evident, for they are (1) the most common, (2) the most
convincing, (3) less subject to subtlety, and (4)
stronger than opposing proofs of other types.[358]
Houteville's case for Christianity is based upon the
miraculous facts of the gospel and upon fulfilled
prophecy.

The proof from miracles presupposes the following
four principles: (1) God would not deceive or allow
deception, (2) in miracles God acts most strikingly,
(3) thus, when a miracle occurs, one may know that God
is acting, and (4) a doctrine authorized by miracles is
therefore a doctrine authorized by God.[359] These
assumptions provide the framework necessary to
determine the divinity and significance of any miracle.
The question now is to establish the facticity of the
gospel miracles. Houtteville sets down seven
pre-requisites which a fact must meet if it is to be
incontestable:[360] (1) It must be without absurdity or
contradiction. (2) Many eyewitnesses must testify to
it. (3) These witnesses should be enlightened, honest,
and forthright. (4) The fact should be interesting and
public. (5) The fact must be bound up in a context of
other facts that are inexplicable without the fact in
question. (6) The testimony to the fact should be
unanimous. (7) The transmission of the reports of the
fact should be without alteration. The remainder of
volume one of Houtteville's work is a demonstration of

how the miraculous events of the gospels fulfill all
these conditions.

   Eighteenth century German development of the
historical argument for Christianity.   The experience
of England and France was repeated on a lesser scale in
Germany. As the influence of English and French Deism
made itself felt in Germany, along with the orthodox
treatises against it, it evoked the same defense of
revealed religion on the basis of historical facts.[361]
Prior to 1741, German interest in Deism was purely
academic.[362] But in that year Tindal's Christianity as
old as the Creation was translated into German, and
during the latter half of the eighteenth century the
controversy that had raged in England and France
replayed` itself on German soil.   The tide of
theological influence at this time flowed from England
to Germany, and German apologists were cast more in the
mold of the English divines rather than of the French.
They stressed the rationality of the Christian religion
and the historical facts that proved it. But they were
perhaps less rationalistic than the English in that the
inner witness of the Holy Spirit was given an important
role complementary to that of rational evidences.

   A good example of the sort of historical
apologetics evoked by imported Deism is Johann
Friedrich Kleuker, Neue Prüfung und Erklärung der
vorzüglichsten Beweise für die Wahrheit und den
göttlichen Ursprung des Christenthums   (1785).[363]
According to Kleuker, there are two types of truth in
Christianity: dogmatic and historical. To prove the
truth of Christianity by its dogma alone would be an a
priori demonstration; this Kleuker deals with in the
second volume of his work. But in order to establish
the truth of Christianity historically, one must

conduct   an   a posteriori   investigation   of   its
origins.[364]   In   order   to   show   the   divine   origin   of
Christianity, one must discover certain signs or
Merkmalen.   Predictably, Kleuker finds these in the
miracles of Christ.   The early apologists were too
influenced by Neo-platonic philosophy to employ such a
proof, he says.   Besides, since their opponents
believed in magic, the proof from miracles had little
efficacy; all they could do was show that Christianity
matches the best that paganism can offer.   Presumably
since these disadvantages no longer beset men, the way
was   now   clear   for   a   historical   vindication   of
Christianity from miracles.   According to Kleuker,
miracles serve in the Bible as decisive signs or proofs
of divine activity.[365]   Christ's miracles therefore
show the divine origin of Christianity; in particular
the resurrection confirms all of Christian life and
activity.[366]   Kleuker therefore spends the remainder of
his time defending the gospel miracles.

An even better example of the historical approach
by perhaps the finest German apologist of this period
was Gottfried Less's Wahrheit der christlichen Religion
(1758).   Less was professor of theology at Göttingen,
home of the Göttingen school of history and the chief
seat of historical studies in Germany during the
eighteenth century.   He wrote in sharp protest to the
Deism streaming into Germany from England and France,
which threatened to undermine Christianity in the
eighteenth century.   There have arisen in our century,
he declares, horrible enemies of the faith who are
destroying the belief of many.   The problem has become
so serious, Less complains, that people are rejecting
the Christian faith merely because they have heard that
works against it were being published in England.[367]

Less specifically names as the source of this evil
Herbert of Cherbury, Hobbes, Toland, Collins, Woolston,
Morgan, Tindal, Mandeville, Chubb, Bolingbroke,
Shaftesbury, Hume, and the French thinkers Montesquieu,
Rousseau, and Voltaire.[368] In his defense of revealed
religion, Less does not bother to prove the existence
of God, which he says is so obvious it needs no proof,
but rather concentrates on proving that a specifically
Christian theism is true, that is to say, that God has
revealed Himself in the world as related in the
gospels.[369]

To prove Christianity, one must demonstrate that
Christianity has divine origins and that it alone is
true.[370] There are several different methods of
demonstration: metaphysical or mathematical proof,
scientific proof, and historical proof. Christianity
is proved via the third method through witnesses,
indeed through a witness of God himself. God can give
either an internal witness through his Spirit or an
external witness through miracles. The inner witness
can by itself give personal certainty of Christianity's
truth, but it will be of no help in convincing others
that Christianity is true.[371] Hence, one must rely
only on objective, external evidences to demonstrate
the truth of the Christian religion. But before one
examines the objective evidence for miracles, one
should ask whether there is in the religion under
investigation anything absurd or contrary to reason,
for if there is, then we may be spared the effort of
further examination, since it cannot in that case be
true.[372] Although this test would not eliminate the
Christian religion, it would disqualify, for example,
Islam.

Now the entire content of Christianity can be

summed up under two heads: facts, as the foundation,
and teaching, as the building.   In demonstrating the
facticity of Christianity, Less follows a three-step
proof: (1) Reliable writers in the first few centuries
testify that the New Testament books were written in
the first century by their alleged authors; (2) these
books have been faithfully transmitted to us today; and
(3) the authors of these books have all the required
characteristics of reliable witnesses.[373]   This having
been shown, three major facts need to be proved: (1)
Jesus of Nazareth came in fulfillment of prophecy, (2)
Jesus performed miracles and himself rose from the
dead, and (3) Jesus predicted accurately future
events.[374]   Less's arguments for the second major fact
of Christianity will be the focus of our attention in
this study.

In Germany, therefore, as in England and France,
the Deist attack on revealed religion in general and on
the Scriptures in particular called forth a defense of
Christianity based on historical facts.   Such a defense
was made possible by the rise of the historical method
and was evoked into being by the Deists' denial of
revealed religion.   The two medieval signs of
credibility, miracle and prophecy, were adopted and
made the objects of historical investigation.   The
historical argument for the resurrection of Jesus
evolved as this event, the greatest of miracles, was
brought into play as a decisive proof of God's
revelation in Christ.

Epistemological common ground
between Deism and orthodoxy

Theological rationalism

Having examined the instigating factor of the
Deist challenge that brought forth historical
apologetics and with it the historical argument for the
resurrection, we may now wish to specify more precisely
the epistemological common ground on which the dispute
was fought.   It was, in a word, rationalism; more
precisely, theological rationalism.   Though few of the
disputants in this controversy were philosophical
rationalists, after the manner of Descartes or Spinoza,
nearly all were theological rationalists, that is to
say, they held that the justification of religious
belief was exclusively rational in character and that
in the absence of such rational justification, one
ought not to believe.

There were exceptions to this, of course: Henry
Dodwell, in his Christianity Not Founded on Argument
(1742), attacked theological rationalism as inimical to
true Christianity.   Contending that the adjudication of
religion lies outside the province of reason, Dodwell
argued: (1) that reason cannot possibly be the faculty
intended by God to lead us to true faith, primarily
because faith cannot hold its breath while reason
cautiously weighs and re-weighs arguments, (2) that the
Scriptures do not teach that the way to God is by means
of the intellect, but by means of the heart, and (3)
faith is the gift of the Holy Spirit.[375]   According to
Dodwell Christianity is based on authority, not the
arbitrary authority of the church, but the inner light
of a constant and particular revelation imparted
separately and supernaturally to every individual.   By
Dodwell's time, however, English Deism had passed full
flower and had begun to wilt away.[376]   His subjectively
based Christianity appears to have generated no
following, and he stands as something of an anomaly.

Indeed, it has been questioned by some whether Dodwell
was not himself an unbeliever using subjective appeals
as a subterfuge to undermine the rationality of
religious belief. In this case he would stand in the
tradition of theological rationalism after all.

There is also a line of subjective French
apologetics running from Pascal's "reasons of the
heart" through Rousseau's "lumière intérieure"; but it
is only after Rousseau that this stream of influence
widens into prominence. Even Pascal supplemented his
subjectivism with objective evidences, and for Rousseau
reason, conscience, and the senses all combined in
leading man to truth. In Germany, too, there were
exceptions to theological rationalism, such as Less,
who saw the witness of the Holy Spirit as a complement
to the rational persuasion of the evidence.

By and large, however, Deist and Christian alike
were committed to theological rationalism. On the
basis of reason, Deists constructed natural religion
and assailed revealed religion; on the basis of reason
the orthodox defenders of Christianity argued that
revealed religion was every bit as rational as natural
religion. This was the Age of Reason, and the
religious controversy bears all the marks of that age.
Reason--a sort of common sense sharpened by logic and
science--was made the judge over the question of
revelation.

Roots of theological rationalism

This magisterial use of reason in questions of
religion appears to have come about as a result of
forces set in motion by the Protestant Reformation
concerning the question of authority. We have seen
that the Reformers challenged the authority of the

Church in the name of Scripture and reason. They blasted away at the Catholic notae ecclesiae as insufficient and spurious warrant for the Church's claim to authority. The Counter-Reformers attacked in their turn the Protestant criteria as essentially private or faulty. In doing so they took up the newly rediscovered Pyrrhonism as a weapon against the Protestant appeal to reason.[377] In 1562 Henri Estienne published the text of Sextus Empiricus partly as a cure for the impious philosophers of his day; in 1569 Gentian Hervet, a leading French Catholic, published the text of Sextus as an answer to the Calvinists. It was believed that by undermining reason, one could demonstrate that there was no recourse in matters of religious truth but the authority of the Church. According to Montaigne, as we have seen, the Pyrrhonian living by nature and custom would naturally embrace Catholicism. Therefore, Catholic theologians adopted Montaigne's method in their anti-Protestant polemic. Montaigne's disciple Charron wrote his Les trois véritez (1594) in specific rebuttal of Mornay's Traité de l'Eglise (1578), charging that Calvinists make the Christian religion rest on precarious human judgement rather than the sure tradition and authority of the Church.[378] Charron's method of doubt, on the other hand, leaves us "blank, naked, and ready" before God to receive His revelation by faith.[379] Camus, another follower of Montaigne, adopted scepticism and fideism precisely out of fear of Calvinist rationalism. He asserted that only religion based on faith alone has secure enough foundations; to develop a rational defense of the faith would only lead to Protestant errors.[380] The ardent Counter-Reformationist Veron reduced Calvinsism to Pyrrhonism by arguing that our

rational faculties cannot serve as the foundation for
the faith, which is properly based on the "Word of God
alone set forth by the Church."[381]   Unlike Montaigne,
Veron's scepticism was not directed at reason as such,
but only against its replacing the authority of the
Church as the infallible interpreter of Scripture and
promulgator of doctrine. He presses an eight-point
case against the Calvinists: (1) Scripture does not
contain the conclusions of the Reformers drawn by
inference. (2) Scripture does not draw these
inferences itself. (3) In reasoning inferentially from
Scripture, one makes reason, not Scripture, the judge
of religious truth. (4) Reason can err. (5) Scripture
does not teach that doctrines reached inferentially are
articles of faith. (6) The Reformers' conclusions were
not held by the Fathers. (7) These conclusions can be
only probable and are fallacious. (8) Not even a true
conclusion inferred from Scripture can be an article of
faith. The thrust of Veron's attack was to show that
if reason, rather than the infallible Church, is made
the interpreter of Scripture, then, since reason is a
fallible guide, all we are left with is uncertainty.
Thus, in the attempt to destroy the Calvinist rule of
faith, the Counter-Reformers wedded Pyrrhonism to
Catholicism. Popkin comments,

> For about seventy-five years after the Council of
> Trent, there seems to have been an alliance
> between the Counter-Reformers and the 'nouveaux
> pyrrhoniens,' an alliance aimed at annihilating
> Calvinism as an intellectual force in France. The
> success of this entente cordiale was, no doubt,
> due to the fact that during this period the
> dominant views in Catholic theology in France were
> primarily negative and Augustinian; they were
> against scholasticism, rationalism, and Calvinism,
> rather than for any systematic and coherent
> intellectual defense of the faith.[382]

The challenge of the Catholic-Pyrrhonic alliance stimulated the development of French Calvinist rationalism and Protestant rational apologetics. Noting that some persons say that the appeal to reason is neither licit nor expedient, Mornay states:

> The first say: it is futile to dispute with those who deny the Principles. And in this way, as soon as a Principle is denied to them they cut short the conversation, as if all means of conferring were removed. This is certainly a very true maxim, but, in my judgement, very misunderstood. It is futile to dispute against those who deny the Principles by means of the very Principles they deny. This is only too true. But there can remain other Principles common to us and to the others, and on the basis of these Principles one can usefully dispute with them and very often by means of these common Principles prove and verify one's own. This is what we claim to do in this work.[383]

At this point Mornay proposes to appeal to various common grounds depending upon the disputants involved; he will use philosophy and history to prove the deity of Christ to unbelievers. Other persons, he notes, object to the use of reason in proving faith because faith is above reason. Mornay readily agrees that faith goes beyond reason; "But we say that human reason can lead us to this point: that it is necessary to believe, even beyond reason, things, I say, to which all the capacity of man cannot attain."[384] Even revealed mysteries absolutely beyond reason are rendered credible (croyable) by reason. Rather than lowering faith, reason mounts us, as it were, upon her shoulders that we might see faith and appropriate it. Already in Mornay, then, we see the preeminent place given to reason that would so characterize later apologetic treatises. The pattern of the signs of

credibility is also evident. Calvinist, rationalistic,
and scholastic, Mornay was the exact counter-point to
the Catholic Pyrrhonism of his adversaries. Thus,
while Catholic polemics remained for a time fideistic,
Protestant apologetics under the influence of Mornay
followed the path of theological rationalism.

The cause of Calvinist rationalism was further
advanced by the Scotsman John Cameron, whom Mornay
called to the Academie de Saumur in 1618. Cameron not
only attacked the blind authoritarianism of the
Catholic church, but more importantly for the present
consideration, he also developed an epistemological
analysis of religious belief that served to foster
theological rationalism. The rational soul according
to common opinion possessed the twin faculties of
intellect and will. It was the function of the
intellect first to discern a matter for consideration
and second to judge of its truth. The function of the
will was to give adherence to the truth. Conservative
Calvinists maintained that in conversion God acted upon
a man's intellect to convince him of the truth of the
gospel and upon his will to bring about adherence to
the gospel. Both operations were necessary, lest a man
be intellectually convinced of the truth of the
Christian doctrine but not moved in his rebellious
heart to embrace it. Cameron, by contrast, maintained
that since the intellect and will are indissolubly
united, two separate, divine operations are
unnecessary; rather in acting upon the intellect, God
acts upon the will. The upshot of this view was that
since the will is posterior to and follows the divinely
influenced intellect, reason,. as that which is
appropriate to the intellect, becomes the avenue to
truth and salvation. Walter Rex explains,

The most important implications of his theology can be stated quite simply: because for Cameron conversion was effected solely through the intellect, and faith was a demonstration involving the faculty of reason, inevitably rational demonstration assumed an importance far greater for him than it did for the conservative theologians who considered that demonstration was not the sole means to conversion, who assumed, in fact, that this demonstration was sometimes incapable of effecting conversion and maintained that the will had to be inclined by the direct action of God.[385]

Cameron's rationalism obviously accentuated the centrality of the role of rational apologetics in effecting conversion, a viewpoint which became widespread under the influence of his disciples at Saumur such as Moise Amyrault and David Blondel. In his De l'élévation de la foy et de l'abaissement de la raison (1640), Amyrault championed the method of examination by reason in matters of religious truth and maintained that in conversion the heart adores because of the force of the demonstration to the intellect. Blondel in his Esclaircissements familiers de la controverse de l'eucharistie (1635) insisted that truths of theology cannot contradict those of philosophy and in effect subordinated even the authority of Scripture to that of reason. These thinkers, while not apologists for Christianity per se (though certainly for Protestantism), helped to create the sort of rationalistic climate that encouraged the rise of modern apologetics among Protestants at the same time that Catholic Pyrrhonism delayed its appearance in the Roman Church.

Theological rationalism of
Descartes and Locke

We noted that the Pyrrhonism which had attracted
both Catholic polemicists and the libertins érudits
elicited several refutations by those who sought to
safeguard knowledge, among them Herbert of Cherbury.
But the most significant figure who attempted to turn
back the force of scepticism and to found a system of
certain knowledge was the French mathematician René
Descartes. Convinced on the basis of a dream
in 1618 that he was destined to provide the
epistemological foundation for a unified view of the
sciences based on mathematics, Descartes sought to
establish deductively a body of certain truth arising
from indubitable first principles. Descartes's
interest in the crise pyrrhonienne appears to have been
awakened in 1628 during a discussion at the home of
Cardinal Bagni in Paris in which Descartes vigorously
opposed the moderate Pyrrhonism of one M. Chandoux, who
proposed to base scientific knowledge of the world on
probabilities. Encouraged by Cardinal Bérulle to
pursue these thoughts, Descartes went into seclusion in
Holland in order to discover by introspection and
meditation those foundational truths invulnerable to
scepticism. Descartes borrowed the "method of doubt"
from the Pyrrhonists themselves in order to pare away
all dubitable beliefs he possessed from those he could
not question. In his Discours de la méthode, which
resulted from this thought-experiment, Descartes lays
down four epistemological rules, the first of which he
describes as follows:

> The first of these was to accept nothing as true
> which I did not clearly recognise to be so: that
> is to say, carefully to avoid precipitation and
> prejudice in judgments, and to accept in them
> nothing more than what was presented to my mind so
> clearly and distinctly that I could have no

occasion to doubt it.[386]

Descartes took this rule very seriously indeed, entertaining levels of doubt never reached by the sceptics. Not only did he adopt the usual pyrrhonical arguments concerning the deceptiveness of sense experience, such that one cannot even be certain that there is an external world at all, but in his Méditations he outstrips all his contemporary pyrrhonists in supposing that some "evil genius," a superhuman being of evil intent, has deceived him into believing such apparently self-evident truths as 2 + 3 = 5 or a square never has more than four sides, although these propositions are false.[387] Given the hypothesis of the evil genius, everything becomes uncertain, for the most indubitable truths may appear such to me only because this diabolical genius has so affected my mind. Descartes probably never really doubted the certainty of these mathematical truths nor even the existence of the external world--these doubts are, as he says, hyperbolical--, but it is only by pushing Pyrrhonism to its absolute limits that it could be successfully overcome. As Popkin remarks, "In doubting to the limits of human capacity, the force of the cogito could emerge as a tidal wave, sweeping away the crise pyrrhonienne and carrying the newly illumined person into the realms of solid unshakeable truth."[388]

By means of the method of doubt, Descartes was able to arrive at a truth that could in no wise be doubted: cogito ergo sum. In the Discourse, Descartes relates that he determined to regard everything that entered his mind as no more true than the illusions of his dreams;

But immediately afterwards I noticed that whilst I

thus wished to think all things false, it was
absolutely essential that the 'I' who thought this
should be somewhat, and remarking that this truth
'I think, therefore I am' was so certain and so
assured that all the most extravagant suppositions
brought forward by the sceptics were incapable of
shaking it, I came to the conclusion that I could
receive it without scruple as the first principle
of the Philosophy for which I was seeking.[389]

Not even the supposition of the evil genius could
overturn this truth, as Descartes explained in the
Meditations:

> . . . I was persuaded that there was nothing in
> all the world, that there was no heaven, no earth,
> that there were no minds, nor any bodies: was I
> then not likewise persuaded that I did not exist?
> Not at all; of a surety I myself did exist since I
> persuaded myself of something [or merely because I
> thought of something]. But there is some deceiver
> or other, very powerful and very cunning, who ever
> employs his ingenuity in deceiving me. Then
> without doubt I exist also if he deceives me, and
> let him deceive me as much as he will, he can
> never cause me to be nothing so long as I think
> that I am something. So that after having
> reflected well and carefully examined all things,
> we must come to the definite conclusion that this
> proposition: I am, I exist, is necessarily true
> each time that I pronounce it, or that I mentally
> conceive it.[390]

Because Descartes's argument from the cogito is a sort
of transcendental argument, not an inferential one, the
evil genius cannot find a foothold for deception.
Descartes does not reason, "Whatever thinks is; I
think, therefore I am"; rather the point appears to be
that one's own existence is the precondition for all
thought whatsoever, such that even doubt of one's
existence presupposes one's existence. Descartes
replied to his critics,

> But when we become aware that we are thinking

beings, this is a primitive act of knowledge
derived from no syllogistic reasoning. He who
says, 'I think, hence I am, or exist,' does not
deduce existence from thought by a syllogism, but,
by a simple act of mental vision, recognizes it as
if it were a thing that is known per se.[391]

My own existence is thus indubitable, for in doubting
it I presuppose it.

From this undeniable truth, Descartes erects his
philosophical system. Having discovered one
indubitable truth, he examines that truth in order to
discover what it is that makes it indubitable. The
only answer would seem to be that the truth is
perceived with such clarity and distinctness that the
mind cannot but assent to it.[392] Hence, things that
are conceived in such a clear and distinct manner are
true. The problem with this criterion, however,
according to Descartes, is that it might be that God
has so constituted me that I perceive falsehoods to be
clear and distinct. Therefore, the existence of a God
who is not a deceiver must be proved. He serves as the
guarantor of my clear and distinct conceptions and
constitutes, as it were, the bridge from the inner
world of the self to the external world. Since the
existence of the external world is in doubt, Descartes
must take as his starting point the idea of God in
one's mind. The argument to which he turns at this
point is not, however, the apriori ontological argument
of Anselm, but a sort of cosmological argument which
moves from one's idea of God as the infinite and
perfect being to the existence of God as the only
sufficient cause of that idea.[393] Since God is the
supremely perfect being, it follows that he cannot be a
deceiver, since deceit is an imperfection.[394] Whence
then arise errors in my knowledge? According to

Descartes, error results when the will, which is wider in range than the understanding, affirms as true things which I do not understand with sufficient clarity and distinctness. "But if I abstain from giving my judgment on anything when I do not perceive it with sufficient clearness and distinctness, it is plain that I act rightly and am not deceived."[395] On this basis, Descartes is able to justify not only mathematical truths, but he is also able to move to the external world and give us a scientific knowledge of sensible things.

Descartes's epistemological rationalism promoted theological rationalism and the rational approach to apologetics. For his method of doubt seemed to imply that the existence of God could be doubted and therefore needed to be demonstrated by rational argumentation. In the dedication to his Meditations, Descartes does seem to suggest an arational knowledge of God's existence is possible, though such knowledge is useless in commending the faith:

> . . . although it is absolutely true that we must believe that there is a God, because we are so taught in the Holy Scriptures, and, on the other hand, that we must believe the Holy Scriptures because they come from God (the reason of this is, that, faith being a gift of God, He who gives the grace to cause us to believe other things can likewise give it to cause us to believe that He exists), we nevertheless could not place this argument before infidels, who might accuse us of reasoning in a circle.[396]

Descartes observes that the doctors of theology themselves affirm that not only is God's existence demonstrable, but that knowledge of God is much clearer than knowledge of creatures. This affirmation Descartes interprets in line with his philosophy:

> . . . all that which can be known of God may be
> made manifest by means which are not derived from
> anywhere but from ourselves, and from the simple
> consideration of the nature of our minds. Hence I
> thought it not beside my purpose to inquire how
> this is so, and how God may be more easily and
> certainly known than the things of the world.[397]

The statement expresses Descartes's procedure in moving
from the idea of God to His existence and thence to a
knowledge of the external world. Indeed, the stated
object of the Meditations is to prove the existence of
God and the mind/body distinction. So even if
Descartes was sincere in his statement that God may be
known simply through the gift of faith, nevertheless
his procedure implied that the existence of God was in
need of rational demonstration, thus promoting
theological rationalism. We have already noted how the
classic French apologists from Malebranche through
Abbadie stood in this Cartesian tradition and how
Cartesian rationalism in Spinoza's mold affected the
course of French Deism during the remainder of the
seventeenth century.

When we turn to the eighteenth century,
undoubtedly the most significant influence for
theological rationalism upon both English and French
Deism was Locke. According to Cragg, "The importance
which he attached to reason and the general character
of his treatment of it were authoritative for the
eighteenth century."[398] His empiricism replaced the
epistemological innatism of Descartes while manifesting
an even more vigorous adherence to the primacy of
reason in matters of religion. Like Descartes, Locke
also held that the existence of God may be demonstrated
by reason: "Though God has given us no innate ideas of
himself; . . . yet having furnished us with those
faculties our minds are endowed with, he hath not left

himself   without   witness;   since   we   have   sense,
perception, and reason, and cannot want a clear proof
of him as long as we carry ourselves about us."[399]
Locke believed that the existence of God was "the most
obvious   truth   that   reason   discovers,"   having   an
evidence "equal to mathematical certainty."[400]   Like
Descartes he also begins with the undeniability of
one's own existence, but he reasons from that existence
to an eternal, powerful, knowing being, not from the
idea of God, as had Descartes.

When one moves beyond these matters of reason and
into the realm of faith, Locke is insistent that any
purported revelation must not only be in harmony with
reason, but must itself be guaranteed by appropriate
rational proofs that it is indeed divine; otherwise one
degenerates into irresponsible enthusiasm:

> Reason is natural revelation, whereby the eternal
> Father of light, and Fountain of all knowledge,
> communicates to mankind that portion of truth
> which he has laid within the reach of their
> natural faculties.   Revelation is natural reason
> enlarged by a new set of discoveries communicated
> by God immediately, which reason vouches the truth
> of by the testimony and proofs it gives that they
> come from God.   So that he that takes away reason
> to make way for revelation, puts out the light of
> both; and does much-what the same as if he would
> persuade a man to put out his eyes, the better to
> receive the remote light of an invisible star by a
> telescope.[401]

So   although   Locke   rejected   the   philosophical
rationalism of Lord Herbert and Descartes in favor of
empiricism, he remained very decidedly a theological
rationalist.   After Locke, in France as well as in
England, the theological rationalism that reigned was
empiricist rather than Cartesian.   The crucial question
was the factual evidence supporting the historicity of

the miraculous events of the gospel. Locke maintained in his Reasonableness of Christianity and Discourse on Miracles that Christ had brought clear teachings and palpable miracles as proof of his divine mission. Stephen remarks,

> Here, then, is the thesis laid down by the typical
> thinker of the age, to be incessantly attacked and
> defended through the next century. . . A
> rationalist to the core, [Locke] does not even
> contemplate as possible an appeal to any authority
> but that of ordinary reason. The truth of
> Christianity was to be proved like the truth of
> any historical or philosophical theory. It was
> simply a question of the evidence, and especially
> of the overwhelming evidence of the Christian
> miracles.[402]

The Deists readily accepted Locke's dictum that reason must judge any purported revelation.[403] We have already noted Toland's attempt to extend Locke's thought so as to eliminate all mysteries in religion. Collins, friend of the elderly Locke, argues in his Discourse on Free-Thinking that free-thinking is a right that cannot be restricted, since only thinking could restrict thinking, and that free-thinking is a right because it is an indispensable means to human purposes. On the basis of the free use of reason, Collins espoused an ardent anti-supernaturalism. Tindal argued eloquently for the ultimacy of reason in religious matters:

> . . . the Use of those Faculties, by which Men are
> distinguish'd from Brutes, is the Only Means they
> have to discern whether there is a God; and
> whether he concerns himself with human Affairs, or
> has given them any Laws; and what those Laws are?
> And as Men have no other Faculties to judge with,
> so their using These after the best Manner they
> can, must answer the End for which God gave them,
> and justify their Conduct: For

If God will judge Mankind as they are
accountable, that is, as they are rational; the
Judgement must hold an exact Proportion to the Use
they make of their Reason. And it wou'd be in
vain to use it, if the due use of it wou'd not
justify them before God; and Men wou'd be in a
miserable Condition, indeed, if whether they us'd
it, or not, they shou'd be alike criminal. And if
God design'd all Mankind shou'd at all Times know,
what he wills them to know, believe, profess, and
practise; and has giv'n them no other means for
this, but the Use of Reason; Reason, human Reason,
must then be that Means; for as God has made us
rational Creatures, and Reason tells us, that 'tis
his Will, that we act up to the Dignity of our
Natures; so 'tis Reason must tell when we do so.
What God requires us to know, believe, profess,
and practise, must be in itself a reasonable
service; but whether what is offer'd to us as
such, be really so, 'tis Reason alone which must
judge; as the Eye is the sole Judge of what is
visible, the Ear of what is audible, so Reason of
what is reasonable.⁴⁰⁴

This is a fine statement of theological rationalism
from a Deist author: the universality of God's demands
upon men implies that the characteristic that makes
them men at all, namely, reason, must be the means to
discerning the truth about God, and if one sincerely
follows the path of reason he will be justified, since
more he could not do. Reason will sanction faith in a
natural religion, but revealed religion cannot pass the
bar of reason. The Christian apologists may declaim
the reasonableness of Christianity all they please, but
they cannot mask its absurdities. Christianity is thus
excluded. Woolston remarks,

There has nothing been a more common Subject of
Declamation among the Clergy than the
Reasonableness of Christianity, which must be
understood of the History of Christ's Life and
Doctrine, or the Application of the Word
Reasonableness to the Christian Religion is
impertinent. But if I proceed, . . . I shall shew
Christianity to be the most unreasonable and

absurd Story, that ever was told. . . . [405]

Hence, the Deist authors only too gladly adopted theological rationalism in order to eradicate Christianity.

For their part, however, the orthodox defenders of the faith were equally faithful to Locke's theological rationalism. A triumphant Leland boasts, "They have appealed to the bar of reason; the advocates for Christianity have followed them to that bar, and have fairly shown that the evidences of revealed religion, are such as approve themselves to impartial reason, and if taken together they are fully sufficient to satisfy an honest and unprejudiced mind."[406] This was indeed the procedure of the orthodox defenders of Christianity. When Bentley attacked Collins's Discourse, his target was not his rationalism, but his anti-supernaturalism. Bentley said that he himself accepted the right of free-thinking and that everyone always had; this was not the issue. The question was whether reason justifies or precludes belief in revealed religion. Here he defended the orthodox cause. Thus, as Lechler points out, Bentley as well as the other opponents of Collins all agreed that Collins's formal principle of free-thinking was perfectly correct, but they rejected the use that he put it to.[407] States Lechler,

> Bentley, as well as Abbot and Clarke agree with Locke and his pupils Toland and Collins concerning the fundamental principle that reason is to be accorded full freedom of thought, even in questions of religion and revelation, that reason and revelation cannot possibly come into contradiction, that on the contrary reason is a natural revelation and revelation is reasonable, that reason is the essential foundation and subjective condition for the recognition of

religion and revelation, and that the knowledge of
the reality of revelation as well as of its form
is dependent upon reason.[408]

The Deist controversy was thus waged very much upon a
common battlefield between opponents employing the same
weapons. Theological rationalism was presupposed by
both sides; as Cragg states, "The supremacy of reason,
was universally accepted. . . . It took complete
possession of the field of theology: argument became
the method, proof became the goal of everyone who
discussed religious topics."[409] The only question at
issue was whether reason would justify or demolish
faith in the Christian gospel.

Overview of the history
of the Deist controversy

Early French development

At this juncture, it would perhaps be useful to
provide a brief overview of the course of the Deist
controversy during the seventeenth and eighteenth
centuries. We have seen that Deists were identified by
that name and their tenets described in terms
applicable to eighteenth century Deists by Viret,
probably in France, as early as 1563. Philippe de
Mornay in his Vérité of 1581 seems to have had similar
opponents in mind, whom he styled as Epicureans, a name
also applied to Deist thinkers by Amyraut in his Traité
of 1631. The first major Deist work was Lord Herbert's
De veritate, penned in 1624 and published in France
largely in response to the nouveaux pyrrhonisme which
he encountered during his diplomatic sojourn at the
French court. In an attempt to thread its way between
orthodoxy's Christological doctrines and Deism's

wholesale abandonment of revealed religion, Socinianism drafted a rationalistic apologetic for supernaturalism based on the miracles and resurrection of Jesus. Drawing upon the works of his predecessors and having received a copy of Lord Herbert's treatise from the author's hand, Grotius expanded his own De veritate in 1627 and so advanced the historical argument for the resurrection as a basis for Christian belief. In his unfinished Apologie, Pascal specifically attacks Deists and espouses evidentialism as well as championing the reasons of the heart. Drawing upon the insights of Hobbes and ibn Ezra, Spinoza's Tractatus of 1670 is the most important Deistic work of the century, attacking miracles philosophically and greatly accelerating biblical criticism, as evident in the ensuing debate between Simon and Le Clerc. Two years after the publication of Spinoza's Tractatus, Filleau de la Chaise in response to the attacks on Mosaic authorship of the Pentateuch inaugurated the methodology of proof "by the facts" in his Discours. So begins a fruitful period in French apologetic literature, crowned by the Traité (1684-9) of Abbadie, a widely influential historical defense of Christianity and the resurrection of Jesus. This period came to an abrupt end in the scepticism and purported fideism of Bayle, whose Dictionnaire of 1696 served as the guiding beacon for the French Deists of the eighteenth century.

Course of the English
Deist controversy

Blount to Sherlock. Strict censorship prevented Deism from coming to full boil in France during the seventeenth century; works of Deist sentiments had to be published in Holland. In England, however, religious toleration and the gradual relaxation of the press laws permitted Deism to erupt in full force. Blount published his Life of Apollonius Tyaneus in 1680, his Religio laici in 1683, and a collection of his miscellaneous works was published posthumously in 1695. Leslie's Short and Easie Method in 1697 took aim specifically at the "execrable Charles Blount"[410] and like the Discours of de la Chaise laid down the method of proof by matters of fact which guided the orthodox disputants of the next century. Even more significant, of course, was the figure of Locke, who espoused empiricism and theological rationalism in his Essay of 1689 and brought these to the defense of revealed religion in the Reasonableness of Christianity in 1695. Deists, such as Toland in Christianity Not Mysterious (1696), appealed to Locke for his rationalism in religious matters, while orthodox thinkers followed Locke in his defense of revealed religion on the basis of miracles. Thus, Clarke in his Boyle lectures of 1705 also defended Christian revelation on the basis of Christ's miracles, while Collins in his Discourse on Free-Thinking (1713) adopts many of Locke's arguments from his letters on toleration to support his Deism. Collins's Discourse whipped up the Deist controversy, drawing down upon himself 20 replies in the same year, the most noteworthy being the meticulous and crushing examination by Bentley, Remarks upon a late Discourse of Free Thinking. Collins's Ground and Reason, which appeared in 1724, was the most significant attack on the proof from prophecy, denying a literal interpretation and fulfillment of Old Testament prophecies. This time Collins's work evoked 35 refutations, the soundest and most esteemed being

Bishop Thomas Sherlock's The Use and Intent of Prophecy in 1725.

Woolston vs. Sherlock on the resurrection. Between 1727 and 1729 Woolston in his Six Discourses ridiculed the proof from miracles, attacking especially the historicity of Jesus's resurrection. Woolston, who eventually went mad, was one of the most vitriolic of the Deists; his works ". . . were written with a coarseness and irreverence so singular, even in the attacks of that age, that it were well if they could be attributed to insanity. They contained the most undisguised abuse which had been uttered against Christianity since the days of the early heathens."[411] Woolston's works were apparently quite popular. According to Voltaire, Woolston sold from his own home between 1727-9 three editions of his Discourses of 20,000 copies each.[412] Among the sixty replies to Woolston particularly influential was Sherlock's Tryal of the Witnesses in 1729, which opened up the debate concerning evidence for the resurrection. This on-going debate was so important that a fuller word should be said here of Woolston's attack and Sherlock's response.

According to Woolston, orthodox defenders of Christianity, distressed with the proof from prophecy, were seeking refuge in miracles. He will therefore exhibit the weakness of this proof by demonstrating three propositions: (1) healing miracles do not prove Messiahship, (2) the literal history of miracles implies absurdities, improbabilities, and incredibilities and should therefore be understood as prophetic or parabolical narratives of what Christ would do, and (3) when Christ appealed to miracles as proofs, he meant the mystical ones which he would do in

the Spirit.[413]   In his fifth discourse, he prepares for
his attack on Jesus's resurrection by lampooning the
resurrections of Jairus's daughter, the widow of Nain's
son, and Lazarus.[414]   In his final discourse, Woolston
charges specifically that the literal story of Jesus's
resurrection consists of absurdities, improbabilities,
and incredibilities.   Under the guise of a letter
received from a rabbi friend, Woolston denounces the
resurrection as the "most notorious and monstrous
imposture that was ever put upon Mankind."[415]   Woolston
argued that the Pharisees and the disciples entered
into a pact to test Jesus's Messiahship by setting a
guard and sealing the tomb and then waiting until the
third day to see if Jesus would rise as he predicted.

> The Condition of the seal'd Covenant was, that if
> Jesus arose from the dead in the Presence of our
> Chief Priests upon their opening the seals of the
> Sepulchre, at the Time appointed; then he was to
> be acknowledg'd to be the Messiah: But if he
> continued in a corrupt and putrified state of
> mortality, then he was to be granted to be an
> Imposter: Very widely and rightly agreed![416]

Had the apostles stood by this agreement, Christianity
would have been nipped in the bud.   But in an act of
perfidy, they stole the body, as proved by the broken
seal, and faked the resurrection, inventing the
resurrection appearances.   Woolston refutes three
objections to this theory: (1) The guard would have
prevented the theft.   Woolston answers that if it is
even possible for the disciples to have evaded the
guard, the objection loses its force.   And in fact,
such evasion was "easy, feasible, and practicable."[417]
The guard might have fallen asleep, or the disciples
could have made them drunk or bribed them.   (2) The
resurrection was later made evident to the priests.   He

never, in fact, appeared to them, responds Woolston, and we have only the word of the imposter disciples to go on. (3) Belief in the resurrection could not arise without the event. Woolston retorts the whole affair was an imposture. It should not be thought remarkable that the disciples became martyrs. For many other criminals and cheats have gone to their death proclaiming their innocence.[418]

In Sherlock's popular reply to Woolston, the Bishop of London imagines a mock trial to determine the question, whether the witnesses of the resurrection of Christ were guilty of giving false evidence.[419] It is interesting that Woolston's attorney is made the prosecutor; the apostles are innocent until proven guilty. In other words, the presupposition is that the biblical accounts ought to be regarded as accurate until some discrepancy can be proved.[420] The burden of proof rests with those who would disprove, not prove, the reliability of the gospels. The counsel for Woolston urges two basic objections against the evidence for Jesus's resurrection: (1) the resurrection itself was a fraud and (2) the testimony for the resurrection was fabricated or unreliable.

With regard to the first objection, Woolston's attorney argues that Jesus contrived to become the Messiah to rule the Jews, but when plans went awry, he predicted his death and resurrection, so that his disciples could carry on his legacy by faking a resurrection through theft of the body.[421] Sherlock counters that there is no evidence that Jesus was involved in any plot. On the contrary, Jesus's acts and words ran against the current Messianic expectations of the Jews; Jesus did not build upon the foundation of the people's idea of the Messiah as a

victorious King.[422]   Because Jesus predicted his
resurrection, he must have been either an enthusiast or
an imposter. But enthusiasm alone will not suffice to
explain the resurrection; either it was a fraud or a
miracle.[423] There is no evidence Jesus was involved in
such a fraud; could the disciples, however, have been
so involved?   Sherlock urges several considerations
against it: (1) since the guards were supposedly
asleep they could not testify as to what actually
happened, (2) it would be impossible to break into the
tomb and steal the body without disturbing the guard,
and (3) it was contrary to the disciples' weak
character to invent and execute such a scheme.[424]
Responding to the objection that the resurrection did
not occur after three days as predicted, Sherlock
explains that the Jews reckoned parts of a day as a
whole day, so that the resurrection did occur on the
third day.[425] He also observes that according to Acts,
neither the Roman nor Jewish councils ever accused the
disciples of being involved in any fraud; Gamaliel even
allows that what they proclaim may be of God.[426] Thus,
the evidence runs counter to the suggestion that the
resurrection was a fraud perpetrated by either Jesus or
his disciples.

As to the second objection, Woolston's counsel
first argues that because the resurrection violates the
course of Nature, no human testimony could possibly
establish it, since it has the whole witness of Nature
against it.[427] We shall examine Sherlock's reply when
we discuss the debate over miracles.

Woolston's attorney also argues that the
resurrection accounts often give the impression that
Christ's appearances were not bodily, but visionary.
Sherlock replies that (1) it is a misinterpretation of

the passages to read them as implying Christ had no
physical body; (2) a physical body can be made to
disappear by natural means (for example, intercepting
all light rays reflected therefrom); and (3) in any
case, the properties ascribed to Christ's resurrection
body may simply be miraculous, but the body is no less
physical for that.[428]

When the opposition further queries why Jesus did
not appear to more persons and especially to the Jews,
Sherlock counters:[429] (1) During his earthly ministry
Jesus, after being rejected by the Jews, pronounced
woes upon them and declared that they would see him no
more until they were better disposed to receive him (Mt
23.39). (2) The objection allows of no logical
stopping point; if Jesus should appear also to the
Jews, why not to all nations in every age? The
testimony we have is sufficient evidence of the
resurrection; it is unreasonable to sit down and
imagine what sort of evidence would please us and then
make the want of this an objection to facts which are
well-established. (3) The resurrection appearances
were designed chiefly to give a new commission to the
apostles to bear testimony to the world, but other
persons saw Jesus as well (Lk 24.33; Acts 1.21-2; I Cor
15.6).

The counsel for Woolston ridicules the evidence
based on the testimony of silly women, to which
Sherlock rejoins: (1) they had eyes and ears, too, and
moreover were not gullible, but actually disbelieving;
(2) they were never employed as witnesses to the
resurrection; and (3) the testimony of the men is not
any worse for having the testimony of the women as
well.[430]

Sherlock concludes by observing that the apostles

died to affirm the truth of what they proclaimed: this
is   certain   testimony   to   their   sincerity.[431]
Furthermore, the apostles themselves performed miracles
to   confirm   their   testimony.[432]   These   miracles
establish the authority of the apostles to bear witness
to the resurrection, for a miracle is directly a proof
of the authority of the person performing it and thus
indirectly of what he says.[433] This evidence of the
resurrection, which was good in the first century, is
equally cogent today.[434]   The jury, convinced of this,
after a brief deliberation returns a verdict of "not
guilty."   The issue was not so easily resolved in
reality, however, and a long, vitriolic debate over the
historicity of the resurrection followed this exchange
betwen Woolston and Sherlock.

      Tindal to Hume. The high point of English Deism
came in 1730 with Tindal's publication of Christianity
as Old as the Creation, to which 150 answers were
published, the most renowned of these being Bishop
Butler's The Analogy of Religion, Natural and Revealed,
to the Constitution and Course of Nature (1736).   The
following year saw the publication of Morgan's The
Moral Philosopher, which ascribed the corruption of
primitive, natural religion to the influence of the
clergy. In 1739 Thomas Chubb in his The True Gospel of
Jesus Christ Asserted portrayed the actual Jesus as a
Deist; other of Chubb's many pamphlets criticizing
revealed religion were collected and published in 1748
as The Posthumous Works of Thomas Chubb. Dodwell broke
with theological rationalism in 1742 with Christianity
Not Founded on Argument, which reinforced the
scepticism concerning natural reason generated by
Butler's Analogy.   Peter Annet joined the debate
concerning the resurrection of Jesus in 1744 with The

Resurrection of Jesus Considered and followed it up
with several sequels as well as an attack on the
character of the apostle Paul in The History and
Character of St. Paul (1747). Hume's epochal essay "Of
Miracles" in which he proffered an in principle
argument against the identification of any miracle in
history appeared in 1748. Although his posthumously
published Dialogues Concerning Natural Religion (1779)
reveal Hume to have been more agnostic than a Deist,
nevertheless his Enquiries, of which the essay is a
part, and his Natural History of Religion (1757) are
consistent with a Deist viewpoint. Even in these
works, however, Hume undercuts natural as well as
revealed religion in his atomistic analysis of sense
impressions and attendant denial of any perception of
necessary connection in cause-effect relationships,
thus undermining any inductive argument for theism, and
in his affirmation that monotheism is a late
development of primitive polytheism. Therefore,
although Hume in his critical side allies himself with
Deism in its critique of revealed religion, his thought
also tended to the dissolution of Deism, even prior to
the publication of the Dialogues, by strengthening the
scepticism concerning the self-sufficiency of reason
and the possibility of a natural religion. Hume's
essay on miracles was actually eclipsed by Middleton's
Free Inquiry published in 1749, in which the author
criticized ecclesiastical miracles by the criteria of
testimony and credibility. The principal Deist works
came to a close with the posthumous publication of Lord
Bolingbroke's Works in 1754. Deist works continued to
appear sporadically during the rest of the century,[435]
but the fire of the controversy had gone out.

    Gibbon and Paley. But if Deism as a school of

thought had ceased to exist in England, nevertheless
Deist attitudes persisted. These found eloquent
expression in Gibbon's naturalistic and often satirical
explanation of the rapid growth of the Christian church
in volume one of his monumental Decline and Fall of the
Roman Empire (1776). Though espousing no formal Deist
creed, Gibbon had been permanently affected by French
sceptical thought, having lived in Paris where he had
intercourse with thinkers like D'Alembert, Diderot,
Raynal, Helvetius, and D'Holbach. In his treatment of
early Christianity exclusively in terms of natural
causes, Gibbon helped to generate scepticism concerning
the supernatural origin of the Christian faith, thus
undermining its claim to be a divinely revealed
religion. Though the sphere of Gibbon's remarks is
properly the post-apostolic period, his account of the
advance of early Christianity could not but cast doubts
on its miraculous origin. His reading of Middleton had
convinced him that the ecclesiastical miracles and the
miracles of the New Testament stand or fall together.
Thus, when he writes, "The scanty and suspicious
materials of ecclesiastical history seldom enable us to
dispel the dark cloud that hangs over the first age of
the church,"[436] this may be taken by implication to
refer to the gospel history as well. Technically,
nothing that Gibbon writes attacks directly the
credibility of the gospel accounts; it is all by
implication. Oliphant Smeaton in his notes on Gibbon's
work wrote,

> The main question, the divine origin of the
> religion, is dexterously eluded or speciously
> conceded, his plan enabling him to commence his
> account in most parts below apostolic times, and
> it is only by the strength of the dark colouring
> with which he has brought out the failings and the

follies of succeeding ages, that a shadow of doubt
or suspicion is thrown back on the primitive
period of Christianity. Divest this whole passage
of the latent sarcasm betrayed by the subsequent
tone of the whole disquisition, and it might
commence a Christian history₄,₃₇written in the most
Christian spirit of candour.

Thus, Gibbon readily grants that the primary cause of
the victory of the Christian religion over the
established religions was "the convincing evidence of
the doctrine itself" and "the ruling providence of its
great Author."438   But, he insists, what were the
secondary causes of the rapid growth of the church?
Five factors effectually favored and assisted in the
church's rise: (1) the inflexible and intolerant zeal
of the Christians, derived from the Jewish religion but
purified of the anti-Gentile spirit; (2) the doctrine
of a future life; (3) the miraculous powers ascribed to
the early church; (4) the pure and austere morals of
Christians; and (5) the union and discipline of the
Christian republic, which gradually formed an
independent and increasing state in the heart of the
Roman Empire.439

     With regard to (1) Gibbon points out that
primitive Christianity was thoroughly Jewish in
character and possessed the same zeal that wrought in
Jews hatred of Gentiles and foreign religions. After
the destruction of Jerusalem these Jewish Christians
were squeezed out of the church as heretics (Ebionites)
as they had been forced out of the synagogue as
apostates. But their zeal remained in Christianity's
aversion to all forms of paganism and idolatry as
demonic.

     As for (2) the Greeks possessed the doctrine of
the immortality of the soul, but this belief was
weakened because (a) their mythology had no proofs for

the doctrine, (b) the portraits of the nether world had been abandoned as the fancy of poets and painters, and (c) the belief in a future state was not a fundamental article of faith. Christianity on the other hand not only promised a heavenly state, but also warned of the imminent end of the world, accompanied by the fiery judgement of God.

Concerning (3), Gibbon relates the glossalalia, exorcism, and miraculous healings reported in the early church. Noting that Middleton in "a very free and ingenious inquiry" has attacked the miracles of the church, Gibbon observes that since there is an unbroken chain of miracles stretching from the earliest fathers to the latest popes, any proponent of the cessation of miracles will be at a loss to specify when the miraculous powers of the apostles ceased, for at any point he will have to contradict the historical testimony of contemporaries of that period who affirm the occurrence of such miracles.[440] The implication is that if the testimony of men like Eusebius and Augustine concerning miracles of their day can--indeed, must--be set aside, then one may also disregard the testimony of the evangelists for the gospel miracles. According to Gibbon, it was the credulity of the early church that ensured their acceptance of the gospel miracles: "The real or imaginary prodigies, of which they so frequently conceived themselves to be the objects, the instruments, or the spectators, very happily disposed them to adopt with the same ease, but with far greater justice, the authentic wonders of the evangelic history. . . ."[441]

In (4) Gibbon attributes the Christians' austere morality to their repentance for past sins and their desire to preserve the reputation of the Christian

society. His satirical wit is at its sharpest here as
he pokes fun at the sexual mores of the Church fathers
and the extravagant attempts to preserve chastity in
the face of temptation. In (5) Gibbon examines the
emergence of the institutional church. Its success was
due to its acquisition of the two most efficacious
instruments of government: rewards and punishments, to
be meted out by the church.

Given these five factors along with the decline in
zeal for paganism, the success of Christianity was all
but inevitable; in fact almost any superstition that
had come along would have displaced the decayed
paganism of that era.[442] As if to cut short those who
would defend Christianity against the implied charge of
superstition by pointing to the historical testimony of
the evangelists, Gibbon notes that the gospels were
written at a considerable geographical and temporal
distance from the events concerned, being composed in
Alexandria, Antioch, Rome, and Ephesus during the
reigns of Nero and Domitian.[443] Besides that, probably
no more than one-twentieth of the Empire became
Christians, and those that did belonged generally to
the ignorant masses. The sages of Greece and Rome
generally turned a blind eye toward the manifold
wonders which purportedly accompanied Christ's ministry
and death. The reader is left to draw his own
conclusion.

In his next chapter, Gibbon treats of the early
martyrs of the church.[444] He wants to explode the idea
that the church was profusely watered by the blood of
the martyrs, and he seeks to establish: (1) that a
considerable time elapsed before the Christians became
an object of interest to Roman authorities; (2) that
the authorities were cautious in the conviction of

accused Christians; (3) that these authorities were
moderate in their use of punishments of the convicted;
and (4) that the church enjoyed many intervals of
peace. We need not examine each point in detail;
however, Gibbon's conclusion is of interest. He
observes that it is a melancholy fact that Christians
have suffered more at their own hands than at the hands
of infidels, for example, in the Catholic persecutions
of the Reformers. According to the learned Grotius, in
Holland alone under Charles V, some 100,000 persons
were executed, a figure far in excess of all those who
died in three centuries of Roman rule. Then comes the
tour de force: if we do not believe the eminent
Grotius, suspecting him of exaggeration, then why
should we believe the ecclesiastical writers of
antiquity who wrote with equal incentive for
exaggeration and whose reports we have no means of
checking? The same point could be urged by implication
against the accounts of the miraculous origin of
Christianity by the gospel writers.

        According to Stephen, Gibbon struck not merely a
heavy blow against Christianity, but he struck by far
the heaviest blow which it had yet received from a
single hand.[445] Gibbon did not explain the origin of
Christianity, but he had reduced it to the realm of the
explicable. His implication was that the gospel
accounts of the miraculous origin of Christianity are
as unreliable as the solemnly attested stories of
ecclesiastical miracles, and their acceptance may be
written off to the credulity of antiquity. Gibbon did
not attempt to prove this thesis, but from the greatest
English historian of the eighteenth century, an
authority of vast erudition and eloquence, mere
implication was enough.

The immediate response to Gibbon was faltering, and it was not until 1794 that a sophisticated defence of the miraculous origin of Christianity was forthcoming. In that year William Paley's two volume <u>A View of the Evidences of Christianity</u> appeared, a work which became so popular that it remained compulsory reading for any applicant to Cambridge University up until the twentieth century. Drawing, like Gibbon himself, upon the work of Nathaniel Lardner, Paley's work is primarily a studious investigation of the historical evidence for Christianity from miracles, plus a consideration of auxiliary evidences and a refutation of important objections. Prior to his historical inquiry, he engages in a critical discussion of Hume's objections to miracles, arguing that neither the in principle argument nor the in fact arguments can preclude a historical investigation of the miraculous origin of Christianity. He then attempts to establish two propositions: (1) that the original witnesses of Christian miracles passed their lives in labor and suffering in attestation to the truth of the accounts they proclaimed and for the same reason submitted to new rules of conduct, and (2) that a parallel case does not exist in history. In support of the first proposition Paley will demonstrate: (a) that Jesus and the apostles did what the proposition states and (b) that they did it in attestation to the miraculous account found in the gospels. Since they were neither enthusiasts nor charlatans, the miraculous account which they proclaimed must therefore be true. This circumstance is shown in the second proposition to be unique in all of history. The auxiliary evidences and refutation of objections comprise the second volume. Paley's argument for the miraculous origin of

Christianity constitutes the high water mark of the
English response to the Deist challenge and was the
last great treatment of Christian evidences during this
period.

The French Deist controversy

    Influence of English Deism. Meanwhile, in France
between   about   1708   to   1734   English   thought
predominated. As Lechler puts it, English Deism owed
its origin to French free-thought, and now England was
paying back its debt to France--with interest.[446] The
works of the English Deists from Blount on began to
appear in French editions. Desmaizeaux, Rousset, and
Garrigue translated works of Collins and Wollaston;
Diderot translated Shaftesbury; Toland, Woolston,
Tindal, Hume, and others also became available in
French. At the same time, the writings of the
opponents of English Deism were also translated. De
Marmande, Mazel, and Lémoine translated the works of
Sherlock on the immortality of the soul, the evidence
for the resurrection, and the proof from prophecy
respectively. Ricotier made the works of Clarke
accessible to French thinkers, among whom, as we have
seen, they exercised considerable sway. Ditton's work
on the resurrection of Christ was translated into
French by de la Chapelle as La vérité de la religion
chrétienne demontrée par la résurrection de Jésus
Christ. Thus, the whole English Deist controversy was
dropped back into the lap of French thinkers.
According to Farrar, "In no stage of French history has
English literature possessed so powerful an
influence."[447] Cardinal Fleury lamented the literary
influence of the English Deists in France during the
first part of the eighteenth century:

> Long before this time, people in England, who
> brought unbelief into a system, had published
> works in which the appearance of uncertainty and
> doubt concerning the truths of Christianity was
> quite deliberately spread abroad. -- Appeal was
> made to the rights of reason and common sense,
> etc. -- During the time of the Regency that
> multitude of scandalous books came over the sea,
> and France became inundated with them; or rather
> all of those among us who laid claim to power of
> the mind or a comprehensive understanding were
> poisoned, for these books were swallowed by them.
> Soon thereafter, since the French are irrationally
> prejudiced against all establishment, due to the
> pride of an inflexible spirit which disdains any
> submission, a great number of the same were led
> astray by the allure of godlessness, and almost
> all fine minds, all who through auspicious talents
> have brought our contemporaries close to the
> Ancients with regard to cultivation and good
> taste, studied the books of the English, who
> proclaimed Deism. From this time on, the
> so-called philosophers disputed, now under this,
> now under that pretext, [448] and sometimes point-blank,
> divine and human laws.

Add to this influx of polemical literature the personal
contact of many French thinkers with England, and the
influence of the English debate was multiplied. [449]
Diderot wrote to Catherine II in 1775, "It is obvious
to all who have eyes in their head, that if it had not
been for the English, reason and philosophy would still
be in the most pitiable and rudimentary condition in
France." [450]

In addition to these specific influences, there
was, as Orr points out, almost a sort of infatuation in
France with nearly everything English. [451] Oppressed by
the lack of freedom of thought and expression and
dominated by the authoritarian institutions of the
ancien régime, the French admired the relatively great
civil and religious liberty enjoyed by the English.
Voltaire's enthusiasm for England's religious,
economic, political, philosophical, and cultural

achievements, popularized in his Lettres philosophiques
(1733; = Letters Concerning the English Nation) after
his return from England, helped to undermine the
institutions of the ancien régime and to create a
climate favorable to the growth of French Deism.

Rousseau and Voltaire. Undoubtedly the central
lights of eighteenth century French Deism were Rousseau
and Voltaire. Both thinkers espoused a constructive
and a critical Deism. Rousseau especially seems to
have been a man of sincere religious sentiments, truly
moved by the perplexities of reconciling faith with
reason and conscience, a refined esprit vastly
different from the coarse Woolston or Annet.[452] Such
sentiments already find expression in Julie's
profession of faith in La Nouvelle Héloïse (1761).[453]
But the fullest treatment of Rousseau's religious
beliefs is found in the "Profession de foi du Vicaire
Savoyard" in Emile (1762). A convert to Catholicism
from the Genevan Protestantism of his childhood,
Rousseau had begun to lose faith through his personal
contact with the Parisian philosophes. He was now
guilt-ridden by the memory of five illegitimate
children he had sired while in Paris, all of whom were
abandoned to a foundlings' home. In the midst of doubt
and anxieties, compounded by physical suffering,
Rousseau felt he had to reach a decision concerning
matters of faith lest he should die in uncertainty of
the most vital human questions. Hence, in the
'Profession de foi' he formulates both a positive creed
of natural religion and presses a critique of revealed
religion.

His positive statement of natural religion is
directed mainly against the philosophes (Helvetius's
defense of materialism De l'Esprit had just appeared in

1758). While it is true that the church is too
dogmatic in its pronouncements, the philosophes, in
Rousseau's opinion, are equally dogmatic in their
pretended scepticism.[454] The diversity of opinion
concerning the nature of ultimate reality stems from
the insufficiency of the human mind and pride. If
truth were found, the philosophes would be too vain to
be interested and too proud to admit someone else had
found it. Therefore, the source of religious truth
must be found in "la lumière intérieure."[455] This
inner light, of which we shall say more in the sequel,
appears to be an intuitive perception of truth
springing from a blend of conscience and common sense.
It does not preclude argument but seems to supplement
and clinch it. Thus, Rousseau presents an argument for
God and against materialism based on motion. Arguing
that movement is not essential to matter, Rousseau
states that we observe two kinds of motion: voluntary,
or spontaneous, and communicated. I know voluntary
motion exists because I sense it every time I will to
move my arm, and my arm moves. Matter in itself has no
spontaneity of motion. This not only implies that my
spontaneous motion issues from an immaterial agent, but
also that the motion in the world must have a
transecendent cause, since positing an infinite regress
of communicated causes explains nothing. "I therefore
believe that a will moves the universe and animates
nature. This is my first dogma, or my first article of
faith."[456] Rousseau's second article of faith is that
the laws in the universe evince an intelligence.
Appealing to the analogy of the watch and the
watchmaker, Rousseau exclaims, "Let us compare the
particular ends, the means, the ordered relations of
every sort, then let us listen to the inner feeling;

what sane mind could resist its testimony?   To whose
unprejudiced eyes does not the sensible order of the
universe announce a supreme intelligence?"[457]   The
materialists' hypothesis of chance can explain neither
the order we see nor thought and intelligence.
Rousseau calls this intelligent, powerful, volitional
being who moves the universe God and gives him the
attribute of goodness.   But nothing more can be known
about him.   Whether the world is eternal or created is
a matter of complete indifference to Rousseau, and it
is evident that for him God need not be conceived as
the creator or sustainer of the universe.   Rousseau's
third article of natural religion is that man is free
in his actions and is animated by an immaterial
substance.   After all, a machine does not think; the
materialists who reduce mind to matter are completely
deaf to the voix intérieure.   Having established these
three articles of faith, it only remains for Rousseau
to explain the ethical duties of man on earth by which
he might merit immortality and happiness.   These, he
believes, are inscribed on the heart of every man, and
we have only to follow conscience to do the right.
"Too often reason deceives us . . . ; but conscience
never deceives; it is the true guide of man. . . . "[458]
Conscience is a divine instinct, an immortal and
heavenly voice, an infallible judge which renders man
like unto God.   Related to this exaltation of
conscience would appear to be Rousseau's firm
conviction that if one is honest and sincere in one's
beliefs concerning God, then he cannot be condemned for
errors of all too fallible reason.   If I err, says the
Vicar, it is out of good faith, and therefore it cannot
be condemned as a crime.[459]   Though Rousseau thus
leaves aside the central doctrines of revealed

Christianity, he affirms that he is a true believer. I
am a Christian, he proclaims, according to the doctrine
of the Gospel.[460] In essence that doctrine is that one
ought to love God and one's neighbor as himself.
Rousseau thus substitutes for salvation by faith an
immortality earned by the ethical life. The
preparation for death is a good life. Julie professes;
"je n'en connais point d'autre."[461]

    Rousseau's critique of revealed religion is based
squarely on the "authority of reason"[462] and, apart
from its socio-political aspects, appears to hinge on
two elements: the lack of immediacy in revealed
religion and the impossibility of miracles. The first
difficulty arises from the particularity of revealed
religion. Since its historical revelation is
restricted in time and place, I can know it only
through the mediation of others, which not only
excludes many from its benefits but also deprives me of
an immediate testimony from God, thus leaving me in
uncertainty:

> God has spoken! This is certainly a great word.
> And to whom has he spoken? He has spoken to men.
> Why then do I not hear anything? He has charged
> other men to deliver his word to you. . . . I
> would rather have heard God himself; it would not
> have cost him anything more, and I would have been
> sheltered from seduction. He guarantees it to you
> in manifesting the mission of his messengers. How
> so? By prodigies. And where are these prodigies?
> In the books. And who made the books? Men. And
> who saw these prodigies? The men who attest to
> them. What! always human witnesses! always men
> who report to me what other men have reported![463]
> Nothing but men between God and me!

According to Rousseau the historical investigation
necessary to determine the reliability of the gospel
accounts would be so mammoth an undertaking requiring

such erudition that it becomes practically impossible
for men to assess reasonably the truth claim of
revealed religion.

In addition to this, the miracles which are
supposed to verify revealed religion are themselves
simply unbelievable. Rather than an evidence for
faith, they have actually become an obstacle. It is
the unalterable course of nature that proves God, not
the exceptions. I believe too much in God, declares
Rousseau, than to believe in so many miracles so little
worthy of him.[464] Rousseau also presses the problem of
false miracles: does one prove the doctrine by the
miracle or the miracle by the doctrine? In attempting
to do both, the evidentialist defender of Christianity
involves himself in a vicious circle.[465] In Rousseau's
Lettres écrites de la montagne, he extended his case
against miraculous evidences. A miracle, he states, is
"an immediate act of divine power, a sensible change in
the order of nature, a real and visible exception to
its laws."[466] That being so, two questions present
themselves: (1) Dieu peut-il faire des miracles?--
that is to say, could God depart from the laws he has
established?--and (2) Dieu veut-il faire des
miracles?-- that is to say, is there any reason for God
to perform miracles? In answer to (1) Rousseau quickly
responds that it would be absurd and impious to assert
that God cannot perform miracles, a fact which nobody
denies. But Rousseau returns a negative answer to (2)
on the basis that miracles would have no evidential
value. Rousseau's Enlightenment scepticism comes to
the fore at this point. Miracles are simply
unbelievable; Rousseau would not believe in a miracle
even if the witnesses numbered a thousand.[467] He also
presses Spinoza's objection that identification of a

miracle would require knowledge of all the laws of
nature, for the alleged miracle could be merely a magic
trick or a scientific marvel. With regard to the
gospel miracles, Rousseau contends that Jesus knew more
of the powers of nature than the people of his day, who
later exaggerated his acts. Hence, there are some
things in the gospels which cannot be taken literally
without abandoning good sense. And yet, admits the
Vicar of Savoy, the gospels are too sublime to be cast
aside without regard: "I confess to you as well that
the majesty of the Scriptures astounds me, that the
holiness of the Gospel speaks to my heart."[468] The
gospels could not have been fabricated by conspiracy;
they also go beyond anything the Jews could have
produced.

> . . . the gospel has characteristics of truth so
> great, so striking, so perfectly inimitable that
> its inventor would be more astounding than the
> hero. With all that, this same Gospel is full of
> unbelievable+ things, things which revolt reason
> and of which it is impossible for any sensible man
> to conceive or admit.
> _____
> + inconceivable[469]

What to do? We must neither accept nor reject the
gospel miracles. Rousseau insists that nowhere does he
take a stand against miracles; he just refuses to
affirm them.[470] He asserts that miracles are
uncertain, unnecessary, prove nothing, and that he
never denied them.[471] Left in this "scépticisme
involontaire," one must simply submit to the grand Etre
who alone knows the truth.[472] Thus, Rousseau's
critique of revealed religion returns him full circle
to his constructive natural religion of Deism.

Voltaire, the other leading French Deist, also had

both a constructive and critical side to his Deism.[473]
Though generally acknowledged today to be a shallow and
unoriginal thinker, Voltaire's literary abilities,
which he brought to the attack upon Christianity, were
influential and deadly weapons unmatched by any
opponent of his day. James Westfall Thompson remarks,

> For sixty years this sparkling little Frenchman
> bestrode Europe like a Colossus, lashing fools
> with his sarcasm, pouring acid on bigots, fighting
> obscurantism with unmatched irony. His literary
> output was prodigious; his correspondence alone
> fills eighteen volumes. Poet and philosopher,
> essayist and dramatist, novelist and historian,
> Voltaire, though frequently superficial, was
> incapable of writing a dull page. He was read,
> imitated, flattered, hated, and talked[474] about by
> intellectuals on two continents. . . .

Like Rousseau, Voltaire also opposed the atheism
of the philosophes, arguing for the existence of God on
the basis of cosmological and teleological proofs.[475]
He maintains that no person has ever found or will find
a demonstrative proof of God's non-existence. On the
other hand, it would be the most enormous absurdity and
most revolting folly that ever entered the human mind
to deny the evident adaptation of means to ends in the
universe, for example, in the eye or the ear. Against
the materialists, Voltaire urges that intelligence can
only come from intelligence, not from inert matter.
There must exist therefore a supreme artificer of the
world. But whether he is infinite, omnipresent, and so
forth, cannot be determined. Human speculations on
this score he compares to a mole and an ant arguing
whether a garden shed was constructed by a mighty mole
or an ant of great genius. Nor is Voltaire's God any
more than Rousseau's the creator of the universe: "My
reason alone proves to me a being who has arranged the

matter of this world; but my reason is unable to prove
to me that he made this matter-that he brought it out
of nothing."[476]   Voltaire was deeply troubled by the
problem of evil, as his poem on the Lisbon earthquake
and Candide make evident, but he refused to surrender
his theism despite the fact that he could not explain
the presence of evil in the world to his satisfaction.
He insisted that when it has been proved that a great
edifice has been built by an architect, then we ought
to believe in that architect even if his edifice be
stained with blood and polluted by our crimes. Thus,
Voltaire advocated the establishment of a cult of
worship to the grand Etre complete with a priesthood.
Between atheism and superstition (read, the church), he
held, there exists a mean which is God and wise laws.
Anything else leads to crimes against humanity.

        We have already mentioned Voltaire's virulent
attack upon the Christian religion. He argued that by
dying Christ made more disciples than had he lived and
that seventy men convinced of his innocence could
easily win over others as well.[477]   He attributes the
doctrines of Christianity to the encrustations with
which the church overlaid the simple teachings of
Jesus, who, he said, never preached a single dogma of
Christianity.[478] Voltaire's scepticism toward miracles
has already been described. He presented this dilemma
to Christian thinkers: if a miracle is impossible for
nature, it is for God as well, since nature is the
eternal order of things; if a miracle is an effect with
an unknown cause, then everything becomes a miracle.
The arguments are a reformulation of Spinoza. Voltaire
also laid down nearly impossible conditions for the
historical proof of a miracle, for example, that it had
been prophesied and its fulfillment verified under oath

by the heads of the nation and that it be as public as
a fore-announced eclipse. Even if a miracle could be
identified, he continues, it would prove nothing, since
false miracles can be performed by deceivers, who may
even preach good morality, the better to deceive. (It
is interesting that Voltaire quotes at length from
Woolston, of whom he speaks quite highly; we have
mentioned Middleton's influence as well.)

The Deism of which Rousseau and Voltaire were
leading lights became ubiquitous in France during the
last half of the eighteenth century right up through
the French Revolution (1789). Robertson points out
that prior to the Revolution the intelligensia of
France were either Deist, pantheist, or atheist; for
example, the writers Diderot, d'Holbach, D'Alembert,
Helvetius, and Condorcet being a rung below Voltaire;
below them Volney and Dupuis; the men of science
Laplace, Lagrange, Lalande, Délambre; to these may be
added Montesquieu, Buffon, Chamfort, Vauvenargues, La
Mettrie, Cabanis, Condillac, Destutt de Tracy, Raynal,
André Chenier, Turgot, Mirabeau, Danton, Desmoulins,
and Robespierre.[479] Against this tide stood the lonely
Bergier. Robertson concludes, "Thus the cause of
Christianity stood almost denuded of intellectually
eminent adherents in the France of 1789."[480]

Orthodox response. The challenge of a
reinvigorated Deism in France produced the same flood
of apologetic literature as it had in England, as
Monod's table illustrates.[481] (See Figure 1) The merit
of the French orthodox response is a moot question.
Typically it is said that Deism triumphed in France
while it failed in England because it did not meet in
France the same rigor of intellectual apologetic that
it had in England. Robertson disputes this, however,

maintaining that the French response was every bit as
good as the English and that both were mediocre.[482]
Monod agrees with the general mediocrity of the French
response and attributes the rise in violent religious
persecution after the mid-point of the century to the
lack of orthodox success with the pen.[483] By the time
of Rousseau, he states, the apologists had had so
little effect that it is difficult to find a notable
Frenchman of that age who was at the same time a man of
ésprit and a Christian.[484]   And it would get worse.
The Christians grew progressively weaker right up until
the Revolution crashed in upon them.

But while this general picture may be accurate,
there were nevertheless exceptionable instances. Abbé
Claude Francois Houteville's La religion chrétienne
prouvée par les faits, issued in an expanded form in
1740, is the best empirical defense of Christianity by
the facts since Abbadie. Houteville's defense of the
resurrection of Jesus compares quite favorably with
that of Sherlock. But the best apologetic treatise of
the century, which stands on a par with any English
work is Jean Alphonse Turrettin and Jacob Vernet's
multi-volume   Traité de la vérité de la religion
chrétienne (1730-88). Turrettin, an esteemed professor
of theology at Geneva, wrote the first volume in Latin;
Vernet, part of the Protestant Refuge and from 1756
also professor of theology at Geneva, translated
Turrettin's volume and added nine of his own. The
resultant work is a sophisticated and informed response
to French Deism based upon internal and external
evidences.

The first are drawn from the very beauty of the
religion,   from its accord with right reason and
with conscience, from the rapport it has with our

condition and our needs, from its utility and the
comfort it furnishes us.--The second type of proof
is drawn from the external marks with which a
religion is clothed, such as miracles, prophecies,
testimony which is not suspect, the success it has
had, and the effects it has produced.[485]

Turrettin and Vernet, writes Monod, were moderate
theologians of broad mind whom travel and commerce with
great minds had lifted above the narrowness of school
or church, and their scholarship and piety equipped
them well for the defense of the faith during their
century.[486]   Finally, one might mention the various
works of Sylvestre Bergier, a Catholic thinker of
comparable standing with English divines, who almost
single-handedly faced the ubiquitous Deism of the
latter eighteenth century. His response to Rousseau,
Le Déisme réfuté par lui-même (1765) was a great
success. In 1780 he published his massive Traité
historique et dogmatique de la vraie religion. He also
attempted to refute d'Holbach in Christianisme devoilé
(1767) and the Système de la Natur in Examen du
matérialisme (1771). But by this time it was far too
late to turn back the wave of anti-Christian sentiment
sweeping France.

The French orthodox response was thus not without
its lights. But even these dim in comparison to the
literary, if not intellectual, abilities of men like
Voltaire and Rousseau; no orthodox pen could match
their wit and expression.

Even more important, however, in the differing
outcomes of the English and French Deist controversies
was the different intellectual-cultural milieu in which
they took place. Farrar writes,

What was the cause why English deists wrote and
taught their creed in vain, were despised while

living and consigned to oblivion when dead,
refrained almost entirely from political
intermeddling, and left the church in England
unhurt by the struggle; while on the other hand
deism in France became omnipotent, absorbed the
intellect of the country, swept away the church,
and remodelled the state? The answer to this
question must be sought in the antecedent history.
It is a phenomenon political rather than
intellectual. It depended upon the soil in which
the seed was sown, not on the inherent qualities
of the seed itself.[487]

In England religious toleration enabled the Deist
controversy to dissipate in the open air of rational
debate, whereas in France the attempt of the
authoritarian church-state structure to repress dissent
only served to make the inevitable explosion more
devastating. Christianity and its institutions
appeared to be backward-looking structures restraining
the forward-looking mood of free inquiry and progress.
"In the state and church all was authority; all was of
the past: in the world of literature and philosophy
all was criticism, activity, hope in the future."[488]
England had the freedoms the French desired; it had
survived a civil war and established constitutional
liberty and religious toleration. Thus, the Deist
victory, given the movement's commitment to the
authority of reason and conscience over against that of
the church and the state seemed ensured. By contrast
to the decay of faith in France, the latter half of the
eighteenth century in England saw the Great Awakening
under Wesley and Whitefield. According to Cragg, these
revivals were probably more significant in the demise
of Deism in terms of immediate effect than even the
scepticism of David Hume.[489] While rationalism reigned
in France, the evangelical revivals, together with the
attacks on rationalism by Law, Berkeley, and Butler,

and Hume's scepticism, served to undermine the
exclusive authority of reason in religion on which
Deism was built.[490]

Related to this is the fact that in the French
Eclaircissement the sentiment against miracles seems to
have been much more deeply ingrained. English divines
might adopt theological rationalism and then defend the
miraculous origin of Christianity as the decisive
refutation of Deism, and such an approach seemed to be
acceptable to the readers. In France, however, this
"short and easy method" fell on deaf ears. The
enlightened ésprit simply no longer believed in
miracles; therefore, all the evidence in the world
could not convince him--it was strictly irrelevant.
Diderot remarked, "I have occasionally read Abbadie,
Huet, and the rest. I am sufficiently well-acquainted
with evidences of my religion, and I admit that they
are important; but were they a hundred times more so,
Christianity would not be demonstrated to me to be
true."[491] Alluding to the resurrection, he declared,

> I should have no difficulty in believing a single
> honest man who should tell me that His Majesty had
> just won a complete victory over the allies; but
> if all Paris were to assure me that a dead man had
> come to life at Passy, I should not believe a word
> of it. That a historian should impose on us, or
> that a whole nation should be deluded--there is no
> miracle in that![492]

It was impossible in principle to establish a miracle
according to the method par les faits, for no amount of
evidence could persuade an enlightened man to believe
in what is intrinsically incredible. Monod comments,

> Now the unbeliever, after having demanded a
> demonstration by the facts, declares: facts can
> prove nothing contrary to reasoning. Were they

established one hundred times more than they are,
we would not believe them because they are
impossible a priori. If I should see a miracle, I
should sooner deem myself mad than allow it, for
nothing is outside of nature, that is to say,
outside of its order.[493]

Given the a priori impossibility of miracles, the
evidentialist argument for Christianity could not even
get off the ground. Of course, men like Houtteville
and Vernet argued philosophically for the possibility
of miracles but again their arguments fell like water
on a stone, for the ésprit fort had already outgrown
such superstition as belief in miracles.

The German Deist controversy

Influence of English and French Deism.   Germany
was the third nation to inherit the Deist controversy,
first from England and then through a fresh influx from
France.   Again the translation of works by English
Deists and their opponents proved the decisive
influence.   Tholuck in his survey of modern apologetic
literature notes,

> Writings in defense of revelation and its docu-
> ments against the enemies of Christianity begin in
> Germany with the start of the 18th century. From
> this time on complaints among theologians grow
> concerning the increase of 'Deism' and 'Natura-
> lism.' The writings of free-thought which flowed
> in from England and were disseminated in numerous
> translations ought to be taken as the principal
> source. . . .[494]

Up until 1741, the German interest in Deism, as we have
seen, was primarily historical.   In that year, however,
Tindal's Christianity as old as the Creation was
translated by Schmidt, and now Deism became a real and
frightening menace.   Gawlick reports, "The publication
of   Beweis, dass das Christenthum so alt als die Welt

sey constitutes in all events a turning point in the
history of the influence of English Deism. It was the
first German edition of a work of this slant, and it
opened a breach through which the spirit of religious
criticism poured in a wide stream."[495]   According to
Lechler, the translations of Tindal and other English
Deists were taken up with rapturous awe and enthusiasm
in Germany.[496]   In his autobiography Laukhard describes
the impact his reading Tindal had upon him:

> God! with what pleasure and encouragement I read
> this noteworthy book, how my thoughts over
> mysteries and revelation have suddenly changed!
> All doubts left me at once and have not come again
> to my soul.   I was convinced with almost
> mathematical certainty: that mysteries cannot be
> the substance of faith, that Jesus and the
> apostles also did not teach this, but rather
> simple natural religion, embellished here and
> there with metaphors from the ancient oriental
> metaphorical language.[497]

Shaftesbury's ethical work was translated in 1745 by
Spalding, and its author enjoyed greater reputation in
Germany than he had in England. His complete works
were available by 1776. Bergman translated writings of
Bolingbroke in 1758.   Hume's Natural History of
Religion became available in 1768 and his Dialogues
concerning Natural Religion in 1781.   In addition to
these translations (as well as others available in
French, such as Collins's Discours sur la liberté de
penser), secondary literature on Deism was abundant.
One need think only of Baumgarten's eight volume
Nachrichten von einer Hallischen Bibliothek (1748-51),
Trinius's Freidenkerlexikon (1759), and especially
Thorschmid's four volume account of English Deism
Versuch einer vollständigen Engellandischen
Freidenkerbibliothek (1765-67). Probably one of the

most effective means of propagating Deist ideas was the
journal Allgemeine Deutsche Bibliothek founded in 1765
and published by F. Nicolai. At its inception it had
50 contributors and at the height of its influence 130,
including such prominent Deists as Mendelssohn and
Lessing. Finally, the responses of English apologists
were made available in German translation; Lechler
provides this list:[498]

> Addison, Zeugnisse der Heiden, usw., trans.
>   Spreng. Zürich: 1745.
> Bentley, Phileleutherus Lipsiensis, trans.
>   Rambach. Halle: 1745.
> G. West (contra Annet), trans. Sulzer. Berlin:
>   1748.
> Lyttleton, Vertheidigung des Paulus, trans. Hahn.
>   Hannover: 1748.
> Ditton on the Auferstehung Jesu, trans. Gotten.
>   1749.
> Stackhouse, Apologie, trans. Lemker. 1750.
> Lardner contra Woolston, trans. Meyenberg. 1751.
> Sherlock contra Woolston, trans. Schier. 1751.
> Warburton, göttliche Sendung Mosis, trans.
>   Schmidt. 1751-53.
> Lowman contra Morgan, trans. Steffens. 1755.
> Leland, Abriss deistischer Schriften, trans.
>   Schmidt & Meyenberg. 1755-56.
> Butler, Bestätigung, usw., trans. Spalding. 1756.
> Leland contra Morgan, trans. Masch. 1756.
> Skelton, Deism Revealed, trans. Mittelstedt. 1756.
> Chapman & Hallet contra Morgan, trans. Steffens.
>   1759.
> Conybeare contra Tindal. Berlin: 1759.
> Benson contra Dodwell, trans. Bamberger. 1761.
> Doddridge contra Dodwell, trans. Rambach. 1764.
> Addisous, Apologie. 1782.

The abundance of Verteidigungschriften from
England apparently occasioned little joy among orthodox
German divines, however, for to them, accustomed as
they were to theological precision, English
latitudinarianism, which formed the backdrop for nearly
all the anti-Deist works, smelled strongly of

heterodoxy. Hence, Johann August Ernesti in a review
in the Neue theologische Bibliothek muses that some
people comfort themselves with the thought that
although Deist writings are invading Germany at least
the refutations of them are also being translated. In
fact, however, the Deists have little to fear from
these apologists, for they are agreed on the essential
point: the difference and superiority of revealed to
natural religion is a matter of advantages, motives,
and hopes being better disclosed. "This is the
ordinary system of those bepraised English writers: in
fact they are Socinians. The Deists do not understand
their own interests, if they set themselves much to
disparage these works, yea, if they be not very well
contented with them. In the great essential, the two
parties are agreed."[499] Thus, revealed religion really
does turn out to be a republication of the religion of
nature.

One immediately thinks of John Locke in this
connection, whose influence in Germany was widespread.
Tholuck observes that for Locke Christianity surpasses
natural religion in four respects: (1) Jesus gave the
most complete teaching concerning God and the ethical
life, (2) Jesus simplified worship from external
ceremonies to that of the heart, (3) Jesus gave
motivation to virtuous living by promising immortality,
(4) Jesus promised his Spirit to help us in the fight
against vice.[500] Tholuck comments, "Ein so dünn
gewordenes Christenthum konnte wohl jeder Deist
verschlingen, ohne den Magen beschwert zu fühlen."[501]
The English apologists after Locke, Tholuck complains,
forget man's sinfulness and so maintain that man's
reason must without rebirth (of which they say
absolutely nothing) recognize Christian truth, which

has been drastically watered down, and never mention redemption.[502] Tholuck recognizes that they supply good refutations of individual points and marshal the evidences effectively (Lardner, for example), but they ignore the central truths of the Christian faith.[503] Thus,   "Die meisten englischen Apologeten sind jedem tollen Hausvater ähnlich, der über die Diebe Mord und Zeter schreit, während er seinen besten Hausrath selbst zum Fenster hinauswirft."[504]

Given their overriding concern for protecting orthodox theology, the latitudinarian route did not seem to be a serious alternative for orthodox German divines.   Either one defended orthodoxy in its doctrinal essentials or one positively departed from it.   The English method of defending a watered-down Christianity as revealed probably thus held little appeal.   Hence, the anti-Deist works available in German translation apparently proved to be little impediment to the spread of Deist ideas in Germany. According to one observer, the English vindications of Christianity "involved so much of timid apology and unchristian concession, that they rather aided than obstructed the progress of infidelity."[505]

The French influence for Deism came somewhat later and centered about the Prussian court of Friedrich der Grosse, where he had gathered a covey of French free-thinkers, including Diderot, La Mettrie, D'Argens, Maupertius, and the illustrious Voltaire himself. Although Tholuck and Noack maintain that French Deism, based as it was chiefly upon satire and condemnation rather than intelligent argument, made less impression upon Germans than did English Deism, Tholuck nevertheless admits that despite their ridicule and slippery arguments the French Deists were believed and

that for example, the German apologist Less is never
read while Voltaire is both read and remembered.[506]

   Deists and their opponents. Perhaps the first
strictly Deist work of any importance to appear in
Germany was Johann Christian Edelmann's Moses mit
aufgedecktem Angesicht (1740). [507] He attacked
miracles, including the resurrection of Jesus, and
charged that the Bible had been corrupted by priests
and filled with lies. Among the other names associated
with German Deism, such as Basedow, Bahrdt, Steinbart,
and Mendelssohn, certainly those of Herrmann Samuel
Reimarus and Gotthold Ephraim Lessing rank as the most
significant.

   A professor of oriental languages in Hamburg,
Reimarus in his published work always sought to show
the accord of Christianity with natural reason. In
private, however, he struggled with gnawing doubts
about the truth of biblical revelation, and from 1730
to 1768 he wrote down his objections and sought
evidence to confute them. His search only served to
reconfirm his doubts, and his writing evolved into an
enormous, 4,000 page critique of the biblical
revelation. He was bothered by the many contradictions
he found in the Bible and could not accept the stories
of the flood, the crossing of the Red Sea, and the
resurrection of Jesus. He was appalled by the
immorality of many Old Testament saints and offended by
the exclusivity of the Judaeo-Christian revelation,
which left most of mankind damned. Even in his
published apologetical work Die vornehmsten Wahrheiten
der natürlichen Religion (1754), cracks appear in his
orthodox facade: he contends that miracles contradict
the order of creation and that therefore it is
impossible for a rational man to believe in them.[508]

Reimarus came to believe in a purely natural religion of reason, which falsified the biblical revelation, which stood in contradiction to it. Most of Reimarus's objections to Christianity had already been voiced by English Deists before him; perhaps his only original contribution was his portrayal of Jesus as a political Messiah figure whom the disciples later exalted to the status of a spiritual ruler.

Reimarus did not deem that the time was right for the publication of his radical views and showed the manuscript of his critique of Christianity, entitled Apologie, order Schutzschrift fur die vernünftigen Verehrer Gottes, only to a few close friends and to two of his children. Lessing, who lived in Hamburg between 1766 to 1769 as a critic of the theater, met Reimarus, and after her father's death Elise Reimarus lent him the manuscript of the Apologie. Appointed librarian for the Duke of Braunschweig at Wolfenbüttel, Lessing in 1774 began to publish excerpts from the Apologie, which he passed off as an anonymous work found by him in the library, in Beiträge zur Geschichte und Literatur as "Wolfenbuttler Fragmente eines Ungenannten." In order to point the finger of suspicion away from Reimarus, Lessing speculated that the author may have been the late J. Lorenz Schmidt, a Deist who had published in 1735 an annotated Pentateuch with rationalist notes and translated in 1741 Tindal's Christianity as old as the Creation; the last ten years of his life (d. 1749) were spent in obscurity under assumed names to avoid persecution, and he had died in humiliation at Wolfenbüttel. Among the extracts published by Lessing was the selection "Über die Auferstehungsgeschichte" (1777), a frontal attack on the resurrection narratives in which Reimarus supports

the conspiracy hypothesis that the resurrection was a
hoax perpetrated by the disciples. This fragment
constituted sections 10-32 of the longer selection "Vom
Zwecke Jesu and seiner Jünger," published by Lessing
the next year, in which Reimarus explains Jesus's
political aspirations and the disciples's transformation of him to a spiritual Messiah.

In publishing the fragments, Lessing did not
commit himself to their viewpoint, but cast himself in
the role of a champion of free speech and open inquiry.
As his letters of 11 November, 1774; 20 March, 1777;
and 25 May, 1777 reveal, Lessing's strategy was to take
the part of the traditional orthodoxy, since it was
more manifestly in conflict with reason and thus more
easily overthrown.[509]   To the collection of five
fragments published in 1777, Lessing appended his
"Gegensätze des Herausgebers," in which he separated
the inward truth of Christianity from the external
traditions received in the New Testament. Reimarus's
critique could only affect the latter, he maintained,
but could not touch the former. Lessing's publication
of the Wolfenbüttel fragments aroused a storm of
outrage and confusion. Refutations of Reimarus came
from every hand.[510]   But the bitterest denunciations
came from the pastor of Hamburg's St. Katharinen,
Johann Melchior Goeze, who became embroiled in an
on-going dispute with Lessing himself.[511]   Although
Goeze has usually been portrayed as a shrill and
ignorant reactionary, this verdict is, as Chadwick
reminds us, pronounced from Lessing's viewpoint. "If
we do not read Goeze through Lessing's spectacles, we
find a sincere and compassionate pastor of his flock,
not without some claim to learning, who seeks to
protect his people from disturbing doubts and

questionings with which they are ill-equipped to
deal."[512]   --hence Goeze's claim that Lessing should
have published the fragments, if at all, in Latin, so
that they might be weighed by theologians rather than
cast into the public arena. Indeed, Goeze, despite his
polemical tone, was a clear-sighted opponent. He was
more concerned with Lessing's counter propositions than
the fragments. He was not far off the mark when he
suspected that Lessing was himself a Deist after the
manner of Toland or Tindal. And he rightly perceived,
unlike the other apologists of the time, that it was
not Reimarus, but Lessing himself who was the real
threat to orthodoxy. But his ad hominem attacks and
warnings to Christians were no match for Lessing's
satirical wit.[513]   Elise Reimarus wrote, "All Germany
has directed its attention to these fencers who come
just short of drawing blood. Among us, the hate
against Goeze has done far more for the truth than
truth itself."[514]

     Lessing's initial response to Goeze came in the
form of a parable in which was described a magnificent
palace of unusual architecture.[515]   Many claimed to
possess the plans of the original architects and
disputed their authenticity among themselves. Others
claimed the plans were unimportant; what was important
was the palace itself. One night a fire was reported
in the palace, and each disputant strove, not to save
the palace from burning, but to rescue his own plan,
and had the fire not been a false alarm the palace
would have actually burned down. Lessing, in a
subsequent vindication of his counter-propositions,
coined the word "Bibliolatry" to describe Goeze's
position. Thereafter a stream of eleven vituperative
pamphlets under the title Anti-Goeze issued from

Lessing's pen.[516]   When Goeze demanded from Lessing
exactly what he understood by Christianity, Lessing
adroitly avoided making a personal profession, but
simply answered historically that the content of the
creed   is   the   <u>regula fidei</u>   and   so   defines
Christianity.[517]   On 9 August, 1778 an exultant Lessing
wrote to Elise Reimarus,

> Since he has made the tactical error of wishing to
> know not what I believe of the Christian religion
> but what I understand by the Christian religion, I
> have scored a victory, and the one half of
> Christendom must defend me in my fortification
> against the other half. Thus Paul divided the
> Sanhedrin, and I need only try to prevent . . .
> the Papists from becoming Lutherans and the
> Lutherans Papists.[518]

On 13 July, 1778, the Duke of Braunschweig officially
clamped down on Lessing, thus bringing the heated
controversy to an end.   Not to be outdone, Lessing
wrote to his brother on 11 August, 1778, that he would
play a trick on the theologians even more annoying than
ten fragments: he would return to his former pulpit,
the theatre.[519]

So   in   1779   Lessing   couched   his   theological
opinions in the form of a play, <u>Nathan der Weise</u>, the
story of Nathan the Jew, Saladin the Moslem, and the
Knight Templar the Christian.   The climax of the play
comes in Lessing's appropriation of the story of the
"Three Rings" from Boccaccio's <u>Decameron</u>:   An ancient
Oriental possessed a ring which gave its wearer favor
with God and man.   The ring was passed down from father
to son until it came to a man who had three sons whom
he loved equally.   Unable to decide to whom to give the
ring, the father had two copies made and gave each of
the three sons a ring.   After their father's death, the

three sons argued among themselves who possessed the
real ring, and the dispute was taken before a judge.
His decision was that none of the brothers could
rightly claim to possess the true ring; these may be
three replicas of the now lost original. But, the
judge adds, each should try to show by brotherly love
and virtue that he wears the authentic ring. Only in
this way could the identity of the true ring possibly
be determined.[520] Lessing thereby argues for religious
indifference and toleration, since any revealed
religion may be but a replica of the true religion.
But more than that, he insists by the judge's final
comment that the essence of true religion consists, not
in doctrinal formulations, but in love for one's fellow
man and the ethical life. Lessing allows that one of
the rings could be genuine, but emphasizes that only
through practical conduct could this be proved.[521]
This is the same message as Lessing's _Testament
Johannis_: "Little children, love one another."[522]
". . . this alone, this alone, if it is done, is
enough, is sufficient and adequate."[523] Again, Lessing
plays off the practical against the doctrinal: it is
enough, he says, to keep to Christian love; it does not
matter what becomes of the Christian religion. The
dogmas of the Christian religion are one thing, and
practical Christianity, which consists in love, is
another.[524] Lessing wanted to preserve the spirit of
Christianity, but without the letter.

Thus, Lessing would have had no trouble
subscribing to the Deist viewpoint of the existence of
God and a religion of the ethical life guided by love.
But at some point in his life, Lessing apparently left
Deism for Spinoza's pantheism. There are already
indications of this in his "Das Christentum der

Vernunft" (1753), in which Leibniz's pre-established
harmony is blended with Spinoza's metaphysics, and in
"Über die Wirklichkeit der Dinge ausser Gott," in which
Lessing breaks down the distinction between God and the
contingent world.[525] Though he does not commit himself
to Spinozism, by the time of his Erziehung des
Menschengeschlechts (1780), there seems to be no need
in his philosophy for a transcendent God at all.[526]
F.H. Jacobi in his Über die Lehre des Spinoza in
Briefen an den Herrn Moses Mendelssohn (1785) reported
that in July of 1780, seven months before Lessing's
death, Lessing told him that the old ideas of Deity
were no longer viable for him and that he accepted
completely Spinoza's pantheism.[527] Although Jacobi's
disclosure generated a heated debate, there seems no
reason to doubt the accuracy of his report [528] or the
fact that Lessing had finally, like Toland before him,
slid from Deism into pantheism.

The response of German orthodox apologists to
Deism followed the English model of presenting
evidences for a supernatural revelation. Thus it was
not the apologetic method of the English which they
disdained, but the latitudinarian theology which it
supported. The same method could be used to defend a
more rigorously orthodox system of doctrine. There
were few orthodox Christian defenders of greatness in
Germany during the eighteenth century. Tholuck
observes that while in England and France there were in
addition to the school theologians and professional
apologists many defenders of the faith who were leading
minds in their nations, in Germany the leading thinkers
had written little in defense of Christianity, even
when they held to it privately.[529] Pre-eminently,
there was, of course, the genius Leibniz, whose

Theodicy was a direct reponse to Bayle's deliberations
on the problem of evil. But as a philosophical
rationalist, he gave no place to historical
argumentation for the truth of Christianity. One of
the best historical defenders of the faith was Kleuker
whose three volumn Neue Prüfung und Erklärung der
vorzüglichsten Beweise für die Wahrheit und den
göttlichen Ursprung des Christenthums (1785) Tholuck
rated among the best, though most neglected, German
apologists.[530] Of greater reknown and rigor was Less,
who presented a sophisticated historical defense of
miracles and the resurrection in Wahrheit der
christlichen Religion (1758) and Auferstehungsgeschichte Jesu (1779). An army of defenders arose to
turn back the attacks of Reimarus and Lessing.[531]
Apologists who specifically defended the resurrection
of Jesus against Reimarus's attack included C.F.
Wiegmann, Versuch eines Beweises Religion aus der
Auferstehung Christi (1778); J.H. Ress, Die Auferstehung Jesu Christi ohne Widersprüche gegen eine Duplik
(1779); J.F. Plessing, Die Auferstehungsgeschichte
unseres Herrn Jesu Christi (1786); and J.G. Herder, Von
der Auferstehung als Glaube, Geschichte und Lehre
(1794). The most influential rebuttal came from the
great biblical critic J.S. Semler, who replied to
Reimarus in his Beantwortung der Fragmente eines
Ungennannten insbesondere vom Zweck Jesu und seiner
Jünger (1779). His reply held particular weight, as
Buchanan explains:

> Although Semler was not alone in his attempt to
> 'kill' R, he was so well known as a scholar that
> his conclusions were widely and uncritically
> accepted. Furthermore, orthodox Christians had
> been left confused and shocked by the fragments.
> They felt a strong need for an authority on whom

they could rely to justify their desire to ignore
the fragments.[532] Semler offered his services to
that end.

According to one reviewer in the Allgemeine Deutsche
Bibliothek of 1795, the fragmentist had by that time
been forgotten.[533] Thus, it would appear that European
Deism as a movement, having been born in France and
come of age in England, finally expired in late
eighteenth century Germany. Such a conclusion would,
however, be too rash, for in Semler's reaction to Deism
we see, not the typical response of the old orthodoxy,
but a radical departure from it and the appropriation
of Deist insights and theological perspective into
German biblical criticism. But that story is reserved
for the sequel. After 1789, according to Tholuck, the
apologetic represented in the works of men like Kleuker
and Less disappeared, and it is not until 1829 with the
appearance of Sack's Christliche Apologetik that it
resurfaces.[534] But now there is a difference: Sack
proceeds under the influence of what his master
Schleiermacher conceived apologetics to be, and the
traditional, evidentialist approach has passed away.

This historical overview serves to delimit the
scope of our study of the historical argument for the
resurrection; our Schwerpunkt will be the eighteenth
century apologetic arguments for the historicity of
Jesus's resurrection. This overview also helps us to
gain a familiarity with the principal figures and
phases of the controversy, for in the ensuing
discussion our interest will not so much be the
historical development of the dispute, but rather the
principal arguments concerning miracles and the
resurrection, apart from their immmediate historical
context. In other words, our interest is in the

cogency of the arguments themselves, not in their
historical genesis. I shall treat the subject
thematically, drawing upon authors of different phases
to discern their contribution to the issue at hand.
Therefore, it is helpful to have had such an overview
of the controversy before we proceed.

The Problem of Miracles

The attack upon miracles

Foundational to the eighteenth century orthodox
defense of the historicity of the resurrection of Jesus
was the question concerning the possibility of
miracles.[535] Though the principal targets of Christian
thinkers in this regard were Spinoza and Hume, the
backdrop for the debate was the Newtonian mechanical
world-view. Under Newton's pervasive influence, [536]
the creation had come to be regarded as the
world-machine governed by eternal and inexorable laws.
Indeed, this complex and harmoniously functioning
system was thought to constitute the surest evidence
that God exists. Diderot wrote,

> It is not from the metaphysician that atheism has
> received its most vital attack. . . . If this
> dangerous hypothesis is tottering at the present
> day, it is to experimental physics that the result
> is due. It is only in the works of Newton, of
> Muschenbroeck, of Hartzoeker, and of Nieuwentit,
> that satisfactory proofs have been found of the
> existence of a reign of sovereign intelligence.
> Thanks to the works of these great men, the world
> is no longer a God; it is a machine with its
> wheels, its cords, its pulleys, its springs, and
> its weights.[537]

Given such a picture of the world, it is not surprising
that miracles were characterized as violations of the

laws of nature. During the Middle Ages, Aquinas had
argued that miracles, while apart from nature, were not
contrary to nature; but with the advent of the
Newtonian world-machine that viewpoint was forgotten,
and miracles were regarded as contradictions to the
divinely established laws of the universe.

The philosophical attack on miracles, however,
antedated Newton's Principia (1687). As early as 1670
Spinoza in his Tractatus theologico-politicus had
argued against the possibility of miracles and their
evidential value.[538] He attempts to establish four
points: (1) nothing happens contrary to the eternal
and unchangeable order of Nature; (2) miracles do not
suffice to prove God's existence; (3) biblical
"miracles" are natural events; and (4) the Bible often
uses metaphorical language concerning natural events so
that these appear miraculous. The first two
contentions bear closer exposition. (1) Spinoza argues
that all that God wills or determines is characterized
by eternal necessity and truth. Because there is no
difference between God's understanding and will, it is
the same to say God knows or wills a thing. Thus, with
the same necessity with which God knows something, God
wills it. Therefore the laws of Nature flow from the
necessity and perfection of the divine nature. So
should some event occur which is contrary to these
laws, that would mean the divine understanding and will
are in contradiction with the divine nature. To say
God does something contrary to the laws of Nature is to
say God does something contrary to his own nature,
which is absurd. Therefore, everything that happens
flows necessarily from the eternal truth and necessity
of the divine nature. What is called a miracle is
merely an event that exceeds the limits of human

knowledge of natural law. (2) Spinoza maintains, in rationalist tradition, that a proof for the existence of God must be absolutely certain. But if events could occur to overthrow the laws of Nature, then nothing is certain, and we are reduced to scepticism. Miracles are thus counter-productive; the way in which we are certain of God's existence is through the unchangeable order of Nature. Since these follow from the divine nature, the more we learn about these laws the better we understand God. By admitting miracles, which break the laws of Nature, warns Spinoza, we create doubts about the existence of God and are led into the arms of atheism! And at any rate, an event contrary to the laws of Nature would not warrant the conclusion to God's existence: the existence of a lesser being with enough power to produce the effect would suffice. Finally, a miracle is simply a work of Nature beyond man's ken. Just because an event cannot be explained by us, with our limited knowledge of Nature's laws, does not mean that God is the cause in any supernatural sense.

If Spinoza attacked the possibility of the occurence of a miracle, Hume attacked the possibility of the identification of a miracle. In his essay "Of Miracles," which constitutes the tenth chapter of his Enquiry, Hume presses a two-pronged attack against the identification of a miracle in the form of an "Even if..., but in fact..." counterfactual judgement.[539] That is to say, in the first portion of the essay, he argues against the identification of any event as a miracle while granting certain concessions, then in the second half he argues on the basis of what he thinks is in fact the case. We may differentiate the two prongs of his argument by referring to the first as his "in

principle" argument and to the second as his "in fact"
arguments. The wise man, he begins, proportions his
belief to the evidence. To decide between two
hypotheses, one must balance the experiments for each
against those for the other in order to determine which
is probably true; should the results be one hundred to
one in favor of the first hypothesis, then it is a
pretty safe bet that the first is correct. When the
evidence makes a conclusion virtually certain, then we
may speak of a "proof", and the wise man will give
whole-hearted belief to that conclusion. When the
evidence renders a conclusion only more likely than
not, then we may speak of a "probability," and the wise
man will accept the conclusion as true with a degree of
confidence proportionate to the probability. So it is
with human testimony. One weighs the reports of others
according to their conformity with the usual results of
observation and experience; thus, the more unusual the
fact reported, the less credible the testimony is.
Now, Hume argues, even if we concede that the testimony
for a particular miracle amounts to a full proof, it is
still in principle impossible to identify that event as
a miracle. For standing opposed to this proof is an
equally full proof, namely the evidence for the
unchangeable laws of nature, that the event in question
is not a miracle. "A miracle is a violation of the
laws of nature, and as a firm and unalterable
experience has established these laws, a proof against
a miracle, from the very nature of the fact, is as
entire as any argument from experience can possibly be
imagined."[540] Thus the testimony of the uniform
experience of mankind stands on one side of the scales
against the testimony in any particular case that a
transgression of that experience has occurred. Thus,

proof stands against proof, and the scales are evenly
balanced. Since the evidence does not incline in
either direction, the wise man cannot believe in a
miracle with any degree of confidence. Indeed, Hume
continues, no testimony could establish that a miracle
has taken place unless the falsehood of that testimony
would be an even greater miracle than the fact it seeks
to establish. And even then the force of the evidence
would only be the difference between the two. So with
regard to the resurrection, Hume comments,

> . . . it is a miracle, that a dead man should come
> to life; because that has never been observed in
> any age or country.
> . . . When any one tells me, that he saw a
> dead man restored to life, I immediately consider
> with myself, whether it be more probable, that
> this person should either deceive or be deceived,
> or that the fact which he relates, should really
> have happened.[541]

Hume later leaves no doubt as to what his answer would
be: should all historians agree that on the first of
January, 1600, Queen Elizabeth died, that she was
pronounced dead by her physicians and seen by all the
court, that she was buried and her successor installed,
but that after a month she reappeared, resumed the
throne, and governed England for three more years, Hume
confesses he would not have "the least inclination" to
believe so miraculous an event.[542] He would only hold
the death to have been pretended, and would prefer to
believe the most extraordinary hypothesis for such a
foolish charade than to admit of so singular a
violation of the laws of nature. Thus, even if the
evidence for a miracle constituted a full proof, the
wise man would not believe in miracles.

But in fact the evidence for miracles does not

amount to a full proof. Indeed, the evidence is so poor, it does not amount even to a probability. Therefore, the decisive weight falls on the side of the scale containing the full proof for the regularity of nature, a weight so heavy that no evidence for a purported miracle could hope to counter-balance it. Hume supplies four reasons, which are a catalogue of typical Deist objections to miracles, why in fact the evidence for miracles is so negligible: (1) No miracle in history is attested by a sufficient number of men of good sense and education, of unimpeachable integrity so as to preclude deceit, of such standing and reputation so that they would have a good deal to lose by lying, and in sufficiently public a manner. (2) People crave the miraculous and will believe absurd stories, as the multitude of false miracles shows. (3) Miracles only occur among barbarous peoples. (4) All religions have their own miracles and therefore cancel each other out in that they support irreconcilable doctrines. Hume adduces three examples: Vespasian's healing of two men as related by Tacitus, a healing reported by Cardinal de Reutz, and the healings at the tomb of the Abbé Paris. The evidence for miracles, therefore, does not even begin to approach the proof of the inviolability of nature's laws. Hume concludes that miracles can never be the foundation for any system of religion. For just as we would not believe Queen Elizabeth's purported resurrection, neither ought we to believe in such an event just because it is ascribed to a divine Being within a system of religion. For we can only know the actions of such a Being from his regular actions in the course of nature, so that we must still weigh the testimony to miracles against the evidence for the laws of nature. Experience teaches that testimony to religious miracles is more likely to be false than that a miracle has occurred. Thus miracles cannot serve as the foundation for a religious system. "Our most holy religion is founded on Faith, not on reason," pontificates Hume, no doubt trying to conceal a smile;

> . . . the Christian Religion not only was at first
> attended with miracles, but even at this day
> cannot be believed by any reasonable person
> without one. Mere reason is insufficient to
> convince us of its veracity: And whoever is moved
> by Faith to assent to it, is conscious of a
> continued miracle in his own person, which
> subverts all the principles of his understanding,
> and gives him a determination to believe what is
> most contrary to custom and experience.[543]

The defense of miracles

What was the response to the objections of Spinoza and Hume, as well as to the popular Newtonian world view in general? Let us consider first some of the replies to Spinoza's arguments against the impossibility of miracles and then some of the responses to Hume's case against the identification of miracles.

We have seen that in his Sentimens de quelques théologiens (1685) Jean Le Clerc attempted to present an apologetic for Christianity that would be invulnerable to Spinoza's criticisms. He not only tried to answer Spinoza's biblical criticism but also his philosophical objections. Against these Le Clerc maintains that the empirical evidence for the miracles and resurrection of Christ is more perspicuous and evidently true than Spinoza's abstract reasoning.[544] Le Clerc's point would seem to be that the back of this a priori, philosophical speculation is simply broken under the weight of the evidence. For Le Clerc

empirical argument takes precedence over speculative
argument.   But   he   also   rebutts   Spinoza's   specific
tenets.   Against   the   allegation   that   miracles   are
simply natural events, the hard-headed Le Clerc
responds that no one will be convinced that Jesus's
resurrection and ascensison could happen as naturally
as a man's birth.   Nor is it convincing to say these
could   be   the   result   of   unknown   natural   laws,   he
continues, for why, then, are no more of these effects
produced and how is it that at the very instant Jesus
commanded a paralyzed man to walk "the Laws of Nature
(unknown to us) were prepared and ready to cause the
. . . Paralytic Man to walk"?[545]   Both   of   these
considerations show that the miraculous facts of the
gospel, which can be established historically, are
indeed of divine origin.

Considerable analysis to the concept of miracle
was brought by Samuel Clarke in his Boyle lectures A
Discourse_concerning_the_Unchangeable_Obligations_of
Natural_Religion_and_the_Truth_and_Certainty_of_the
Christian_Revelation (1705).   He points out that to the
power of God all events--miraculous or not--are alike.
Furthermore,   it   is   possible   that   created   beings
including angels and demons, may have the power to
produce any event, with the sole exception of creatio
ex_nihilo.[546]   Reflecting Newtonian influence, Clarke
asserts that matter has only the power to continue in
its present state, be it rest or motion.   Anything that
is done in the world is done either by God or by
created intelligent beings.   The   so-called   natural
forces of matter, such as gravitation, are properly
speaking the effect of God's acting on matter at every
moment.   The implication of this is that the so-called
"course of nature" is a fiction; what we discern as the

course of nature is nothing else than God's will,
producing certain effects in a continual and uniform
manner.[547]   Thus, a miracle is not against the course
of nature (which really does not exist) except only
insofar as it is an unusual event which God does.[548]
Thus, the regular "works" of nautre prove the being and
attributes of God, and miracles prove the interposition
of God into the regular order in which he acts.[549]   Now
from the miracle itself as an isolated event, it is
impossible to determine whether it was performed
immediately by God or by an angel or by a demonic
spirit.   Clarke insists that miracles done by demonic
spirits are "true and real" miracles that occur because
God does not restrain the demonic spirit from acting at
that point.[550]   The means of distinguishing between
demonic miracles and miracles wrought mediately or
immediately by God is the doctrinal context in which
the miracle occurs:

> If the doctrine attested by Miracles, be in
> itself impious, or manifestly tending to promote
> Vice; then without all question the Miracles . . .
> are neither wrought by God himself, nor by his
> commission; because our natural knowledge of the
> Attributes of God, and of the necessary
> difference between good and evil, is greatly of
> more force to prove any such doctrine to be false,
> than any Miracles in the World can be to prove it
> true. . . .[551]

Should the doctrine be neutral in itself, but another
person performs greater miracles within a context of
doctrine contrary to the first, then the latter is to
be accepted as the miracle of divine origin.[552]   Thus,
the correct theological definition of a miracle is
this: "a work effected in a manner unusual, or
different from the common and regular Method of
Providence, by the interposition either of God himself,

or of some Intelligent Agent superior to Man, for the
proof or Evidence of some particular Doctrine, or in
attestation to the Authority of some particular
Person."[553]   The relationship between doctrine and
miracle is that miracle proves that a higher power is
involved, and the doctrinal context of the miracle
enables us to discern the source of the miracle as
either God or Satan.   Thus, the miracles prove the
docrtrine, but ". . . at least the _indifferency_ of the
Doctrine, [is] a necessary Condition or Circumstance,
without which the _Doctrine_ is not capable of being
proved by any Miracles."[554]   When applied to Jesus's
miracles, this criterion proves that Jesus was "a
Teacher sent from God" and that he had "a Divine
Commission."[555]

     In   his   _Traité de la vérité de la religion
chrétienne_ (1730-88), Jacob Vernet also seeks to answer
the objection that any miracle is impossible because it
is contrary to the order of Nature.[556]   He defines a
miracle as "a striking work which is outside the
ordinary course of Nature and which is done by God's
all-mighty will, such that witnesses thereof regard it
as extraordinary and supernatural."[557]   Vernet does
not, like Clarke, deny that there is a course of
Nature, but he does insist that the so-called course or
order of Nature is really composed of incidental states
of events, not necessary or essential states.   They
depend on the will of God, and it is only the constant
and uniform procession of the normal course of Nature
that leads us to think it is invariable.   God does not
change Nature's course entirely, but can make
exceptions to the general rules when He deems it
important.   These miracles serve to show that the
course of Nature "is not the effect of a blind

necessity, but of a free Cause who interrupts and
suspends it when he pleases."[558]   It might also be
objected that the miracles are the result of a yet
undiscovered operation of Nature itself.[559]   Vernet
replies that when the miracles are diverse and
numerous, this possibility is minimized because it is
hardly possible that all these unknown, marvelous
operations should occur at the same time.   Perhaps a
single, isolated miracle might be so explained away,
but not a series of miracles of different sorts.

       In Claude François Houtteville's La religion
chrétienne prouvée par les faits (1740), the Abbé
argues against Spinoza that miracles are possible.[560]
A miracle he defines as "a striking action superior to
all finite power," or more commonly, as "a singular
event produced outside the chain of natural causes."[561]
Given the existence of God, one sees immediately that
miracles are possible, for a perfect Being who created
the world also conserves it in being, and all the laws
of its operation are directed by his sovereign hand.
Against Spinoza's charge that miracles are impossible
because natural law is the necessary decree of God's
nature and God's nature is immutable, Houtteville
rejoins that natural law is not necessary, that God is
free to establish whatever laws He wills.   Moreover,
God can change His decrees when He wishes.   And even if
He could not, miracles could be part of God's eternal
plan and decree for the universe just as much as
natural laws, so that the occurrence of a miracle in no
way represents a change of mind or decree on God's
part.   Houtteville even suggests that miracles are not
contrary to nature, but only to what we know of nature.
From God's perspective they may conform to certain laws
unknown to us.

Thus, the orthodox response to Spinoza's objections was quite multi-faceted. Hume's objections also elicited a variegated response. Although it was against Woolston's attacks on miracles that Thomas Sherlock wrote his Tryal of the Witnesses, the counsel for Woolston presents an argument against miracles that is anticipatory of Hume. Woolston's attorney argues that because the resurrection violates the course of Nature, no human testimony could possibly establish it, since it has the whole witness of Nature against it. To which Sherlock replies: (1) If testimony is admitted only when the matter is deemed possible according to our conceptions, then many natural matters of fact would be excluded.[562] For example, a man living in a hot climate would never believe in that case testimony from others that water could exist in a solid state as ice.[563] (2) The resurrection is simply a matter of sense perception.[564] If we met a man who claimed to have been dead, we would be suspicious. But of what? Not that he is now alive, for this contradicts all our senses, but that he was ever dead. But would we say it is impossible to prove by human testimony that this man died a year ago? Such evidence is admitted in any court of law. Conversely, if we saw a man executed and later heard the man had come to life again, we would suspect, not that he was not dead, but that he was alive again. But could we say that it is impossible for human testimony to prove that a man is alive? The reason we are suspicious in these cases is not because the matter itself does not admit of being proved by evidence, but only because we are more inclined to believe our own senses rather than reports of others which go contrary to our pre-conceived opinions of what can and cannot happen. Thus,

considered as a fact, the resurrection requires no
greater ability in the witnesses than to be able to
distinguish between a dead man and a living man.
Sherlock does admit that in such miraculous cases we
may require more evidence than usual, but it is absurd
to say that such cases admit of no evidence. (3) the
resurrection contradicts neither right reason nor the
laws of Nature.[565] Sherlock takes yet a third course
from Clarke and Vernet. The so-called course of Nature
arises from the prejudices and imaginations of men.
Our senses tell us what the usual course of things is,
but we go beyond our senses when we conclude that it
cannot be otherwise. The uniform course of things runs
contrary to resurrection, but that does not prove it to
be absolutely impossible. The same Power that gave
life to dead matter at first can give it to a dead body
again; the latter feat is no greater than the former.

Gottfried Less in his Wahrheit der christlichen
Religion (1758) discusses at length Hume's objections
to miracles. Less defines a miracle as a work beyond
the power of all creatures.[566] Of course, a miracle is
such only in a context; healing itself, for instance,
is no miracle, but when no natural means are employed
then healing is miraculous. There are two types of
miracles: (1) first degree miracles, which are wrought
by the immediate power of God, and (2) second degree
miracles, which are above any human power but are
wrought by finite spiritual beings such as angels.
First degree miracles are incapable of being proved
because we never know whether a finite spiritual being
might not be at work. Thus, only second degree
miracles can be proved to have occurred. Less
enumerates five marks of a divine miracle:[567] (1) A
truly divine miracle must be executed by an

unobjectionable person. This person must be
unobjectionable with regard to his intelligence, his
conduct, and his station in life. If these conditions
are not fulfilled, the miracle is either a fraud or an
effect of evil spiritual beings. (2) Truly divine
miracles must be repeatedly executed freely and
publicly. (3) A truly divine miracle must also occur
in a respectable and frank manner. Less intends to
eliminate here mere spectacles and shows. (4) A truly
divine miracle must happen in confirmation of a
teaching that is appropriate to God but previously
unknown to men. (5) A truly divine miracle must exceed
the power of all creatures or at least all men.

So understood, miracles are possible.[568] Because
God is the Lord of Nature and can make events happen,
it follows that miracles are physically possible. And
because miracles are a part of God's eternal plan to
confirm His teaching, they are morally possible. How
does one prove that a miracle has occurred?[569] There
are two steps: one must determine (1) the historicity
of the event itself and (2) the event's being a
miracle. Although Hume discounts the testimony of the
apostles because they were unlearned men, it is clear
that to prove merely that something happened (for
example, a disease's being healed by sheer verbal
command), one need be no scholar, but simply have five
good senses and common sense. In fact, the New
Testament witnesses fulfill even Hume's conditions for
credibility of reports of miracles.[570] (1) A miracle
should have a sufficient number of witnesses. Jesus's
miracles were seen by hundreds of friends and enemies
alike. (2) These witnesses should be of such
doubtlessly good intelligence, upbringing, and learning
as is required to assure us that they themselves were

not bedazzled. The apostles were admittedly unlearned men, but all they needed was healthy senses to testify to what they saw and heard. (3) The reporter of a miracle should be of such doubtless honesty and sincerity, as is necessary to set him above suspicion of fraud. Jesus's disciples were of such a character that this condition is eminently fulfilled. (4) People should be of such credit, good standing, and respect in the eyes of men that they would have lost a great deal if they were found out to be involved in any fraud. The disciples, being of low estate, had little to lose materially, but they had comfort and life itself to lose. (5) These persons should bear witness to such things as were executed in so public a manner and in so famous a part of the world as is necessary to make the discovery of fraud unavoidable. The gospel accounts are of events in Jerusalem, the capital city of the Jews, in the civilized part of the world under the Roman Empire. Thus, even Hume should concede the historical certainty of the gospel miracles. Less then answers the objections in Hume's essay point by point.[571] Hume's principal argument is that testimony to miracles has the experience of the world and the centuries against it. In response, Less argues: (1) Because Nature is the freely willed order of God, a miracle is just as possible as any event. Therefore, it is just as believable as any event. (2) Testimony to an event cannot be refuted by experiences and observations. Otherwise we would never be justified in believing anything outside our present experience; no new discoveries would be possible. (3) There is no contradiction between experience and Christian miracles. Miracles are different events (Contraria) from experience in general, but not contradictory

events (Contradictoria) to experience in general.[572]
The contradiction to the testimony that under the reign
of Tiberius Caesar, Jesus raised certain persons from
the dead and himself so rose three days after his death
must necessarily be the exact opposite of this
statement, namely, that Jesus never raised anyone from
the dead and never himself so rose. This latter has to
be proved to destroy the gospel testimony. It is
hardly enough to assert that experience in general says
that dead men do not rise, for with this the Christian
testimony is in full agreement. Only when the exact
opposite is proved to be true can Christian testimony
be said to contradict experience. Hume's other
objections are easily dismissed: (1) No miracle has a
sufficient number of witnesses. This has been shown to
be false with regard to the gospel miracles. (2)
People tend to believe and report miraculous stories
without proper scrutiny. This shows only that our
scrutiny of such stories ought to be cautious and
careful. (3) Miracles originate among ignorant and
barbaric peoples. This cannot be said to describe
Jesus's miracles in Jerusalem and Judea. (4) All
religions have their miracles. This is in fact not
true, for no other religion purports to prove its
teachings through miracles, and there are no religious
miracles outside Jewish-Christian miracles. Less later
examines in considerable detail the miracles alleged by
Hume to have equal footing with Christian miracles,
particularly the miracles at the tomb of the Abbé
Paris.[573] In all these cases, the evidence that
miracles have occurred never approaches the standard of
the evidence for the gospel miracles. Therefore, none
of Hume's objections can overturn the evidence for the
gospel miracles.

William Paley's A View of the Evidences of Christianity (1794) is, as we have mentioned, primarily a studious investigation of the historical evidence for Christianity from miracles, and Paley's preliminary considerations to his investigation constitute an across the board refutation of Hume's objections. Paley makes it clear from the beginning that he presupposes the existence of the God proved by the teleological argument.[574] Given the existence of God, miracles are not incredible.[575] For why should it be thought incredible that God should want to reveal Himself in the natural world to men, and how could this be done without involving a miraculous element? Any antecedent improbability in miracles adduced in support of revelation is not such that sound historical testimony cannot surmount it. This, says Paley, suffices to answer "a modern objection to miracles," which he later identifies as that of David Hume.[576] The presupposition of Hume's argument, he continues, is that ". . . it is contrary to experience that a miracle should be true, but not contrary to experience that testimony should be false."[577] Like Less, Paley argues that the narrative of a fact can be said to be contrary to experience only if we, being at the time and place in question, were to see that the alleged event did not in fact take place. What Hume really means by "contrary to experience" is simply the want of similar experiences. (To say a miracle is contrary to universal experience is obviously question-begging.) But in this case, the improbability arising from our want of similar experiences is equal to the probability that, given the event as true, we should also have similar experiences. But suppose Christianity was inaugurated by miracles; what probability is there then

that we today must also have such experiences? It is
clear that any such probability is negligible; hence,
any improbability arising from our lack of such
experiences is also negligible. A miracle is not like
a scientific experiment capable of being subsumed under
a law and repeated, for then it would not be contrary
to nature as such and would cease to be a miracle. The
objection to miracle from want of similar experiences
presupposes either (1) that the course of nature is
invariable or (2) that if it can be varied, these
variations must be frequent and general. But if the
course of nature be the agency of an Intelligent Being,
should we not expect him to interrupt his appointed
order only seldom on occasions of great importance? As
to the cause of miracles, this is simply the volition
of Deity, of whose existence and power we have
independent proof. As to determining whether a miracle
has in fact occurred, Paley considers Hume's account of
the matter to be a fair one: which in any given case
is more probable, that the miracle be true or that the
testimony be false? But in saying this, Paley adds, we
must not take the miracle out of the theistic and
historical context in which it occurred, nor can we
ignore the question of how the evidence and testimony
arose. The real problem with Hume's scepticism becomes
clear when we apply it to a test case: suppose twelve
men, whom I know to be honest and reasonable persons,
were to assert that they personally saw a miraculous
event in which it was impossible that they had been
tricked; further, the governor called them before him
for an inquiry and told them that if they did not
confess the imposture they would be tied up to a
gibbet; and they all went to their deaths rather than
say they were lying. According to Hume, I should still

not believe them. But such incredulity, states Paley, would not be defended by any sceptic in the world.

Paley maintains against Hume's matter of fact argument that no parallel to the gospel miracles exists in history.[578] Paley examines in considerable detail Hume's three examples and concludes that it is idle to compare such cases with the evidence for the miracles of the gospels.[579] In none of these cases is it unequivocal that a miracle has occurred. Even in other unexplained instances, it is still true that there is no evidence that the witnesses have passed their lives in labor, danger, and suffering voluntarily undergone in attestation to the truth of the accounts they delivered. Thus, the circumstance of the gospel history is without parallel.

Spinoza's arguments for the impossibility of miracles and Hume's arguments against the identification of miracles were thus contested from various standpoints. It is noteworthy that virtually all of the Christian thinkers presupposed the existence of God in their argument. It was not a case of theism versus atheism, but of Christian theism versus Deism. In that sense they did not try to found a system of religion on miracles; rather they argued that given the existence of God, miracles are possible, because of His omnipotence (Clarke), His constant conservation of the world in being (Houtteville), and His sovereign freedom to act as He wills (Less). Moreover, the existence of God was not always simply assumed: Clarke and Paley provided sophisticated arguments to justify their theism. The question was, given the existence of God, are miracles possible? Against the mechanistic Newtonian conception of the course and laws of Nature, they argued that the course of Nature is really only

the regular pattern of God's will (Clarke) or that it
is subject to God's freedom to alter it (Vernet,
Houtteville, Less, Paley) or even that it may include
within itself the capacity of allowing miraculous
events (Sherlock, Houtteville). Against Spinoza's two
objections, they urged: (1) Miracles do not contravene
God's nature because the laws of nature do not flow in
necessitarian fashion from the being of God, but are
freely willed and therefore alterable (Vernet), and
miracles as well as the laws could be willed according
to God's plan from eternity, so that their occurence
represents no change in God's decrees (Houtteville,
Less). (2) Miracles are not proof of the existence of
God, but of the existence of the Christian God. Hence,
it is correct to say that the regular order of Nature
proves God's existence; but it is equally true to say
that a miracle proves the action of that God in the
world (Clarke, Paley). The Christian protagonists
sometimes freely granted that it could not be proved
that God or a lesser being was at work in a miracle;
but here they urged that it was the religious,
doctrinal context that allowed one to determine if a
miracle was divine (Clarke, Less; cf. Aquinas, Socinus,
Grotius, Pascal). Against Spinoza's charge that
perhaps an unknown law of Nature is operating in the
case of a "miracle," they responded that it then
becomes inexplicable why such events do not recur and
why these mysterious laws operated coincidentally at
the moment of Jesus's command (LeClerc) and that when
numerous and various miracles occur this possibility is
negligible (Vernet), or they granted that this could be
God's means of acting within the course of Nature
(Sherlock, Houtteville). Against Hume's in principle
argument, they maintained: (1) Given God's existence,

miracles are as possible as any other event (Less), and the probability that God would reveal Himself nullifies any improbability inherent in the concept of miracle itself (Paley). (2) A miracle is a matter of sense perception as much as any other event and is therefore capable of being supported by historical testimony (Sherlock, Bergier). (3) A miracle is not contrary to experience as such, and therefore the testimony to a miracle cannot be overturned by the testimony to the regular order of other experiences (Less, Campbell, Paley). (4) The improbability that a miracle should accur uniquely in the past is equal to the probability that we should experience such miracles s well, which is slight or non-existent (Paley). (5) Hume's argument if applied equably would eliminate many natural matters of fact as well as miracles (Sherlock, Less). (6) Hume's principle results in unrealistic and exaggerated scepticism concerning matters amply established by reliable testimony (Paley). In response to Hume's matter of fact arguments the orthodox protagonists simply sought to prove that in the case of the gospel miracles and the resurrection of Jesus, the factual evidence is sufficiently strong to warrant the conclusion that these events really occurred in contrast to other stories of purported miracles (Less, Campbell, Paley). Thus, there can be no objection to the resurrection of Jesus because it entails a supposedly "impossible" miracle.

The Use of Historical Methodology

Another interesting feature of the eighteenth century argumentation, which we have seen to be the product of the rise of historical consciousness, is the

use of historiographical principles to show that a
miracle is established by the same canons of history
that make the facticity of ordinary events probable.
The point was to show that the Bible could be shown to
be true by the same tests that are used to establish
the veracity of other historical documents. This
involved a very fundamental change in one's approach to
Scripture.   For now the biblical writings had to be
regarded, not as inspired revelation, since this was
precisely the point of contention, but as ordinary
documents of antiquity to be handled like any other
ancient work. Already in Grotius we see a doctrine of
attenuated inspiration, plenary inspiration not being
necessary for historical works.   If few followed
Grotius in this doctrine, nearly all followed him
methodologically, that is to say, they professed to
proceed as if the biblical documents were merely human
historical works.   Given the pervasive theological
rationalism of the day, such a procedure was
inevitable, since apart from reason, no avenue of
discerning revelation was open.   A claim to an
immediate inner testimony from God would have been
dismissed as empty enthusiasm.   Hence, since the
Scripture purports to be a historical revelation, the
task of weighing its claim must fall to reason in its
a posteriori function. Thus, we find an emphasis on
proving Christianity by the facts in accord with
historiographical principles. Leslie's "short and
easie method" was almost universally adopted: one lays
out several historiographical principles, uses these to
establish the gospels' accuracy, and then presents the
dilemma of either accepting the gospel history or
abandoning all other history which is equally or less
attested.

For example, Vernet insists that in the
investigation of the historicity of a miracle we must
employ no other methodology than that normally employed
in investigating historical material.[580] He declares,
"The portion of religion which can be called
philosophical is proved by philosophical reasoning, and
the historical portion is proved by well-attested
facts. What could be more reasonable than this
method!"[581] He then elaborates some of this
methodology. The very best sources will always be the
written reports of eyewitnesses. Once the source has
been determined as authentic, the temporal distance of
the source is incidental.[582] Now there are two
requisite conditions for reliable testimony: first,
the witness must not be himself mistaken, and second,
the witness must not be intentionally trying to
deceive.[583] With regard to the first condition, the
witness must be a man of good sense and must be
well-informed concerning that of which he testifies.
As to the second condition, the witness should be
generally known as honest and, more specifically,
should be disinterested in that to which he bears
testimony. Finally, Vernet concludes, the more
witnesses there are to an event, the better.[584] Vernet
wants to prove that the evidence for the gospel
miracles fulfills these criteria, and therefore to
reject it would be to cast doubts on all of history.[585]
He cautions that with a subject of this nature we can
have neither mathematical proof nor direct observation
nor precisely the same certainty that we have
concerning present events. What we can have is a
historical certainty. And with regard to the evidence
for the gospel miracles this certainty is of such a
degree that we can demand no more from any other fact

of history.

In the same spirit Less remarks that there are
several different methods of demonstration:
metaphysical or mathematical proof, scientific proof,
and historical proof.[586] Christianity is proved
through the third method by means of witnesses. In
investigating the gospels' historicity, we must use no
other rules than those normally employed in historical
inquiry.[587] Because Christianity is grounded in
historical events, it can only be proved historically.
But this proof reaches such a degree of certainty that
we are confronted with this dilemma: either accept the
gospel accounts as historically accurate or throw out
the rest of history with them.[588]

The eighteenth century authors thus recaptured the
dilemma presented by Eusebius. Either we abandon all
of history or we allow the miraculous events of the
gospels to enter arm in arm with natural events of the
past. Any attempt to draw a dichotomy between the two
only evidences a dogmatic bias against miracles. As
Leland states,

> What can be a plainer proof of the power of their
> prejudices, than to advance rules in judging of
> the truth and credibility of Scripture-history,
> which would be absolutely rejected and exploded if
> applied to any other history in the world; and to
> reject the evidence as insufficient with regard to
> the facts recorded in the gospel, which they
> themselves would count sufficient with regard to
> any other facts done in past ages?[589]

The correct procedure, the orthodox thinkers contended,
is to apply to the gospels the same historiographical
principles used in the investigation of secular
history. Although this involved treating the gospels
as ordinary historical documents instead of revealed

Scripture, the defendants of this view were confident that the biblical narrative could be established to a high degree of probability.

The Case for the Resurrection

Both Deist and orthodox thinkers alike understood that Jesus's resurrection lay at the heart of the Christian religion and constituted the greatest Biblical miracle. It was inevitable therefore that it should become the centerpiece of the controversy between them. Leland wrote, "The resurrection of Christ is an article of vast importance, which lieth at the foundation of Christianity. If this faileth, the Christian religion cannot be maintained, or may be proved to be false. . . On the other hand, if this holdeth good, the divine mission and authority of the blessed Founder of our holy religion is established." [590] What then was the case which they presented for the historical resurrection? Generally speaking, it could be schematized as follows:

1. The gospels are authentic.
2. The text of the gospels is substantially pure.
3. The gospels are reliable.
   a. The disciples were neither deceivers nor deceived.
   b. The origin and growth of the Christian church confirm the reliability of the gospels.
4. Objections are unsound.

Let us attempt to fill out this schema step by step with the arguments employed by the proponents of the historical argument for the resurrection.

The authenticity of the gospels

Internal evidence

The first step in the case was proving the authenticity of the gospels, that is, that the gospels actually stem from the apostolic pens. Paley underlines the importance of this step, for, he points out, if the gospels are authentic apostolic writings, then quite simply either these accounts are true or they are lies. If only one gospel can be shown to be apostolic, then this is enough to confirm the truth of the original miraculous events contained therein.[591] Vernet contends that the authenticity of the gospels can be established through the use of both internal and external criteria. Turning first to internal criteria he observes:[592] (1) The style of writing in these books is simple and alive, which gives them the mark of authenticity. In the same vein, Less notes that these are the works of simple men, not philosophers, and appear to be empirical reports of what they saw and heard.[593] (2) Since the book of Acts was written before the death of Paul, the gospel of Luke must have been composed still earlier. (3) The gospels evince an intimate knowledge of Jerusalem before its destruction, indicating that they were written before that catastrophic event. With regard to Jesus's prophecies of Jerusalem's destruction, these must have been written before the event, for otherwise the church would have separated out the apocalyptic element from the prophecies so that the destruction of the city would not seem bound up with the destruction of the world. (4) The gospels are full of references to proper names, dates, cultural details, historical events, and opinions and customs of the time. (5) The

stories of Jesus's weaknesses and the faults of the
disciples are earmarks of authenticity. (6) It would
have been impossible for forgers to put together so
consistent a narrative as that which we find in the
gospels. (7) The gospels do not try to suppress
apparent discrepancies, which bespeaks their
originality. (8) There is no attempt at harmonization
between the gospels; each produces his own order of
events. (9) The style of writing is proper to what we
know of the peculiar personality of each author. Less
brings forth one more argument: (10) The gospels do
not contain anachronisms; the writers appear to have
been first century Jews who were witnesses of the
events.[594]   Paley suggests an additional consideration:[595] (11) The Hebraic and Syriac idioms that mark
the gospels are appropriate to their received authors.
He concludes that there is no more reason to doubt that
the gospels come from their received authors than do
the works of Philo or Josephus from their authors,
except the gospels contain supernatural events.

External evidence
        Turning   next   to   external   criteria, Vernet
argues: [596] (1) The disciples must have been forced to
leave some writings, engaged as they were in giving
lessons and counseling believers geographically
distant; but what could these writings be, if not the
gospels and epistles themselves? And the apostles must
have used writings in instruction, which could only be
the books now in the New Testament. Ditton maintains
that not only is it highly probable that the early
disciples would leave writings, but also that as long
as the original apostles were still alive, nothing
contrary to their doctrine could be forged as

proceeding from them.[597] In fact so long as the autographs of their writings endured, the same would be true. Paley urges that eventually the apostles would have needed to publish accurate narratives of Jesus's history, in which case any spurious attempts would be discredited and the genuine gospels preserved.[598] (2) There were many eyewitnesses still alive when the books were written who could testify as to whether they came from their alleged authors. (3) The external testimony of extra-biblical sources unanimously ascribes these works to their respective authors. No finer presentation of this point can be found than Paley's extensive eleven point argument:[599] (a) The gospels and Acts are cited by a series of authors beginning with those contemporary with the apostles and continuing in regular and close succession.[600] This is the strongest form of historical testimony, a procedure regularly employed in secular historiography. When applied to the gospels and Acts, it establishes unquestionably their authenticity. The epistle of Barnabas quotes the gospel of Matthew as Scripture; Clement of Rome also cites words of Jesus found in Matthew. The Shepherd of Hermas contains allusions to Matthew, Luke and John. Ignatius clearly alludes to Matthew and John. His contemporary Polycarp, who knew the apostle John and other eyewitnesses of Jesus's ministry, refers about 40 times to New Testament books. Papias, who also heard the apostle John, specifically ascribes Matthew and Mark to their respective authors and in an incidental way that assumes that this fact was generally known. Justin Martyr who came 20 years later, frequently cites the gospels, and that without specific references, which shows that these gospels were the only ones in existence. Irenaeus, who knew

Polycarp and claimed to be able to reckon up the
succession of bishops in all the principal churches
back to the first, specifically names the four
evangelists as the respective authors of the gospels.
Paley traces this chain of testimony all the way to
Eusebius in AD 315. Less furnishes this convenient
summary:[601]

>Matthew: Papias, various sources cited by
>Eusebius, Justin Martyr, Tatian, Irenaeus,
>Athenagoras, Theophilus, Clement of Alexandria,
>Tertullian, Ammonius, Julius Africanus, Origen,
>and all ancient writers without exception known to
>Eusebius; possible references also in Barnabas,
>Clement, Ignatius, and Polycarp.

>Mark: Papias, various sources cited by Eusebius,
>Justin Martyr, Tatian, Irenaeus, Clement of
>Alexandria, Tertullian, Ammonius, Origen, and all
>ancient writers known to Eusebius; possible
>references also in Clement and Ignatius.

>Luke and Acts: various sources cited by Eusebius,
>Justin Martyr, Tatian, Irenaeus, Clement of
>Alexandria, Tertullian, Ammonius, Julius
>Africanus, Origen, and all writers known to
>Eusebius; possible references also in Clement,
>Ignatius, Polycarp, and correspondence of the
>churches of Lyon and Vienne.

>John: various sources cited by Eusebius, Justin
>Martyr, Tatian, Irenaeus, Theophilus, Clement of
>Alexandria, Tertullian, Ammonius, Origen, and all
>writers known to Eusebius, possible reference also
>in the correspondence of the churches of Lyon and
>Vienne.

Both Vernet and Less emphasize that many of these men,
such as Origen and Eusebius, were scholars in their own
right, who had studied the works of Homer, Aeschylus,
Plato, Aristotle, and others, who would want to
determine with accuracy the authenticity of writings
foundational to their religion.[602] Less concludes that
there is better testimony for the authenticity of the

New Testament books than for _any_ classical work of
antiquity.[603]   (b) The Scriptures were quoted as
authoritative and _sui generis_. Again citations from
Theophilus, the writer against Artemon, Hippolitus,
Origen and many others make the point abundantly
clear.[604] (c) The Scriptures were very early collected
into a distinct volume.[605]   Ignatius alludes to
collections known as the Gospel and the Apostles, what
we today call the gospels and the epistles. According
to Eusebius, Quadratus about 60 years after the
appearance of the gospels distributed them to converts
during his travels. Irenaeus and Melito refer to the
collection of writings we know as the New Testament.
Clement of Alexandria and Tertullian also refer to the
division of Scripture into the Gospel and Apostles.
And Eusebius refers to the four gospels collected
together as a volume. (d) These writings were given
titles of respect.[606]   Polycarp, Justin Martyr,
Dyonisius, Irenaeus, and others call them Scriptures,
divine writings, and so forth. (e) These writings were
publicly read and expounded.[607] Quotations from Justin
Martyr, Tertullian, Origen, and Cyprian go to prove the
point. (f) Copies, commentaries, and harmonies were
written on these books.[608] Worthy of mention here is
Tatian's Diatessaron, a harmony of the four gospels
from about AD 170. Other writings include those by
Pantaenus, Clement of Alexandra, Tertullian, and so on.
With the single exception of Clement's commentary on
the Revelation of Peter, no commentary was ever written
during the first 300 years on any book outside the New
Testament. (g) The Scriptures were accepted by all
heretical groups as well as by orthodox Christians.[609]
Examples include Basilides, the Valentinians, the
Carpocratians, and many others. (h) The gospels, Acts,

13 letters of Paul, I John, and I Peter were received
without doubt as authentic by those who doubted the
authenticity of other books now in the canon.[610] Caius
about AD 200 reckoned up 13 of Paul's letters, but
insisted that Hebrews was not written by Paul. Origen
about 20 years later cites Hebrews to prove a
particular argument; he observes that some might
dispute the authority of Hebrews, but the same point
could be proved from the undisputed books of Scripture
and proceeds to quote Matthew and Acts. Though he
expresses doubt concerning some books, Origen states of
the four gospels that they alone were received without
dispute by the whole church of God under heaven.
Eusebius, too, while reporting doubt concerning some
books, states that the four gospels were universally
recognized as authentic. (i) The early opponents of
Christianity regarded the gospels as containing the
accounts upon which the religion was founded.[611]
Celsus admits that the gospels were written by the
disciples. Porphyry attacked Christianity as it is
found in the gospels. The Emperor Julian acted
similarly. (j) Catalogues of authentic scriptures were
published, which always contained the gospels and
Acts.[612] Citations from Origen, Athanasius, Cyril, and
others are brought forth in support. (k) The so-called
apocryphal books of the New Testament were never so
treated.[613] It is a simple fact that during the first
300 years, with one exception, no apocryphal gospel is
even quoted by any known writer. In fact there is no
known evidence that any inauthentic gospel whatever
existed in the first century, in which all four of the
gospels and Acts were extant. The apocryphal gospels
were never quoted, not read in Christian assemblies,
not admitted into a volume, not listed in the catalogs,

not noticed by Christianity's adversaries, not appealed
to by heretics, not the subject of commentaries and
collations, but were nearly universally rejected by
Christian writers of succeeding ages.

Therefore, Paley concludes, the evidence strongly
confirms the authenticity of the gospels.[614]   Even
should it be the case that the names of the authors
assigned to the gospels are somehow mistaken, it cannot
be denied in light of all the foregoing arguments that
the gospels, whoever their authors might be, do contain
the story which the original apostles told and for
which they labored and suffered.

Taken together, therefore, both internal and
external criteria serve to confirm the first step of
the argument, that the gospels are authentic.   The
implications of this fact for the credibility of the
resurrection narratives will become clear in step
three.

The textual purity
of the gospels

The second step often taken by the Christian
thinkers was the demonstration that the text of the
gospels is substantially pure. Vernet in favor of this
point argues:[615]   (1) Because of the need for
instruction and personal devotion, these writings must
have been copied many times. (2) No other ancient work
was available in so many copies and languages, and yet
they all conform in content. (3) The text of these
works remains unmarred by heretical conflations. (4)
The abundance of manuscripts over wide geographical
distribution demonstrates that the text has been
transmitted with only trifling discrepancies. (5) The

differences that do exist are quite minor and are the
results of unintentional errors. (6) The text of the
books of the New Testament is every bit as good as the
classical works of antiquity. To these arguments, Less
adds:[616] (7) The quotations of the New Testament books
in the early church fathers and the different versions
of the books all coincide. (8) The gospels could not
have been corrupted without a great outcry of protest,
as the example of the writer against Artemon, recorded
by Eusebius, shows: the writer had accused the
followers of Artemon of having changed the Scriptures
and of being unable to authorize this by any old
copies. Against the notion that there has been a
deliberate falsifying of the text, Houtteville
argues:[617] (9)(a) No one--pagans, Jews, or
Christians--could have corrupted all the manuscripts.
(b) There is no precise time when the corruption could
have occurred, since the biblical writings are
continuously cited by ecclesiastical writers. The
writings could not have been falsified before all
external testimony, since then the authors were still
alive and would check any alteration. (c) There was no
motivation on anyone's part to falsify these writings.
Against the suggestion that the text has been corrupted
by transcriptional errors, Houtteville urges: (10)(a)
Surely at least one uncorrupted manuscript would
survive. (b) The correct copies would prevail over the
errant ones. (c) The transcriptional changes that have
occurred are of no great weight. Hence, Ditton
concludes that to reject the text of the New Testament
is to reject all books whose text cannot be
demonstrated to be purer, which no one would do.[618] In
sum, Vernet asserts that it is certain that the text of
the New Testament is as pure and complete as that of

any ancient book, so much so that to deny the point
would be to reverse all the rules of the art of
criticism and to reject all that we know of
antiquity.[619]

Again the dilemma posed in this second step of the
case is clear: renounce the texts of classical
antiquity or else admit the text of the gospels as
equally pure.   The Christian thinkers were attempting
to secure a place for the gospels along side of and as
unshakeable as any other work of antiquity.

The reliability of
the gospels

The apostles neither
deceivers nor deceived

Having demonstrated that the gospels are authentic
and that their text has been transmitted to us
substantially without corruption, the proponents of the
historical argument were now prepared to argue that the
gospels are reliable.   Again the argument boiled down
to a fundamental dilemma: if there were no miracles
and resurrection, then the apostles were either
deceivers or deceived.[620]   These were in fact the
explanations proferred by the Deists themselves.
Leland accurately sums up the alternatives propounded
by Deist thinkers:

> Sometimes the apostles are represented as
> hot-brain'd enthusiasts, who really believed
> themselves to be inspired of God, and were so mad
> as to imagine that they wrought miracles, and had
> extraordinary gifts of the Holy Ghost, when there
> was no such things.   At other times they are
> represented as artful imposters, who formed a
> scheme of wordly power and grandeur under

spiritual pretences, and forged facts and
evidences which they knew to be false.[621]

Since, according to the defenders of biblical
Christianity, both of these alternatives could be shown
to be extremely unlikely, it followed that the miracles
and resurrection of Jesus actually took place.

Let us turn first to the arguments presented
against the second horn of this dilemma: that the
disciples could not have been deceived. This
alternative embraces all those hypotheses which hold
that the miracles and resurrection of Jesus did not in
fact occur, though the disciples sincerely believed
that they did. Clarke argues: (1) The miracles were
so great, so many, so public, and so evident that they
could not be the result of any human manipulation,
chance, or fallacy.[622] Less points out:[623] (2) The
New Testament authors lived at the time and place of
the events they record. They could therefore confirm
or disconfirm the truth of the facts they recorded.
The eyewitnesses were still alive and could be
questioned. With specific regard to the resurrection,
Ditton maintains:[624] (3) The witnesses of the
appearances were well-qualified. (a) There were many
witnesses to this event. (b) They had personal
knowledge of the matter, since Jesus appeared to them
over a period of several weeks. There is no room for
the hypothesis of imagination or dream. (c) The
disciples were not religious enthusiasts, as is
apparent from their balanced behavior and doctrine,
even in the face of extreme situations. Against the
charge that the evidence based on the testimony of
silly women is unreliable, Sherlock responds:[625]
(4)(a) They had eyes and ears, too, and were not
gullible, but actually disbelieving. (b) They were

never employed as witnesses to the resurrection. (c)
The testimony of the men is none the worse for having
the testimony of the women as well. Paley answers the
charge that the resurrection appearances were the
result of "religious enthusiasm" (="subjective visions"
in modern parlance):[626]   (5) The theory fails on
several counts: (a) Not just one person but many saw
Christ appear. (b) They saw him not individually, but
together. (c) They saw him not once but several times.
(d) They not only saw him, but touched him, conversed
with him, and ate with him. These considerations are
decisive, but the most fundamental reason for rejecting
the religious enthusiasm hypothesis is (e) the
non-production of the body. It is impossible that
Jesus's followers could believe that he was raised if
the corpse were there before them. But it is equally
incredible to suppose that the disciples would have
stolen the body and perpetrated a fraud. Moreover,
Christianity was founded at Jerusalem, and this would
have been impossible if the body of Jesus were to be
found. The Jewish authorities could certainly have
produced it as the shortest and completest answer to
the whole story. But all they could do was assert that
the disciples had stolen the corpse. Thus, the
hypothesis of religious enthusiasm, in failing to
explain the absence of Jesus's body, ultimately
collapses back into the hypothesis of fraud, which,
Paley remarks, has been pretty much given up in view of
the obvious sincerity of the apostles, as well as their
character and the dangers they underwent.

Given these factors, it is not feasible to explain
away the resurrection accounts on the grounds that the
apostles had been misled into believing that Jesus was
risen. With Paley's last remark we return to the first

horn of the dilemma: that the disciples were deceivers.   This alternative includes all hypotheses which hold that the apostles knew that the miracles and resurrection of Jesus did not take place, but that they nevertheless said that they did.   One of the most popular arguments against this theory was the obvious sincerity of the disciples as attested by their suffering and death.   No more eloquent statement of the argument can be found than Paley's: he seeks to show that the original witnesses of the miraculous events of the gospels passed their lives in labors, dangers, and sufferings, voluntarily undertaken in attestation to and as a consequence of the accounts which they delivered.   Paley argues first from the general nature of the case. [627]   We know that Christian religion exists.   Either it was founded by Jesus and the apostles or by others, the first being quiet and silent.   The second alternative is quite incredible. If the disciples had not zealously followed up what Jesus had started, Christianity would have died at its birth.   If this is so, then a life of missionary sacrifice must have been necessary for those first apostles.   Such a life is not without its own enjoyments, but they are only such as spring from a true sincerity.   With a consciousness at bottom of hollowness and falsehood, the fatique and strain would have become unbearable.   There was probably difficulty and danger involved in the propagation of a new religion.   With regard to the Jews, the notion of Jesus's being the Messiah was contrary to Jewish hopes and expectations; Christianity lowered the esteem of Jewish law; and the disciples would have had to reproach the Jewish leaders as guilty of an execution which could only be represented as an unjust and cruel

murder. As to the Romans, they could have understood
the Kingdom of God only in terms of an earthly kingdom
and thus a rival. And concerning the heathen,
Christianity admitted no other god or worship. While
the philosophers allowed and even enjoined worship of
state deities, Christianity could countenance no such
accommodation. Thus, even in the absence of a general
program of persecution, there were probably random
outbursts of violence against Christians. The heathen
religions were old and established and not easily
overthrown. These religions were generally regarded by
the common people as equally true, by the philosophers
as equally false, and by the magistrates as equally
useful. From none of these sides could the Christians
expect protection. Finally, the nature of the case
requires that these early apostles must have
experienced a great change in their lives, now involved
as they were in preaching, prayer, religious meetings,
and so forth.

What the nature of the case would seem to require
is in fact confirmed by history.[628] Writing 70 years
after Jesus's death, Tacitus narrates the persecution
of Nero about 30 years after Christ, how the Christians
were clothed in the skins of wild beasts and thrown to
dogs, how others were smeared with pitch and used as
human torches to illuminate the night, while Nero rode
about Rome in the dress of a charioteer, viewing the
spectacle. The testimonies of Suetonius and Juvenal
confirm the fact that within 31 years after Jesus's
death, Christians were dying for their faith. From the
writings of Pliny the Yonger, Martial, Epictetus, and
Marcus Aurelius, it is clear that the believers were
voluntarily submitting to torture and death rather than
renounce their religion. This suffering is abundantly

attested in Christian writings as well. Christ had been killed for what he said; the apostles could expect the same treatment. Jesus's predictions in the gospels of sufferings for his followers were either real predictions come true or were put into his mouth because persecution had in fact come about. In Acts, the sufferings of Christians is soberly reported without extravagance. The epistles abound with references to persecutions and exhortations to steadfastness. In the early writings of Clement, Hermas, Polycarp, and Ignatius, we find mentioned the sufferings of the early believers historically confirmed.

It is equally clear that it was for a miraculous story that these Christians were suffering.[629] After all, the only thing that could convince these early Christians that Jesus was the Messiah was that they thought there was something supernatural about him. The gospels are a miraculous story, and we have no other story handed down to us than that contained in the gospels. Josephus's much disputed testimony can only confirm, not contradict, the gospel accounts. The letters of Barnabas and Clement refer to Jesus's miracles and resurrection. Polycarp mentions the resurrection of Christ, and Irenaeus relates that he had heard Polycarp tell of Jesus's miracles. Ignatius speaks of the resurrection. Quadratus reports that persons were still living who had been healed by Jesus. Justin Martyr mentions the miracles of Christ. No relic of a non-miraculous story exists. That the original story should be lost and another replace it goes beyond any known example of corruption of even oral tradition, not to speak of the experience of written transmission. Moreover, the rites and rituals

known to be practiced by the early Christians come
right out of the New Testament documents, which
demonstrates that it was these narratives that the
early Christians had received. Furthermore, it is
clear from the gospels themselves that the Christian
story was already well-known and that the gospels were
not originating something new. These facts show that
the story in the gospels was in substance the same
story which Christians had at the beginning. This
means, for example, that the resurrection of Jesus was
always a part of this story. Were we to stop here,
remarks Paley, we have a circumstance unparalleled in
history: that in the reign of Tiberius Caesar a
certain number of persons set about establishing a new
religion, in the propagation of which they voluntarily
submitted to great dangers, sufferings, and labors, all
for a miraculous story which they proclaimed wherever
they went, and that the resurrection of a dead man,
whom they had accompanied during his lifetime, was an
integral part of this story.

Since it has been already abundantly proved that
the accounts of the gospels do stem from their
apostolic authors, Paley concludes, then the story must
be true. For the apostles could not be deceivers. He
asks,

> Would men in such circumstances pretend to have
> seen what they never saw; assert facts which they
> had no knowledge of; go about lying to teach
> virtue; and, though not only convinced of Christ's
> being an imposter, but having seen the success of
> his imposture in his crucifixion, yet persist in
> carrying on; and so persist, as to bring upon
> themselves, for nothing, and with full knowledge
> of the consequence, enmity and hatred, danger and
> death?[630]

The question is merely rhetorical, for the absurdity of

the hypothesis of deceit is all too clear.

A second popular argument against the apostles' being deceivers was (2) the evidence of the disciples' character precludes their being liars. Ditton notes:[631] (a) The proclamation of the resurrection was frequent, public, solemn, and devout. (b) The apostles were men of unquestioned moral uprightness. (c) The disciples were simple, common men, not cunning deceivers. (d) They had absolutely no worldly interest in view in preaching this doctrine. (e) They had been raised in a religion vastly different from that which they preached. Especially foreign was the notion of the death and resurrection of the Jewish Messiah. (f) The Jewish laws against deceit, especially forgery and false testimony, were very severe. (g) The disciples were obviously sincere about what they proclaimed. Now in view of these facts, Ditton asks bluntly, why not believe the testimony of these men?

Other arguments include (3) the hypothesis of a conspiracy among the disciples is ridiculous. Vernet thinks it inconceivable that one of the disciples would suggest to the others that they say their Master was risen when he and they both knew exactly the contrary to be true.[632] How could he possibly rally his bewildered colleagues into so detestable a project? And are we then to believe these men would stand before judges declaring the truth of this product of their imaginations? Houtteville maintains that the disciples could never have invented nor carried out a conspiracy of such unmanageable proportions as would be necessary to fake the resurrection.[633] Ditton asserts that had there been a fraud, it would have been detected by the disciples' enemies, who had great interest and requisite power to expose any falsehood.[634] The common experience of the world shows that such intrigues are inevitably exposed where the chances of doing so are much less than in the case of the resurrection. (4) The gospels were in such temporal and geographical proximity to the events themselves that it was almost impossible to fabricate events. Moreover, the record could be checked by any one. Were the gospel authors inventing stories, they would never have made them of such a nature that their truth could be so easily investigated and confirmed or disconfirmed.[635] The fact that the disciples proclaimed the resurrection in Jerusalem itself a few weeks after the crucifixion and that their enemies were silent shows that what they proclaimed was true; for the disciples could never have preached the resurrection under these circumstances if it had never occurred.[636] (5) The theft of the body from the tomb by the disciples was not possible. Ditton states that the Jews had the ability (through the agency of the guard) to prevent the body's being stolen; either they took advantage of this or they did not. If not, why not? It was in their interest and power to do so. Hence, the disciples could not have stolen the corpse had they wanted to, on account of the guard. Furthermore, the story of their stealing the body while the guard was asleep is ridiculous, since sleeping men can bear no witness as to the identity of the robbers. To this Houtteville adds that the disciples could never have stolen the body without waking the guard.[637] Nor could the disciples have persuaded someone else to steal the corpse, for they were too poor to offer any bribe and too prudent to trust anyone else with this secret.[638] Ditton concludes that a Deist must believe: (a) that twelve poor fishermen were able to change the world through a

plot laid so deep that no one has ever been able to
discern where the cheat lay, (b) that these men
divested themselves of the pursuit of happiness and
ventured into poverty, torments, and persecutions all
for nothing, (c) that dispirited men should suddenly
grow so resolute as to force the sepulchre and steal
the body, (d) that in the theft they should take the
time to nicely fold the grave clothes prior to
departure, and (e) that these imposters should furnish
the world with the greatest system of morality that
ever was.[639]   (6) Even the enemies of the Christians
acknowledged Jesus's resurrection. The Jews did not
publicly deny the disciples' allegation concerning the
bribing of the guard. Had this allegation been false,
the normal reaction would have been to openly denounce
and refute it.[640]   (7) The change in the disciples
shows that they were absolutely convinced Jesus had
risen from the dead. They went from the deepest doubts
to a certainty of such height that they boldly
proclaimed the resurrection openly and suffered for it
bravely.[641]   (8) The disciples were convinced of the
resurrection despite every predisposition to the
contrary and every sceptical doubt.[642]

These considerations combine to make the
hypothesis of deceit simply out of the question. But
if the disciples were neither deceivers nor deceived,
then it becomes impossible to deny that what they wrote
in the gospels is true. Therefore, the resurrection of
Jesus must be a historical fact.

The origin and growth
of the church

But in addition to this, the Christian defenders

of the resurrection argue that apart from the
resurrection the origin and growth of the Christian
church cannot be adequately explained. Suppose, says
Vernet, that no resurrection or miracles ever occurred:
how could a dozen men, poor, coarse, and apprehensive,
turn the world upside down?[643] If Jesus did not rise
from the dead, states Ditton, then either we must
believe that a small, unlearned band of deceivers
overcame the powers of the world and preached an
incredible doctrine over the face of the whole earth,
which received this fiction as the sacred truth of God;
or else, be they not deceivers but enthusiasts, we must
believe that these extremists, carried by the impetus
of extravagant fancy, managed to spread a falsity which
statesmen and philosophers, as well as the common
people, embraced as sober truth.[644] According to
Houtteville, without the miracles and resurrection, two
facts cannot be explained:[645] (1) Twelve men went out
preaching the good news of what they had seen and
heard, and in less than two centuries the world had
been changed: "Il étoit Idolatre, & le voilà
Chrétien." (2) Great numbers of educated men who lived
during the sub-apostolic period went steadfastly to
martyrdom for the truth of what they had received.
Thus, the old argument from the origin and growth of
Christianity found an important place in the eighteenth
century apologetic, too.

Refutation of objections

The privacy of Jesus's appearances
        Finally, step four, objections to the historicity
of the resurrection are unsound. One typical objection
that had to be answered was that Jesus only appeared to

his disciples, not publicly. Ditton remarks that this
objection is intended to imply either that Jesus did
not rise at all or that the proof of his resurrection
would have been much stronger had he risen publicly.[646]
But if the first is implied, then one must refute all
the evidence that he <u>did</u> rise and provide an alternative explanation, which has not been forthcoming. If
the second is intended, then the answer is that an
infinitely wise God, whom the Deists acknowledge, knows
what sort of appearances are best. Furthermore, the
evidence for the resurrection is no less perspicuous or
convincing than that from natural revelation, allowed
by every Deist. And had Jesus appeared publicly, we
today should still be dependent on the same sort of
evidence that we already have: written testimony. The
fact that the Deists deny the multitude of public
miracles performed by Jesus, which were never denied in
any early writings of unbelievers, shows that they
would still reject the resurrection, even had it
occurred publicly as well. At any rate, the objection
is somewhat beside the point: the issue is whether the
evidence we <u>have</u> proves that Jesus rose from the dead.
The Deists have failed to offer any convincing
alternative to the resurrection. In answer to the same
objection, Vernet believes that, judging from the Jews'
rejection of Christ's miracles, had Jesus appeared to
them, they would have explained it away as an
imposture.[647] And, Vernet asks, would it have really
made that much difference historically had four more
Pharisees come to faith as opposed to one Apostle Paul?
Vernet explains that Jesus appeared to his own
primarily to commission them to carry the gospel to the
world. To this Sherlock adds that others outside the
apostolic circle did see Jesus risen (Lk 24.33; Acts

1.21-22; I Cor 15.6).[648]   He also notes that Jesus had
pronounced woes upon the Jews and declared that they
would see him no more until they were better disposed
to receive him (Mt 23.39).   He and Vernet concur that
the objection knows no logical stopping point; if Jesus
should have appeared to the Jews in Jerusalem, why not
also in Nazareth and Capernaum, and so forth, to all
nations of all ages?[649]   Houtteville seeks to turn the
objection back upon the Deist: why is God's existence
not so plain to all that no one could deny it?[650]   The
answer is that we must not complain of want of more
evidence, but profit from that which we have, which is
sufficient to convince reasonable men.   In the same way
the evidence for the resurrection is sufficient.   The
facts concerning the resurrection have positive
evidential value; what they could have been, but are
not, does not nullify what they are.   Similarly
Sherlock states that it is unreasonable to sit down and
imagine what sort of evidence would please us and then
make this an objection to facts which are well
established.[651]

The inconsistencies in the
resurrection narratives

     One of the thorniest problems for the proponents
of the historical argument for the resurrection was the
obvious discrepancies in the resurrection narratives.
In this connection it is interesting to follow the
debate that succeeded Sherlock's Tryal of the
Witnesses.   When the Tryal had gone through ten
printings, a refutation appeared entitled The
Resurrection of Jesus Considered by Peter Annet,[652] a
pamphlet which Leland pronounced to be "one of the

boldest and openest attacks that was ever made upon
that grand article of the Christian faith, the
resurrection of our Lord Jesus Christ."[653] A rather
low-brow work employing the arguments of the village
atheist,[654] Annet's book nevertheless raises a few
important objections to the historical reliability of
the gospel accounts of the resurrection.[655] For
example, Annet argues that Jesus's predictions of the
resurrection were probably written back into the text
by the disciples.[656] He observes that although Jesus
is said to have clearly predicted his resurrection
privately to his disciples five times, never once did
he do so publicly. Only the vague "sign of Jonah"
saying (Mt 27.63) was delivered in the hearing of the
Pharisees. The upshot of this is that the disciples
should have anticipated Jesus's resurrection and the
Pharisees not. But according to the accounts, the
exact opposite is true: the disciples had absolutely
no inkling that Jesus would rise from the dead, while
the Jewish leaders were so well-informed thereof that
they asked Pilate for a guard to prevent a fraudulent
fulfillment of Jesus's prediction. The implication
would seem to be that Jesus made no predictions of his
resurrection at all. In that case, the Matthean story
of the guard at the tomb must be false; indeed, none of
the other gospel writers mention it, and it appears to
be an interpolation. Even at face value, the story is
ridiculous: surely the Jewish leaders could have
invented a better excuse than that the guard fell
asleep! And had the guard actually been so terrified
as to become as dead men, could a bribe really have
shut them up from telling what actually happened?
Annet does not draw the conclusion that since the story
of the guard is false, the disciples probably stole the

body; he simply drops the point here and does not
explain how (or if) the tomb became empty. His second
major contribution is an attempt to discount the
resurrection appearances by exhibiting the manifold
contradictions between them.[657] The first appearance
to Mary is contradictory with regard to the persons,
the place and time, the manner, and the message
delivered. The second appearance on the road to Emmaus
is doubtful because the travellers did not recognize
their companion as Jesus. The third appearance to all
the apostles is contradictory as to time and place,
among other factors. Fourthly, the appearances
mentioned by John and Paul either contradict or are
unconfirmed by the synoptics and are therefore of no
consequence. Fifthly, the accounts (or lack thereof)
of the ascension are mutually contradictory. Annet
concludes that no man would wager five shillings upon
such evidence as is thought material enough to support
the resurrection of Christ.[658]

Among the many who responded to Annet's objections
was Charles Moss, whose The Evidence of the Resurrection Cleared, &c (1744)[659] was revised by Thomas
Sherlock and became known as The Sequel of the Tryal of
the Witnesses of the Resurrection.[660] Against Annet,
he argues that some of Jesus's predictions of his
resurrection were probably made to larger bodies of
disciples (Mt 16.13; Mk 8.27; Lk 9.18 and Mt 17.19; Mk
9.29) as opposed to others made specifically to the
Twelve (Mt 20.17ff; Mk 10.32ff; Lk 17.31ff and Mt
26.20; Mk 14.17) and that it was from members of this
wider group that the Jewish leaders could have learned
of Jesus's prediction.[661] Moreover, the sign of Jonah
saying in light of other sayings like Jn 7.33, 34
provide clear enough indication of the resurrection.[662]

Or again, it is not impossible that Judas told the
Jewish leaders of Jesus's prediction of his rising
again issued at the Last Supper.[663]   Thus, it is
possible that the priests and Pharisees should know of
Jesus's prediction while the disciples failed to
understand its import.   This would account for the
setting of the guard at the tomb.   That only Matthew
records the story in no way implies that the other
evangelists contradict it.[664]   Since Matthew's gospel
was published in Judea with a Jewish audience in mind,
any falsehood would have been immediately detected, as
many were probably still living who knew of this
transaction.[665] As to the behavior of the soldiers, we
must remember they had no Jewish conceptions of the
Messiah or Israel's God, and therefore they would be
ready to accept easy money to report a false story.[666]
As for the chief priests, of course they acted
foolishly and wickedly, but do not men ever so act?[667]

Moss then attempts to show how the resurrection
narratives actually complement each other.[668]   If we
take Matthew's account through verse 8 and Mark's
account to the separate appearance to Mary Magdalene,
then the Synoptics are consistent, Luke simply omitting
the appearance.   If we take John as picking up where
Luke leaves off, then it is evident that Mary went
twice to the tomb.   Luke records only Mary's first
visit and ends with Peter's setting out, where John
begins.   Matthew and Mark through verse 8 also record
only the first visit; what happened in verses 9 and
following occurred at her second visit recorded by
John.   As to the time of this appearance, it may be
that the women having seen the angels went to find the
disciples; finding only Peter and John, Mary and
whoever was with her returned with them to the tomb

before having found the other disciples, intending to
find them later.   Thus, Matthew might record the
appearance as occurring while they were still engaged
in carrying the first message.[669]   At any rate,
Matthew's description may give only a general order of
the events.[670]   This description of the appearances is
confirmed by the Emmaus account, for it reports the
first visit of the women and that of Peter and John,
but knows of no appearance to Mary, the travellers'
having left Jerusalem before this took place.[671]   This
shows that Matthew's account actually contains two
separate incidents not simultaneously reported;
otherwise the two going to Emmaus would have known of
it.   The difficulty that John mentions only Mary
whereas Matthew records that Jesus appeared to more
than one is dissolved by Mary's words in John, We know
not where they have laid him.   Hence, the gospel
accounts are not contradictory.   Moss furnishes this
order of the appearances: (1) to Mary Magdalene and
other women, (2) to the two disciples going to Emmaus,
(3) to Peter the same day, (4) to the Eleven the
evening of the same day, (5) to the Eleven with Thomas
eight days later, (6) to the disciples at the Sea of
Tiberius, (7) to the disciples in Galilee mentioned
only by Matthew (but cf. Acts 1.4), (8) to the
disciples in Jerusalem before the ascension.[672]   The
appearance to the 500 mentioned by Paul was probably in
Galilee.[673]   Thus, each separate gospel account, though
abbreviated, is entirely consistent with the synthetic
picture of what probably occurred.

     Yet another refutation of Annet's objections was
Samuel Chandler's The Witnesses of the Resurrection of
Jesus Christ Re-examined (1744).   He maintains that the
disciples understood the meaning of Jesus's predictions

that he should die and rise again, but that they, like
the Pharisees, could not understand how this should
come to pass, since it contradicted fundamentally what
the Jews believed concerning the Messiah.[674]   Because
of their pre-conceptions, they could not accept or
believe Jesus's predictions, and thus, neither the
disciples   nor   the   Pharisees   expected   Jesus's
resurrection. But the Jewish leaders, amply warned by
the sign of Jonah sayings, set a watch at the tomb to
prevent any exhumation and faked resurrection.   The
resurrection's having occurred, the Jews had no
recourse but lying and bribery; the lie they invented
was as good as any, since to claim that the disciples
had come with clubs and swords and scattered the guards
would have been even stupider, there being no wounds
and bruises to show for the fracas.[675]   Chandler
proposes a somewhat different reconciliation of the
resurrection narratives than Moss.[676]   Taking John's
account of the appearance to Mary to be dislocated, he
argues that when the women visited the tomb and saw the
angels, Mary lingered behind, whereupon Jesus appeared
to her alone. She then ran to rejoin her companions,
and as they were going to tell the disciples, Jesus
appeared to the group, as related by Matthew.   Peter
and John upon hearing the women's report then run to
the tomb, as recorded by John and alluded to by Luke.
Chandler summarizes the order of appearances so: (1)
to Mary alone, (2) to the company of women, (3) to
Peter, (4) to the Emmaus disciples, (5) to the Eleven
without Thomas, (6) to the entire Eleven, (7) to the
disciples in Galilee at the Sea of Tiberius, (8) to the
Eleven on the mount in Galilee, (9) to the 500
brethren, probably also in Galilee, (10) to James, (11)
to a broad company of disciples (Lk 24.46-51; Acts

1.4-9; I Cor 15.7), (12) to Stephen, and (13) to Paul.

Undoubtedly the most extravagant attempt at harmonization of the resurrection narratives in answer to Annet's charges of inconsistency was that undertaken by Gilbert West in his Observations on the History and Evidence of the Resurrection (1747). He presents this order of events:[677] (1) Mary Magdalene, the other Mary, and Salome come to the tomb early (i.e., before the time agreed upon with Joanna and the others) to survey the tomb and the stone. (2) Seeing the stone rolled back, Mary Magdalene runs to inform Peter and John, leaving her companions to meet Joanna. (3) Mary and Salome enter the sepulchre, see the angel, and flee without speaking to anyone. (4) Peter and John arrive to inspect the tomb. (5) After they depart, Mary Magdalene lingers behind, sees two angels in the sepulchre, and then beholds Jesus himself. (6) After this Jesus appears to the other Mary and Salome still fleeing from the tomb. (7) Joanna and the other women arrive at the tomb with spices for the body and find the two angels. (8) Joanna runs and tells the now assembled disciples, who dismiss her story; but Peter goes again to the tomb and seeing only the grave clothes departs. (9) Jesus appears to two disciples on the road to Emmaus who had heard only Joanna's report. (10) Before they return to Jerusalem, Jesus also appears to Peter. (11) Upon their return, Jesus appears to the disciples, rebuking them for not believing the report of the two from Emmaus.

The limited conversion
of the Jews

Paley attempts to answer the objection that most

of the disciples' contemporaries were not converted, thereby implying that the miracles and resurrection did not take place. He makes a distinction between the reactions of the Jews and the heathen.[678] He points out that for a Jew, although he might recognize the reality of miracles, there was still a good way to go before he could persuade himself to recognize Jesus as the Messiah. The gospels themselves are filled with examples of Jews who admitted Jesus's miracles, but refused to bow the knee to him. How can this be explained? Paley names two factors: (1) the expected Jewish Messiah was utterly unlike Jesus, and (2) the Jews firmly believed in the reality and agency of demons in the world, by which they could explain away Jesus's miracles. And as for the Gentile reaction to Christianity, it generally followed the pattern of contempt prior to investigation. Christianity shared at first in the low esteem given to Judaism. The relative silence of Tacitus and Pliny concerning what was then widespread Christianity can only be accounted for as the result of ignorance and apathy. With these obstacles in mind, we can appreciate how amazing it was that this new faith did in fact spread so rapidly throughout the empire.

The nature of the
resurrection body

A final objection is handled by Vernet.[679] It sometimes appears that in the gospels the disciples saw only a spectre and not a truly resurrected body of Jesus. Vernet explains that the resurrection body, while preserving a sort of identity and likeness to the mortal body, is nevertheless a glorified body with capacities far exceeding those of our present bodies. But Jesus was no mere spectre, for he gave clear signs of corporeality to the disciples.

Summary

In summary, then, against their Deist apponents, who denied the special revelation of God in the physical universe, the orthodox thinkers argued that both internal and external evidence confirms the authenticity of the gospels, so that the reports we have of the resurrection stem from the apostles themselves or the apostolic circle. Therefore, if these accounts are not true, then their authors and the disciples were either deceivers or deceived. But the perspicuity of the events of the resurrection makes it impossible for the disciples to have been misled into thinking that Jesus had been raised from the tomb when in fact he had not. And it is equally futile to try to dismiss the apostles as base charlatans who had conspired together to invent the whole affair. Therefore, the accounts must be true, and Jesus did rise from the dead and appear to his disciples, leaving an empty grave behind him. This fact alone allows us to account for the otherwise unexplainable phenomena of the origin, spread, and steadfastness of primitive Christianity. Objections to the evidence for the resurrection can be refuted; in particular the resurrection narratives can be shown to be complementary, not contradictory, in nature. Therefore, the resurrection of Jesus is firmly established as a historical fact.

The argumentation of the eighteenth century was thus strongly marked by a historical approach to the events of the New Testament. The Christian authors were fond of emphasizing that the principles of historiography which they employed were the same used by any historian. The epistemolgical framework within which they built their case was the demonstration that the events of the gospels were on a level with the ordinary events of history, so that the dilemma arises: either accept the events narrated in the gospels or reject the record of all history. They insisted on treating the Scriptures as one would ordinary historical documents; they made no appeal in their argument to the divine authority of Scripture. Gone, too, was even the scholastic framework of the "signs of credibility:" though the eighteenth century thinkers retained miracle and prophecy as their principal evidences, they at least aspired to approach the problem of the miracles and resurrection inductively. Rather than take Scripture as a whole and adduce signs on behalf of it, these thinkers tried to prove that the evidence shows that the miracles and resurrection occurred, further that there is no convincing natural explanation for these events, and that therefore their cause must be supernatural; given the doctrinal context authorized by these acts, their cause must be divine. Now it must be admitted that probably most of these men personally believed in the divine origin and authority of Scripture--they would probably have accepted almost any harmonization rather than admit an error in the gospels--but the point is that epistemologically this belief played no role in the argument. It only affected perhaps the rigor with which they carried it out.

Because their Deist opponents accepted only natural revelation and rejected all special revelation,

the orthodox could not appeal to Scripture authority to
found the Christian religion, but rather proceeded from
the common ground of natural reason in its a posteriori
function.   This resulted in an apologetic by the facts
for special revelation.   The orthodox as well as the
Deists were products of the Age of Reason, and most
shared the common presupposition that reason and
revelation cannot contradict each other.   But even in
France, where the contenu of the faith was reckoned to
appear contrary to reason, it was staunchly insisted
that the contenant of the faith was nevertheless not
only in accord with the empirical facts, but could also
be established by the facts.   Hence, aposteriori
natural reason provided the basis for Christian belief.
The orthodox maintained that the same reason which
leads one to belief in a Creator on the basis of the
evidence of design in nature also demonstrates that He
has revealed Himself in the world on the basis of the
evidence of miracles in history.   In the former
instance, a posteriori reason constructs a
philosophical proof, and in the latter a historical
proof, each compelling according to the principles of
the subject matter involved.

The Decline of the Historical Argument
for the Resurrection

Paley's case for Christianity in his View of the
Evidences constitutes the high water mark of the
historical apologetic for Christianity based on
evidences like Jesus's miracles and resurrection.
During the nineteenth century this evidentialist
approach dramatically recedes and almost disappears.
Certainly it loses altogether the place of prominence

that it enjoyed during the eighteenth century, and it
is difficult to find a significant and influential
nineteenth century figure arguing for the truth of the
Christian religion on the grounds of the historical
evidence for the resurrection. Although our center of
interest lies in the arguments employed by the
eighteenth century apologists for the resurrection, it
would nevertheless be worthwhile to say something
concerning the final outcome of the Deist controversy
and the factors which served to undermine the
traditional apologetic.

The Advance of Biblical Criticism

The late 18th century
crisis in German theology

If in England the Deist controversy subsided and
in France was cut short by the catastrophe of the
Revolution, then in Germany it was transferred to a
higher plane. There is a direct link between Deism and
the advance in biblical criticism which began in
Germany in the latter half of the eighteenth
century.[680] Prior to the beginning of the eighteenth
century two factors predominated in the shape of German
religious life. First, from the passing of the Formula
of Concord (1577) and the Synod of Dort (1618) German
theology took the form of a sort of Protestant
scholasticism based on the authority of Holy Scripture.
The system was characterized by a rigid view of
biblical verbal inspiration and by an extreme
authoritarianism. Second, there arose following the
close of the Thirty Years' War in reaction to dead
Lutheran orthodoxy a revival of personal religious

experience in the movement of Pietism. Emphasizing the
devotional, practical side to Christian piety in
opposition to mere intellectual assent to doctrinal
orthodoxy, Pietism flourished as a movement under the
leadership of Philipp Jacob Spener (1635-1705) and his
successor August Herrmann Francke (1663-1727).
According to Tholuck, by 1750 there were as a result of
the influence of this movement more pious pastors and
laymen in Germany than ever before.[681]

By this time, however, the factors that were to
bring crisis into German theology and religious life
had already begun to be introduced:[682]

1.   The influence of Wolffian philosophical
theology: Standing in the rationalist tradition of
Leibniz, Christian Wolff (1679-1754) attempted to cast
his mentor's philosophy into a rigid geometrical system
in which the whole of cosmology, psychology, and
natural theology might be deduced a priori from the
twin principles of the law of contradiction and the
principle of sufficient reason. Wolff founded theology
upon reason, and though he did not attempt to deduce
any theological truths beyond the existence of God, he
did hold that the principles requisite for the ethical
life might be established on the basis of reason alone.
The influence of Wolff's philosophy was two-fold.
First his genius for systematization and penchant for
a priori deductivism inspired the formulation of
dogmatic theology in imitation of his model. Noack
points out that after 1740 all candidates in theology
were by royal decree recommended to study Wolff's
philosophy.[683] The end result was that theology
became arid and unreal, detached from the empirical
world. Second, his rationalism tended to undercut
those truths of theology not deducible from first

principles alone, as Tholuck comments:

> Much more detrimental was the influence of the
> distinction reintroduced especially through Wolff
> between natural and revealed religion, and
> particularly with the stipulation that the former
> can be demonstrated while the latter can only be
> believed. What was more natural than that one
> should stick with what could be demonstrated,
> especially when the English Deists then came along
> and showed that what was to be believed by and
> large was unbelievable.[684]

Wolff, who was Professor of Philosophy at Halle, so
outraged the Pietist sentiments there that they secured
his dismissal from the university by Friedrich I in
1723. Their victory was merely temporary, however, and
upon the accession of Friedrich II Wolff was called
back to Halle in 1740. In the meantime Wolff's
rationalism had become pervasive in German universities, and when Johann Semler came to Halle to study
theology it was the spirit of rationalism that he
imbibed.

     2. The influence of English Deism: Although the
threat of Deism was noticed in Germany as early as 1680
in Kortholt's De tribus impostoribus, this threat did
not become a reality until the translation of Tindal's
work in 1741, as we have seen. Tindal's work produced
a general consternation in German theological thought,
which was only augmented by the scores of refutations
issued against him. Gawlick believes that Tindal's
greatest impact in Germany may have been upon Reimarus,
who incorporated many arguments of the English Deists
into his Apologie and seems most closely related
intellectually to Tindal.[685] In any case, Brandl has
demonstrated the influence of English Deism upon
Reimarus, for Reimarus mentions by name Collins,
Woolston, Morgan, Shaftesbury, and Hume.[686] When

Lessing published portions of Reimarus's work between
1774-78, he brought the inflammatory thought of English
Deism into public view, earning himself the reputation
of Brandstifter. Furthermore, English Deism stimulated
the development of German biblical criticism.[687]
According to Salvatorelli, the new theology which
sprang up in Germany under the leadership of J.S.
Semler did so under the influence of Deism.[688]   It was
through S.J. Baumgarten, the chronicler of the course
of Deism in his Nachrichten von einer Hallischen
Bibliothek (1748-51) and Semler's teacher at Halle,
that Semler became open to Deist influences.[689]
Salvatorelli explains the result:

> Semler's distinction [between the essential and
> permanent element in religion and the formulation
> of it, varying with time and place], evidently
> suggested to him by the efforts of the deists to
> find the original nucleus of the rational and
> moral essence of Christianity, represents the
> first development in an historical direction of
> the rationalistic method of deism. From this came
> a radical transformation of the conception of
> inspiration and finally the new method of
> conceiving of the New Testament as formed
> gradually from diverse and even opposite elements
> blended into a final synthesis.[690]

J.D. Michaelis, the other seminal figure in German New
Testament criticism, also absorbed Deist influences
through his sojourn in England.[691]   Locke had a
profound influence in Germany, and Baumgarten, Semler,
Ernesti, and Michaelis all believed that much could be
learned from him in dogmatics, exegesis, and
philosophy.[692]   The Deist controversy, coming on the
heels of Wolffian rationalism, helped to shatter the
structure of German orthodoxy, fragmenting it into
schools of thought spanning the theological spectrum.

3. The influence of French free-thought: We have

already noted the influence of French Deism and of the
French free-thinkers whom Friedrich gathered at the
Prussian court. Though not as significant as English
thinkers, these men of enlightenment helped to promote
a spirit of scepticism and incredulity in Germany,
especially concerning the miraculous.[693]

These three influences helped to produce a crisis
in German theological thought during the second half of
the eighteenth century. As we have seen, Deism
consisted primarily in an attack upon revealed religion
in favor of the natural religion of reason. In Germany
such an attack was particularly acutely felt because of
the historically dogmatic attitude toward the
inspiration and authority of Scripture and the
pietistic distrust of reason unguided by revelation.
One might respond to these attacks on Scripture by
defending the reliability of the biblical accounts;
such was the procedure of those who adopted a
historical apologetic for the Christian faith. But
others, who felt more deeply the force of the Deist
objections, had either to abandon the Christian
religion or else radically re-interpret its relation to
the biblical narratives so that the truth of
Christianity was not bound up with the historical truth
of the narratives; it was out of this group that modern
New Testament criticism evolved.

The fundamental hermeneutical change

Neologians and Rationalists

This latter group of scholars is usually referred
to as Neologians, proponents of Neologie, or the new
theology. They adhered like the orthodox to the
reality of God's revelation, but they broke with the

traditional view of the verbal inspiration of the
Scriptures. Instead, they took a critical approach to
the Bible, refusing to accept as historical anything
contrary to reason or as inspired anything that
offended one's moral sense. They generally rejected
like the Deists miraculous elements in biblical
narratives, since these were contrary to the order of
nature. Refusing to bring a dogmatic interpretive
framework to Scripture, they claimed to discover
divinely inspired truths inductively from Scripture.

Sometimes the Neologians are classed under a more
all-embracing description as Rationalists. Here,
however, clarification would be helpful. The term
"Rationalist" as it is used of German biblical
criticism at the end of the eighteenth century has no
inherent connection with what I have called
philosophical rationalism and theological rationalism.
A defender of orthodoxy might well be a philosophical
rationalist in the Leibnizian tradition and/or a
theological rationalist after the manner of John Locke.
"Rationalism" as it is applied to German theology and
biblical criticism during the late eighteenth and early
nineteenth centuries is not an epistemological term,
but is an umbrella description used to cover a whole
spectrum of thinkers chiefly characterized by their
opposition to the miraculous in Scripture and history.
In this sense, a Rationalist was anybody who opposed
Supernaturalism, which affirmed that the miraculous
events described in the Bible were literal, divine
interventions in history. Under such a negative
characterization, Rationalists might be called Deists,
but generally such a designation would be thought
misleading, since it ignores the peculiar flavor of
German Rationalism. For this movement was, after a

fashion, actually an attempt to come to grips with
Deism and defend Christianity in light of its attacks.
Rationalism was not a lay movement, as was Deism, but
the response of scholars within the biblical and
theological disciplines to preserve Christian belief
while adopting a critical approach to the Scriptures.
Farrar explains,

> This form of rationalism differed from the English
> deism and French naturalism, in not regarding the
> Bible as fabulous in character, and the device of
> priestcraft; but only denied the supernatural. By
> them the apostles had been regarded as imposters;
> and scripture was not only not received as divine,
> but not even respected as an ordinary historical
> record; whereas rationalism was intended as a
> defence against this view. It denied only the
> revealed character of scripture, and treated it as
> an ordinary history; and, distinguishing broadly
> between the fact related and the judgement on the
> fact, sought to separate the two, and explained
> away the supernatural element, such as miracles,
> as being orientalisms in the narrative, adapted to
> an infant age, which an enlightened age must[694]
> translate into the language of ordinary events.

So although Rationalists adopted the Deists'
anti-supernaturalism, it would be unfair to classify
German Rationalists as Deists tout simple, for they
probably perceived themselves for the most part as
defenders of the Christian religion. Nevertheless, it
must be admitted that what some more extreme
Rationalists conceived Christianity to be differed
little in substance from the Deism of, say, Rousseau,
and it is in this sense that one can properly speak of
the Rationalists as the heirs of Deism. A closely
related term would be "naturalism," which is again a
broad term used to designate all those who believed in
the sufficiency of natural as opposed to revealed
religion.[695] Naturalists are sometimes classified as

philosophical or theological. The former denied any
revealed religion whatsoever and were thus Deists; the
latter held to revelation, but regarded it as a
republication of nature and thus generally coincided
with Rationalists. A thinker could therefore be called
a Rationalist insofar as he affirmed the sufficiency of
natural religion. But it would be possible to hold to,
say, theological Naturalism and yet deny Rationalism, a
position to which Semler ostensibly retreated. As I
shall use these terms, then, we have a spectrum of
theological beliefs in late eighteenth-early nineteenth
century Germany, ranging from the orthodox Supernaturalism on one extreme to Deism at the other, and spanning
a wide middle field of Rationalists and Naturalists in
which Neology stands between orthodoxy and the more
extreme forms of Rationalism and philosophical
Naturalism.

Now what the Neologians perceived was that if
Christianity was to be rescued from the Deist assault,
one had to somehow cut loose the truth of the Christian
religion from the beleaguered biblical document. Thus,
as Hans Frei argues in his study The Eclipse of the
Biblical Narrative, there occurred in the late
eighteenth century a radical change in the
hermeneutical approach to the Scriptures.[696] Prior to
the Deist controversy, virtually everyone identified
the "history-likeness" of the text with the actual
historicity of the text. Thus, a debate over the
historicity of a text was essentially a dispute over
genre: is the narrative meant to be a historical-type
text or is it really an allegory whose true meaning
transcends the historical form? Once one allowed that
the account was a historical-type text, its meaning and
historicity were given. No one dared to maintain that

the text was of the historical genre, but nevertheless
false--that is, until the Deist critique. Men such as
Collins, Woolston, Annet, Chubb, and Reimarus were bold
enough to argue or imply that the factual, historical
claim was the true meaning of the biblical narratives
and that they are false, so that rightly understanding
the stories was equivalent to knowing that they are
factually erroneous and religiously meaningless, if not
nefarious. Now one of the chief differences between
the English Deists and the German Rationalists of the
eighteenth century is that the German scholars almost
to a man held the Bible, and especially the New
Testament, to be a rich embodiment of religious truth.
Only Reimarus despised the Bible as a valuable source
of religious insight. Since by that time the
"spiritual" interpretation of Scripture had lost all
credit, it became incumbent upon the Rationalists, if
one was not to slide into Deism, to establish a new
hermeneutical approach to Scripture that would not
violate the historical genre of the text but would
preserve intact the religious truth expressed therein.
They had to detach the broader religious meaning of the
text from the historicity of the events related.
Hence, the Deists found themselves opposed
overwhelmingly on all points of the theological
spectrum, by Supernaturalists who held to the
historical meaning of the text and its truthfulness and
by various shades of Rationalists who sometimes denied
the historicity of the events but affirmed the
religious meaningfulness of the text. The Rationalists
thus sought a middle-ground in the tension between the
positions of Deism and Supernaturalism. All parties
agreed that the Scriptures are in large measure of the
genre of history. Deists argued that the miraculous

events never happened and that therefore Christianity
is false, while the Supernaturalists maintained that
the events in question did occur and that therefore
Christianity is true. The Rationalists would not yield
to either camp, but insisted that whether or not the
events happened, nevertheless Christianity is true.
The religious truth of Christianity transcends the
historical particularity of the events, and instead of
appealing to external evidences, Rationalists appealed
to a leap of faith in the miracle of redemption,
regardless of any corroboration by an investigation of
the life of the actual historical Jesus. These early
biblical critics thus sought to adopt the Deists'
critical attitude toward the text, but were unwilling
to follow them in abandoning the Christian religion.
Frei comments,

> The specter now barely visible on the horizon was
> that important, indeed hitherto central portions
> of the Bible, no matter if they made referential
> sense, did not make abiding religious or moral
> sense at all, so that they are in effect really
> obsolete. And the accounts concerning Jesus as
> Messiah might be among these. What appeared, but
> not even sufficiently distinctly to be noticed by
> anyone except a few Deists who were mostly
> regarded as disgruntled cranks, was the suspicion
> that the accounts mean what they say, but that
> what they say is not an untrue or unverifiable but
> is an insignificant claim as well--except as an
> ancient superstition about miraculous and personal
> divine intervention. That is to say, for
> instance, that the tests concerning unique
> redemption exclusively through Jesus cannot . . .
> be demythologized, because they have no other
> meaning than what they say. And what they say may
> no longer mean anything religiously significant.
> To explicate them properly is to erect a
> formidable barrier to any possible applicative
> sense. That was the impossible option which no
> thinker across the religious spectrum would have
> countenanced then. . .

Unwilling to embrace either Deism or Supernaturalism, the Rationalists attempted to separate the a-historical, religious meaning of the text from the facticity of the events described.

Such an attitude allowed them to criticize the text with impunity and thus advance the science of biblical criticism. For although the Supernaturalists advocated in many instances treating the biblical documents like ordinary history, scarcely any really did so. Thus Johann August Ernesti, for example, championed the historical-grammatical as opposed to dogmatic interpretation of the New Testament, but because of his commitment to biblical inerrancy, he laid down the principle that when contradictions or difficulties in the text appear, then the critic should not treat the Scriptures as he would a human writing, but either infer a lack of insight on his part or attempt a reconciliation.[698] This was the actual, if not admitted, procedure of most of the apologists for Christianity, a procedure which Rationalist critics abandoned without compunction.

Johann Salomo Semler

His view of Scripture

The key figure in the genesis of this new approach was Johann Salomo Semler, whose Abhandlung von freier Untersuchung des Canon (1771) constitutes a turning point in the history of biblical criticism. A conservative Rationalist, or Neologian, Semler preferred to describe himself as a "Christian naturalist", by which he meant that he bound the power of Christianity to its spiritual truths rather than to the external forms of these or those books of the Old

and New Testament.[699]   In order to do this, Semler
distinguished sharply between the moral and the merely
local truths expressed in Scripture. By moral
(moralisch) truths, he did not mean simply ethical
truths, but rather the whole sphere of spiritual
doctrines which have a lasting significance for man.[700]
According to Semler, such concepts as God, Spirit of
God, Kingdom of God, Son of God, Messiah, Christ,
justice of God, sin, grace, faith, redemption,
reconciliation, and new creation are all part of the
essential moral truths of Christianity. Hornig
comments,

> . . . Semler wants to stress by the use of the
> adjective 'moral' that certain concepts signify a
> spiritual reality which cannot without further ado
> be experienced empirically or established through
> the senses. In this sense 'moral' and 'spiritual'
> are for Semler equivalent. According to Semler,
> precisely the moral concepts present an integral
> component of the Christian religion. They mediate
> the power of God and should be proclaimed at all
> times   and   assimilated   in   the   faith   by
> Christians.[701]

These truths possess a universal value and applica-
bility to men of all ages and stand over against those
elements in the Bible which are cultural, relative, and
of purely local interest. The central content of the
Scriptures is Christ's reconciliation of men with God,
and this is not a physical occurence, but a moral,
spiritual reality.[702]
       Now it was Semler's conviction that only these
moral truths can be properly called the Word of God:

> Holy Scripture and Word of God must certainly be
> differentiated because we know the difference. . .
> To the holy scripture, as this historical,
> relative term came to be used among the Jews,
> belong Ruth, Esther, [Ezra,] Song of Songs, etc.,

but to the <u>Word of God</u>, which makes all men in all times wise unto salvation, [to the divine <u>instruction</u> for all men,] not all of these <u>books</u> called <u>holy</u> belong.[703]

Semler justified his distinction between the Word of God and Scripture on the basis of two facts: (1) the uncertainties generated by textual and historical criticism make it evident that the text itself cannot be the Word of God, and (2) not all parts of Scripture proclaim equally the universal, moral truths of Christianity.[704] Only the moral truths contained in the books of Scripture can be said to be the Word of God:

It is incomprehensible to me how it can occur that thoughtful Christians and even teachers, who according to their profession should help salutary knowledge to grow, [even today] can still go astray and always confuse <u>holy books</u> or writings of the Jews and the <u>Word of God</u> or general moral instruction [for all men], which is here and there, not through and through, contained, shared, and clothed therein. Moreover, it is also astonishing that scarcely a few scholars of our time have perceived and taught this and that so many on the contrary want by all means to assert that <u>all books</u> of the Jews and all parts of the same are the pure and simple <u>Word of God</u>![705]

This identification of the Bible with the Word of God Semler simply could not accept. The stories of the twelve tribes of Israel, their wars, the good or bad behavior of the kings, the condition of Judah and Samaria, and so forth, "contain absolutely nothing" of divine import that make these events more significant than the events in the histories of other peoples.[706] Such stories can only be regarded, therefore, as provincial or family histories wherein there lies really nothing of moral significance with regard to the needs of other men.

Since only the moral truths contained in the Bible are the Word of God, Semler held the Scriptures as a whole can no longer be regarded as a divinely inspired revelation. Why should we regard the book of Ruth as inspired, he asked, when it has no moral significance and is just a piece out of the genealogy of David?[707] It has always been presupposed that all of these books and all of their parts have a divine origin and as a revelation of God are intended for all men of all ages. "Dies," writes Semler, "halte ich geradehin für unerweislich. . ."[708] Rather than regard the books of the Bible as parts of a homogeneous whole, it would be better to recognize that the foundation and content of Judaism with all its flaws and obstacles does not constitute the foundation and content of Christianity, so that every Christian in different times and places need not accept these Jewish tales as divine instruction. Against those who use Jesus and the apostles' citation of the Old Testament to prove its divine origin, Semler replies, "The reason why Jesus and the apostles cite such books from time to time to prove and support their teaching among the Jews is mainly this: because the Jews already held these books to be the source of religious truths and furthermore because such citations were useful to Jesus and the apostles' purpose at the time."[709]

This introduces another important element of Semler's view of Scripture: the theory of accommodation.[710] According to Semler, the purely local elements in Scripture represented God or Jesus's accommodation to the then prevailing Jewish thought forms in order to communicate the transcendent moral truths. Hence, Semler insists,

[. . . whether Jesus and the apostles] <u>themselves</u>,
according to their own judgement, <u>according to
their own certain knowledge</u>, [and in order to
support the new Christian teaching generally and
<u>for all men</u>,] ascribed a similar divine origin [to
all the books of the Jews] and at the same time
confirmed them, [according to my honest
judgement,] can not in and of itself be[711]
demonstrated from these <u>allegations</u>.

Semler applied the theory of accommodation equally to
miracle, prophecy, and doctrine. Miracles and
fulfilled prophecy as related in the gospels are
unnecessary, and these stories represent an
accommodation to the Jewish craving for the miraculous.
Semler unequivocally rejected the miraculous element in
Scripture and believed many apparent miracles could now
be explained in scientific terms.[712] For example,
Semler viewed demon possession as most likely epilepsy
and insanity, but he held that Jesus accommodated
himself to the Jewish belief in this matter. Semler,
under the influence of C.G. Heyne, introduces the
concept of mythology as a primitive, pictorial way of
speaking of divine things in anthropomorphic terms as
the explanation for Jewish belief in the devil and
demonic beings.[713] Semler believes that the Synoptic
evangelists accommodate themselves to this mythological
world-view and the Jewish interest in miracles in their
miracle stories. This desire for miracles Semler
identified with the σάρξ and contrasted to it purely
spiritual doctrine, not based on miracles and history,
which was πνεῦμα . But Semler also saw doctrinal
accommodation in the New Testament in the differing
outlook between Jewish-Christian and Gentile-Christian
books and sought to classify the New Testament writing
by this criterion. He played off the more universal
principles of Pauline, Gentile Christianity against the

relative and local, Petrine, Jewish Christianity.
Nevertheless, portions of Paul's letters, he admitted,
such as his use of Stoic wisdom or his expectation of
an imminent return of Christ, represent an
accommodation to his readers and contain nothing for us
today.

Thus, Semler's attitude toward the books of the
New Testament was the same as toward those of the Old.
He does not think it incumbent upon the Christian to
believe that all four gospels are divinely inspired.[714]
As a student and critic of Simon's writings, Semler
would have been aware of the debate between Simon and
Le Clerc over inspiration, and it is interesting that
Semler adopts a similar position to that which Le Clerc
had argued: that historical writing need not be
inspired.[715]   Semler maintains that to write a
historical description of an event no divine
inspiration is required.   Therefore, the Christian
today, who experiences the divine power of the
universal moral truths of Christianity need not be
concerned with the extent of the inspiration of these
historical narratives. Semler believes that the main
reason behind the doctrine of verbal inspiration is
religio-psychological: the believer wants to have an
absolutely certain basis in Scripture for his faith.[716]
But given his view of revelation, Semler feels no such
need. Since the Word of God is not identical with the
historical form of the narrative, the proof that
certain events are unhistorical is irrelevant to divine
truths.   If John 8, for example, were to drop out of
sacred Scripture in its _forma externa_, Semler asserts,
nothing would be lacking in the Word of God.

Semler's view of the canon was the logical
extension of his views on inspiration. He argued that

canonicity was arbitrarily determined in the early
church by church officials on the basis of which books
were publicly read.[717] The idea of a homogeneous canon
equally inspired throughout and universally relevant in
all respects is now obsolete. We must, he emphasizes,
distinguish between the Word or instruction of God and
the collection of books of Jews and Christians which is
called the Holy Scriptures.[718] Therefore, every
Christian is free, indeed, duty-bound, to investigate
the books of the Bible to find for himself the true
Word of God contained therein. There will never be a
universal, unchangeable certainty with regard to the
books in the Bible, but there always remains a general
and unchangeable certainty with regard to the moral
truths of the Christian religion.

"With all these ideas, Semler is the founder of
the historical study of the New Testament," writes
Kümmel; "For him the Bible as a book is no longer
inspired and can therefore be viewed impartially with
the eyes of the historical investigator, without
endangering the Word of God, which he wishes at all
costs to safeguard."[719] By differentiating between the
historicity of the narratives and the universal
religious meaning they contain and by renouncing the
inspiration of the former, Semler charted a new course
for biblical criticism. " . . . with his Abhandlung
von freier Untersuchung des Canon Semler delivered the
fatal wounds to the orthodox teaching of verbal
inspiration and broke the ground for historical-
critical research of the Bible."[720]

His Auseinandersetzung with Reimarus. Given
Semler's rejection of miracles as accommodations to the
Jewish thought-world, it is evident why a historical
apologetic for the resurrection of Jesus could find no

place in his system. It is therefore somewhat
surprising to find that in 1779, after Lessing's
release of the Wolfenbuttel fragments, Semler actually
did write a direct refutation of Reimarus and defended
the resurrection of Christ.[721] By all accounts, Semler
was a personally pious man and had no desire to use his
critical methods to undermine the doctrines of
Christian orthodoxy, as did extremists like Bahrdt.[722]
Thus, he seemed anxious to reaffirm his orthodoxy in
this work. Hornig points out that since Semler held
the death and resurrection of Christ to be part of
Christian Heilsglaube, he had to defend the
resurrection against Reimarus as a real event.[723]

At this point, in order to grasp the significance
of Semler's reply, it would be helpful to exposit in
greater detail Reimarus's case against the resurrection
which was causing all the commotion. Reimarus's
critique of Christianity reflects the influence of
Wolff.[724] According to Wolff, any claimant to
revelation must fulfill two criteria: (1) it must
reveal something not attainable by natural reason, and
(2) it must not be logically contradictory. Reimarus
will accordingly try to show that the resurrection is
naturally explicable and that the biblical evidence for
it is self-contradictory. His full argument was
published by Lessing in two separate fragments, which
must be reunited to see the scope and context of
Reimarus's objections. He has already argued that
Jesus had only claimed to be a worldly Messiah, and,
having tried to establish his rule and failed, he was
executed.[725] The disciples claimed, of course, that he
was resurrected and was therefore really the Messiah.
Reimarus recognizes that " . . . for all Christianity
the truth of the narrative of the resurrection of Jesus

from the dead is first and foremost."[726]   Therefore,
Reimarus must refute the historicity of this claim.
The evidence for the resurrection consists of three
facts: the witness of the guard at the tomb, the
apostles' witness, and the fulfillment of Old Testament
prophecies. Reimarus will seek to discredit each fact.

Against the testimony of the guard, Reimarus
presses objections similar to those of Annet.[727]   Why
does Matthew alone relate this story, if it is true?
Why did not the apostles obtain the guards' names and
refer to them as witnesses? Why did they not obtain
from Pilate a written document concerning the setting
of the guard for use in Roman courts? Why was this
apologetic not widely used against the Jews? Reimarus
thinks that Matthew really invented the story, but that
others did not find the apologetic convincing and so
disdained to use it; hence, the story's confinement to
Matthew's gospel. Reimarus thinks it "entirely
possible," indeed, "highly probable," that the
disciples stole the body of Jesus, since they had free
access to the garden and there was no guard to stop
them.[728]   In a manner reminiscent of Woolston, he
contends that Jesus's rising so far in advance of his
prediction smacks of deceit, for the disciples should
have arranged in advance to go with the Jews to the
tomb on the third day to watch for the resurrection.
And if Jesus subsequently appeared to the disciples for
forty days, why did he not show himself to the chief
priests?

Besides all this, Matthew, in spinning the story
out of his head for want of a better answer to the
Jews, has filled the story with contradictions: (1)
the disciples knew nothing of Jesus's resurrection in
advance, so how could the chief priests know, so as to

set a guard? (2) It is improbable that the chief
priests would go in procession to Pilate on the first
day of Passover. (3) It is more likely that they would
have sent a couple of delegates than all go together.
(4) Why should they have gone to Pilate at all to
secure heathen guards instead of their own? (5) It is
ridiculous to think all the Sanhedrin were such rogues
as to agree to the stupid story of the guards' falling
asleep. (6) If the story is true, then why do the Jews
still hold to the theft hypothesis while no other
apostles mention the Sanhedrin's deceit? In addition
to these internal contradictions, the other evangelists
presuppose that there was no guard at the tomb. The
story of the women going to anoint the body and their
discovery of the empty tomb is incompatible with the
guards' still being there, the earthquake, and so
forth.

Having discredited the guard story, Reimarus now
turns to the second support of the resurrection: the
apostles' testimony.[729] In order to undermine the
evangelists' witness to the resurrection, Reimarus
wants to capitalize on the many inconsistencies and
contradictions in the narratives. The inconsistencies
remove any positive, evidential value in the
evangelists' reports: "And I am definitely assured
that if today in court four witnesses were heard in a
case and their testimony was as different in all
respects as is that of our four evangelists, the
conclusion would at least have to be made that no case
could be constructed on such conflicting testimony."[730]
Reimarus adduces ten inconsistencies: (1) The names
and number of the women visiting the tomb differ. (2)
The women's intention in visiting the tomb is different
in the various gospels. (3) John and the Synoptics

differ on the number of times Mary went to the tomb.
(4) Only John speaks of Peter and John's inspection of
the tomb. (5) The angel's message varies among the
evangelists. (6) Jesus's words to Mary are different
in Matthew and John. (7) Only Mark and Luke refer to
the Emmaus appearance. (8) The location of the
appearances are inconsistent. (9) Jesus's words are
not identical in the various gospels. (10) John and
Matthew are silent about the ascension. Such
inconsistencies, concludes Reimarus, would invalidate
testimony in any court of law. "How then can anyone
want the whole world and all mankind to base their
religion, faith, and hope of salvation at all times and
in all places upon the testimony of four such varying
witnesses?"[731]

In addition to these inconsistencies, there are
unquestionable contradictions, of which Reimarus will
list only the ten most obvious: (1) Mark and Luke are
contradictory on the time of the buying of the spices.
(2) John contradicts Mark and Luke on the completeness
of Jesus's burial and need for further anointing. (3)
Matthew contradicts the other evangelists on the
circumstances of the tomb's discovery. (4) The number,
position, and words of the angel(s) are contradictory.
(5) John and Luke contradict each other concerning the
time of Peter's visit to the tomb. (6) Matthew and
John are mutually incompatible on the appearance to
Mary. (7) Matthew and John differ on the touching of
Jesus. (8) The Galilee and Jerusalem appearances are
irreconcilable. There would be no purpose to the
disciples' traveling back and forth. (9) The Galilean
appearances in Matthew and John conflict. (10) The
circumstances of the appearance in Galilee are
contradictory: (a) it is first in Matthew, but third

in John; (b) it is expected in Matthew, but a surprise
in John; (c) Jesus's speeches in Matthew and John are
different.

If these inconsistencies and contradictions were
not enough, there is also the overriding problem of the
privacy of Jesus's appearances. If he had appeared
only once in the temple before the people and
Sanhedrin, visibly, audibly, tangibly, the whole Jewish
nation would have believed. Millions of souls
throughout history would have been saved from hell.
Thus, this single objection, that he did not appear
publicly, is enough to cast the evangelists'
credibility aside. "It is foolishness to sigh and
complain about mankind's disbelief if one cannot
furnish men with the persuasive evidence that the
matter demands, based on a healthy reason."[732]

Having demolished the guards' and apostles'
testimony, Reimarus makes short shrift of the proof
from prophecy.[733] Stephen gave no Scripture proofs at
all for the resurrection; it was a pity, muses
Reimarus, that all those 70 enlightened men did not
have so clear a vision as Stephen so that they could
see Jesus as he claimed to. Paul's attempts to prove
the resurrection from Scripture in Acts 13 involved
strained interpretations. And the whole procedure begs
the question anyway by assuming that Jesus was raised
from the dead and that therefore these predictions
apply to him! Besides, even if he were raised from the
dead, that fact proves nothing. "Even if he had really
been awakened from the dead it does not necessarily
follow logically that he would be the savior, because
we read in the scripture also of others whom God had
aroused who were, after all, not thereby designated
messiah to the people."[734] The third support for the

resurrection thus falls away. "So it is completely clear and unequivocal that the proof for the resurrection of Jesus from the scripture can never in eternity survive before the judgement seat of sound reason . . . ."[735]

In conclusion, Reimarus summarizes his case against the historicity of the resurrection:

> (1) the guard story is very doubtful and unconfirmed, and it is very probable the disciples came by night, stole the corpse, and said afterward Jesus had arisen; (2) the disciples' testimony is both inconsistent and contradictory; and (3) the prophecies appealed to are irrelevant, falsely interpreted, and question-begging.[736]

Reimarus believes that the disciples enjoyed the easy life of preaching they had had with Jesus, so they transformed him into a purely spiritual Messiah with a future, coming kingdom. Thus, Christianity, far from embodying universal, spiritual truths, was quite simply a fraud.

Upon the publication of the fragments, Semler took it upon himself to refute them in his lengthy der Fragmente eines Ungenannten. In a sense, Reimarus had forced Semler into a somewhat awkward position. Semler had agreed with the Deist critique of miracles and sought an explanation in accommodation to mythological thought-forms, which, one would think, could be equally applied to the incarnation and resurrection. But Semler held the incarnation and resurrection to be important, if not essential, elements in Christianity. He does not want to let these slide into the sphere of mythology, lest the content of the Christian Heilsglaube be lost. Indeed, the dilemma of affirming the positivity of these events without thereby affirming a physical miracle was one that plagued

Neology, as Frei explains:

> 'Positivity' is not identical with 'miracle'
> conceived as disruption of natural law or uniform
> experience. But there are obvious parallels
> between them. For positivity is the affirmation
> of a direct or unmediated intervention of the
> Godhead in the finite realm, even though not
> necessarily one to be known directly in the chain
> of physical events. Increasingly, Christian
> theologians, who continued to affirm that the New
> Testament claimed the historical positivity of
> revelation by virtue of the unique status of
> Jesus's being and dignity, located the claim in
> the moral and personal qualities that bespoke his
> being. They insisted on these qualities as the
> description of an authentic, factual history. For
> these men miracle did not mean seemingly or really
> contranatural physical events in connection with
> Jesus, but rather the qualitative, immanently
> inexplicable uniqueness of his being, on which an
> equally mysteriously originated faith in him was
> totally dependent. Positivity thus became
> anchored in 'miracles' not of a physical but of a
> peculiarly historical, inward, or moral sort,
> perhaps one should say miracles of character, and
> in this way one would hopefully avoid some of the
> more awkward questions about miracles.[737]

Reimarus's attack on the resurrection, however, forced
the issue in a dramatic way, and Semler apparently drew
back toward the orthodox end of the spectrum.

> Several of the Neologians, including . . . Semler,
> had recourse to the accommodation theory,
> bespeaking at the hermeneutical level their
> inclination toward the notion of positivity as
> 'character' rather than physical miracle,
> expressed most adequately in its truth content
> rather than its sheer occurrence character. Yet
> when men like Semler were confronted by a flat
> denial of the factuality of the events narrated
> (the position of Reimarus on the resurrection), or
> a denial of their religious significance as
> supernaturally caused occurrences (the position of
> rationalists like K.F. Bahrdt and J.B. Basedow),
> they drew back in the direction of the importance
> of positivity as factual happening, and therefore

of the texts' meaning as deriving from the
miraculous occurrence character of the narrated
events. And this included, specifically, the
resurrection of Jesus.[738]

Hence, in the <u>Beantwortung</u> Semler rails against
Rationalism's attempt to prescribe what we may and may
not believe if we are to remain enlightened
(<u>aufgeklärte</u>) men. Although miracles are not necessary
as a foundation for faith, some men have believed on
the basis of miracles, and so they are not incidental
for everyone.[739] Indeed, in order to believe in the
resurrection, one must believe that God can do
miracles.[740] At the same time, however, Semler
undercut the apologetic significance of miracles.
Since Deists deny miracles, he asserts, one cannot
convince them of the truth of Christianity through
miracles.[741] In response to Reimarus's claim that a
single public miracle by Jesus would have convinced the
Jews of his divinity, Semler states that this
contradicts the fragmentist's contention that a miracle
cannot prove that someone has spoken the truth.[742] By
opting for this response instead of the traditional
apologetic, Semler appears to imply that miracles have
no evidential value for doctrine. In fact, he goes on
to say that human nature is such that the world, even
when confronted with a palpable miracle, would not have
to believe; there are other explanations of the fact,
so that people can always find a way out.[743] And he
still seems to hold miracles to be accommodations to
Jewish thought-forms. For when Reimarus charges that
if one must appeal to miracle in order to prove
doctrine, then the doctrine must have no inner truth
and so they must appeal to miracles.[744]

With specific regard to the resurrection, Semler
appears to affirm its facticity, but he emphatically

subordinates it to the teaching of Jesus and removes
from it any apologetic importance. Christianity,
according to Semler, consists chiefly of the doctrines
taught by Christ, which describe a spiritual, perfect
worship of God for all men, and also of motifs and
promises of important benefits.[745] The content of both
is the same, but their presentation differs. The
doctrinal teachings of Jesus are the criterion by which
all other motifs are judged.

> Thus one cannot say flatly that all parts of the
> history of Jesus, all the circumstances of the
> same in and of themselves, even the resurrection
> in and of itself, belong to the essential
> principles of Christianity, or that they
> themselves simply constitute it, but rather when
> they stand in a true connection [Zusammenhang] to
> the teaching of Jesus about our restoration and
> welfare.[746]

The fragmentist thinks that by refuting the three
purported grounds for the resurrection, he has thereby
struck down the essential, foundational truths of
Christianity. Not at all, replies Semler. In the
first place, belief in the resurrection is not
essential to being a Christian. Semler furnishes the
example of Bishop Synesius, who did not believe in the
resurrection, but was nevertheless a Christian. Schutz
notes that for Semler a person can be a Christian even
if he cannot bring himself to believe in the
resurrection; if he can, this will be consoling, but
those who cannot should not be held to be blasphemous
or ungodly.[747] Secondly, the truth of Christ's
teaching is the basis for belief in the resurrection,
not vice versa. For Semler the spiritual teachings of
Christ are always primary. "Christianity originates
from the teachings of Jesus, who taught this in his

life, not merely from the report that he is risen, apart from the teachings."[748]   The belief in the resurrection is the result of the connection of this event to Jesus's teaching. " . . . the resurrection of Jesus hangs together with Jesus's life and goal; whoever has experienced his teachings will also believe that God has raised him from the dead."[749]   The Christians believed that Jesus was risen as a consequence of Jesus's teaching (als eine Folge der Lehre Jesu).[750]   Indeed, Semler will go so far as to call the teaching of Jesus the proof of the resurrection. We must, he insists, distinguish the substance (Sache) from the proof (Beweis) thereof. If a proof which was convincing in the second century (the three proofs attacked by Reimarus) is no longer convincing today, it does not follow that I have no proof. Rather the proof is the teaching of Jesus, which surpasses any doctrines in Jewish or pagan religions.[751]   The truth of the teaching of Jesus is apparently evident by its spiritual superiority and proves the resurrection, an event not essential in itself, because of the connection of that event with the teaching. Semler thus stands the traditional apologetic completely on its head. Instead of the empirical evidence for the historicity of the resurrection serving as the proof of the divinity of Christ's doctrine, the doctrine by its self-evident truth now becomes the basis for belief in the per se incidental event of the resurrection. Schmittner correctly observes,

> Semler does not regard the resurrection as a proof for the divine mission of Jesus; faith needs no visible support, but holds to the Word alone, the teaching of Jesus . . . Belief in the resurrection is, according to Semler, not the ground, but

> rather the consequence of faith in the divine
> mission of Jesus . . . Not the historical fact,
> which indeed as such is no longer accessible, but
> rather the Word of proclamation grounds faith.[752]

Semler's defense of the resurrection against Reimarus
therefore actually served to undermine the historical
argument for the resurrection. Not only was the
resurrection as a historical event made to appear
somewhat superfluous in comparison with the
a-historical, spiritual doctrines of Jesus's teaching,
but it also had no power to ratify that teaching, being
instead actually dependent upon the teaching for its
own validity.

Not only this, but Semler in his refutation of
Reimarus offers no positive evidence for the
resurrection, but assumes a purely defensive stance.
Even this characterization is perhaps too strong;
Semler actually admits all three of Reimarus's
objections, he only denies their relevance. We have
seen that for Semler the resurrection has a connection
with the teaching of Jesus, but, he maintains,
Christianity has no necessary connection with the Roman
guard, the testimony of witnesses, or the fulfilled
prophecies.[753] We believe in the resurrection because
of the teaching, but the particular circumstances
surounding the resurrection are unimportant.[754] He
later underlines the point: " . . . the resurrection
does not depend on this or that series of
circumstances."[755] Reimarus, it will be remembered,
had attacked the resurrection narratives chiefly upon
the basis of their abundant inconsistencies and
contradictions. These had led the orthodox apologists,
who accepted verbal inspiration, into elaborate
attempts to harmonize the accounts. But such
difficulties did not disturb Semler, for he had already

abandoned the doctrine of verbal inspiration in his
Freie Untersuchung. Because he actually did, and not
merely as a methodological device, regard the gospels
as human historical documents, he was able to freely
admit all the errors alleged by Reimarus and yet deny
that these disproved the event of the resurrection.
Hence, he is at pains to emphasize that the fact of the
resurrection does not hang on the accuracy of all the
circumstantial details surrounding it.

    With specific regard to Matthew's guard at the
tomb, Semler asserts that the guard story is
unimportant.[756] As for the inconsistent testimony of
the evangelists, Semler points out that the great part
of the contradictions among the evangelists hangs
together with the doctrine of inspiration.[757] Over
against this, Semler holds that the gospels were
written after a 30 year period on the basis of
traditions handed down during that time. During this
period only the preaching of the resurrection was
extant; there were no contradictions because none of
the circumstances were given. Later, writings were
made, and no consternation was caused if the incidental
details of the accounts conflicted. Finally, the
gospels appeared, and now the contradictions became
evident. But, Semler adds, these are of no importance
because Lessing was right: the religion existed before
the books did, and therefore the books are not
necessary.[758] As for the proof from fulfilled
prophecy, Semler has recourse to his theory of
accommodation. This proof was appropriate to the
people of that time, but it is not so for us.[759] Thus,
Paul in citing the Psalm of David in application to the
resurrection of Jesus is actually disputing ex
concessis.[760] In his response to Reimarus, Semler thus

grants all three of the fragmentist's major objections,
but he denies that they have the force attributed to
them. Since the accounts are purely human stories
based on 30 years of tradition, we can expect to find
conflicts in them concerning the secondary details, but
these do not affect the heart of the matter: the
resurrection of Jesus. At the same time, Semler never
provides any historical reason to believe that the core
of the story is any more reliable than the
circumstantial details. The fact of the resurrection
ought to be accepted, it seems, simply because of its
connection with the teachings of Jesus.

Semler's defense of the resurrection thus seems to
give with one hand and take back with the other. While
insisting that the resurrection ought to be accepted as
a historical event and that contradictions in the
circumstances do not affect its facticity, he at the
same time admits that belief in the resurrection is not
essential to being a Christian, he provides no
historical reason to accept the reliability of the
gospel accounts in regard to this event, he denies to
the resurrection any confirmatory power with regard to
the doctrine of Jesus, and he subordinates the fact of
the resurrection to the doctrinal teaching of
Christianity, making the latter the proof of the
former.[761] Semler's position was thus fraught with a
certain instability. Buchanan speculates, "His answer
to the fragmentist may have arisen partly because of an
unconscious need to turn the attack of the orthodox
away from himself and even gain their approval. At any
rate it was not an objective, dispassionate, scholarly
appraisal of the fragmentist."[762] Tholuck, too, calls
Semler's refutation "superficial" and charges that in
his private views, he became even more unorthodox.[763]

Schmittner likewise thinks that despite his struggles
to the contrary Semler could not avoid slipping into a
purely natural theology.[764]

His Letztes Glaubensbekenntnis. This allegation
would appear to be confirmed by Semler's Letztes
Glaubensbekenntnis über natürliche und christliche
Religion (1792). In this work, in answer to the
question, What is the Christian Religion? Semler
distinguishes between external religion (äussere
Religion) and private religion (Privat-Religion).[765]
The first involves the public forms of worship, while
the latter is subjective and embodies personal,
spiritual beliefs. Now the Jews came to differentiate
themselves from all other nations in an external way
and called themselves the people of God. But the
fundamental truth of Christianity is that God does not
look upon the external forms of religion, but upon
one's personal religion:

> . . . but certainly the first and foremost
> principle of the new, Christian religion is that
> one and the same God is the Lord and Father of all
> men and peoples, that he does not look upon the
> external circumstances by which Jews distinguish
> themselves from other peoples in an immoral way,
> but rather judges the conduct of men according to
> the standard of their knowledge of Good and Evil.
> In Christ, or according to the pure teaching of
> Christ concerning the equal footing of all men
> generally before God [von dem allgemeinen gleichen
> Verhältnis Gottes über allen Menschen], this false
> distinction, which the Jews had introduced to the
> advantage of[766] their nation, was completely
> abolished. . .

According to Schutz, apart from this one principle,
Semler "did not allow any so-called Fundamen-
talartikel of Dogmatics to count as a necessary article
of faith which must by all means be accepted and

affirmed if one does not wish to renounce the name of
'Christian' . . . ."[767] Of course, it does not hurt
the true spirit of Christianity if one wished to also
affirm these doctrines, but they are not necessary.
Already in the Beantwortung, Semler had indicated such
an outlook. He wrote, "But we cannot and should not
compel every true admirer of natural religion to think
and believe exactly like us with regard to the Trinity,
reconciliation, and satisfaction--this is neither
possible nor necessary."[768] In this work he states
that the difference between a Deist and a Christian is
that Christians do not abandon the teachings of
Jesus.[769] In the Letztes Glaubensbekenntnis, the
teaching of Jesus has been so reduced that the above
statement could hold only in the sense that Christians
held to the truths as teachings of Jesus whereas Deists
may have held to them on reason alone. Schutz thinks
that Semler would not have withheld the name of
"Christian" to those naturalists who held to the moral
teaching of Christ and the participation of all men in
God's grace, not on the basis of authority, but on the
basis of reason.[770] Indeed, Semler himself calls
natural religion "a true worship of God" (eine wahre
Verehrung Gottes).[771] The Christian religion is
different in its expressly new or greater content--but
this, we have seen, not to be fundamentally necessary
for belief. Christianity also differs from natural
religion in that the latter lacks any public forms of
worship like the Christian religion.[772] Schutz remarks
that Semler mainly opposed the naturalists because he
thought they wanted to impose their views forcefully
and jettison the orthodox forms of public worship.[773]
But insofar as the content of beliefs is concerned,
Semler saw no contradiction in the designation

"Christian naturalist"[774]--indeed, we have seen that he applied the term to himself. Hence, it would seem that Semler in the end differentiated Christianity from natural religion in its best forms only in that the former embraced certain additional, but non-essential, beliefs and practices.

Semler stands therefore as a pivotal figure in the demise of the historical argument for the resurrection. He exemplifies the radical hermeneutical change in late eighteenth century Germany whereby the truth of Christianity was cut loose from the historicity of the events related in Scripture, so that the former might be preserved even while the latter was denied. In Semler we see the elevation of the Word of God to the position of prominence and the subordination of the historical to the non-essential, a situation which has characterized German theology until recent years. He absorbed the anti-supernaturalism of the Deists against miracles, a presupposition which, had he applied it consistently, would have eliminated the fact of the resurrection, as later thinkers were to see. Since the truth content of Christianity consisted of spiritual doctrines, abstracted from all historical particularity, it would be a short step for later rationalists to affirm the spiritual truths of Christianity while denying the miraculous events of the gospels, including the resurrection, which Semler did not wish to deny. Insofar as he affirmed that event, he did so only in virtue of its connection with the spiritual teachings of Jesus. In itself it was non-essential. No positive historical reasons could be given in favor of Jesus's resurrection, although the accounts of that event could not be impugned simply because they involve inconsistencies and contradictions

in the secondary details. Semler's bouleversement of
the traditional apologetic consisted in his assertion
that the resurrection had no evidential value for the
truth of Jesus's doctrine, but that on the contrary the
doctrine by its own inner truth is actually the proof
of the resurrection. That doctrine in its fundamental
principle is virtually indistinguishable from a refined
natural religion. Semler's views were widely accepted,
as we have seen, and the traditional historical
argument for the resurrection soon fell into disfavor.

Gottfried Ephraim Lessing
     The rift between truth and biblical historicity.
The crucial separation which Semler had wrought between
the   truth   of   Christianity   and   the   historical
particulars described in the Bible was reinforced by
Lessing's "Gegensätze" appended to the Reimarus
fragments   and   by   his   subsequent,   influential,
theological writings.   He consoled those who were
disturbed at Reimarus's attacks by distinguishing the
essence of Christianity from the Bible.   The true
Christian need not be troubled by Reimarus's disproofs
because for him Christianity is simply a fact--he feels
it to be true and is blessed in it.   "In short, the
letter is not the spirit, and the Bible is not
religion.   Consequently, objections to the letter and
to the Bible are not also objections to the Spirit and
to religion."[775]   Moreover, the Bible contains much
that is inessential to religion, and in these matters
it need not be infallible.   Furthermore, religion
existed before the Bible, and Christianity existed
before the New Testament, since some years elapsed
after Jesus's appearance before the evangelists and
apostles wrote.   So the Bible is not essential to the

Christian religion. "The religion is not true because the evangelists and apostles taught it; but they taught it because it is true. The written traditions must be interpreted by their inward truth and no written traditions can give the religion any inward truth if it has none."776 The impact of Lessing's remarks was to widen the rift between historical event and spiritual truth. Talbert explains,

> Orthodox and Deists alike assumed that the truth of the Christian religion depended upon the veracity of the biblical accounts, upon their facticity. Put in its barest form: Christianity is true if the Gospel narratives are accurate in their reporting of events. In this context, Reimarus, following Wolff, said that the truth of Christianity was established if the New Testament accounts of the historical origins of Christianity satisfied the criteria established by reason to test every alleged revelation. Reimarus concluded that the application of the two criteria of necessity and consistency proved Christianity to be based on fraud.
>   Lessing . . . separated the question of the faciticity of Christian origins from that of the truth of the Christian religion. . . . Even if Reimarus's objections were unanswerable and the factual claims of the Christian religion unsupportable and the biblical accounts hopelessly contradictory, Christianity contains an intrinsic truth, immediately grasped by the believer, which retains its validity whether or not Jesus actually arose from the tomb after three days.777

It must be kept in mind, however, that Lessing's statements in this regard are mere palliatives, as his letters reveal, and that he himself did not believe that Christianity had some sort of inward truth that could stand while the Bible disintegrated under the hammers of criticism.

Perhaps this is best seen in Lessing's attitude toward Neology. He had only scorn for Semler's

Abhandlung and the liberal theology he represented.
While the old orthodoxy was plainly absurd, the new
theology had an air of rationality about it that could
deceive one into thinking it credible. In a letter to
his brother Karl, Lessing compared Neology to orthodoxy
as liquid manure to impure water. As Sierig notes,
Lessing saw only a graduated difference between the two
because they both still stood on the basis of
revelation.[778] Lessing's attack was on the reality of
revelation itself, and Neology was only an incomplete
break from orthodoxy, an accommodation to reason, but
for that fact all the more dangerous and deceptive.
"He was exercised--the longer, the more so; the longer,
the more clearly and decidedly---with putting through a
religion of reason, a natural theology and knowledge of
God, that lies behind all historical and earthly
appearances of religion."[779]

Lessing's essay, "Die Erziehung des
Menschengeschlechts," probably expresses this most
clearly. In this work, though Lessing uses Christian
terminology, the idea of revelation is domesticated to
become simply the process of man's education, a
historical process of increasing understanding of
reality.[780] What education is to the individual man,
revelation is to the whole human race; revelation
simply is the education of the human race. Lessing
states that there was a primitive monotheism which was
then corrupted into polytheism and idolatry.[781] In the
historical process, the various religions are
apparently returning to their source: "Why are we not
more willing to see in all positive religions simply
the process by which alone human understanding in every
place can develop and must still further develop
instead of either ridiculing or becoming angry with

them?"[782] In the growth from infancy to manhood, the
religions develop into a religion of pure reason by
means of a process in which later stages replace
earlier stages, preserving their truth and throwing off
their childish elements, until maturity is attained.
Thus, if we are led to a better conception of the
divine being by a religion whose historical truth has
now become dubious, so much the better.[783] Eventually,
all these will become superfluous, and man will be
fully guided by reason alone.

Lessing thus sought to relativize Christianity and
the Bible such that both orthodoxy and Neology would be
undercut. The religion of reason owes nothing in the
end to revelation, except insofar as particular
religions serve as stages along the way to its
Vollendung.

The impossibility of historical proofs for truths
of faith. Lessing not only forwarded the hermeneutical
change of separating the truth of Christianity from the
historical reliability of the biblical narratives, but
he also helped to undermine the evidentialist approach
to the truth of Christianity as well. In his essay,
"Über den Beweis des Geistes und der Kraft" (1777),[784]
he states that the problem with the traditional proofs
from prophecy and miracle is that the report of a
fulfilled prophecy is not itself a fulfilled prophecy,
nor is a report of a miracle itself a miracle.[785]
Since the events themselves now lie in the past, the
only proof we can have of them is historical in nature,
and historical proofs for anything are uncertain. Now
a less certain truth cannot be a proof for a more
certain truth. Lessing like Leibniz and Wolff
apparently accepted the classification of truths as
either truths of reason (necessary propositions,

deducible from self-evident truths, based on the law of
contradiction) and truths of fact (contingent
propositions, the opposite of which is possible). The
truths of religion in its mature expression he
identifies with truths of reason. Hence, the problem
with a historical apologetic is simply this:
<u>contingent truths of history can never become the proof
of necessary truths of reason</u>.[786] Therefore, religion
can never be proved by historical enquiry. But Lessing
has a second major objection to the evidentialist
approach, which might be roughly stated: one cannot
infer from historical events a trans-historical
meaning.[787] Suppose I do accept that Jesus rose from
the dead. What am I warranted to conclude therefrom?
Lessing's answer is that from a historical truth only
another historical truth can be inferred. But one
cannot infer a trans-historical truth such as "Christ
is the Son of God," especially when this flies in the
face of reason. To infer from historical truths other
truths of a different class is to commit a category
mistake. Now the usual response to this objection, as
we have seen, would have been to argue that given
Jesus's doctrinal teachings, one is warranted in
inferring from the resurrection that Jesus's doctrine
was true and that therefore he was the Son of God.
Hence, Lessing puts this response in the mouth of an
objector: "The Christ of whom on historical grounds
you must allow that he raised the dead, that he himself
rose from the dead, said himself that God had a Son of
the same essence as himself and that he is this
Son."[788] Lessing does not deny that the inference is
now warranted, but rather responds, "This would be
quite excellent! if only it were not the case that it
is not more than historically certain that Christ said

this."[789]   We thus seem to return to the first
objection, that contingent truths cannot support truths
of reason.   If the objector should now respond that it
is more than historically certain that Christ said this
because it is asserted by an inspired historian who
cannot err, Lessing will retort that this fact as well
is only historically certain.   The fundamental problem
thus remains that contingent historical truths cannot
be the basis for necessary truths of reason such as the
truths of natural religion.   "This, then, is the ugly,
broad ditch which I cannot get across, however often
and however earnestly I have tried to make the
leap."[790]   Hence, historical apologetics must
necessarily fail.

       Lessing thus undercut a historical argument for
the resurrection in two ways: (1) negatively, in
making the truth of Christianity independent of
historical facts and (2) positively, in arguing that no
historical facts could provide the basis for truths of
religion.   His wide literary influence helped to turn
the general thought of the day against the traditional
apologetic approach.

The hermeneutic of
natural explanations

Karl Bahrdt and Karl Venturini

       Rationalism subsequent to Semler evolved
explanations of ever-increasing ingenuity to eliminate
the miraculous element in the gospels by means of
natural accounts of the facts described.   Salvatorelli
explains,

       This exegesis, in brief, adhered firmly to the
       letter of the New Testament writings, especially

the gospels, and interpreted their meaning and
their connection not according to the general
content and the thought of the writers,
objectively ascertained, but according to the
demands of a naturalistic explanation acceptable
to the rationalism of the end of the eighteenth
century.[79]

Thus, Karl Bahrdt in his <u>Ausführung des Plans und
Zwecks Jesu</u> (1784-92) explains the feeding of the 5,000
by postulating a secret store of bread which Jesus and
his disciples distributed to the multitude; Jesus's
walking on the water was effected by a platform
floating just beneath the surface; his raising the dead
was actually reanimation from a coma, thus preventing
premature burial. This last explanation provided the
key to explaining Jesus's own resurrection. By the end
of the eighteenth century, the theft hypothesis, so
dear to Deism, had apparently pretty much lost
conviction, and a new explanation was needed. This
German rationalism found in the apparent death
(<u>Scheintod</u>) theory. According to Bahrdt, Jesus
belonged to a secret order of Essenes, dedicated to
disabusing Israel of her wordly Messianic expectations
in favor of spiritual, religious truths. In order to
gain a hearing from the people, Jesus claimed to be the
Messiah, the plan being to spiritualize the concept of
Messiah by engineering his death and resurrection. To
bring this about, Jesus provoked his arrest and trial
by his triumphal entry into Jerusalem. Other members
of the order, who secretly sat on the Sanhedrin,
ensured his condemnation. By means of drugs, Luke the
physician had prepared Jesus's body to withstand the
rigors of crucifixion for an indefinite time. By his
loud cry and slumped head, Jesus feigned his death on
the cross, and a bribe to the centurion guaranteed that
his legs would remain unbroken. Taken to a cave by

Joseph of Arimathea, another member of the order, Jesus
was resuscitated by his ministrations. On the third
day, they pushed aside the stone over the mouth of the
cave, and Jesus went forth, frightening away the guard
and appearing to Mary and subsequently his other
disciples. Thereafter, he lived in seclusion among the
members of the secret order.

Similar to Bahrdt's theory was the reconstruction
of Jesus's life by Karl Venturini in his Natürliche
Geschichte des grossen Propheten von Nazareth
(1800-02). As a member of a secret society, Jesus
sought to persuade the Jewish nation to substitute for
their conception of a worldly Messiah the idea of a
spiritual Messiah. But his attempt back-fired; he was
arrested, condemned, and crucified. However, he was
taken down from the cross and placed in a tomb alive,
where he revived. A member of the society, dressed in
white, frightened away the guard, and Jesus was taken
from the tomb by other society members. During forty
days thereafter, he appeared to various disciples,
always to return to the secret place of the society;
finally, his energy spent, he retired permanently.

Heinrich Eberhard Gottlob Paulus

But the dean of the natural explanation school was
certainly H.E.G. Paulus, professor of theology at
Heidelberg. In his Philologisch-kritischer und
historischer Kommentar über das neue Testament
(1800-02), Das Leben Jesu, als Grundlage einer reinen
Geschichte des Urchristentums (1828), and Exegetisches
Handbuch über die drei ersten Evangelien (1830), he
perfected the art of explaining naturally the
miraculous elements in the gospels while retaining a
close adherence to the letter of the text. A pantheist

who accepted Spinoza's dictum "Deus sive Natura,"
Paulus rejected all miracles a priori. Although he
staunchly insisted that the main point of his Leben
Jesu was not to explain away miracles,[792] it is
nevertheless true that he expended a great deal of
effort doing precisely this, and it is chiefly for this
effort that he is remembered. According to Paulus,
miracles are not the important thing, but rather the
spirit of Jesus as seen in his thought and actions.[793]
It is the person of Jesus in his moral character and
courage that is truly miraculous. "Das Wunderbare von
Jesus ist Er selbst."[794]   The true meaning of
Christianity is to be found in the teachings of Jesus,
which, Paulus says, are self-evidently true, as
demonstrated by their inner spirituality. In any case,
literal miracles, even if they had occurred, would
contribute nothing toward the grounding of Christian
truth. "The main point is already certain in advance,
that the most inexplicable changes in the course of
Nature can neither overturn nor prove any spiritual
truth, since it cannot be seen from any event of Nature
for what spiritual purpose it should so happen and not
otherwise."[795] Once a person has grasped the spiritual
truth of Jesus's person and teaching, miracles become
superfluous anyway. "The proof from miracles itself
always demands first, as it must, that the claims
should be worthy of God and not contrary to reason. If
this be the case, then a miracle is no longer necessary
as a proof for them."[796] Paulus's a priori rejection
of the miraculous is perhaps best seen in his response
to the objection, Why all this effort to explain away
the extraordinary as something within the order of
nature?[797]   He answers, in order to find the more
probable explanation; and, he adds, the more probable

explanation is that which can be made easier to believe. Since for post-Enlightenment thinkers, miracles had ceased to be believable, a natural explanation would always be preferred. There are two types of faith, he continues: one glories in holding without reflection to what is the most unbelievable, while the other has a ground for faith which makes it credible to believe. Paulus quite evidently accepts only the second. "For true believing is only that which holds fast the most tenable."[798]   Apart from reason, faith cannot be protected from superstition.[799] When Paulus states further that probability always depends on whether an effect can be derived from the causes at hand,[800] then the presuppositional nature of his anti-supernaturalism becomes clear. For now the most probable explanation is seen by definition to be a purely natural explanation; hence, his efforts to explain away the miraculous.

In approaching the subject of the resurrection, Paulus distinguishes between the juridical method of procedure and the psychologico-historical approach.[801] Under the first methodology, the resurrection cannot be proved, but according to the second it has all possible credibility. The juridical procedure cannot establish the resurrection because the women were too rattled to give reliable testimony and the remaining witnesses of the resurrection appearances were all partisan followers of Jesus. The aim of the juridical method is to protect the innocent and deems it better to let ten quilty men go free than to convict one innocent person. Hence, it is unsuitable for proving positive facts. Therefore, we must use the psychologico-historical approach to establish the resurrection. According to Paulus, some criminals who are, according to

psychologico-historical standards, certainly guilty get
off scott-free because they cannot be proved
juridically to be guilty. The same is true of the fact
of the resurrection. Paulus's comments on this matter
are very interesting because they show just how much
attitudes toward the credibility of the Scriptures had
changed from the days of the traditional apologetic.
One hundred years earlier in England, Thomas Sherlock
had employed the juridical procedure by putting the
apostles on trial for their testimony concerning the
resurrection, and had assumed them innocent until
proven guilty. The gospels were taken as true until
proven false. Paulus's approach appears to be
precisely the opposite: no longer are the gospels
assumed to be reliable, rather this is the fact to be
proven. For Paulus, proving the gospels true is
equivalent to proving a criminal guilty. The
implication seems to be that as a criminal is assumed
innocent until proven guilty, so the gospels are
assumed false until proven true. The burden of proof
has completely shifted in contrast to the approach of
the old apologetic, and Paulus cannot carry that
burden.

Therefore, he resorts to the psychologico-
historical approach in order to furnish grounds that
render the resurrection credible, if not strictly
proven. He lists five such grounds:[802] (1) The
radical change in the disciples in the 50 day period
following Jesus's death implies the resurrection. (2)
The change in the opponents of Christianity also points
to the resurrection. During his lifetime Jesus was
opposed by the Pharisees, but after his death, the
Sadduccees became the chief enemies of Christianity,
the Pharisees actually standing by and defending the

Christians because they shared belief in the
resurrection (Acts 5.34-9; 23.9). (3) The appearances
of Jesus were entirely contrary to the expectation of
the disciples, so that they cannot be attributed to the
disciples' fantasy. (4) There were many and varying
witnesses and circumstances for the appearances. (5)
Mere apparitions do not have continuity in space and
time as did the resurrection appearances. On the basis
of these appearances the apostles concluded that God
had raised Jesus from the dead.

But Paulus reinterprets the resurrection so that
it is no longer a miraculous event. Paulus
reconstructs Jesus's death and resurrection by means of
purely natural explanations.[803] The darkness at the
crucifixion was caused by dense fumes which normally
precede an earthquake, such as occurred that afternoon.
These fumes made it all the more difficult for Jesus to
breathe, and his expiration could be clearly seen, as
his final gasps were heavier. The guards watching
Jesus were filled with awe and so did not administer
the leg-breaking. One of the guards pierced Jesus's
side to see if his body had grown completely stiff.
The lance may have been a small javelin, and there is
no way to know where Jesus's side was pierced. The
wound was not designed to kill, only to test for
feeling. The "water and blood" did not flow or gush
out, but merely "came" out and may have been a reddish
lymph fluid. There was no time to embalm the body, so
it was simply smeared with ointment and wrapped in a
sheet, then placed in the tomb.

Now to all appearances Jesus was certainly dead.
In fact, Paulus would perhaps even say that Jesus was
clinically dead. Hence, he rejects the appellation
Scheintod. But, he asks, was he really dead in his

innermost life forces? How many times have doctors thought someone dead only to find him alive? Death by crucifixion requires a considerable length of time, but Jesus expired too quickly. He was probably in a deep syncope, but he was not simply unconscious. Only the inner-most life forces remained. Precisely how he revived cannot be known, whether it was the fresh coolness of the new tomb, the wrapping of the body in stimulating spices and astringents, the quaking of the earth, the electric power of the lightning, or other secret powers of Nature which served to bring him back to life; but without these factors Jesus would never have risen.[804] God raised Jesus by the conspiration of powers and means at hand in the divine order of world, and there was no need for God to intervene in His work to effect this end, as men must intervene in theirs for its correction or improvement.[805] Since Jesus appeared alive from the dead, not in a glorified body, but in the same, earthly body that was crucified--a point Paulus underlines again and again--, there is no need to posit some unknown, creative force at work.

Having thus ascribed the "resurrection" of Jesus to purely natural causes, Paulus proceeds to clarify the rest of the resurrection narratives in this light. Matthew's guard story he dismisses as a fairy-tale, for the now familiar reasons.[806] He ascribes its origin to the Jews, who fabricated the guard and their falling asleep as an unverifiable story in order to explain away the resurrection. Matthew knew the disciples had not stolen the body, but he was unaware that the rest of the story was fictitious as well, so he only refuted the charge of theft. Reimarus had argued against the guard story to make room for the theft hypothesis, but according to Paulus, Jesus's resurrection is so

historically certain that the guard story is now
entirely unnecessary. By eliminating the guard, Paulus
is able to avoid the fanciful theories of Bahrdt and
Venturini to explain why they did not interfere with
Jesus's escape when the earthquake rolled back the
stone. When Jesus appeared to Mary, he forbad her
touching him because his body was still aching from the
suffering he endured. Jesus himself was quite amazed
to be alive; hence, his exclamation of surprise, "I am
not yet ascended to the Father!" When he appeared to
the Emmaus disciples, he was unrecognized because his
countenance had been changed by his suffering, but when
the disciples saw the familiar bread-breaking and his
wounded hands, they recognized him. They made so much
commotion that Jesus withdrew and went back to
Jerusalem; so quickly did he depart that they referred
to it as his disappearing. Jesus then appeared to the
disciples in Jerusalem, showing his corporeality by his
wounds and by eating. The disciples thought at first
that they were seeing a glorified body, that is, a body
which is refined, sensibly intangible, and not
nourished by physical sustenance, so Jesus had to show
that his was the same earthly, crucified body. Paulus
apparently equates physicality with an unglorified
state, such that a proof of Jesus's physical
appearances entails that his resurrection was actually
a Wiederbelebung, a resuscitation. He thinks that Paul
teaches a more spiritualized resurrection in I Cor. 15,
but this concerns the future resurrection of Christians
and is actually predicated in contrast to the physical
"resurrection" of Jesus.[807] During the weeks following
his resurrection, Jesus greatly exerted himself through
his many appearances. Finally, as was inevitable with
a body that had been so mistreated, his powers were

exhausted. He led the disciples out to the Mount of
Olives and, sitting before them, taught them. Then,
rising up and lifting his hands in blessing, he
withdrew from them. A cloud, which at that time of
year usually forms in early morning in this region,
enveloped him, so that he could no longer be seen.
"What else could He be from now on but the one taken up
to God in highest blessedness."[808]

So understood, states Paulus, the resurrection of
Jesus is credible. "The fact of the resurrection of
Jesus is after all this an undeniable event according
to psychologico-historical examination. . . ."[809] But
the event has now been reduced to a natural occurrence
and emptied of any religious significance whatever. In
these respects, Paulus stands as a progenitor of later
liberal theology. Indeed, it is noteworthy that
Schleiermacher, the father of modern theology, followed
Paulus's lead in these regards.[810] Schleiermacher
remained rationalistic with respect to the denial of
miracles, and he attached no religious importance to
the resurrection of Jesus. In his lectures of 1832,
Der Christus des Glaubens und der Jesus der Geschichte,
he passively accepts Paulus's theory of Jesus's merely
apparent death, stating that it is unimportant whether
the death and resurrection of Christ were real or
apparent. Schleiermacher himself believed that Jesus's
resurrection was only a resuscitation and that he
continued to live physically with the disciples for a
time after this event.

The hermeneutic of
mythological interpretation

The resolution of the
traditional dilemma

Just three years after Schleiermacher's lectures, however, a work appeared which sounded the death knell for the natural explanation school: David Friedrich Strauss's Das Leben Jesu. In its consistent application of mythological explanations to the New Testament, Strauss's work constitutes a watershed in the history of critical methodology, to which modern form and redaction criticism can be traced. Kümmel's judgement is no exaggeration: 1835 marks a turning point in the history of the Christian faith.[811]

Strauss's approach to the gospels, and to the resurrection in particular, can be seen as an attempt to forge a third way between the horns of the dilemma proposed by the traditional apologetic: if the miracles and resurrection of Jesus are not historical facts, then the apostles were either deceivers or deceived, both of which are impossible. Reimarus had chosen to defend the first horn, arguing that the disciples had stolen Jesus's corpse and fabricated the resurrection. Paulus, rejecting the theory of Reimarus, attempted instead to defend the second horn of the dilemma, that the disciples were mistaken in their attribution to divine agency of events which possessed entirely natural causes. What Strauss perceived was that neither of these alternatives could pass as a plausible explanation and that therefore the dilemma had to be dissolved by constructing a third alternative.

Strauss rejected the conspiracy theory of Reimarus
as typical of the eighteenth century's simplistic,
naive approach to matters of religious belief. In his
helpful treatise Herrmann Samuel Reimarus und seine
Schutzschrift für die vernünftigen Verehrer Gottes
(1861), he describes the prior century's reductionistic
attitude toward revealed religion: "All positive
religions without exception are works of deception:
that was the opinion that the eighteenth century
cherished within its heart, even if it did not always
pronounce it as frankly as did Reimarus."[812]   Thus,
whenever miraculous events were encountered in the
Scriptures, these were facilely explained away as lies
or hoaxes deliberately perpetrated by the persons
involved. The explanation for the resurrection was
obvious: "If Jesus was not wakened miraculously from
the dead and yet the tomb was empty on the third
morning, then, to be sure, his disciples must have
stolen the corpse away."[813]   This sort of explanation
completely misunderstands the nature of religious
commitment and devotion, charges Strauss. Only the
eighteenth century could have conjoined deliberate
deception with the apostles' religious zeal:

> The apostles are supposed to have known best that
> there was not one single word of truth in the news
> of their master's resurrection, since they
> themselves spirited his corpse away, yet
> regardless of this, they are supposed to have
> spread the same story with a fire of conviction
> that sufficed to give the world a different form.
> These are incompatible things that only the
> eighteenth century was in a position to harmonize.
> All founders of religion are deceivers: that was
> the open or secret doctrine of the eighteenth
> century. The nineteenth, on the contrary,
> considers it a foregone conclusion that no
> religion that has attained historical permanency
> was ever founded through deception, but that all

were founded by people who were themselves convinced.[815]

According to Strauss, all religions therefore contain divine and human elements. Christianity cannot be passed off simply as a hoax. When Reimarus says that Christianity is not a divine revelation, but a human fraud, we know today that this is an error, that Christianity is not a fraud.[815] But the rejection of Reimarus's hypothesis does not entail embracing the supernaturalists' explanation. Reimarus's "Nein" to the traditional view remains "Nein," but his "Ja" to deception must yield to a better answer.

That answer was not to be found in the natural explanation school epitomized by Paulus. The contrived and artificial character of so many of these explanations was painfully apparent, and the profferred explanations were no more believable than the miracles themselves. The attempt to explain Jesus's resurrection was in particular doomed to failure:

> It is impossible that a being who had stolen half-dead out of the sepulchre, who crept about weak and ill, wanting medical treatment, who required bandaging, strengthening and indulgence, and who still at last yielded to his sufferings, could have given to his disciples the impression that he was a Conqueror over death and the grave, the Prince of Life, an impression which lay at the bottom of their future ministry. Such a resuscitation could only have weakened the impression which he had made upon them in life and in death, at the most could only have given it an elegiac voice, but could by no possibility have changed their sorrow into enthusiasm, have elevated their reverence into worship.[816]

Strauss not only believed that the natural explanations of rationalism could not provide a convincing account of the facts, but he also objected that this approach

lost the true meaning of the text. The natural system
of interpretation, while it seeks to preserve the
historical certainty of the narrative, nevertheless
loses its ideal truth. For example, if the
transfiguration were, as Paulus claimed, an accidental,
optical phenomenon and the two men either images of a
dream or simply unknown persons, then what is the
significance of the narrative? What was the motive for
preserving in the church's memory a story so void of
ideas and barren of inference, resting upon a delusion?
As Frei points out, Strauss is concerned to preserve
the ideal truth of the narrative even when its
historical facticity must be denied, and in this way he
reflects the hermeneutical change spearheaded by
Semler.

> In their own way the iconoclastic rebels against a
> historically uncritical adoration of the Bible as
> dogmatic truth were fully as zealous in their
> defense of the Bible's meaningfulness as their
> supernaturalist and pietist opponents. Among
> German New Testament critics, D.F. Strauss . . .
> was one of the most radical, and many a solemn
> mind reproached him not only for the substance but
> the irreverent tone of his attacks upon the
> credibility of the gospel story and its scholarly
> defenders. Nonetheless, Strauss was genuinely
> surprised by the virulence of the reaction to his
> Life of Jesus. For it appeared to him, his
> detractors quite to the contrary, that his
> negative historical results about the reliability
> of the narrative reports concerning the messianic
> uniqueness of Jesus opened the way for a genuinely
> positive reestimation of the religious meaning of
> the gospels. . . . Strauss was simply part of a
> tradition that combined liberation from biblical
> orthodoxy with a lively sense for the Bible as a
> valuable source of religious insight.[817]

Strauss believed that the natural explanation school
abandoned the substance to save the form, whereas his
alternative would, by renouncing the historical

facticity of the narrative, rescue and preserve the idea which resides in it and which alone constitutes its vitality and spirit.

This alternative Strauss found in the mythological interpretation of the gospels. According to this view, the miraculous events recorded in the gospels, such as the resurrection, never occurred, but are the product of religious imagination and legend, and, hence, require no historical explanation as the Supernaturalists, Deists, and Rationalists assumed.

> In the view of the church, Jesus was miraculously revived; according to the deistic view of Reimarus, his corpse was stolen by the disciples; in the rationalistic view, he only appeared to be dead and revived; according to our view the imagination of his followers, aroused in their deepest spirit, presented their Master revived, for they could not possibly think of him as dead. What for a long time was valid as an external fact, first miraculous, then deceptive, finally simply natural, is hereby reduced completely to the state of mind and made into an inner event.[818]

But the fact that the resurrection is mythological does not denude it of religious significance. The history of religion has taught us that a truth can be revealed to men within the husk of a delusion, where it nevertheless may possess the value and effectiveness of a truth. Jesus's resurrection was a delusion that in fact contains a good deal of truth, namely, that the true and important thing is not the earthly realm, but the spiritual.

Johann Eichhorn, Johann Gabler, and Georg Bauer

The idea of applying mythological motifs to the

gospels was, of course, not original to Strauss. He
himself says that Reimarus had prepared the way for him
in his explanation of Old Testament miracles as due to
the Jewish stylus theocraticus.[819]   We have already
seen that Semler explicitly ascribes the angelology and
demonology of the gospels to a mythological world view.
J.G. Eichhorn and his pupil J.P. Gabler also employed
mythological explanation in this way. Eichhorn, whose
Einleitung in das Alte Testament (1780-83) initiated
the succession of modern introductions, had adopted the
concept of myth from his teacher C.G. Heyne, a
classical philologist at Gottingen, and he applied this
form first to the Old Testament narratives and then to
those of the New Testament in order to explain the
miraculous events they record. A good example of this
method is Eichhorn's comments on Peter's deliverance
from prison in his essay "Versuch über die
Engel-Erscheinungen in der Apostelgeschichte."
According to Eichhorn, the story itself contains in
essence nothing except that Peter was suddenly
awakened, his fetters were released, he wrapped himself
in his coat and half-drunk with sleep followed his
guide from one door to another, and found himself, as
soon as he was on the street, abandoned and alone. His
confusion, drowsiness, and consternation precluded any
clear apprehension of what had happened. All that he
remembered was being shaken from sleep, the removal of
his bonds, his clutching his coat, and the easy
springing open of the outer door. From this story,
notes Eichhorn, it follows that we can find no
historical report of the actual manner of his
deliverance, but only an explanation of the same based
on Jewish concepts:

> The visible hand of Providence had freed him:
> Peter must have concluded this from the whole
> occurrence.   Jewish theology, which always
> furnishes Providence with a multitude of angels
> for carrying out its purposes, could express this
> in no other way than that an angel of the Lord
> brought him out of prison.   As soon as this
> expression was chosen, so also the shaking, the
> speaking, the guidance, everything that happened,
> must have been done by an angel of the Lord.   One
> must therefore carefully distinguish between
> substance and Jewish wording; then the story will
> proceed in a natural, easy course, uninterrupted
> by any miracle.[820]

Gabler, too, sought to explain the demonology of the
Bible as a category of a mythological world view. For
example in his analysis of the temptation of Jesus,[821]
he attributes the personification of the temptations in
the form of the devil to the myths adopted by Judaism
from Persian and Babylonian thought.   In reality,
Jesus's temptations arose out of individual, sensual
desires, and his triumph over these came through firm,
rational principles.   But the story became clothed in
the mythological thought-forms of the ancient world,
and so the evangelists delivered it.   Building upon the
work of Eichhorn and Gabler, G.L. Bauer sought to
isolate all the myths in the Old and New Testaments
through comparison with Greek and Roman mythology as
well as that of other religions.[822]   He specifically
ascribed the story of the virgin birth of Christ to
mythological formation.   Bauer laid down four criteria
for discernment of myth: (1) accounts of the origin of
the universe or the earth, (2) ascriptions of events to
the activity of gods or heavenly beings who act
personally and directly, rather than to natural causes,
(3) accounts in which thoughts of men are represented
sensibly as words and actions, and (4) accounts of
events that neither happen today nor can happen in the

regular order and course of nature.[823]   Bauer's fourth
point makes it quite clear that any miraculous account
cannot in principle be historical, but is a priori
mythological.

David Friedrich Strauss

But although Strauss had his predecessors in
employing the concept of myth to explain particular
elements in the Scriptural narratives, he was the first
to compose a wholesale account of the life of Jesus
utilizing mythological explanation as the key
hermeneutical method. According to Strauss himself, up
until the time of his writing myth had been applied to
the childhood and ascension stories of Jesus's life,
but not to the life of Jesus itself; this yielded a
framework in which " . . . the entrance to the gospel
history was through the decorated portal of mythus, and
the exit was similar to it; whilst the intermediate
space was still traversed by the crooked and toilsome
paths of natural interpretations."[824]   In his Leben
Jesu, Strauss sought to show in detail how all
supernatural events in the gospels can be explained as
either myth, legend, or redactional additions.

Strauss claimed to operate without any religious
or dogmatic presuppositions; he ascribed this
neutrality to the influence of his philosophical
studies. To the objection that this absence of
presupposition was unchristian, Strauss rejoined that
the presence of orthodox presuppositions was
unscientific. Nevertheless, it is clear that Strauss
did operate on the basis of certain philosophical (if
we wish not to call these religious or dogmatic)
presuppositions, such as the impossibility of miracles.
As an acknowledged pantheist and in later life a

materialist, Strauss proceeded, like Bauer and others
before him, from the assumption that miracles are
impossible in principle. According to Strauss, this is
not a presupposition requiring proof; on the contrary,
to affirm that miracles are possible is a
presupposition which requires proof.[825] God acts
immediately on the universe only as a Whole, but not on
any particular part; on any particular part he acts
only mediately through the causal laws of all the other
parts of nature.[826] Hence, with regard to the
resurrection, God's interposition in the regular course
of nature is "irreconcilable with enlightened ideas of
the relation of God to the world."[827] Thus, any
purportedly historical account of miraculous events
must be dismissed out of hand; "Indeed no just notion
of the true nature of history is possible, without a
perception of the inviolability of the chain of finite
causes, and of the impossibility of miracles."[828]
Thus, although Strauss rejected the rationalist
hermeneutic of natural explanation in favor of the
mythological, he remained rationalistic in his
rejection of the miraculous.

Strauss's application of the category of myth to
the miraculous element in the gospels proved a decisive
turning point. According to Schweizer in his history
of the Life of Jesus movement Von Reimarus zu Wrede
(1906), the critical study of the life of Jesus falls
into two periods with Strauss. "The dominant interest
in the first is the question of miracles. What terms
are possible between a historical treatment and the
acceptance of a supernatural event? With the advent of
Strauss, this problem found a solution, viz., that
these events have no rightful place in history, but are
simply mythical elements in the sources."[829] By the

mid-1860's the question of miracles had lost all importance. Schweizer explains,

> That does not mean that the problem of miracles is solved. From the historical point of view it is really impossible to solve it, since we are not able to reconstruct the process by which a series arose, or a series of historical occurrences were transformed into miracle stories, and these narratives must simply be left with a question mark standing against them. What has been gained is only that the exclusion of miracle from our view of history has been universally recognized as a principle of criticism, so that miracle no longer concerns the historian either positively or negatively. Scientific theologians of the present day who desire to show their 'sensibility,' ask no more than that two or three little miracles may be left to them--in the stories of the childhood perhaps, or in the narratives of the resurrection. And the miracles are, moreover, so far scientific that they have at least no relation to those in the text, but are merely spiritless, miserable little toy-dogs of criticism, flea-bitten by rationalism, too insignificant to do historical science any harm, especially as their owners honestly pay the tax upon them by the way in which they speak, write, and are silent about Strauss.[830]

Until Strauss it had been pretty generally agreed that the events in question had actually occurred--it was just a matter of explaining how they took place. But with Strauss, the miraculous events recorded in the gospels never in fact happened: the narratives are unhistorical tales determined by myth and legend.

Strauss believed that the chief problem in applying the mythical interpretation to the New Testament is that the first century was no longer a mythical age.[831] But although it was a time of writing, if there was a long period of oral transmission during which no written record existed, then marvelous elements could begin to creep in and

grow into historical myths. Strauss recognized as well
that adherence to this theory necessitated denying the
contemporary authorship of the gospels and the
influence of eyewitnesses.[832]   Hence, Strauss regarded
it as "the sole object" of his book to examine the
internal evidence in order to test the probability of
the authors' being eyewitnesses or competently informed
writers.[833]   Strauss gave short shrift to the external
testimony to the gospels: he believed Mark to be
compiled from Matthew and Luke and hence not based on
Peter's preaching; the Matthew mentioned by Papias is
not our Matthew; Acts so contradicts Paul that its
author could not be his companion; the earliest
reference to John is in 172, and the gospel's
authenticity was disputed by the Alogoi.[834]   Nor could
living eyewitnesses prevent the accrual of legend: (1)
the legends could have originated in areas where Jesus
was not well-known; (2) the apostles could not be
everywhere at once to correct or suppress unhistorical
stories; and (3) eyewitnesses themselves would be
tempted to fill up the gaps in their own knowledge with
stories.[835]   Strauss argues that the Jews lagged behind
the Romans and Greeks in their historical
consciousness; even Josephus's work is filled with
marvelous tales. Myths about the Messiah had already
arisen between the exile and Christ's day. All that
was wanting was the application of these myths with
some modification to Jesus by the Christian
community.[836]

      According to Strauss, the non-historical portions
of the gospel may be regarded as either: (1) myths, of
which there are three kinds: (a) evangelical myths:
narratives of Jesus arising from an idea of his
followers; (b) pure myths: a Messianic idea plus a

modifying personal impression of Jesus; and (c) historical myths: definite facts entwined with the mythical idea of Messiah; (2) legends, which are the natural result of oral tradition; and (3) additions of the author, which are purely individual contribu-tions.[837] Strauss then furnishes the criteria for the detection of these elements: (1) The negative criterion: an account is not historical if (a) " . . . the narrative is irreconcilable with the known and universal laws which govern the course of events," for example: (i) the law that the chain of secondary causes is undisturbable; (ii) the law of succession that things follow an order of decrease and increase (e.g., "If . . . we are told of a celebrated individual that . . . if the transition from the deepest despon-dency to the most ardent enthusiasm after his death is represented as the work of a single hour; we must feel more than doubtful whether it is a real history which lies before us"); (iii) psychological laws that a person should think and act according to character (e.g. the Jewish leaders would sooner believe the guards' story than accuse them of falling asleep); (b) the alleged historical account contradicts itself or other accounts.[838] (2) The positive criterion: legend is recognizable in form and substance: (a) it has a poetic form, and (b) its substance accords with the prevailing ideas. When these factors combine, we see myth.[839]

In his examination of the gospel miracles, Strauss points out contradictions, legendary developments (from Matthew to Luke to Mark, that is), and Old Testament parallels accounting for the origin of the gospel accounts. With regard to the resurrection, Strauss regards Jesus's predictions as

post eventum interpretations.[840]   The miraculous events
attending Jesus's death are mythical or symbolic
offspring.[841]   As for the burial, if the body was
embalmed and wrapped, he asks, why do the women return
for this purpose?   And was the body placed in the tomb
because it was Joseph's or because it was near?[842]   The
story of the guard is unhistorical, for (1) the Jews
could not have known Jesus's prediction, (2) the women
would have known of the guard, (3) Pilate would not
have consented, nor would the guards tell a story for
which they could be executed, and (4) the Jews spoke
only of theft, so the Christians invented the guard.[843]
In the empty tomb narratives the discrepancies are
irreconcilable.   The angels are later embellishments.
Matthew reproduces the message of the angel in an
appearance of Jesus himself.   John betrays a tendency
to subordinate Peter to John.[844]   With regard to the
appearances, Strauss demands why Jesus should command
the disciples to stay in Jerusalem while he went to
Galilee?   And why tell them to go to Galilee when he
was going to appear to them in Jerusalem?   Acts
contradicts Luke with regard to the duration of the
appearances.   For these reasons no credence need be
given to the gospel stories of the discovery of the
empty tomb and the resurrection appearances of Jesus.

        Despite all this, Strauss admits that Paul's
challenge in I Corinthians 15 concerning living
witnesses of an appearance of Jesus to over 500
brethren makes it certain that persons were alive at
that time who believed they had seen the risen
Christ.[845]   How then can one most satisfactorily
explain the supposed resurrection of Christ?   Certainly
not by supernatural intervention, for this is
unenlightened;

> The proposition: a dead man has returned to life,
> is composed of two such contradictory elements,
> that whenever it is attempted to maintain the one,
> the other threatens to disappear. If he has
> really returned to life, it is natural to conclude
> that he was not wholly dead; if he was really
> dead, it is difficult to believe that he has
> really become living . . . . Hence the cultivated
> intellect of the present day has very decidedly
> stated that following dilemma: either Jesus was
> not really dead, or he did not really rise
> again.[846]

But that Jesus never died is the worn-out old warhorse
of rationalism and must be rejected. Therefore, Jesus
did not rise again. What about the appearances of
Christ? Paul's own personal experience makes it clear
that these appearances, which Paul places all on an
equal level, were not external to the mind.[847] This
enables us to reconstruct the origin of the
resurrection narratives. The disciples were impressed
that Jesus was the Messiah. So subsequent to his
death, they later began to search the scriptures. They
found the dying and glorified Messiah of Isaiah 53.
How then could Jesus fail to reveal himself to them out
of his glory? Soon they would see him, especially the
women. They would naturally infer that the grave must
be empty, and as they had gone back to Galilee, there
was no closed tomb to refute them. By the time they
began to preach the resurrection in Jerusalem, which
was certainly not as soon as Pentecost, as a time
interval must be allowed for the process described
above, it was no longer possible to be refuted by the
body of Jesus. In this way the idea of the
resurrection of Jesus came into being.

Strauss, who was denied either academic post or
pulpit because of his views, concluded that although
the resurrection never occurred, it is nevertheless

uncultivated to denounce a theologian as a hypocrite because he preaches the resurrection without believing in the historical event.[848]   The essence of the Christian faith stands perfectly independently of historical criticism.   The resurrection remains an eternal truth, whatever doubts may be cast on it as a historical event.

The impact on the
traditional apologetic

Strauss's work, states Farrar, completely altered the whole tone and course of German theology.[849]   By rejecting on the one hand the conspiracy theory of Reimarus and on the other the natural explanation theory of Paulus, and by proposing a third explanation of the gospel narratives in terms of myth, legend, and redaction, Strauss in effect dissolved the central dilemma of the eighteenth century apologists' argument for the resurrection of Jesus. The evangelists were now seen to be neither deceivers nor deceived, but rather they stood at the end of a long process in which the original events were re-shaped through mythological and legendary influences. The dissolution of the orthodox dilemma did not logically imply that the supernaturalist view was therefore false. But this Strauss not only took to have been shown by the Reimarus-inspired objections concerning contradictions and inconsistencies in the narratives, but for him this was simply given by definition in the criteria for discerning mythological motifs, which were in turn predicated upon the a priori presupposition of the impossibility of miracles. Any event which stood outside the inviolable chain of natural causes and

effects was _ipso facto_ unhistorical and therefore to be
mythologically explained. This was the legacy which
Strauss bequeathed to his successors.[850] As Frei says,
reasons for rejecting as unhistorical reports which run
contrary to our general experience of natural,
historical, or psychological occurrences "have become
standard explanations of the criteria that go into
making unprejudiced ('presuppositionless') assessments
of what is likely to have taken place in the past, and
what is not."[851] Such a perspective makes it
impossible even to regard the resurrection as an event
of history, much less to establish it as such.

It was not, therefore, simply the advance of
biblical criticism that destroyed the historical
argument for the resurrection. Historical-critical
studies in the second half of the present century have
demonstrated at least the compatibility of that
methodology and the resurrection as an object of
historical research.[852] Rather it seems to have been
the Deist presupposition against miracles, taken up
into criticism by Rationalism, which precluded a
historical inquiry into that event, miraculously
conceived. Strauss used the Hegelian term "_aufgehoben_"
to describe the relationship of the Deism of Reimarus
to subsequent biblical criticism:

> Hegel would have said that Reimarus's viewpoint
> has been absorbed into that of the contemporary
> science of religion. For him . . . taking things
> into a higher unity was admittedly not merely an
> abolishing but at the same time a preservation, as
> we know. What has been taken up into a higher
> unity is indeed no longer what sets the tone and
> represents the exclusive and ultimate validity; it
> has been deposed for the moment by something
> higher that developed out of it. But this higher
> thing would not be such if it were itself merely a
> one-sided abstraction, if it were bent on

destroying what has been taken up in it or making
it ineffective; rather it preserves it within
itself, even if only with relative validity. It
is exactly the same with Reimarus's views.[873]

As Strauss himself then points out, it was Reimarus's
anti-supernaturalism which was preserved and only his
conspiracy theory which was abolished. Had it not been
for this presupposition, there would seem to be no
inherent reason why the demise of the historical
argument for the resurrection had to accompany the
advance in the science of biblical criticism. For if,
as Semler argued, contradictions in the secondary
details do not disprove the fact of the resurrection,
then it would have been theoretically possible to argue
for the historicity of the event itself, while
admitting the contradictions. But given the
impossibility of miracles, such an avenue was closed in
advance. And given the transcendent truth of
Christianity regardless of the historicity of the
gospel records, such an apologetic was simply
pointless.

The Tide of Subjectivism

During roughly the same period as that described
in the foregoing section there arose in Europe a
reaction to the Age of Reason in which the pendulum
swung away from the objective and rational to a
reappreciation of the subjective and sentimental. The
theological rationalism which had constituted the
common ground for the Deist controversy was swept away
by a romanticism emphaisizing the subjective
apprehension and appropriation of religious truth.

Subjectivism in England

Theological Complacency

Though this backlash of subjectivism was to have
the most far-reaching ramifications for theology in
Germany, it also swept over England and France as well.
In England after Paley, a sort of theological
self-complacency set in: the work had been done, the
foe of Deism had ostensibly been crushed, the final
word had been pronounced. There seemed little more to
be said concerning the historical evidences for faith.
There were still evidential, apologetic treatises
written, more so in England than in France or Germany,
but they were fewer in number and more mediocre than
those of the previous century. For example, the
Scottish churchman Thomas Chalmers (1780-1847) composed
The Miraculous and Internal Evidences of the Christian
Revelation (n.d.), but this is a disappointing rehash
of Paley and his predecessors. Richard Whately's
Historic Doubts Relative to Napoleon Bonaparte (1819)
is an entertaining attempt to show how Hume's in
principle argument against miracles would, if applied
equably, eliminate the historicity of Napoleon, but
Whately's work is restricted to the refutation of
Hume's essay and furnishes no positive evidence for
Christian revelation. Undoubtedly much of this
complacency in English theology during the first half
of the nineteenth century was due to ignorance of the
revolution in biblical criticism going on in German
lands. English theology was isolated, and the majority
of English divines were utterly ignorant of the
advances in biblical criticism on the Continent.[854]
They were unaware of the new challenge this posed for
Christian faith; for them the threat had been met and

conquered by Paley's apologetic approach, and the
argument could not be stated much more effectively.
There were few great theological thinkers in England
during this time and few great works written. The most
important religious figures of the time were Coleridge
and Newman; but the latter was something of a solitary
figure, while the former was not even a theologian.
And both were deeply influenced by Romanticism such
that their approach to religion was heavily
subjectivistic.

Religious revival

At the same time that this theological and
apologetic complacency prevailed, there arose the
counter-reaction to the Age of Reason of Romanticism
and religious subjectivism. As Cragg points out, there
was in eighteenth century England an ineradicable fear
of fanaticism, such that any display of religious
emotion or zeal was considered unseemly and
dangerous.[855] "Enthusiasm" was the bête noire of the
age. Religion became dry, academic, and ethical. Thus
when the Wesleys and Whitefield began to preach the
need for personal, spiritual rebirth and renewal, they
were denounced by churchmen as ugly enthusiasts. But
their message opened fresh springs for the dry souls of
the English laity. In so doing, they helped to prepare
the ground for the change in mood of the next century.

> Indirectly . . . Methodism had an influence upon
> the theology of the succeeding century . . . .
> after the rationalistic methods of the eighteenth
> century had proved their impotence, it was seen
> that a wider spiritual vision was needed, if a
> theology was to grow up, adequate to religious
> experience. This wider vision Wesley and
> Whitefield helped to create, and they did so by
> restoring to the emotions their place in religion.

Religion for the average man, and for the uneducated in particular, can never be founded on argument. Its basis must be laid deeper, in an appeal to the heart and the will. But, broadly speaking, we are right in saying that it was just this appeal which was lacking in the teaching of the English clergy at this period. Their sermons, for the most part, were moral essays, or logical demonstrations, and were addressed to the head, not the heart. Christian morality was taught, but its practice was advocated from prudential motives. There was an absence of fire. 'Enthusiasm' was a thing to be avoided at all costs.[856]

Wesley reacted against the theological rationalism of his day, re-introducing the inner witness of the Spirit in the life of the believer, but he did not, it must be said, depreciate reason itself.[857] "When you despise or depreciate reason, you must not imagine that you are doing God service; least of all, are you promoting the cause of God when you are endeavouring to exclude reason out of religion."[858] Rather he emphasized the restrictedness of reason in furnishing truths about God and religion. If man is to know anything more about God than his mere existence, revelation is absolutely necessary. This Wesley found in the Bible, which he regarded as the inspired Word of God to men. It was to be interpreted by reason and confirmed by experience through the inner witness of the Holy Spirit. This confirmation by experience represents the new and subjective contribution of Methodism to religious consciousness. Later evangelicals, unlike Wesley, did betray a tendency to depreciate intellectual effort in favor of religious experience.[859] They conceived of religion as an individualistic, subjective relation of the soul to God brought about by the inner work of the Holy Spirit upon the heart of an individual. Their interest lay primarily in spiritual religion, and

fields of study that lay outside this concern were
viewed with indifference or hostility. Even in the
realms of theology and exegesis they produced no great
work. During the early years of the nineteenth
century, the evangelicals were the strongest influence
in the Church of England, and their religious
subjectivism helped to usher in the Romantic Age and to
undercut the traditional, objectivist apologetic.

Romanticism

Following the religious revivals of the
eighteenth century came the literary revival. Storr
remarks, ". . . the literary and poetic revival which
had begun in the preceding century, and was now in
progress in England, owed not a little to the religious
revival. The religious awakening, effected in the
eighteenth century by Methodism and Evangelicalism,
provided a general atmosphere of emotion which formed a
stimulus for fresh, creative literary effort."[860] The
strivings of the Romantic Age were first felt in a
re-appreciation of nature and its beauty. The
formalism and descriptive objectivity of the
conventional treatments of nature was replaced by a
feeling for the living and spiritual beauty of nature,
with a recognition of the spiritual ties between man
and nature. These sentiments reach their highest
expression in the poetry of Wordsworth, for whom nature
is invested with a spiritual beauty and religious
significance such that it becomes the manifestation of
God himself. Romanticism rebelled against the
rationalizing tendencies of the Enlightenment and
rediscovered the emotional and intuitive facets of
human nature. The mysterious and the wondrous, not
subsumable under rational categories of thought,

allured the mind of the Romantic. Coleridge, the most
influencial of the English Romantic religious thinkers,
differentiated in this regard between the faculties of
understanding and reason. The former grasped all those
truths known by the scientific empiricism of the
Enlightenment, while reason he re-defined to be the
higher faculty which is the source of religious beliefs
and personal ideals. Coleridge had absorbed the spirit
of German idealism and Romanticism during his visit to
Germany in 1798. Not only did he thus imbibe Romantic
idealism, but equally important for our purposes, in
his theological discussions with Eichhorn's followers
at Gottingen he confronted for the first time German
biblical criticism. In England the Bible was still
regarded as inspired and reliable in all respects. The
argument from design established the existence of God,
and miracle and prophecy proved the Bible to be His
revelation. But Coleridge's faith in this approach was
shaken by his encounter with German criticism. The
arguments against infallibility he judged to be
insurmountable. But he did not therefore abandon the
Bible. Rather under the influence of Lessing, whose
work he met during his sojourn in Germany, he
maintained that the truth of Scripture lay not in
the letter, but in the spirit. He advises, read the
Bible as you would any other book and you will find
that it is better than any other book because it
speaks to the deepest needs and aspirations of human
nature.[861] ". . . the Bible and Christianity," he
declares, "are their own sufficient evidence."[862] Here
Coleridge's Romanticism with its subjective and
self-attesting warrant for Christianity supplants the
old, objectivist apologetic:

THE RESURRECTION OF JESUS

> I more than fear the prevailing taste for books of
> natural theology, physico-theology, demonstrations
> of God from nature, and the like--Evidences of
> Christianity! I am weary of the word. Make a man
> feel the want of it; rouse him, if you can, to the
> self-knowledge of his need of it; and you may
> safely trust to its own evidence.[863]

For Coleridge the appeal of Christianity lay not in its
intellectual superiority, but in its fulfillment of
human needs and aspirations. Therefore, the typical
evidentialist approach was just misguided.

Under the influence of Romanticism and the
pressure of criticism, the traditional, objective,
evidentialist apologetic of the previous century was
supplanted by the subjective approach of Coleridge:

> Romanticism . . . has, working here together with
> the historical method, called into being a new
> apologetic. The apologetic of the last half of
> the eighteenth century, and of the earlier years
> of the nineteenth, was narrowly evidential. The
> standing arguments were those from miracle and
> prophecy, or from the trustworthiness of the New
> Testament writers, as proved by their readiness to
> die for their beliefs. Elaborate schemes were
> drawn up in defense of Christianity. They were
> based upon a false theory of the inspiration of
> the Bible, were often dry and technical, requiring
> for their appreciation a detailed knowledge of the
> scriptural narratives. It was an apologetic which
> lacked a spiritual appeal. The newer apologetic,
> which, after it had received its initial impulse
> from Coleridge, gradually gathered force in
> England in the nineteenth century, was very
> different in aim and method. It found in
> Christianity a message for the whole nature of
> man. The appeal to human needs and their
> satisfaction in Christ became a dominant feature
> of apologetic writings . . . . The argument from
> prophecy . . . recedes into the background when
> biblical criticism begins to show the true
> character of the prophet's work. Miracles are no
> longer regarded as the main evidence for the truth
> of Christianity. The greatest miracle of all is
> seen to be the Person of Christ, whose claim to be
> Way, Truth, and Life has been justified in the

continuous   experience   of   the   Christian
consciousness.[864]

This turn toward subjectivism obviated the need for and
the appeal of a historical argument for the
resurrection of Jesus, since this truth could be known
through Christian experience. Thus, although, for
example, the great exegete B.F. Wescott authored two
books on the resurrection of Jesus, The Gospel of the
Resurrection (1866) and The Revelation of the Risen
Lord (1881), neither deals with the historical
question, but the first leans toward amateur
philosophizing, while the second is largely devotional
in character.[865] As the impact of German biblical
criticism led by Strauss and Baur made itself
increasingly felt in Britain, the appeal of the
subjective approach, which did not depend on
establishing historically the miraculous events of the
gospels, became even stronger. One of the few
exceptions to this general subjectivizing of
apologetics was the Scottish divine A.B. Bruce, whose
Apologetics (1892), Dulles deems "the most
distinguished apologetical manual in English" during
its time, a "highly successful piece of work" which
with some updating "could still be serviceable
today."[866] But Bruce himself, remarking on the advance
of nineteenth century unbelief over the simple fraud
hypothesis of the eighteenth century, admits that
contemporary Christian apologetic divorces Christianity
from history.[867] Thus, the old Hastings' Encyclopedia
of Religion and Ethics reported, "The bitter attack
upon miracles in the nineteenth century has caused
recent apologists to seek some line of proof that
should be independent of this confident assault. It is
on the moral aspects of Christianity that the chief

stress is now laid."[868]

Subjectivism in France

Post-revolutionary subjectivism

The same subjectivism that dominated England also
swept France after the Revolution. The Revolution had
been the brainchild of the Age of Reason, this fact
being perhaps most poignantly symbolized by the
substitution of a Cult of Reason at the Cathedral of
Notre Dame in the place of Christianity. On November
9, 1793 an actress in the guise of Reason led in
procession from the Convention to the cathedral where
she was elevated upon the altar. The Christian week
with its Sunday was to be replaced by a ten-day week,
holy days abolished, and the calendar revised such that
years be computed from the date of the establishment of
the Republic as year one. But the Reign of Terror
masterminded by Robespierre produced a bitter backlash,
which ended in his death. For more than 20 years the
favorite theme of the philosophes had been the tyranny
and persecution of the church; now suddenly the roles
had been reversed. One had been led to believe that
the reign of the disciples of the philosophes would be
one of liberty, equality, and fraternity. But the
facts proved otherwise, as Duvoisin observed:

> Experience has judged the systems, and now one
> knows what becomes of a nation which lets itself
> be governed by philosophers. This terrible lesson
> will not be lost on posterity. Already
> anti-religious prejudices are beginning to die out
> . . . . One finally understands that there cannot
> be morality without religion, nor religion without
> a public form of worship and those not blinded by
> philosophical fanaticism recognize that the
> Christian religion is the only one which can bring[869]
> morality back into the family and society.

In 1795 the religious press reappeared, and in 1796 the
doors of the churches reopened. In 1801 Napoleon, who
had become First Consul of France, negotiated the
Concordat with Rome, which reestablished Catholicism as
the religion of the majority of Frenchmen. On April 11
of the next year, some eight years after the Cult of
Reason had been inaugurated at Notre Dame, the
Christian Sunday was reinstated in a public ceremony at
the cathedral. But the religion which emerged
chastened from the Revolution had been purged of the
theological rationalism of the preceding century. The
end result of the Age of Reason had been the Terreur,
bringing disenchantment with the approach of
rationalism. Moreover, not all the ground which had
been lost by the Catholic faith had been taken over by
reason: many had turned to spiritism and mysticism,
astrology, divination, and theurgy. Given these
circumstances, the success of the subjectivist
apologetic of Chateaubriand was assured.

François de Chateaubriand's Le génie du
christianisme; ou, beautés de la religion chrétienne
(1802) was the first significant apologetic work to
appear after the Revolution, and it stamped the era to
follow with a decidely subjective approach to
Christianity. Farrar writes,

> The spiritual tone of such a writer as Chateau-
> briand, similar to that of the Romantic literature
> of Germany, awakened in France early in the
> century the conceptions of a world of spirit, of
> chivalrous honour, of immortal hope, of divine
> Providence; and led mankind to feel that there was
> something in them nobler than mere material
> organism, even a spirit that yearned for the world
> invisible. Chateaubriand showed . . . that
> Christianity was not merely suited to a rude age,
> but was the friend of art, of intellect, of
> improvement.[870]

As a young man Chateaubriand was a Deist and disciple
of Rousseau, and while in London in 1792 he published
his   Essai historique, politique et moral sur les
révolutions, in which he sought to show that truth is
attained not by philosophical reasoning but by an inner
light or feeling.   Though the death of his mother
brought him back to Catholicism, the impress of
Rousseau's subjectivism never left him.   The
subjectivism, therefore, which shaped nineteenth
century French apologetics was actually the legacy of
Rousseau handed on by Chateaubriand.

Historical antecedents

        This makes it worthwhile to survey the background
and nature of Rouseau's subjectivism.   From Pascal
there runs through French apologetics a subjective
stream emphasizing so-called "reasons of the heart,"
the inherent beauty and truth of the Christian religion
which impress themselves immediately upon the heart of
the sincere inquirer, furnishing him with an inner and
spiritual certainty not dependent upon external
evidence.   In thinkers like Pascal and Abbadie, the
internal and external proofs of Christianity are wed
together to provide both rational and spiritual
conviction of Christianity's truth.   But due in part to
the influence of Pietism, the external proofs sometimes
dropped away, leaving only the apologetic of internal
experience.   The most important precursor of Rousseau
in this respect is Marie Huber.

        Marie Huber.   She is, according to Monod, the
principal representative of a line of "pietistic
rationalists" who increasingly internalize religion
and, rejecting all external authority, recognize only

the authority of conscience and experience of the soul.[871] Pietism, which had spread itself throughout French Switzerland, tended to identify religion with inner, individual piety rather than with theology or the church. It was oriented toward experience rather than ideas and so opened a door to unorthodox theology. Hence, writes Monod, "The orthodox Spener counts among his authentic decendants Rousseau, Kant, and above all Marie Huber."[872] Born into a Pietist family in Geneva in 1695, she moved to Lyon in 1711 with her family, where they maintained relationships with German, Swiss, and English mystics. At the age of 22 Marie left on a mission to convert the city of Geneva, but was very badly received by the clergy. Doubting the authority of the church, she departed ever further from orthodox Christianity between the years of 1722 and 1731. Then she began to publish her works on pietistic natural religion. In Le monde fou préféré au monde sage, en vingt-six promenades (1731), she upholds conscience as the only guide of life and test for religious truth. She escapes the Baylean dilemmas posed in ascribing this role to conscience simply by refusing to argue about them: the pietist cannot answer the difficulties, but he knows his own experience. Conscience is invariable in itself, the true light and key to knowledge, but men play upon it, arguing about conscience rather than listening to their own. This appeal to conscience leads to a religious relativism and universalism. Two people of equally upright will may, due to the external circumstances in which they were raised, come to believe different religions. Since these factors are beyond their control, they are not responsible and, hence, not culpable for their beliefs. "We may conclude from this that one is no less agreeable to God than the other and that though they have different names one is a Jew or a Christian only externally."[873] This constitutes "the essence of Christianity."[874]

But what of the Scriptures? To answer this question, she differentiates two sorts of truths: one is united to the Truth inseparably like the rays of the sun, while the other is like objects which the sun illuminates. Of the latter class are historical facts, including those of the Old and New Testaments. The Scriptures, she says, are not the Truth, but only a witness to the Truth. "The Scripture is a tableau, a rough and imperfect image of invisible things."[875] The Truth bears witness to itself both as cause and object, directly as cause within conscience and indirectly as object in the Holy Scriptures. It is the will in each individual man which determines how his understanding will apprehend the Truth. She depicts in a fable warring religious sects as people wearing glasses which make objects appear differently to each of them.[876] The point would seem to be that if people would listen to the inner voice of conscience rather than concentrate on the external objects pointing to the Truth, then they would all discover the Truth. In fact, Marie Huber reduces Christianity to natural religion:

> I understand by religion not only what was manifested to men by the Law or by the Gospel, but that which is called natural Religion, that which men can know of the Truth from without by the testimony of Nature and from within by that of Conscience. This Religion is the foundation of the Christian Religion; the Christian Religion adds nothing to it, basically and essentially, but it serves to develop and show to men the use to which they can put it.[877]

With this expression of Deist sentiments, we see
clearly the religious affinities of Marie Huber with
Jean-Jacques Rousseau. The appeal to the authority of
conscience with its attendant universalism, the attempt
to retain the spiritual teaching of Scripture while
denying its literal, historical truth and authority,
and the reduction of Christianity to natural religion
are chords which are all echoed by Rousseau. He read
and annotated Huber's work, probably during his sojourn
in Geneva [878], such that Monod can call her "la mère
spirituelle du Vicaire savoyard."[879]

Jean-Jacques Rousseau. We have already discussed
the rationalistic side of Rousseau's religion, but this
picture would be a distortion if it were not completed
by the strong subjectivism of Rousseau. For him reason
was but one factor in the mind's apprehension of truth.
In addition to this are nature and conscience. "Look
at the spectacle of nature, listen to the inner voice.
Has not God said all to our eyes, to our conscience, to
our judgement?"[880] It is significant that the
'Profession de foi" is set upon a high hill overlooking
the Po with the Alps visible along the horizon and the
sun's rays bathing the countryside. It is as if nature
were displaying before our eyes all its magnificence in
order to offer the text for our conversation, writes
Rousseau.[881] Only after contemplating these objects in
silence does the Vicar begin to speak. Nature provides
the proper context and backdrop for the discussion of
God and spiritual truths. For Rousseau nature speaks
to man of the existence of God, and the inner response
of man's conscience confirms the impression which
nature makes upon him. "Let us compare the particular
ends, the means, the ordered relations of every kind,
then let us listen to the inner feeling; what sound

mind can reject its testimony? To what eyes not
blinded does the sensible order of the universe not
announce a supreme intelligence?[882] The testimony of
nature without is complemented and confirmed by the
testimony of conscience within. Over and over again,
some 20 times in the "Profession de foi," "Lettre à M.
de Beaumont," and "Lettres de la montagne," Rousseau
stresses this subjective proof from the inner voice.
Whether he calls it les lumières primitives, la lumière
intérieure, le sentiment intérieur, la voix intérieure,
it all comes to the same thing: the subjective,
arational conviction of a truth presented to the mind.
Grimsley comments, "Rousseau tirelessly insists upon
the essential principle of inwardness. The term 'inner
light' does not denote any kind of mystical
illumination, but simply expresses the intuitive
certainty of immediate consciousness."[883] Insofar as
this inner voice operates in the ethical realm to
prescribe rules of conduct for personal behavior,
Rousseau calls it conscience.[884] This he elevates
above reason, calling it the true guide of man, a
divine instinct, an immortal and celestial voice, an
infallible judge of good and evil. When the Vicaire
savoyard finishes his discourse, his young companion,
states Rousseau, could have made many objections, but
he did not chiefly because the priest had spoken
according to his conscience and the young man's
conscience also felt persuaded.[885] Rousseau's
subjectivism comes clearly to the fore here. The Vicar
has used rational argument, but in the end, as the
young man says, "It is the inner feeling which must
lead me to your example . . . ."[886] Interestingly, it
is when he turns to his critique of revealed
religion that Rousseau is most rationalistic: here he

says, "For the rest give me only the authority of
reason . . ." and demands reasons to submit his reason
to revelation.[887]   Nevertheless, even here his
subjectivism triumphs in the end:

> I also confess to you that the majesty[+] of the
> Scriptures astound me, that the holiness of the
> Gospel speaks to my heart. Look at the books of
> the philosophers with all their pomp: how small
> they are next to that book! Could it be that a
> book so sublime and at the same time so simple is
> the work of men? Could it be that the one whose
> history it tells is but a man himself? Do we find
> there the tone of an enthusiast or of an ambitious
> sectary?   What sweetness, what purity in his
> morals!   What touching grace in his teachings!
> What elevation in his maxims!   What profound
> wisdom in his discourses! What presence of mind,
> what finesse and what correctness in his answers!
> What control of his passions!

————————

[+]sublimity[888]

Rousseau contrasts Jesus with Socrates, especially in
their deaths, concluding, "Yes, if the life and death
of Socrates is that of a sage, the life and death of
Jesus is that of a God."[889]   These reasons of the heart
counterbalance the rational absurdities of the
Scriptures so that one is left in a sort of involuntary
scepticism in which the biblical religion is not
declared to be either true or false.   The essence of
Christianity consists in loving God and your neighbor
as yourself.[890]

     According to Monod, one of the curious results of
Rousseau's work was that almost all of his opponents
came to adopt the subjective proof of inner experience
for the faith.[891]   Misinterpreting Pascal's approach to
be one-sidedly subjectivistic, they revived his
apologetic of the reasons of the heart for use against

Rousseau. Bergier, as we have seen, refuted Rousseau in Le Déisme réfuté par lui-même (1765) from an objectivist standpoint, but despite this, few apologists escaped the influence of Rousseau's subjectivism. When in his Examen du matérialisme (1771), Bergier places his final reliance on proofs of God from sentiment, Rousseau's triumph is complete. By winning even his enemies to the mode of his approach, Rousseau set the stage for the anti-intellectualism and subjectivism of the next century.

François René de Chateaubriand

French Romanticism was more sentimental than the German, and nowhere is the subjectivistic, feeling-oriented apologetic for Christian belief better expressed than in Chateaubriand's Le génie du christianisme.[892] Because the traditional apologetic approach to Christianity on the basis of evidences has failed to carry conviction, Chateaubriand declares that he will employ a different approach: proving Christianity is true because it is excellent. In part one he expounds the exalted doctrines of Christianity: the Trinity, incarnation, sacraments and so forth. In part two he shows how the Christian religion has stimulated and enriched the dramatic and poetic arts, as, for example, in the works of Dante and Milton. In the third part of his work, Chateaubriand discusses the benefits of Christianity to the fine arts and literature. In music, art, architecture, oratory, and history Christianity has given birth to the greatest works of man. It is especially interesting that in philosophy, Chateaubriand lauds Malebranche's Recherche de la vérité, Clarke's Treatise on the Existence of God, and Leibniz's Theodicy, all works of philosophical

rationalism in which reasoning by the empirical facts
plays virtually no role. This leap-frogging of a whole
century of empirically oriented thought to return to
the apriori rationalism of old underlines his rejection
of the traditional evidentialist apologetic. Finally
part four praises the Catholic church in its liturgy,
priesthood, and mission to the world. Through his
subjectivist apologetic, Chateaubriand shaped at its
inception the Christian thought of France during the
nineteenth century. Dulles remarks,

> Chateaubriand's apologetic, while it may have
> proved next to nothing, succeeded in presenting
> Christianity in colors that appealed enormously to
> French readers of the day . . . . By calling
> attention to the many blessings brought into the
> world by Christianity he helped to restore the
> morale of a Church that had been too long on the
> defensive, and thus he evoked an enthusiastic
> response among a people eager for a restoration of
> the glories of ancient France.[893]

Under the influence of the subjectivism of Rousseau and
Chateaubriand, French apologetics turned away from the
evidential approach and the historical argument for the
resurrection of Jesus.

When the impact of biblical criticism eventually
began to make itself felt in France, the subjective,
feeling-oriented approach found that it could sleep
comfortably in the same bed with the new, sceptical
criticism. Ernst Renan's Le vie de Jesus (1863) was
the most popular life in the nineteenth century Life of
Jesus movement and the first to be written by a
Catholic.[894] It is a syrupy work, gushing with
sentimentality, whose gentle Jesus, beautiful Mary, and
fair Galileans Schweizer aptly compared to the
figurines in the shop window of an ecclesiastical art
emporium in the Place de St. Sulpice.[895] Though

Renan's Jesus is purely human, a tragic and disappointed martyr whose life ends in crucifixion, Renan still praises him because his religion of love will go on and his story will call forth endless tears. Sentimentality thus finds in Christianity the truth of which historical criticism would threaten to rob it.

During the period of the Restoration, there also occurred a return to the rigid authoritarianism of the Catholic church, which commanded by right of divine and infallible authority. Authoritarian traditionalists like Maistre and Bonald had no more use for an evidentialist apologetic than did the subjectivists. Spurned therefore by both the authoritarians and the Romantics, the objectivist, evidentialist apologetic was relegated to the obscurity of Catholic seminary manuals on apologetics.[896]

Subjectivism in Germany

Immanuel Kant

In Germany, too, the tide of subjectivism prevailed. The key seminal figure in the turn from objective arguments and evidences for faith to an inward, subjective justification is Immanuel Kant. Kant's approach to religious epistemology has both a negative and a positive face, the one inspired by the scepticism of Hume and the other by the subjectivism of Rousseau. Kant tersely summarized the entire project of his Kritik der reinen Vernunft (1781) in terms of these two aspects: "I have therefore found it necessary to deny knowledge in order to make room for faith."[897]

The elimination of speculative metaphysics. Kant had been educated under Martin Knutzen at the

University of Königsberg in the rationalist tradition
of Leibniz as systematized by Wolff, which Kant called
"dogmatism" (since it proceeded into metaphysics on the
basis of reason without a previous criticism of the
powers of reason).[898]   Some years later, prior to the
first Critique, Kant encountered the sceptical
empiricism of David Hume.

The Scottish philosopher in his A Treatise of
Human Nature (1738-40) and An Enquiry Concerning Human
Understanding (1751) had conducted an examination of
the powers of reason, with decidely negative results.
According to Hume, "All the objects of human reason or
enquiry may naturally be divided into two kinds, to
wit, Relations of Ideas and Matters of Fact."[899]
Belonging to the first class are mathematical and other
sorts of proposition intuitively or demonstratively
certain, while the second class is comprised of all
propositions dependent upon sense experience for their
truth value. Truths expressing relations of ideas are
purely formal in nature and communicate no knowledge of
the real world, being true by definition. To deny them
is to involve oneself in logical contradiction. By
contrast matters of fact are not true by definition and
thus can be negated without contradiction. Since they
are dependent upon sense experience for the
determination of their truth value, they are genuinely
informative about reality. Since matters of fact are
based on sense experience, it follows that no matter of
fact can be the subject of demonstration, for its
opposite always remains logically possible.

> It seems to me, that the only objects of the
> abstract sciences or of demonstration are quantity
> and number, and that all attempts to extend this
> more perfect species of knowledge beyond these
> bounds are mere sophistry and illusion . . . . All

other enquiries of men regard only matter of fact
and existence; and these are evidently incapable
of demonstration. Whatever is may not be. No
negation of a fact can involve a contradiction.
The non-existence of any being, without exception,
is as clear and distinct an idea as its existence.
The proposition, which affirms it not to be, however false, is no less conceivable and intelligible than that which affirms it to be . . . . The
existence, therefore, of any being can only be
proved by arguments from its cause and its effect;
and these arguments are founded entirely on
experience.[900]

But the causal relation is itself incapable of
demonstration. For the essence of the causal relation
consists in some necessary connection between the cause
and its effect,[901] but this connection is given neither
a priori by definition nor a posteriori in experience.
The proposition that 'whatever begins to exist has a
cause' is neither intuitively obvious nor demonstrable,
for we can conceive of an object as non-existent and
then as existent without conceiving of its cause.[902]
This means that it is only on the basis of experience
that we can infer the existence of one object from
another. But, Hume argues, experience provides no such
warrant. For simply because we have always observed
two objects in constant conjunction does not entail the
idea of a necessary connection between them. Moreover,
we have no assurance that the future will resemble the
past, that these objects will be constantly conjoined
in the future.[903] Hume is therefore driven to the
conclusion that the idea of necessary connection is
subjective, derived from the propensity of the mind to
pass from one object to another which is observed to be
constantly conjoined with the first.[904] Since all
reasoning in matters of fact beyond mere reports of
immediate sense impression are based on the causal
relation, this leads Hume into scepticism concerning

almost all statements informative about reality. He
recognized, however, that such a Pyrrhonical philosophy
was practically untenable. The chief and most
confounding objection to this excessive scepticism is
that no durable good can ever result from it, so long
as it remains in full force and vigor. A Pyrrhonian
"must acknowledge, if he will acknowledge anything,
that all human life must perish, were his principles
universally and steadily to prevail. All discourse,
all action would immediately cease; and men remain in a
total lethargy, till the necessities of nature,
unsatisfied, put an end to their miserable
existence."[905] But nature will not allow such an end:

> Most fortunately it happens, that since reason is
> incapable of dispelling these clouds, nature
> herself suffices to that purpose, and cures me of
> this philosophical melancholy and delirium, either
> by relaxing this bent of mind, or by some
> avocation, and lively impression of my senses,
> which obliterate all these chimeras. I dine, I
> play a game of back-gammon, I converse, and am
> merry with my friends; and when after three or
> four hour's amusement, I wou'd return to these
> speculations, they appear so cold, and strain'd,
> and ridiculous, that I cannot find in my heart to
> enter into them any farther. Here then I find
> myself absolutely and necessarily determin'd to
> live, and talk, and act like other people in the
> common affairs of life.[906]

Nevertheless, despite this admission, Hume saw value in
a sort of mitigated scepticism, which, while allowing
one to go confidently about the affairs of everyday
life such as nature would constrain him to undertake,
would remain nonetheless an effective check against
abstract philosophical reasonings.[907] Hume leaves no
doubts about the effect of his mitigated scepticism
upon theology:

> When we run over libraries, persuaded of these
> principles, what havoc must we make? If we take
> in hand any volume; of divinity or school
> metaphysics, for instance; let us ask, <u>Does it
> contain any abstract reasoning concerning quantity
> or number? No. Does it contain any experimental
> reasoning concerning matter of fact and existence?
> No. Commit it then to the flames: for it can
> contain nothing but sophistry and illusion.</u>[908]

Kant tells us in his <u>Prolegomena zu einer jeden
künftigen Metaphysik</u> (1783) that it was Hume that
"first interrupted my dogmatic slumber and gave my
investigations in the field of speculative philosophy a
quite new direction."[909] Unwilling to embrace either
dogmatism or scepticism, Kant sought to forge a new
alternative, which he called criticism. He proposed to
undertake a critique of pure reason in order to
discover what and how much reason can know apart from
all experience.[910] He believed he could enunciate and
justify a class of propositions that fell into neither
of Hume's divisions of relations of ideas or matters of
fact. Like Hume, he began by distinguishing two types
of knowledge: knowledge which is absolutely
independent of all experience so far as its truth value
is concerned he called <u>a priori</u> knowledge; knowledge
which is based on experience with regard to its truth
value he termed <u>a posteriori</u> knowledge.[911] A priori
propositions, being independent of all experience, are
characterized by universality and necessity, and these
twin properties serve to distinguish them from <u>a
posteriori</u> judgements. But Kant also distinguished
between what he called analytic and synthetic
statements. In an analytic proposition the predicate
is connected to the subject by a relation of identity
and merely serves to explicate the subject more fully,
while in a synthetic judgement the predicate adds to

the subject a concept which no amount of analysis could
have derived from it.[912]   Analytic propositions are
based on the law of contradiction, whereas the denial
of a synthetic proposition, though perhaps false, does
not entail a logical contradiction.[913]

By employing these two sets of distinctions, Kant
was able to generate four classes of propositions:
analytic a priori, analytic a posteriori, synthetic a
priori, and synthetic a posteriori. But not all of
these are possible: it is absurd, says Kant, to posit
analytic a posteriori propositions, since no appeal to
experience is necessary to determine the truth of an
analytic statement. Any analytic statement must
therefore be a priori and any a posteriori statement
must be synthetic. That leaves the synthetic a priori
judgement, and here we come to the issue that lies at
the heart of the Critique. Kant now stood at Hume's
fork: on the one hand lay the path of analytic a
priori knowledge, on the other that of synthetic a
posteriori knowledge. The one road led to dogmatism,
the other to scepticism. But Kant would not travel
either road; instead he struck out in a new direction
on a path that he thought would lead to necessary and
universal truths that are at the same time genuinely
informative about reality--the path of synthetic a
priori knowledge.

The question is, how can statements about the
world of sense experience ever be universal and
necessary? Kant answered this question by means of a
bold move which he declared to be a Copernican
revolution in epistemology. Hitherto, he says, it has
always been assumed that our knowledge must conform to
objects, but as this has always led to scepticism in
the past, we must now inquire whether better progress

might not be made if we assume that objects must
conform to our knowledge.[914] Just as Copernicus found
that better progress in astronomy could be made by
supposing that it was the earth that was in motion and
not the fixed stars, so better progress in epistemology
can be achieved by supposing that it is the objects
that conform to the mind and not the mind to the
objects. Kant's Copernican revolution constitutes the
foundation of his critical philosophy; indeed, he
himself states in the preface to the second edition of
the Critique that his attempt to prove the Copernican
revolution was "the main purpose" of the Critique.[915]

According to Kant's analysis, the mind structures
objects in two fundamental respects; first, the
sensibility, or the faculty whereby sense experience is
given to the percipient, structures the formless sense
data into the forms of time and space, and secondly,
the understanding, or the faculty whereby intelligent
thought conceives objects, structures the intuitions
given it by the sensibility into twelve categories
fundamental to logical thought. The sensibility and
the understanding Kant called the two stems of human
knowledge: "Through the former, objects are given to
us; through the latter, they are thought."[916] If
intelligible experience is to arise, both faculties
must be involved. "Without sensibility no object would
be given to us, without understanding no object would
be thought. Thoughts without content are empty,
intuitions without concepts are blind."[917]

In his discussion of the role of the sensibility
in sense perception, Kant distinguished between the
matter and the form of any sensory appearance to the
mind.[918] The matter corresponds to the sensation, and
the form is that which allows the sensations to be

ordered into certain relations. The matter is given to the percipient a posteriori, but the form of the appearances is imposed a priori by the mind's faculty of sensibility. Kant identified the two forms of the sensibility as time and space. The upshot of this view is that time and space are not characteristics of reality, of things in themselves, but only subjective forms which the mind imposes on sense experience. Because this is so, Kant could hold that the truths of mathematics and Newtonian physics are synthetic a priori propositions, genuinely descriptive of the world of the senses and yet universal and necessary because the mind structures all sense appearances in terms of them. But it is the world of appearance only that is so structured; reality in itself remains unknown to us.[919]

In order to determine what a priori factor the understanding brings to experience, Kant turned to logic for the clue, for all thought in order to be intelligible must be cast in logical form. He therefore compiled what he believed to be an exhaustive and irreducible list of all the logical forms which statements may assume. In order to make these judgements, Kant reasoned, the mind must be equipped with certain primitive forms of thoughts, or categories, and he attempted to correlate a category to each of the logical forms of judgement which would enable the mind to conceive that judgement. For example, in order to cogitate a hypothetical judgement "If p then q," the mind must have a category of causality and dependence, or cause and effect; otherwise, it could only conceive of p and q in terms of temporal succession, not ground and consequent. Kant derived in this manner a list of twelve categories

essential to thought. But are these categories
objective, a priori features of the mind? Kant argued
that they are, for if an object is to become an object
of thought for me, I must think of it in terms of
logical judgements, which in turn presuppose the
requisite categories in order to be framed. Unless the
categories were objective features of the mind, thought
could never arise.

> Now I maintain that the categories . . . are
> nothing but the conditions of thought in a[^4]
> possible experience, just as space and time are
> the conditions of intuition for that same
> experience. They are fundamental concepts by
> which we think objects in general for appearances,
> and have there a priori objective validity.

---

[^4] enthalten [920]

If the mind were not equipped with these categories,
then intelligible thought could never arise; since we
do have such thought, the categories must objectively
exist as its precondition.

Kant then introduced two crucial restrictions on
the categories. First, the categories have no
application beyond the realm of sense data. Since the
categories remain empty, so to speak, or mere forms of
thought without content, until impinged upon by sense
intuitions from the sensibility, they cannot operate
outside the purely empirical realm.[921] Hence, we can
have no knowledge of such non-sensible entities as God,
the soul, or freedom on the basis of speculative
reason. Indeed, Kant spent the next major division of
the Critique reinforcing this restriction by showing
the problems involved in the metaphysical employment of
reason. Secondly, the categories give us no knowledge
of things in themselves. In the same way that the

forms of space and time are imposed on sense data by
the sensibility, so the categories are imposed upon
sense intuitions by the understanding. Appearances
therefore must be structured in terms of the
categories, for example, the cause-effect relation,
thus overcoming Hume's scepticism. But once again,
Kant provides certainty concerning only the world of
appearances and this at the expense of leaving reality
in itself utterly unknown to us.[922] In this sense,
although his avowed aim was to overcome sceptical
philosophy, Kant's first Critique itself constitutes a
milestone in the history of scepticism.

   The substitution of subjective justification of
religious belief. It would appear at this point that
Kant like Hume would be prepared to consign books on
divinity or school metaphysics to the flames as nothing
but sophistry and illusion. But here Kant's program
takes a positive turn in the direction of Rousseau's
subjectivism. During his lifetime, Rousseau, whose
portrait graced the wall of Kant's study, had an even
greater influence in Germany than he did in France.
His emphasis on the role of conscience as the true
guide in matters of religion struck a sympathetic chord
in Kant's pietism. This movement, it will be
remembered, had begun after the Thirty Years' War had
ended. Spener, the father of Pietism, aspiring to
bring revival to the German church, began to hold Bible
studies and prayer meetings in his home in Frankfurt.
The movement grew in influence, and in 1694 through the
support of the elector Friedrich III of Brandenburg,
Spener helped to nominate the faculty to the newly
founded university at Halle, which became a center of
Pietist views, Francke his successor later holding the
chair of theology there. In Spener's Pia desideria,

oder, _herzliches_ _Verlangen_ _nach_ _Gottgefälliger_
Besserung _der_ _wahren_ _Evangelischen_ _Kirchen_ (1675), he
outlined the essential tenets of Pietism: (1) the
Bible should be studied more earnestly in a spirit of
devotion; (2) the laity should participate more fully
in the life and governance of the church; (3) it should
be recognized that Christianity is essentially
concerned with practice and not merely with
intellectual assent to doctrines; (4) a new style of
apologetics should be adopted that seeks to woo the
unbeliever to faith rather than condemn him; (5)
theological education in the universities should place
a higher premium on the practical and devotional life;
and (6) preaching should be revitalized to inculcate
piety in the listeners rather than to display
rhetorical eloquence.[923]   Clearly Pietism emphasized
the subjective, practical, and devotional aspects of
Christianity rather than the intellectual and
doctrinal.   In this the movement was akin to the
Methodist awakening in England, and in fact
contributory to it, for it was through his contact with
Moravian missionaries to America that Wesley first
sensed his need of spiritual regeneration.   Count
Nikolaus von Zinzendorf (1700-60), leader of the
Moravians, was a godson of Spener and pupil of Francke
at Halle, and although Wesley eventually broke with the
Moravians, he was indebted to Zinzendorf and maintained
good relations with him.   Indirectly then, this
remarkable movement, although already past the height
of its power by the middle of the eighteenth century,
through Wesley in England, Marie Huber in France, and
Kant in Germany helped to bring about a new period of
subjectivism in the nineteenth century which supplanted
the Age of Reason.

Pietism exercised a profound influence upon Kant's life and teaching. Both his parents were devout members of a Pietist church, his father a simple and upright man, his mother a woman deeply devoted to God and moved by his handiwork in creation. The family's pastor Franz Albert Schultz was a leading light of Pietism whose influence extended the life of that movement in Königsberg while it was declining elsewhere. He often visited and assisted the Kant family, taking a special interest in Immanuel. It was he who persuaded his parents to send the boy to the Collegium Fredericianum. Though a Pietist school, the college was infected by religious hyprocrisy and affected emotionalism, which apparently put Kant off permanently from being a Pietist. After eight years there, Kant entered the University of Königsberg where his teacher Knutzen turned his interest toward philosophy. Himself a pupil of Schultz, Knutzen was a faithful Pietist while at the same time a Wolffian philosophical rationalist. Kant would have seen in him the best synthesis of a man of piety and intellect. Though no longer a genuine Pietist himself, Kant retained many features of his Pietist upbringing and education. Theodore Green remarks,

> The fundamental pietist precepts which had been taught by his parents and drilled into him at the Collegium were reinforced at the University by Schultz's lectures and, we may imagine, by Knutzen's pietist theology. These essential ideas became and remained identified in his mind with the Christianity of the Bible. It is invariably the pietist version of Christianity that he seems to have in view in his later writings. True, he had early disassociated himself from certain aspects of pietism, but its emphases on the moral or practical side of religious life and on the doctrines of sin, rebirth, atonement, and the

like, became determinants that gave form to his
own mature attempt to build within the limits of
reason, the structure of his theology.[924]

Kant never divested himself of Pietism's subjectivism
and emphasis on the moral life. These elements were
underlined by Rousseau's religious philosophy and
produced a positive counterpoint to Kant's negative
restrictions on the use of theoretical reason.

In his Grundlegung zur Metaphysik der Sitten
(1785) and his Kritik der praktischen Vernunft (1788),
Kant sought to restore by means of practical reason
what he had robbed from theoretical reason. By
practical reason he meant reason insofar as it is
concerned with moral choices, with the grounds of the
determination of the will.[925] Already in the first
critique he had indicated that this would be the path
he would follow.[926]

As his starting point, Kant appeared to take moral
experience as a sort of "given":

> I assume that there really are pure moral laws
> which determine completely a priori . . . what is
> and is not to be done . . . . I am justified in
> making this assumption, in that I can appeal not
> only to the proofs employed by the most
> enlightened moralists, but to the moral judgment
> of every man . . . .[927]

Anticipating a possible objection at this point, Kant
states, "The only point that may seem questionable is
the basing of this rational belief on the assumption of
moral sentiments."[928] He admitted that to a man "who
is completely indifferent with regard to moral laws,"
no argument can be given that could "compel the most
stubborn scepticism to give way."[929] But, he believed,
the human mind naturally takes an interest in morality,
and if we confirm and increase this interest, we shall

find reason very teachable and amenable to the uniting
of speculative with practical interests. So just as
Kant had begun his inquiry into theoretical reason with
the assumption that we do, indeed, have intelligible
experience, so he begins his investigation into
practical reason with the assumption of moral
experience.

"Nothing," Kant observed, "can possibly be
conceived in the world, or even out of it, which can be
called good without qualification, except a Good
Will."[930] He meant that while other attributes and
virtues may be misused, a good will is always good,
regardless of circumstances or results. Even if the
good will fails to achieve its desired end, by "virtue
of the volition" itself, it is good.[931] More
specifically, a will which acts for the sake of duty is
a good will. A truly good will does not look to the
results to justify its acts; rather it merely asks,
"What is my duty in this situation?" regardless of
consequences.

Kant drew three conclusions. (1) To have moral
worth, an action must be done from duty. It must not
be simply in accordance with duty, but motivated from
duty itself.[932] (2) The action done from duty derives
its moral worth, not from the foreseen consequences,
but from the maxim or principle of volition by which it
takes place so that if the foreseen results do not
occur, the worth of the action is not diminished.[933]
(3) Consequently, duty is the necessity of acting out
of respect for the law. To act out of duty is the same
as acting out of sheer respect for the law itself.[934]

But since law is essentially universal, admitting
no exceptions, Kant concluded that "I am never to act
otherwise than so that I could also will that my maxim

should become a universal law."[935] As an example, Kant
asked, "May I when in distress make a promise with the
intention not to keep it?"[936] The answer is, "No."
Universal lying would be self-destructive:

> . . . I can by no means will that lying should
> become a universal law. For with such a law there
> would be no promises at all, since it would be in
> vain to allege my intention in regard to my future
> actions to those who would not believe this
> allegation . . . . Hence my maxim . . . would
> necessarily destroy itself.[937]

But this principle must confront man as a command,
an imperative, because "the will does not in itself
completely accord with reason"--laws must appear to
such a will as obligations.[938] Now imperatives can be
either hypothetical (a command with a view to the
results obtained) or categorical ("that which
represented an action as necessary of itself without
reference to another end.")[939] The categorical
imperative "commands a certain conduct immediately,
without having as its condition any other purpose to be
attained by it."[940] But such an imperative commands
action apart from all conditions; it expresses the same
conformity of maxims to a universal law that was shown
previously. Thus, there is but one categorical
imperative: "Act only on that maxim whereby thou canst
at the same time will that it should become a universal
law."[941]

But does this principle hold for all rational
beings? To do so, there must exist something of
absolute value, an end in itself, that would be the
source of the categorical imperative. Kant found this
in man: ". . . man and generally any rational being
exists as an end in himself, not merely as a means to
be arbitrarily used by this or that will . . . ."[942]

Rational beings are <u>persons</u> and are ends in themselves,
objects of respect. The foundation of the categorical
imperative is thus: "rational nature exists as an end
in itself."[943]   The categorical imperative can be
reformulated: "<u>So act as to treat humanity, whether in
thine own person or in that of any other, in every case
as an end withal, never as means only.</u>"[944]

From this Kant derived his principle of the
autonomy of the will. This principle, implicit in the
categorical imperative, states that "every human will
is <u>a will which in all its maxims gives universal laws</u>
. . . ."[945] The justification for this principle is
that for the imperative to be truly categorical, it
must be unconditioned by any interest or constraint;
the will that obeys it does so simply from duty. Thus,
that will is autonomous, and being autonomous, it
legislates the moral law from itself. It is subject to
laws only of its own giving, though they must at the
same time be universal.[946]   So instead of being
subjected to some transcendent moral law, the will is
the source of the law, which it legislates.

Because rational beings are ends in themselves and
the source of the moral law, we may regard them
collectively as a kingdom of ends.[947] Kant defined
this as a "systematic union of rational beings by
common objective laws."[948]

Kant then asked, "<u>How is a Categorical Imperative
Possible?</u>"[949] His answer formed the first postulate of
practical reason: the categorical imperative is
possible only upon the condition of freedom. The
concept of freedom is the key to explaining the
autonomy of the will.[950]   For that I ought to do
something implies that I can. So, although freedom
cannot be demonstrated by theoretical reason, it is

nevertheless necessary according to practical reason.
Kant concluded, ". . . therefore our knowledge is
extended beyond the limits of that (sensible) world--a
pretension which the critique of pure reason declared
to be futile in all speculation."[951] Kant called this
the "enigma of the critical philosophy," that what is
denied to knowledge through supersensible use of the
categories is admitted with respect to the postulates
of practical reason.[952]

     Kant regarded the concept of freedom to be the
"keystone" to the further postulates of immortality and
God.[953] But in passing to these, it is important to
explain Kant's idea of the summum bonum. In the first
Critique he had argued that although all men seek
happiness, morality is to be found in seeking to make
oneself worthy of happiness.[954] The supreme good to
which practical reason strives is a synthesis of
happiness and virtue, the former apportioned to the
latter:

> Now inasmuch as virtue and happiness together
> constitute the possession of the summum bonum in a
> person, and the distribution of happiness in exact
> proportion to morality (which is the worth of the
> person, and his worthiness to be happy) constitute
> the summum bonum of a possible world; hence, this
> summum bonum expresses the whole, the perfect
> good, in which, however, virtue as the condition
> is always the supreme good, since it has one
> condition above it . . ."[955]

     But we seem to encounter an antinomy here. On the
one hand, happiness cannot be the motive for virtue
(only duty fulfills this role), yet on the other hand,
virtue does not seem to produce happiness in this all
too human world. The solution to the antinomy lies in
the fact that while the first alternative is
"absolutely impossible," the second is only

"<u>conditionally</u> false."[956] That is to say, it is false
only upon the assumption of the mortality of the soul.
Here Kant introduced his second postulate: the
immortality of the soul.   Two considerations require
the soul's immortality.   First, if happiness is to be
apportioned to virtue, as it must be, this must take
place after life in this world has terminated, and
thus, the soul must be immortal.   But second, in order
for our imperfect wills to achieve the <u>summum bonum</u>,
they   must   attain   perfect   accordance   with   the   moral
law--but   this   would   take   eternity.   Thus,   the
immortality of the soul, being "inseparably connected
with the moral law,"[957] is the second postulate of
practical   reason--not   demonstrable,   but   "an
inseparable   result   of   an   unconditional   <u>a priori</u>
<u>practical</u> law."[958]

But this leads inevitably to the third postulate
of practical reason: the existence of God.   He is the
"necessary condition of the possibility of the <u>summum</u>
<u>bonum</u>."[959] God is the one who apportions happiness to
virtue   in   impartial   adjudication.   Happiness   for   a
rational being occurs when everything goes according to
his wish; but since we are finite, we cannot bring this
condition to pass.   Therefore, there must exist a being
capable of uniting happiness to virtue.   Kant said,

> Accordingly,   the   existence   of   a   cause   of   all
> nature,   distinct   from   nature   itself,   and
> containing   the   principle   of   this   connexion,
> namely,   of   the   exact   harmony [960] of   happiness   with
> morality, is also <u>postulated</u>.

This being must be capable of acting according to law
and   thus   possesses   intelligence;   he   is   able   to   act
causally and therefore exercises will; in other words,
He is God.[961]   So, according to Kant, it becomes

"morally necessary to assume the existence of God."[962]

It is important to recall that we still do not possess knowledge of God's existence. This is the first Critique denied:

> No one, indeed, will be able to boast that he
> knows that there is a God, and a future life; if
> he knows this, he is the very man for whom I have
> long (and vainly) sought . . . . No, my conviction
> is not logical, but moral certainty; and since it
> rests on subjective grounds (of the moral
> sentiment), I must not even say, 'It is morally
> certain there is a God, etc.,' but 'I am morally
> certain, etc.' In other words, belief in a God
> and in another world is so interwoven with my
> moral sentiment that as there is little danger of
> my losing the latter, there is equally little
> cause for fear that the former can ever be taken
> from me.[963]

Again in his second Critique, Kant underlined the point: the moral necessity of God's existence is subjective, not objective, for there cannot be a duty to suppose the existence of anything.[964] God is apprehended by "a pure rational faith."[965] In so affirming the existence of God, Kant believed he could "sever the root" of materialism, fatalism, atheism, free-thinking, fanaticism, superstition, idealism, and scepticism.[966] To repeat his words, "I have therefore found it necessary to deny knowledge, in order to make room for faith."[967]

The implication for the historical approach to religion. Kant's denial of theoretical knowledge of God and his entire reliance on practical reason blew the traditional apologetic to bits and replaced it with a purely subjective justification of religion. Negatively, it was no longer possible to provide proofs for God or indeed anything supernatural. It must be emphasized that Kant's is not a moral argument for theism, though he appeared to be moving in that direction in the Opus postumum;[968] rather one merely postulates God as a necessary condition for morality, without knowing whether He actually exists. Historical proofs for Christianity fared no better in his critical philosophy than did the traditional ontological, cosmological, and teleological arguments for God's existence. In Die Religion innerhalb der Grenzen der blossen Vernunft (1793), Kant applies his critical approach to Christianity. In his second general observation he treats the subject of miracles, and while not denying their existence, he makes it quite clear that they play no role in a religion delimited only by reason. According to Kant, "Reason does not dispute the possibility or the reality of the objects of these ideas; she simply cannot adopt them into her maxims of thought and action."[969] This is because reason cannot operate in the realm of the supernatural, since ". . . our use of the concept of cause and effect cannot be extended beyond matters of experience, and hence beyond nature."[970] When we seek to introduce miracles into religion, the result is superstition. Kant calls this "illusory faith," since it involves overstepping the bounds of reason in the direction of the supernatural, which is not an object of either theoretical or practical reason.[971] Kant admits that when an ethical religion replaces a religion of mere rites and observances, then it is appropriate, though not necessary, for it to be accompanied with miracles to attract the adherents of the old religion.[972] But once the religion is established, miracles are entirely superfluous, since it stands by the authority of practical reason alone. "If this be so it is quite useless to debate those narratives or interpretations;

the true religion, which in its time needed to be
introduced through such expedients, is now here, and
from now on is able to maintain itself on rational
grounds."[973] Kant also objected positively to miracles
because their admission would disrupt rational
investigation of the universe.[974] If we assume that
God at certain times allows nature to deviate from its
laws, then since we know of no operating laws governing
when and why God so intervenes, reason is crippled in
respect to its dealings with known laws. Kant allows
that there may occur so-called natural wonders,
sufficiently attested and yet irrational events not
conforming to the known laws of nature, but these are
no problem so long as they are held to be natural. But
should such an event be really miraculous, then reason
would be of no use in such a bewitched world and the
proclamation of such an event would undermine
confidence in all that we do know. To the reply that
miracles occur seldomly and thus are not disruptive,
Kant retorts, how seldom? Since there is no way of
answering this question, we must, Kant seems to argue,
be prepared to accept their occurence daily or not at
all. Since the first alternative controverts reason,
the second must be adopted, but, Kant makes it clear,
only as a maxim of reason, not a theoretical assertion:
the rational man "does not incorporate belief in
miracles into his maxims (either of theoretical or
practical reason), though, indeed, he does not impugn
their possibility or reality."[975]

On the subject of the resurrection, Kant wastes
few words. But he does add this interesting note
concerning Christ's death:

> With which the public record of his life ends
> . . . The more secret records, added as a sequel,

of his <u>resurrection</u> and <u>ascension</u>, which took
place before the eyes only of his intimates,
cannot be used in the interest of religion within
the limits of reason alone without doing violence
to their historical valuation.[976]

This is not, however, due to its supernatural
character, but because of its materialism. Kant thinks
that the resurrection entails both that personality can
exist only as conditioned always by the same body and
that this body must exist in a material world to come.
Because Kant believes spiritual survival to be eminently more rational (not only because of the materialist
view of mind implied by resurrection, but also because
reason "can neither take an interest in dragging along,
through eternity, a body . . . for which, in life, it
never achieved any great love; nor can it render
conceivable that this calcareous earth, of which the
body is composed, should be in heaven . . .,"[977] the
resurrection cannot be admitted within the limits of
rational religion as a historical event. So it is
quite clear that for Kant, the traditional, historical
apologetic for the resurrection was both unnecessary
and impossible.

Positively, in the place of historical
argumentation for Christianity, Kant reinterpreted
Christianity in terms of an ethical system whose truth
was self-evident to practical reason. He contrasts a
historical faith with the faith of practical reason:

Every faith which, as an historical faith, bases
itself upon books, needs for its security a
<u>learned public</u> for whom it can be controlled, as
it were, by writers who lived in those times, who
are not suspected of a special agreement with the
first disseminators of the faith, and with whom
our present-day scholarship is connected by a
continuous tradition. The pure faith of reason,
in contrast, stands in need of no such documentary

authentication, but proves itself.[978]

Kant did not in fact believe Christianity met the
control test for a historical faith; but no matter, for
it is the ethical truth which it embodies which is its
essence. Religion for Kant thus reduces to morality.
He reinterprets the gospels along ethical lines as the
triumph of the principle of good over evil. All
historical   particularity   is   dissolved   into
philosophical truths. The historical Jesus he replaces
by an idea of pure reason which represents the epitome
of the moral man acting according to the demands of
practical reason. The resurrection has validity only
as an idea of reason signifying the commencement of
another life. Historical particulars are irrelevant:
it is only the timeless truths of moral reason that
Jesus exemplified that are important. Thus, for Kant,
to live as a Christian means to regard the ethical
structures of the categorical imperative as divine
commands and to live accordingly.

In his detaching the truth of Christianity from
its historical moorings, Kant clearly resembles Semler,
but there is no evidence Kant knew of his work. Kant
was familiar with the Wolfenbüttel fragments, and,
though he differed from Reimarus in his positive
evaluation of Jesus and the nature of his kingdom, yet
he spoke of the fragmentist with respect and
admiration.[979] But according to Greene, "To the
development of biblical interpretation and criticism in
the eighteenth century he seems to have given virtually
no attention."[980] Nonetheless, his severing the truth
of Christianity from the question of historicity was
all of a piece with the developments in German theology
at that time and served to further it. As Dieter
Heinrich has pointed out, Kant's critical philosophy

had an important impact upon New Testament criticism, for the young Kantians took up Semler's methods of biblical criticism to show that Jesus's true message was actually Kant's moral philosophy expressed "in the spirit of the time," and they thus helped to lead to the Tübingen school of criticism in the next century.[981] In his reduction of religion to ethics Kant also served as the forerunner for nineteenth century liberal theology.[982]

The move toward subjectivism in apologetics

Friedrich Daniel Ernst Schleiermacher.   Kant's turn to subjective justification of belief, together with the influence of volatile German Romanticism, many of whose principal figures such as Goethe, Schiller, and Schelling drew inspiration from Kant's philosophical work, helped to effect a transformation of Christian apologetics in the nineteenth century. Probably the principal figure in this transformation is Friedrich Schleiermacher, whose Der christliche Glaube (1821-2; rev. 1830-1) has been called the most important work, with the exception of Calvin's Institutes, covering the whole field of Protestant theology, thus establishing him as the father of modern theology.[983] Like Kant, Schleiermacher sprang from a Pietist background which helped to mould his conception of religion. He was educated in a Moravian school at Nisky and at a Moravian college in Barby. In 1787 he left Barby to enter the University of Halle, which had by that time become a seed-bed for rationalism under the influence of J.S. Semler. There Schleiermacher deeply imbibed the spirit of Kant and Spinoza, particularly admiring the latter's pantheistic conception of God. A personal friend of Schlegel, Schleiermacher was later also deeply affected by Romanticism. The combination of all these influences reaching back to Pietism and extending to contemporary Romanticism and undergirded intellectually by the pantheism of Spinoza and the critical philosophy of Kant, produced in Schleiermacher a determined proclivity to subjectivism in theology.

According to Schleiermacher, piety considered in itself is neither a knowing nor a doing, but a modification of feeling or of immediate self-consciousness.[984] If knowledge were piety, then the most learned master of Christian dogmatics would be the most pious Christian, which no one would admit. On the other hand, if action were piety, the piety could not reside in the content of the action, for things both abominable and admirable are done piously. So the piety must rest in the form of the action, as either the motive or the goal. But no one would judge the piety of an action by the measure of success in attaining its goal, so the piety must rest in the motive. But this leads to the conclusion that an action is pious only insofar as the determination of self-consciousness or feeling is pious. Hence, knowing and doing pertain to but do not constitute the essence of piety. ". . . piety in its diverse expressions remains essentially a state of feeling."[985]

Furthermore, the essence of piety consists in this: the consciousness of being absolutely dependent, or, which is the same thing, of being in relation to God.[986] In all self-consciousness there is both a consciousness of the subject for itself and of its co-existence with the other distinct from itself. To

the former element corresponds receptivity of
self-consciousness, to the latter its activity. The
common element of receptive self-consciousness is a
feeling of dependence, that of active self-consciousness a feeling of freedom. The total self-consciousness made up of both will therefore be one of
reciprocity between the subject and the other. When
this is taken as a totality, we arrive at the notion of
the world set over against self-consciousness. But in
addition to this reciprocal relationship to the world,
we have a feeling of absolute dependence that
accompanies our whole existence: ". . . it is the
consciousness that the whole of our spontaneous
activity comes from a source outside us in just the
same sense in which anything towards which we should
have a feeling of absolute freedom must have proceeded
entirely from ourselves."[987]   The source of our
existence implied in this self-consciousness is God.
Thus, to feel absolutely dependent and to be conscious
of being in relation to God are one and the same thing.
Piety, then, is to be ascribed to an individual to the
degree that he possesses this God-consciousness.

All religions that have appeared in history
express different stages in the development of this
God-consciousness.[988]   Monotheism represents the
highest stage of development because it fosters the
deepest sense of dependence.[989]   Christianity stands
apart from other monotheisms in that it takes as its
central tenets man's need of redemption, that is,
release from God-forgetfulness which constrains the
feeling of absolute dependence, and the fact of that
redemption through Jesus of Nazareth.[990]
Schleiermacher emphasizes that there is nothing
supernatural in Christ's appearance;[991] he is like all

men in virtue of the identity of human nature, but distinguished from them all by the constant power of his God-consciousness, which, Schleiermacher says, was a veritable existence of God in him.[992]   Jesus's God-consciousness determined his self-consciousness so continually and exclusively that we can say that the Supreme Being dwelt in his inmost self.   He is the redeemer in that he evokes in us the movement toward God-consciousness in our own lives; his redemptive activity is his pervasive influence which one receives as one responds freely to its attraction.[993]

Schleiermacher, like Kant, loses the historical Jesus by reducing him to a pure idea,[994] not indeed of the ideal ethical man, but of the ideal pious man.   His Christianity is entirely subjective and feeling-oriented in character.   Accordingly, he also radically re-interpreted the task of apologetics. Schleiermacher will have nothing to do with providing proofs for Christianity:

> . . . it is obvious that an adherent of some other faith might perhaps be completely convinced by the above account that what we have set forth is really the peculiar essence of Christianity, without being thereby so convinced that Christianity is actually the truth, as to feel compelled to accept it. Everything we say in this place is relative to Dogmatics, and Dogmatics is only for Christians. . . . We entirely renounce all attempt to prove the truth or necessity of Christianity; and we presuppose, on the contrary, that every Christian, before he enters at all upon enquiries of this kind, has already the inward certainty that his religion cannot take any other form than this.[995]

Hence, apologetics "needs to be refashioned for these present times."[996]   In Schleiermacher's view, philosophy of religion is the critical presentation of

the different existing forms of religion in the world,
and apologetics starts from there and lays down as a
foundation a description of the peculiar essence of
Christianity and its relation to other faiths. Thus,
apologetics is purely descriptive in character. In his
Kurze Darstellung des theologischen Studiums zum Behuf
einleitender Vorlesung (1830) Schleiermacher proposes
that the discipline of philosophical theology precede
the other branches of theology.[997] Taking the findings
of philosophy of religion, it would seek to display the
uniqueness of Christianity. Philosophical theology
would be comprised of polemics and apologetics. The
task of polemics is to detect and remedy deviations
from the Christian faith; the aim of apologetics is to
discover and show the distinctiveness of the Christian
religion. The goal of apologetics to not to persuade
people to embrace the faith--that is the task of
practical theology. Now Schleiermacher recognizes that
the task of philosophy of religion has not been
completed, but apologetics cannot wait. Therefore,
apologetics provisionally determines that Christianity
is a monotheism and is essentially distinguished from
other such faiths in that everything in it is related
to the redemption accomplished by Christ.[998] But as we
have seen this in no way proves that Christianity is
true.[999]

Schleiermacher could not be more explicit in his
rejection of the traditional, evidential apologetic.
Between the preaching of the Church and the response of
faith in the hearer comes no intermediary:

> . . . in shutting up the whole process between
> these two points, the witness or testimony and its
> effect, our proposition is intended to make an end
> of everything which, in the form of demonstration,
> is usually brought to the aid of the proper

witness or even substituted for it. This refers
principally to the attempts to bring about a
recognition of Christ by means of the miracles
which He performs, or the prophecies which
predicted Him, or the special character of the
testimonies originally born to Him, regarded as
the work of divine inspiration.[1000]

Schleiermacher's fundamental objection to miracles is
that miracles cannot produce faith but rather
presuppose it. Taken in itself, a purportedly
miraculous event proves nothing. For even Scripture
itself testifies to the occurence of false miracles,
but gives no basis for distinguishing false from true
miracles. Moreover, in any other context than that of
faith, if we encounter a fact which we cannot explain
naturally, we never have recourse to miracle, but defer
explanation until we have a better understanding of the
fact and the laws of nature. But in the realm of
faith, we think immediately of miracle; the only
problem is that each man regards as genuine only that
miracle confirming his own faith, and sets the others
down as false. Hence, in the absence of at least an
incipient faith in Christ, Jesus's miracles would be
pronounced as either false or else judgement would be
reserved until a natural explanation were forthcoming.[1001] Schleiermacher concludes that if faith in
the revelation of God in Christ has not already arisen
in the direct way through experience as the
demonstration of the Spirit and of power, then miracles
cannot produce it.[1002]

Schleiermacher also argues generally that miracles
as supernatural events are not necessary to
religion.[1003] Miracles are not demanded by our
religious emotions; on the contrary, where nature is
best known and miracles are seldom, there the feeling
of absolute dependence is greatest. Schleiermacher

refutes five possible reasons for the necessity of miracles: (1) They are necessary manifestations of omnipotence. Why is omnipotence shown to be greater in intervening into nature than in establishing its original, immutable course? To intervene in nature's course implies some imperfection either in it or in God. (2) It is God's privilege to perform miracles. This assumes there is something not ordained by God which can offer Him resistance, thus destroying our feeling of absolute dependence (presumably because absolute dependence is a correlate of God's absolute freedom, which would be here negated). (3) By miracles God compensates for the effects of free causes on the course of nature. Divine preservation would achieve this without miracles. Besides, the biblical miracles were not of this sort. (4) Answers to prayer necessitate miracles. The prayers and their answers are part of the original divine plan carried out by God's preservation, so that it is wholly meaningless to say something else might have happened in the absence of prayer. (5) Regeneration is miraculous. The revelation of God in Christ is not necessarily something absolutely supernatural, so neither is regeneration, which flows from it. Finally, in addition to these points, Schleiermacher argues that miracles would destroy the whole system of nature. For the chain of finite causes would be severed at the point of divine intervention. But we could never be certain where those points are. Thus the interests of natural science and religion combine to prompt us to abandon the idea of the absolutely supernatural. If everything that happens is allowed to be a matter of scientific research, then it does not matter if a certain event which evokes a pious feeling is explained. This frees us from the insoluble problem of how to distinguish divine from false miracles, for neither are admitted.

As for Christ's miracles, Schleiermacher holds that the arrival in him of a new stage of self-consciousness was accompanied by the ability to effect things in nature.[1004] Yet these events were not truly miraculous, for our understanding of the influence of the mind upon nature is limited and capable of being extended. These events served to draw attention to Christ, but with increasing distance in time and space, their efficacy is lost and no longer exists today.[1005] But this is actually to our advantage, says Schleiermacher, for now our attention is drawn to the Person of Christ. Miracles do not evoke faith;[1006] rather Christ elicited faith by the direct impression of his Person. Others have wrought external miracles comparable to Christ's, but no one equals the "great spiritual miracle" of his Person.

Schleiermacher paid scant attention to the resurrection of Jesus. Not only would he ascribe no apologetic value to this event, but he went even further and denied to it any doctrinal significance as well. "The facts of the Resurrection and the Ascension of Christ . . . . can not be laid down as properly constituent parts of the doctrine of His Person."[1007] This is because these events are superfluous to the recognition of God's being in Christ, this being manifest simply from the extent of his God-conscious-ness.

Schleiermacher's subjectivistic, anti-miraculous Christianity and his consequent reinterpretation of apologetics turned away nineteenth century defenders of the faith from historical argumentation. When Karl

Sack's <u>Christliche Apologetik</u> appeared in 1829 he began
in Germany a new movement in apologetics based on
Schleiermacher's subjectivism.[1008]   Unlike
Schleiermacher, he does view apologetics as a defense
of the truth of Christianity, but the justification he
offers is entirely subjective.   He argues for the
religious deficiencies of other faiths in contrast to
Christianity and exalts Christ as the source of
redemption.   He appeals to moral, religious, and
spiritual benefits of Christianity. No proof is to be
found concerning the historical evidences for Jesus's
miracles and resurrection.   Other apologists followed
suit.[1009]   C.H. Stirm in his <u>Apologie des Christentums,</u>
<u>in Briefe für gebildete Leser</u> (1836) devotes five
letters to inner evidences of Christianity, two to its
impact on world history, two to its moral effects, one
to its religious superiority, and finally only two
letters to its revelatory character evidenced by
Jesus's claims, miracles, and disciples' testimony.
Karl Ullmann's apologetic works exemplify a devotional
approach, his most famous piece <u>Die Sündlosigkeit Jesu</u>
(1828) being an argument for Christ as the sinless
redeemer on the basis of the gospel portrait of Jesus.
The Catholic apologist J.S. von Drey was about the only
significant defender of the faith who was able to shake
off Schleiermacher's influence and argue historically
for Christianity in his <u>Die Apologetik als</u>
<u>wissenschaftliche Nachweisung der Göttlichkeit des</u>
<u>Christentum</u> (1843), and his impact was but in a corner.

      <u>Friedrich August Gottreu Tholuck</u>. But what is
perhaps most significant is that not only did the
mainstream of German theology follow Schleiermacher's
subjectivism, but so did the conservative element as
well.   The prime example here is Friedrich August

Tholuck, the most popular and effective of nineteenth century German apologists.[1010] Tholuck was brought to a personal faith in Christ through the witness of Pietist believers, and he sought to combine the best of biblical scholarship with a warm, devotional faith in Christ. His early work Die Lehre von der Sünde und vom Versöhner (1823), to which we shall return, is deeply pietistic and contains autobiographical material in its presentation of two German university students. The saintly Pietist elder in the book is doubtlessly Tholuck's own spiritual father Baron H.E. von Kottwitz, and the student's conversion mirrors Tholuck's own spiritual experience.[1011] Tholuck came to personal faith in Christ as a theology student under Neander in Berlin, where he then taught on the faculty with his former teacher and with Schleiermacher. In 1826, having become a defender of theology with a Pietist cast, he took a position at Halle, which by this time had become entrenched in rationalism. He assumed his position under a protest from the theological faculty there, and Tholuck needed a military guard to protect him and his house from attacks by radical students who opposed his appointment. But during his 30 years there, he grew to be recognized as the most attractive and beloved professor at the university. His stress on the necessity of a personal, devotional, religious faith and the practical service of theology to the church shaped the thinking of a generation of students who followed him.

    Tholuck was well acquainted with and in many ways sympathetic to the apologetics of the last century, and therefore his critique of that approach should be most revealing. In his essay "Über Apologetik und ihre Litteratur," he makes these observations on the historical argumentation of the traditional apologists:

It was believed that one could prove in a
historical way that Christianity appeared in the
world through an extraordinary revelation,
without knowing in advance what Christianity was.
Wherein lay the fundamental error in this
procedure? We find it in this: one overlooked
that faith in religious facts, that is, facts
which ground the divinity of a religion, is
dependent upon the religious and moral disposition
and orientation of men. It was thought that when
the same quantity of evidence was produced for the
archetypal moral purity of Jesus, for his
resurrection, and for the authenticity of the
biblical books as for the military campaign of
Alexander or for the violent death of Caesar, then
a faith equally firm would arise in those
religious facts as in these facts. . . .
The common proverb says: "What a man wishes,
that he believes"; daily experience confirms it.
Herein lies the reason why the historical evidence
concerning historical facts in which our interest
has a stake has, depending on our interest,
varying power of demonstration. He who is utterly
unacquainted with the content of Christianity and
who set about to test the historical facts would
either hold some religion or no religion to be
true. In the latter case he would be an
Indifferent or a Free-thinker, and as such he
would from the beginning be disinclined to admit
the divinity of the Christian religion. In the
former case he would out of partiality to his
religion also bring along a bias against the
Christian religion. Now by this remark do we want
to show that even the most compelling historical
facts of Christianity would make no impression at
all on such men, that they would be utterly
incapable of taking them aback and confounding
them? Not at all. To take aback, to confound,
these facts can do; but to effect conviction and
unshakeable faith? That is another question!
--Now let us think of another man, who is
acquainted with the teaching of the New Testament
about sin and the divine plan of salvation in
Christ, without knowing of Christ's prophecies and
miracles, without being acquainted with the
evidence for the authenticity of the New Testament
writings; but through the influence of the divine
Spirit those truths of faith have been confirmed

to him to be true, and this confirmation increases
with every new experience of life. Would not such
a man also immediately grasp the historical facts
to be credible, and would not this faith heighten[1012]
as the truths in his inner being hold good?

The problem with the apologetics of the last century,
says Tholuck, is that the difference between fides
historica and viva was forgotten. He chides the
traditional apologists for overemphasizing the external
and the miraculous over against the essential ethical
and dogmatic truths of the Christian revelation.[1013]
It is evident that Tholuck was not opposed to
objective, evidentialist apologetics as such, but he
did regard them as ineffective apart from the context
of the proclamation of Christian truths which would
arouse a sense of sin and guilt in the hearer and point
him to the way of salvation through faith in Christ.

Tholuck therefore took upon himself the task of
re-awakening the unbeliever to his spiritual bankruptcy
and need of redemption in Christ. His afore-mentioned
Die Lehre von der Sünde und vom Versöhner, oder die
Weihe des Zweiflers was written in reaction to De
Wette's Theodor; oder, des Zweiflers Weihe (1822), in
which the author portrayed religion as an innate urge
of man, recommended salvation through self-effort, and
countenanced the ordination of agnostics. Tholuck's
book takes the form of letters between Guido and
Julius, two university students in theology and
philosophy respectively, describing their search for
truth. Tholuck's description of Guido's professors at
university provides a good survey of the points of view
which Tholuck rejects: (1) there were those who spoke
coldly and profanely of the characters of the New
Testament and brought the Scriptures down to a
terrestrial level; (2) there were those whose method it

was to uphold the doctrines of Christianity by historical proofs, each of which by itself, they confessed, had little weight, but when taken together had sufficient force of argument; and (3) there was one professor who based his system on the authority of the church, demanding unconditional submission of belief.[1014] None of these views satisfied Guido's doubts; in his spirit he sensed that there was more, and he could perceive a mysterious dialogue of another spirit with his own. Thereby Tholuck introduces his own alternative to the typical theology. This is advanced by a sudden letter from Julius stating that he had undergone regeneration and had learned what the truth was by the most indubitable experience.[1015] Julius's advice to his friend is clearly Tholuck's own: look into the interior of your own being, descend into the abyss of self-knowledge to discover one's selfishness so that one may in turn ascend to the heights of the knowledge of God. The letter ends, "Oh, that you knew Him, Guido!"

The letter awakens in Guido a sense of his own evil as he turns the eye of the spirit from foreign subjects to the spirit itself. This discovery of the hitherto unexperienced realm of the spirit leaves him disenchanted with the lifeless theology taught at the university. Tholuck's own emotions express themselves as Guido writes back to Julius:

> And it is this misuse of science which so disgusts me in that shallow school of theologians. They lack the internal power to mount upwards, or to descend into the depths, for which they fain would compensate by spreading themselves over an immense extent of surface, and make miserable attempts at constructing their spiritual life out of phrases and criticisms . . . . How am I shocked, when I see around me, hundreds of those who are preparing

to take the care of souls, instead of building a
compact edifice, merely heaping stones together;
instead of laying a foundation, sweeping rubbish!
O Julius! Tell me, when the salt hath lost its
savor, wherewith shall it be salted? I am silent,
and weep. [1016]

Despite the awakening of spiritual conscience, Guido is
uncertain of the doctrine of redemption. Tholuck puts
in his mouth the anti-historical sentiments which we
have seen expressed in Kant, Schleiermacher, and
others: "Especially I find it irksome to retain what
is historical and matter-of-fact in it: I would rather
contemplate it as a beautiful sublime idea."[1017] But
Tholuck will have none of this; though he minimizes
historical apologetics, he wants to preserve the
historicity of the events of redemption. Liberal
theology, he writes, is scarcely better than Islam. He
cannot assent to the rationalist view that the
connection between Christ's crucifixion and forgiveness
of sins is merely accidental.[1018] Tholuck's Pietism
becomes explicit in describing how Guido comes to
faith. More than theological speculations or inquiry
it was his acquaintance with certain true disciples of
Christ that drew him to the Savior. He had heard them
ridiculed as mystics, bigots, or pietists, but he found
them to have a true knowledge of God. Particularly
influential was the example of one man, reputedly a
Moravian, who ministered to both the physical and
spiritual needs of those he touched. In the end Guido
decides that one must take the name "Pietist" for
oneself, and he sees the dawn of a spiritual
re-awakening in Germany, such that in a few decades
perhaps no one will not wish to be called a
Christian.[1019]

The story of Guido and Julius illustrates the

subjectivistic, spiritual mode of apologetics
championed by Tholuck. Extremely popular, the book
went through nine printings during Tholuck's lifetime
and helped shape the conservative apologetics of the
nineteenth century. Although this subjective side of
Tholuck's thinking weighs for him most heavily, the
fact that he was not averse to historical defenses of
Christianity is evident from his own Glaubwürdigkeit
der evangelischen Geschichte (1836), published in
response to Strauss's mythological interpretation.
This treatise is an attempt to defend the historical
credibility of Luke-Acts against the Straussian
hypothesis. Tholuck charges that Strauss came to his
study with his mind already made up that miracles are
impossible, which is an illegitimate procedure.[1020] He
also argues that the contradictions and inconsistencies
in the gospels cannot overturn their general reliability: ". . . the circumstance that the synoptical
evangelists, in some points, vary from or contradict
each other, affords no reason whatever for regarding
the great features in which they agree, or the facts
recorded only by a single evangelist, as substantially
unhistorical and mythical."[1021] He points out that in
secular history which is generally accepted as
reliable, there are yet contradictions and omissions,
for example, the history of Alexander or Hannibal.
Tholuck's defense at this point is significant because
he departs from the harmonizing method of the
traditional apologetic and seems willing to allow for
errors in the gospels, but challenges his opponent to
show how this undermines the credibility of the whole
gospel history.

     Tholuck begins his case by considering the
authorship and date of Luke-Acts. On the basis of

external testimony and Paul's letters and Acts, Tholuck
argues that the author was Paul's companion. Acts ends
prior to Paul's trial; with any normal historian we
would conclude that it was written prior to that event,
so why not also with Luke? We know Luke was with Paul
in Rome, and this would have afforded the perfect
opportunity to write. So Acts was probably written
about A.D. 63-4 and Luke's gospel even earlier. This
has great import for Luke's credibility:

> Such being the case, we are introduced at once, in
> the author of the Gospel, whatever may have been
> his name, to an individual who lived in immediate
> contact with apostles and disciples of Jesus, with
> those who were eyewitnesses and hearers of his
> public life and teachings. We are at once placed,
> in short, on the firm ground of historical data,
> which, as we feel it solidly beneath us, in the
> progress of our inquiries, it will be impossible
> for us to regard as the mere Fata Morgana of the
> mythical hypothesis.[1022]

Tholuck then argues that Luke was both willing and able
to record the truth about Jesus. He compares Luke's
prologue to that in Josephus's Jewish War and contends
that Luke stands on a par with Josephus in his
competent handling of historical information in Acts.
The "we" passages in Acts shows that he had great
intercourse with eyewitnesses; while in Jerusalem he
would have had first hand contact with disciples who
had been with Jesus. Since the gospel of Luke was
written prior to Paul's death, Paul must have seen it
and agreed with its accuracy. Tholuck then expounds at
length the detailed historical accuracy of Acts. All
this goes to establish Luke's credibility, and if his
reliability is established then so is the general
credibility of the other evangelists.

It is interesting that Tholuck avoids dealing

specifically with Jesus's miracles and resurrection,
which formed the heart of the traditional apologetic.
His only allusion to them is the remark, that if Jesus
never performed miracles, then why did the disciples
come to ascribe them to themselves?[1023]   He argues for
these events only by implication, in demonstrating
Luke's historical reliability.   So even in this
historical apologetic, Tholuck does not return to the
explicit argument for Christianity from Jesus's
miracles and resurrection that predominated in the last
century.

The impact on the
traditional apologetic

     Tholuck's apologetic, therefore, illustrates how
even the conservative element in German theology during
the nineteenth century became disenchanted with the
traditional, objectivist apologetic.[1024]   Though
conservatives could and did defend the general
reliability of Scripture against critics like Strauss
and Bauer, they were now on the defensive, and their
main positive emphasis in commending the Christian
faith lay in subjective reasons of the heart, the moral
and spiritual excellence of Christianity.   Thus, in
Germany as in France and England, the historical
argument for the resurrection of Jesus was eclipsed
during the nineteenth century by the new, subjective,
inwardly-oriented apologetic, but now with much more
far-reaching consequences.   For Germany had by now
emerged and would remain the leader of the theological
world, and thus the subjectivism which came to dominate
the approach to the truth of the Christian religion in
German theology would have a lasting impact on theology

up to the present day.

Summary

In conclusion, then, the historical argument for the resurrection of Jesus, which had formed the centerpiece of the evidentialist apologetics so popular in the eighteenth century, was supplanted in the nineteenth century by an inwardly-oriented apologetic through the advance in biblical criticism and the tide of subjectivism which swept Europe. The Deist antipathy to miracles was taken up into criticism by men like Semler, Paulus, Strauss, and others, while the hermeneutical change pioneered by Semler and Lessing, which severed the transcendent, spiritual truth of Christianity from the historical record thereof, permitted them either to explain away the miraculous character of certain events or to deny the historicity of the events altogether, while at the same time retaining the truth of the Christian religion. The fact that these spiritual truths were taken to be self-evident precluded the need for any positive Christian apologetic. Stauss's mythological explanation finally broke the dilemma of the traditional apologists, while the presupposition of miracles disqualified the supernaturalist option from consideration. Meanwhile, a growing backlash of subjectivism to the Age of Reason turned men from the rational to the sentimental and moral. The Romanticism of persons like Wordsworth, Coleridge, Chateaubriand, Goethe, Schiller, and Schelling overwhelmed the dry and lifeless rationalism of the Enlightenment. The indirect but strategic influence of Pietism through figures like Wesley, Marie Huber and Rousseau, Kant,

Schleiermacher, and Tholuck was a major factor in
undermining the traditional apologetic and replacing it
with subjective concerns. Rousseau's appeal to the
inner light and to conscience bore fruit in
Chateaubriand and in Kant. Kant's critical philosophy
constituted a turning point in the history of thought,
eliminating theoretical knowledge of supersensible
entities and postulating them for faith by ethical
considerations. Schleiermacher redefined the nature of
Christianity in subjective terms and reinterpreted the
function of apologetics for the nineteenth century.
Even the conservative element in theology followed the
pattern of turning away from objective to subjective
justifications of religious belief. Through all these
powerful forces, the historical argument for the
resurrection of Jesus was eclipsed.

SECTION III

ASSESSMENT OF THE EIGHTEENTH CENTURY
DEBATE OVER THE RESURRECTION OF JESUS

In Part III of this work, I wish to look back over
the classical debate concerning the historicity of the
resurrection with a view toward evaluating the
arguments both pro and con and assessing their worth
for contemporary research. At the same time we shall
want to take note of the status of the issues among
twentieth century theologians and exegetes.

The Problem of Miracles

We have seen that foundational to the attempt to
prove the resurrection historically was the argument
for the possibility of miracles. Undoubtedly it was
the arguments of Spinoza, Hume, and the Deists which
posterity gave an eye to, for during the next century
Strauss was able to proceed on the a priori assumption
that miracles were impossible. This same assumption
underlies the influential work of Rudolf Bultmann in
our century.[1] Bultmann's approach to the New Testament
was guided by two underlying presuppositions: (1) the
existence of a full-blown pre-Christian Gnosticism and
(2) the impossibility of miracles. While he sought to
present evidence in support of (1), he simply assumed
(2). Like Strauss he seemed to regard the
impossibility of miracles as a presupposition not
requiring proof, and many contemporary scholars would
also appear to accept a similar position. Pesch, for
example, asserts that the central task of dogmatic
theology today is to show how Jesus can be the central

figure of God's revelation without presupposing "a 'theistic-supernaturalistic model of revelation and mediation,' which is no longer acceptable to our thought."[2] "The talk of the resurrection of Jesus is then an expression of the believing confession to the eschatological meaning of Jesus, his mission and authority, his divine legitimation in face of his death."[3]

Probably the Marburg theologian Hans Grass most clearly exemplifies the critical scepticism concerning the empty tomb and physical resurrection of Jesus which is born out of philosophical presuppositions against the miraculous. It is part of Grass's historical methodology that anything which smacks of the miraculous is immediately excised as unhistorical.[4] Grass, therefore, inveighing against the "massiven Realismus" of the gospel resurrection narratives, constructs an elaborate and lengthy case against the empty tomb, impressive in its scope but defective in its details, and rejects all physical appearances of Jesus in favor of visions of the risen Jesus caused by God in the minds of the disciples. It is difficult to exaggerate the extent of Grass's influence. John Alsup remarks that " . . . no other work has been so widely used or of such singular importance for the interpretation of the gospel accounts . . . as Grass' 'Easter Event and Easter Reports.'"[5] But, Alsup protests, Grass's insistence that the heavenly vision type of appearance underlies the physical appearances of the gospels "is predicated upon the impossibility of the material realism of that latter form as an acceptable answer to the 'what happened question' . . . . Grass superimposes this criterion over the gospel appearance stories and judges them by their conformity or diver-

gence from it."[6] Though few scholars have been willing
to join Grass in denying the historicity of the empty
tomb, since the empirical evidence seems to incline in
the opposite direction, one not infrequently finds
statements that because the resurrection body does not
depend upon the old body, we are not compelled to
believe in the empty tomb,[7] and it is everywhere
asserted, even by those who staunchly defend the
empty tomb, that the spiritual nature of the
resurrection body precludes physical resurrection
appearances such as are narrated in the gospels.[8]
Alsup comments, ". . . the contemporary spectrum of
research on the gospel resurrection appearances
displays a proclivity to the last century (and Celsus
of the second century) in large measure under the
influence of Grass' approach. In a sense the gospel
stories appear to be something of an embarrassment;
their 'realism' is offensive."[9] The physical
resurrection of Jesus is an offense because it clashes
so rudely with Deist presuppositions held, perhaps
subconsciously, by many scholars.[10] The presupposition
against miracles appears to have been wedded oft times
with a Platonizing tendency on the part of many
theological minds concerning the physical body.
Instructive is the heated reaction that Cullmann's
Immortality of the Soul or Resurrection of the Dead met
with when he defended as biblical the physical
resurrection of the dead. Cullmann responded, "The
attacks provoked by my work would impress me more if
they were based on exegetical arguments. Instead I am
attacked with very general considerations of a
philosophical, psychological, and above all sentimental
kind."[11] This might lead one to conclude that the
opponents of miracles had won the debate. But is this

really the case?

Natural Law

It will be remembered that the world view that
formed the backdrop to the Deist controversy was a
model of the universe as a Newtonian world machine that
bound even the hands of God. Twentieth century
scientists, however, have abandoned so ironclad a view
of natural law.[12] Natural law is now understood
essentially as <u>description</u>, not <u>prescription</u>. This
does not mean that it cannot serve as a basis for
prediction, for it does; but our formulation of a
natural law is never so certain as to be beyond
reformulation under the force of observed facts.
Einstein wrote,

> The belief in an external world independent of the
> perceiving subject is the basis of all natural
> science. Since, however sense perception gives
> information of this external world indirectly, we
> can only grasp the latter by speculative means.
> It follows from this that our notions of physical
> reality can never be final. We must always be
> ready to change these notions in order to do
> justice to perceived facts in the most logically
> perfect way.[13]

Thus an event cannot be ruled out simply because
it does not accord with the regular pattern of events.
The advance of modern physics over the Newtonian world
machine is not that natural law does not exist, but
that our formulation of it is not absolutely final.
After all, even quantum physics does not mean to assert
that matter and energy do not possess certain
properties, such that anything and everything can
happen, for even indeterminacy has parameters and in
any case concerns only the microscopic level. On the

macroscopic level, firm natural laws do obtain.[14] But
the knowledge of these properties and laws is derived
from and based on experience. The laws of nature are
thus not "laws" in the rigid, prescriptive sense, but
inductive generalizations.

This would appear to bring some comfort to the
modern believer in miracles, for now he may argue that
one cannot rule out a priori the fact that a certain
event has occurred which does not conform to known
natural law, since our formulation of natural law is
never final and so must take account of the fact in
question. It seems to me, however, that while this
more descriptive understanding of natural law re-opens
the door of possibility to certain anomalous events in
the world, it does not help much in settling the
question of miracles. The advantage gained is that one
cannot rule out the occurrence of a certain event a
priori, but the evidence for it must be weighed. The
defender of miracles has thus at least gained a
hearing. But one is still operating under the
assumption, it would appear, that if the event really
did run contrary to natural law, then it would be
impossible for it to have occurred. The defender of
miracles appeals to the fact that our natural laws are
only inductive generalizations and so never certain, in
order to gain admittance for his anomalous event; but
presumably if an omniscient mind knew with certainty
the precise formulations of the natural laws describing
our universe, then he would know a priori whether the
event was or was not actually possible, since a true
law of nature, being a universal generalization, could
not be violated.

For as Bilynskyj argues, whether one adopts a
regularity theory of natural law, according to which

laws are simply descriptive of events and have no
special modal quality, or a necessitarian theory,
according to which natural laws are not merely
descriptive but possess a special sort of modality
determining gnomic necessity/possibility, still so long
as natural laws are conceived of as universal inductive
generalizations the notion of a "violation of a law of
nature" is incoherent.[15] For on the regularity theory,
since a law is a generalized description of whatever
occurs, it follows that an event which occurs cannot
violate a law. And on the necessitarian theory, since
laws are universal generalizations which state what is
physically necessary, a violation of a law cannot occur
if the generalization is to remain truly universal. So
long as laws are conceived of as universal
generalizations, it is logically impossible to have a
violation of a true law of nature. Suppose that one
attempts to rescue the situation by introducing into
the law certain ceteris paribus conditions, for
example, that the law holds only if either (1) there
are no other causally relevant natural forces
interfering, or (2) there are no other causally
relevant natural or supernatural forces interfering.
Now clearly, (1) will not do the trick, for even if
there were no natural forces interfering, the events
predicted by the law might not occur because God would
interfere. Hence, the alleged law, as a purportedly
universal generalization, would not be true, and so a
law of nature would not be violated in such a case.
But if, as (2) suggests, we include supernatural forces
among the ceteris paribus conditions, it is equally
impossible to violate the law. For now the statement
of the law itself includes the condition that what the
law predicts will occur only if God does not intervene,

so that if He does the law is not violated. Hence, so
long as natural laws are construed as universal
generalizations about events, it is incoherent to speak
of miracles as violations of such laws.

The upshot of Bilynskyj's discussion is that
either natural laws ought not to be construed as
universal generalizations about events or that miracles
should not be characterized as violations of nature's
laws. He opts for the first alternative, arguing that
laws of nature are really about the dispositional
properties of things based on the kinds of things they
are.[16] He observes that most laws today when taken as
universal generalizations are literally not true. They
must include _ceteris paribus_ clauses about conditions
which seldom or perhaps never obtain, so that laws
become subjunctive conditionals conerning what would
occur under certain idealized conditions. But that
means that laws are true counterfactuals with no
application to the real world. Moreover, if laws are
merely descriptive generalizations, then they do not
really explain anything; rather than telling why some
event occurs, they only serve to tell us how things
are. Bilynskyj therefore proposes that natural laws
ought to be formulated as singular statements about
certain kinds of things and their dispositional
properties: Things of kind A have a disposition to
manifest quality F in conditions C, in virtue of being
of nature N.[17] Laws can be stated, however, as
universal dispositions; for example, "All potassium has
a disposition to ignite when exposed to oxygen." On
this understanding, to assert that an event is physically impossible is not to say that it is a violation
of a law of nature, since dispositional laws are not
violated when the behavior disposed toward them does

not occur; rather an event E is physically impossible
if and only if E occurs at time t and E is not produced
at t by the powers (dispositions) of the natural agents
which are causally relevant to E at t.[18] Accordingly,
a miracle is a physically impossible act of God which
is religiously significant.[19] On Bilynskyj's version
of the proper form of natural laws then, miracles turn
out to be physically impossible, but not violations of
those laws.

I have a great deal of sympathy for Bilynskyj's
understanding of natural law and physical
impossibility. So as not to create unnecessary
stumbling blocks, however, the defender of miracles
might ask whether one might not be able to retain the
standard necessitarian theory of natural law as
universal generalizations, while jettisoning the
characterization of miracles as "violations of the laws
of nature" in favor of events which lie outside the
productive capacity of nature. That is to say, why may
we not take a necessitarian theory of natural law
according to which laws contain ceteris paribus
conditions precluding the interference of both natural
and supernatural forces and hold that a miracle is not,
therefore, a violation of a law of nature, but an event
which cannot be accounted for wholly by reference to
natural forces? Natural laws are not violated by such
events because they state what will occur only if God
does not intervene; nevertheless, the events are still
naturally impossible because the relevant natural
causal forces do not suffice to bring about the event.
Bilynskyj's objections to this view do not seem
insuperable.[20] He thinks that on such a view it
becomes difficult to distinguish between miracles and
God's general providence, since according to the latter

doctrine every event has in a sense a supernatural cause. This misgiving does not seem insurmountable, however, for we might construe God's providence as Bilynskyj himself does, as God's conservation of all secondary causes and effects in being, while reserving only His immediate causal activity in the world for inclusion in a law's ceteris paribus conditions. Bilynskyj also objects that the physical impossibility of a miracle is the reason we attribute it to supernatural causation, not vice versa. To define physical inpossibility in terms of supernatural causation thwarts the motivation for having the concept of physical impossibility in the first place. But my suggestion is not to define physical impossibility in terms of supernatural causation, but, as Bilynskyj himself does, in terms of what cannot be brought about wholly by natural causes. One may argue that some event E is not a violation of a natural law, but that the event is naturally impossible. Therefore, it requires a supernatural cause. It seems to me, therefore, that even on the necessitarian theory of natural law, we may rid ourselves of the incoherent notion of "violation of the laws of nature" and retain the concept of the naturally impossible as the proper characterization of miracle.

Thus, those who would defend miracles solely on the basis of a descriptive understanding of natural laws as universal inductive generalizations rather than a priori: prescriptions, without adopting the qualifications suggested above, would appear to be still operating under the assumption that events which really do transcend the dispositional properties of matter and energy cannot occur. But the difficult question remains for such a defender of miracles: how can

events occur which do not conform to those properties
of matter and energy which have been determined on the
basis of empirical evidence to a reasonably high degree
of certainty? In such a case, one would seem compelled
to admit either that such an event could not occur or
that what one thought was a law of nature was not such
after all. The resurrection of Jesus is a case in
point. For the fact that a man should be raised from
the dead and so transformed as to possess the powers
attributed to Jesus's resurrection body by the gospels
and Paul is so disparate to what we know of the normal
processes of decay that one may safely say that such an
event lies outside the productive capacity of the
natural causal nexus. The point is not whether such an
event has a statistical chance of occurring given
sufficient time. The probability concerns, not the
series of events or the properties of matter and
energy, but our attempted formulations of law-like
statements on the basis of those events or properties.
If physics establishes to a high degree of certainty
that dead men do not of themselves have the capacity to
rise from the dead in a transformed existence, then we
may be reasonably certain that any such hypothetical
event lies outside the productive capacity of the
natural causal nexus. Therefore, the defender of
miracles who appeals only to the descriptive character
of natural laws without adopting the distinctions
suggested above seems to be caught in the dilemma of
either denying the historicity of the resurrection of
Jesus or denying well-established natural laws.

The proper course would be to abandon the
incoherent notion of miracle as a "violation of a law
of nature" in favor of "an event which is naturally
impossible." The proper question concerning miracles

is thus whether an event can occur which has no physical or human causes. If the event were, on the one hand, wholly the product of the properties of matter and energy, then we should have no reason to call it miraculous; it would be a natural event. But on the other hand, it also cannot be the effect of the human mind. For unless one is a materialist, the effect of my willing to lift my arm is an event the cause of which lies outside the physical causal nexus. The effects of the mind's cognition and volition on the physical world, including my own body, are not produced by a combination of physical causes alone. Yet we should not want to describe my lifting my arm as miraculous (unless we were a materialist deriding the view of his opponent). Therefore, the miraculous ought to exceed the productive capacity of the human mind as well as physical causes. If we hold to a materialist view of mind, of course, this added qualification is unnecessary, and the question need only be whether an event can occur without a physical cause.

So although an initial advantage has been won by the construal of natural laws as descriptive, not prescriptive, this advantage evaporates unless one abandons the characterization of a miracle as a "violation of a law of nature" and adopts instead the notion of an event which is naturally impossible. Now the question which remains to be asked is how an event could occur which lies outside the productive capacity of natural causes.

It would seem to be of no avail to answer with Clarke that matter has no properties and that the pattern of events is simply God's acting consistently, for contrary to his assertion, physics does seem to have established that matter possesses certain

properties and that certain forces such as gravitation
and electro-magnetism are real operating forces in the
world. Bilynskyj points out that Clarke's view entails
a thorough-going occasionalism, according to which fire
does not really burn nor water quench, which runs
strongly counter to common sense.[21] Nor will it seem
to help to answer with Sherlock and Houtteville that
nature may contain within itself the power to produce
events contrary to its normal operation, for this would
not seem to be the case when the properties of matter
and energy are sufficiently well-known so as to
preclude to a reasonably high degree of certainty the
occurrence of the event in question. Moreover, though
this might secure the possibility of the event, so as
to permit a historical investigation, it at the same
time reduces the event to a freak of nature, the result
of pure chance, not an act of God. It seems most
reasonable to agree with medical science that an event
like Jesus's resurrection really does lie outside the
capability of natural causes.

But that being admitted, what has actually been
proved? All that the scientist conceivably has the
right to say is that such an event is naturally
impossible. But with that conclusion the defender of
miracles may readily agree. We must not confuse the
realms of logical and physical (or natural)
possibility. As Nagel argues, while there may be a
gain in clarity by interpreting the necessity of
natural laws in terms of logical necessity,
nevertheless this position faces formidable
difficulties:

> In the first place, none of the statements
> generally labeled as laws in the various positive
> sciences are in point of fact logically necessary,

since their formal denials are demonstrably not
self-contradictory. Accordingly, proponents of
the view under discussion must either reject all
these statements as not cases of 'genuine' laws
(and so maintain that no laws have yet been
discovered in any empirical science), or reject
the proofs that these statements are not logically
necessary (and so challenge the validity of
established techniques of logical proof). Neither
horn of the dilemma is inviting. In the second
place, if laws of nature are logically necessary,
the positive sciences are engaged in an incon-
gruous performance whenever they seek experimental
and observational evidence for a supposed law.
The procedure appropriate for establishing a
statement as logically necessary is that of
constructing a demonstrative proof in the manner[22]
of mathematics, and not that of experimentation.

It would thus seem necessary to distinguish between
logical necessity and natural or physical necessity.
Is the occurrence of a miracle logically impossible?
No, for such an event involves no logical contradiction. Is the occurrence of a miracle naturally
impossible? Yes, for it cannot be produced by natural
causes; indeed, this is a tautology, since to lie
outside the productive capacity of natural causes is to
be naturally impossible.

It might be urged that some miracles, such as
Aquinas's third category of miracles, lie within the
capacity of nature. But what this fails to see is that
every third order miracle would seem to involve of
necessity a first order miracle. To use Aquinas's
example, both God and nature can cause it to rain; but
if at a particular time the cause is God, then at some
point a first order miracle has occurred to set the
natural process in motion. Otherwise, the notion of
third order miracles simply reduces to God's general
providence, which is not technically speaking in the
realm of miracle. Considered abstractly, such events

are naturally possible, but given their historical
context they are naturally impossible. Thus, a miracle
by definition entails natural impossibility.

The question is, what could conceivably transform
a miracle as a logical possibility into an actual,
historical possibility? Clearly, the answer is, the
personal God of theism. For if a personal God exists,
then He serves as the transcendent cause to produce
events in the universe which are incapable of being
produced by causes within the universe (that is to say,
events which are naturally impossible). But it is to
such a personal, transcendent God that the orthodox
proponents of the argument for the resurrection
appealed. Given a God who conserves the world in being
moment by moment (Aquinas, Vernet, Houtteville), who is
omnipotent (Clarke), and free to act as He wills
(Vernet, Less), the orthodox thinkers seem to be
entirely justified in asserting that miracles are
really possible. The question is whether given such a
God miracles are possible, and the answer seems
obviously, yes. It must be remembered that even their
Deist opponents did not dispute God's existence, and
Clarke and Paley offered elaborate defenses for their
theism. And the widespread contemporary disdain for
proofs of the existence of God notwithstanding, the
ontological, teleological, and cosmological arguments
as a basis for theism all find eloquent, philosophically sophisticated proponents today.[23] In this way,
one could justify the possibility of miracles. For if
the existence of such a God is even possible, then
miracles are possible. Only an atheist can deny the
possibility of miracles, for even an agnostic must
grant that if it is possible that a transcendent,
personal God exists, then it is equally possible that

He has acted in the universe. Hence, it seems that the orthodox protagonists in the classical debate argued in the main correctly against their Newtonian opponents and that their response has been only strengthened by the modern understanding of natural law.

Spinoza

First Objection

With regard to Spinoza's objections to miracles, the orthodox thinkers seem to have again argued cogently. Turning to his first objection, that nothing happens contrary to the eternal and unchangeable order of Nature, it must be remembered that Spinoza's system is a pantheistic one, in which God and Nature are interchangeable terms. When we keep this in mind, it is little wonder that he argued against miracles on the basis of the unchangeable order of Nature, for, there being no ontological distinction between God and the world, a violation of nature's laws is a violation of the being of God. But, of course, the question is not whether miracles are possible on a pantheistic basis, but whether they are possible on a theistic basis. If God is personal and ontologically distinct from the world, there seems to be no reason why even a total alteration of the laws of nature should in any way affect God's being. Since natural law ought not to be construed as logically necessary, as we have seen, there would seem to be no reason why God could not have established a different set of laws for this universe nor why He could not now change them. As Aquinas urged against the necessitarian emanationism of the Arabic philosophers that God acts by His free will in determining the course of nature, so Vernet correctly

argues against Spinoza that nature's laws are freely
willed by God and are therefore subject to change.
Contrary to Spinoza, the properties of matter and
energy do not flow from the being of God with
inexorable necessity, but are the result of His choice.
Hence, He does not violate His own nature should He
choose to produce an event in the world which is not
the result of the immanent causes operating in the
universe.   Houtteville and Less also argued soundly
against Spinoza that if God willed from eternity to
produce a miracle at some point in time, then there is
no change on God's part, either in His being or
decrees. Thus, Spinoza's objection to miracles on the
basis of the unchangeableness of Nature is system-
dependent upon his pantheism. And we need be little
troubled by that, for, being a rationalistic system
unfolded by geometric deductions, Spinoza's conclusions
are hidden in his axioms and definitions, waiting to be
unpacked.   Deny his definition of substance as that
which is in itself and conceived through itself and the
whole edifice collapses.

Second Objection

Spinoza's second objection, it will be remembered,
was that miracles do not suffice to prove God's
existence. So stated, the objection found no foothold
in the apologies of most orthodox thinkers, for
virtually all of them used miracles, not as a proof for
the existence of God, but as a proof for His action in
the world.   Thus, the objection was strictly speaking
irrelevant.   But Spinoza's supporting reasoning was
pertinent to their arguments. His main point appears
to have been that a proof for God's existence must be
absolutely certain.   Since, therefore, we conclude to

the existence of God on the basis of the immutable laws
of nature, anything that impugned those laws would make
us doubt God's existence. Underlying this reasoning
would appear to be two assumptions: (1) a proof for
God's existence must be demonstratively certain and (2)
God's existence is inferred from natural laws. The
Christian apologists denied respectively both of these
assumptions. The first is based upon Spinoza's
rationalism, which prevents him from recognizing the
cogency of an argument unless he can affix his Q.E.D.
at the argument's conclusion. His more empirically
minded opponents, however, saw no reason to think that
an argument which was not absolutely demonstrative
could not provide sufficient warrant for theism.
Paley, for example, tried to give overwhelming
empirical evidence in his Natural Theology for God as
the designer of the universe; though not achieving
demonstrative certainty, the argument's aim was to make
it much more plausible to believe in God than not. The
demise of Spinozistic rationalism seems to be
sufficient testimony that subsequent generations have
not shared Spinoza's concern for geometric certainty.
Hence, one could argue for God's existence using a
modern, inductive conception of natural law instead of
a Spinozist conception (if this type of argumentation
works at all). The second assumption, for its part,
would not have relevance for someone who argued for
God's existence by other means. For example, Clarke,
while espousing the same concern for demonstrative
certainty as Spinoza, based his theism on cosmological
and ontological arguments. Hence, the objection that
miracles rendered natural law uncertain, even if true,
would not strike against Clarke.

But is the objection in fact true? Spinoza seemed

to think that the admission of a genuine miracle would
serve to overthrow the natural law pre-empted by the
miracle. If one retains the old "violation" concept of
miracle, this is certainly true. But if we abandon
that notion, as I have suggested, in favor of the
naturally impossible, then we can see that Clarke and
Paley were correct in arguing that a miracle does not
serve to abrogate the regularity of nature in general;
it only shows the intervention of God at that point in
the causal nexus. As Swinburne has argued, a natural
law is not abolished because of one exception; the
counter-instance must occur repeatedly whenever the
conditions for it are present.[24] If an event occurs
which is contrary to a law of nature and we have
reasons to believe that this event would not occur
again under similar circumstances, then the law in
question will not be abandoned. One may regard an
anomalous event as repeatable if another formulation of
the natural law better accounts for the event in
question. It would do this if it not only predicts all
other phenomena as accurately as the original law, but
also predicts the event in question, and if it is no
more complex than the original law. If any doubt
exists, the scientist may conduct experiments to
determine which formulation of the law proves more
successful in predicting future phenomena. In a
similar way, one would have good reason to regard an
event as a non-repeatable counter-instance to a law if
the reformulated law were much more complicated than
the original without yielding better new predictions or
by predicting new phenomena unsuccessfully where the
original formulation predicted successfully. If the
original formulation remains successful in predicting
all new phenomena as the data accumulate, while no

reformulation of the law does any better in predicting
the phenomena and explaining the event in question,
then the event should be regarded as a non-repeatable
counter-instance to the law. Hence, a miraculous event
would not serve to upset the natural law:

> We have to some extent good evidence about what
> are the laws of nature, and some of them are so
> well-established and account for so many data that
> any modifications to them which suggest to account
> for the odd counter-instance would be so clumsy
> and _ad hoc_ as to upset the whole structure of
> science. In such cases the evidence is strong
> that if the purported counter-instance occurred it
> was a violation of the laws of nature.[25]

Swinburne unfortunately retains the violation concept of
miracle, which would invalidate his argument, but if we
conceive of a miracle as a naturally impossible event,
he is on target in reasoning that the admission of such
an event would not lead to the abandonment of a natural
law.

Spinoza's fear, therefore, that miracles would
destroy natural laws seems unjustified. In fact
Spinoza's argument, if taken seriously, would prove a
positive impediment to science, for on his principles
not even repeatable counter-instances to a natural law
could be allowed, since these would impugn the present
natural law. In other words, Spinoza assumes we have
the final formulation of the natural laws known to us.
While he will admit that there may be unknown natural
laws, he cannot permit the revision of known laws. But
such a position is unscientific. If one adjusted
Spinoza's position to admit the possible revision of a
natural law by repeatable counter-instances, then any
argument for miracles based on those laws would, of
course, share in the uncertainty of our formulations.

If, however, we were confident that a particular
formulation of a law were genuinely descriptive of
reality, then the occurrence of an event shown by the
law to be naturally impossible could not overthrow
this law.   Rather than lead us away from God, such a
situation could lead us to see the hand of God in that
event, for there is no other way it could be produced.
And that was precisely the position of the orthodox
defenders of miracles.

     Spinoza's sub-contention that a miracle need not
prove God's existence, but only the existence of a
lesser being was not effective against most proponents
of the argument for the resurrection quite simply
because they were not trying to prove the existence of
God.   Having either proved or presupposed the existence
of God, they used miracles chiefly to prove Christian
theism was true.   On the other hand, the protagonists
in the classical debate over miracles were greatly
concerned about the possibility of demonic miracles and
how to identify a truly divine miracle.   Their answer
to this problem constitutes one of their most important
and enduring contributions to the discussion of
miracles.   They argued that the doctrinal context of
the miracle makes it clear whether the miracle is truly
from God.   Thus, they drew attention to the context in
which the miracle occurred as the basis for the
interpretation of that miracle.   This is extremely
important, for a miracle without a context is
inherently ambiguous.   This is the problem with Hume's
example of the revivification of Queen Elizabeth: the
event lacks any religious context and appears as a bald
and unexplained anomaly.   Hence, one feels a degree of
sympathy for Hume's scepticism.   But in the case of
Jesus's resurrection the context is dramatically

different: it occurs in the context of and as the
climax to Jesus's own unparalleled life, teaching, and
personal claim to authority, and it produced a profound
effect on his followers, including his own brothers and
the chief persecutor of the infant church, such that
they called him LORD and proclaimed salvation for all
men in his name.   Here is a context of events that, as
Paley rightly emphasized, is unique in the history of
mankind.   It ought, therefore, to give us serious
pause, whereas the hypothetical resuscitation of
Elizabeth might occasion only curiosity.   In this way
the religious context of a miracle furnishes us with
the proper interpretation of that miracle.

Spinoza's concern with lesser divine beings, such
as angels and demons, would probably not trouble too
many twentieth century minds.   It would be very odd,
indeed, were an atheist to grant the resurrection of
Jesus as a historical and miraculous event and yet
assert that perhaps only an angel raised him from the
dead.   Finite spirit beings are usually conceived to
exist only within a wider theistic framework, such that
to infer directly that God raised Jesus from the dead,
if the resurrection is a miraculous event, would not
appear to many to be an unwarranted inference.   In this
way, then, contrary to Spinoza's allegation, miracles
taken within their religious context could, it seems,
provide an adequate justification for a Christian
theism and perhaps even for theism itself.

Spinoza's final sub-point, that a miracle may
simply be the effect of an unknown cause in nature,
does not properly strike against the possibility of the
occurrence of a miracle, but against the identification
of the occurrence of a miracle.   Granted that miracles
are possible, how can we know when one has occurred?

This is admittedly a very thorny problem, and
undoubtedly most of our reserve over against purported
miracles stems from an underlying suspicion that the
event is somehow naturally explicable, even though we
do not know how. The problem has been persuasively
formulated in modern times by Antony Flew:

> Protagonists of the supernatural, and opponents
> too, take it for granted that we all possess some
> natural (as opposed to revealed) way of knowing
> that and where the unassisted potentialities of
> nature (as opposed to a postulated supernature)
> are more restricted than the potentialities which,
> in fact, we find to be realized or realizable in
> the universe around us.
>   This is a very old and apparently very easy
> and tempting assumption . . . . Neverthless, the
> assumption is entirely unwarranted. We simply do
> not have, and could not have, any natural (as
> opposed to revealed) criterion which enables us to
> say, when faced with something which is found to
> have actually happened, that here we have an
> achievement which nature, left to her own unaided
> devices, could never encompass. The natural
> scientist, confronted with some occurrence
> inconsistent with a proposition previously
> believed to express a law of nature, can find in
> this disturbing inconsistency no ground whatever
> for proclaiming that the particular law of nature
> has been supernaturally overridden.[26]

The response of Sherlock and Houtteville that an
unknown law of nature may be God's means of acting is
surely inadequate, for it may equally be the case that
the event in question is no act of God at all, but a
product of entirely natural but unknown causes.
Leclerc and Vernet have taken a better tack: when the
miracles occur precisely at a momentous time (say, a
man's leprosy vanishing when Jesus spoke the words, "Be
clean") and do not recur regularly in history and when
the miracles in question are various and numerous, the
chance of their being the result of unknown natural

properties seems negligible. If the miracles were
naturally caused, one would expect them to occur
repeatedly and not by coincidence at just the proper
moments in Jesus's ministry. In this sense Baur's
ridicule of Hase's explanation of Lazarus's
revivification as due to plötzlich wirkende Heilskräfte
seems justified. And it must be remembered that the
argument for the resurrection of Jesus was almost
always part of a wider argument for the historicity of
Jesus's miracles; often other arguments such as
fulfilled prophecy were adduced as well. The issue at
hand was not the occurrence of an isolated miracle, but
of the supernatural character of Jesus's entire
ministry. One thus had several convergent lines of
probability all pointing to the divine origin of
Jesus's power. In this sense, focusing exclusively on
the resurrection limits the scope of the evidence.
Though an isolated miracle might be dismissed as the
effect of an unknown operation of nature, Vernet seems
to be correct in regarding this possibility as minimal
when the entire scope of Jesus's miracles is surveyed.

But since our attention is focused on the
resurrection itself, it ought to be asked whether on
the basis of the resurrection alone, we would be
justified in inferring that a miracle has truly
occurred. Here the overwhelming majority of people
would undoubtedly say, yes. For the question here is
not whether the empty tomb and appearances could be
explained in another way (for example, theft,
subjective visions, and so forth). The question is, if
it were proved beyond reasonable doubt that Jesus
actually did rise from the dead, would we be justified
in inferring a divine act? For most people the answer
would be in the affirmative; those who argue against

the resurrection attempt to explain the facts of the
case without Jesus's rising. But I know of no critic
who argues that the historical evidence shows that
Jesus did rise, but that this was a purely natural
occurrence. This would appear as a somewhat desperate
obstinacy. Two factors undergird this judgement: (1)
The resurrection is so unnatural an event that it seems
best to attribute it to a supernatural cause. Both the
orthodox and their sceptical opponents acknowledged
Jesus's resurrection to be the biblical miracle par
excellence. It was always viewed as the greatest of
the gospel miracles associated with Jesus. Hume
himself acknowledged that it has never in the history
of the world been heard of that a truly dead man (in
Jesus's case two nights and a day) has been raised from
the dead. But more than that: we must keep in mind
that the resurrection of Jesus as portrayed in the
gospels and described by Paul was not simply the
resuscitation of a corpse; it was the transformation of
the body to a new mode of reality which Paul characterized as powerful, glorious, imperishable, and
Spirit-directed (I Cor 15.42-44). It simply strains
the credibility too far to attribute such an event to
purely natural causes. If Jesus's resurrection were
the result of natural factors, then its singularity in
the history of mankind is difficult to understand. And
in the nearly 2,000 years since that unique event, no
natural causes have been discovered that could account
for it. On the contrary, the advance of science has
only served to confirm that such a resurrection is
naturally impossible. (2) The supernatural explanation
is immediately given in the religious context in which
the event occurred. Jesus's resurrection was not merely an anomalous event occurring without context, but

took place as the climax to Jesus's own life and teachings. As Pannenberg explains,

> The resurrection of Jesus acquires such decisive meaning, not merely because someone or anyone has been raised from the dead, but because it is Jesus of Nazareth, whose execution was instigated by the Jews because he had blasphemed against God.
>   Jesus's claim to authority, through which he put himself in God's place, was . . . blasphemous for Jewish ears . . . . If Jesus really has been raised, this claim has been visibly and unambiguously confirmed by the God of Israel, who was allegedly blasphemed by Jesus.[27]

If Jesus claimed to have a unique relationship of Sonship with the Father, as seen in his use of the familiar "Abba,"[28] and if he made a claim to divine authority[29] and if his disciples proclaimed that it was God who raised him from the dead, then why not accept the religious explanation as the most satisfactory answer to the question of the cause of his resurrection?

A final remark on Spinoza's reasoning ought to be made. The objection does not, like Hume's, spring from the nature of historical investigation; rather it could be pressed by witnesses of Jesus's miracles and resurrection appearances themselves. But in this case, the objection loses all conviction: for can we imagine, say, doubting Thomas, when confronted with the risen Jesus, studiously considering whether some unknown natural cause might have produced what he experienced? There comes a point when the back of scepticism is broken by the sheer reality of a wonder before us.[30] At any rate, had Jesus himself been confronted with such scepticism, would he not have attributed it to hardness of heart in his opponent? To that extent, an answer to Spinoza's objection is

perhaps superfluous. Having shown the resurrection of
Jesus to be the most plausible explanation of the
facts, a proponent of this argument should perhaps
simply leave the question of its miraculous nature to
be settled between his hearer and God. Perhaps Pascal
was right in maintaining that God has given evidence
sufficiently clear for those with an open heart, but
sufficiently vague so as not to compel those whose
hearts are closed.

Hume

'In principle' argument

Hume's in principle argument against the
identification of a miracle, for its part, seems either
question-begging or mistaken. To say that uniform
experience is against miracles is to implicitly assume
that the miracles in question did not occur. Otherwise
the experience could not be said to be truly uniform.
Thus, to say uniform experience stands against miracles
begs the question. If, however, we relax the term
"uniform" to mean simply "general" or "usual," then the
argument fails of cogency. Hume seems to confuse the
realms of science and history: the general experience
of mankind has allowed us to formulate certain laws
which describe the physical universe. That dead men do
not rise is a generally observed pattern in our
experience. But at most this only shows that a
resurrection is naturally or physically impossible.
That is a matter of science. But it does not prove
that such a naturally impossible event has never
occurred. That is a matter of history. As Less and
Paley pointed out, the testimony in history for the
general pattern of events cannot overturn good

testimony for any particular event. Since, as Sherlock
argued, a miracle is just as much a matter of sense
perception as any other event, it can be proved by
historical testimony in the same way as an non-
miraculous event. Qua history, they stand exactly on
the same par. But it is contrary to sound historical
methodology to suppress particular testimony out of
regard for general testimony. As Isaiah Berlin
explains:

> Whereas in a developed natural science we consider
> it more rational to put our confidence in general
> propositions or laws than in specific phenomena
> . . . this rule does not operate successfully in
> history . . . . If . . . a historian were to
> attempt to cast doubt on--or explain away--some
> piece of individual observation of a type not
> otherwise suspect, say, that Napoleon had been
> seen in a three-cornered hat at a given moment
> during the battle of Austerlitz; and if the
> historian did so solely because he put his faith .
> . . in a theory or law according to which French
> generals or heads of state never wore
> three-cornered hats during battles, his method,
> one can safely assert, would not meet with
> universal or immediate recognition from his
> profession. Any procedure designed to discredit
> the testimony of normally reliable witness, or
> documents as, let us say, lies or forgeries, or as
> being defective at the very point at which the
> report about Napoleon's hat occurred, would be
> liable to be regarded as itself suspect, as an
> attempt to alter the facts to fit a theory . . . .
> It seems clear that . . . in history we tend, more
> often than not, to attach greater credence to the
> existence of particular facts than to general
> hypotheses . . . .[34]

In the case of the resurrection, if the testimony which
we have makes it probable that Jesus's tomb was really
found empty on the first day of the week by some of his
women followers and that he later appeared to his
disciples in a non-hallucinatory fashion, then it is

bad historical methodology to argue that this testimony
must be somehow false because historical evidence shows
that all other men have always remained dead in their
graves.   Nor can it be argued that the testimony must
be false because such an event is naturally impossible,
for it may well be the case that history proves that a
naturally impossible event has, in fact, occurred.   As
Paley contended, Hume's argument could lead us into
situations where we would be led to deny the testimony
of the most reliable witnesses to an event because of
general considerations, a situation which results in an
unrealistic scepticism.   In fact, as Sherlock and Less
correctly contended, this would apply to non-miraculous
events as well.   There are all sorts of events which
make up the stuff of popular books on unexplained
mysteries (such as levitation, disappearing persons,
spontaneous human combustions, and so forth) which have
not been scientifically explained, but, judging by
their pointless nature, sporadic occurrence, and lack
of any religious context, are not miracles.   It would
be folly for a historian to deny the occurrence of such
events in the face of good eyewitness evidence to the
contrary simply because they do not fit with known
natural laws.   Yet Hume's principle would require the
historian to say that these events never actually
occurred.   The fact is, the historian can determine the
facticity of a historical event without knowing how or
whether it accords with natural laws.   Finally, it
might be urged against Hume's in principle argument, if
God's existence is possible, then as Paley argued, He
may have chosen to reveal Himself decisively in history
at one point, and there is no probability that we
should experience the same events today.   Hence, the
occurrence of those events uniquely in the past cannot

be dismissed because such events are not experienced at
other times. As long as God's existence is possible,
then it is equally possible that He has acted uniquely
at a point in history, in which case the question
simply becomes whether such an event did take place.
But then it is a question of evidence, not of
principle, as Hume maintained.

Antony Flew has sought also to defend Hume's in
principle argument against the identification of a
miracle:

> . . . it is only and precisely by presuming that
> the laws that hold today held in the past and by
> employing as canons all our knowledge--or presumed
> knowledge--of what is probable or improbable,
> possible or impossible, that we can rationally
> interpret the detritus of the past as evidence and
> from it construct our account of what actually
> happened. But in this context, what is impossible
> is what is physically, as opposed to logically,
> impossible. And 'physical impossibility' is, and
> surely has to be, defined in terms of inconsis-
> tency with a true law of nature . . . .
> . . . Our sole ground for characterizing [a]
> reported occurrence as miraculous is at the same
> time a sufficient reason for calling it physically
> impossible.[32]

Now this objection actually seems to be inconsistent
with the final point of Spinoza's second objection
against miracles, which Flew also sought to defend.
There, it will be remembered, it was asserted that our
knowledge of nature is so incomplete that we can never
regard any event whatsoever as miraculous, since it
could be the effect of an unknown law of nature. This
would compel us to take a totally open attitude toward
the possibility of any given event, for virtually
anything would be possible in nature. We should never
be entitled to say any event is naturally impossible.
But now Hume's objection asserts precisely the

opposite, namely, that our knowledge of natural law is
so complete that we can not only determine which events
would be naturally impossible, but we are able to
impose this over the past to expunge such events from
the record. The two positions are incompatible. Flew
thus seems to have worked himself into a dilemma:
either naturally impossible events can be specified or
not. If they can, then such an event's occurring could
be identified as a miracle. If they cannot, then we
must be open to anything's happening in history. Flew
cannot have it both ways: he cannot line up behind
both Spinoza and Hume. Now I have contended that
naturally impossible events can sometimes be specified
and that an event such as Jesus's resurrection ought to
be regarded as naturally impossible. Does that mean
therefore, as Flew alleges, that it must be regarded a
priori as unhistorical? Not at all; Flew has made an
unjustifiable identification between natural (or in his
terms, physical) possibility and actual, historical
possibility. The assumption here is that the naturally
impossible cannot occur, or in other words, that
miracles cannot happen, which is question-begging,
since this is precisely the point to be proved.
Historical possibility and impossibility, insofar as
such terms are suitable to historical study, ought not
to be defined in terms of scientific law, but in terms
of the factual evidence: hence, it is historically
impossible that the Crusaders re-conquered and subdued
all the lands previously lost by Christianity to Islam;
it is historically possible that Jesus healed people
miraculously. Flew's argument really boils down to the
assertion that in order to study history, one must
assume the impossibility of miracles. This question
will be taken up below.

In recent times the classical debate over the identification of miracles has continued in the dispute over principles of historical methodology. It has been contended that the historical method is inherently restricted to non-miraculous events; for example, D.E. Nineham asserts,

> It is of the essence of the modern historian's method and criteria that they are applicable only to purely human phenomena, and to human phenomena of a normal, that is non-miraculous, non-unique, character. It followed that any picture of Jesus that could consistently approve itself to a historical investigator using these criteria, must a priori, be of a purely human figure and it must be bounded by his death.[33]

On what basis can it be said that the historical method applies only to non-miraculous phenomena? According to Carl Becker, it is because that method presupposes that the past is not dissimilar to our present experience:

> History rests on testimony, but the qualitative value of testimony is determined in the last analysis by tested and accepted experience . . . . the historian knows well that no amount of testimony is ever permitted to establish as past reality a thing that cannot be found in present reality . . . . In every other case the witness may have a perfect character--all that goes for nothing . . . .
>   . . . We must have a past that is the product of all the present. With sources that say it was not so, we will have nothing to do; better still, we will make them say it was so.[34]

Becker's historical relativism allows him to reshape the past with impunity so that it is made to accord with our experience of the present. The result is that miracles such as the resurrection must be expunged by the historian, for these are not found in the experience of his own generation.[35] Thus, Makoto

Yamauchi, arguing that the resurrection is not
historically ascertainable because we must work with
the presupposition that there are no acts of gods in
history, roundly concludes,

> Now one can say with all assurance that the
> assumption from which the historical approach sets
> out, i.e. that the resurrection is an objectively
> ascertainable object of knowledge and accessible
> to impartial observation, is fundamentally
> incorrect. The resurrection of Jesus is actually
> not a point on the historic plane to which one
> could conceivably have an objective relation.[36]

According to this outlook, historians must adopt as a
methodological principle a sort of "historical
naturalism" that excludes the supernatural.

This viewpoint is simply a restatement of Ernst
Troeltsch's principle of analogy.[37]   According to
Troeltsch, one of the most basic of historiographical
principles is that the past does not differ essentially
from the present. Though events of the past are of
course not the same events as those of the present,
they must be the same in kind if historical investigation is to be possible. Troeltsch realized that this
principle was incompatible with miraculous events and
that any history written on this principle will be
sceptical with regard to the historicity of the events
of the gospels.

F.H. Bradley formulated a historiographical
principle similar to Troeltsch's principle of analogy:
the principle of uniformity. He maintained that the
presupposition of critical history is the uniformity of
nature and that testimony running contrary to this
ought not to be believed:

> We have seen that history rests in the last resort
> upon an inference from our experience, a judgement

> based upon our own present state of things, . . .
> and that this is the sole means and justification
> which we possess for holding and regarding
> supposed events as real . . . . When therefore we
> are presented . . . with so-called 'historical
> facts,' the like of which seem to stand in no
> relation to all that we now have in heaven and on
> earth; when we are asked to affirm the existence
> in past time of events, the effects of causes
> which confessedly are without analogy in the
> world in which we live, and which we know--we are
> at a loss for any answer but this, that . . . we
> are asked to build a house without a foundation
> . . . . And how can we attempt this without
> contradicting ourselves?[38]

For Bradley the present is the foundation for any view
of the past and to construct a view that denies the
foundation is fundamentally self-contradictory.

What may be said of Bradley's principle of
uniformity and Troeltsch's principle of analogy? R.G.
Collingwood has effectively criticized Bradley's
principle as precluding the possibility of our learning
anything new from history:

> His view is that the historian brings to his work
> a ready-made body of experience by which he judges
> the statements contained in his authorities.
> Because this body of experience is conceived of as
> ready-made, it cannot be modified by the
> historian's own work as an historian; it has to be
> there complete, before he begins his historical
> work.[39]

Because the present determines the past for Bradley
(which is, in fact, exactly the opposite of what occurs
in reality), we cannot learn anything from history
except what we already know from the present. But such
a situation is intolerable, especially when one
reflects on the fact that the present does not
ontologically determine the past and, therefore, ought
not to be allowed to do so epistemologically. Simply

because something does not happen in the present does
not mean it did not happen in the past. Therefore, to
assume as a methodological principle that the past
cannot differ in any respect from the present risks
giving us a distorted picture of the past. Collingwood
proceeds to query whence Bradley's ready-made store of
knowledge comes; the answer appears to be from
scientific law:

> . . . this experience is not regarded as
> consisting of historical knowledge but as
> knowledge of some other kind, and Bradley in fact
> conceives it as scientific knowledge, knowledge of
> the laws of nature. This is where the positivism
> of his age begins to infect his thought. He
> regards the historian's scientific knowledge as
> giving him the means of distinguishing between
> what can and what cannot happen; and this
> scientific knowledge he conceives in the
> positivistic manner, as based on induction from
> observed facts on the principle that the future
> will resemble the past and the unknown the
> known.[46]

Here again we have the confusion between the realms of
science and history. Science is being used to dictate
to history what can and cannot have happened. But this
is methodologically impermissible. At the very most
Bradley would be justified in claiming that certain
events are naturally impossible--and that is not the
same as saying they never happened. It could be the
case that historical evidence supports the facticity of
certain events which cannot be explained by reference
to natural causes. Nor need one fear that this
admission will overthrow the natural law in question;
the fact that such events are so rare and do not accord
with scientific experimentation nor facilitate
prediction provides good reason for assigning them to
the categories of either scientifically unexplained or

unexplainable events.[41]

Pannenberg has persuasively argued that neither can Troeltsch's principle of analogy be legitimately employed to banish from the realm of history all non-analogous events.[42] Properly defined, analogy means that in a situation which is unclear, the facts ought to be understood in terms of known experience; but Troeltsch has elevated the principle to constrict all past events to purely natural events. But that an event bursts all analogies cannot be used to dispute its historicity. When, for example, myths, legends, illusions, and the like are dismissed as unhistorical, it is not because they are unusual, but because they are analogous to present forms of consciousness having no objective referent. When an event is said to have occurred for which no analogy exists, its reality cannot be automatically dismissed; to do this we should require an analogy to some known form of consciousness lacking an objective referent that would suffice to explain the situation. Pannenberg has thus upended Troeltsch's principle of analogy such that it is not the want of an analogy that shows an event to be unhistorical, but the presence of a positive analogy to known thought forms that shows a purportedly miraculous event to be unhistorical. Thus, he has elsewhere affirmed that if the Easter traditions were shown to be essentially secondary constructions analogous to common comparative religious models, the Easter appearances were shown to correspond completely to the model of hallucinations, and the empty tomb tradition were evaluated as a late legend, then the resurrection would be subject to evaluation as unhistorical.[43] In this way, the lack of an analogy to present experience says nothing for or against the historicity of an event.

Troeltsch's formulation of the principle of analogy
succumbs to the same criticism as Bradley's principle
of uniformity: it attempts to squeeze the past into
the mold of the present without providing any warrant
for doing so. As Richard Niebuhr has protested,
Troeltsch's principle really destroys genuine
historical reasoning, since the historian must be open
to the uniqueness of the events of the past and cannot
exclude a priori the possibility of events like the
resurrection simply because they do not conform to his
present experience.[44]   But Pannenberg's use of the
principle preserves the analogous nature of the past to
the present or to the known, thus making the investigation of history possible, without thereby sacrificing
the integrity of the past or distorting it.

     This means that there seems to be no in principle
philosophical objection to establishing the occurrence
of a miracle like the resurrection of Jesus by means of
historical research. It is hard to understand the
resistance of so many theologians, even those who argue
quite persuasively for the historical credibility of
the resurrection, to this conclusion. Very typical is
the reasoning of Künneth with regard to the empty tomb:
"The fact of the empty tomb as such . . . does not have
any power to prove the resurrection, since the latter
in itself is wholly independent of any substratum of a
material kind, so that Paul, too, like the rest of the
New Testament, does not adduce the fact of the empty
tomb as a specific argument."[45]   Whether the
resurrection body is wholly independent of a material
substratum, even for Paul, is a moot point.[46] But that
aside, the fallacy of this oft-repeated reasoning would
seem to lie in confusing necessary with sufficient
conditions. One may grant for the sake of argument

that the empty tomb may not be a necessary condition
for the resurrection, but it may still be a sufficient
condition for the resurrection. More simply put, it is
illogical to argue that because the resurrection does
not require the empty tomb, therefore the empty tomb
does not require the resurrection. If it can be shown
that it is historically probable that Jesus's tomb was
found empty and that alternative explanations (for
example, theft of the body by the disciples) are
implausible, then the empty tomb could become a
sufficient condition for inferring the resurrection of
Jesus as the most plausible explanation. (The same is
true of the appearances; they are not necessary
conditions of the resurrection, but should alternative
explanations prove unlikely [for example, subjective
visions on the part of the disciples], then they become
a sufficient condition for inferring the resurrection
of Jesus as the most reasonable explanation.)

       This also seems to reveal the flaw in the
reasoning of Wilckens, who says, "How the grave of
Jesus became empty is a question that cannot be . . .
answered in a historical way," but nevertheless thinks
that all naturalistic alternative explanations can be
refuted.[47] If no plausible natural explanation for the
empty tomb is forthcoming, then why not accept the
explanation given in the religious context of the event
itself? Wilckens's reserve does not seem to be due to
lack of evidence; rather he insists that it is
inherently impossible to prove the resurrection
historically because it is an eschatological event.[48]
Clearly the problem here seems to be not historical,
but theological. Wilckens and others of like
persuasion recoil from the New Testament's portrayal of
the resurrection as a historical event every bit as

objective as the crucifixion, and they substitute
instead the notions of an "eschatological event" or a
"meta-historical event."[49]   But it needs to be asked
whether such expressions are not in fact nonsensical
when applied to Jesus's resurrection.   An eschatological event is an event at the end of history, which
has not yet occurred; but Jesus's resurrection has
occurred.   Thus it is not literally an eschatological
event.   If one takes the expression more loosely to
mean Jesus's resurrection was an event of the same
character as some end-time event, an event fraught with
divine   or   existential   significance,   then   the
impossibility of historically verifying or falsifying
it qua event does not seem to exist, since as an event
it has already occurred in advance and is therefore
susceptible to historical inquiry.   A meta-historical
event, for its part, seems to be a contradiction in
terms.   For an event is that which happens.   Thus, to
be an event is to be part of history.   To speak of an
event that is not part of history is therefore to speak
of an event which has not happened.   The resistance,
therefore, of many modern theologians to a historical
approach to the resurrection of Jesus seems to be
unwarranted.   If naturalistic explanations cannot
plausibly account for the full scope of the New
Testament data, then these data do seem to become a
sufficient condition for inferring the resurrection of
Jesus.

Certain contemporary theologians, such as Berthold
Klappert, have agreed that the resurrection occurred in
space and time and left a historical margin accessible
to research (for example, the empty tomb), but maintain
that the resurrection itself is not verifiable because
the historian cannot consider causes outside history.[50]

There seems, however, to be a flaw in this reasoning:
Klappert appears to confuse the event of the resurrection with the cause of the resurrection. The event of
the resurrection purportedly occurred within history,
but the cause of the resurrection is said to be outside
human history. Thus, even on Klappert's historiography, the resurrection (=Jesus's rising transformed
from the dead) is susceptible to historical proof,
since to affirm it is to say nothing about its cause.
The hypothesis of the resurrection is thus both
verifiable and falsifiable: verifiable through
establishing the facts concerning the empty tomb, the
appearances, and the origin of the Christian Way;
falsifiable by either disproving the above or providing
naturalistic explanations of them. The real problem
comes when we inquire concerning the cause of the
resurrection. According to Klappert's historiography,
the historian qua historian could conclude that the
best explanation of the facts is that "Jesus rose from
the dead," but he could not conclude "God raised Jesus
from the dead." But may I submit that the historian
"in his off-hours," to paraphrase Bertrand Russell,
that is, the historian as a man, may indeed rightly
infer from the evidence that God has acted here in
history? The situation is somewhat analogous to the
scientist and creatio ex nihilo. The astrophysicist
pushes back to an event for which there are no
empirical antecedents, the beginning of the universe;
similarly, the historian discovers an event for which
there is no historically antecedent cause, the
resurrection of Jesus. Qua scientist or historian, he
may halt his inquiry, lacking empirical data; but I
submit that as human beings searching for meaning and
significance for our lives and the universe, we must go

further. This is especially so for the resurrection,
given the religious context in which it occurred: the
life, teachings, and claims of Jesus and the effect on
those who followed him. They saw in it the key to
human life and salvation (Rom 10.9). We would be
foolish to ignore their claims.

But more than this, the methodological principle
that prohibits the historian from adducing a
supernatural cause for an event is not incapable of
being challenged. For what basis is there for this
principle? Science can neither bar gnomically
impossible events from history nor force us to
assimilate anomalous events to natural law. Philosophy
cannot preclude either the occurrence or identification
of a miracle. Therefore, so long as the existence of
God is possible, it seems that such events' being
caused by God cannot be ruled out. The historian ought
first, as a methodological principle, to seek natural
causes; but when no natural cause can be found that
plausibly accounts for the data and a supernatural
hypothesis presents itself as part of the historical
context in which the event occurred, then it would not
seem to be illicit to choose the supernatural explanation.[51] As C.F.D. Moule urges,

> If the coming into existence of the Nazarenes, a
> phenomenon undeniably attested by the New
> Testament, rips a great hole in history, a hole
> the size and shape of the Resurrection, what does
> the secular historian propose to stop it up with?
> . . . the birth and rapid rise of the Christian
> Church . . . remain an unsolved enigma for any
> historian who refuses to take seriously the only
> explanation offered by the Church itself.[52]

One should not suspend judgement forever. Naturalism
has had nearly 2,000 years to explain the resurrection

of Jesus. Should it be judged to have failed to do so,
then the rational man can hardly be blamed if he now
infers that at the tomb of Jesus on that early Easter
morning a divine miracle has taken place.

'In fact' arguments

If then, there seems to be no in principle
argument against establishing the resurrection of Jesus
by means of the historical method, what may be said
concerning Hume's four in fact arguments against
miracles? All of Hume's arguments have force; but the
fact remains that these general considerations cannot
be used to pronounce on the historicity of any
particular miracle. They only serve to make us
cautious in our investigation. Hume's fourth point
does seek to preclude any investigation by asserting
that the miracles of various religions cancel each
other out. But it still remains an _empirical_ question
whether a miracle supporting a counter-Christian claim
is equally or better attested than Jesus's
resurrection. There is no way to settle the issue
apart from an investigation. Less, Campbell, and Paley
argued fairly convincingly, I think, against at least
Hume's examples of purported miracles. And it must be
said that we may be spared the effort of investigating
every single miracle story known; for if the
resurrection of Jesus were shown to be historical, the
overwhelming number of miracles in support of a
counter-Christian claim are so minor in character that
they could not stand against the miracle of the
resurrection, but could rightly be regarded as
inauthentic or as yet unexplained natural events.

Hence, one of the most important contributions of
the orthodox protagonists in the classical debate that

remains of lasting value is their insistence that the
presupposition of the impossibility of miracles should
play no role in determining the historicity of any
event. And although many scholars, especially in the
first half of this century, have continued to operate
under this presupposition, there seems now to be a
growing recognition that such a presupposition is
illegitimate. The presupposition against the
possibility of miracles survives in theology only as a
hangover from an earlier Deist age and ought to be once
for all abandoned.

The Historical-Critical Method

We have already seen how the Deist controversy
helped to stimulate the rise of the modern
historical-critical approach to the Bible. The
critical doubts raised by Hobbes and especially Spinoza
concerning Mosaic authorship of the Pentateuch served
to arouse early, particularly in Simon and LeClerc, the
historical-critical spirit. Though the Deists did not
advance in any significant way the science of
criticism, they helped to remove the aura of sanctity
surrounding the Scriptures and to dethrone it from its
privileged place of authority. Perhaps the key figure
in the transition to the modern approach to the Bible
was Semler, who abandoned the doctrine of verbal,
plenary inspiration for a purely historical approach to
the documents. The force of the Deists' attacks on
Scripture helped to lead him to jettison that doctrine
as untenable, while his Pietism helped him to preserve
the truth of Christianity notwithstanding. After
Semler the approach to Scripture as inspired documents
fell increasingly into disfavor while the historical-

critical approach gained ascendancy. Deist influence
fostering the historical-critical approach was also
mediated through Lessing, who accepted the historical
criticisms of Reimarus and proposed to regard the
evangelists as merely human authors. Indirectly then
the Deists did serve to promote the rise of the
historical-critical method.

While the Deist contribution in this regard is
widely recognized, perhaps it is not so often
appreciated how indebted the historical-critical
approach is to the orthodox defenders of Christianity.
For it was they who staunchly insisted that an
objective, open-minded investigation of the biblical
documents, regarded not as inspired accounts but as
ordinary historical records, would justify
Christianity. No matter that they were not entirely
objective themselves in carrying out this investigation: for they encouraged a purely human approach to
the documents, free from all presuppositions concerning
divine authorship and inerrancy, and others would carry
out their program more rigorously. Nor was this for
most of them a retreat or concession on their part: we
have seen how such an approach grows naturally out of
the medieval signs of credibility once historical
consciousness is awakened. Vives and Mornay already
begin to argue historically for their faith; Grotius
nearly 50 years before Spinoza argues that the
historical books of the Scriptures need not be regarded
as inspired, but only as reliable. Not that the
orthodox thinkers would have developed such an approach
wholly on their own: without the stimulus of
opposition the apologetic enterprise does not thrive.
But surely this is precisely the point: the orthodox
Christians were not forced to retreat into this

position, as though they were retrenching theologically. Rather this approach to the Scriptures arose in the realm of apologetics, and it was assumed for the most part as a positiion of strength. It was thought that by adopting a position that presupposes nothing of the divine nature of Scripture, one might argue more convincingly for it, since this avoids any circularity in the argument. Thus, throughout the eighteenth century Deist controversy, the Christian apologists claimed to be able to establish the truth of the Christian religion from the historical facts alone, without begging the question by apppealing to the inspiration or authority of Scripture. In this way, they actually pointed the way to the historical-critical approach to the documents.

It hardly needs to be said that this approach has been overwhelmingly adopted by modern biblical scholars. In investigating and interpreting the biblical documents, the modern critic does not view them as inspired and therefore sui generis. Rather he treats them as he would any other ancient text. The same historiographical principles govern an investigation of the biblical events as of any other "secular" events. As Van Harvey notes, "Believers have no distinctively Christian justificatory warrants for ascertaining whether Hitler was mad, Constantine wrote the famous Donation, Luther nailed his theses to the cathedral door, or, for that matter, whether Jesus was raised from the dead."[53] That the adoption of the historical-critical approach seems to necessitate abandonment of the doctrine of biblical inspiration does not seem to have been appreciated by the defenders of Christianity during the Deist controversy, with the exception of perhaps Grotius and LeClerc. The majority

seem to have thought that they could believe in the
doctrine of inspiration and yet at the same time, as a
sort of methodological principle in apologetics,
suspend this belief in favor of viewing the biblical
accounts as merely human documents. In this way they
could justify them as revelation. They never really
succeeded in escaping the influence of their belief in
biblical inspiration, as I have said, but this is not
the chief difficulty, for none of us succeeds in
approaching the text from a wholly neutral standpoint.
Rather the difficulty seems to lie in the fact that the
historical-critical approach and the doctrine of
biblical inspiration appear to pull in opposite
directions. For the historical-critical approach
assumes of necessity that the biblical documents are to
be treated like any other human writings, while the
doctrine of divine inspiration holds them to be
precisely not that. For someone who believes in divine
inspiration, therefore, the historical-critical
approach necessarily falsifies the nature of the
documents. This leads to the odd hermeneutical
approach of an Ernesti, who held that the historical-
critical method ought to govern our approach to the
Scriptures until difficulties are encountered. Then
the doctrine of inspiration is introduced to preserve
the infallibility of the text. The Christian
apologists might retort that the historical-critical
method ought to govern the inquiry into whether the
Scripture is divine revelation, and once that has been
established by the evidence for miracle and prophecy,
then theology ought to proceed on the basis that this
divine revelation is inspired and therefore inerrant.
While logically consistent, however, this approach, if
carried out honestly, would probably lead to the

awkward circumstance that the defender of Christianity
would have to hold that certain aspects of the gospel
accounts ought to be judged to be unhistorical on the
basis of the historical-critical method, but that
nevertheless he believes them to be true anyway on the
basis of divine inspiration! At best, his second
affirmation would probably appear strained and
unconvincing; at worst, he could give the appearance of
holding to a double-truth theory. Thus, the position
of the Christian apologists was fraught with a terrible
instability. They advocated treating the Scriptures as
ordinary, human documents and yet wanted in the end to
affirm their status as divinely inspired and inerrant
revelation. The modern science of criticism has
followed them in their first recommendation, but could
not turn a blind eye to the difficulties unearthed
through such an approach so as to affirm their second
conclusion. The only reason the Christian apologists
did not generally encounter this situation themselves
is probably because they were not ruthlessly objective
in their historical investigations.

The Argument for the Resurrection

We now turn to a consideration of the historical
argument for the resurrection as formulated by its
proponents. The general logic of their argument, it
will be remembered, took the form of a dilemma: either
accept the resurrection of Jesus as an event of
history or else reject all other events equally
attested. Probably the main objection to such
reasoning today would be that the resurrection as a
miraculous event cannot be susceptible to historical
proof. This objection, as we have already seen, seems

not to be cogent. It might be insisted that the
resurrection and another equally attested ordinary
event are not on a par, since a miraculous event must
have stronger supporting evidence than a non-miraculous
event. Even if this condition were granted, however,
it would not affect the fundamental dilemma that the
evidence for the resurrection is better than for many
commonly accepted, non-miraculous events and therefore
cannot be denied without renouncing much of secular
history.

Within the framework of this dilemma the Christian
apologists, as we have seen, presented this case:

1. The gospels are authentic.
2. The text of the gospels is substantially pure.
3. The gospels are reliable.
   a. The disciples were neither deceivers nor
      deceived.
   b. The origin and growth of the Christian
      church confirm the reliability of the
      gospels.
4. Objections are unsound.

Now during the Deist controversy, step one was
virtually undisputed. Friend and foe alike were
persuaded that the gospels did stem from their received
authors. This meant that a Deist had to argue either
that the text had been utterly corrupted and changed by
the church or that the apostles were liars or
enthusiasts. Though some thinkers like Collins did
argue for a corrupted text, it was obvious that this
alone could not explain the gospel accounts. Modern
textual criticism has justified this conviction, so
that step two of the argument is no longer a point of
contention. Therefore, the Deists had to argue that
the disciples were either deceivers or deceived with
regard to the resurrection of Jesus. The first

alternative is represented by the conspiracy theory,
which held that the disciples stole Jesus's corpse and
fabricated the resurrection; the second alternative is
represented by the apparent death theory, which held
that Jesus did not die on the cross at all. Now it
almost goes without saying that these alternatives, so
construed, have been decisively rejected by modern
scholarship. Although Rudolf Pesch has asserted that
the empty tomb "permits all possible explanations" as
shown by the Jewish polemic and anti-Christian
rationalism,[54] this simply does not seem to be true.
The old rationalistic explanations have, in the
judgement of modern scholarship, thoroughly failed to
provide plausible historical explanations of the facts,
and no one today would seriously defend Reimarus's or
Paulus's hypotheses.[55] When the arguments of the
Christian apologists are weighted against the
alternatives offered by their Deist opponents, the
orthodox thinkers undoubtedly had the more plausible
case. Lawton concludes that ". . . within the very
narrow corridor in which they argued their case they
may be deemed to have carried their point. . . . it
becomes fair to say that, in so far as the
historico-critical demands of their day went, the
evidentialists did present a prima facie case for the
supernatural origin of Christianity; an adequate
springboard, so to speak, for the act of faith."[56]

Dissolution of the Orthodox Dilemma

That does not mean that theology was ready to
embrace supernaturalism. What has happened instead is
that biblical criticism since Strauss has sought to
dissolve the evidentialists' dilemma altogether and

thus forge a third way between its horns. It has done
this by denying the ground on which the dilemma was
formulated: the authenticity of the gospels. The
dilemma propounded by the orthodox thinkers was based
on the apostolic authorship of the gospels and on the
gospels' having been faithfully transmitted down to
their day. They argued that given these two points,
one is reduced to two alternatives concerning the
apostolic witness: they were either liars or mistaken,
neither of which is plausible. Their opponents usually
did not think to deny either of the two foundational
points and so embraced one of the two horns of the
dilemma. But Strauss broke the hammerlock of the
orthodox apologists' dilemma by arguing that the
gospels are not authentic, but the result of a long
period of transmission and development during which
mythological influences reshaped the facts. Strauss
thus rendered naive the simple "deceivers or deceived"
dilemma, and the interpretation of the resurrection
narratives as unhistorical legends remains the
alternative embraced by modern critics who deny the
historicity of that event. It is also to the credit of
Strauss that he saw the key role played by Paul in the
evidence for the resurrection, a role that has become
predominant in current studies on the resurrection, and
acknowledged that Paul's testimony indicates that
people were about who definitely believed that they had
seen Jesus alive from the dead. Strauss's argument
that since Paul places all the appearances on a level
with his own experience, all the resurrection
appearances were therefore visions has been adopted by
a great many contemporary critics.[57] His explanation
of this in terms of the effect made upon the disciples
by the personality of Jesus has also had a lasting

influence and remains one of the debated questions in resurrection research today.[58] The contemporary critic who wishes to deny the historicity of Jesus's resurrection usually employs some variant of Strauss's subjective vision/legendary development theory to explain the evidence of Paul and the gospels. That is his lasting contribution.

Strauss's denial of the gospels' authenticity and his explanation of them in terms of an evolutionary development throws a new light on the dilemma of the orthodox apologists. To take the alternative that the disciples were deceived, for example; since in the opinion of most modern criticism, none of the gospels stems from any eyewitness, the possibility of the disciples' being deceived or at least giving a wrong interpretation to their experience becomes a more real possibility. To say, for example, that the disciples could not have been mistaken because Jesus appeared to them over several weeks (Ditton) or because they talked and ate with Jesus (Paley) assumes that these narratives are not legends or theologically shaped statements. Not that anyone would defend today, say, the apparent death hypothesis; but some, for example, Bultmann or Marxsen, do find the subjective vision hypothesis a real option. Since Paul does not differentiate among the appearances in I Cor 15.3-8 and since the appearance to him was a heavenly vision, it is argued, perhaps the other appearances were also visions, visions of a subjective sort brought on by a crisis of faith. The physicalism of the gospels is a later development--perhaps as an apologetic against Docetism. In this way the alternative that the disciples were "deceived" receives fresh life.

The new outlook of modern criticism also affects

profoundly the other horn of the dilemma, that the
disciples were deceivers. Not that any modern critic
would be so rash as to assert that the original Twelve
were deliberate hoaxers: to that extent the modern
critic agrees with the arguments of Paley, Ditton,
Vernet, and others that the suffering of the disciples,
their sincere character, the absurdity of a conspiracy
among them, and the evident change in their lives
preclude that they were deceivers. That no longer
comes into question. But the discovery of theology in
the gospels has had a deep effect on how the modern
critic assesses the historicity of the resurrection
narratives. Since these narratives do not flow fresh
from the pen of an eyewitness, but are products of a
later time, the modern exegete is reluctant to equate
theological reshaping of a tradition with deliberate
deceit. For example, if Luke out of anti-docetic
motives takes a tradition of resurrection visions and
re-works it into physical appearances, the modern
critic would not label this as deliberate deceit on
Luke's part. Rather it simply reflects his theological
Sitz im Leben, the needs of the believing community for
whom he wrote, and his own theological perspective. In
this way, the modern critic regards many aspects of the
resurrection narratives as redactional additions or
reshapings of tradition and as therefore unhistorical.
The classical proponents of the historical argument for
the resurrection would have called this deceit, but due
to its theological motivation the modern critic rejects
that appellation and along with it the argument against
the evangelists' being deceivers.

Some Arguments of Enduring Worth

At the same time, however, it must be said that several of the arguments developed by the classical defenders of the resurrection would still have force even against these reformulated objections. For example, Paley's arguments against the subjective vision hypothesis retain their worth today as Grass's refutation of this hypothesis shows.[59] Paley contends that the theory of hallucinations cannot account for the plurality of separate witnesses to these appearances, the group nature of some of the appearances, the repetition of the appearances, and the empty tomb. Many contemporary scholars still find these arguments convincing. On the basis of Paul's citation of the pre-Pauline formula in I Cor 15, most critics grant that the disciples did have some sort of visionary experiences of Jesus risen from the dead. Thus, Norman Perrin, though like Grass denying the empty tomb, says of the appearances: "The more we study the tradition with regard to the appearances, the firmer the rock begins to appear upon which they are based."[60] But if this is so, then as Grass argues, the subjective vision theory encounters several difficulties. For from Paul's list of witnesses alone, we know that different individuals and groups on different occasions and no doubt in different places and circumstances saw appearances of Jesus. But it seems unlikely that hallucinations could be experienced by so many various persons and groups under so many varied conditions. The possible suggestion that there was a chain reaction of hallucinations among the disciples does not alleviate this difficulty because neither James nor Paul stood in the chain. Hence,

Paley's objections to this theory are not without weight even today.

And it must be said that Grass and Perrin notwithstanding most scholars have come to agree with Paley's viewpoint on the historicity of the empty tomb. Several of Paley's arguments in support of the empty tomb still seem to be cogent: that the disciples could not have believed in the resurrection without an empty tomb, that the origin of the church in Jerusalem requires an empty tomb, that the Jews would have produced the body had the tomb not been empty, and that early Jewish polemic presupposes the empty tomb. With regard to the first point, for a first century Jew a resurrection would have automatically entailed an empty tomb, whether the resurrection be conceived as a mere resuscitation or as a transformation to a glorified body.[61] The idea that Jesus rose from the dead with a new body while the old body lay in the grave is a purely modern conception. As Bode points out, Jewish mentality would never have accepted a division of two bodies, one in the tomb and one in the risen life. Therefore, the disciples' belief in Jesus's resurrection could not have survived in the face of Jesus's closed tomb. The tomb was therefore probably empty. About the only way to resist this conclusion is to deny the historicity of the burial tradition and maintain that Jesus's burial place was unknown or lost. This, however, is very difficult to carry through plausibly, since the burial tradition is widely recognized to be one of the most reliable of the traditions about Jesus.[62] This is significant, for, as Grass admits, if the burial story of Jesus is basically reliable, then the site of Jesus's tomb must have been known to Jew and Christian alike. In that case,

however, it is very difficult to understand how the
first disciples could have come to believe in Jesus's
resurrection were the tomb not empty.

Paley's second argument makes a similar point:
the locus of the early church was in Jerusalem, the
very place where Jesus was executed and buried. Had
the tomb not been empty, this palpable fact would have
been obvious to all. When therefore the disciples
began to preach the resurrection in Jerusalem, and
people responded, and the religious authorities stood
helplessly by, the tomb must have been empty. This
conclusion would not seem to be substantially altered
by any uncertainty as to the precise time that the
disciples began to preach, as Pesch alleges.[63] The
point would remain, when the disciples returned from
Galilee to Jerusalem, preaching the resurrection, the
tomb by that time at least must have been empty in
order for their message to meet sympathetic and
believing reception, whenever that may have been. The
fact that the Christian fellowship, founded on the
belief in Jesus's resurrection, could come into
existence and flourish in the very city where he was
executed and buried remains a positive piece of
evidence in favor of the empty tomb.[64]

The third argument is also not without force.
Even if the disciples in their enthusiasm had not
bothered to check Jesus's tomb--itself an unlikely
hypothesis--, then surely the Jews could have been
guilty of no such oversight. Exhuming the corpse may
seem to be a rather drastic counter-measure, but it is
interesting that in the medieval Jewish polemic the
Jewish authorities are made to do precisely this. In
any case, they would no doubt have pointed to the
closed tomb of Jesus as ample evidence that he had not

risen. This seems especially evident if the tomb of Jesus was well-known; but even if Jesus had been buried in the criminals' common graveplot, it is not even then obvious why the authorities could not have located a newly dug grave, even after six weeks, and pointed to Jesus's resting place. The Jewish inability to produce or point to the body of Jesus, particularly in light of the credibility of the burial narrative, does count in favor of the empty tomb--especially when the next point is considered.

Paley's fourth point was that the early Jewish polemic presupposes the empty tomb. This is perhaps one of the most persuasive confirmations of the empty tomb tradition. From Matthew's story of the guard at the tomb, we learn that the current anti-Christian polemic did not deny that Jesus's tomb was empty. Although Matthew's guard story is nearly universally rejected by modern critics,[65] his incidental remark concerning the Jewish allegation of body-snatching on the disciples' part provides an important clue to the historicity of the empty tomb. For it shows that the enemies of Christianity were involved in an effort to explain away Jesus's empty tomb. This not only confirms that the tomb was apparently known, but that it was also empty. Many contemporary critics consider this a weighty argument in favor of Jesus's empty tomb.[66]

Thus, some of the arguments of the classical apologists for the empty tomb still have weight today in the mind of contemporary scholars. Together with other evidences,[67] they seem to furnish an adequate historical basis for affirming the historicity of the empty tomb. Van Daalen concludes that it is very difficult to object to the fact of the empty tomb on

historical grounds; most objectors do so out of
theological or philosophical considerations.[68] But, as
I have argued, these ought not to be allowed to dictate
to history what has or has not happened. And interestingly more and more New Testament scholars seem to be
realizing this. According to Kremer, "By far most
exegetes hold firmly . . . to the reliability of the
biblical statements concerning the empty tomb . . .,"
and he lists 28 prominent scholars in support: Blank,
Blinzler, Bode, von Campenhausen, Délorme, Dhanis,
Grundmann, Hengel, Lehmann, Léon-Dufour, Lichtenstein,
Mánek, Martini, Mussner, Nauck, Rengstorff, Ruckstuhl,
Schenke, Schmidt, K. Schubert, Schwank, Schweizer,
Seidensticker, Strobel, Stuhlmacher, Trilling, Vögtle,
and Wilckens.[69] Besides Kremer's own name, at least 17
others could be added to his list: Benoit, Brown,
Clark, Dunn, Ellis, Gundry, Hooke, Jeremias, Klappert,
Ladd, Lane, Marshall, Moule, Perry, J.A.T. Robinson,
and Schnackenburg. Even the Jewish scholars Lapide and
Vermes have defended the historicity of the empty tomb,
the former going so far as to declare on the basis of
the evidence that Jesus probably did rise from the
dead.

The fact of the empty tomb together with the
foregoing considerations do serve to create significant
reservations with regard to the subjective vision
hypothesis, as the classical apologists contended. Not
only does the theory seem to encounter real difficulties in explaining the appearances, but it also cannot
in any way account for the empty tomb and must
therefore be conjoined with some other hypothesis to
explain the disappearance of Jesus's body. So not all
of the arguments for the resurrection pressed against
this theory during the Deist controversy have been

rendered obsolete.

The same may be said of some of the apologists' arguments against the second horn of the dilemma, that the disciples were deceived. Paley's general consideration, for example, that the period of time between the occurrence of the events and the writing of the gospels is too short to allow for the legendary development of a non-miraculous into a miraculous story still has force. Roman historian A.N. Sherwin-White remarks that in classical history the sources are usually biased and removed at least one or two generations or even centuries from the events, but historians still reconstruct with confidence what happened.[70] In the gospels, by contrast, the tempo is "unbelievable" for the accrual of legend; more generations are needed.[71] The writings of Herodotus enable us to test the tempo of mythmaking, and the tests suggest that even two generations are too short a span to allow the mythical tendency to prevail over the hard historic core of oral tradition.[72] In the same vein, Julius Müller writing in response to Strauss, challenged scholars of his day to show where in thirty years a great series of legends, the most prominent elements of which are fictitious, have anywhere gathered around an important historical individual and become firmly fixed in general belief.[73] His challenge has never been met. This would suggest that the burden of proof does not rest solely on the critic who would affirm the historicity of a particular tradition, but equally on him who would dispute it.

A second consideration that still has weight today is the temporal and geographical proximity of the origin of the belief in Jesus's resurrection with the original events. The Christian thinkers rightly

emphasized the controlling presence of living
eyewitnesses on the development of the tradition.
Vincent Taylor has chided overly sceptical critics on
their neglect of this factor, observing that if these
critics were right, then the disciples "must have all
been translated into heaven immediately after the
Resurrection."[74] The witnesses listed by Paul in I Cor
15 continued to live and move in the early community
and would exercise a control on the appearance
traditions. As Plummer observes, those who had seen
Christ after the resurrection would soon become "marked
men."[75] Similarly, if persons like Mary Magdalene and
the women did not discover the empty tomb, then it is
difficult to see how the early tradition could arise,
in opposition to the better knowledge of first
generation believers, that they did. It is also
difficult to imagine how fictitious stories could
become widespread so long as the apostles were still
alive or that the true story should be supplanted by a
false. Though Strauss was certainly correct that the
apostles could not be everywhere at once, nevertheless
they did exercise an authoritative control on the basic
traditions, so that it is difficult to imagine how
generally accepted tradition concerning Jesus's
resurrection might arise contrary to their witness.
Künneth remarks,

> It is extremely difficult to see how the Gospel
> accounts of the resurrection could have arisen in
> opposition to the original apostolic preaching and
> that of Paul . . . . The authority of the
> apostolic eye-witnesses was extraordinarily
> strong. It would be inconceivable how there
> should have arisen in opposition to the
> authoritative witness of the original opostles a
> harmonious tradition telling of an event that has
> no basis in the message of the eye-witnesses.[76]

Discrepancies in secondary details could exist, and the theology of the evangelists could affect the traditions, but one must doubt whether the basic traditions themselves could have been legendary so long as the disciples were alive and directed the church's preservation of its traditions.

Therefore, even if from the perspective of a modern biblical critic, the classical dilemma is no longer cogent, it nevertheless remains true that some of the arguments brought forth in support of the resurrection are not thereby invalidated. On the contrary, many contemporary critics have found some of the arguments still cogent within a redaction-critical outlook and have adopted or reformulated them in order to defend the substantial historicity of the resurrection traditions.

The Origin of the Christian Way

It will be recalled that in addition to the dilemma argument, the defenders of the historical resurrection also had recourse to the ancient argument from the origin and rapid growth of early Christianity. This is not an argument from the success of Christianity, for counter-examples of successful movements opposed to Christianity (for instance, Islam) come all too easily. The question rather is how one can account for the coming into existence of the Christian Way apart from the historical resurrection. The argument is logically independent of the authenticity of the gospels and still finds supporters today.[77] As R.H. Fuller notes, even the most sceptical critic must posit some mysterious x to get the movement going.[78] But what was that x?

Contemporary defenders of this argument emphasize
that the Christian Way cannot be seen simply as a
logical extension of Judaism.[79] For Christian belief
in Jesus's resurrection differed radically from the
popular Jewish belief in resurrection in two ways. (1)
The Jewish belief always concerned an eschatological
resurrection, not a resurrection within history, and
(2) the resurrection in Jewish thought always concerned
the people as a whole, not an isolated individual. In
contradistinction to this, Jesus's resurrection was
both within history and concerned one individual
person. With regard to the first point, the Jewish
belief was that at the close of history, God would
raise the dead and receive them into a state of eternal
blessedness. There are, to be sure, examples in the
Old Testament of resuscitations of the dead, but this
was merely a return to the earthly life, so that
eventually these persons would die again. The
eschatological resurrection alone was to eternal life
and glory. The notion that a true resurrection might
occur prior to God's bringing the eschatological
Kingdom would have been foreign to the disciples, and
it is interesting that Mark portrays them as stumbling
over this very point (Mk 9.9-13). Jeremias explains,

> Ancient Judaism did not know of an anticipated
> resurrection as an event of history. Nowhere
> does one find in the literature anything
> comparable to the resurrection of Jesus.
> Certainly resurrec-tions of the dead were known,
> but these always concerned resuscitations, the
> return to the earthly life. In no place in the
> late Judaic literature does it concern a
> resurrection to δόξα as an event of history.[80]

The disciples, therefore, confronted with Jesus's
crucifixion and death, would probably have only looked

forward to the eschatological resurrection and have carefully preserved their master's tomb as a shrine, where his bones could rest until the resurrection. It seems doubtful that they would have come upon the idea that he was already raised.

With regard to the second point, the Jewish conception of the resurrection always concerned a general resurrection of the dead, not of an isolated individual. It was the righteous or the people of Israel as a whole which God raised up in the resurrection. Moreover, in Jewish thought, there was simply no concept of the people's resurrection in some way hinging on the Messiah's resurrection. Yet this is precisely what is said to have occurred in Jesus's case. Wilckens explains,

> For nowhere do the Jewish texts speak of the resurrection of an individual which already occurs before the resurrection of the righteous in the end time and is differentiated and separate from it; nowhere does the participation of the righteous in the salvation at the end time depend on their belonging to the Messiah, who was raised in advance as the 'First of those raised by God' [87] (I Corinthians 15.20).

Once again the disciples would probably not have conceived from Jewish influences or background that Jesus alone had been raised from the dead. They would probably have waited with longing for that day when he and all the righteous of Israel would be raised by God to glory. These two considerations strongly suggest that the disciples' belief in Jesus's resurrection cannot be accounted for in terms of the influences of Jewish beliefs.

Much of the early Christian movement's zeal and theology may be explained in light of its belief that

God had raised Jesus from the dead. Indeed, one may
rightly say that belief in Jesus's resurrection brought
the movement into being. But how does one explain the
origin of that belief? In an exchange of letters with
Don Cupitt, C.F.D. Moule repeatedly presses this
point.[82] With regard to the resurrection, Moule
contends, there is historical evidence for a belief for
which nothing in the scope of prior historical facts
can account. In support he argues: (1) a large number
of people all shared tenaciously a conviction
organically connected with their way of life; (2) this
conviction cannot be derived from the Old Testament or
Pharasaism; and (3) this conviction persisted until
they were squeezed out of the synagogue for this
belief. These facts cannot be plausibly explained
unless the resurrection of Jesus was a historical
event. Thus, the old argument from the origin of the
Christian Way still seems to have considerable weight.
Even according to the strictest use of the
dissimilarity criterion, it seems we ought to accept
the basis in historical fact for the Christian Way's
adherence to the resurrection, for this belief cannot
apparently be explained from the side of Judaism, nor
can it be explained from the side of the church, since
it is itself the ground of the church. Therefore, it
seems that it ought to be explained in terms of
historical fact.

Refutation of Objections

The final step of the classical argument for the
resurrection was the refutation of objections. Today
these objections do not seem to be so weighty as they
once were. For example, far from wondering why Jesus

only appeared to his disciples and not publicly, many
contemporary theologians are scandalized by the
objectivity of the gospels' portrayal of the
appearances, such that unbelievers would have seen the
risen Lord had they been present.[83] At any rate Ditton
was certainly right in reminding his objectors that the
question is the sufficiency of the evidence as we have
it, not as it could have been. The objection that most
Jews remained unconverted also occasions little worry
today; perhaps more remarkable is the fact that so many
were. The final objection we mentioned in our
discussion of the classical debate shows how far modern
discussions have moved from past concerns: whereas
Vernet felt obliged to emphasize that the gospels do
portray a physical resurrection body of Jesus, despite
its extraordinary properties, modern critics are often
offended by the all too apparent physicalism of the
gospels and attempt to play them off against Paul in
favor of a more "spiritual" conception of the
resurrection body.[84] In this sense, the physicalism of
the gospels has become something not to be defended,
but to be got rid of. Hence, most of the objections
that once occasioned vigorous responses from defenders
of the resurrection would hardly raise an eyebrow
should any sceptic press them today.

On the other hand, the verdict of modern
scholarship is that the Deists carried the objection
concerning the inconsistencies and contradictions in
the resurrection narratives. Reimarus, it will be
remembered, based his entire case against the
resurrection on the many contradictions in the gospel
accounts of the resurrection. Although some of these
are probably more imagined than real (for example, the
time of the buying of the spices or Matthew vs. John on

the touching of Jesus), others have occasioned great
difficulty (for example, Galilee vs. Jerusalem
tradition of appearances). Although the orthodox
defenders sought to harmonize the accounts, modern
scholarship has sided with Reimarus and Annet and
rejected the harmonizing approach as unconvincing and
artificial. Thus, C.F. Evans in his study on
resurrection in the New Testament concludes that the
gospel accounts are impossible to harmonize and that
their discrepancies are not the result of legendary
developments stemming from the differing reports of
witnesses, but rather the result of rational reflection
and apologetic.[85]   To this extent at least modern
criticism has supported Reimarus.

But this being said, modern scholarship seems to
deny the significance which Reimarus attributed to this
objection. For what does it prove?--certainly not
Reimarus's theory that the disciples stole the corpse
and faked the resurrection, for this has been rejected
as absurd by subsequent scholarship. Most critics
would today probably grant Reimarus's point that the
accounts contain contradictions, but at the same time
be very little troubled by such an admission. Such a
concession would only cause consternation to those who
regard the gospel narratives as divinely inspired and
therefore inerrant accounts. No doubt this is why the
defenders of the resurrection did feel compelled to go
to such lengths at harmonization. But the modern
biblical critic who regards the narratives as ordinary
historical documents is generally prepared to sort
through the difficulties in order to determine the
historical core; he will not jettison the historicity
of, say, the empty tomb merely because the various
gospel accounts of its discovery differ or even

contradict in some respects.   Historian Michael Grant
comments,

> . . . the historian . . . cannot justifiably deny
> the empty tomb.   True, this discovery, as so
> often, is differently described by the four
> Gospels--as critical pagans early pointed out.
> But if we apply the same sort of criteria that we
> would apply to any other ancient literary sources,
> then the evidence is firm and plausible enough to
> necessitate the conclusion that the tomb was
> indeed found empty.[86]

The gospel resurrection narratives are, in fact,
remarkably harmonious in their cores and mainly differ
in circumstantial aspects.   Thus, the presence of
contradictions is not usually held to be of very great
moment.   Although Strauss's rejection of the
resurrection narratives was ostensibly based on the
contradictions in the accounts, more profoundly it was
founded rather upon the impossibility of miracles.   And
Strauss was certainly mistaken when he said this
presupposition required no proof.[87]   That miracles are
possible is, as it were, neutral ground between the
opposing claims that miracles are necessary and that
miracles are impossible.   Since the proposition,
"miracles are impossible" is a claim to knowledge, it
is quite definitely an assertion requiring proof.
Similarly, when a critic like Marxsen asserts that a
synchronizing harmony of the gospel accounts is
impossible and then concludes from this that the
evangelists "unequivocally" mean to say that the mode
of the resurrection is not an essential ingredient of
faith in the risen Jesus,[88] he almost certainly seems
to overdraw his conclusion.   At the most Marxsen has
shown that the correct chronological and geographical
sequence of the appearances is not an essential

ingredient of faith in the resurrection. So although
modern criticism has rejected harmonizing in favor of
Reimarus, the impact of this has probably not been very
great in terms of the argument for the historicity of
the resurrection. In fact, ironically, it has actually
served to make the defender's task a bit easier, for
now he may readily admit some aspect of a tradition is
contradictory   without   thereby   abandoning   the
historicity of the entire tradition nor being forced
into harmonizing exegesis. Contrary to Annet, there
seem to be a good number of critics who would be quite
willing to lay down five shillings that the historical
evidence, contradictions and all, is material enough to
support the resurrection of Jesus.

Summary and Conclusion

In summary, then, it appears that modern criticism
agrees that the Christian apologists argued more
effectively than did their Deist opponents. The idea
that the disciples were deceivers or deceived, in the
Deist understanding of those expressions, has been
decisively rejected by modern criticism. Though the
alternative of Strauss was later to dissolve this
dilemma, the eighteenth century apologists argued
effectively against the opponents of their day. I
think it is quite unfortunate that these thinkers are
so often denigrated as shallow apologists, biased for
Christianity and ignorant of the methods of criticism;
for such a characterization is both unfair and
anachronistic. Of course they were biased for
Christianity--just as the Deists were biased against
it--, but this need not affect the worth of their
arguments. Moreover, it would be anachronistic to

expect them to employ historical-critical tools not yet available to them. The question is simply which side of the debate provided the most plausible account of the evidence. Though modern scholarship was to advance beyond the simple dilemma posed by the Christian apologists, thus nullifying much of their argumentation, nevertheless this dilemma was effective against the opponents of their day, and modern criticism agrees that the Deist explanations of the resurrection are, indeed, untenable. It must be remembered that during the heyday of this controversy, proponent and opponent alike were agreed that the gospel accounts of the resurrection were penned by the apostolic authors themselves. In fact the defenders of the resurrection often argued at length to the best of their ability utilizing the tools of their time that the evidence, primarily though not exclusively external testimony, did prove apostolic authorship. It is anachronistic to expect them to deal with problems of source, form, or redaction criticism before these arose. Given then the apostolic authorship of the gospels, the issue boiled down to two alternatives to the resurrection: the apostles were either deceivers or deceived. Although viewed from the perspective of modern biblical criticism, this dilemma is not valid, nevertheless it was decisive taken within the historical context of the period we are considering, and it can be said that with regard to the resurrection of Jesus the Christian apologists argued more effectively than their Deist opponents.

Moreover, we have seen that some of the arguments they propounded on behalf of the resurrection have retained a lasting value. They correctly argued, I think, that miracles are both possible and identifiable. They emphasized the importance of using ordinary tools of historical study in investigating the historicity of the gospel narratives. And they adduced evidence for the resurrection that still merits consideration today: the inadequacy of the subjective vision hypothesis, the witness of the earliest enemies of Christianity to the empty tomb, the lack of sufficient time for the accrual of legend, the temporal and geographical proximity of the origin of the belief in Jesus's resurrection to the original events, and the inexplicability of the origin of the Christian Way apart from the historical resurrection of Jesus.

In closing I should like to make some brief remarks on how, in light of what we have learned from the classical debate, a historical argument for the resurrection might look today. The general framework of the argument would take the form of an epistemological dilemma: one must accept the resurrection of Jesus as a historical event or else reject all other events in history for which the evidence is of comparable weight. It is presumed that any reasonable man who is not being tendentious will not be prepared to scrap great portions of history, particularly classical history. The argument, thus, does not purport to reach an apodeictic certainty; rather it seeks to establish that insofar as reasonable and open-minded men are willing to accept the facticity of certain events in the past, so ought they to be ready to acknowledge the historicity of Jesus's resurrection, should it be supported by evidence of comparable quality. The argument would have no force to a person who is ready to reject all possibility of historical knowledge; such an individual would first have to be shown the unrealistic and unliveable nature of such historical scepticism. The thrust of a historical argument for the resurrection would be to show that the evidence for that event is just as compelling as the evidence for a great many events in history which we all quite naturally accept and that therefore it ought to be equally accepted as a historical event.

Such a formulation of the argument would necessitate a defense of the possibility of the occurrence and identification of miracles. To prove the possibility of the occurrence of a miracle, it will be enough to show that if it is possible that a personal, transcendent God exists, then it is possible that He has caused an event in history. The identification of the resurrection as a genuine miracle may be won through its naturally impossible character and especially its historical-religious context of the life, teachings, and personal claims of Jesus. At this point it should be emphasized, I think, that the identification of the resurrection as an act of God also involves a certain spiritual openness on the part of the investigator; the evidence may be sufficient without being coercive.

Given this framework, the real historical work would now have to be done. The evidence concerns basically three facts: the empty tomb, the appearances, and the origin of the Christian Way. Procedurally, the historical investigator will have to begin with the evidence of Paul. He will need to assess the credibility of Paul's testimony concerning the witnesses of the resurrection appearances and ask whether Paul gives any information concerning the nature of those appearances. He will have to determine Paul's understanding of the nature of the resurrection body, as this may have an important effect upon the

historicity of the gospel accounts of the empty tomb
and resurrection appearances. He will then need to
comb the gospel narratives, separating tradition from
redaction insofar as this is possible. Then these
traditions and additions will have to be weighed to
determine their historical plausibility. Here many of
the points raised in the classical debate must be kept
in mind. The investigator will want to examine the
Jewish backdrop against which the gospels were written
in order to understand the Jewish conception of
resurrection vis à vis the Christian.

Finally, if the investigator, as a result of this
research, determines that the tomb of Jesus was
probably found empty, that the original disciples saw
appearances of Jesus on several occasions and under
various circumstances, and that Christian belief in the
resurrection of Jesus is sharply dissimilar to the
Jewish notion, he will have to assess various
hypotheses that could be offered to explain these
facts. He may dispense with the old rationalistic
hypotheses such as conspiracy of the disciples or
Jesus's apparent death; but he will have to come to
grips with Strauss's theory of subjective visions which
were later elaborated into the gospel accounts of the
empty tomb and appearances. If then he comes to the
conclusion that the hypothesis which best fits all the
facts is that Jesus actually rose from the dead, then
as a historian he ought to accept that explanation as
the most reasonable reconstruction of what took place.

NOTES TO SECTION I

[1] Rudolph Bultmann, "New Testament and Mythology," in Kerygma and Myth, 2 vols., ed. Hans-Werner Bartsch, trans. R.H. Fuller (London: SPCK, 1953), 1:42.

[2] Schubert Ogden, Christ Without Myth (London: Collins, 1962), p. 102.

[3] James M. Robinson, A New Quest of the Historical Jesus, SBT 25 (London: SCM Press, 1959), p. 42.

[4] Willi Marxsen, "The Resurrection of Jesus as a Historical and Theological Problem," in The Significance of the Message of the Resurrection for Faith in Jesus Christ, ed. C. F. D. Moule, SBT 8 (London: SCM Press, 1968), p. 17.

[5] On the pre-Pauline formula contained in these verses see note 85.

[6] For a discussion of resurrection formulas, see Grant Osborne, "History and Theology in the Resurrection Narratives: a Redactional Study," (Ph.D. thesis: University of Aberdeen, 1974), pp. 79-144.

[7] Gerhard Koch, Die Auferstehung Jesu Christi, BHT (Tübingen: J. C. B. Mohr, 1959), p. 25.

[8] Justin Martyr Dialog with Trypho 108; Testament of the Twelve Patriarchs (Levi) 16.3.

[9] For discussion, see I. Broer, Die Urgemeinde und das Grab Jesu, SANT 31 (München: Kösel Verlag, 1972), pp. 69-78; F. Neirynck, "Les Femmes au tombeau: Etude de la rédaction mathéenne," New Testament Studies 15 (1968-9): 168-90. On the independence of Matthew from Mark, see E. Rückstuhl and J. Pfammatter, Die Auferstehung Jesu Christi (Lucerne and München: Rex, 1968).

[10] See B. A. Johnson, "The Empty Tomb in the Gospel of Peter Related to Mt. 28.1-7," (Ph.D. dissertation, Harvard University, 1966), p. 17.

[11] See Paul Rohrbach, Die Berichte über die Auferstehung Jesu Christi (Berlin: Georg Reimer, 1898), p. 79.

[12] Contrary to Hans Grass, Ostergeschehen und

Osterberichte, 4th ed. (Göttingen: Vandenhoeck &
Ruprecht, 1970), p. 23, this proclamation alone could
have evoked the Jewish response that the disciples had
stolen the body, if it was also the case that Jesus's
empty tomb was known. Indeed, the Jewish polemic is
perhaps best understood as an attempt to explain away
the empty tomb. The Jewish response need not
presuppose that the Christians were using the empty
tomb itself as an apologetic argument.

[13]As was thought by H. E. G. Paulus, Das Leben
Jesu, 2 vols. (Heidelberg: C. F. Winter, 1828), 2:264.

[14]Mahoney denies this, contending that the Jews
argued as they did only because it would have been
"colorless" to say the tomb was unknown or lost.
(Robert Mahoney, Two Disciples at the Tomb, TW 6 [Bern:
Herbert Lang, 1974], p. 100.) But here Grass seems to
be correct: if the grave were unknown or lost, then
the preachers of the resurrection would have been
greeted with the jeers of Acts 2.13: "They are filled
with new wine." It seems doubtful that the Jewish
leaders so feared being "colorless" that they preferred
to invent the empty tomb for the Christians. And if
the burial place of Jesus was known, as seems likely
(Josef Blinzler, "Die Grablegung Jesu in historischer
Sicht," in Resurrexit, ed. Edouard Dhanis [Rome:
Libreria Editrice Vaticana, 1974], pp. 94-6, 101-2),
the reaction of the Jews becomes even more
problematical: for instead of pointing to the tomb of
Jesus or exhibiting his corpse, they entangled
themselves in a series of hopeless absurdities trying
to explain away the absence of his body. The fact that
the enemies of Christianity felt obligated to explain
away the empty tomb shows not only that the tomb was
known, but that it was also empty.

[15]Rudolf Bultmann, Die Geschichte der synoptischen
Tradition, 8th ed., FRLANT 29 (Göttingen: Vandenhoeck
& Ruprecht, 1970), p. 309.

[16]Wolfgang Nauck, "Die Bedeutung des leeren Grabes
für den Glauben an den Auferstandenen," Zeitschrift für
die Neutestamentliche Wissenschaft 47 (1956): 243-67.

[17]See M. Rosh Ha-Shanah 1.8; M. Shebuoth 4.1;
Josephus Antiquities of the Jews 4.8.15; Numbers Rabbah
10.159b; T J Yoma 6.2; and references in Paul
Billerbeck, Kommentar zum Neuen Testament aus Talmud
and Midrasch, 6 vols., ed. Hermann L. Strack (München:
Beck, 1922-63), 2: 441; 3: 217, 251, 259. The fact

that women and not male disciples are made to discover
the empty tomb is perhaps one of the strongest
evidences of its historicity.

[18]Plutarch Antonius 2; Cicero Orationes
Philippicae 2.7.17; Philo Against Flaccus 10.83.

[19]Quintillian Declamationes maiores 6.9.

[20]Grass, Ostergeschehen, p. 174; M. J. Lagrange,
Evangile selon saint Marc (Paris: Librairie Lecoffre,
1966), p. 441; Vincent Taylor, The Gospel According to
St. Mark, 2d ed. (London: Macmillan: 1966), pp.
600-1; Blinzler, "Grablegung," p. 59.

[21]Note the classical touches in the use of
ἐπειδηπερ (inasmuch as) and the second aorist
παρέδοσαν (de-livered) instead of the more common first
aorist παρέδωκαν.

[22]D. E. Nineham, "Eye-witness testimony and the
gospel tradition," Journal of Theological Studies 11
(1960): 254.

[23]According to Roman historian A. N.
Sherwin-White, Luke's chronology is deliberate and in
Lk 3.1 cannot be challenged for accuracy. Luke also
tries to date the beginning and end of Christ's life
and ministry and to date the narrative of the mission
in Galilee through a fourfold mention of Herod. (A. N.
Sherwin-White, Roman Society and Roman Law in the New
Testament [Oxford: Clarendon Press, 1963], pp.
166-67.)

[24]See also F. F. Bruce, The Apostolic Defense of
the Gospel: Christian Apologetic in the New Testament
(London: Inter-Varsity Fellowship, 1959); Barnabas
Lindars, New Testament Apologetic: The Doctrinal
Significance of the Old Testament Quotations
(Philadelphia: Westminster Press, 1961); Michael
Green, Evangelism in the Early Church (London: Hodder
& Stoughton, 1970), pp. 78-143; Avery Dulles, A History
of Christian Apologetics, TR (London: Hutchinson,
1971), pp. 1-21.

[25]Ulrich Wilckens, Die Missionsreden der
Apostelgeschichte, 2d ed., WMANT 5 (Neukirchen-Vluyn:
Neukirchner Verlag, 1963), p. 148; cf. 145-50, 68-69,
144.

[26]Allison A. Trites, The New Testament Concept of

Witness (Cambridge: Cambridge University Press, 1977), pp. 128-33.

[27]Ibid., p. 135.

[28]Ibid., pp. 128,138.

[29]Ibid., p. 138.

[30]For a good discussion of this difficult word see John E. Alsup, The Post-Resurrection Appearance Stories of the Gospel Tradition, CTM A5 (Stuttgart: Calwer Verlag, 1975), pp. 77-8.

[31]Daniel Fuller has argued that the purpose of Acts 20-28 is precisely to establish the fact of the resurrection on the basis that the origin of the Gentile mission cannot be explained without it. (Daniel P. Fuller, Easter Faith and History [London: Tyndale Press, 1968], pp. 208-41.) For a short critique of Fuller's hypothesis see C. F. Evans, Resurrection and the New Testament, SBT 2/12 (London: SCM Press, 1970), pp. 114-5.

[32]Trites, Witness, pp. 78-90.

[33]Wilckens sadly misunderstands the passage as showing that true faith is not that of those who came to Jesus through miracles but of those who recognized him as the sent one of God. (Ulrich Wilckens, Auferstehung, TT4 [Stuttgart and Berlin: Kreuz Verlag, 1970], p. 73.)

[34]An additional apologetic motif is sometimes discerned in John's three-fold repetition of Mary's fear that someone had taken the body of Jesus (20.2, 12, 15). (Hans Freiherr von Campenhausen, Der Ablauf der Osterereignisse und das leere Grab, 3d rev. ed., SHAW [Heidelberg: Carl Winter, 1966].) Presumably this is meant to counteract the rumor that the disciples had stolen the body. The reference to the gardener's having carried the body away is supposed to be designed to quell another Jewish allegation, noted later by Tertullian, that the gardener had transferred the body to another place. But it is difficult to understand how Mary's saying these things in any way counts against them. The gardener hypothesis especially would be unaffected by the fact that Mary mistook Jesus for the gardener. So it seems doubtful that this is deliberate apologetic; better is Grass's judgement that the Jewish polemic may be in fact a

reaction to Christian tradition such as John's. (Grass, Ostergeschehen, p. 59).

[35]Wolfhart Pannenberg, "Ist Jesus wirklich auferstanden?" in Ist Jesus wirklich auferstanden? Geistliche Woche fur Südwestdeutschland der Evang. Akademie Mannheim vom 16. bis 23. Februar 1964 (Karlsruhe: Evangelische Akademie Mannheim, 1964), p. 24.

[36]C. H. Dodd, "The Appearances of the Risen Christ: a study in form-criticism of the Gospels," More New Testament Studies (Manchester: University Press, 1968), p. 128. Cf. Berthold Klappert, "Einleitung," in Diskussion um Kreuz und Auferstehung, ed. idem (Wuppertal: Aussaat Verlag, 1971), p. 10.

[37]Wolfhart Pannenberg, Jesus--God and Man, trans. L. L. Wilkins and D. A. Priebe (London: SCM Press, 1968), p. 89.

[38]Hans Conzelmann, Der erste Brief an die Korinther, KEKNT 5 (Göttingen: Vandenhoeck & Ruprecht, 1969), pp. 294-5, 313. Conzelmann asserts that because the credo is accepted in Corinth, Paul does not want to prove that Christ is risen, but to draw out the meaning "from the dead" (Ibid., p. 295.) But Paul never does seem to draw out the meaning of this phrase, which is not even found in the formula; the "from the dead" does not seem to play any special role in Paul's argument. It is the fact that Christ is risen that makes the difference and provides the key to the argument (v. 20), for if he is risen, we shall rise also. The fact that Christ is risen is supported by the empirical evidence of vs. 5-7. If Paul does not wish to provide evidence for the resurrection, why does he continue to pile up witnesses in vs. 6,7 after the formula ends in v. 5? Conzelmann thinks that if the extra names were listed as evidence for the resurrection, this would contradict vs. 12ff. There Paul argues, "If . . . , then . . ." because the Corinthians accept the resurrection of Christ. This is, says Conzelmann, no formallogische Konsequenzmacherei. The point is to show that the resurrection is temporally removed from us, as is the Parousia, and that we live in the Zwischenzeit. (Ibid., pp. 304, 314.) But this alleged contradiction seems illusory. The "if . . . then" argumentation spells out the disastrous consequences of the Corinthian error; but the evidence of vs. 5-7 secures the fact of v. 20. Therefore, the disastrous results will not follow. The naming of extra witnesses

is important to secure v. 20; but it would not be
necessary to prove that we live in the
Zwischenzeit--Paul could have stopped with the 500
brethren.

[39]Johannes Weiss, Der erste Korintherbrief, 9th
ed., KEKNT 5 (Göttingen: Vandenhoeck & Ruprecht,
1910), p. 355.

[40]Chiefly three in number: (1) Christian faith
would be in vain and we would still be in our sins.
(2) The apostles would be liars.   (3) Christian loved
ones who have died would be no more (cf. I Thess
4.13-18).

[41]For an analysis, see Manfred Kwiran, The
Resurrection of the Dead, Theologische Dissertationen 8
(Basel: Friedrich Reinhardt Kommissionsverlag, 1972),
pp. 235-325;   Adriaan Geense, Auferstehung und
Offenbarung, FSOT 27 (Göttingen: Vandenhoeck &
Ruprecht, 1971), pp. 13-33.

[42]Karl Barth, The Resurrection of the Dead, trans.
H. J. Stenning (London: Hodder & Stoughton, 1933), p.
138.   "Verses 5-7 have nothing whatever to do with
supplying a historical proof . . ." (Ibid., p. 150.)

[43]Ibid., p. 140.

[44]Ibid., p. 147.

[45]Ibid., pp. 150-51.

[46]Ibid., pp. 146-7.   "Of what these eyes see it
can really be equally said that it was, is, and will
be, never and nowhere, as that it was, is, and will be,
always and everywhere possible." (Ibid., p. 143.)

[47]Rudolf Bultmann, Faith and Understanding I, 6th
ed., trans. L. P. Smith, ed. with an Introduction by
Robert W. Funk, Library of Philosophy and Theology
(London: SCM Press, 1969), pp. 83-4.

[48]Ibid., p. 83.

[49]Rudolf Bultmann, "Reply to the Theses of J.
Schniewind," in Kerygma and Myth, 1:   112.

[50]Rudolf Bultmann, Theology of the New Testament,
2 vols., trans. K. Grobel (London: SCM Press, 1952),
1:    295; cf. 1:   305.   Referring specifically to Acts

17.31 and I Cor. 15.3-8 he admits, "Yet it cannot be
denied that the resurrection of Jesus is often used in
the New Testament as a miraculous proof." (Rudolf
Bultmann, "New Testament and Mythology," in Kerygma and
Myth, 1: 39.) The post-Bultmannian James M. Robinson
disagrees: ". . . Paul explicitly recognized the
rejection of such signs as inherent in the existential
meaning of the kerygma (I Cor. 1.17-25)." (Robinson,
Quest, p. 51.) When Paul does discuss the signs
legitimizing himself in II Cor. 10-13 he begins by
listing the facts which demonstrate his
superiority--"but all under the admission 'I am
speaking as a fool' i.e. such a method is contrary to
the kerygma;" but then he shifts to speaking of his
humiliation, the only Christian way of speaking of
one's self. (Ibid.) But Paul in no way rejects
legitimizing signs for the kerygma, and in fact appeals
to them as its factual foundation. In I Cor.
1.17-2.13, Paul is not denying that his preaching has
either miraculous attestation or wisdom; rather he is
rejecting the ability of the natural man to reach God
by his own religious or intellectual efforts (cf. I
Cor. 3.18-21). To the eye of unregenerate man the
simple gospel of faith appears to be foolishness, and
the notion of a crucified Messiah is a stumbling block.
Nevertheless it is true, and Paul does not "dress it
up" in any way to make it appear more respectable. But
this does not mean Paul will not argue for its truth
(cf. Acts 17.16-34) nor adduce signs on its behalf (I
Cor. 15.3-8). Indeed in the very passage in question,
Paul says that his preaching was "in demonstration of
the Spirit and power" (I Cor. 2.4), which were the
apostolic miracles: "The signs of a true apostle were
performed among you in all patience, with signs and
wonders and mighty works" (II Cor. 12.12; notice he
says this after speaking of his humiliation)
Robinson's assertion that Paul's interjection "I am
speaking as a fool" means that the method of
legitimizing signs as contrary to the kerygma is
groundless; Paul simply recognizes that self-centered
boasting of one's own worth is contrary to the
"meekness and gentleness of Christ" (II Cor. 10.1-2)
and therefore to Christian character (II Cor. 10.12,
18; 12.11). But furnishing signs to legitimate the
truth of the content of preaching has nothing at all to
do with selfish boasting (as I Cor. 1.31-2.5 shows) and
is not at all opposed to humility. Look at Paul's
juxtaposition of the two: "Last of all, as to one
untimely born, he appeared also to me. For I am the
least of the apostles, unfit to be called an apostle,
because I persecuted the church of God" (I Cor.

15.8,9). Indeed, the legitimation of the kerygma by
Jesus's resurrection focuses the attention on God's
act: " . . . we testified of God that he raised Christ
. . ." (I Cor. 15.15b). Robinson is reading his
existentialist kerygma into and not out of Paul.

[51]R. H. Fuller, The Formation of the Resurrection
Narratives (London: SPCK, 19972), pp. 18-30.

[52]Paul's argument may be exhibited in a simple
syllogism (p = The dead are raised; q = Christ is
raised; r = Rueful consequences result):

   $\sim p \supset \sim q$
   $\sim q \supset r$
   q
   $\therefore p$
   $\therefore \sim r$

The last step does involve a logical fallacy. Paul
implicitly assumes $q \supset \sim r$. But Paul may be forgiven for
not making this explicit. It is logically equivalent
to saying: if the car has an engine, it will run; the
car does not have an engine; therefore it will not
run--technically fallacious, but hardly offensive in
ordinary discourse. Paul naturally assumes that if
Christ is raised, then we are not the most pitiable of
men because he has redeemed us.

[53]See also Archibald Robertson and Alfred Plummer,
First Epistle of Saint Paul to the Corinthians, 2d ed.,
ICC (Edinburgh: T & T Clark, 1967), p. 346. Contrast
Marxsen's understanding of the argument. (Marxsen,
Resurrection, pp. 108-09)

[54]Dodd, "Appearances," pp. 127-28.

[55]See the standard treatments by Hans Conzelmann,
"Zur Analyse der Bekenntnisformel I. Kor. 15:3-5,"
Evangelische Theologie 25 (1965): 1-11; Joachim
Jeremias, Die Abendmahlsworte Jesu, 4th ed. (Göttingen:
Vandenhoeck & Ruprecht, 1967), pp. 95-98. For a
wonderfully thorough discussion, see Karl Lehmann,
Auferweckt am dritten Tag naach der Schrift, QD 38
(Freiburg: Herder, 1968). Jeremias and Conzelmann
adduced five major arguments for a formula here: (1)
The words παραλαμβάνειν and παραδιδόναι correspond to
the technical rabbinical terms used for transmission of
tradition. (2) The subsequent verses contain many
non-Pauline expressions. (3) Similar formulas are
found elsewhere in the New Testament. (4) The contents
of these verses are appropriate to a formula. (5) What

is cited in these verses exceeds what needs to be proved, viz., the resurrection.

[56]See Ernst Bammel, "Herkunft and Funktion der Traditionselemente in I. Cor. 15, 1-11," Theologische Zeitschrift 11 (1955): 401-19 and the therein cited literature.

[57]According to Dodd, the earliest form of the resurrection appearances was that of a list, whose purpose "seems to have been to provide interested inquirers with a guaranteed statement of the sources of evidence upon which the affirmations of the kerygma were founded." (Dodd, "Appearances," p. 131.) Dodd should say the earliest we know of, since he holds that the gospel pericopae are not expansions from such a list and could therefore represent a parallel tradition even so old.

Fuller had disputed that the kerygma entailed the naming of witnesses. (Fuller, Formation, pp. 12-14.) Drawing attention to the curious repetition of ὅτι before each of the four main statements in I Cor 15.3-7, he, in dependence on Wilckens (Ulrich Wilckens, "Der Ursprung der Überlieferung der Erscheinungen des Auferstandenen," in Dogma und Denkstrukturen, ed. W. Joest und W. Pannenberg [Göttingen: Vandenhoeck & Ruprecht, 1963], pp. 56-95; Wilckens, Missionsreden, pp. 74-80.), believes that ὅτι (that) serves the function of modern quotation marks. Usually ὅτι is regarded simply as typical of credal formulas, but in the only example of this (I Thess 4.13-17) the three occurrences of ὅτι combine quite separate elements (a credal formula in 4.13, a dominical logion in 4.15, and an apocalyptic elaboration in 4.16) and therefore are used as quotation marks to combine different traditions. From this it follows that in I Cor 15 we also have four different traditions combined by ὅτι. The first three statements summarize basic incidents in the act of salvation, whereas the fourth validates the third. The Semitized Greek suggests Damascus as the origin of the first three; the mention of Cephas and James suggests that Paul received the fourth while visiting Jerusalem. Thus the first three formulas are kerygmatic and catechetical, while the fourth consists of information gathered by Paul. The upshot of this is that the appearances formed no part of the primitive kerygma or catechesis. The earliest church did not prove the reality of the resurrection from appearances; it simply affirmed it kerygmatically (I Thess 1.9). Paul began the use of witnesses as evidence. Now a deductive chain of reasoning is only as strong as its weakest link, and Fuller's argument seems strained in many points: (1) Wilckens has shown only the bare possibility, by no means the necessity, of taking ὅτι as serving the function of quotation marks in I Thess 4.13-17. As Karl Lehmann has observed, ὅτι serves so many different functions that it is extremely questionable whether one can infer very much from its multiple occurrence. (Lehmann, Auferweckt, pp. 73-77.) He suggests that it would be better to leave the question open than to embrace interpretations which are very difficult to prove, but which carry with them decisive consequences. Certainly Wilckens and Fuller are guilty in this sense of trying to rest a pyramid on its point. (2) Neither Wilckens nor Fuller has justified the subsequent application, much less the probability, of the function of ὅτι in question to I Cor 15.3-8. If the combination of quite separate elements is the criterion for discerning this function of ὅτι , then I Cor 15.3-8 may well be intended, as Werner Kramer and Franz Mussner have suggested, simply to emphasize the equal importance of each successive event. (Werner Kramer, Christos, Kyrios, Gottessohn, ATANT 44 [Stuttgart and Zürich: Zwingli Verlag, 1963], p. 15; Franz Mussner, Die Auferstehung Jesu, BH 7 [München: Kösel Verlag, 1969], pp. 60); cf. Joseph Schmitt, "Le 'milieu' littéraire de la 'tradition' citée dans I Cor, XV, 3b-5, "in Resurrexit, ed Edouard Dhanis [Rome: Liberia Editrice Vaticana, 1974], p. 178.) Embarrassing for Fuller is that in his third edition of Missionsreden, Wilckens declared himself convinced that this interpretation is correct! (Ulrich Wilckens, Die Missionsreden der Apostelgeschichte, 3d ed., WMANT 5 [Neukirchen-Vluyn: Neukirchner Verlag, 1974], p. 228.) (3) The first three formulas cannot be placed over against the fourth as salvific, for in no sense can the burial of Christ be called a basic incident in the event of salvation (Cf. Rom 4.24-25). Unlike the crucifixion and resurrection, it has no redemptive significance, certainly no more than the appearances so as to exclude the latter. (4) The names James and Cephas in no way prove the fourth statement was not also used in Damascus. They only show that the formula could be no later than Paul's Jerusalem visit, since then he would have heard from Cephas and James themselves what took place. (See the remarks of Grass, Ostergeschehen, p. 95.) It is naive to think that the content of the first three formulas could be delivered to the believers in Damascus without mentioninng the names of Jesus's disciples or that, given the free flow of information among the primitive Christian churches

(Acts 9.13; Gal 1.22-23), these two leaders of the Jerusalem church could remain unknown in Damascus. (5) It is highly unlikely that the formulas ever existed separately, for no conceivable function could be served by the bald statement "He was buried" in isolation from the other statements. While one could imagine the first and third, and even the fourth, formula existing alone, Fuller's schema is shipwrecked on what Barth called the "unambiguous banal historical fact", "that he was buried." (Barth, Resurrection, p. 142.) It is much more plausible that the early church formulated a tradition that related in smooth succession the principal events of Jesus's death and resurrection, just as Paul delivers it, with all the events interconnected and complementary. (6) The remainder of the New Testament evidence indicates that the primitive church did not simply preach the resurrection without adducing the testimony of witnesses. (See note 89.) I Thess 1.9 does contain kerygmatic traces (as is evident from comparing it with Acts 14.15-17; 17.22-31; this is developed by Wilckens, Missionsreden, pp. 86-88; Wilckens, "Ursprung," pp. 58-59.), but does not pretend to be a complete kerygmatic summary, since then the death of Christ would also have to be excluded from the kerygma. Hence, one cannot conclude that Paul's preaching failed to mention the witnesses to the resurrection. It is important to remember that what Paul says in I Cor 15.3-8 is a reminder of what he preached to the Corinthians on his missionary tour which took him through Thessalonica, Athens, and Corinth. There is no reason to doubt his word that the gospel that he, as well as the other apostles, preached in all these cities included the fact that "he appeared to Cephas, then to the twelve . . ."

Wilckens himself pursued a somewhat different line of reasoning than Fuller. (Wilckens, Missionsreden, pp. 73-81; Wilckens, "Ursprung," pp. 70-81; Wilckens, Auferstehung, pp. 26, 29.) As we have seen, he took the fourfold ὅτι as the indication for separate traditions. But he further argues that the appearance formula itself is not a unity, but a fusion of principally two legitimation formulas sanctioning the authority of the leaders of the church. The appearance to the 500 did not belong to the original formula because it alone contains the words ἐπάνω and ἐφάπαξ is less exact in content, and cannot be confirmed through comparison with other material. That leaves two parallel sets of appearances, each containing an appearance to an individual and then to a group. Because this obvious pattern is not likely to be chronological, we have here two independent traditions

which probably arose consecutively as a historical
description of the leadership of the Jerusalem church.
Paul has brought these originally independent formulas
together.   The upshot of this is that the naming of
witnesses was not, therefore, part of the early
kerygma: "Thus the appearances were handed down, not
really as witnesses to the resurrection, but much more
as legitimations of the men who, because of their
divine commission, had standing authority in the
church." (Wilckens, Auferstehung, p. 147.) Wilckens
analyzes I Cor 15.3-7 into six separate levels of (I)
kerygmatic tradition and (II) catechetical tradition:

    Ia.   I Cor 15.3   formula on Christ's
                          substitutionary death for
                          our sins plus proof-text
     b.   15.4a   mention of the burial
     c.   15.4b   missionary preaching formula
                          constituting the central
                          point
    IId.   15.5   oldest legitimation formula
                          for Peter as the leader
     e.   15.6   Paul's own summary of the
                          legend of the founding of
                          the first church
     f.   15.7   legitimation formula from a
                          somewhat later time when
                          James was the leader

But Wilckens's argument fares no better than Fuller's.
(1) For it, too, stands on the pebble of the fourfold,
and once this is removed the whole mass topples. With
Wilckens's afore-mentioned repudiation of his ealier
interpretation, points a-d in the analysis must all
belong to the same formula, so that at least the
appearances to Peter and the Twelve belonged to the
kerygmatic tradition. The truth seems to be that in
this context, the appearances were regarded primarily
as authentications of the resurrection and only
secondarily as legitimations of the men who saw them.
(2) Wilckens may well be correct that the 500 brethren
did not belong to the original formula, but his
arguments for this are quite contrived: (a) the
mention of "more than" and "at one time" provides no
clue whatsoever of the appearance's not belonging to
the formula, especially when one considers that the
appearance to the apostles includes   πᾶσιν ; (b) to
say this appearance is less exact than the others,
especially the vaguely characterized group mentioned
last, is just silly; (c) neither can the appearance to
James or all the apostles be definitely confirmed
through comparison. (3) Paul goes to great lengths to
spell out the chronological sequence of appearances.

The appearances follow the chronological pattern of the death, burial, and resurrection of Christ and are guided by the pattern εἶτα . . . ἔπειτα . . . ἔπειτα . . . εἶτα and conclude with ἔσχατον δε πάντων. Clear-ly Paul holds these appearances to be strictly chronological. (Von Campenhausen, Ablauf, p. 11.) Now when we keep firmly in mind the astounding fact, at which we cease to wonder because of its familiarity, that we have here the testimony of a man who actually talked with Jesus's brother and one of his principal disciples, both of whom claimed to have personally seen Jesus risen again from the dead, during a two-week period in Jerusalem about six years after the event, then it must become clear that Paul makes no mistake here with regard to the succession of events. The order is chronological, and no theoretical discernment of patterns can overthrow this conclusion. But this drastically undermines the legitimation theory: (a) For the only rationale for such a theory is the perception of the individual/group pattern in the appearances. But the mention of James and the apostles could stem, like the 500 brethren, from single bits of information which Paul then arranged chronologically. Any pattern could be either simply fortuitous or the result of intentionally leaving out other single bits of information, such as the appearance to the women. (b) But what is absolutely devastating for Wilckens's theory is that Paul says, last of all to me. For this means that the appearances to James and the apostles occurred before Paul's conversion, that is before James became prominent (cf. Acts 8.14; 12.17b; Gal 1.19; 2.1, 9) and before any later body not comprised principally of the first apostles could arise and assume their name. (4) The age of the formula militates against its being a historical description of the leadership of the Jerusalem church. When Paul visited Jerusalem and spoke with Cephas, James was there. Fourteen years later he had become with Peter and John one of three pillars of the church (Gal 2.1, 9). Even then he does not appear to be the sole leader of the church. But this takes us practically right up to the time of writing of I Cor. Since Paul's formula is very old, the notion of a legitimation formula for James is difficult since the formula threatens to ante-date James's ascension to power. Indeed, if Grass is correct that the formula can be no later than Paul's first visit, then a historical description of the church's leadership is simply excluded. To this may be added that if the formula is a late legitimation formula, it becomes impossible to identify any group associated with James that could be called "all the

apostles." That this is a later body of missionaries
looking to James for authority is not only purely
speculative, but against it counts the consideration
that the church would not be likely to lend much
credibility to a supposed appearance so many years
distant from the originals. (5) It needs to be asked
whether the notion of a legitimation formula has
anything at all to do with historical reality, but
rather is a modern fiction. In the early church not
everyone who saw a resurrection appearance was invested
with authority (the 500 brethren) and not everyone who
was called an apostle had seen an appearance
(Andronicus and Junias [Rom 16.7], Barnabas [I Cor 9.5,
6]). John and Luke are strikingly in accord in stating
that a disciple belonged to the Twelve, not so much
because he had seen the risen Jesus, but because he had
been with Jesus from the beginning (Jn 15.27; Acts
1.21, 22). Paul did not explicitly ground his
apostleship in the fact that Jesus had appeared to him,
but rather that Jesus had commissioned him through this
appearance (Rom 1.1-5; 15.15, 16; I Cor 1.1; 3.10; 9.1,
2, 16, 17; 15.8-11; II Cor 1.1; 2.17; 5.18; Gal 1.1;
2.15-16; Col 1.1, 23-25; I Thess 2.4-6; cf. Eph 3.7-8).
For Paul, apostleship was a spiritual gift (I Cor
12.28; cf. Eph 4.11), which was confirmed by signs and
wonders (Rom 15.19; II Cor 12.12). In justifying his
apostleship he usually appeals to his labors and
sufferings, not to the fact that he had seen an
appearance of Christ (I Cor 15.8-10; II Cor
11.1-12.13). All this makes it very suspect whether
so-called legitimation formulas based on who had seen
an appearance of Christ ever existed. The concept of
legitimation and authority in the early church was much
more complex than that.

58The problem of the accuracy of Luke's
reconstruction of the kerygma is still very hotly
debated. (For histories of the problem consult A. J.
Matill, Jr., "Luke as a Historian in Criticism since
1840" [Ph.D. Dissertation, Vanderbilt University,
1959]; W. Ward Gasque, A History of the Criticism of
the Acts of the Apostles, Beiträge zur Geschichte der
biblischen Exegese 17 [Tübingen: Mohr 1975].) Martin
Kahler was one of the first researchers who sought to
demonstrate that the words of Peter's speeches were not
Lukan, but went back to a Palestianian origin. (Martin
Kähler, "Die Reden des Petrus in der
Apostelgeschichte," Theologische Studien und Kritiken
46 [1873], pp. 492-536.) C. C. Torrey championed the
thesis that the first fifteen chapters of Acts are so
filled with Aramaisms that it is probable that Luke has

simply translated an early document into Greek and then
added the final chapters himself. (C. C. Torrey,
Composition and Date of Acts, Harvard Theological
Studies 1 [Cambridge, Mass.: Harvard University Press,
1916].) J. de Zwaan critically reviewed Torrey's
thesis and, although finding it exaggerated, did
conclude that Torrey had a strong case for Acts 1-5.16
and 9.31-11.18. (J. de Zwaan, "The Use of the Greek
Language in Acts," in The Beginnings of Christianity,
Part I: The Acts of the Apostles, ed. F. J. Foakes
Jackson & Kirsopp Lake [London: Macmillan & Co.,
1922], II: 44-65.) C. H. Dodd concluded that the
Petrine speeches are based on material from the
Aramaic-speaking church at Jerusalem. He observes that
in Acts 10 the Greek is "notoriously rough and
ungrammatical," "scarcely translatable," but when
translated back into Aramaic becomes "grammatical and
perspicuous;" therefore the speech to Cornelius is
probably a translation of an Aramaic original and
represents the "form of the kerygma used by the
primitive church in its earliest approaches to a wider
public." (C. H. Dodd, The Apostolic Preaching and its
Developments, 3d ed. [London: Hodder & Stoughton,
1967], p. 26.) Meanwhile Martin Dibelius had drawn
attention to the primitive Christology of the speeches
and to their harmony with Paul's summary of the kerygma
as evidence of their great age. He argued that the
earliest kerygma included an account of Jesus's life,
sufferings, and resurrection, mostly under the emphasis
of the disciples' role as witnesses (meist unter
Betonung der Zeugenschaft der Jünger). He believed not
only the outline, but even core sentences of the
kerygma, such as in I Cor 15, were at Luke's disposal.
(M. Dibelius, Die Formgeschichte des Evangeliums, 3d
ed. [Tübingen: Mohr, 1959], pp. 12-18; M. Dibelius,
Aufsätze zur Apostelgeschichte, ed. H. Greeven, FRLANT
60 [Göttingen: Vandenhoeck & Ruprecht, 1953], p. 142.)
The arguments of Dodd and Dibelius still constitute the
principal case for the historical authenticity of the
speeches of Acts: (1) the abundant Semitisms, (2) the
primitive Christology, and (3) the harmony with the
Pauline kerygma. Each of these questions is contested:
(1) Critics of the Aramaic source theory contend that
the Semitisms of Acts are really Seputagintisms, i.e.,
expressions borrowed by Luke from the LXX to give the
speeches an intentionally authentic coloring. (H. F.
D. Sparks, "The Semitisms in Acts," Journal of
Theological Studies, NS 1 [1950]: 16-28; Ernst
Haenchen, "Schriftzitate und Textüberlieferung in der
Apostelgeschichte," Zeitschrift für Theologie und
Kirche 51 [11954]: 153-67; Ernst Haenchen, The Acts of

the Apostles, 14th ed.; trans. B. Noble, G. Shinn, and
R. Mc L. Wilson [Oxford: Basil Blackwell, 1971], pp.
73-77.) The question cannot be pronounced settled, for
scholars remain divided on the problem: Grasser makes
the interesting observation that the issue of Aramaisms
in Acts is handled in Anglo-Saxon research with as
great an optimism as it is in German research with
scepticism!   (Erich Grässer, "Acta-Forschung seit
1960," Theologische Rundschau 41 [1976]: 181.) For the
most outstanding recent work on the problem, consult
Max Wilcox, The Semitisms of Acts (Oxford: Clarendon
Press, 1965).   (2) Wilckens has argued vigorously that
the so-called primitive Christology of the speeches is
really Luke's own, although Luke may occasionally use a
traditional title to his own purposes.   (Wilckens,
Missionsreden, 3d ed., pp. 156-78, 237-40; cf. C. F.
Evans, "The Kerygma," Journal of Theological Studies,
NS 7 [1956]:   25-41.)   The majority of scholars,
however, do see in the speeches evidence of an early
christological tradition.   (For a critique of Wilckens
and Evans, see John A. T. Robinson, "The Most Primitive
Christology of All?" Journal of Theological Studies,
NS 7 [1956]:   177-89; Jacques Dupont, "Les discours
missionaires des Actes des Apôtres d'après un ouvrage
récent," Revue biblique 69 [1962]:   37-60.) This would
tend to support the antiquity of the tradition in the
speeches.   (3) Wilckens has also attempted to sharply
differentiate the Pauline kerygma from that of Acts.
(Wilckens, Missionsreden, pp. 72-81; see note 59.)   So
influential has Wilckens's argument been that Haenchen
took it for granted that "Ulrich Wilckens . . . has
proved against Dibelius and Dodd that Peter's speeches
in the first part of Acts do not contain any old
pattern of Jewish-Christian missionary preaching."
(Haenchen, Acts, pp. 129-30.) But in the third edition
of Missionsreden Wilckens did an about face, and took
back all his objections to Dibelius's thesis.
(Wilckens, Missionsreden, p. 195; see note 59.) Nor is
he alone in this; according to Grasser, the more recent
research on the speeches of Acts has undisputedly come
to the conclusion that Luke's bond with tradition,
including in the resurrection formulas, is stronger
than has been allowed. (Erich Grässer, "Acta-Forschung
seit 1960," Theologische Rundschau 42 [1977]:   50.)
Stuhlmacher, for example, has argued that Acts 10 is
not simply Luke's own gospel, but follows a pattern of
presentation (Darbietungsschema) that grows out of the
same tradition as I Cor 15.   (Peter Stuhlmacher, Das
paulinische Evangelium I: Vorgeschichte,   FRLANT 95
[Göttingen: Vandenhoeck & Ruprecht, 1968], pp.
197-98.) Bovon also researches the speech to Cornelius

and finds a Christian kerygmatic tradition for a Jewish
audience (François Bovon, "Tradition et rédaction en
Acts 10.1-11.18," Theologische Zeitschrift 26 [1970]:
42.), as does Burchard (Christoph Burchard, Der
dreizehnte Zeuge, FRLANT 103 [Göttingen: Vandenhoeck &
Ruprecht, 1970], p. 139.). As a result of these and
other studies, it seems fair to say that the weight of
the evidence supports the Dodd/Dibelius thesis that
Luke has accurately reproduced the substance of
primitive Christian preaching.

[59]It is extremely instructive to survey the
development of Wilckens's assessment of this question.
He first attempted to drive a wedge between the kerygma
of I Cor 15 and that of Acts: (1) Paul's kerygma
stresses that Christ died "for our sins," while Acts
sees Jesus's death merely as the Jews' evil mishandling
of Jesus; (2) Paul has "Christ," not "Jesus" as the
subject of the kerygma; (3) Paul makes no mention of
the sufferings of Christ; (4) Paul recounts no life of
Jesus in the kerygma; (5) What is "according to the
scriptures" is different: for Acts it is the fact, but
for Paul it is the meaning of the fact; (6) Paul
mentions "on the third day," a phrase found only in
Acts 10, probably under the influence of a formula such
as Paul's; and (7) Luke knows only the formula of the
appearance to Peter (Lk 24.34) in isolation from the
others. Thus, it cannot be said that I Cor 15 and Acts
mutually confirm one another as to the content of the
early preaching. In fact, in I Thess 1 and Heb 6 we
find a totally different kerygma; the only common
element is the resurrection, but even it has a
different meaning: in I Thess it is the ground for
Jesus's coming again as Savior. This other kerygma is
duplicated in Acts 14 and 17 and consists in (1) a call
to the true God from lesser gods, (2) God's overlooking
the past of ignorance, and (3) the resurrection as the
basis for Jesus's coming as Judge. If this represents
the true kerygmatic tradition, then it at once raises
the question whether the type of preaching prior to
Acts 14 is not then simply Luke's own invention.
Wilckens answers in the affirmative. He contends, in
dependence on Conzelmann's conception of Luke's
program, that Luke's theological purpose is to ground
the church age in the time of Jesus, and he does this
through the instrumentality of eyewitnesses. Thus, the
schema of the Jewish-Christian preaching is Lukan.
(Wilckens, Missionsreden, pp. 72-100.)

        "The theory of the twelve apostles as 'witnesses'
    directly commissioned by the Risen One in virtue

of extensive eyewitness experience is conceived by
Luke himself; the generalizing mention of the
appearances, through which the witnesses are
legitimized in salvation history, is also Lukan.
. . .The apostolic speeches of the Acts are in an
outstanding way summaries of his theological
conception; they cannot be valued as witnesses of
old or especially the oldest primitive Christian
theology, but of Lukan theology of the expiring
first century." (Ibid., pp. 150, 186.)

Now Wilckens's premises in this series of deductions
seem to be very fragile indeed.   (1) That his
differences between the kerygma of I Cor 15 and that of
Acts are often exaggerated and artificial is painfully
obvious.   For example, difference (2) is simply
trivial, and (3), (4) cannot be rigidly assumed because
of the summary character of the formula cited by Paul.
Difference (5) has more substance; but it is doubtful
that Paul's second reference to "according to the
scriptures" explicates the meaning and not the event of
the resurrection (contrast Rom 4.25), and it is not
clear that the first reference does not also include
the event of the death as well as its meaning.
Meanwhile, in Acts it is sometimes the meaning of an
event that is clarified by the scriptures.   (Acts
2.34-36;   10.43;   13.33).   Difference (6) is
question-begging, since both I Cor 15 and Acts 10 could
reflect an element of the primitive kerygma.
Difference (7) only shows that Luke did not have a
story to go with the appearance to Peter and,
therefore, quotes only the kerygmatic exclamation. But
he did have a story about the appearance to the Twelve
and so is independent of the kerygma at this point.
The order of events and appearances in Luke and I Cor
15 are in complete harmony.   This leaves difference
(1), which is really the major discrepancy between I
Cor 15 and Acts.   Two things may be said here: (a)
There can be no doubt that the kerygma did include
Christ's dying "for our sins," for (i) the very age of
the formula shows that this doctrine was held in the
early church, (ii) this is a theme that is widespread
in the New Testament and not of Pauline origin (Rom
3.25; 5.9; Eph 1.7; Col 1.20; Heb 9.12; 10.19; I Pet
1.19; Rev 1.5; 5.9), and (iii) otherwise we should have
no choice but to say that Paul was quite simply lying
when he asserts that this gospel is preached by all the
apostles and was received by him and was approved by
the Jerusalem apostles (Gal 2.2, 9; this included the
substitutionary death of Christ as the basis of
breaking down the wall of partition between Jew and

Gentile). (b) Luke does give hints of the death of
Christ "for our sins," most obviously in the account of
the Lord's Supper and in Acts 20.28 (interestingly a
Pauline speech), which even Haenchen admits echoes the
doctrine of vicarious atonement. (Haenchen, Acts, p.
92.) The Christological title "Servant" may reflect Is
53, from which this doctrine could be inferred (cf.
Acts 8.32-35). Indeed, the Acts speeches inevitably
include an offer of forgiveness of sins through Jesus
(Acts 2.38; 2.38; 3.19; 4.12; 5.31; 10.43; 13.38-39),
so that this doctrine may lie just beneath the surface.
The difference between the kerygma of Acts and I Cor 15
may therefore be simply one of emphasis; it alone
cannot overturn the conclusion that Luke and Paul are
remarkably compatible in their representation of the
early kerygma. (2) The "totally different" kerygmatic
tradition inferred from I Thess 1 and Heb 6 is a
different cast of the same kerygma. Heb 6 is so
sketchy that no kerygmatic inference at all is
warranted; I Thess 1 and Acts 14 and 17 appear to
represent a form of the kerygma appropriate to a
Gentile pagan audience. It is noteworthy that the
resurrection remains God's decisive act of vindication
of Jesus, and even in the Jewish speeches, the
magisterial and apocalyptical elements are clearly
present (Acts 3.20-21; 10.42). There is no
justification in taking the Jewish preaching as a Lukan
invention and the Gentile preaching as the genuine
kerygmatic tradition. Rather these represent different
methods of approach, suited to the audience to be
addressed. (Thus there is absolutely no reason to
believe that Paul could not have given a speech like
that of Acts 13 as well as that of Acts 17. Indeed,
the correlation between the former speech and I Cor 15
is astounding: every element of the formula is
explicitly mentioned except the "for our sins," and
this seems implicit in Acts 13.38. That Paul was also
familiar with the kerygmatic approach of the Jews'
mishandling of Jesus is evident from I Thess 2.14-15.)
(3) Because Wilckens's interpretation of Luke's
emphasis on eyewitnesses is dependent upon Conzelmann's
construction of Luke's understanding of history,
insofar as Conzelmann's construction succumbs to
criticism, Wilcken's interpretation is undermined.
Even Haenchen, who accepts Conzelmann's "Mitte der
Zeit" construction, rebukes Wilckens for reading too
much theory of history into Luke's work; a mighty arch
of God's saving plan stretches from Abraham to the
Parousia--" . . . there is no deep caesura between the
time of Jesus and that which follows." (Haenchen,
Acts, p. 132.) (4) The decisive consideration against

Wilckens's interpretation is that the emphasis on witnesses is not at all exclusive Lukan property. That the Twelve apostles are not a Lukan construction erected to serve as official witnesses is secured by Rev 21.14, as well as Mk 6.7, 30; Mt 10.1, 2, 5, 19 (cf. Haenchen, Acts, pp. 124-25). We have already seen Paul's use of confirmatory witnesses in preaching the resurrection. We have also seen that John has an emphasis on witnesses nearly as great as Luke's (an emphasis perhaps overlooked by Wilckens because of his unfortunate misunderstanding of the Thomas pericope). Gerald O'Collins underscores this point well:

> "Luke and John . . . clearly interpret the post-Easter encounters of these witnesses as different in principle from experiences of the risen Lord which later Christians might enjoy. Luke represents Christ as ascending into heaven . . . The events of the forty days (in which the risen Lord met, spoke and ate with that privileged group) differed fundamentally from all later encounters. John also carefully discriminates other Christians from those disciples to whom the risen Christ appeared. Thomas came to belief when he saw the Lord. His road to faith differed from that of later Christians . . . The official witnesses to the resurrection did not enjoy some privileged form of faith. But they played a unique role in testifying to the 'signs,' so that others might 'believe that Jesus is the Christ, the Son of God' (John 20.29-31). . . . John invites those 'who have not seen' to believe in reliance on eye-witness testimony." (Gerald O'Collins, The Easter Jesus [London: Darton, Longmann & Todd, 1973], p. 80.)

This invitation is especially clear in I John, which in the Muratorian canon follows directly upon John as a postscript (while II and III John appear much later): "That . . . which we have seen with our eyes, which we have looked upon and touched with our hands, . . . that which we have seen and heard we proclaim also to you . . ." (I Jn 1.1, 3). There are many remarkable parallels between John and Luke on the problem of the resurrection, and this mutual emphasis on eyewitness testimony as evidence is one of the most noteworthy. We also find the same concern in II Pet 1.16: "For we did not follow cleverly devised myths when we made known to you the power and coming of our Lord Jesus Christ, but we were eyewitnesses of his majesty." Thus it is quite clear that Luke did not--out of any motive,

theological or otherwise--invent the theory of the
disciples as witnesses to the resurrection. Rather
what Paul and Luke affirm seems to be the truth: that
the original apostolic preaching really did include as
an important note the appeal to eyewitness testimony as
historical evidence for the resurrection.

Most interesting is that in his third edition of
Missionsreden Wilckens completely surrenders his case.
Under the influence of O. H. Steck's investigation of
Old Testament Jewish preaching (O. H. Steck, Israel und
das gewaltsame Geschick der Propheten, WMANT 23
[Neukirchen-Vluyn: Neukirchner Verlag, 1967].),
Wilckens concedes that the kerygmatic outline of the
Acts speeches is not Lukan, but belongs to
Jewish-Christian tradition. (Wilckens, Missionsreden,
p. 3.) The speeches directed to the Gentiles are
created from a broad hellenistic-Jewish tradition of
apologetic-missionary activity to pagans that goes back
to the oldest time of hellenistic missionary work,
since Paul refers to it. (Ibid., pp. 190-93.) The
speeches to the Jews, which Wilckens formerly ascribed
to the creative hand of Luke, are now acknowledged to
stem from the early traditions underlying I Cor 15.
(Ibid., pp. 193-200.) The seven differences between
the kerygma of Acts and I Cor 15 now, says Wilckens,
really resolve into only one: Paul sees saving
significance in Christ's death, while Luke regards it
as the last abuse of the Jew's maltreatment of Jesus.
But this tension may be explained as a result of the
Sitz im leben: for Paul the catechetical viewpoint of
the salvific meaning of Jesus's death; for Luke the
tradition, also found in the gospels, of the course of
events of the passion and resurrection, showing the
contrast between the Jews' mistreatment and God's
vindication of Jesus. The firm conclusion is that I
Cor 15 and the kerygma of Acts presuppose a similar
outline, which stems out of the passion and Easter
reports, which is then filled out according to the
respective Sitz im Leben. But more than that: in
dependence on Steck, Wilckens proceeds to argue that
Luke's employment of this material in the context of
the Acts speeches is not his own, but reproduces the
Christianized form of Jewish preaching. (Ibid., pp.
200-08.) "Luke did not himself construct the pattern
of the apostolic preaching addressed to the Jews as
such, but took it over from the tradition of Jewish,
Deuteronomic repentance preaching as mediated by the
Christians." (Ibid., p. 205.) This being the case,
there seems to be no grounds left for denying that the
mention of confirmatory witnesses to the resurrection
was an integral part of the earliest Christian

preaching.   If Paul   and   Luke   represent   twin
developments of the same tradition, and despite their
differences in emphasis concerning the meaning of the
events, they both testify that the apostolic preaching
climaxed   in   the   proclamation   of   the   resurrection
confirmed by eyewitnesses, then we have no reason to
doubt the authenticity of this feature of the primitive
kerygma.

[60]Mussner, Auferstehung, p. 58.

[61]Dulles, History, p. 19.

[62]That is not to say the resurrection was not
mentioned.   Ignatius wrote of Jesus,

> "Who was truly born, both ate and drank, was truly
> persecuted   under   Pontius   Pilate,   was   truly
> crucified and died in the sight of those in heaven
> and on earth and under the earth; who also was
> truly raised from the dead, when his Father raised
> him up, as in the same manner his Father shall
> raise up in Christ Jesus us who believe in him,
> without whom we have no true life."   (Ignatius
> Adversus Trallians 9.1-2.)   See also Epistle of
> Barnabas 15; I Clement 24; Ignatius Adversus
> Magnesians II; Ignatius Adversus Smyrneans 2-3;
> Polycarp para. 2, 12; Aristides Apology (Greek)
> 15; Justin Martyr Apology 1.21.   These are not,
> however arguments for the resurrection.

[63]Dulles, History, pp. 22-3.

[64]Justin First Apology 30.

[65]Ibid., 31; 50.   Contrary to the impression given
by Brown, the adjunct use of prophecy was not a sort of
retreat associated first with Origen, but prophecy was
the predominant proof over miracles from the first
Apologists.   (Colin Brown, Miracles and the Critical
Mind [Grand Rapids, Mich.:   Wm. B. Eardmans, 1984], pp.
4-6.)

[66]Justin First Apology 2; 20; 53; 54; 57; 58.

[67]Justin Dialog with Trypho the Jew 108.   Eusebius
also mentions such a report in his commentary on Isaiah
18.1.

[68]Tertullian Apologeticus 21.   Eusebius concurs
concerning this (Eusebius History 2.2.)

[69] Tertullian De spectaculis 30.

[70] Tertullian De resurrectione carnis 3.

[71] Ibid. 1.

[72] Ibid. 4.

"For this reason heretics immediately begin operations and lay their foundations and afterwards erect their scaffolding with those materials by which they know it is easy for them to entice men's minds, the popularity of the ideas making things favourable for them. Is there anything a heretic says, which a gentile has not already said, and said more frequently? Is there not, forthwith and throughout, reviling of the flesh, attacks upon its origin, its material, its fate, its whole destiny, as being from its first beginning foul from the excrement of the earth, more foul thereafter because of the slime of its own seed, paltry, unstable, reproachable, troublesome, burdensome, and (following on the whole indictment of its baseness) fated to fall back into the earth from whence it came and to be described as a corpse, and destined to perish from that description too into no description at all from thenceforth, into a death of any and every designation? 'Do you then, as a philosopher, wish to persuade us that this flesh, when it has been ravished from your sight and touch and remembrance--that it is sometime to recover itself to wholeness out of corruption, to concreteness out of vacuity, to fullness out of emptiness, in short to something out of nothingness, and that even the funeral pyre or the sea or the bellies of wild beasts or the crops of birds or the intestines of fishes or the peculiar gluttony of time itself will give it back again? And is this same flesh which has disappeared to be an object of hope simply that the lame and the one-eyed and the blind and the leprous and the palsied may revert, so as to wish they had not returned, to what they were before? . . . In that case the hope of the recovery of the flesh will amount to just this, the desire to escape from it a second time.' Now I have expressed this somewhat more decently, out of respect for my pen: but how much licence is given even to foulspeaking, you may find out for yourselves in these people's discussions, whether they be gentiles or heretics." (Tertullian, Tertullians's Treatise on the Resurrection, trans. with an Introduction and Commentary by Ernest Evans [London: SPCK, 1960].)

[73] Justin Martyr First Apology 8.

[74] Ibid. 19.

[75] Justin Dialogue with Trypho 69.

[76] Ibid. 80.

[77] Athenagoras Supplicatio 36.

[78] Theophilus Ad Autolycum 1.8. "He formed you out
of a small moist matter and a tiny drop, which itself
previously did not exist. It was God who brought you
into this life . . . Then do you not believe that the
God who made you can later make you over again?"
(Theophilus of Antioch, Ad Autolycum, trans. R. M.
Grant [Oxford: Clarendon Press, 1970].)

[79] Ibid. 1.7.

[80] Ibid. 1.13.

[81] Ibid. 1.14.

[82] Irenaeus Adversus haereses 5.7.1.

[83] Ibid. 5.1-2; 5.14.1.

[84] Ibid. 5.6.1; 5.7.1; 5.9.1-4; 5.10.2.

[85] Ibid. 5.3.2.
"But that He is powerful in all these respects, we
ought to perceive from our origin, inasmuch as God,
taking dust from the earth, formed man. And surely it
is much more difficult and incredible, from
non-existent bones, and nerves, and veins, and the rest
of man's organization, to bring it about that all else
should be, and to make man an animated and rational
creature, than to reintegrate again that which had been
created and then afterwards decomposed into earth (for
the reasons already mentioned), having thus passed into
those [elements] from which man, who had no previous
existence, was formed." (Irenaeus Against Heresies, 2
vols., trans. Alexander Roberts and W. H. Rambaut,
Ante-Nicene Christian Library [Edinburgh: T & T Clark,
1869].)

[86] Ibid. 5.4.

[87] Ibid. 6.1.

"Now the soul and the spirit are certainly a part
of the man, but certainly not the man; for the

perfect man consists in the commingling and the
union of the soul receiving the spirit of the
Father, and the admixture of that fleshly nature
which was moulded after the image of God."

[88]Tertullian Apologeticus 48.

[89]Tertullian De resurrectione carnis 3.

[90]Ibid. 5-10.

[91]Ibid. 11-13.

[92]Cf. Apologeticus 48, where Tertullian argues
that since God brought one into existence from nothing
in the first place He can do it again. In fact it is
easier to make a man be again what he once was than to
make him initially what he never was.

[93]Tertullian De resurrectione carnis 11.

"For if out of nothing God has built up all
things, he will be able also out of nothing to
produce the flesh reduced to nothing: or if out
of material he has contrived things other than it,
he will be able also out of something other than
it to recall the flesh, into whatsoever it may
have been drained away. And certainly he who has
made is competent to remake, seeing it is a
greater thing to make than to remake, to give a
beginning than to give back again. Thus you may
believe that the restitution of the flesh is
easier than its institution."

[94]Ibid. 12.

"To put it in one word, the whole creation is
recurrent. Whatsoever you are to meet with has
been: whatsoever you are to lose will be.
Nothing exists for the first time. All things
return to their estate after having departed: all
things begin when they have ceased. They come to
an end simply that they may come to be: nothing
perishes except with a view to salvation.
Therefore this whole revolving scheme of things is
an attestation of the resurrection of the dead.
God wrote down resurrection in works before he put
it in writing, he preached it by acts of power
before he told of it in words."
Cf. Apologeticus 48, where he appeals to the creation
of the universe, the constellations, night and day, the

seasons, and so forth as natural analogies of the
resurrection.

[95] Tertullian _De resurrectione carnis_ 13. "But
shall men die once for all, while birds of Arabia are
assured of their resurrection?"

[96] Ibid. 14-17. Cf. _Apologeticus_ 48 where he
states the reason for the resurrection is the judgement
which God has appointed.

[97] Tertullian _De resurrectione carnis_ 14.

"Therefore since it is most appropriate for one
who is God and Lord and Maker to appoint for man
judgement concerning precisely this, whether or
not he has taken care to acknowledge and respect
his Lord and Maker, and since the resurrection
will bring that judgement into actuality, this
will be the whole purpose, yea the necessity, of
the resurrection, such a provision of judgement as
is most appropriate to God."

[98] Ibid. 17. But contrast the earlier _Apologeticus_
48, where the contrary is asserted.

[99] Tertullian _De resurrectione carnis_ 57-61.

[100] This ascription is usually held to be in error
(R. M. Grant, "Athenagoras or Pseudo-Athenagoras,"
Harvard Theological Review 47 [1954]: 121-9), chiefly
because the objection from cannibalism does not appear
prior to Origen.

[101] Athenagoras _De resurrectione_ 1.3.

[102] Ibid. 2.3.

[103] Ibid. 3.1-92.

[104] Ibid. 3.1.
"As to power, the creation of our bodies shows
that God's power suffices for their resurrection.
For if when he first gave them form, he made the
bodies of men and their principal constituents
from nothing, he will just as easily raise them up
again after their dissolution, however it may have
taken place. For this is equally possible for
him." (Athenagoras, Legatio _and_ De Resurrectione,
ed. William R. Schoedel, Oxford Early Christian
Texts [Oxford: Clarendon Press, 1972].)

[105]Ibid 4.1-4.

[106]Ibid. 7.4.

[107]Ibid. 10.-11.2.

[108]Ibid. 12.1-17.4.

[109]Ibid. 13.2 "the reason then for man's creation guarantees his eternal survival, and his survival guarantees his resurrection, without which he could not survive as man." Cf. 15.6.

[110]Ibid., 18.1-25.5.

[111]Irenaeus Adversus haereses 5.13.1.

[112]Origen Contra Celsum 2.62.

[113]Ibid., 2.48.

[114]Ibid., 2.54.

[115]Ibid., 2.55.

[116]Ibid., 2.56.

[117]Ibid., 2.59.

[118]Ibid., 2.60.

[119]Ibid., 2.61.

[120]Ibid., 2.62. Origen's demurring to defend the resurrection of the flesh made him the target of treatises such as Athenagoras De resurrectione and Methodius De resurrectione. The belief in a literal, physical resurrection was associated with belief in a literal millenium, and Origen rejected both doctrines (Ibid. 5. 15, 22.) See Henry Chadwick, Early Christian Thought and the Classical Tradition (Oxford: Clarendon Press, 1966), pp. 78-9.

[121]Origen Contra Celsum 2.63.

[122]Ibid., 2.64-67.

[123]Ibid., 5.56.

[124]Ibid., 3.22.

[125]Ibid., 3.24.

[126]See discussions in Walther Volker, Das Bild vom nichtgnostischen Christentum bei Celsus (Halle: 1928), p. 74; R. Bader, Der Alethes des Kelsos, TBAW 33 (Stuttgart and Berlin: 1940), p. 79; Carl Andresen, Logos und Nomos: Die Polemik des Kelsos wider das Christentum, AKG 30 (Berlin: Walter de Gruyter, 1955), pp. 47-51.

[127]Even in 8. 45 his comment that "Life is full of such experiences" could mean only that one hears always about such goings-on.

[128]Origen Contra Celsum 3.2.

[129]Ibid., 3.26.

[130]Ibid., 3.31.

[131]Ibid., 3.32.

[132]Andresen, Logos und Nomos, p. 49.

[133]Origen Contra Celsum 3.23.

"However, let the stories about them be examined side by side with that of Jesus. Does Celsus want to make out that their stories are true, while those of Jesus are inventions, although they were recorded by people who were eyewitnesses, and showed in practice their clear apprehension of the one whom they saw, and proved their sincerity by the persecutions which they willingly suffered for his doctrine?"

[134]Ibid., 3.27.

[135]Brown, Miracles, p. 6.

[136]"Sed qui ea conspicati sunt fieri et sub oculis suis viderunt agi, testes optimi certissimique auctores, et crediderunt haec ipsi et credenda posteris nobis haud exilibus cum adprobationibus tradiderunt." (Arnobius Adversus nationes 1.54.)

[137]Ibid., 1.55.

[138]Eusebius Demonstratio evangelica 3.4.

[139]Ibid.

[140]Ibid., 3.5.

[141]Origen Contra Celsum 1.42.
". . . the endeavor to show with regard to almost
any history, however true, that it actually occurred,
and to produce an intelligent conception regarding it,
is one of the most difficult undertakings that can be
attempted, and is in some instances an impossibility.
For suppose that someone were to assert that there
never had been any Trojan War, chiefly on account of
the impossible narrative interwoven therewith, about a
certain Achilles being the son of a sea-goddess Thetis
and of a man Peleus, or Sarpeolon being the son of
Zeus, or Ascalaphus and Ialmenus the sons of Ares, or
Aeneas that of Aphrodite, how should we prove that such
was the case, especially under the weight of the
fiction attached, I know not how, to the universally
prevalent opinion that there really was a war in Ilium
between Greeks and Trojans?"

[142]Ibid.

[143]Origen In evangelium Johannis 2.34 (28). 87.
14-20.

"Christ's stupendous acts of power were able to
bring to faith those of Christ's own time, but
. . . they lost their demonstrative force with the
lapse of years and began to be regarded as
mythical. Greater evidential value than that of
the miracles then performed attaches to the
comparison which we now make between these
miracles and the prophecy of them; this makes it
impossible for the student to cast any doubt on
the former."
(Origen, Origen's Commentary on the Gospel of John, The
Ante-Nicene Fathers, vol. 9, ed. Allan Menzies [New
York:- Christian Literature Co., 1896], p. 342.)

[144]Origen Contra Celsum 2. 50-51; Arnobius Adversus
nationes 1. 43, 55; Eusebius Demonstratio evangelica
3.3,6.

[145]Beryl Smalley, Historians in the Middle Ages
(London: Thames & Hudson, 1974), p. 25.

[146]Ibid., p. 19. Many were, however, proficient
in Hebrew, which they could learn from neighboring Jews
for the study of the Old Testament. But in New
Testament studies, non-Byzantine scholars depended on
the Vulgate. (Beryl Smalley, The Study of the Bible in

the Middle Ages, 1d ed. [Notre Dame, Ind.:   University
of Notre Dame Press, 1970], pp. 360-64.) Some medieval
exegetes, notably Andrew of St. Victor pursued the
historical interpretation of a scripture text in
preference to spiritual, allegorizing exegesis; but
they did not investigate historically the events
themselves related in the text.

[147] Anselm Cur Deus homo 2. 22.

"All things which you have said seem to me
reasonable and incontrovertible. And by the
solution of the single question proposed do I see
the truth of all that is contained in the Old and
New Testament. For, in proving that God became
man by necessity, leaving out what was taken from
the Bible, . . . you convince both Jews and Pagans
by the mere force of reason. And the God-man
himself originates the New Testament and approves
the Old. And, as we must acknowledge him to be
true, so no one can dissent from anything
contained in these books."

[148] Augustine Epistolae 28. 3,5.

[149] Ibid. 82. 3; cf. 22. According to Polman, for
Augustine not even the universal council of the Church
is infallible, for infallibility belongs exclusively to
the Holy Scripture. (A. D. R. Polman, Word of God
according to St. Augustine [Grand Rapids: Wm. B.
Eerdmanns, 1961], p. 66.)

[150] Augustine De civitate dei 21.6.1.

[151] Hans Küng, Infallible? An Enquiry (London:
Collins, 1972), pp. 173-4.

[152] Augustine De libero arbitrio 2.1.6.

[153] Augustine De vera religione 24.45. Cf. Contra
academicos 3. 43.

[154] Augustine Sermons 43.

[155] Frederick Copleston, A History of Philosophy, 9
vols., vol. 2: Mediaeval Philosophy, pt. 1: Augustine
to Bonaventure (Garden City, N.Y.:   Doubleday, Image
Books, 1962), pp. 63-4.

[156] Augustine De vera religione 25.46.

[157]Gerhard Strauss, Schriftgebrauch, Schriftaus-
legung und Schriftbeweis bei Augustin, Beiträge zur
Geschichte der biblischen Hermeneutik 1 (Tübingen: J.
C.G. Mohr, 1959), p. 7. As Gilson acknowledges,

". . . even the faith of an Augustinian
presupposes a certain exercise of natural reason.
We cannot believe something, be it the word of God
Himself, unless we find some sense in the formulas
which we believe. And it can hardly be expected
that we will believe in God's Revelation, unless
we be given good reasons to think that such a
Revelation has indeed taken place. (Etienne
Gilson, Reason and Revelation in the Middle Ages
[New York: Charles Scribner's Sons, 1938], pp.
17-18.)

[158]Augustine De vera religione 25.46.

[159]Strauss, Schriftgebrauch bei Augustin, p. 7.

[160]Ibid., p. 42.

[161]Albert Lang, Die Entfaltung des apologetischen
Problems in der Scholastik des Mittelalters (Freiburg:
Herder, 1962), p. 16.

[162]Augustine Epistolae 147.

[163]Augustine De vera religione 25.46.

[164]Augustine De libero arbitrio 2.1.5.

[165]Dulles, History of Apologetics, pp. 61-2.

[166]Augustine De vera religione 3.4.

[167]Ibid. 3.5; cf. Augustine De civitate dei 22.5.

[168]Augustine De vera religione 24.47.

[169]Augustine De civitate dei 22.5.

[170]Lang, Entfaltung des apologetischen Problems,
pp. 64-79. From the foregoing Lang's contention that
the question of the basis of Scripture authority was
not raised prior to this time seems to be in error.

[171]Thomas Aquinas Summa contra gentiles 1.3.

[172]Ibid., 4.1.

[173]Ibid., 1. 5.

[174]Ibid., 1. 3.

[175]Ibid., 1.9; Aquinas Summa theologiae 1a.32.1.

[176]Ibid., 1. 6; 3. 154.

[177]Thomas Aquinas Summa Theologiae 2a2ae. 1. 4 ad
2.

"Then they are indeed seen by the one who
believes; he would not believe unless he saw that
they are worthy of belief on the basis of evident
signs or something of this sort." (Blackfriars'
translation.)

[178]Aquinas Summa contra gentiles 3. 154.

"Since . . . the proffered speech [of the
apostles] needs confirmation that it may be
accepted, unless it be manifest in itself; and
whereas things that are of faith are not clear to
human reason: it was necessary to provide some
means of confirming the utterances of those who
preached the faith. But they could not be
confirmed by being demonstrated from principles of
reason, since matters of faith are above reason.
Therefore the preachers' words needed to be
confirmed by some kind of signs, whereby it was
made evident that their words were from God, and
that the preacher should do such works as healing
the sick, and performing other deeds of power,
which God alone can do. . . .

There was also another manner of confirmation in
that when the heralds of truth were found to speak
the truth about such hidden things as could
subsequently be made manifest, they were believed
because they spoke truthfully of things beyond the
ken of man. Hence the necessity of the gift of
prophecy, whereby through divine revelation they
were able to know and announce to others, the
things that were to happen, and such things as are
commonly hid from man's knowledge . . ."

[179]Ibid., 1. 6.
"For divine Wisdom Himself . . . by suitable
arguments proves His presence, and the truth of
His doctrine and inspiration by performing works
surpassing the capability of the whole of nature,

namely, the wondrous healing of the sick, the
raising of the dead to life, a marvellous control
over the heavenly bodies, and what excites yet
more wonder, the inspiration of human minds, so
that unlettered and simple persons are filled with
the Holy Ghost, and are in one instant endowed
with the most sublime wisdom and eloquence. And
after considering these arguments, convinced by
the strength of the proof, and not by the force of
arms, nor by the promise of delights, but--and
this is the greatest marvel of all--amid the
tyranny of persecutions, a countless crowd of not
only simple but also of the wisest men, embraced
the Christian faith, which inculcates things
surpassing all human understanding, curbs the
pleasures of the flesh, and teaches contempt of
all worldly things."

[180]Aquinas Summa theologiae 3a. 43. 4.

[181]Aquinas Summa contra gentiles 1. 9.

[182]Alois Van Hove, La doctrine du miracle chez
Saint Thomas (Paris: 1927), pp. 249-52; Lang,
Entfaltung des apologetischen Problems, pp. 115-19.

[183]Aquinas Summa contra gentiles 3. 101.

[184]"Haec autem praeter ordinem communiter in rebus
sstatutum quandoque divinitus fiunt, miracula dici
solent." (Aquinas Summa contra gentiles 3. 101.)

[185]Ibid., 3. 99.

[186]Ibid., 3. 100.

[187]Ibid., 3. 101. Cf. Aquinas Summa theologiae
1a. 105. 8 and Thomas Aquinas De pontentia Dei 6. 2. ad
3.

[188]Aquinas Summa contra gentiles 3. 102.

[189]Ibid., 3. 103.

[190]Aquinas Summa theologiae 3a. 43. 1.
"A man is empowered by God to work miracles . . .
principally, in order to confirm the truth of what
he teaches. For since what is of faith surpasses
human reason, it cannot be proved by human
reasoning, but must be proved by the argument of
divine power: so that when a man does works that

God alone can do, we may believe that what he says
is from God . . .

Secondly, in order to make known God's presence in
a man by the grace of the Holy Spirit . . ."
Cf. Aquinas 1 Sententia 3. 3. ad 2; 3 Sententia 24.
1.2.

[191]Ibid., 3a. 43. 3. "Christ wrought miracles in
order to confirm his teaching, and in order to
demonstrate the divine power that was his."

[192]Ibid., 3a. 43. 4.

[193]Ibid., 3a. 55. 6.

[194]Dulles, History, p. 111. Dulles is speaking of
14 and 15th century scholastics, but it applies to
Aquinas as well. Lang remarks,
    "Scholastic theology occupied itself . . . greatly
    with the possibility and presuppositions of the
    proof from miracles, hence, with the theory of
    miracle. It expended less effort on laying the
    historical foundations of the proof from miracles.
    One was satisfied with a brief allusion to the
    miracles wrought by Christ without attempting a
    thorough historical-critical demonstration of
    them." (Lang, Entfaltung des apologetischen
    Problems, p. 141.)

[195]Aquinas Summa contra gentiles 1. 6.
"Now such a wondrous conversion of the world to
the Christian faith is a most indubitable proof
that such signs did take place, so that there is
no need to repeat them, seeing that there is
evidence of them in their result. For it would be
the most wondrous sign of all if without any
wondrous signs the world were persuaded by simple
and lowly men to believe things so arduous, to
accomplish things so difficult, and to hope for
things so sublime."

[196]Oddly enough, this most fundamental of
arguments is overlooked by Brown. He contends that the
Patristic and Medieval thinkers were not fideistic in
their approach to miracles, since they argued for
miracles on the basis of (1) the historical
trustworthiness of Scripture, (2) the analogy of
contemporary miracles, and (3) the conceivability of
miracles. (Brown, Miracles, pp. 18-19.) But (1) was
chiefly Patristic, (2) of minimal importance, and (3)

irrelevant to establishing that a miracle has occurred.
Rather the most important argument for biblical
miracles during the Medieval Period was the miracle of
the church itself. Brown also misunderstands the
medieval's notion of "sign," playing it off against
"proof." A sign's main function, he asserts, is to
direct us to that to which it points. (ibid., p. 19.)
But as we have seen, for the medievals a miracle is a
sign precisely because it is a proof of a person's
claim to speak or act for God; if it were not a proof
it would be incapable of functioning as a sign.

[197]Lang,   Entfaltung des apologetischen Problems,
p. 128.

[198]Similarly, John Duns Scotus provides an
extensive ten point apologetic for the credibility of
scripture: (1) Praenuntiatio prophetica: the
prophecies of the Old Testament are fulfilled in the
New, a feat made possible only by God.   (2)
Scripturarum concordia: despite its different authors
and times of composition, the scripture is harmonious
throughout. (3) Auctoritas scribentium: the authors
guarantee the reliability of the contents, which they
often introduce by "thus saith the Lord."   (4)
Diligentia recipientium: the scripture was
scrupulously preserved and handed down by Jews and
Christians alike. (5) Rationabilitas contentorum: the
ethical teachings of scripture are in accord with
reason, and even truths of faith, such as the
incarnation and Trinity, contain nothing absurd.   (6)
Irrationabilitas errorum: by contrast the doctrines of
heretics and pagans are full of absurdities.   (7)
Ecclesiae stabilitas: the church endures as is
promised in scripture, while the sects are transient.
(8) Miraculorum limpiditas: not only the miracles
recorded in the scripture but the miracle of the
triumph of Christianity itself through a few unlearned
men (Scotus refers here to Augustine De civitate Dei
22. 5) testifies to the truth of the revelation in holy
scripture. (9) Testimoniam non fidelium: Josephus and
Sybille also confirm the accuracy of scripture.   (10)
Promissorum efficacia: God confirms the truth of
scripture by giving salvation to all who truly seek it,
which He does not do for the sects. (John Duns Scotus
Ordinatio prologus 2. 1; cf. Reinhold Seeberg, Die
Theologie des Johannes Duns Skotus, SGTK 5 [Leibzig:
1900; rep. ed.: Aalen: Scientia Verlag, 1971], pp.
116-18; Josef Finkenzeller, Offenbarung und Theologie
nach der Lehre des Johannes Duns Skotus, BGPTM 38
[Munster: Aschendorffsche Verlagsbuchhandlung, 1961],

pp. 38-42.) Clearly for Scotus as for Aquinas
Scripture is not to be accepted blindly by the sheer
weight of authority alone; rather it is authoritative
because it is Scripture, and there are good grounds
(even historical ones!--e.g., [4], [8], [9]) for
holding it to be Scripture, i.e., revelation.

[199]Lang, Entfaltung des apologetischen Problems,
pp. 148-51.

NOTES TO SECTION II

[1]John   Orr,   English Deism: its Roots and its
Fruits (Grand Rapids: Wm. B. Eerdmans, 1934), p. 172.

[2]Avery Dulles, A History of Apologetics, Theological Resources (London: Hutchinson: 1971; New York:
Corpus, 1971), p. 157.

[3]Pierre   Bayle,   Dictionnaire historique et
critique, 3d ed. (Rotterdam: n.p., 1715), s.v. "Viret,
Pierre."

[4]John M. Robertson, A Short History of Freethought
Ancient and Modern (London: Swan, Sonnenschein, & Co.,
1899), p. 341.

[5]Ibid., p. 296.

[6]Charles   Blount,   Miscellaneous Works of Charles
Blount (n.p.:   n.p., 1695); idem, The Two First Books
of Philostratus (London: Nathaniel Thompson, 1680).

[7]John   Toland,   Christianity Not Mysterious; or, a
Treatise shewing That there is Nothing in the Gospel
Contrary to Reason, nor above it; and that no Christian
Doctrine can be properly Called a Mystery (London:
n.p., 1702).

[8]The first Boyle lecturer was Richard Bentley, who
spoke on The Folly Atheism and What is Now Called Deism
and later became the opponent of Deist Anthony Collins.
In Boyle's day Deism was often called "theism."

[9]See partial list in Robertson, History, pp.
303-4.

[10]Philippes de Mornay, De la vérité de la religion
chrestienne (Anvers: Imprimerie de Christofle Plantin,
1581), pref. Yet another Huguenot divine Moise Amyraut
in   his   Traité des religions contre ceux qui les
estiment indifférentes published at Saumur in 1631
names as his opponents the Epicureans, who deny God's
providence, along with the philosophers, who deny
supernatural revelation, and the indifferent, who
acknowledge revelation but do not bind men to any
particular religion. Both of the first two parties
could be classed as Deists. Pascal like Viret also
associates by name Deism with Epicureanism (Blaise
Pascal, Oeuvres, vols. 12-14: Pensées, new ed., ed.

Leon Brunschvicg [Paris: Librairie Hachette, 1904;
rep. ed.:   Vaduz: Kraus Reprint, 1965], pensée 556,
14:1-7.)   Notice, too, that in the progressive listing
of infidels from atheists to Mohometans in Mornay's
subtitle, the Epicureans occupy the slot logically
reserved for and in later lists actually occupied by
Deists.

[11]Pascal, Pensées, pensée 556, 14:5.

[12]Hugo Grotius De veritate religionis christianae
1.1.   ". . . and there are never wanting profane
persons, who, upon   occasion, are ready to scatter
their poison amongst the weak and simple, which fear
had forced them to conceal: against all which evils,
my desire was to have my countrymen well fortified
. . . ."   (Clarke translation.)

[13]Ibid., 1.11.   "And they are under a very great
mistake, who confine this providence to the heavenly
bodies. . . ."

[14]Ibid.   "Nor is their error less, who allow the
universe to be governed by him, but not the particular
things in it."

[15]Ibid., 1.13.
"But the most certain proof of Divine Providence
is from miracles, and the predictions we find in
histories: it is true, indeed, that a great many
of those relations are fabulous; but there is no
reason to disbelieve those which are attested by
credible witnesses to have been in their time, men
whose judgment and integrity have never been
called in question."

[16]Edward   Lord   Herbert   of   Cherbury,   The
Autobiography of Edward Lord Herbert of Cherbury,   ed.
with an Introduction, and a Continuation of the Life by
Sidney Lee, 2d ed.   (London: George Routledge & Sons,
1906), p. 133.

[17]Pascal, Pensées, pensée 556, 14:2-3, 6.

[18]He writes,
". . . I shall not undertake here to prove by
natural reasons either the existence of God or the
Trinity or the immortality of the soul or anything
of that nature, not only because I should not feel
myself sufficiently able to find in nature
arguments to convince hardened atheists, but also

because such knowledge without Jesus Christ is
useless and barren." (ibid., pensée 556, 14:4)

[19]Jacques Abbadie, Traité de la vérité de la
religion chrétienne (The Hague: Jean Neaulme, 1771),
pp. 122-67.

[20]Harry Elmer Barnes, A History of Historical
Writing, 2d rev. ed. (New York: Dover Publications,
1962), p. 136.

[21]For a fuller account see ibid., pp. 138-47; Paul
Hazard, The European Mind [1680-1715], trans. J.L. May
(New York: New American Library, 1963), pp. 3-28.
These travels might even be purely imaginary; see Paul
Hazard, European Thought in the Eighteenth Century,
trans. J.L. May (New Haven, Conn.: Yale University
Press, 1954), pp. 6-8.

[22]La Bruyère, Les Caractères (Paris: Michallet,
1689), Pensée 4. The reference is to Tavernier, Voyage
en Turquie, en Perse et aux Indes (1676-79) and
Chardin, Voyage en Perse (1686).

[23]La Bruyère, Caractères, Pensee 16.

[24]Grotius De veritate 1.1.
"For my design was to undertake something which
might be useful to my countrymen, especially
seamen; that they might have an opportunity to
employ the time which in long voyages lies upon
their hands, and is usually thrown away:
wherefore I began with an econium upon our nation,
which so far excels others in the skill of
navigation; that by this means I might excite them
to make use of this art, as a peculiar favour of
heaven; not only to their own profit, but also to
the propagating of the Christian religion; for
they can never want matter, but in their long
voyages will every where meet either with Pagans,
as in China or Guinea; or Mohometans, as in the
Turkish or Persian empires, and in the kingdoms of
Fez and Morocco; and also with Jews, who are the
professed enemies of Christianity, and are
dispersed over the greatest part of the world
. . .: against all which evils my desire was to
have my countrymen well fortified: that they, who
have the best parts, might employ them in
confuting errors, and that the other would take
heed of being seduced by them."
Grotius's work enjoyed an enormous popularity, being

translated not only into many European languages, but into Persian, Arabic, Malayan, and Chinese as well.

[25] Denis Diderot, "Philosophical Thoughts," in Diderot's Early Philosophical Works, trans. Margaret Jourdain, Open Court Series of Classics of Science and Philosophy 4 (Chicago: Open Court, 1916), Pensée LXII.

[26] Leslie Stephen, History of English Thought in the Eighteenth Century 2 vols., 3d ed. (New York: Harcourt, Brace & World; Harbinger Books, 1962), 1: chaps. 3,4. Though Stephen separates these elements chronologically, they are perhaps best seen in the two halves of Rousseau's "Profession du foi de Vicaire Savoyard" in his Emile, ou de l'éducation (1762). The vicar's profession of faith, which is Rousseau's own, was explained by Rousseau in his "Lettre à M. De Beaumont":

> "The Profession of the vicar of Savoy is comprised of two parts: the first, which is the larger, the more important, the more full of new and striking truths, is designed to combat modern materialism, to establish the existence of God and natural religion with all the force of which the author is capable . . . .
>
> The second, much shorter, less regular, less deep, proposes some doubts and difficulties about revelations in general, nonetheless giving to ours its true certainty in the purity, the holiness of its doctrine and in the divine sublimity of him who is its author. (Jean-Jacques Rousseau, "Lettre à M. De Beaumont," in Rousseau: Religious Writings, ed. Ronald Grimsley [Oxford: Clarendon Press, 1970], pp. 300-1.)

Rousseau's attitude toward Christianity is not unlike that of Matthew Tindal, Christianity as old as the Creation: or the Gospel a Republication of the Religion of Nature (1730).

[27] Charles Leslie, A short and Easie Method with the Deists, 2d ed. (London: C. Brome, E. Poole, & Geo. Strahan, 1699), p. 2.

[28] Thomas Woolston, A Third Discourse on the Miracles of Our Saviour, 3d ed. (London: author, 1728), p. 66.

[29] Jean-Jacques Rousseau, "Profession de foi du Vicaire savoyard," in Religious Writings, pp. 180-8. So also Voltaire, who went so far as to assert that if intelligent beings exist on other worlds then they,

too, must be Deist. (See Hazard, European Thought, p. 116.)

[30]Rousseau, "Profession de foi," pp. 187-8.

[31]Ibid., p. 191.

[32]Stephen, English Thought, p. 68. For a good example of this, see Matthew Tindal, Christianity as old as the Creation: or the Gospel a Republication of the Religion of Nature, with an Introduction by Gunter Gawlick (London: 1730; rep. ed.:   Stuttgart-Bad Canstatt: Friedrich Frommann Verlag, 1967), pp. 404-5. Tindal cites Leibniz and Huet in testimony to the Chinese's moral superiority to Christians, also a missionary named Navarette, who said, "It is God's special Providence, that the Chinese did not know what is done in Christendome; for if they did, there wou'd be never a Man among them, but wou'd spit in our Faces."   (Navarette, Acco. of China, Christianity of old as the Creation, p. 405.)

[33]Marie François Arrouet de Voltaire, Dictionnaire philosophique (Paris: Garnier,   1967),   s.v. "Christianisme."

[34]Ibid.

[35]Rousseau, "Profession du foi," p. 188.

[36]Ibid., pp. 184-5.

[37]Tindal, Christianity as old as the Creation, p. 5.

[38]Tindal concludes,
". . . Men, if they sincerely endeavour to discover the Will of God, will perceive, that there's a Law of Nature, or Reason; which is so call'd, as being a Law, which is common, or natural, to all rational Creatures; and . . . this Law, like its Author, is absolutely perfect, eternal, and unchangeable; and . . . the Design of the Gospel was not to add to, or take from this Law; but to free Men from that Load of Superstition, which had been mix'd with it: So that TRUE CHRISTIANITY is not a Religion of Yesterday, but what God, at the Beginning, dictated, and still continues to dictate to Christians, as well as to Others." (ibid., p. 8.) Notice the important phrase, "as well as to Others."

[39] Günter Gawlick, "Einleitung," to Tindal, Christianity as old as Creation, pp. 14-15. David Friedrich Strauss wrote,

"Long enough people had held the Jewish and Christian religions alone of all religions true and divine; all others, the so-called heathen religions, such as the Mohammedan, had been held to be false . . . . This inequality was unbearable for the eighteenth century because of its expanded historical and geographical perspective. It was that century's firm assumption that intra muros things could not differ basically from what was extra muros, for surely there were both within and without men with the same nature, the same talents and powers, weaknesses and passions. Hence, either the heathen religions, together with Islam, were divine revelations (but how was that possible with such demonstrable error and contradiction which the eighteenth century thought it found in them? and anyway how was a miraculous revelation consistent with this century's concept of God and the world?), or also Judaism and Christianity were products of human deception on the one hand and human superstition and foolishness on the other." (David Friedrich Strauss, Hermann Samuel Reimarus und seine Schutzschrift für die vernünftigen Verehrer Gottes [Leipzip: F.A. Brockhaus, 1862], pp. 270-1.)

[40] Tindal, Christianity as old as the Creation, p. 13.

[41] Orr, Deism, p. 28.

[42] Klaus Scholder traces the roots of the rise of biblical criticism to Galileo's separation of science and religion with respect to biblical authority. While Scripture is inerrant in religion, it does not speak to science; on the contrary science is binding upon Scripture. After Galileo, nature and its laws needed no interpretation, whereas the Scripture had to be interpreted in light of science. When the two conflicted, it was Scripture that had to yield. Tradition and authority were now opposed by reason and experience, and this development constitutes the watershed between the medieval and modern periods. (Klaus Scholder, Ursprünge und Probleme der Bibelkritik im 17. Jahrhundert, Forschungen Zur Geschichte und Lehre des Protestantismus 10/33 [München: Chr. Kaiser Verlag 1966], pp. 73-8.) On the centrality of Galileo's contribution in the history of thought, see

E.A. Burtt, <u>The Metaphysical Foundations of Modern Physical Science</u>, 2d rev. ed. (Garden City, N.Y.: Doubleday & Co.; Anchor Books, 1954), pp. 103-4.

[43] Stephen, <u>English Thought</u>, p. 69.

[44] Voltaire, <u>Dictionnaire</u>, s.v. "Miracles."

[45] Ibid.

[46] Ibid.

[47] Ibid.

[48] Richard Popkin, "Scepticism, Theology, and the Scientific Revolution in the Seventeenth Century," in <u>Problems in the Philosophy of Science</u>, ed. Imre Lakatos & Alan Musgrave, Proceedings of the International Colloquium on the Philosophy of Science, 1965, vol. 3 (Amsterdam: North-Holland Publishing Co., 1968), pp. 17-18. Agreeing with Popkin's assessment of La Peyrère is Scholder, <u>Ursprünge und Probleme der Bibelkritik</u>, pp. 98-104.

[49] [La Peyrère], <u>Prae-adamitae. sive exercitatio super versibus duodecimo, decimotertio, & decimoquarto, capitis quinti Epistolae D. Pauli ad Romanos. quibus inducuntur [sic] primi homines ante Adamum conditi</u> (n.p.: n.p., 1655), pp. 6-7.

[50] Ibid., pp. 21-2

[51] "Peccatum Adami fuisse retro imputatem primis hominibus ante Adam conditis: & damnationem mortis ex illo peccato, retro regnavisse in illos." (ibid., p. 45.)

[52] Ibid., p. 58. According to Scholder, La Peyrère's turn to empirical justification was even more dangerous than his exegesis. He brought forth proofs from the Bible itself and from the histories of other peoples to back up his conclusions from Rom 5. His collection of critical arguments to support an ancient earth, says Scholder, later served as a resource from which French Free-thinkers and English Deists drew to fill their arsenals for the attack upon Christianity. (Scholder, <u>Ursprünge und Probleme der Bibelkritik</u>, p. 100.) On La Peyrère's influence see D.R. McKee, "Isaac de La Peyrère: a precursor of 18th century critical Deists, "<u>Publications of the Modern Language Association of America</u> 59 (1944): 471-85.

[53]La Peyrère, Rélation de Groenland (Paris: L. Billaine, 1663).

[54]Popkin, "Scepticism, Theology and the Scientific Revolution," pp. 21,23.

[55]Isaac Newton, Mathematical Principles of Natural Philosophy, trans. Andrew Motte, 3d ed., rev. Florian Cajori (Berkelely: University of California Press, 1947).   See also Encyclopedia of Philosophy, s.v. "Newton, Isaac," by Dudley Shapere; Encyclopedia of Philosophy, s.v. "Newtonian Mechanics and Mechanical Explanation," by Dudley Shapere.

[56]Voltaire, Dictionnaire, s.v. "Miracles."

[57]Hugo Grotius Votum pro pace ecclesiastica, p. 672.

"For there was no need that the histories should be dictated by the Holy Spirit. It was sufficient that the writer had a good memory concerning the things he had seen or that he was careful in transcribing the ancient records . . . . If Luke had written by the dictation of divine inspiration, then he would have drawn his authority from that, as the prophets do, rather than from witnesses, whose credit he follows. . . ."

[58]"As a writer he is so bold as to treat the Scriptures as if they were no more than a mere literary work.   He approaches them as he would any work of classical antiquity."   (W.S.M. Knight, The Life and Works of Hugo Grotius, Grotius Society Publications 4 [London: Sweet & Maxwell, 1925], p. 250.)

[59]Grotius De veritate 3.1-6.

[60]Ibid., 3.7, 8.

[61]Ibid. 3.13.

". . . this very thing ought to acquit these writers of all suspicion of deceit; because they who bear testimony to that which is false, are used to relate all things so by agreement, that there should not be any appearance of difference. And if, upon the account of some small difference, which cannot be reconciled, we must immediately disbelieve whole books; then there is no book, expecially of history, to be believed; and yet Polybius, Halicarnassensis, Livy, and Plutarch, in whom such things are to be found, keep up their

authority amongst us in the principal things."
(Clarke trans.).

[62] Ibid. 3.16.

[63] Albert Monod, De Pascal à Chateaubriand: Les
défenseurs français du Christianisme de 1670 a 1802
(New York: Burt Franklin, 1916; rep. ed.: 1971), p.
506.

[64] Houtteville, whom we shall meet later, reported
that of all the Spinozists he interviewed, all admitted
that they did not really understand Spinoza but adhered
to him because he denied God. (Houtteville, "Discours
historique et critique sur la méthode des principaux
auteurs qui ont écrit pour et contre le christianisme
depuis son origine," in idem, La religion chrétienne
prouvée par les faits, 2d ed., 3 vols. [Paris:
Mercier & Boudet, 1740], 1:189.) Voltaire, after a
half-hearted stab at refuting Spinoza in his article on
"God," brushed him aside, commenting that Spinoza is
not so dangerous: he is confusing because he really is
confused, he has written in bad Latin, and there are
not ten persons in Europe who have read him from
beginning to end. (Voltaire, Dictionnaire, s.v.
"Dieu.")

[65] Adam Storey Farrar, A Critical History of Free
Thought (New York: D. Appleton, 1863), p. 113.
According to Monod, it was difficult after Spinoza to
write an apology without consecrating long chapters to
the defense of Old Testament authenticity and the
refutation of objections to miracles. (Monod, De
Pascal à Chateaubriand, p. 36).

[66] Thomas Hobbes Leviathan 32.

[67] Ibid. 33.

[68] Ibid. 34.

[69] Ibid.

[70] Ibid. 12.

[71] Ibid.; cf. 34.

[72] In his verse autobiography, Hobbes relates how
on his third trip to the Continent, he came to accept
Galileo's view that bodies are naturally in motion and
will so continue unless acted upon by some outside

force. Galileo's theory of inertia as well as his
heliocentric cosmology thus destroyed the foundations
of the traditional Aristotelian proof of God from
motion. See Encyclopedia of Philosophy, s.v. "Hobbes,
Thomas," by R.S. Peters.

[73]Hobbes Leviathan 32.

[74]Ibid.

[75]Ibid. 33.

[76]Ibid.

[77]Benedict de Spinoza Tractatus theologico-
politicus praef. Spinoza penned the Tractatus, he
says, to show that piety can flourish in a tolerant
society and indeed cannot exist without it.

[78]Ibid. 8.

[79]Ibid. 10;11.

[80]As Monod points out, the starting point of the
work is a fundamental rationalism, allowing only the
universal light of reason and conscience to the
exclusion of any privileged revelation. Prophecy and
miracles are likewise excluded. Religion reduces to
the practice of justice and charity. The Bible is a
book of morality and piety, not philosophy and science.
It is a book historically conditioned like all others
and should be studied by the same methods. Since
Scripture allows reason to be free, philosophy has
absolute independence from it. Freedom of conscience
is a natural right entailing freedom of speech, of
which every man may avail himself. (Monod, De Pascal à
Chateaubriand, p. 30.) The Deist tone of the treatise
is most evident in Spinoza's list of the seven dogmas
of the universal faith: (1) that a just and merciful
God exists, (2) that He is one, (3) that He is
omnipresent, (4) that He has supreme dominion over all
things, (5) that worship of God consists only in
justice and love of one's neighbor, (6) that only those
who obey God by their manner of life are saved, and (7)
that God forgives the sins of those who repent.
(Spinoza Tractatus theologico-politicus 14).

[81]Jean Le Clerc, Five Letters Concerning the
Inspiration of the Holy Scriptures (London: n.p.,
1690), pp. 125-6.

[82] Richard Simon, _A Critical History of the Old Testament_, trans. H.D. (London: Jacob Tonson, 1682), 1.7. See also John Woodbridge, "The Reception of Spinoza's _Tractatus theologico-politicus_ by Richard Simon (1638-1712)," to be published by the Lessing Akademie, Wolfenbuttel, West Germany.

[83] He states,
". . . This principle which I have laid down, concerning the way how the Holy Scriptures which we have at present have been collected, we having only an abridgement of the Acts which were preserv'd intire in the Registry of the Republic; This principle, I say is of great use for the resolving of many difficult questions concerning Chronology and the Genealogies." (Simon, _History of the Old Testament_, pref.)

[84] Ibid.

[85] Ibid.

[86] Richard Simon, _Traité de l'Inspiration des livres sacrés_ (Rotterdam: Renier Leers, 1687), pp. 43-9.

[87] Le Clerc knew Grotius well, for he wrote a series of annotations on Grotius's _De veritate_ and cites him on several occasions in the _Sentimens_.

[88] Jean Le Clerc, _Letters_, p. 8. Note once again how closely the dispute is associated with Deism.

[89] Ibid., pp. 14-15. Compare Hobbes's discussion of the same in Hobbes, _Leviathan_ 32.

[90] Le Clerc, _Letters_, p. 114.

[91] Ibid., pp. 46-7.

[92] Ibid., p. 29.

[93] Ibid., pp. 30-1.

[94] Ibid., p. 31.

[95] Ibid., p. 33.

[96] Ibid., p. 34.

[97] Ibid., p. 36.

[98]Ibid., p. 114.

[99]Ibid., pp. 126-7.

[100]Ibid., p. 227.

[101]Ibid., p. 232.

[102]Ibid., p. 235.   Le Clerc himself evidently understood these objections quite well, for he goes on to offer specific refutation of these, an exposition of which I shall defer to our discussion of the problem of miracles.

[103]Richard   Simon,   Histoire critique du Texte du Nouveau Testament (Rotterdam: 1689; rep. ed.: Frankfurt; Minerva, 1968), p. 192. See also Richard Simon, Réponse au livre intitulé Sentimens de quelques théologiens de Hollande sur l'Histoire critique du Vieux Testament (Rotterdam: Renier Leers, 1686), p. 128.

[104]Simon,   Histoire critique du Texte du Nouveau Testament, p. 208.

[105]Le Clerc, Sentimens, p. 158; cf. Jean Le Clerc, Défense des Sentimens de quelques théologiens de Hollande sur l'Histoire Critique du Vieux Testament contre le prieur de Bolleville (Amsterdam: Henri Desbordes, 1686), p. 245.

[106]Le Clerc, Sentimens, pp. 171-3.

[107]See   Simon's   Réponse au livre intitulé: Sentimens de quelques théologiens de Hollande (1686). Le Clerc responded to Simon in Défense des Sentimens de quelques théologiens de Hollande (1686); Simon struck back in his De l'inspiration des livres sacrés avec une réponse au livre intitulé Défense des Sentimens, etc. (1687).

[108]Monod, De Pascal à Chateaubriand, p. 201.   So also Luigi Salvatorelli, "From Locke to Reitzenstein: The Historical Investigation of the Origins of Christianity," Harvard Theological Review 22 (1929): 271.

[109]On   Collins's   contribution   to   biblical hermeneutics, see Hans W. Frei, The Eclipse of the biblical Narrative: a Study in Eighteenth and Nineteenth Century Hermeneutics (New Haven and London:

Yale University Press, 1974), pp. 66-85). According to
Frei, Collins's chief contribution lay in his taking
account of the human author as an independent factor.

[110]Anthony Collins, A Discourse of Free-Thinking,
Occasion'd by the Growth of a Sect call'd Free-Thinkers
(London: n.p., 1713), p. 58.

[111]Phileleutherus Lipsiensis [Richard Bentley],
Remarks Upon a Late Discourse of Free-Thinking (London:
n.p., 1737). On the debate see Gerald Cragg, Reason
and Authority in the Eighteenth Century   (Cambridge:
Cambridge University Press, 1964), p. 74.

[112]Anthony Collins, A Discourse on the Ground and
Reason of the Christian Religion (n.p.: n.p., [1724]),
pp. 135-6.

[113]Ibid., pp. 14, 20.

[114]Monod, De Pascal à Chateaubriand, p. 204.
Cragg would agree:
    "The Deists were trying to evolve a critical
    approach to the Bible, but they lacked the
    necessary tools--historical understanding and
    technical skill . . . . Both Tindal and Collins
    quoted the great French critic R. Simon, but they
    saw only the destructive potentialities latent in
    his theories.

    [1]Tindal, Christianity as Old, p. 46; Collins, The
    Scheme of Historical Prophecy Considered   pp.
    71-2." (Cragg, Reason and Authority, p. 84.)

[115]Stephen, English Thought, p. 176. Stephen's
charge that Bentley undermined the theory of verbal
inspiration by admitting errors in the transmitted text
and the necessity of a critical apparatus is curious,
since the defenders of that doctrine maintained that
only the autographs were free from error.

[116]John Leland, A View of the Principal Deistical
Writers that have appeared in England in the last and
present Century with Observations upon them and some
Account of the Answers that have been published against
them (London: for B. Dod at the Bible and Key, 1754),
pp. 394-5. Already in 1697 Leslie complains that the
sacred Scriptures, especially the histories of Moses
and Christ, is turned into ridicule. (Leslie, Short and
Easie Method, p. 2.)

[117] Monod, De Pascal à Chateaubriand, p. 31. For a good example, see Voltaire, Dictionnaire, s.v. "Genese," in which he refers to ibn Ezra, Spinoza, and Astruc.

[118] Translator's preface to Le Clerc, Sentimens, p. 7.

[119] Ibid.

[120] Orr, English Deism, pp. 21-5.

[121] Lord Edward Herbert of Cherbury, The Antient Religion of the Gentiles, and Causes of their Errors Considered (London: John Nutt, 1705), pp. 3-4. In De veritate the principles read: (1) Esse aliquod supremum numen. (2) Numen illud coli debere. (3) Virtutem cum pietate conjunctam optiman esse rationem cultus divini. (4) Resipiscendum esse a peccatis. (5) Dari proemium vel poenam post hanc vitam transactam. The principle most often disputed by subsequent Deists was the fifth.

[122] Herbert of Cherbury, Antient Religion, p. 364.

[123] Ibid., p. 318.

[124] Rousseau, "Profession de foi," pp. 131-2, 134, 144.

[125] Ibid., pp. 137-8, 147.

[126] Ibid., pp. 152, 160-1.

[127] Ibid., p. 168.

[128] Rousseau, "Lettre à M. De Beaumont," p. 303. Voltaire scribbled in the margin, "On a trouvé cette plaisanterie mauvaise, elle me parait fort bonne."

[129] Rousseau, "Profession de foi," p. 169.

[130] Jean-Jacques Rousseau, Contrat Social: "De la religion civile," in Religious Writings, p. 209.

[131] Ibid.

[132] Ibid., p. 212.

[133] Ibid.

[134]Voltaire, Dictionnaire, s.v., "Religion."

[135]Ibid., s.v. "Dieu."

[136]Ibid., s.v. "Religion."

[137]Ibid., s.v. "Miracles."

[138]Ibid., s.v. "Christianisme."

[139]Ibid., s.v. "Religion."

[140]Thomas Woolston, A Discourse on the Miracles of Our Saviour, 5th ed. (London: author, 1728), p. 2. Many writers on the history of the Deist controversy seem to share a similar view.   They suggest that from the a priori reasoning of Clarke, there is a turning to the empirical evidences.   When the proof from prophecy is destroyed, apologists turn to miracles.   With the further attack upon miracles, they rally around the resurrection.   This account, however, seems mistaken. It is inaccurate to speak of a departure from the a priori arguments of Clarke, for Clarke as a rationalist stands as something of an anomaly in post-Lockean Britain.   He belongs much more to the tradition of Continental rationalism.   If one takes Locke as a more representative point of departure, then it is not evident that apologetics experiences so fundamental a shift toward empiricism after the start of the eighteenth century.   Certainly this is the great century of Christian evidences, but that involves an increasing sophistication in the approach already popular in the seventeenth, not a shift from it. Besides, this is to leave wholly out of account Clarke's own evidentialism in his Boyle lectures of 1705, which serve as a sequel to his 1704 lectures on the existence of God.   In proving the truth of Christianity, he employs the proofs from fulfilled prophecy and miracle, characteristic of apologies before and after him.   It needs to be remembered that Clarke's a priori reasoning concerned only God's existence; but the only way to prove Christian theism was by the facts.   Since in the Deist controversy, it was unnecessary to prove God's existence, apologists focused their efforts on strengthening the factual case for Christian theism; Hence, the appearance of increasing empiricism.

As to Woolston's contention, it is incorrect to think orthodox divines turned to miracles to support Christianity when the bottom fell out of the proof from prophecy.   Miracle was always one of the two signs of

credibility with prophecy. The proof from prophecy,
however, enjoyed the advantage that it was simply a
matter of matching up prophecy and fulfillment in the
two testaments, whereas the proof from miracles, if it
was not to be question-begging, required at least a
sense of historical methodology. During the
seventeenth century, we see the proof from miracles
assume an important role in evidential apologetics.
Grotius elevates it over the proof from prophecy.
Pascal appeals to miracles and prophecies. Abbadie
argues at length for the historicity of Christ's
miracles as proof of Christianity. Locke employs the
proof from miracles to demonstrate the reasonableness
of Christianity. Leslie's "short and easy method" is
the proof from miracles. Clarke, we have said, used
both proofs. Thus, it seems incorrect to say that
apologists turned to the proof from miracles after
Collins's attack, for they had been vigorously
employing it all along. Rather what they emphasized
was that, in the formulation of Bullock, because of the
argument from miracles the proof from prophecy is not
necessary to a rational defense of the Christian
religion and that in any case the proof from prophecy
does provide such a rational foundation also.
(Bullock, The Reasoning of Christ and His apostles
vindicated [1728]; cf. Leland, A View of the Principal
Deistical Writers, p. 123.) Collins's attack on
prophecy provoked more than 30 replies, and the debate
over prophecy raged from about 1724 to 1728. (See
Gotthard Victor Lechler, Geschichte des englischen
Deismus [Stuttgart & Tübingen: 1841; rep. ed.:
Hildesheim: Georg Olms, 1965], pp. 266-88.) The best
of these was Sherlock's The Use and Intent of Prophecy
(1725), which Frei judges to be "a perfectly reasonable
defense of typology or figuration" (Frei, Eclipse of
the biblical Narrative, p. 70). "Though [Collins]
referred to Sherlock's essay frequently and
respectfully, he did not come to grips with the thrust
of his thought." (Ibid., p. 72). Then came Woolston's
attack. Since the Deist controversy was primarily a
reflexive movement consisting of replies and counter-
replies, this new attack turned the focus of the debate
to new grounds.
     It hardly needs to be added that the historical
argument for the resurrection did not only then take on
primary importance. The apologies of Grotius, Le
Clerc, and Ditton depend entirely on the evidence for
the resurrection, and this event was crucial in the
evidences of Abbadie and others. It just happens that
when Woolston in his sixth discourse attacked the
resurrection of Jesus, Sherlock replied, and so began

the controversy over the resurrection narratives.

[141]Woolston, First Discourse, p. 4.

[142]Thomas Woolston, A Sixth Discourse on the
Miracles of our Saviour (London: author, 1729), p. 50.
The Earl of Shaftesbury even went so far as to declare
ability to survive ridicule to be one of the tests of
truth.   But ridicule as a weapon was never more
skillfully employed than by Voltaire.   Woolston used
mockery like a bludgeon, Voltaire wielded satire like a
rapier.   Even the most soberly orthodox reader of
Voltaire may find himself trying to repress a smile at
the Frenchman's carefully barbed wit.   Rousseau, too,
could employ ridicule to good advantage.   Consider his
treatment of the Gaderene demoniac:
    "Jesus asks a group of demons what their names
    are.   What?   Demons have names?   Angels have
    names? Pure spirits have names? Probably for use
    among themselves or to hear when God calls them?
    But who gave them these names?   In what language
    are the words?   Which are the mouths which
    pronounce these words, the ears that their sounds
    strike?   The name is Legion, for they are many,
    which apparently Jesus did not know.   These
    angels, these sublime intelligences in evil as in
    good, these celestial beings who could revolt
    against God, who dare to combat his eternal
    decrees, lodge as a pack in the body of a man!
    Forced to abandon this unfortunate man, they ask
    to cast themselves upon a herd of swine; they get
    this; the swine precipitate themselves into the
    sea.   And these are the august proofs of the
    mission of the Redeemer of the human race, the
    proofs which have to attest to all peoples of all
    ages, and of which no one should doubt under pain
    of damnation! Good God! The head swims; one does
    not know where one is.   These, sirs, are the
    foundations of your faith?   Mine has surer ones,
    it seems to me." (Jean-Jacques Rousseau, "Lettres
    écrites de la montagne," in Religious Writings, p.
    363.)

[143]Thomas Woolston, A Second Discourse on the
Miracles of Our Saviour, 3d ed. (London: author,
1728), p. 67.   The teasing use of sexual imagery was a
favorite device among free-thinkers.   Similar to
Woolston's satire here is Voltaire's observation that
Cleopatra, when told by the Jews of our resurrection at
the last day, asked if we should rise again quite
naked. (Voltaire, Dictionnaire, s.v. "Christianisme,"

ibid., s.v. "Resurrection.") Voltaire in his article
on miracles speaks warmly of Woolston, calling him a
learned member of the University of Cambridge, and
quotes him at length. (Voltaire, Dictionnaire, s.v.
"Miracles.")

[144]For an account see B. Robert Kreiser, Miracles,
Convulsions, and Ecclesiastical Politics in Early
Eighteenth Century Paris (Princeton: Princeton
University Press, 1978); for literature on current
assessment of these healings, see Colin Brown, Miracles
and the Critical Mind (Grand Rapids, Mich.:   Wm. B.
Eerdmans, 1984), p. 336.

[145]Marie   Huber,   Lettres sur la religion
essentielle a l'homme, distinguée de ce qui n'en est
que l'accessoire, 3d ed. (London: Nourse, 1756),
Intro.

[146]Diderot,   Philosophical Thoughts,   Pensées
LI-LIV.

[147]Conyers Middleton,   Free Inquiry into the
Miraculous Powers, Which are supposed to have subsided
in the Christian Church (London: R. Manby & H.S. Cox,
1749).

[148]See discussion in Brown, Miracles, pp. 64-72;
Stephen, English Thought, pp. 222-7, for an analysis of
Middleton's contribution.

[149]David   Hume,   An Enquiry concerning Human
Understanding   in   Enquiries concerning Human
Understanding and concerning the Principles of Morals,
ed. with an Introduction by L.A. Selby-Bigge, 3d ed.,
ed. P.H. Nidditch (Oxford: Clarendon Press, 1975),
10.2.96, pp. 124-5.

[150]Rousseau, "Lettre à M. De Beaumont," p. 293.

[151]On Voltaire's dependence on Middleton at this
point, see Norman L. Torrey, Voltaire and the English
Deists (New Haven, Conn.:   Yale University Press,
1930), pp. 159-63.

[152]Voltaire, Dictionnaire, s.v. "Miracles."

[153]See   bibliography   in   Monod,   Pascal à
Chateaubriand, p. 351; See also note 144.

[154]Stephen,   English Thought,   p.   227;   Brown,

Miracles, pp. 65, 72.

[155]Martin Luther De servo arbitrio in Werke
(Weimar: 1908), 18:603-10.

[156]Jean Calvin Institutio Christianae religionis
1.7-8.

[157]See Gustave Thils, Les Notes de l'église dans
l'apologétique depuis la réforme, Universitas Catholica
Lovaniensis 2:30 (Gembloux: J. Duculot, 1937); René
Voeltzel, Vraie et fausse église selon les théologiens
protestants français du XII siècle (Paris: Presses
universitaires, 1955).

[158]Bellarminus Disputationem . . . De Controver-
siis Christianei Fidei,   adversus huis temporis
Haereticos 2:80A.

[159]Pierre Du Moulin, Nouveauté du Papisme, opposée
a l'antiquité du vray christianisme (Geneva: Pierre
Chouet, 1627), pp. 160-1.

[160]Michel de Montaigne, Journal de voyage, 2d ed.,
ed. with an Introduction by Louis Lautrey (Paris:
Hachette, 1909).

[161]Raimundus Sabundus Liber creaturarum 68; 208.

[162]Michel de Montaigne, "Apologie de Raimond
Sebond," in Les essais de Michel de Montaigne, new ed.,
ed. Pierre Villey (Paris: F. Alcan, 1922), 2:148-9.

[163]Ibid., p. 150.

[164]Ibid., pp. 329-49.

[165]Ibid., p. 325.

[166]Ibid., pp. 353-66.

[167]Ibid., pp. 366-7.

[168]Ibid., pp. 236-7.

[169]Ibid., pp. 238-9. (Translation by D.M. Frame.)

[170]Richard Popkin, The History of Scepticism from
Erasmus to Descartes, rev. ed. (New York: Harper &
Row; Harper Torchbooks, 1968), pp. 53-4.

171 Ibid., p. 55.

172 Ibid., p. 111. This was the group, it will be remembered, among whom Hobbes sojourned while in France.

173 Herbert of Cherbury, Antient Religion, p. 357.

174 John Locke An Essay concerning Human Understanding 1.3.15-19. "Though I allow these to be clear truths, and as such, if rightly explained, a rational creature can hardly avoid giving his assent to; yet, I think, he is far from proving them innate impressions in foro interiori descriptae. . . ." (ibid. 1.3.15.)

175 William Chillingworth, The Religion of Protestants, A Safe Way to Salvation, in The Works of William Chillingworth (London: M. Clark, 1704).

176 John Tillotson, A Discourse against Transsubstantiation, in The Works of Dr. John Tillotson, 10 vols., ed. Thomas Burch (London: Richard Priestly, 1820): 2:407-52.

177 Stephen, English Thought, pp. 65-6; that is to say, the assumptions shared by Catholics and Protestants (eg., special revelation) were attacked by Deists on the basis of the same rationalist principles on the basis of which Protestants attacked Catholics.

178 Walter Rex, Essays on Pierre Bayle and Religious Controversy, International Archives of the History of Ideas 8 (The Hague: Martinus Nijhoff: 1965), p. xii.

179 Pierre Bayle, Pensées diverses sur la comète, 2 vols., ed. with an Introduction and Notes by A. Prat (Paris: Librairie E. Droz, 1939).

180 Ibid., 1:248-9; 2:118.

181 Ibid., 1:332-3.

182 Rex, Essays, p. 51.

183 Ibid., p. 35.

184 Pierre Jurieu, Examen de l'eucharistie de l'Eglise Romaine (Rotterdam: Renier Leers, 1682), pp. 278-92.

[185]Pierre Bayle, Commentaire philosophique sur ces paroles de Jésus-Christ "Contrain-les d'entrer",   in Oeuvres diverses de Mr. Pierre Bayle, 4 vols. (The Hague: 1727-31), 2:367A.

[186]Ibid., 2:368A.

[187]Rex, Essays, p. 158. Taken in isolation, he muses, the paragraph sounds like a preliminary sketch of the frontispiece to the Encyclopedie: "Is there not a hint at least of those gracious allegorical figures of the Enlightenment depicting Lady Reason gently but resolutely preparing to press an iron bit into the charming mouth of Lady Revelation who kneels before her?" (Ibid., pp. 158-9.)

[188]Jean Daillé, Apologie des Eglises Réformées, où est monstrée la nécessité de leur séparation d'avec l'Eglise Romaine; Contre ceux qui les accusent de faire Schisme en la Chrestienté (Paris: Louis Vendosme, 1633), pp. 39-49.

[189]Jurieu, Examen, pp. 108-20.

[190]Bayle, Commentaire philosophique, p. 430B.

[191]Richard Popkin, "Introduction," in The Philosophy of the 16th and 17th Centuries, ed. R. Popkin, Readings in the History of Philosophy (New York: Free Press, 1966), pp. 21-2.

[192]Cited in Elisabeth Labrousse, Pierre Bayle, 2 vols., International Archives of the History of Ideas I (The Hague: Martinus Nijhoff, 1963), 1:255.

[193]Pierre   Bayle,   Dictionnaire historique et critique, 3d ed. s.v. "Bunel, Pierre."

[194]Pierre Bayle, "Réponse aux questions d'un provincial," in Oeuvres diverses, ed. with Notes by Alain Niderst, Les classiques du peuple (Paris: Editions sociales, 1971), p. 156.

[195]Bayle, Dictionnaire, s.v. "Acosta, Uriel."

[196]Ibid., s.v. "Pyrrhon."

[197]Ibid., s.v. "Acosta."

[198]Ibid., s.v. "Charron, Pierre."

[199] Ibid., s.v. "Maniche'ens"; c.f. "Pauliciens."

[200] Ibid., s.v. "Maniche'ens."

[201] Ibid., s.v. "Pauliciens."

[202] Ibid., s.v. "Marcionites."

[203] When Jacquelot defended the coherence of
Christian theism in Conformité de la foi avec la raison
(1705), Bayle tightened the argument from evil in his
Réponse aux questions by challenging Jacquelot to show
how the doctrines of God and sin (viz., [1] God,
infinitely powerful and good, possesses eternally a
glory which can neither be augmented nor diminished.
[2] God freely chooses from among all possible beings
those He wants to exist. [3] He created man with a
free will so that he might obey or disobey. [4] Man
sinned and incurred condemnation to misery, physical
death, eternal damnation, and an inclination to sin.
[5] God chose to deliver and save a small number of men
from this fate. [6] God foresaw all this and governs
everything such that nothing happens against His will.
[7] He offers grace to those He knows will not accept
it, thereby increasing their condemnation, and urges
them ardently to accept it, while withholding the grace
that would make this possible.) Can be brought into
accord with the following philosophical maxims: (1)
Since God has all glory, His act of creation can only
be because of His goodness, not a desire to augment His
glory. (2) His goodness is infinite, such that a
greater goodness is inconceivable. (3) He made known
His perfections in the world only in order that
creatures could find their happiness in knowledge of
them. (4) His blessings which are given to creatures
tend only to their happiness. (5) He could not give
creatures free will if He knows they will use it such
that they become unhappy. If He gives free will, He
will ensure it is used properly. If He cannot, He will
remove this faculty, rather than let it cause
unhappiness. (6) One may just as effectively kill a
man by giving him a silk ribbon which one knows he will
use to strangle himself as stabbing him oneself; it
would be especially wrong to put all the blame on him.
(7) A true benefactor will give his gift quickly rather
than make the recipient first suffer a long time. If
he can achieve good directly, he will do so, rather
than indirectly by allowing evils. (8) A Master's
greatest glory is to maintain virtue, order, peace, and
happiness among his subjects. (9) The greatest love of
virtue a Master could show would be to see it practiced

with no mixture of vice. (10) The greatest hatred of
vice is to prevent its ever appearing, rather than to
permit it a long time and then punish it. (11) A
Master interested in the virtue and good of his
subjects will do all he can to see that they never
disobey his laws; if he must punish, it will only be to
remedy the inclination to evil and to restore the
dispostion to good. (12) It is a great fault to allow
disorder in one's state; it is especially contemptible
if one secretly foments it oneself so that one can
receive glory in saving the state. (13) It is
excusable to permit an evil if the attempt to remedy it
would introduce a greater evil; but if one has the
power to remedy not only the evil but any others which
might arise, to permit it is inexcusable. (14) Since
an infinite being controls all physical objects and all
thoughts, physical and moral evil could not be
permitted unless a greater evil would result from their
absence. (15) One is equally the cause of an event by
moral as by physical means. (16) It is impossible for
a being to be free with regard to that to which it is
already determined. (17) When a great people have
rebelled, it is not merciful to save a tiny part and
execute all the rest. (18) If a doctor has many
remedies for a disease and he chooses to administer the
one which he knows the patient will reject, he really
has no desire to heal him. (Bayle, Réponse aux
questions, pp. 166-71.)

[204] Bayle, Dictionnaire, s.v. "Maniche'ens."

[205] Ibid., s.v. "Pauliciens." He reiterates these
sentiments in Réponse aux questions, pp. 154-55. Once
you admit Scripture, he says, the dispute is over; the
problem of evil cannot arise.

[206] Bayle, Dictionnaire, s.v. "Maniche'ens."

[207] Ibid., s.v. "Pauliciens." Cf. Bayle, Réponse
aux questions, p. 156.

[208] Bayle, Dictionnaire, s.v. "Maniche'ens."

[209] Ibid., s.v. "Pyrrhon."

[210] Bayle scholars remain divided on this issue.
Maintaining the view that Bayle was an irreligious
sceptic are Howard Robinson, Bayle the Skeptic (New
York: 1931); E.D. James, "Scepticism and Fideism in
Bayle's Dictionnaire," French Studies 16 (1962):
307-24; H.T. Mason, "Pierre Bayle's Religious Views,"

French Studies 17 (1963):   205-17.   Challenging the
Enlightenment   view   of   Bayle   and   interpreting   his
fideism sympathetically are W.H. Barber, "Bayle: Faith
and Reason," in _The French Mind: Studies in Honour of
Gustav Rudler_, ed. W.G. Moore, R. Sutherland, and E.
Starkie (Oxford: Clarendon Press, 1952), pp. 109-25;
Richard   Popkin,   "The   Sceptical   Precursors   of   David
Hume," _Philosophy and Phenomenological Research_ 16
(1955):   61-71; Elisabeth Labrousse, _Pierre Bayle_,,   2
vols., vol. 2:   _hêterodoxie et rigorisme_, Archives
Internationales   d'Histoire   des   Idées   1   (The   Hague:
Martinus Nijhoff, 1964); K.C. Sandberg, "Pierre Bayle's
Sincerity in His Views on Faith and Reason," _Studies in
Philology_ 61 (1964):   74-84; Walter Rex, _Essays on
Pierre Bayle and Religious Controversy_,   International
Archives   of   the   History   of   Ideas   8   (The   Hague:
Martinus Nijhoff, 1965).

[211]Cited in Labrousse, _Pierre Bayle_, 1:269.

[212]Bayle, _Dictionnaire_, s.v. "Pyrrhon."

[213]For example, Anthony, Earl of Shaftesbury,
Characteristics of Men, Manners, Opinions, Times, etc.,
2 vols. (London: Grant Richards, 1900), 1:109-11, 151;
2:61, 189-94, 227; Collins, _Discourse_, pp. 91-9; idem,
Ground and Reason, pp. 104-05; Bernard de Mandeville,
The Fable of the Bees; or Private Vices Public Benefits
(London: Allen and West; Edinburgh: J. Mundell,
1795), pp. 87-90, 228; Thomas Woolston, _Free Gifts to
the Clergy_, in _The Works of Thomas Woolston_, 5 vols.
(London: J. Roberts, 1733), vol. 3; Thomas Chubb, _The
Posthumous Works of Mr. Thomas Chubb_, 2 vols. (London:
R. Baldwin, 1748), 1:41-55; 2:57-60, 221; Voltaire,
Dictionnaire, s.v. "Dieu."

[214]Cragg, _Reason and Authority_, p. 76.

[215]Voltaire, _Dictionnaire_, s.v. "Dieu."

[216]Ostervald, _Traité de la corruption_ (Neuchatel:
1700), pp. 16-17, cited in Monod, _De Pascal à
Chateaubriand_, p. 211.

[217]Rousseau, "Profession de foi," pp. 170-1.   Cf.
the comment of Diderot:
    "I hear cries against impiety on every side.   The
    Christian is impious in Asia, the Mussulman in
    Europe, the papist in London, the Calvinist in
    Paris, the Jansenist at the top of the rue St.
    Jacques, the Molinist at the bottom of the

Faubourg St. Médard. What is an impious person
then? Either everybody, or nobody." (Diderot,
"Philosophical Thoughts," Pensée XXXV.)

[218]See James Westphal Thompson, The Wars of
Religion in France, 1559-1576; the Huguenots, Catherine
de Medici, Philip II (New York: F. Ungar, 1957).

[219]G.A. Rothrock, The Huguenots: A Biography of a
Minority (Chicago: Nelson-Hall, 1979), pp. 94-5.

[220]Lechler, Geschichte des englischen Deismus, pp.
29-35.

[221]Robertson, Short History, p. 282.

[222]John Locke, "A Letter Concerning Toleration,"
in The Works of John Locke, 11th ed., 10 vols.; vol. 6:
Letters on Toleration (London: W. Olridge & Son,
1812), pp. 13-19.

[223]Ibid., pp. 10, 45, 47; idem, "A Third Letter
for Toleration," in Works, vol. 6: Letters on
Toleration, p. 212.

[224]Locke, "A Letter Concerning Toleration," p. 40.

[225]Rothrock, Huguenots, pp. 172-8.

[226]Spinoza Tractatus praef.

[227]Stephen, English Thought, p. 71.

[228]Voltaire, Dictionnaire, s.v. "Dieu."

[229]Ibid., s.v. "Religion."

[230]Ibid.

[231]Rousseau also believed that love of God and
neighbor is the essence of true Christianity and
declared himself a sincere Christian ("Comme il ment!"
Voltaire scribbled in his margin). The most true
religion is also the most humane and social.
(Rousseau, "Lettre à M. De Beaumont," pp. 264, 273.)
But Rousseau worked himself into a Baylean paradox when
it came to civil religion. For in the very preceding
paragraph to his remarks on the one negative doctrine
of civil religion's being intolerance, he declares,
        "There is thus a profession of faith purely civil
whose articles are to be fixed by the sovereign,

not precisely like dogmas of religion, but like
feelings of sociability without which it is
impossible(i) to be either a good citizen or loyal
subject.   Not being able to oblige anyone to
believe them, he can banish from the State anyone
who does not believe them; he can banish them, not
as impious, but as unsociable, as incapable of
sincerely loving the laws and justice and of
sacrificing out of necessity his life to his duty.
If someone, after having publicly recognized these
same dogmas, behaves as not believing them, he
shall be punished by death: he has committed the
greatest of crimes; he has lied before the laws.

_____

(i)
. . ."(Rousseau, "De la religion civile," p.
212.)

He later adds that those who believe that outside the
church there is no salvation should be chassé de
l'Etat.   (ibid., p. 213.)   The intolerance of
Rousseau's tolerance is thus the reverse side of
Bayle's tolerance of intolerance.

[232]Leland,   A View of the Principal Deistical
Writers, p. iii.

[233]Ibid., p.v.

[234]Herbert of Cherbury, Antient Religion, p. 366.
Curiously enough, Lord Herbert rather inconsistently
claimed to have himself heard a sign from God which
encouraged him to publish De veritate.   (Edward Lord
Herbert of Cherbury, Autobiography, pp. 133-4.)

[235]Hobbes, Leviathan, p. 200.

[236]Lechler, Geschichte des englischen Deismus, p.
107.

[237]Toland, Christianity not Mysterious, p. 6.

[238]Ibid., p. 37.

[239]Ibid., p. 108.

[240]Stephen, English Thought, p. 88.

[241]Between 1690 and 1700 a bitter dispute over
Trinitarianism raged in England.   In 1712 Clarke
published the Scripture Doctrine of the Trinity in

which he claimed to substitute a scriptural Trinity for a metaphysical Trinity, contending that both Athanasians and Arians were wrong. According to a story told by Voltaire, this lost him the Archbishopric of Canterbury, for when Queen Anne was about to bestow it upon him, Gibson discreetly intervened, remarking to Her Majesty that Clarke lacked but one thing to qualify as Archbishop: to be a Christian. (Voltaire, "Anti-Trinitarians," in Works, 39:220-1).

[242]Thomas Sherlock, Serm. for the prop. of the Gosp. in for. Parts, pp. 10, 13, cited by Tindal on the title page of Christianity as old as the Creation.

[243]Tindal,   Christianity as old as the Creation, pp. 367-8.

[244]Ibid., p. 375.

[245]Ibid., p. 370.

[246]Ibid., p. 378.

[247]Leland,   A View of the Principal Deistical Writers, p. 3.

[248]Rousseau, "Profession de foi," p. 124. Bergier, Rousseau's orthodox réfutateur, mocked his adulation of Clarke: So since not all people perceive natural revelation, we had to wait, did we, 6,000 years for Clarke? (Sylvestre Bergier, Le Déisme réfuté par lui-meme, ou examen, en forme des lettres,   des principes d'incrédulité répandus dans les divers ouvrages de J.-J. Rousseau, new ed. [Besançon: Imprimerie de Outhenin-Chalandre Fils, 1842], p. 38.)

[249]Voltaire, "Anti-Trinitarians," in Works, 39:220.

[250]Rousseau, "Profession de foi," p. 168.,

[251]James W. Thompson and Bernard J. Holm, A History of Historical Writing, 2 vols. (Gloucester, Mass.: Peter Smith, 1967), 2:3.

[252]Ibid., 2:94.

[253]J.A. Dorner, System der christlichen Glaubens- lehre, 3 vols., 2d ed. (Berlin: Wilhelm Hertz, 1886), 1:77-89.

[254]Hugo Grotius De veritate religionis Christianae
1.1.

[255]It is interesting to compare Mornay's work with
the precedent set by Calvin in the apologetic chapters
of the Institutes. Although Calvin appeals to miracles
and prophecy in confirmation of the Old Testament's
credibility, such proofs of the New Testament are
conspicuously absent, being supplanted by proofs based
on the harmony and majesty of the New Testament writers
and by proofs from the existence and universality of
the church. (Jean Calvin Institutio Christianae
religionis 1.5,8.)

[256]Philippe de Mornay, De la vérité de la religion
chrestienne (Anvers: Imprimerie de Christofle Plantin,
1581), pp. 1-61, 493-509, 547-80, 648-81, 681-784.

[257]Ibid., p. 835.

[258]Ibid., preface.

[259]Ibid.

[260]Ibid., p. 836.

[261]Ibid., pp. 836-7.

[262]Ibid., pp. 843, 845-6.

[263]Dulles, History, p. 122.

[264]Pablo Graf, Luis Vives commo Apologeta:
Contribución a la Historia de la Apologética, trans.
Jose M. Millas Vallicrosa (Madrid: Consejo Superior de
Investigaciones Científicas, 1943), p. 135; cf. p. 153.

[265]Ibid., pp. 69-72.

[266]Juan Luis Vives De veritate fidei christianae
8.

[267]Ibid. 9.

[268]Ibid. 18.

[269]Otto Zöckler, Geschichte der Apologie des
Christentums (Gütersloh: Bertelsmann, 1907), p. 317.

[270]Graf, Vives pp. 144-7.

[271] According to Grotius, he had read both ancient and modern apologetic treatises and culled out the weightiest arguments. (Grotius De veritate 1.1.)

[272] Adolf von Harnack, Lehrbuch der Dogmengeschichte, 3 vols., 4th ed., Sammlung theologischer Bücher 1, vol. 3: Die Entwicklung des kirchlichen Dogmas II, III (Tübingen: J.C.B. Mohr, 1909), pp. 785, 774.

[273] Catechesis Ecclesiarum quae in Regno Poloniae, etc. 5.7.

[274] Ibid. 5.8

[275] Ibid.

[276] Ibid. 5.1.

[277] Ibid. 4.1.

[278] Ibid. (1680 version)

[279] Ibid. 5.8. (1680 version)

[280] Ibid. 6.

[281] Ibid. 7.

[282] Ibid. 1.2. (1680 version)

[283] Ibid. (1680 version)

[284] Harncack, Entwicklung des Dogmas, p. 787. It is not the first attempt to establish the authority of Scripture without appealing to faith, as we have seen; but it may be the first attempt which considered the alternate approach by faith to be illicit. According to Knox, "More than any other group the Socinians were the precursors of the outlook which made rationality the decisive test of what was acceptable in religion." (R. Buick Knox, "The History of Doctrine in the Seventeenth Century," in A History of Christian Doctrine, ed. Hubert Cunliffe-Jones [Philadelphia: Fortress Press, 1980], p. 440.)

[285] Ibid. 1.1. In the 1680 version, appeal is also made to the great multiplicity of copies made in different places and languages in order to refute the charge of textual corruption.

[286] Ibid. 1.1. "For, as he asserted that he

wrought miracles by a divine power, it is evident,
since God after his crucifixion restored him to life,
that what he declared was true -- namely, that his
miracles were divine." In the 1680 version, it is also
argued that the holiness of Jesus's doctrine makes it
impossible to ascribe his miracles to the devil.

[287] Rees adduces the testimony of one Dr.
Smallbrook, bishop of St. David's, to the effect that
Grotius was dependent upon a work by Socinus De
auctoritate sancti scripturale (Latin ed. 1611), but I
have not been able to pursue this assertion. (Thomas
Rees, Notes to Racovian Catechism [London: Longman,
Hurst, Rees, Orme, and Brown, 1818], p. 10.)

[288] See especially 2.7, 18; note also the Socinian
emphasis on Christ's exaltation's being proved by his
bestowal of miraculous gifts; cf. 2.1.

[289] For example, in 1614 he wrote his Defensio
fidei catholicae de satisfactione Christi, in which he
attacks Socinus's theory of the atonement. But
Grotius's own theory, unlike Anselm's, lacks any
rationale for Christ's being God as well as man.

[290] Grotius De veritate 2.1.

[291] Bayle praised it in his Dictionnaire, s.v.
"Grotius"; Leibniz in his fifth letter to Burnet said
he preferred it to all modern apologies.

[292] Grotius De veritate 2.2.

[293] Ibid., 2.3,4.

[294] Ibid., 2.5.

[295] Ibid., 2.6.

[296] Ibid., 2.7.

[297] Ibid., 2.8.

[298] Ibid., 2.9.

[299] Ibid., 2.7.

[300] Tholuck observes that Grotius's work served as
the model and instigator of countless other apologetic
works in England, France, and Germany. (August
Tholuck, "Über Apologetik und ihre Litteratur," in

Vermischte Schriften grösstentheils apologetischen
Inhalts, 2 vols. [Hamburg: Friedrich Perthes, 1859],
1:157.

[301] Blaise   Pascal,   Les Pensées,   in   Oeuvres
complètes,   3   vols.,   ed.   with   a   Biography,
Introductions, Notes, and Tables by Fortunat Strowski
(Paris: Albin Michel, 1931), 3:18, 219.   See also
Fortunat Strowski, Pascal et son temps, Histoire du
sentiment religieux en France au XVIIᵉ siècle (Paris:
Plon-Nourrit, 1907).

[302] Blaise Pascal, "Le Miracle de Sainte Epine," in
Oeuvres, 2:435, 439.

[303] Ibid., 2:447-8.

[304] Ibid., 2:440.

[305] Ibid., 2:452.

[306] Pascal, Pensées, 3:25.

[307] Ibid., 3:236.

[308] Monod, De Pascal à Chateaubriand, p. 61.

[309] Ibid.

[310] Ibid., p. 65.

[311] Filleau de la Chaise, "Discours sur les preuves
des livres de Moise," in idem, Discours sur les pensées
de M. Pascal, ed. with an Introduction by Victor
Giraud, Collection des chefs-d'oeuvre méconnues (Paris:
Editions Bossard, 1922), p. 105.

[312] Ibid., pp. 104-5.

[313] Monod, De Pascal à Chateaubriand, p. 16.

[314] Malebranche,   Conversations chrétiennes, dans
lesquels on justifie la vérité de la religion et de la
morale de Jésus-Christ, ed. with an Intrtroduction by
L. Bridet (Paris: Librairie Garnier Freres, 1929).

[315] For a good statement, see ibid., pp. 24-5; cf.
Nicolas Malebranche, Dialogues on Metaphysics and
Religion, trans. Morris Ginsberg (London: George Allen
& Unwin, 1923), pp. 177-201.   According to Malebranche,
"That which is the cause of suffering is neither the

soul which feels nor the thorn which pricks; it is a
superior power." (Malebranche, Conversations
chrétiennes, p. 25). This is God, who, knowing the
occasion of the thorn prick, causes pain. Such
implications helped to catapult Bayle, who was much
influenced by Malebranche, into insoluble difficulties
concerning the problem of evil.

[316]Malebranche, Conversations chrétiennes, pp.
157-66.

[317]Petri Danielis Huetii Demonstratio evangelica
(Lipiae: J. Thomam Fritsch, 1694). Monod ridicules
the "gaucherie philosophique de Huet." (Monod, De
Pascal à Chateaubriand, p. 86.)

[318]Jacques-Benigne Bossuet, Discourse on Universal
History, trans. Elborg Forster, ed. with an
Introduction by Orest Ranum, Classic European
Historians (Chicago: University of Chicago Press,
1976); on the fulfillment of Messianic prophecies, see
pp. 177-202.

[319]Pierre Bayle, Nouvelles de la République des
Lettres 2 (1684): 309. When Bussy wrote to Madame de
Sevigne that "We are presently reading it and find
there is no other book in the world to be read"
(Lettre, 5 juillet, 1688), she replied, "It is the most
divine of all books; this estimation is general. I do
not think that anyone has ever spoken of religion like
that man." (Lettre, 13 aout, 1688) See Monod, De
Pascal à Chateaubriand, pp. 100-1 for more accolades
showered upon Abbadie.

[320]Monod, De Pascal à Chateaubriand, p. 517.

[321]Jacques Abbadie, Traité de la vérrité de la
religion chrétienne (The Hague: Jean Neaulme, 1771),
2:1.

[322]Ibid., 2:3-30.

[323]Ibid., 2: 31-135.

[324]Ibid., 2: 32-3.

[325]Ibid., 2: 36-41.

[326]Ibid., 2: 41-59.

[327]Ibid., 2: 47-8.

[328]Ibid., 2: 50-4.

[329]Ibid., 2: 54-9.

[330]Ibid., 2: 136-53.

[331]Ibid., 2: 153-71.

[332]Ibid., 2: 167-8.

[333]Ibid., 2: 171-86.

[334]Ibid., 2: 203-4. The truth of these principles may be readily seen, says Abbadie, by stating them negatively and observing how patently false they then appear.

[335]Monod, De Pascal à Chateaubriand, p. 185.

[336]See the very interesting discussion on faith and reason in Locke, Essay, 4.18.

[337]In Locke's words, "And therefore no proposition can be received for divine revelation, or obtain the assent due to all such, if it be contradictory to our clear intuitive knowledge, because this would be to subvert the principles and foundations of all knowledge, evidence, and assent whatsoever . . . . faith can never convince us of any thing that contradicts our knowledge, because, though faith be founded on the testimony of God (who cannot lie) revealing any proposition to us, yet we cannot have an assurance of the truth of its being a divine revelation greater than our own knowledge . . . ." (Locke, Essay 4.18.5.)

[338]Ibid., 4.18.10.

[339]John Locke, The Reasonableness of Christianity, Works 7: 135-9, 148-51.

[340]John Locke, A discourse on Miracles, in Works, 9: 256-64; cf. idem, Essay 4.19.15. In Reasonableness of Christianity he also emphasizes fulfilled prophecy.

[341]Locke, Essay, 4.17.23; 4.18.7.

[342]Adam Storey Farrar, A Critical History of Free Thought in Reference to the Christian Religion (New York: D. Appleton, 1863), p. 140.

[343] Leslie, Short and Easie Method, pp. 6-7.

[344] Ibid., pp. 7-8.   The rules are printed in old English characters, perhaps thereby to enhance their air of authority.

[345] Charles Leslie, "Tract on Private Authority and Judgement," in Theological Works (Oxford: 1832), 1:390, cited in Stephen, English Thought, p. 166.

[346] Leslie, Short and Easie Method, p. 36.

[347] Stephen, English Thought, p. 169.

[348] Lewis   White   Beck,   "Introduction,"   in 18th-Century Philosophy, Readings in the History of Philosophy (New York: Free Press, 1966), p. 3.

[349] "Dieu ne peut nous révéler, et nous ne pouvons croire que ce qui est démontré vrai."   (Bergier, Le Déisme réfuté par lui-même, pp. 4-5.)

[350] Ibid., p. 8.

[351] Ibid., p. 12.

[352] Ibid., p. 18.

[353] Ibid., p. 30.

[354] Ibid., p. 69.

[355] Ibid., p. 80.

[356] Houtteville, La religion chrétienne prouvée par les faits, 3 vols. (Paris: Mercier & Boudet, 1740), 1: preface.

[357] Ibid., 1:5.

[358] Ibid., 1:6-18.

[359] Ibid., 1:21-2.

[360] Ibid., 1:29-31.

[361] See August Tholuck, "Über Apologetik und ihre Litteratur" in idem, Vermischte Schriften grössten-theils apologetischen Inhalts, 2 vols. (Hamburg: Friedrich Perthes, 1859), 1:311-76.

362Lechler, Geschichte des englischen Deismus, p. 447.

363Johann Friedrich Kleuker, Neue Prüfung und Erklärung der vorzüglichsten Beweise für die Wahrheit und den göttlichen Ursprung des Christenthums, 3 vols. (Riga: Johann Friedrich Hartknach, 1787). Tholuck says of Kleuker that he is on a level above almost all other German apologists, but has remained unrecognized. (Tholuck, "Apologetik," pp. 365-6.)

364Kleuker, Neue Prüfung, pp. 14-15.

365Ibid., p. 284.

366Ibid., pp. 297-8.

367Gottfried Less, Wahrheit der christlichen Religion, 4th ed. (Göttingen and Bremen: Georg Ludewig Forster, 1776), Einleitung, 2.

368Ibid., Einleitung, 3.

369Ibid., Einleitung, 5.

370Ibid.

371Ibid., Einleitung, 6. Less does, however, include an appendix to his work on the proof for Christianity from experience or the inner witness of the Holy Spirit, which indicates that this witness has value as a supplement to objective evidences. (ibid., pp. 665-81.)

372Ibid., Einleitung, 6. This sharply differentiates Less from the French approach.

373Ibid., Einleitung, 8.I.

374Ibid., Einleitung, 8.II.

375Henry Dodwell, Christianity Not Founded on Argument; and the True Principle of the Gospel-Evidence Assigned, 3d ed. (London: M. Cooper, 1743), pp. 7-8.

376Of Dodwell's book, Lechler writes, "We consider this work to be epochal, as marking an essentially new standpoint, and we take it as the beginning of a new period in Deism, namely its collapse into Scepticism." (Lechler, Geschichte des englischen Deismus, p. 412.) Similarly, Stephen believes that the chief result of

Dodwell's tract was to strengthen the indolent scepticism that came to characterize the second half of the century. (Stephen, English Thought, p. 148.)

[377]On the following, see Popkin, History of Scepticism, pp. 44-88.

[378]Pierre Charron, Les Trois véritez (Paris: J. Du Corroy, 1595), pp. 554-8.

[379]Pierre Charron, La Sagesse,, in idem, Toutes les oeuvres de Pierre Charron (Paris: J. Villery, 1635), 2:22.

[380]Jean-Pierre Camus, "Essay sceptique," in idem, Les Diversitez de Messire Jean Pierre Camus, Evesque & Seigneur de Bellay, Prince de l'Empire (Paris: E. Foucault, 1610), 4: 274v, 278r.

[381]François Veron, Méthodes de traiter des controverses de religion (Paris: Louys de Heuquiville, 1638), 1: 170.

[382]Popkin, History of Scepticism, p. 68.

[383]Mornay, De la vérité de la religion chrest-ienne, pref.

[384]Ibid.

[385]Rex, Essays, p. 97.

[386]René Descartes, "Discourse on the Method of Rightly Conducting the Reason and Seeking for Truth in the Sciences," in The Philosophical Works of Descartes, 2 vols., trans. E. S. Haldane and G. R. T. Ross (Cambridge: Cambridge University Press, 1973), 1: 92.

[387]Rene Descartes, "Meditations on the First Philosophy in which the Existence of God and the Distinction between Mind and Body are Demonstrated," in Philosophical Works, 1: 147-9.

[388]Popkin, History of Scepticism, p. 193.

[389]Descartes, Discourse, 1: 101.

[390]Descartes, Meditations, 1: 150.

[391]René Descartes, "Objections urged by certain Men of Learning against the preceding Meditations; with

the Author's Replies," in Philosophical Works, 2:38.
Descartes elsewhere does admit that a major premiss is
implicit, but denies that it plays any role in the
thinking of Cogito, ergo sum (René Descartes, Oeuvres
de Descartes, 13 vols., ed. C. Adam and P. Tannery
[Paris: 1897-1913], 5. 147.). Copleston remarks,
> "But his general position is this. I intuit in my
> own case the necessary connection between my
> thinking and my existing. That is to say, I
> intuit in a concrete case the impossibility of my
> thinking without my existing. And I express this
> intuition in the proposition Cogito, ergo sum.
> Logically speaking this proposition presupposes a
> general premiss. But this does not mean that I
> first think of a general premiss and then draw a
> particular conclusion. On the contrary, my
> explicit knowledge of the general premise follows
> my intuition of the objective and necessary
> connection between my thinking and my existing.
> . . . it is discovered as latent in or
> intrinsically implied by the intuition."
> (Frederick Copleston, A History of Philosophy,
> vol. 4: Modern Philosophy: Descartes to Leibniz
> [Garden City, N.Y.: Doubleday & Co.; Image Books,
> 1963], p. 102.)

See also Jaakko Hintikka, "Cogito, ergo sum:
"Inference or Performance?" Philosophical Review 71
(1962): 3-32.

[392]Descartes, Discourse, 1: 102.

[393]Descartes, Meditations, 1: 162-70.

[394]Ibid., 1: 171.

[395]Ibid., 1: 176.

[396]Ibid., 1: 133. It might be wondered whether
this is merely a concession to the doctors of theology
at the Sorbonne in order to win the Privilegio et
Approbatione Doctorum.

[397]Ibid., 1: 134.

[398]Cragg, Reason and Authority, p. 8; also Hazard:
"I can call to mind no thinker who exerted a profounder
influence on his contemporaries than Locke." (Hazard,
European Thought, p. 41.)

[399]Locke, Essay, 4.10.1.

[400]Ibid.

[401]Ibid., 4.19.4.

[402]Stephen, English Thought, pp. 83-4.

[403]Cragg comments,
"More decisive still was the authority of John
Locke. With vociferous and embarrassing enthusiasm,
the Deists insisted that they derived all their
principles from him. Locke indignantly repudiated the
inferences which they drew from his position.
Everybody, of course, appealed to Locke. He certainly
differed from the Deists on many crucial points, but he
created the atmosphere in which Deism could flourish
and established the presuppositions to which its
leaders invariably appealed." (Cragg, Reason and
Authority, p. 66).

[404]Tindal,   Christianity as old as the Creation,
pp. 5-6.

[405]Thomas Woolston, A Third Discourse on the
Miracles of Our Saviour, 3d ed. (London: author,
1728), p. 66.

[406]Leland,   View of the Principal Deistical
Writers, pp. 391-2.

[407]Lechler, Geschichte des englischen Deismus, pp.
231, 457.

[408]Ibid., p. 239.

[409]Cragg, Reason and Authority, p. 28.

[410]Leslie, Short and Easie Method, p. 45; cf.
preface.

[411]Farrar,   Critical History of Free Thought, p.
137. Voltaire declared, "Never was Christianity so
daringly assailed by any Christian." (Voltaire,
Dictionnaire, s.v. "Miracles.")

[412]Voltaire, Dictionnaire, s.v. "Miracles."

[413]Thomas Woolston, A Discourse on the Miracles of
Our Saviour, 5th ed. (London: author, 1728), p. 4.

[414]Thomas Woolston, A Fifth Discourse on the
Miracles of Our Saviour, 2d ed. (London: author,

1728).

[415]Thomas Woolston, A Sixth Discourse on the Miracles of Our Saviour (London: author, 1729), p. 5.

[416]Ibid., pp. 15-16.

[417]Ibid., p. 19.

[418]Ibid., p. 27.

[419]Thomas Sherlock, The Tryal of the Witnesses of the Resurrection of Jesus (London: J. Roberts, 1729), p. 87.

[420]See remarks by Stephen, English Thought, p. 161. He asserts that the apologists transferred the principle of English law "innocent until proven guilty" to an inappropriate sphere. But it is not at all clear that the application of this principle to history is inappropriate. Indeed, the question of burden of proof is a hotly contested issue in gospel criticism.

[421]Sherlock, Tryal, pp. 15-18.

[422]Ibid., pp. 23-6.

[423]Ibid., p. 31.

[424]Ibid., pp. 42-4.

[425]Ibid., pp. 45-8.

[426]Ibid., pp. 49-51.

[427]We have here an anticipation of Hume's argument which Burns takes as evidence for a pre-Humean version, much closer than any parallel in known Deist works, which Hume adopted. (R.M. Burns, The Great Debate on Miracles [London: Associated University Presses, 1981], pp. 89, 122.)

[428]Sherlock, Tryal, pp. 65-73.

[429]Ibid., pp. 74-80.

[430]Ibid., p. 81.

[431]Ibid., pp. 81, 104.

[432]Ibid., pp. 82-4.

[433]Ibid., pp. 107-8.

[434]Ibid., pp. 108-9.

[435]See list in Robertson, Short History, p. 320.
Even Robertson, who is anxious to display the
continuing influence of freethought, acknowledges that
the "main line of Deistic propaganda," apart from the
works of Hume and Bolingbroke, ends with Dodwell in
1743. (ibid., p. 320.) Similarly, Mossner, while
insisting that Deism neither died, faded away, nor was
vanquished, nevertheless asserts that with Bolingbroke,
the course of British Deism "had pretty well been
played out," though there always remained "opportunity
for remorseless repetition and intensified publicity."
(Encyclopedia of Philosophy, s.v. "Deism," by E.C.
Mossner.) His statement on the longevity of Deism can
only be correct in the sense that Deism moved from
England to France and Germany, for in England, it
certainly did fade away.

[436]Edward Gibbon, The Decline and Fall of the
Roman Empire, Modern Library (New York: Random House,
n.d.), 1: 382.

[437]Oliphant Smeaton, Notes to Gibbon, Decline and
Fall, 1: 383.

[438]Gibbon, Decline and Fall, 1: 383.

[439]Ibid.

[440]Ibid., 1: 408-10.

[441]Ibid., 1: 410.

[442]Gibbon asserts,
"So urgent on the vulgar is the necessity of
believing, that the fall of any system of
mythology will most probably be succeeded by the
introduction of some other mode of superstitiion.
Some deities of a more recent and fashionable cast
might soon have occupied the deserted temples of
Jupiter and Apollo, if, in the decisive moment,
the wisdom of Providence had not interposed a
genuine revelation fitted to inspire the most
rational esteem and conviction, whilst, at the
same time it was adorned with all that could
attract the curiosity, the wonder, and the
veneration of the people. . . . Those who are
inclined to pursue this reflection, instead of

viewing with astonishment the rapid progress of
Christianity, will perhaps be surprised that its
success was not still more rapid and still more
universal." (ibid., 1: 432.)

[443]Ibid.

[444]Ibid., 1: 444-504.

[445]Stephen, English Thought, p. 380. Compare the
judgement of J.B. Bury that Gibbon's critique had more
impact on subsequent generations than even Voltaire's
attacks on Christianity (J.B. Bury, A History of the
Freedom of Thought, Home University Library of Modern
Knowledge [London: Williams & Norgate, n.d.], p. 166.)

[446]Lechler, Geschichte des englischen Deismus, p.
444.

[447]Farrar, History of Free Thought, p. 168.

[448]Cardinal Fleury, cited in Friedrich Christoph
Schlosser, Geschichte des achtzehnten Jahrhunderts und
des neunzehnten bis zum Sturz des französichen
Kaiserreichs [Heidelberg: Mohr, 1836-48], 1: 523; cf.
521-2.

[449]Voltaire was exiled in England during 1726-29
and there developed the philosophical and religious
ideas that were to serve him the rest of his life.
Norman L. Torrey, Voltaire and the English Deists (New
Haven: Yale University Press, 1930), contends that the
influence of Bolingbroke upon Voltaire has been
overdrawn and emphasizes the decisive influence of
Collins, Woolston, Tindal, Middleton, and Annet, with
whose writings Voltaire became later acquainted. In
the Encyclopedia of Philosophy, s.v. "Voltaire,
Francois-Marie Arouet de" by Norman L. Torrey, however,
he notes that Voltaire's early poem Epitre à Uranie
(1722) already evinces Deist sentiments prior to the
English visit; therefore, Torrey appears ready to
ascribe a more decisive influence of the English years
on the maturation of Voltaire's thought.

[450]D. Diderot, cited in Philosophical Works, p. 2.

[451]Orr, English Deism, p. 188.

[452]See P.M. Masson, La religion de J.-J. Rousseau,
3 vols. (Paris: Librairie Hachette, 1916); Albert
Schinz, La pensée religieuse de J.-J. Rousseau et ses

récents interprètes (Paris: F. Alcan, 1927).

453

"O great Being! Eternal Being, supreme intelligence, source of life and felicity, creator, conserver, father of man and king of nature, God very powerful, very good, whom I never doubt for a moment and beneath whose eyes I would always live! I know, I rejoice that I shall appear before thy throne. In not many days my soul, free from its mortal remains, will begin to offer you more worthily that immortal hommage which will constitute my happiness throughout eternity." (Jean-Jacques Rousseau, "La nouvelle Héloise," in Religious Writings, p. 93.)

454 Rousseau, "Profession de foi", p. 122.

455 Ibid., p. 123; cf. p. 120:   "des lumières primitives."

456 Ibid., pp. 131-2.

457 Ibid., p. 134.

458 Ibid., p. 153; cf. pp. 160-1.

459 Ibid., p. 119; similarly Julie professes that God will not condemn someone for sincerely following what his best reason told him. (Rousseau, La Nouvelle Héloise, p. 93.)

460 Rousseau, "Lettre à M. De Beaumont," p. 264. "Comme il ment!" snorted Voltaire.

461 Rousseau, La Nouvelle Héloise, p. 93.

462 Rousseau, "Profession de foi," p. 167; cf. his later remark on reason's alleged duty to submit to revelation: " . . . il me faut des raisons pour soumettre ma raison." (ibid., p. 171.) No miracle could suffice to demonstrate a doctrine which is absurd or unreasonable. (Rousseau, "Lettre à M. De Beaumont," p. 295; cf. idem, "Profession de foi," pp. 176-9.)

463 Rousseau, "Profession de foi," pp. 171-2.

464 Ibid., p. 173.

465 Ibid., p. 174; see also Rousseau, "Lettres écrites de la montagne," pp. 364, 367.

[466]Rousseau, "Lettres écrites de la montagne," p. 356.

[467]Ibid., p. 357.

[468]Rousseau, "Profession de foi," p. 188.

[469]Ibid., p. 190.

[470]Rousseau, "Lettres écrites de la montagne," p. 367.

[471]Ibid., p. 371.

[472]Rousseau, "Profession de foi," p. 190.

[473]On Voltaire's religious thought, consult René Pomeau, La religion de Voltaire (Paris: 1956); Norman L. Torrey, Voltaire and the English Deists (New Haven: Yale University Press, 1930.)

[474]Thompson, A History of Historical Writing, p. 66; see also Hazard, European Thought, pp. 402-15.

[475]In his Eléments de la philosophie de Newton (1738), Voltaire describes his awe at the Newtonian cosmos which grounded his belief in a Supreme Intelligence. See also Voltaire, Dictionnaire philosophique, s.v. "Dieu"; idem, "On the Existence of God," in Works, 38: 238-44.

[476]Voltaire, "Dieu."

[477]Voltaire, Dictionnaire philosophique, s.v. "Christianisme;" cf. idem, "Religion."

[478]Voltaire, Dictionnaire philosophique, s.v. "Miracles."

[479]Robertson, Short History, pp. 343-4.

[480]Ibid., p. 344.

[481]Monod, Pascal à Chateaubriand, p. 4.

[482]Robertson, Short History, pp. 342-3.

[483]Monod, De Pascal à Chateaubriand, p. 366.

[484]Ibid., p. 402.

485 J. Alph. Turrettin, Traité de la vérité de la religion chrétienne, 2d ed., 7 vols., trans. J. Vernet (Geneva: Henri-Albert Gosse, 1745-55), 2:x.

486 Monod, De Pascal à Chateaubriand, pp. 347-8.

487 Farrar, History of Free Thought, p. 164.

488 Ibid., p. 167.

489 Cragg, Reason and Authority, p. 153.

490 Gerald R. Cragg, The Church and the Age of Reason, 1648-1789, Pelican History of the Church 4 (Harmondsworth: Penguin Books, 1972), p. 167.

491 Diderot, Pensées philosophiques, pensée LIX.

492 Ibid., pensée XLVI. Diderot's attitude is that of Hume's, that a genuine miracle is always more incredible than that the witnesses, regardless of reliability or number, should be mistaken.

493 Monod, De Pascal à Chateaubriand, p. 228.

494 August Tholuck, "Über Apologetik und ihre Litteratur," in Vermischte Schriften grösstentheils apologetischen Inhalts, 2 vols. (Hamburg: Friedrich Perthes, 1859), 1:362.

495 Gawlick, "Einleitung," to Tindal, Christianity as old as Creation, p. 37.

496 Lechler, Geschichte des englischen Deismus, p. 451.

497 Laukhard, cited in August Tholuck, "Abriss einer Geschichte der Umwalzung, welche seit 1750 auf dem Gebiete der Theologie in Deutschland statt gefunden," in Vermischte Schriften, 2:31-2; also in Gawlick, "Einleitung," to Tindal, Christianity as old as Creation, p. 37.

498 Lechler, Geschichte des englischen Deismus, p. 450.

499 Johann August Ernesti, Neue theologische Bibliothek, 1:115, cited in Tholuck, "Geschichte der Umwalzung," 2:31. Translation of John Pye Smith.

500 Tholuck, "Apologetik," 1:164-5.

^{501}Ibid., 1:165. Cf. similar remarks by Stephen,
English Thought, pp. 81-4, who accuses Locke of making
Christianity to be a legislative reform of moral law.
See also Orr, English Deism, pp. 91-103.

^{502}Tholuck, "Geschichte der Umwalzung," 2:29.

^{503}Tholuck, "Apologetik," 1:167.

^{504}Ibid., 1:163.

^{505}John Pye Smith, Preface to Guido and Julius, by
Frederick Aug. D. Tholuck (Boston: Gould & Lincoln,
1854), pp. 14-15. Cf. Edward Pusey, An historical
enquiry into the probable causes of the rationalist
character lately predominant in the theology of Germany
(London: C & J Rivington, 1828), pp. 125, 127.

^{506}Noack, Die Freidenker in der Religion, 3:1;
Tholuck, "Geschichte der Umwalzung," 2:6, 24, 35. See
also Robertson, Short History of Freethought, pp.
360-2.

^{507}See Johann Christian Edelmann, Sämtliche
Schriften in Einzelausgauben, vol. 7, pt. 1: Moses mit
aufgedeckten Angesicht (Stuttgart-Bad Cannstatt,
1969-). See also Walter Grossmann, Johann Christian
Edelmann: From Orthodoxy to Enlightenment, Religion
and Society 3 (The Hague: Mouton, 1976).

^{508}Herrmann Samuel Reimarus, Die vornehmsten
Wahrheiten der natürlichen Religion, 4th ed. (Hamburg:
Johann Carl Bohn, 1772).

^{509}See Henry Chadwick, "Introduction" to Lessing's
Theological Writings, trans. Henry Chadwick, Library of
Modern Religious Thought (London: Adam & Charles
Black, 1956), pp. 13-14.

^{510}See literature in Allgemeine Deutsche
Bibliothek 40 (1780); Karl Godeke, Grundriss zur
Geschichte der Deutschen Dichtung, 3d ed. (Dresden: L.
Ehlermann, 1916), 4:436-42.

^{511}Johann Melchior Goeze, Etwas Vorläufiges gegen
des Herrn Hofraths Lessings mittelbare und unmittelbare
feindselige Angriffe auf unsre allerheiligste Religion
und auf den einigen Lehrgrund derselben, die Heilige
Schrift (Hamburg: D.A. Harmsen, 1778); idem, Lessings
Schwächen gezeigt von Johann Melchior Goeze (Hamburg:
D.A. Harmsen, 1778). Goeze's polemical writings

against Lessing have been collected in E. Schmidt, Goezes Streitschriften gegen Lessing (Stuttgart: G.J. Goschen, 1893).

[512]Chadwick, "Introduction," p. 22. Similarly Sierig points out that Goeze was a great theologian of his day and held the resurrection to be a verifiable fact without which Christianity is futile. (Hartmut Sierig, "Die grosse Veränderung," in Vorrede zur Schutzschrift für die vernünftigen Verehrer Gottes, by Herrmann Samuel Reimarus [Göttingen: Vandenhoeck & Ruprecht, 1967], p. 20.)--Hence, his alarmist tones.

[513]See comments by George Wesley Buchanan, "Introduction," to The Goal of Jesus and his Disciples, by Hermann Samuel Reimarus, trans. George Wesley Buchanan (Leiden: E.J. Brill, 1970), pp. 13-14.

[514]H. Sieveking, "Elise Reimarus (1735-1805) in den geistigen Kämpfen ihrer Zeit," Zeitschrift des Vereins für Hamburgische Geschichte 38 (1939): 104.

[515]G.E. Lessing, Eine Parabel nebst einer kleinen Bitte, und einem eventuelen Absagungschreiben an den Herrn Pastor Goeze, in Hamburg (Braunschweig: 1778), pp. 5-11.

[516]G.E. Lessing, Anti-Goeze, with a Preface by Arthur Pfungst (Frankfort am Main: Neuer Frankfurter Verlag, 1905). Lessing's three above-mentioned works are translated in idem, Cambridge Free Thoughts and Letters on Bibliolatry, trans. H.H. Bernard, ed. I. Bernard (London: Trubner, 1862).

[517]G.E. Lessing, "Necessary Answer to a very Unnecessary Question," in Theological Works, pp. 62-4.

[518]G.E. Lessing to Elise Reimarus, 9 August, 1778, in Chadwick, "Introduction," p. 25.

[519]G.E. Lessing to Karl Lessing, 11 August, 1779, in Chadwick, "Introduction," p. 26.

[520]G.E. Lessing, Nathan der Weise, ed. August Thorbecke (Bielefeld and Leipzig: Velhagen & Klasing, n.d.), act 3, sc. 7.

[521]See Sierig, "Die grosse Veränderung," pp. 24-5.

[522]G.E. Lessing, "The Testament of John," in Theological Writings, p. 58.

[523] Ibid., p. 59.

[524] Ibid., p. 60.

[525] G.E. Lessing, "The Christianity of Reason," in Theological Writings, pp. 99-101; idem, "On the Reality of Things outside God," in Theological Writings, pp. 102-3.

[526] G.E. Lessing, "The Education of the Human Race," in Theological Writings, pp. 82-98.

[527] Friedrich Heinrich Jacobi, Über die Lehre des Spinoza in Briefen an den Herrn Moses Mendelssohn (Breslau: G. Lowe, 1785).

[528] So Chadwick, "Introduction," pp. 46-7; Encyclopedia of Philosophy, s.v. "Lessing, Gotthold Ephraim," by Henry Chadwick.

[529] Tholuck, "Apologetik," 1:311.

[530] Ibid., 1:365-6.

[531] See note 488.

[532] Buchanan, "Introduction," pp. 21-2.

[533] Allgemeine Deutsche Bibliothek 16 (1795):41. So also Albert Schweizer, The Quest of the Historical Jesus, with a Preface by F.C. Burkitt (New York: Macmillan Co., 1948), p. 26.

[534] Tholuck, "Apologetik," 1:368; cf. 1:375-6.

[535] In this section, I am interested in the defense of miracles proferred only by those for whom the issue was interconnected with their defense of the historicity of the resurrection of Jesus. For good discussions of the wider debate over miracles consult John Stewart Lawton, Miracles and Revelation (New York: Association Press, [1959]); Burns, Great Debate; Brown, Miracles.

[536] Beck remarks, "'Nature' became a catchword of eighteenth century thought in morals, politics, poetry, and religion, and almost everywhere . . . it was Newton's nature they were talking about." (Beck, "Introduction," 18th Century Philosophy, p. 5). The history of eighteenth century philosophy is the history of the expansion of Newtonian methods to all fields,

with the ideas of Locke.

[537]Diderot, "Philosophical Thought," 18.   Diderot
later abandoned his Deism.   In his "The Letter on the
Blind for the Use of Those who See," the hero
criticizes the teleological argument in Humean fashion
and dies crying "O thou God of Clarke and Newton, have
mercy on me!" (idem, Early Philosophical Works, pp.
108-14.)

[538]Benedict de Spinoza Tractatus theologico-
politicus 6.

[539]David Hume, "An Enquiry concerning Human
Understanding," in David Hume, The Philosophical Works,
4 vols., ed. T.H. Green and T.H. Grose, vol. 4:
Essays, Moral, Political, and Literary,   2   vols.
(London: 1882; rep. ed.:   Aalen: Scientia Verlag,
1964), 2:   88-108.   For a lengthy discussion of this
essay see Burns, Great Debate, pp. 131-75.   Remarkably,
Burns does not see the counterfactual nature of Hume's
reasoning, so that his discussion of the essay tends to
fall into two unconnected halves, with far too much
emphasis on the second half.   The same oversight flaws
the discussion of Brown, Miracles, pp. 79-100.

[540]Hume, "Enquiry," 2:93.

[541]Ibid., 2:94.

[542]Ibid., 2:106.

[543]Ibid., 2:107-08.

[544]Le Clerc, Letters p. 235.

[545]Ibid., pp. 235-6.

[546]Samuel Clarke, A Discourse concerning the
Unchangeable Obligations of Natural Religion and the
Truth and Certainty of the Christian Revelation
(London: W. Botham, 1706), pp. 351-52.

[547]Ibid., pp. 354-55.

[548]Ibid., pp. 356-57.

[549]Ibid., p. 359.

[550]Ibid., p. 361.

[551]Ibid., pp. 362-63. Notice that Clarke does not arbitrarily exclude certain doctrines as incapable of being proved, but he presupposes what he has already argued concerning natural theology and ethics. Cf. his statement:

"Some Doctrines are in their own Nature necessarily and demonstrably true, such as are all those which concern the obligations of plain moral Precepts; and these neither need nor can receive any stronger proof from Miracles, than what they have already . . . from the evidence of right Reason." (ibid., pp. 369-70.)

[552]Ibid., pp. 363-64.

[553]Ibid., p. 367.

[554]Ibid., pp. 368-69.

[555]Ibid., p. 368. The foregoing exposition makes evident how gross a distortion of Clarke's views is presented by Burns, Great Debate, pp. 96-103, who ascribes to Clarke an "extreme evidentialism" whereby miracles divorced from their doctrinal context are proof of Christianity. In fact, Clarke is entirely one with the typical orthodox response to Deism.

[556]J. Alph. Turrettin, Traité de la vérité de la religion chrétienne, 2d ed., 7 vols., trans. J. Vernet (Genève: Henri-Albert Gosse, 1745-55), 5: 235. Vernet has Spinoza particularly in mind here.

[557]Ibid., 5: 2-3.

[558]Ibid., 5: 240.

[559]Ibid., 5: 272.

[560]Houtteville, La religion chrétienne prouvée par les faits, 3 vols. (Paris: Mercier & Boudet, 1740), 1: 32-50.

[561]Ibid., 1: 33.

[562]Thomas Sherlock, The Tryal of the Witnesses of the Resurrection of Jesus (London: J. Roberts, 1729), p. 60.

[563]Originally mentioned by Locke, Essay, 4.15.5 and taken up by Hume in a footnote to his essay on miracles, this example was regarded as the Achilles

heel of Hume's argument, for Hume had to admit that on
his principles the man in the tropics should not in
fact believe the testimony of travellers concerning
ice.

[564]Sherlock, Tryal of the Witnesses, pp. 60-62.
This point is also argued by Bergier, who asserts that
to prove a resurrection one has only to prove two
sensible facts: (1) the death of a man and (2) his
actual life. "This man was dead . . . he is living
today . . . . therefore he has been raised [ressuscité].
. . . . (Bergier, Le Déisme réfuté par lui-meme, pp.
86-7.)

[565]Sherlock, Tryal of the Witnesses, pp. 63-64.

[566]Gottfried Less, Wahrheit der christlichen
religion, 4th ed. (Göttingen and Bremen: Georg Ludewig
Forster, 1776), p. 243.

[567]Ibid., pp. 246-53.

[568]Ibid., pp. 254-60.

[569]Ibid., pp. 260-62.

[570]Ibid., pp. 280-84.

[571]Ibid., pp. 366-75.

[572]Campbell in his Dissertation on Miracles (1762)
makes the same point. "The two thousand instances
formerly known, and the single instance attested, as
they relate to different facts, though of a contrary
nature, are not contradictory. There is no
inconsistency in believing both." (George Campbell,
The Works of George Campbell, 6 vols., vol. 1:
Dissertation on Miracles [London: Thomas Tegg, 1840],
p. 23.)

[573]Less Wahrheit, pp. 471-549; see also discussion
in Campbell, Dissertation, pp. 88-116.

[574]William Paley, A View of the Evidences of
Christianity, 2 vols., 5th ed. (London: R. Faulder,
1796; rep. ed.: Westmead, England: Gregg
International Publishers, 1970), 1: 2-3. Cf. his
concluding remark: "Let the constant recurrence to our
observation of contrivance, design and wisdom in the
works of nature, once fix upon our minds the belief of
a God, and after that all is easy." (ibid., 2:409.)

For Paley's classic exposition of the teleological argument, see his Natural Theology (1802).

[575]Ibid., 1: 3-15.

[576]Ibid., 1: 5, 7.

[577]Ibid., 1: 6.

[578]Ibid., 1: 329-83.

[579]Ibid., 1: 369-83.

[580]Turrettin-Vernet, Traité, 5:   254-55.   Kümmel draws attention to Turrettin's insistence that the Bible be treated like any other historical document as a significant step in the development of biblical criticism, but he does not seem to realize that he was merely one member of a long line of apologists stretching back to Grotius who so insisted.   (Werner Georg Kümmel, The New Testament: The History of the Investigation of Its Problems, trans. S. McLean Gilmour and Howard C. Kee [Nashville: Abingdon Press, 1972], p. 58.)

[581]Turrettin-Vernet, Traité, 5: 10.

[582]Ibid., 5: 14-15.

[583]Ibid., 5: 20.

[584]Ibid., 5: 25.

[585]Ibid., 5: 460.

[586]Less, Wahrheit, Einleitung, 5.

[587]Ibid., p. 3.

[588]Ibid., p. 2.

[589]Leland,   View of the Principal Deistical Writers, pp. 394-5.

[590]Ibid., p. 245.

[591]Paley, Evidences, 1: 142.

[592]Turrettin-Vernet, Traité, 3:23-36.

[593]Less, Wahrheit, pp. 7-14.

594 Ibid.

595 Paley, Evidences, 1: 171.

596 Turrettin-Vernet, Traité, 3:37-75.

597 Ditton, Discourse, pp. 260-67.

598 Paley, Evidences, 1: 162-63. He goes on to assert that if it were so easy to produce works under false names, then we would have more spurious writings attributed to Jesus himself. Moreover, if the gospels are under false names, then it is difficult to explain why they were attributed to obscure persons (such as Matthew, of whom we know almost nothing, or Mark) instead of more celebrated disciples.

599 Ibid., 1: 178-319. Paley draws largely from Nathaniel Lardner's The Credibility of the Gospel History: or the Facts Occasionally Mentioned in the New Testament Confirmed by Passages of Ancient Authors Who were contemporary with our Saviour or his Apostles or Lived near their Time, 2d ed. (London: John Gray,, 1730-55). The result of a lifetime of research, Lardner's voluminous compendium is impressive by any standard. See also idem, A Supplement to the First Book of the Second Part of the Credibility of the Gospel History, 3 vols. (London: n.p., 1756-57).

600 Paley, Evidences, 1: 183-229.

601 Less, Wahrheit, pp. 101-02.

602 Turrettin-Vernet, Traité, 3: 37-75; Less, Wahrheit, p. 110.

603 Less, Wahrheit, p. 110.

604 Paley, Evidences, 1: 230-38.

605 Ibid., 1: 239-46.

606 Ibid., 1: 247-51.

607 Ibid., 1: 252-56.

608 Ibid., 1: 257-67.

609 Ibid., 1: 268-82.

610 Ibid., 1: 283-91.

611Ibid., 1: 292-303.

612Ibid., 1: 304-08.

613Ibid., 1: 309-19.

614Ibid., 1: 320-28.

615Turrettin-Vernet, Traité, 3: 61-76.

616Less, Wahrheit, pp. 113-25.

617Houtteville, Faits, 1: 235-87.

618Ditton, Discourse, p. 273.

619Turrettin, Traité, 3: 76.   Cf. Less, Wahrheit
p. 126.

620This fundamental dilemma is foreshadowed
vaguely in Vives De veritate fidei christianae 18 and
more clearly in Grotius De veritate religionis
christianae 2.6.   Abbadie formulated it more precisely
in his Traité de la vérité de la religion chrétienne,
pp. 3-30.   During the eighteenth century the dilemma
comes fully into view. For example, Clarke states that
to ensure the historical reliability of the testimonies
we have, it must be shown that the disciples could not
have been deceived and that they could not have been
deceivers of others.   (Clarke, Discourse, p. 379.)
Similarly, Sherlock's counsel for Woolston presses two
basic objections against the evidence for the
resurrection: (1) the resurrection itself was a fraud,
and   (2) the testimony for the resurrection was
fabricated or unreliable. (Sherlock, Tryal, p. 87.)
Cf. also Turrettin-Vernet, Traité, 4: 53-79; Paley,
Evidences, 2: 201-08.

621Leland,   View of the Principal Deistical
Writers, p. 399; cf. pp. 447-8.

622Clarke, Discourse, 347-49.

623Less, Wahrheit, pp. 127-43.

624Ditton, Discourse, 281-324.

625Sherlock, Tryal, p. 81.   This exchange
obviously took place in the days of pre-feminist
consciousness!

[626] Paley, Evidences, 2: 201-08.

[627] Ibid., 1: 20-41.

[628] Ibid., 1: 42-105.

[629] Ibid., 1: 106-41.

[630] Ibid., 1: 327-28.

[631] Ditton, Discourse, pp. 290-315.

[632] Turrettin-Vernet, Traité, 5: 145.

[633] Houtteville, Faits, 2: 369-89.

[634] Ditton, Discourse, pp. 325-30.

[635] Less, Wahrheit, pp. 160-62.

[636] Samuel   Chandler,   The Witnesses of the Resurrection of Jesus Christ Re-examined: and their Testimony Proved entirely Consistent (London: J. Noon & R. Hett, [n.d.]), pp. 130-70.

[637] Houtteville, Faits, 2: 269-89.

[638] Ditton, Discourse, pp. 341-62.

[639] Ibid., pp. 362-71.

[640] Ibid., pp. 330-41.

[641] Chandler, Witnesses, pp. 130-70.

[642] Ibid.

[643] Turrettin-Vernet, Traité, 5: 160.

[644] Ditton, Discourse, pp. 362-71.

[645] Houtteville, Faits, 1: 126-41.

[646] Ditton, Discourse, pp. 380-413.

[647] Turrettin-Vernet, Traité, 5: 485.

[648] Sherlock, Tryal, pp. 74-80.

[649] Ibid.; Turrettin-Vernet, Traité, 5: 485.

[650] Houtteville, Faits, 2: 392-416.

[651] Sherlock, Tryal, pp. 74-80.

[652] Peter   Annet,   The Resurrection of Jesus considered; in Answer to the Tryal of the Witnesses (London: author, [n.d.].   The second edition of this work is probably a forgery, perhaps by Thomas Morgan. Woolston also replied in Mr. Woolston's Defence of his Discourses on the Miracles of our Savior (London: author, 1729), but he demurs a refutation of Sherlock for fear of persecution.

[653] Leland,   View of the Principal Deistical Writers, p. 280.

[654] Stephen describes Annet's work in these words: "A man who could believe the evangelists to be deliberate   liars   was   simply   impervious   to Sherlock's logic . . . . Annet is to Sherlock what an abusive Old Bailey barrister is to a dignified advocate.   He cross-examines the evangelists with a cynical audacity.   He spares no imputations, sticks at no cavils, and bullies and browbeats as if he had to deal with convicted felons.   He is as coarse as Woolston and no crazy regard for allegory   muffles   the   force   of   his   blows. Woolston, he says, failed because he granted too much.[2]   Annet, therefore, grants nothing.   The witnesses   are   treated   as   vulgar   cheats   and imposters, acting from the vilest of motives.

[2] 'Collection of Tracts,' p. 271." (Stephen, English Thought, pp. 246-47.)

[655] Of Annet, Orr states, ". . . his criticism of the Resurrection of Jesus and his brief statement of the positive aspect of deism show some shrewd ability and call for more attention to his work than is usually given." (Orr, English Deism, p. 151.)   If it is the case that Reimarus borrowed most of his objections to the resurrection from Annet (they are in large measure identical), which were then published by Lessing in excerpted form, this would be a good illustration of how an apparently minor thinker might indirectly have an enormous impact upon the history of thought.

[656] Annet, Resurrection, pp. 22-49.

[657] Ibid., pp. 49-71.

[658]Ibid., p. 69.

[659]Charles Moss, The Evidence of the Resurrection
Cleared from the Exceptions of a late Pamphlet,
Entitled, The Resurrection of Jesus considered by a
Moral Philosopher; in Answer to the Tryal of the
Witnesses, & c. (London: John and Henry Pemberton,
1744).

[660]Charles   Moss,   The Sequel of the Tryal of the
Witnesses of the Resurrection,   rev.   Thomas   Sherlock
(London: J. Davidson, 1749).   Annet answered Sherlock
again   in   The Resurrection Defenders stript of all
Defense (London: 1745).

[661]Ibid., p. 45.

[662]Ibid., p. 54.

[663]Ibid., pp. 54-55.

[664]Ibid., pp. 78-79.

[665]Ibid., p. 80.

[666]Ibid., pp. 86-88.

[667]Ibid., p. 89.

[668]Ibid., pp. 92-125.

[669]Ibid., pp. 103-05.

[670]Ibid., pp. 105-06.

[671]Ibid., pp. 106-31.

[672]Ibid., pp. 124-25.

[673]Ibid., p. 123.

[674]Chandler, Witnesses,, pp. 10, 24.

[675]Ibid., p. 44.

[676]Ibid., pp. 64-129.

[677]Gilbert   West,   Observations on the History and
Evidence of the Resurrection of Jesus Christ,   3d   ed.
(Dublin: John Smith and Abraham Bradley, 1747), pp.
66-73.   Since he was a layman, West's work was highly

esteemed. Leland wrote that he "hath happily removed
the difficulties and inconsistencies charged upon them,
and hath taken away the very foundation of the
principal objections that have been so often repeated
almost from the beginning of Christianity to this day."
(Leland, View of the Principal Deistical Writers, pp.
283-4). Annet retorted that West harmonizes by
distorting the text and that the whole resurrection
story is made up of dreams and visions, not facts.
(See Lechler, Geschichte des englischen Deismus, pp.
314-15; Stephen, English Thought, pp. 208-13).

[678]Paley, Evidences, 2: 312,.

[379]Turrettin-Vernet, Traité, 5: 476.

[380]See Kümmel, New Testament, pp. 51-62; see also
Luigi Salvatorelli, "From Locke to Reitzenstein: The
Historical Investigation of the Origins of
Christianity," Harvard Theological Review 22 (1929):
263-80; Hazard, European Thought, pp. 65-73; Brown,
Miracles, pp. 107-23.

[681]Tholuck, "Geschichte der Umwalzung," 2: 6.

[682]See ibid., 2. 2-5; Farrar, Free Thought, pp.
214-17.

[683]Noack, Die Freidenker in der Religion, 3: 4.

[684]Tholuck, "Geschichte der Umwalzung," 2:18. See
also excellent comments by T.M. Greene, "The Historical
Context and Religious Significance of Kant's Religion,"
in Immanuel Kant, Religion within the Limits of Reason
Alone (New York: Harper & Row; Harper Torchbooks,
1960), pp. xv-xviii.

[685]Gawlick, "Einleitung," p. 37.

[686]B. Brandl, Die Überlieferung der "Schutzschrift" des Hermann Samuel Reimarus (Pilson: 1907),
pp. 24-6; see also A.C. Lundsteen, Hermann Samuel
Reimarus und die Anfänge der Leben-Jesu Forschung
(Copenhagen: O.C. Olsen, 1939), pp. 110-46.

[687]Orr, English Deism, p. 247-8.

[688]Salvatorelli, "Locke to Reitzenstein," pp.
271-2.

[689]Semler actually assisted in the reading and

translation of Deist literature while at Halle.
Baumgarten, a disciple of Wolff, reviewed almost every
English Deist and apologetiic work.

[690]Salvatorelli, "Locke to Reitzenstein," p. 273.

[691]Kümmel, New Testament, pp. 62, 415.

[692]Tholuck, "Geschichte der Umwalzung," 2: 29.

[693]Ibid.

[694]Farrar, Free Thought, pp. 231-2.

[695]Ibid., pp. 415-16; Lechler, Geschichte des
englischen Deismus, p. 456.

[696]Frei, Eclipse of the Biblical Narrative, pp.
51-65. So also Klaus Scholder:
    "The less credible the particular, historical
    statements of the Scripture appeared, all the more
    theology fled to the 'eternal truths' which it
    believed to find therein and which stood firm
    before the bar of reason. The Bible became a
    handbook of morals and ethics, whose teachings
    were acceptable to every rationally thinking man."
    (Scholder, Ursprünge und Probleme der Bibelkritik,
    p. 171.)

[697]Frei, Eclipse of the Biblical Narrative, pp.
132-3.

[698]Jo. Augusti Ernesti Institutio interpretis Novi
Testamenti (Leipzip: M.G. Wiedemanni et Reichium,
1765), pp. 11-15, 87.

[699]Johann Salomo Semler, Abhandlung von Freier
Untersuchung des Canon, Texte zur Kirchen- und
Theologiegeschichte 5 (Gütersloh: G. Mohn, 1967), p.
68.

[700]See Wolfgang Schmittner, Kritik und Apologetik
in der Theologie J.S. Semlers, Theologische Existenz
heute 106 (München: Chr. Kaiser, 1963), p. 32;
Gottfried Hornig, Die Anfänge der historisch-kritischen
Theologie: Johann Salomo Semlers Schriftverständnis
und seine Stellung zu Luther, Forschungen zur
Systematischen Theologie und Religionspilosophie 8
(Göttingen: Vandenhoeck & Ruprecht, 1961), pp. 106-12.

[701]Hornig, Semlers Schriftverständnis, p. 107.

The equivalence is between moralisch and geistlich.

[702]Schmittner, Kritik und Apologetik Semlers, p. 32.

[703]Semler, Abhandlung, p. 60. Brackets indicate Se-mler's additions after the first edition.

[704]See Hornig, Semlers Schriftverständnis, pp. 84-8; Schmittner, Kritik und Apologetik Semlers, pp. 30-6.

[705]Semler, Abhandlung, p. 43.

[706]Ibid., p. 51.

[707]Ibid., pp. 36-7.

[708]Ibid., p. 54.

[709]Ibid., p. 73.

[710]See Schmittner, Kritik und Apologetik Semlers, pp. 40-6; Hornig, Semlers Schriftverständnis, pp. 211-36.

[711]Semler, Abhandlung, p. 73.

[712]Schmittner, Kritik und Apologetik Semlers, p. 39.

[713]Hornig, Semlers Schriftverständnis, pp. 225-6.

[714]Semler, Abhandlung, p. 83.

[715]Ibid., p. 84.

[716]Hornig, Semlers Schriftverständnis, p. 71.

[717]Semler, Abhandlung, p. 19.

[718]Ibid., p. 91.

[719]Kümmel, New Testament, p. 68.

[720]"Einleitung" to Semler, Abhandlung, p. 6.

[721]D. Joh. Salomo Semler, Beantwortung der Fragmente eines Ungenannten insbesondere vom Zweck Jesu und seiner Junger, 2d ed. (Halle: Verlag des Erziehungsinstituts, 1780).

[722]See J.S. Semler, Antwort auf das Bahrdtische Glaubensbekenntnis (Halle: Hemmerde, 1779); cf. idem, D. Joh. Salomo Semlers aufrichtige Antwort, auf Herrn Basedows Urkunde (Halle: 1780).

[723]Hornig, Semlers Schriftverständnis, p. 200.

[724]Talbert, "Introduction," p. 13; Greene, "Kant's Religion," pp. xviii-xx.

[725]Reimarus, Goal of Jesus, pp. 85-95.

[726]Ibid., p. 96.

[727]Hermann Samuel Reimarus, "Concerning the Intention of Jesus and His Teaching," in Fragments, ed. Talbert, pp. 153-71.

[728]Ibid., pp. 161, 212; cf. Reimarus, Goal of Jesus, p. 100.

[729]Reimarus, "Intention of Jesus," pp. 172-200.

[730]Ibid., p. 174.

[731]Ibid., p. 176.

[732]Ibid., p. 200.

[733]Reimarus, Goal of Jesus, pp. 96-104.

[734]Ibid., p. 100.

[735]Ibid., p. 103.

[736]Ibid., p. 104.

[737]Frei, Eclipse of the Biblical Narrative, pp. 57-8.

[738]Ibid., p. 61.

[739]Semler, Beantwortung, p. 341.

[740]Ibid., p. 342.

[741]Ibid., p. 340.

[742]Ibid., p. 234.

[743]Ibid., p. 235.

[744] Ibid., p. 249.

[745] Ibid., p. 248.

[746] Ibid.

[747] Chr. Gottfr. Schutz, Preface to Letztes Glaubensbekenntnis über natürlicher und christliche Religion, by J.S. Semler (Königsberg: Friedrich Nicolovius, 1792), p. xxiii.

[748] Semler, Beantwortung, p. 250.

[749] Ibid., p. 266.

[750] Ibid., p. 264.

[751] Ibid., p. 251.

[752] Schmittner, Kritik und Apologetik, p. 56.

[753] Semler, Beantwortung, p. 251.

[754] Ibid., p. 259.

[755] Ibid., p. 272.

[756] Ibid., p. 262.

[757] Ibid., p. 267.

[758] Ibid., p. 269.

[759] Ibid., p. 275.

[760] Ibid., p. 284.

[761] And this Brown calls a "profound and effective" rebuttal of Reimarus! (Brown, Miracles, p. 110.)

[762] Buchanan, "Introduction," p. 22. This surmise appears to find support in Semler's own remarks in the preface to the Beantwortung. There Semler says that he never wanted to write a refutation of the fragmentist, but wanted rather to find the unchangeable essence of Christianity. But he decided to write this work because of the uneven judgement on his own work by his contemporaries. People did not, he reflects, expect very much from him against a naturalist. (Semler, Beantwortung, Vorrede a3.)

[763]Tholuck, "Umwalzung," pp. 78-9.

[764]Schmittner, Kritik und Apologetik, p. 68.

[765]J.S. Semler, Letztes Glaubensbekenntnis über natürliche und christliche Religion, with a preface by Chr. Gottfr. Schutz (Königsberg: Friedrich Nicolovius, 1792), pp. 2-5.

[766]Ibid., p. 9.

[767]Schutz, Preface to Letztes Glaubensbekenntnis, by Semler, p. x.

[768]Semler, Beantwortung, Vorrede.

[769]Ibid., pp. 264-5.

[770]Schutz, Preface to Letztes Glaubensbekenntnis, by Semler, p. xi.

[771]Semler, Letztes Glaubensbekenntnis, p. 84.

[772]Ibid., pp. 114-15.

[773]Schutz, Preface to Letztes Glaubensbekenntnis, by Semler, pp. xi, xv.

[774]Ibid., p. xix.

[775]Lessing, "Eidtor's Counter-propositions," in Chadwick, "Introduction," p. 18.

[776]Ibid.

[777]Talbert, "Introduction," pp. 30-1.

[778]Sierig, "Die grosse Veränderung," p. 15.

[779]Ibid., p. 16.

[780]G.E. Lessing, "The Education of the Human Race," in Theological Writings, pp. 82-3.

[781]Ibid., p. 83. This would seem to refute Chadwick's assertion that in this essay Lessing abandons the Deist view of particular religions as corruptions of natural religion for a view of religions as advancing from infancy to maturity.

[782]Ibid., p. 82.

783Ibid., p. 95. Cf. his statement that it is the truth that counts; if a mathematical truth were discovered by a fallacious calculation, should I therefore deny the truth? (G.E. Lessing, "On the Proof of the Spirit and of Power," in Theological Writings, pp. 55-6).

784The logical course of the argument in this essay is quite muddied. Chadwick discerns five ideas which Lessing has fused together: (1) All knowledge of past events based on testimony is uncertain. (2) It would have been easier to believe in Christ if one could have been a contemporary observer of him. (3) The idea that Jesus Christ is the Son of God of one substance with the Father is irrational. (4) Historical events cannot prove moral and metaphysical truths. (5) The realm of historical experience is one of flux, whereas truths of divine revelation are timeless. (Chadwick, "Introduction," p. 31; cf. 32.)

785Lessing, "Proof of the Spirit and of Power," p. 52.

786Ibid., p. 53. The argument so stated thus has no direct bearing on the issue of being a contemporary witness of Jesus, as the problem is sometimes discussed today. This impression arises from Lessing's inconsistent suggestion that had he seen the miracles of Christ himself he would have believed. In point of fact, since even first hand perceptions would be truths of fact, they could not establish the truths of reason. Thus, contemporaneity is irrelevant.

787Ibid., pp. 53-4.

788Ibid., pp. 54-5.

789Ibid., p. 55.

790Ibid.

791Salvatorelli, "Locke to Reitzenstein," p. 275.

792Heinrich Eberh. Gottlob Paulus, Das Leben Jesu, als Grundlage einer reinen Geschichte des Urchristentums, 2 vols. (Heidelberg: C.F. Winter, 1828), 2: pt. 2: XI.

793Ibid., 2: pt. 2: XIV-V.

794Ibid., 2: pt. 2: XI.

[795] Ibid.

[796] Ibid., 2: pt. 2: XIV.

[797] Ibid., 1: 283-4.

[798] "Denn das wahre Glauben ist nur das, welches das Haltbarste fest hält." (ibid., 1: 284.)

[799] Ibid., 2: pt. 2: XV.

[800] Ibid., 1: 284.

[801] Heinrich Eberhard Gottlob Paulus, Philologisch-kritischer und historischer Kommentar über das neue Testament, 3 vols. (Lubeck: Johann Friedrich Bohn, 1800-02), 3: 841-2.

[802] Ibid., 3: 842-52.

[803] Paulus, Leben Jesu.

[804] Ibid., 1: 288.

[805] Ibid., 1: 278-9.

[806] Ibid., 1: 260-4. He lists five objections: (1) Why do the priests know of Jesus's predictions, but not his disciples and why do they not use a Jewish guard? (2) Since the guard needed an excuse before Pilate, they must have been a Roman guard; but the real Pilate would never have granted the Jews' request. (3) The guards would have kept the tomb unsealed so that they could look in on the body. (4) The real Caiphas, upon hearing the guards' report, would have said, "Away with you liars!" and reported them to Pilate and had them executed; and the guards would never have accepted a bribe for spreading a lie that could cost them their heads. (5) The guard would have been prosecuted under Roman law and their false story revealed. In his Kommentar, Paulus goes into even greater detail, listing 15 reasons why the guard story contradicts the historical probabilities of the case. (Paulus, Kommentar, 3: 855-61.)

[807] Paulus, Leben Jesu, 1: 305; idem, Kommentar, 3: 852-3.

[808] Paulus, Leben Jesu, 1: XLIV.

[809] Ibid., 1: 303.

[810]Schweizer, Quest of the Historical Jesus, pp. 64-5; Salvatorelli, "Locke to Reitzenstein," p. 279.

[811]Kümmel, New Testament, p. 121.

[812]David Friedrich Strauss, Herrmann Samuel Reimarus und seine Schutzschrift für die vernünftigen Verehrer Gottes (Leipzig: F.A. Brockhaus, 1862), p. 271. The crucial final three chapters of this work are translated in David Friedrich Strauss, "Hermann Samuel Reimarus and his 'Apology'," in Reimarus: Fragments, ed. Talbert, pp. 44-57, and citations are from this translation.

[813]Strauss, Reimarus und seine Schutzschrift, pp. 273-4.

[814]Ibid., pp. 276-7.

[815]Ibid., pp. 284-5.

[816]David Friedrich Strauss, A New Life of Jesus, authorized trans., 2 vols., 2d ed. (London: Williams & Norgate, 1879), 1: 412.

[817]Frei, Eclipse of the Biblical Narrative, pp. 113-14.

[818]Strauss, Reimarus und seine Schutzschrift, pp. 280-1.

[819]Ibid., p. 286.

[820]Johann Gottfried Eichhorn, "Versuch über die Engels-Erscheinungen in der Apostelgeschichte," in idem, Allgemeine Bibliothek der biblischen Litteratur (Leipzig: Weidmannsche Buchhandlung, 1790), 3: 398-9. Cf. Eichhorn's predisposition against the miraculous in idem, "Ueber die Ausgiessung des Geistes am Pfingstfest," in Allgemeine Bibliothek, pp. 239-44.

[821]Johann Philipp Gabler, "Über den Unterschied Zwischen Auslegung und Erklärung erläutert durch die verschiedene Behandlungsart der Versuchungs-geschichte Jesu," in idem, Kleinere theologische Schriften, ed. T.A. Gabler and J.G. Gabler (Ulm: Stettinische Buchhandlung, 1831), 1: 201-7.

[822]Georg Lorenz Bauer, Hebräische Mythologie des alten und neuen Testaments, mit Parallelen aus der

Mythologies anderer Völker, vornehmlich der Griechen
und Römer, 2 vols. (Leipzig: Weygand, 1802).

[823]Georg Lorenz Bauer, Entwurf einer Hermeneutik
des Alten und Neuen Testaments (Leipzig: Weygan,
1799), p. 156.

[824]David Friedrich Strauss, The Life of Jesus
Critically Examined, trans. George Eliot, ed. with an
Introuction by Peter C. Hodgson, Lives of Jesus Series
(London: SCM Press, 1973), p. 64.

[825]Ibid., p. 80.

[826]Ibid., p. 79.

[827]Ibid., p. 736.

[828]Ibid., p. 75.

[829]Schweizer,   Quest of the Historical Jesus,   p.
10.

[830]Ibid., p. 111.

[831]Strauss, Life of Jesus, p. 57.

[832]Ibid., p. 58.

[833]Ibid., p. 70.

[834]Ibid., pp. 70-3.

[835]Ibid., p. 74.

[836]Ibid., p. 86.

[837]Ibid., pp. 86-7.

[838]Ibid., p. 88.

[839]Ibid., p. 89.

[840]Ibid., pp. 565-82.

[841]Ibid., pp. 692-700.

[842]Ibid., pp. 703-4.

[843]Ibid., pp. 706-9.

[844]Ibid., pp. 711-17.

[845]Ibid., pp. 719-28.

[846]Ibid., pp. 735-6.

[847]Ibid., p. 741.

[848]Ibid., p. 782.

[849]Farrar, Free Thought, p. 266. On the influence of Strauss's work, see pp. 272-86. Subsequent lives of Jesus during the nineteenth century laid little emphasis on the problem of miracles. A particularly representative life was H.J. Holtzmann's Die synoptischen Evangelien, ihr Ursprung und geschichtlicher Charakter (Leipzig: W. Engelmann, 1863), in which he tried to rescue the historical Jesus from Strauss's scepticism. By this time critical studies had developed the "two-source hypothesis" of the priority of Mark and a sayings collection, and liberal theologians sought to discover there the historical Jesus not yet overlaid with layers of myth and legend. The real Jesus was neither an insurrectionist nor an apocalyptic prophet, but a man convinced that the kingdom of God would come as the result of his life and moral teaching. Jesus was willing to die to impress men with his righteous cause. Jesus is therefore the perfect model for mankind, the supreme example of the developing God-consciousness of man. Holtzmann did not want to deny the miracles of Jesus, but he reinterpreted them such that Jesus's healings were the impact of his moral purity upon men and the nature miracles were sublime pictures of ideal truths. Some "miracles" could be result of natural processes as yet unknown to science. As for the resurrection the accounts in the gospels were too conflicting to be of any historical value. In his later Lehrbuch der Neutestamentlichen Theologie (Freiburg: B. & Leipzig: Mohr, 1897), Holtzmann approximated more nearly the position of Strauss: after Jesus's death, Peter was so grief-stricken with guilt that he had a vision of Jesus raised from the dead. This prompted hallucinations by the other disciples. To justify that Jesus was after all the Messiah, the disciples combed the Old Testament for passages describing the suffering and subsequent glorification of the Messiah, which they applied to Jesus in their preaching. Other liberal lives of Jesus followed Holtzmann's pattern.

[850]In Strauss's later Glaubenslehre, he explains
in some detail die Auflösung des Wunderbegriffs,
recounting the arguments of Spinoza, Hume, and Lessing
to show that the concept has now become obsolete.
(David Friedrich Strauss, Die christliche Glaubenslehre
in ihrer geschichtlichen Entwicklung und im Kämpfe mit
der modernen Wissenschaft [Tübingen: C.F. Osiander,
1840; Stuttgart: F.H. Kohler, 1840], pp. 224-53.) The
point was not lost on his successors.   See, for
example, the Auseinandersetzung between Hase and Baur
on miracles.   Baur had reviewed Hase's Leben Jesu in
the Theologisches Jahrbuch of 1854 and accused him of a
rationalistic tendency in his implication that the
death of Lazarus and of Jesus himself was merely a
Scheintod.   Hase retorted, "You know full well that I
cannot regard miracles as possible in the absolute
sense of an overturning of the laws of nature . . .,"
but he reminds Baur that he recognizes "unknown powers,
namely, suddenly effective powers of healing" in Jesus.
(Karl Hase, "Die Tübinger Schule, Eine Sendschreibung
an Herrn Dr. F. Ch. von Baur," in Ferdinand Christian
Baur, Ausgewählte Werke in Einzelausgaben, ed. Klaus
Scholder, vol. 5:   Für und wider die Tübinger Schule
[Stuttgart-Bad Cannstatt: Friedrich Frommann Verlag,
1975], p. 21.)   He accuses Baur of trying to heighten
the gospel miracles in order to discredit their
historicity as Strauss had done.   Sometimes we must
remain ignorant of what really happened, he cautions.
In his scorching reply, Baur excoriates Hase for his
naive handling of miracles.   So you really don't know,
Baur queries, whether Lazarus was dead or not?   On your
own principles you must know.   For unless we regress to
the exegesis of Paulus, there is no indication in the
text of any natural powers at work.   If you want to go
no further than the historical documents themselves,
then you must admit a real miracle.   On the other hand,
since you know full well that no absolute miracle
exists, then Lazarus could not have been dead;
otherwise his resurrection would be a miracle.   The
problem is that you know that he was dead and at the
same time that he could not have been dead.   So in
order to escape this tension, you say that his
resurrection was not a real miracle, but only similar
to a miracle in that suddenly effective powers of
healing brought him back to life at precisely the right
moment!   These powers introduce a new factor not in
your premisses.   Where did they suddenly come from?
Neither the documents nor the concept of miracle
justifies this appeal.   What will become of the gospel
history if one allows free reign to this caprice, that
now here, now there, at exactly the right time and

place, unknown, suddenly effective powers of nature
operated, which onlookers could only regard as a
miracle? What a labyrinth of arbitrary, fanciful
hypotheses await us if this viewpoint ever again gets a
foothold in the gospel history! Nevertheless you are
perfectly right that both hold true: there is no
absolute miracle, and yet according to the historical
documents we must accept real miracles. But why can we
not unite them in this way: one holds for us and the
other holds for the evangelist? Undoubtedly the
evangelist wanted to report the raising of Lazarus as a
real miracle, but does it follow from that that we must
do the same? Only this view can yield consistency and
unity in our world view in our grasp of the gospel
history. (Ferdinand Christian Baur, "An Herrn Dr. Karl
Hase, Beantwortung des Sendschreibens 'die Tübinger
Schule', "in Tübinger Schule, pp. 136-8.) Notice that
neither man even seriously considers that a genuine
miracle could have occurred. Baur blocks any retreat
to the old natural explanation hermeneutic as well.

In a later essay, Baur argues against allowing the
possibility of a real miracle in the gospels because
this would undermine a historical perspective. For the
historical task is to investigate an event in its
context of causes and effects, whereas a miracle has no
natural cause. So how could one prove such an event
occurred? It could only be established historically,
but this would be a petitio principii, since the event
stands in blatant contradiction to all other analogies
of the historical perspective. (idem, "Die Tübinger
Schule und ihre Stellung zur Gegenwart," in Tübinger
Schule, pp. 308-9.)

851Frei, Eclipse of the Biblical Narrative, p.
240.

852See pp. 461-77.

853Strauss, Reimarus und seine Schutzschrift, p.
284.

854See Rosemary Ashton, The German Idea: Four
English Writers and the Reception of German Thought
1800-60 (Cambridge: Cambridge University Press, 1980);
Alec R. Vidler, The Church in an Age of Revolution,
rev. ed., Pelican History of the Church 5
(Harmondsworth: Penguin Books, 1971), pp. 33-5; Vernon
F. Storr, The Development of English Theology in the
Nineteenth Century 1800-60 (London: Longmans, Green, &
Co., 1913), pp. 4-5.

855Cragg, Reason and Authority, p. 30.

856Storr, English Theology, p. 41; see also Lawton, Miracles, pp. 107-13.

857Cragg, Reason and Authority, pp. 158-62.

858John Wesley, The Works of the Rev. John Wesley, 14 vols. (London: 1872), 6: 360.

859Cragg, Reason and Authority, pp. 179-80.

860Storr, English Theology, p. 70; see also Lawton, Miracles, pp. 113-17.

861Samuel Taylor Coleridge, Confessions of an Inquiring Spirit, ed. Henry Nelson Coleridge (Boston: Jame Munroe, 1841), p. 115.

862Ibid., p. 39.

863Samuel Taylor Coleridge, Aids to Reflection in the Formation of a Manly Character, 2d ed. (London: Hurst, Chance, & Co., 1831), p. 399.

864Storr, English Theology, p. 133.

865Brooke Foss Wescott, The Gospel of the Resurrection (London: Macmillan, 1906); idem, The Revelation of the Risen Lord, 3d ed. (London and Cambridge: Macmillan, 1884).

866Dulles, History of Apologetics, pp. 199, 200.

867Alexander Balmain Bruce, Apologetics; or, Christianity Defensively Stated, International Theological Library 3 (Edinburgh: T & T Clark, 1892), pp. 30-31, 351; see also idem, The Miraculous Element in the Gospels (London: Hodder & Stoughton, 1886), pp. 84-95. In this last-named work, he argues against Strauss and Baur's attempts to explain miracles as later accretions to the tradition. In his Ferdinand Christian Baur and his Theory of the Origin of Christianity and of the New Testament Writings, Present Day Tracts 7 (London: Religious Tract Society, n.d.), Bruce argues for an early date for the synoptics of AD 60-70 and for John of AD 80-90, thus disallowing sufficient time for the significant accrual of legendary, miraculous elements.

In his argument for the resurrection, Bruce sought to rebutt all the important alternative explanations of

this event. The resurrection is of fundamental
importance to Christianity, notes Bruce; even Strauss
admits that he must either demonstrate that belief in
the resurrection could have arisen without any
miraculous element or else admit the failure of his
naturalistic approach and retract all that he has
written. Baur was fully aware for his part that
Christianity could never have gotten underway without
at least belief in the resurrection, but he never
provided a naturalistic account of how that belief
originated. If there was no resurrection of Jesus,
then there are basically five rival theories to explain
how that belief came to be: 1. The Theft Theory:
According to Reimarus and certain others, Jesus and/or
the disciples plotted together for the purpose of
propagating the belief that the crucified one had risen
again. This hypothesis, Bruce remarks, is so out of
date that men of all schools in modern times would be
ashamed to identify themselves with it, and it may be
left to the oblivion it deserves. 2. The apparent
Death Theory: Propounded by Paulus and patronized by
even Schleiermacher, this old rationalist hypothesis
contended that since very little blood is lost in
crucifixion, Jesus, being taken down from the cross
after only six hours, was still alive and recovered in
the tomb. Against this theory Bruce urges: (a) There
is unanimous agreement among the evangelists that Jesus
was really dead, not to speak of the Roman soldier's
piercing Jesus's side, as mentioned by John. (b)
Strauss has rightly objected that a pale and half-dead
Jesus who eventually did die could never have convinced
the disciples that he was the conqueror of death and
the Prince of Life, as they later proclaimed him to be.
3. The Subjective Vision Theory: Renan and Strauss
chose to explain the resurrection appearances as
hallucinatory; Renan through the conviction of the
disciples that their adored Master just could not be
dead and Strauss by arguing that Paul's subjective
vision of Jesus was of the same nature as those
experienced by the apostles, as they reflected on what
had happened after their return to Galilee. Several
problems crop up in this theory: (a) Some time is
required to develop the state of mind required, whereas
according to the gospels the appearances began within
three days of the crucifixion. (b) The disciples were
in such a frame of mind that subjective visions were
the least likely thing to befall them; they were
depressed, sceptical, unexpectant, even suspecting that
they saw a spirit, which is exactly the theory of Renan
and Strauss. (c) The appearances were simple, which
would not have been true of subjective visions. (d)

The appearances ceased quickly, which is not true of
visionary experiences, which gradually dwindle in
number after some time. (e) The sudden change in mood
of the disciples is not characteristic of the usual
course of events produced by visions, which generate a
temporary excitement ending in languor and apathy. 4.
The Objective Vision Theory: According to Keim, the
appearances were visions produced by an objective
cause, the Spirit of Jesus who thereby sent a message
of his continuing life.   Thus, the theory is
supernaturalistic, but denies that Christ rose bodily.
Bruce observes concerning this theory: (a) It does not
do justice to the gospel narratives of the empty tomb.
(b) It bases the faith of the disciples on a
hallucination, for certainly the impression was given
that Jesus had risen from the grave through these
appearances.   But is this not deceitful?   Why not
simply a voice from heaven to give the message? 5. The
Legend Theory: The previous theories all assumed that
something occurred which demanded explanation, but
according to the most recent hypothesis, expounded by
Martineau, there was nothing to explain.   The
appearances belong only to the later traditions
reported in the gospels, so that all that needs to be
explained is how the legend of the resurrection arose.
Martineau thinks it resulted from the disciples'
conviction that Jesus "still lives," as Enoch and
Elijah still live. To convey this, they could even say
they had seen Jesus, just as Paul was to say later.
The more substantial appearance stories arose due to
the craving for something better than mere subjective
visions as proof that Christ still lived.   To this
theory, Bruce objects: (a) It ascribes to the
disciples a Greek conception of life as purely
spiritual. The Jew did not believe in an immortality
detached from the physical body, but incorporating it.
Paul's self-defense as an apostle that he had seen
Jesus was intended to place his vision on the same
level as those of the Eleven.   It was to protect
himself aagainst the charge of hallucination that he
associated his experience with that of the apostles.
Modern critics pull the visions of the disciples down
to the supposedly subjective level of Paul's whereas it
was Paul's interest and intention to level his own
vision up to the objectivity of the earlier
appearances. Paul certainly believed that the Eleven,
Peter in particular, had seen a bodily resurrected
Lord, for the expression "on the third day" would have
no sense unless Paul shared the belief that Jesus went
forth bodily from the tomb alive on the third day. (b)
The causality in the legend theory is reversed.   The

faith that Jesus still lived could not have arisen
without the appearances. The appearances are needed to
explain the faith, not vice versa. (c) The theory
collapses to the fraud hypothesis. The apostles could
have easily corrected the misimpressions that were
arising concerning the continuing life of Jesus and the
mistaken notion of a bodily resurrection. The
foregoing shows, Bruce concludes, that all naturalistic
attempts to explain away the resurrection have turned
out to be failure. The physical resurrection remains a
fact--a mysterious one, no doubt, for Jesus's body was
also transformed into a pneumatic body, but in his
resurrection the revivification of the crucified body
and its translation to a spiritual body coincide, the
former being the actual condition of the latter.
(Bruce, Apologetics, pp. 383-97.)

[868]Hastings' Encyclopedia of Religion and Ethics,
s.v. "Apologetics," by T.W. Crafer.

[869]J.B. Duvoisin, Démonstration évangélique
(Brunswick: 1800), pp. 2,3, cited in Monod, Pascal à
Chateaubriand , p. 503.

[870]Farrar, Free Thought, p. 291.

[871]Monod, De Pascal à Chateaubriand, p. 321. On
her life see Metzger, Marie Huber (1695-1753), sa vie,
ses oeuvres, sa théologie (Geneva: 1887).

[872]Monod, De Pascal à Chateaubriand, p. 323.

[873]Marie Huber, Le monde fou préféré au monde
sage, en vingt-six promenades, rev. ed. (London: n.p.,
1744), p. 126.

[874]Ibid.

[875]Ibid., p. 174.

[876]Ibid., pp. 223-48.

[877]Ibid., pp. 164-5.

[878]Masson, Religion de J.J. Rousseau, 1: 207-8;
Eugene Ritter, "Jean-Jacques Rousseau et Marie Huber,"
Annales de Jean-Jacques Rousseau 3 (1907): 207.

[879]Monod, Pascal à Chateaubriand, p. 323.

[880]Rousseau, "Profession de foi," p. 168. Here

the three factors of nature, conscience, and reason are brought together.

[881] Ibid., p. 118.

[882] Ibid., p. 134. Cf. his later remark that sense impressions and the inner feelings lead us to the cause of the world. (Ibid., p. 151.)

[883] Ronald Grimsley, Annotation to Rousseau, "Profession de foi," p. 123.

[884] Rousseau, "Profession de foi," pp. 152-61.

[885] Ibid., p. 166.

[886] Ibid., p. 167.

[887] Ibid., pp. 167, 171; cf. 176-9.

[888] Ibid., pp. 188-9.

[889] Ibid., p. 190. "What is the death of a god!" exclaimed Voltaire. Cf. Rousseau, "Lettre à M. De Beaumont," p. 297.

[890] Rousseau, "Lettre à M. De Beaumont," p. 264.

[891] Monod, De Pascal à Chateaubriand, p. 414. See also Dulles, History of Apologetics, pp. 171-2.

[892] François René De Chateaubriand, The Genius of Christianity, trans. Charles I. White, 2d rev. ed. (Baltimore: J. Murphy, 1856).

[893] Dulles, History of Apologetics, pp. 173-4.

[894] Ernst Renan, Vie de Jesus, 10th ed. (Paris: Michel Levy frères, 1863).

[895] Schweizer, Quest of the Historical Jesus, p. 182.

[896] See the author-title list in Paul de Haes, La résurrection de Jésus dans l'apologétique des cinquante dernières années (Rome: Pontifical Universitatis Gregorianae, 1953), pp. 12-13. The procedure of these apologists remains identical to that of the eighteenth century thinkers.

[897] Immanuel Kant, Immanuel Kant's Critique of Pure

Reason, trans. Norman Kemp Smith (London: Macmillan, 1970), Bxxx, p. 29.

[898]Ibid., Bxxxv, p. 32.

[899]David   Hume,   An Enquiry concerning Human Understanding, in idem, Enquiries concerning Human Understanding and concerning the Principles of Morals, ed. L.A. Selby-Bigge, 3d ed., ed. P.H. Nidditch (Oxford: Clarendon Press, 1975), 4.1.20, p. 25.

[900]Ibid., 12.3.131-2, pp. 163-4.

[901]David Hume, A Treatise of Human Nature, ed. L.A. Selby-Bigge, 2d ed., ed. P.H. Nidditch (Oxford: Clarendon Press, 1978), 1.3.2., p. 77.

[902]Ibid., 1.3.3, pp. 79-80.

[903]Ibid., 1.3.6, pp. 87-9.

[904]Ibid., 1.3.14, pp. 164-9.

[905]Hume, Enquiry, 12.2.128, p. 160.

[906]Hume, Treatise, 1.4.7, p. 269.

[907]Hume, Enquiry, 12.3.129-30, pp. 161-2.   Cf. David Hume, Dialogues concerning Natural Religion, ed. with an Introduction by Norman Kemp Smith, Library of Liberal Arts (Indianapolis: Bobbs-Merrill, 1947), p. 227.

[908]Hume, Enquiry, 12.3.132, p. 165.

[909]Immanuel   Kant,   Prolegomena to Any Future Metaphysic (New York: Bobbs-Merrill Co., 1950), p. 8.

[910]Kant, Critique, A xvii, p. 12.

[911]Ibid., B2, pp. 41-3.

[912]Ibid., A7/B11 - A10/B14, pp. 48-9.

[913]Kant, Prolegomena, pp. 14-15.

[914]Kant, Critique, B xvi-ii, p. 22.

[915]Ibid., B xxii, p. 25.

[916]Ibid., A15/B29, pp. 61-2.

[917]Ibid., A51/B75, p. 93.

[918]Ibid., A20/B34, pp. 65-6.

[919]Kant concludes,
"Time and space, taken together, are the pure
forms of all sensible intuition, and so are what
make a priori synthetic propositions possible.
But these a priori sources of knowledge . . .
apply to objects only insofar as objects are
viewed as appearances, and do not represent things
as they are in themselves." (ibid., A39/B56, p.
80.)

[920]Ibid., A111, p. 138; cf. B143, p. 160.

[921]As Kant explains,
"Knowledge involves two factors: first, the
concept, through which an object in general is
thought (the category); and secondly the intuition
through which it is given. For if no intuition is
given corresponding to the concept, the concept
would still indeed be a thought, so far as its
form is concerned, but would be without any
object, and no knowledge of anything would be
possible by means of it. So far as I could know,
there would be nothing and could be nothing, to
which my thought could be applied. Now . . . the
only intuition possible to us is sensible;
consequently, the thought of an object in
general, by means of a pure concept of the
understanding, can become knowledge for us only in
so far as the concept is related to objects of the
senses . . . . Our conclusion is therefore this:
the categories, as yielding knowledge of things,
have no kind of application, save only in regard
to things which may be objects of possible
experience." (ibid., B146-8, pp. 161-2.)

[922]In the Prolegomena, Kant maintains that the
categories serve only to decipher appearances.
"The principles which arise from their reference
to the sensible world only serve our understanding
for empirical use. Beyond this they are arbitrary
combinations without objective reality, and we can
neither know their possibility a priori nor verify
. . . their reference to objects. . . .
     This, therefore, is the result of all our
foregoing inquiries: 'All synthetical principles
a priori are nothing more than principles of
possible experience' and can never be referred to

things in themselves, but only to appearances as objects of experience." (Kant, *Prolegomena*, p. 60.)
Cf. Kant, *Critique*, B294, p. 256.

[923]Philipp Jacob Spener, *Pia desideria*, trans. with an Introduction by Theodore G. Tappert (Philadelphis: Fortress Press, 1964), pp. 87-122.

[924]Theodore M. Greene, "The Historical Context and Religious Significance of Kant's *Religion*," in Immanuel Kant, *Religion within the Limits of Reason Alone* (New York: Harper & Row; Harper Torchbooks, 1960), p. xxx.

[925]Immanuel Kant, *Critical Examination of Practical Reason*, trans. T.K. Abbott, in *Kant's Critique of Practical Reason*, ed. T.K. Abbott (London: Longmans, Green, & Co., 1963), p. 101.

[926]Kant, *Critique*, A796/B824, p. 629.

[927]Ibid., A807/B835, pp. 636-7.

[928]Ibid., A829/B857, p. 651.

[929]Ibid.

[930]Immanuel Kant, *Fundamental Principles of the Metaphysic of Morals*, in *Kant's Critique of Practical Reason*, trans. T.K. Abbott (London: Longmans, Green, & Co., 1963), p. 9.

[931]Ibid., p. 10.

[932]Ibid., p. 13.

[933]Ibid., p. 16.

[934]Ibid., pp. 16-17.

[935]Ibid., p. 18.

[936]Ibid.

[937]Ibid., p. 19.

[938]Ibid., pp. 29-30.

[939]Ibid., p. 31.

[940]Ibid., p. 33.

[941] Ibid., p. 38.

[942] Ibid., p. 46.

[943] Ibid., p. 47.

[944] Ibid.

[945] Ibid., p. 50.

[946] Ibid., p. 51.

[947] Ibid.

[948] Ibid., p. 52.

[949] Ibid., p. 73.

[950] Ibid., p. 65.

[951] Kant, _Critical Examination_, p. 140.

[952] Ibid., p. 90.

[953] Ibid., p. 88.

[954] Kant, _Critique_, A806/B834, p. 636.

[955] Kant, _Critical Examination_, p. 206.

[956] Ibid., pp. 209-11.

[957] Ibid., p. 219.

[958] Ibid.

[959] Ibid., p. 221.

[960] Ibid.

[961] Ibid., p. 222.

[962] Ibid.

[963] Kant, _Critique_, A829/B857, p. 650.

[964] Kant, _Critical Examination_, p. 222.

[965] Ibid., p. 223.

[966] Kant, _Critique_, B xxxiv, p. 32.

967 Ibid., B xxx, p. 29. The full context reads:
"[From what has already been said, it is evident
that] even the assumption--made on behalf of the
necessary practical employment of my reason--of
God, freedom, and immorality is not permissible
unless at the same time speculative reason be
deprived of its pretensions to transcendent
insight. For in order to arrive at such insight
it must make use of principles which, in fact,
extend only to objects of possible experience, and
which, if also applied to what cannot be an object
of experience, always really change this into an
appearance, thus rendering all practical
extension of pure reason impossible. I have
therefore found it necessary to deny knowledge, in
order to make room for faith." (ibid.)

968 See Norman Kemp Smith, A Commentary of Kant's
"Critique of Pure Reason" (New York: Humanities Press,
1962), Appendix C; Greene, "Kant's Religion," pp.
1xv-vi; cf. G.A. Schrader, "Kant's Presumed Repudiation
of the 'Moral Argument' in the Opus Postumum,"
Philosophy 26 (1951): 228-41.

969 Immanuel Kant, Religion within the Limits of
Reason Alone, trans. with an Introduction and Notes
T.M. Greene and H.H. Hudson with a new essay by J.R.
Silber (New York: Harper & Row; Harper Torchbooks,
1960), p. 48.

970 Ibid.

971 Ibid., p. 79.

972 Ibid.

973 Ibid., p. 182.

974 Ibid., p. 81.

975 Ibid., p. 83.

976 Ibid., p. 119.

977 Ibid.

978 Ibid., p. 120.

979 Greene, "Kant's Religion," p. xviii; cf. Kant,
Religion within the Limits of Reason Alone, p. 76.

[980]Greene, "Kant's Religion," p. xxx.

[981]Dieter   Heinrich,   "Some   Historical
Presuppostions of Hegel's System," in Hegel and the
Philosophy of Religion, ed. with an Introduction by
Darrell E. Christensen (The Hague: Martinus Nijhoff,
1970), pp. 32-7.

[982]Classical liberal theology also tended to
reduce religion to ethics.   Albrecht Ritschl, Die
christliche Lehre von der Rechtfertigung und Versöhnung
(Bonn: A. Marcus, 1870-4), and Wilhelm Herrmann, Der
Verkehr des Christen mit Gott im Anschluss an Luther
(Stuttgart: Cotta, 1903), moralized Jesus's message of
the kingdom of God into a community of love among men.
According   to   Ritschl,   although   Jesus   employed
apocalyptic language, the primary meaning of the
kingdom of God was ethical.   Jesus was absolute in that
he   lived   in   complete   devotion   to   his   vocation   in
founding this kingdom.   He serves therefore as the
model of the ethical life for all men, and the
historical facts of his miracles and resurrection are
irrelevant to any man's fulfilling his role in the
moral kingdom which Jesus established.   Hermann
concurred as to the ethical nature of Jesus's kingdom.
Jesus's complete identification with the moral ideal of
the   kingdom   of   God   makes   him   God's   unique
representative among men.   The resurrection of Jesus is
of minimal importance, since knowledge of any
historical event is shifting and uncertain.   It is
through contacting the inner life of Jesus, which is
available immediately to all men in all ages, that one
experiences the love of God, which is quickened by
loving relationships with other human beings.   Adolf
von Harnack styled true Christianity as simple belief
in the Fatherhood of God and the brotherhood of man,
arguing in his famous Das Wesen des Christentums (1900)
that miracles and the resurrection have no part in the
simple gospel of love preached by Jesus.   Harnack held
that   belief   in   the   resurrection   originated   in   a
post-crucifixion vision seen by Peter which was
prompted by his earlier vision of Christ at the
transfiguration.   For liberal theology there could be
no question about arguing for the historicity of the
gospel miracles or Jesus's resurrection, since these
were irrelevant to the gospel message of love.   In no
sense did the ethically interpreted kingdom of God
among men depend on the historicity of the supernatural
events in the gospels.   In fact such events were worse
than useless; they were actual impossibilities, and
liberal theologians were united in their rejection of

the miraculous:
> " . . . we are firmly convinced that what happens
> in space and time is subject to the general laws
> of motion, and that in this sense, as an
> interruption of the order of Nature, there can be
> no such things as 'miracles.'"   (Adolf von
> Harnack, What is Christianity?, 3d ed. rev.,
> trans. T.B. Saunders, Crown Theological Library 5
> [London: Williams & Norgate, 1912; New York:
> G.P. Putnam's Sons, 1912], p. 27.)

This denial of the supernatural left no room in history
for events such as the resurrection.   Hence, in
liberalism's greatest study of the resurrection
narratives,   The Historical Evidence for the
Resurrection of Jesus by Kirsopp Lake, the author
explains away the empty grave by the "wrong tomb"
hypothesis, largely on the grounds of personal
doctrinal preferences for the immortality of the soul
as opposed to resurrection of the body, and suggests
explaining the resurrection appearances as
psychological phenomena such as those involved in
communication with the dead.   The "unique and
miraculous character of the Resurrection" ought to be
abandoned and the witness of the Spirit heeded instead,
in order to convince men "that on one side of their
nature they are the 'sons of God.'" (Kirsopp Lake, The
Historical Evidence for the Resurrection of Jesus
Christ [London: Williams & Norgate, 1907; New York:
G.P. Putnam's Sons, 1907], pp. 277-9.)   Thus, in its
reduction of religion to morality and its attendant
denial of the supernatural in history, liberal theology
was heir to Kant.

[983]H.R. Mackintosh and J.S. Stewart, "Editors'
Preface," in Friedrich Schleiermacher, The Christian
Faith, 2d ed. (Edinburgh: T & T Clark, 1928), p.v.
This was, of course, prior to Barth's great work.

[984]Friedrich Schleiermacher, The Christian Faith,
2d ed., ed. H.R. Mackintosh and J.S. Stewart
(Edinburgh: T & T Clark, 1928), pp. 5-12.

[985]Ibid., p. 11.

[986]Ibid., pp. 12-18.

[987]Ibid., p. 16.

[988]Ibid., pp. 31-4.

[989]Ibid., pp. 34-9.

[990]Ibid., pp. 52-60.

[991]Ibid., pp. 62-8.

[992]Ibid., pp. 385-9.

[993]Ibid., pp. 424-6.

[994]Salvatorelli comments,
" . . . in accordance with Schleiermacher's extra-temporal, anti-historical, individualistic conception of religion, his Jesus, especially as pictured in the Glaubenslehre, is an entirely abstract being, a dialectic, mystical, and almost vaporous form of the Logos of the Gospel of John . . ., a prototype of humanity, the ideal Man become a reality at a certain moment in history." (Salvatorelli, "Locke to Reitzenstein," p. 278.)

[995]Schleiermacher, The Christian Faith, pp. 59-60.

[996]Ibid., p. 4.

[997]Friedrich Schleiermacher, Brief Outline on the Study of Theology, trans. with an Introduction by T.N. Tice (Richmond, Va.: John Knox Press, 1966), pp. 29-40.

[998]Schleiermacher, The Christian Faith, p. 52.

[999]Schleiermacher adds,
"Perhaps in a universal Philosophy of Religion, to which, if it were properly recognized, Apologetics could then appeal, the inner character of Christianity in itself could be exhibited in such a way that its particular place in the religious world would thereby be definitely fixed. This would also mean that all the principal moments of the religious consciousness would be systematized, and from their inter-connexion it would be seen which of them were fitted to have all the others related to them and to be themselves a constant concomitant of all the others. If, then, it should be seen that the element which we call 'redemption' becomes such a moment as soon as a liberating fact enters a region where the God-consciousness was in a state of constraint, Christianity would in that case be vindicated as a distinct form of faith and its nature in a sense

construed. But even this could not properly be
called a proof of Christianity, since even the
Philosophy of Religion could not establish any
necessity, either to recognize a particular Fact
as redemptive, or to give the central place
actually in one's own consciousness to any
particular moment, even though that moment should
be capable of occupying such a place." (ibid., p.
59.)

[1000] Ibid., p. 71.

[1001] Ibid., pp. 71-3.

[1002] Ibid., p. 75.

[1003] Ibid., pp. 178-84.

[1004] Ibid., p. 72.

[1005] Ibid., p. 448, 71.

[1006] Ibid., p. 71.

[1007] Ibid., p. 417.

[1008] Karl Heinrich Sack, Christliche Apologetik, 2d
rev. ed. (Hamburg: Perthes, 1841).

[1009] See Zöckler, Geschichte der Apologie, pp.
521-36; Dulles, History of Apologetics, pp. 159-64,
179-81, 195-8.

[1010] Theologische Realenzyklopädie,   s.v.
"Apologetik II, Neuzeit," by Karl Gerhard Steck. See
also the chapter on Tholuck in Otto Zöckler, Die
christliche Apologetik im Neunzehnten Jahrhundert
(Gutersloh: C. Bertelsmann, 1904), pp. 11-18.

[1011] Zöckler, Geschichte der Apologie, p. 531.

[1012] Tholuck, "Uber die Apologetik und ihre
Litteratur," 1: 150-2.

[1013] Ibid., pp. 161, 191, 293.

[1014] Friedrich Aug. D. Tholuck, Guido and Julius;
or, Sin and the Propitiator exhibited in the true
consecration of the sceptic, trans. J.E. Ryland, with a
Preface by John Pye Smith (Boston: Gould & Lincoln,
1854), pp. 43-4.

[1015]Ibid., p. 49.

[1016]Ibid., p. 98.   Cf. Tholuck's own comments on
the state of contemporary German theology.   The causes
of current unbelief he attributes to: (1) the lack of
independent and powerful church authorities, but
especially (2) the theoretical orientation toward
scholarship of Germans, who consider it a greater
sacrilege to be inconsistent in scholarship than to
bury the most influential and sacred institutions.   He
thinks a great difference between the early theologians
like Semler and the later like Bauer is that for the
latter the theological consciousness and religious
interest have apparently altogether ceased; they regard
themselves as scholars, but they have no consciousness
that this scholarship ought to stand in the service of
some church, which has made a great practical
difference.   (Tholuck, "Geschichte der Umwalzung," 2:
1, 131.)

[1017]Tholuck, Guido and Julius, p. 101.

[1018]Ibid., p. 148.

[1019]Ibid., pp. 196-220.

[1020]A. Tholuck, The Credibility of the Evangelical
History (London: John Chapman, 1844), p. 52.

[1021]Ibid.

[1022]Ibid., p. 8.

[1023]Ibid., p. 36.

[1024]Cf. the work of Ernst Luthardt, Apologetische
Vorträge über die grundwahrheiten des christenthums
(Leipzig: Dorffling and Franke, 1864), a work which
Steck characterizes as representative of the later
nineteenth century (Theologische Realenzyklopädie, s.v.
"Apologetik II, Neuzeit"), in which the author defends
Christianity wholly upon spiritual, ethical, and
cultural considerations.

NOTES TO SECTION III

[1] Rudolph Bultmann, "New Testament and Mythology," in Kerygma and Myth, 2 vols., ed. Hans-Werner Bartsch, trans. R.H. Fuller (London: SPCK, 1953), 2:1-44. Bultmann's a priori assumption of history and the universe as a closed system is especially evident in idem, "Bultmann Replies to his Critics," in Kerygma and Myth, 1: 197. According to Niebuhr, Bultmann retained uncriticized the nineteenth century idea of nature and history as a closed system, which forces him to insist that the resurrection is only the wonder of faith. (Richard R. Niebuhr, Resurrection and Historical Reason [New York: Charles Scribner's Sons, 1957], pp. 60-1.)

[2] Rudolf Pesch, "Die Entstehung des Glaubens an den Auferstandenen," Theologische Quartalschrift 153 (1973): 227.

[3] Ibid., p. 226. Cf. Marxsen's "Die Sache Jesu geht weiter" as expressing the essence of the resurrection.

[4] See Hans Grass, Ostergeschehen und Osterberichte, 4th ed. (Göttingen: Vandenhoeck & Ruprecht, 1970), pp. 20, 28, 48-9, 81, and his treatment of the gospels in general.

[5] John E. Alsup, The Post-Resurrection Appearance Stories of the Gospel-Tradition (Stuttgart: Calwer Verlag, 1975), p. 32.

[6] Ibid., p. 34.

[7] For example, the popular Catholic scholar Jakob Kremer asserts that because the resurrection body is not dependent on the physical body (all one needs is the genetic code to insure identity) we can today be serious defenders of the church's Easter message and still hold to the thesis that Jesus's grave was probably not empty. (Jakob Kremer, "Zur Diskussion über 'das leere Grab,'" in Resurrexit, ed. Edouard Dhanis [Rome: Libreria Editrice Vaticana, 1974], p. 140; idem, Die Osterevangelien--Geschichten um Geschichte [Stuttgart: Katholisches Bibelwerk, 1977], p. 49.) Cf. the opinion of J.A.T. Robinson: "The bones of Jesus could yet be lying around Palestine and the resurrection still be true." (J.A.T. Robinson, Can We Trust the New Testament? [London & Oxford: Mowbrays, 1977], p. 124.) The fallacy of this

reasoning seems to lie in confusing what God <u>can</u> do
with what God <u>did</u> do. If He did raise Jesus physically
from the tomb, then we would be misrepresenting God
were we to preach that the tomb was not empty.

[8] For example, Robin Scroggs, <u>The Last Adam</u>
(Oxford: Basil Blackwell, 1966), pp. 92-3.

[9] Alsup, <u>Stories</u>, p. 54.

[10] Gundry remarks that Paul's understanding
of σῶμα in relation to the resurrection is as
scandalous to twentieth century man as to the ancient
Greeks and proto-Gnostics. "The scandal is
difficult--imposs-ible--to avoid." (Robert Gundry,
Soma <u>in Biblical Theology</u> [Cambridge: Cambridge
University Press, 1976], p. 168.

[11] Oscar Cullmann, <u>Immortality of the Soul or
Resurrection of the Dead</u> (London: Epworth Press,
1958), pp. 6-7.

[12] See Ernst and Marie-Luise Keller, <u>Miracles in
Dispute</u>, trans. Kohl (Philadelphia: Fortress Press,
1969), pp. 163-76.

[13] Albert Einstein, in P.A. Schilpp, <u>Albert
Einstein: Philosopher-scientist</u>, Library of Living
Philosophers (New York: Tudor, 1951), p. 248.

[14] Even with regard to quantum laws, one may
plausibly speak of events which are naturally
impossible, as Mary Hesse explains:

> At first sight it might be thought that in theory,
> as far as isolated events are concerned, anything
> at all would be consistent with the statistical
> laws of quantum physics, even though perhaps very,
> very highly improbable. In this case, the notion
> of 'violation' of quantum laws by single events
> would lose its meaning. But statistical laws in
> science are in fact regarded as violated if events
> occur which according to them are excessively
> improbable, and in ordinary scientific contexts
> such violation leads to abandonment of the law,
> just as in the case of deterministic theories.
> There is no question that most events regarded as
> significantly 'miraculous' in religious contexts
> would, if they violate Newtonian laws, also be
> excessively improbable on well-established quantum
> laws, and therefore would be regarded as

violations of these also. Thus, if we consider only the currently accepted theories of physics, the credibility of such miracles is no greater than in Newtonian theory."
(Mary Hesse, "Miracles and the Laws of Nature," in Miracles, ed. C.F.D. Moule [London: A.R. Mowbray, 1965], p. 38.)

[15]Stephen S. Bilynskyj, "God, Nature, and the Concept of Miracle," (Ph.D. dissertation, University of Notre Dame, 1982), pp. 10-42.

[16]Ibid., pp. 46-53.

[17]Ibid., p. 117.

[18]Ibid., p. 138.

[19]Ibid., p. 146.

[20]Ibid., pp. 43-4.

[21]Ibid., pp. 86-97; for further criticism see pp. 97-101.

[22]Ernst Nagel, The Structure of Science, 2d ed. (Indianapolis: Hackett Publishing Co., 1979), pp. 53-4.

[23]Alvin Plantinga, The Nature of Necessity (Oxford: Clarendon Press, 1974); idem, God and Other Minds (Ithaca, N.Y.: Cornell University Press, 1967); Stuart C. Hackett, The Resurrectiion of Theism (Chicago: Moody Press, 1957), and many others.

[24]R.G. Swinburne, "Miracles," Philosophical Quarterly 18 (1968): p. 321.

[25]Ibid., p. 323.

[26]Encyclopedia of Philosophy, s.v. "Miracles," by Antony Flew.

[27]Wolfhart Pannenberg, "Jesu Geschichte und unsere Geschichte," in Glaube und Wirklichkeit (München: Chr. Kaiser, 1975), p. 92; idem, Jesus--God and Man, trans. L.L. Wilkens and D.A. Priebe (London: SCM, 1968), p. 67.

[28]Joachim Jeremias, "The Lord's Prayer in Modern Research," in New Testament Issues, ed. Richard Batey

(New York: Harper & Row, 1970), p. 95.

[29]James D.G. Dunn, <u>Jesus and the Spirit</u> (London: SCM Press, 1975), pp. 11-92; Royce Gordon Gruenler, <u>New Approaches to Jesus and the Gospels</u> (Grand Rapids, Mich: Baker, 1982).

[30]There is a delightful passage in Dickens's "Christmas Carol" that vividly illustrates this point. After experiencing several strange phenomena of which he is struggling inwardly to convince himself that they were humbug, Scrooge is confronted with the dreadful apparition of his deceased partner Marley, all bound in chains.

> "'You don't believe in me,' observed the Ghost.
> 'I don't,' said Scrooge.
> 'What evidence would you have of my reality beyond that of your senses?'
> 'I don't know,' said Scrooge.
> 'Why do you doubt your senses?'
> 'Because,' said Scrooge, 'a little thing affects them. A slight disorder of the stomach makes them cheats. You may be an undigested bit of beef, a blot of mustard, a crumb of cheese, a fragment of under-done potato. There's more gravy than of grave about you, whatever you are.' . . .
> . . . 'You see this toothpick?' said Scrooge . . . .
> 'I do,' replied the Ghost . . . .
> . . . 'Well!' returned Scrooge, 'I have but to swallow this, and be for the rest of my life persecuted by a legion of goblins, all of my own creation. Humbug, I tell you! humbug!'
>   At this the spirit raised a frightful cry, and shook its chain with such a dismal and appalling noise, that Scrooge held on tight to his chair, to save himself from falling into a swoon. But how much greater was his horror, when the phantom taking off the bandage round its head, as if it were too warm to wear indoors, its lower jaw dropped down upon its breast!
>   Scrooge fell upon his knees, and clasped his hands before his face.
>   'Mercy!' he said. 'Dreadful apparition, why do you trouble me?'
> 'Man of wordly mind!' replied the Ghost, 'do you believe in me or not?'
>   'I do,' said Scrooge. 'I must.'"
(Charles Dickens, "A Christmas Carol," in idem, <u>Christmas Books</u>, with an Introduction by E.

Farjeon [London: Oxford University Press, 1954],
pp. 18-19.)
Scrooge's studied scepticism becomes unrealistic in
light of the evident reality confronting him.

[31] Isaiah Berlin, "The Concept of Scientific
History," in Philosophical Analysis and History, ed.
W.H. Dray, Sources in Contemporary Philosophy (New
York: Harper & Row, 1966), pp. 16-17.

[32] Encyclopedia of Philosophy, s.v. "Miracles."

[33] D.E. Nineham, "Some Reflections on the Present
Position with Regard to The Jesus of History," CQR 166
(1965):   6-7.

[34] Carl Becker, "Detachment and the Writing of
History," in Detachment and the Writing of History, ed.
Phil L. Snyder (Ithaca, N.Y.:   Cornell University
Press, 1958; Westport, Conn: Greenwood Press, 1972),
pp. 12-13.

[35] Ibid., p. 14.

[36] Makoto Yamauchi, The Easter Texts of the New
Testament: Their Tradition, Redaction and Theology
(Ph.D. Thesis, University of Edinburgh, 1972), p. 29.

[37] Ernst Troeltsch, "Über historische und
dogmatische Methode in der Theologie," in idem,
Gesammelte Schriften (Tübingen: J.C.B. Mohr 1913), 2:
729-53.

[38] F.H. Bradley, The Presuppositions of Critical
History, ed. Lionel Rubinoff (Chicago: J.M. Dent and
Sons, 1968), p. 100.

[39] R.G. Collingwood, The Idea of History, ed. T.M.
Know (Oxford: Oxford University Press, 1956), p. 139.

[40] Ibid.

[41] See Ninian Smart, Philosophers and Religious
Truth (New York: Macmillan Co., 1970), pp. 25-35;
Swinburne, "Miracles,": 320-8.

[42] Wolfhart Pannenberg, "Redemptive Event and
History," in idem, Basic Questions in Theology, 2
vols., trans. G.H. Kehm (Philadelphia: Fortress Press,
1970), pp. 40-50.

[43]Wolfhart Pannenberg, cited in James M. Robinson, "Revelation as Word and as History," in New Frontiers in Theology: vol. 3: Theology as History, ed. James M. Robinson and John B. Cobb, Jr. (New York: Harper & Row, 1967), p. 33.

[44]Niebuhr, Resurrection and Historical Reason, p. 170.

[45]Walter Künneth, The Theology of the Resurrection, trans. J.W. Leitch (London: SCM, 1965), pp. 94-5.

[46]See the excellent discussion in Robert H. Gundry, Soma in Biblical Theology (Cambridge: Cambridge University Press, 1976), pp. 159-83.

[47]Ulrich wilckens, Auferstehung, TT 4 (Stuttgart and Berlin: Kreuz Verlag, 1970), pp. 152-3.

[48]Ibid., pp. 153-4.

[49]This latter term is chosen by R.H. Fuller, The Formation of the Resurrection Narratives (London: SPCK, 1972), p. 23.

[50]Berthold Klappert, "Einleitung," in idem, ed., Diskussion um Kreuz und Auferstehung (Wuppertal: Aussaat Verlag, 1971), pp. 18, 50-1.

[51]Bilynskyj proposes these criteria for identifying some event E as a miracle: (1) The evidence for the occurence of E is at least as good as it is for other acceptable but unusual events similarly distant in time and space from the point of inquiry; (2) An account of the natures and/or powers of the causally relevant natural agents, such that they could account for E, would be clumsy and ad hoc; (3) There is no evidence except the inexplicability of E for one or more natural agents which could produce E; (4) There is some justification for a supernatural explanation of E, independent of the inexplicability of E. (Bilynskyj, "Miracles," p. 222.)

[52]C.F.D. Moule, The Phenomenon of the New Testament, SBT 2d series 1 (London: SCM, 1967), pp. 3, 13.

[53]Van A. Harvey, The Historian and the Believer (New York: Macmillan Co., 1969), p. 242.

[54] Rudolf Pesch, Das Markusevangelium, 2 vols., HTKNT 2 (Freiburg: Herder, 1976-77), 2: 536; so also Kremer, "Grab," p. 139. Contemporary scholarship seems to have a woeful ignorance of the historical debate over the resurrection, despite its indebtedness to the debate, a fact illustrated by Wilckens's bibliography from the "history of the research:" it consists of Woolston, Annet, Reimarus, and Strauss! (Wilckens, Auferstehung, pp. 171-2.)

[55] These are not so much as even mentioned by Grass or von Campenhausen, much less seriously considered.

[56] John Stewart Lawton, Miracles and Revelation (New York: Association Press, 1959), pp. 63, 76.

[57] See Scroggs, Adam, pp. 92-3 for a typical statement.

[58] For defenses of a Straussian position, see Emanuel Hirsch, Jesus Christus der Herr (Göttingen: Vandenhoeck & Ruprecht, 1926), p. 39; Rudolph Bultmann, Offenbarung und Heilsgeschehen, BET 7 (München: Albert Lempp, 1941), pp. 66-8; James McLeman, Resurrection Then and Now (London: Hodder & Stoughton, 1965), pp. 170-90; Howard M. Teeple, "The Historical Beginnings of the Resurrection Faith," in Studies in the New Testament and Early Christian Literature, ed. D.E. Aune (Leiden: E.J. Brill, 1972), pp. 107-20.

[59] Grass argues convincingly that there are no objective historical factors which could create an Easter faith prior to resurrection appearances, neither Jesus's predictions, nor reflection on Old Testament texts, nor the personality of Jesus, nor Messianic beliefs; nor can subjective factors such as religious enthusiasm or guilt complex account for the appearances. See also J.A.T. Robinson, The Human Face of God (London: SCM Press, 1973), p. 131.

[60] Norman Perrin, The Resurrection according to Matthew, Mark, and Luke (Philadelphia: Fortress Press, 1977), p. 80.

[61] See Edward Lynn Bode, The First Easter Morning, AB 45 (Rome: Biblical Institute Press, 1970), pp. 162-3.

[62] For a fine discussion, see Josef Blinzler, "Die Grablegung Jesu in historischer Sicht," in Resurrexit,

ed. Edouard Dhanis (Rome: Libreria Editrice Vaticana, 1974), pp. 56-102. To summarize some of the evidence in favor of the burial: (1) The pre-Pauline formula in I Cor 15 mentions the burial. The four-fold ὅτι , the chronological sequence, and the gospel narratives make it probable that the burial is not meant to underscore the death, but summarizes the tradition of Jesus's burial in the tomb. (2) The burial story is part of the pre-Markan passion story and therefore belongs to the oldest tradition. (3) the story is simple and lacks signs of theological reflection or legendary development. (4) Joseph of Arimathea is probably the historical individual responsible for Jesus's burial. It is unlikely that the Christian tradition would invent a fictional figure and place him on the historical council of the Sanhedrin. (5) Archaeological discoveries confirm the descriptions of the type of tomb used by Joseph. (6) Jesus was probably buried late on the day of Preparation. Jewish custom did not allow a man to hang on the cross overnight or to be buried on the Sabbath. (7) Women probably observed the burial. The reason women are named as witnesses, despite the worthlessness of their testimony, instead of men is probably because they were the historical witnesses. (8) No other burial tradition exists. That no trace of the true story or even a conflicting one should remain is difficult to explain unless the gospel account is substantially true. Grass admits that the historicity of the burial story cannot be denied unless an earlier burial tradition can be discovered and the present account can be shown to contain improbabilities. (Grass, Ostergeschehen, p. 178.) Despite his efforts, Grass does not, I think, succeed in proving either point.

[63]Pesch, "Entstehung," p. 207.

[64]This consideration plays a crucial role in the case argued by Wolfhart Pannenberg, Jesus: God and Man, trans. L.L. Wilkins and D.A. Priebe (London: SCM Press, 1968), pp. 101-2. See also Bode, Easter, pp. 162-3; Kremer, "Grab," p. 157.

[65]For a summary of arguments against the historicity of the guard, see Hans Freiherr von Campenhausen, Der Ablauf der Osterereignisse und das leere Grab, 3d rev. ed., SHAW (Heidelberg: Carl Winter, 1966), p. 29.

[66]See the literature cited in Bode, Easter, p. 158; also Kremer, "Grab," p. 157.

[67]See the outstanding work on the empty tomb by
Bode, Easter, especially pp. 160-3.   Among the
evidences for the empty tomb are: (1) The historical
reliability of the account of Jesus's burial supports
the empty tomb.   For if the site of the tomb were
known, belief in Jesus's resurrection would be
impossible, unless the tomb were empty.   (2) The
pre-Pauline formula of I Cor 15 implies the empty tomb.
For a Jew, the phrase "he was raised" following the
phrase "he was buried" could only imply an empty grave.
Moreover, the expression "on the third day" is probably
a time indicator for the date of the empty tomb's
discovery, using the language of the LXX to signify
God's intervention and victory.   (3) The empty tomb
story was probably part of the pre-Markan passion story
and therefore belongs to the oldest tradition.   This
means it cannot be a late legend.   (4) The use of "on
the first day of the week" instead of "on the third
day" indicates a very ancient tradition.   The empty
tomb tradition appears to antedate the "third day"
motif, which itself probably goes back to within the
first five years of Jesus's death.   The fact that the
phrase is probably a Semitism confirms this.   (5) The
empty tomb story is simple and lacks signs of theological reflection or legendary development.   (6) The
discovery of the empty tomb by women is highly
probable, given their low status and lack of
qualification to serve as legal witnesses.   (7) The
disciples' investigation of the tomb is probable.
Given the disciples' presence in Jerusalem over the
weekend, as attested by the denial of Peter tradition,
it is not unlikely that they should investigate the
women's report.   (8) That Jesus's tomb was not
venerated as a shrine indicates the tomb was empty.
Given the extraordinary interest in Judaism in the
tombs of holy men and prophets, the fact that Jesus's
tomb was not venerated is probably best explained
because it was empty and thus devoid of religious
significance.   To these considerations, Paley's should
be added.

[68]D.H. Van Daalen, The Real Resurrection (London:
Collins, 1972), p. 41.

[69]Kremer, Osterevangelien, pp. 49-50.

[70]A.N. Sherwin-White, Roman Society and Roman Law
in the New Testament (Oxford: Clarendon Press, 1963),
pp. 188-91.

[71]Ibid., p. 189.

[72]Ibid., p. 190. This consideration becomes
especially forceful if one follows critics such as
Guthrie, Reicke, and Robinson in a pre-70 dating of
Luke-Acts. (Donald Guthrie, New Testament
Introduction, 3d ed. rev. [London: Inter-Varsity
Press, 1970], pp. 340-5; Bo Reicke, "Synoptic
Prophecies on the Destruction of Jerusalem," in Studies
in New Testament and Early Christian Literature, ed.
D.E. Aune [Leiden: E.J. Brill, 1972], pp. 121-34; John
A.T. Robinson, Redating the New Testament [London: SCM
Press, 1976], pp. 13-30, 86-117.)

[73]Julius Müller, The Theory of Myths, in its
Application to the Gospel History, Examined and
Confuted (London: John Chapman, 1844), p. 29.

[74]Vincent Taylor, The Formation of the Gospel
Tradition, 2d ed. (London: Macmillan & Co., 1935), p.
41.

[75]Archibald Robertson and Alfred Plummer, First
Epistle of Saint Paul to the Corinthians, 2d ed., ICC
(Edinburgh: T & T Clark, 1967), p. 337.

[76]Künneth, Theology, pp. 92-3.

[77]J.A.T. Robinson, for example, calls the
existence of the Christian church the "strongest
evidence" for Jesus's resurrection. (J.A.T. Robinson,
Can We Trust the New Testament [London and Oxford:
Mowbrays, 1977], p. 127.

[78]Fuller, Formation of the Resurrection Narratives, p. 2.

[79]See S.H. Hooke, The Resurrection of Christ as
History and Experience (London: Darton, Longman &
Todd, 1967), pp. 2-18; Franz Mussner, Die Auferstehung
Jesu, BH 7 (München: Kösel Verlag, 1969), pp. 39-49;
Wilckens, Auferstehung, pp. 109-44; C.F. Evans,
Resurrection and the New Testament, SBT 2/12 (London:
SCM Press, 1970), pp. 14-17, 27-40. The Jewish
doctrine of the resurrection (attested three places in
the Old Testament: Ez 37; Is 26.19; Dan 12.2) flowered
in the intertestamental period (II Macc 7.9-42;
12:43-5; I Enoch 5.7; 22.1-14; 51.1; 61.5; 90.33;
91;9-10; 100.4-5; Testament of the Twelve Patriarchs
(Judah) 25.1,4; (Zebulun) 10.2; (Benjamin) 10.6-18; II
Baruch 30.2-5; 50-1; IV Ezra 7.26-44). It is probably
not the result of Iranian influences, but rather the
logical outworking of Yahweh's power over death and the

future (Ps 16.10; 49.16; Is 25.8; 49.16); the deaths of the Jewish martyrs provided a powerful stimulus to the development of this doctrine.

[80]Joachim Jeremias, "Die älteste Schicht der Osterüberlieferungen," in Resurrexit, ed. Edouard Dhanis (Rome: Libreria Editrice Vaticana, 1974), p. 194.

[81]Wilckens, Auferstehung, p. 131.

[82]C.F.D. Moule and Don Cupitt, "The Resurrection: A Disagreement," Theol 75 (1972): 507-19.

[83]Grass, Ostergeschehen, p. 25; von Campenhausen, Aablauf, p. 29; Walter Grundmann, Das Evangelium nach Matthäus, 3d ed. THKNT 1 (Berlin: Evangelische Verlagsanstalt, 1972), p. 565; Alsup, Stories, p. 117.

[84]See especially Grass, Ostergeschehen, pp. 139-73; also McLeman, Resurrection, p. 202; Ernst Haenchen, The Acts of the Apostles, 14th ed., trans. B. Noble, G. Shinn and R. McL. Wilson (Oxford: Basil Blackwell, 1971), p. 114.

[85]Evans, Resurrection, pp. 128-9.

[86]Michael Grant, Jesus: an Historian's Review of the Gospels (New York: Charles Scribner's Sons, 1977), p. 176.

[87]The same error is made by Schubert Ogden, Christ Without Myth (London: Collins, 1962), p. 158. He charges that those who defend the historicity of miracles are guilty of a petitio principii; they assume miracles are actual because they are possible or assume their historicity in the premisses. The charge seems foundationless; the defenders of miracles argue that miracles are possible in a theistic universe, but whether any have actually occurred is an empirical question to be determined by historical investigation. If we find an event occurring in a significant religious context and no plausible natural causes may be found to account for its occurrence, then it may be regarded as probably a miracle.

[88]Marxsen, Resurrection, pp. 74-8.

TEXTS AND STUDIES IN RELIGION